■ THE RESOURCE FOR THE INDEPENDENT TRAVELER

"The guides are aimed not only at young budget travelers but at the indepedent traveler; a sort of streetwise cookbook for traveling alone."

—The New York Times

"Unbeatable; good sight-seeing advice; up-to-date info on restaurants, hotels, and inns; a commitment to money-saving travel; and a wry style that brightens nearly every page."

—The Washington Post

"Lighthearted and sophisticated, informative and fun to read. [Let's Go] helps the novice traveler navigate like a knowledgeable old hand."

—Atlanta Journal-Constitution

"A world-wise traveling companion—always ready with friendly advice and helpful hints, all sprinkled with a bit of wit."

—The Philadelphia Inquirer

■ THE BEST TRAVEL BARGAINS IN YOUR PRICE RANGE

"All the dirt, dirt cheap."

—People

"Anything you need to know about budget traveling is detailed in this book."

—The Chicago Sun-Times

"Let's Go follows the creed that you don't have to toss your life's savings to the wind to travel—unless you want to."

—The Salt Lake Tribune

■ REAL ADVICE FOR REAL EXPERIENCES

"The writers seem to have experienced every rooster-packed bus and lunar-surfaced mattress about which they write."

—The New York Times

"A guide should tell you what to expect from a destination. Here Let's Go shines."

—The Chicago Tribune

LET'S GO PUBLICATIONS

TRAVEL GUIDES

Alaska & the Pacific Northwest 2003
Australia 2003
Austria & Switzerland 2003
Britain & Ireland 2003
California 2003
Central America 8th edition
Chile 1st edition **NEW TITLE**
China 4th edition
Costa Rica 1st edition **NEW TITLE**
Eastern Europe 2003
Egypt 2nd edition
Europe 2003
France 2003
Germany 2003
Greece 2003
Hawaii 2003 **NEW TITLE**
India & Nepal 7th edition
Ireland 2003
Israel 4th edition
Italy 2003
Mexico 19th edition
Middle East 4th edition
New Zealand 6th edition
Peru, Ecuador & Bolivia 3rd edition
South Africa 5th edition
Southeast Asia 8th edition
Southwest USA 2003
Spain & Portugal 2003
Thailand 1st edition **NEW TITLE**
Turkey 5th edition
USA 2003
Western Europe 2003

CITY GUIDES

Amsterdam 2003
Barcelona 2003
Boston 2003
London 2003
New York City 2003
Paris 2003
Rome 2003
San Francisco 2003
Washington, D.C. 2003

MAP GUIDES

Amsterdam
Berlin
Boston
Chicago
Dublin
Florence
Hong Kong
London
Los Angeles
Madrid
New Orleans
New York City
Paris
Prague
Rome
San Francisco
Seattle
Sydney
Venice
Washington, D.C.

AMSTERDAM 2003

Sarah E. Kramer Editor

Researcher-Writers
Stefan Atkinson
Catherine Burch
Ian MacKenzie

Avra Celine van der Zee Map Editor
Christopher Blazejewski Managing Editor
Chris Clayton Typesetter

Macmillan

HELPING LET'S GO If you want to share your discoveries, suggestions, or corrections, please drop us a line. We read every piece of correspondence, whether a postcard, a 10-page email, or a coconut. Please note that mail received after May 2003 may be too late for the 2004 book, but will be kept for future editions. **Address mail to:**

Let's Go: Amsterdam
67 Mount Auburn Street
Cambridge, MA 02138
USA

Visit Let's Go at **http://www.letsgo.com,** or send email to:

feedback@letsgo.com
Subject: "Let's Go: Amsterdam"

In addition to the invaluable travel advice our readers share with us, many are kind enough to offer their services as researchers or editors. Unfortunately, our charter enables us to employ only currently enrolled Harvard students.

Published in Great Britain 2003 by Macmillan, an imprint of Pan Macmillan Ltd.
20 New Wharf Road, London N1 9RR,
Basingstoke and Oxford
Associated companies throughout the world
www.panmacmillan.com

Published in the United States of America by St. Martin's Press.

ISBN: 1-4050-0084 8
First edition
10 9 8 7 6 5 4 3 2 1

Let's Go: Amsterdam is written by Let's Go Publications, 67 Mount Auburn Street, Cambridge, MA 02138, USA.

Printed in the USA on recycled paper with soy ink.

ADVERTISING DISCLAIMER All advertisements appearing in Let's Go publications are sold by an independent agency not affiliated with the editorial production of the guides. Advertisers are never given preferential treatment, and the guides are researched, written, and published independent of advertising. Advertisements do not imply endorsement of products or services by Let's Go, and Let's Go does not vouch for the accuracy of information provided in advertisements.

If you are interested in purchasing advertising space in a Let's Go publication, contact: Let's Go Advertising Sales, 67 Mount Auburn St., Cambridge, MA 02138, USA.

WHO WE ARE

A NEW LET'S GO FOR 2003

With a sleeker look and innovative new content, we have revamped the entire series to reflect more than ever the needs and interests of the independent traveler. Here are just some of the improvements you will notice when traveling with the new *Let's Go.*

MORE PRICE OPTIONS

Still the best resource for budget travelers, *Let's Go* recognizes that everyone needs the occassional indulgence. Our "Big Splurges" indicate establishments that are actually worth those extra pennies (pulas, pesos, or pounds), and price-level symbols (❶ ❷ ❸ ❹ ❺) allow you to quickly determine whether an accommodation or restaurant will break the bank. We may have diversified, but we'll never lose our budget focus—"Hidden Deals" reveal the best-kept travel secrets.

BEYOND THE TOURIST EXPERIENCE

Our Alternatives to Touism chapter offers ideas on immersing yourself in a new community through study, work, or volunteering.

AN INSIDER'S PERSPECTIVE

As always, every item is written and researched by our on-site writers. This year we have highlighted more viewpoints to help you gain an even more thorough understanding of the places you are visiting.

IN RECENT NEWS. *Let's Go* correspondents around the globe report back on current regional issues that may affect you as a traveler.

CONTRIBUTING WRITERS. Respected scholars and former *Let's Go* writers discuss topics on society and culture, going into greater depth than the usual guidebook summary.

THE LOCAL STORY. From the Parisian monk toting a cell phone to the Russian *babushka* confronting capitalism, *Let's Go* shares its revealing conversations with local personalities—a unique glimpse of what matters to real people.

FROM THE ROAD. Always helpful and sometimes downright hilarious, our researchers share useful insights on the typical (and atypical) travel experience.

SLIMMER SIZE

Don't be fooled by our new, smaller size. *Let's Go* is still packed with invaluable travel advice, but now it's easier to carry with a more compact design.

FORTY-THREE YEARS OF WISDOM

For over four decades *Let's Go* has provided the most up-to-date information on the hippest cafes, the most pristine beaches, and the best routes from border to border. It all started in 1960 when a few well-traveled students at Harvard University handed out a 20-page mimeographed pamphlet of their tips on budget travel to passengers on student charter flights to Europe. From humble beginnings, *Let's Go* has grown to cover six continents and *Let's Go: Europe* still reigns as the world's best-selling travel guide. This year we've beefed up our coverage of Latin America with *Let's Go: Costa Rica* and *Let's Go: Chile;* on the other side of the globe, we've added *Let's Go: Thailand* and *Let's Go: Hawaii.* Our new guides bring the total number of titles to 61, each infused with the spirit of adventure that travelers around the world have come to count on.

CONTENTS

RESEARCHER-WRITERS

Stefan Atkinson *CRW, JP, NZ, Arnhem, Hoge Veluwe, Groningen, Leiden, Utrecht, Flower Country*

Stefan put his knowledge as a European History major to work this summer as he breezed through the city's most historic neighborhoods and the country's oldest cities. His copy was full of hidden and notable facts, whether about a seemingly boring building front or a lesser-known museum. Finally, Stefan swept through the bulk of the city's coffeeshops, with a surprisingly clear head.

Catherine Burch *MV, CCR, RP, LP, DP, Maastricht, Noordwijk, Haarlem, Zaanse Schans*

Katie fell in love with living in Amsterdam. A recent Harvard graduate with a degree in History and Literature, Katie settled down in De Pijp and took on the city alone and confident. Whether on daytrips to Haarlem and Maastricht or when digging her heels into Shopping, Katie always was able to find some exciting addition to the book, with a go-to attitude and a smile on her face.

Ian MacKenzie *J, WO, RLD, OZ, SQ, The Hague, Rotterdam, Delft, Gouda, Wadden Islands*

Ian went above and beyond the call of duty as a researcher. He braved the Red Light District and the seedier neighborhoods of the city with grace and ease. And despite his reputation as an award-winning fiction author, Ian paid scrupulous attention to detail. Whether checking prices or noting the latest political controversy, his prose was on the ball, without losing the quality that comes from a writer's writer.

Susan Frauenhoffer *Proofer*

Genevieve Cadwalader *Brussels*

CONTRIBUTING WRITERS

Margot Kaminski
Margot is a contributing writer for *Lilith Magazine.*

Sasha Polakow-Suransky
Sasha writes for the *American Prospect Magazine.*

ACKNOWLEDGMENTS

SARAH: First, thanks to my RW's—Stefan, for sticking with me in the spring when the times were rough; Ian and Katie, my saviors who jumped in at the last minute and were better than I could ever have hoped for; Ian for making me laugh; Katie for being so happy. All of you cared so much.

Thanks to Blaz—for letting me in on the job, for coming up with plans of attack—however crazy—for the long hours at the computer indexing, and for grappling again and again with daytrips. To the basement: It's a hard-knock life. Scrobins for empathy, the Byrne for hot love, Club F for mood lighting, Kwok for late night philosophy, Eustace for defying all expectations, Antoinette, my Crimson events buddy, Ankur for music.

Alex, for help: Johs Pierce for Alt. to Tour. Amélie Cherlin for noting every error. Especially to Amber Musser for being calm, for charts, for laughing at us silently.

Avra, for being lovely and competent, and for your unexpected knowledge of Dutch. Street names and poste restante would not be the same without you.

The Europe pod, my second home. Jeff and Tabby. Matt for attempting to keep me sane, for being calm yourself, for bad, awkward, theater, for last-minute help. Susan for being an amazing helper and an even better friend. Matthew S. for advice over the phone, Thalia for banners, Meredith for advice in the spring.

Robbie, for taking care of me, for the long treks to the Co-op, for food, your room, and for every good thing that happened this summer.

Jacob and Matthew, my awesome brothers.

And finally, I dedicate this book to my **Parents,** whom I did not thank in my yearbook, but whom I am thanking, here, now. Thanks Mom and Dad, I couldn't have done anything without you.

AVRA: Thanks to the fabulous Amsterdam RWS, Katie, Ian and Stefan, who took on Amsterdam with fervor. Thanks to Mapland, the Map Rave, and Johnnies. Thanks to my roommates. Thanks to Chris for killing the mouse. Thanks to Charlotte for being my career counselor. Thanks to Julie for taking the me out of M.E. Thanks to Blaz for being Blaz. And of course, thanks to Sarah, for braving the stench of the basement, Ankur's monkey purse, and the ridiculous string of consonants and vowels that is the Dutch language. Gefeliciteerd.

Editor
Sarah E. Kramer
Managing Editor
Christopher Blazejewski
Map Editor
Avra van der Zee
Typesetter
Chris Clayton

HOW TO USE THIS BOOK

PRICE RANGES AND RANKINGS. Our researchers list establishments in order of value from best to worst. Our absolute favorites are denoted by the Let's Go thumbs-up (☒). Since the best value does not always mean the cheapest price, we have incorporated a system of price ranges into the guide. The table below lists how prices fall within each bracket.

SYMBOL:	❶	❷	❸	❹	❺
ACCOMMODATIONS	under €30	€30-49	€50-69	€70-99	€100+
FOOD	under €7	€7-10	€11-14	€15-19	€20+

WHEN TO USE IT

TWO MONTHS BEFORE. Our book is filled with practical information to help you before you go. **Planning Your Trip** (p. 265) has advice about passports, plane tickets, insurance, and more. The **Accommodations** chapter (p. 177) can help you with booking a room from home.

ONE MONTH BEFORE. Take care of travel insurance and write down a list of emergency numbers and hotlines to take with you. Make a list of packing essentials and shop for anything you're missing. Make any necessary reservations.

TWO WEEKS BEFORE. Start thinking about your ideal trip. **Discover Amsterdam** (see p. 1) lists the city's top 20 sights and also includes suggested itineraries, our new **walking tours** (complete with maps), Let's Go Picks (the best and quirkiest that Amsterdam has to offer), and the scoop on each of the city's neighborhoods, including what areas to avoid and what you absolutely should not miss.

ON THE ROAD. **Once in Amsterdam** (see p. 23) will be your best friend once you've arrived, with all the practical information you'll need, plus tips on acting like a true Amsterdammer. When you reach Amsterdam, you'll spend most of your time flipping through the following chapters: **Sights, Museums, Food & Drink, Only in Amsterdam** (which includes complete coffeeshop listings), **Nightlife, Entertainment,** and **Shopping.** When you feel like striking out, the **Daytripping** chapter will help: it provides a list of options for one-day and weekend trips away from Amsterdam into The Netherlands, and even as far as Brussels. The **Service Directory** contains a list of local services like laundromats, tourist offices, and dentists. The **Appendix** has a list of useful Dutch words and phrases to help you navigate almost every situation. Finally, remember to put down this guide once in a while and go exploring on your own—take the tram, rent a bike, paddle through the canals, or just go for a stroll—you'll be glad you did.

A NOTE TO OUR READERS The information for this book was gathered by *Let's Go* researchers from May through August of 2002. Each listing is based on one researcher's opinion, formed during his or her visit at a particular time. Those traveling at other times may have different experiences since prices, dates, hours, and conditions are always subject to change. You are urged to check the facts presented in this book beforehand to avoid inconvenience and surprises.

INSIDE:

Discover Amsterdam

Amsterdam emerged from the sea a city created, literally, by its inhabitants. Today, the same beautiful terrain remains: small plots of land surrounded on all sides by canals, lined with elegant houses that lean over the streets as if trying to glimpse at their reflections in the water. The Golden Age of art flourished here, and here it remains—Rembrandt's shadowy portraiture and Vermeer's luminous women, the Modern swirls of Van Gogh's brush and the clean, sharp lines of Mondrian's squares sing an æsthetic lullaby to the dignified sensibilities of the Protestant populace. Yet sleepy gabled houses and calm water combined with art in stately museums are not the soul of the city.

Amsterdam is the hot, bustling capital of northern Europe. It's open attitude towards sex, self-expression, and soft drugs make it a mecca and meeting point for the youth of the Continent and for ex-patriots from all over the world. Its liberal mindset extends back into history, so that now its population is as diverse as any city twice its size. Visit Amsterdam to experiment and party, to club and cruise. Or, begin by taking in the culture of years past and end with the city's bustling gallery scene. See the city from another angle: on bike like a local or on boat from the canals. Use Amsterdam as a starting point for exploring The Netherlands, a country as eclectic as its capital: scattered among beaches and international cities are tulip fields and windmills, and the odd clog can still be found in shops' windows and on natives' feet. As Amsterdam is a city where anything goes, there is no end to the possibilities.

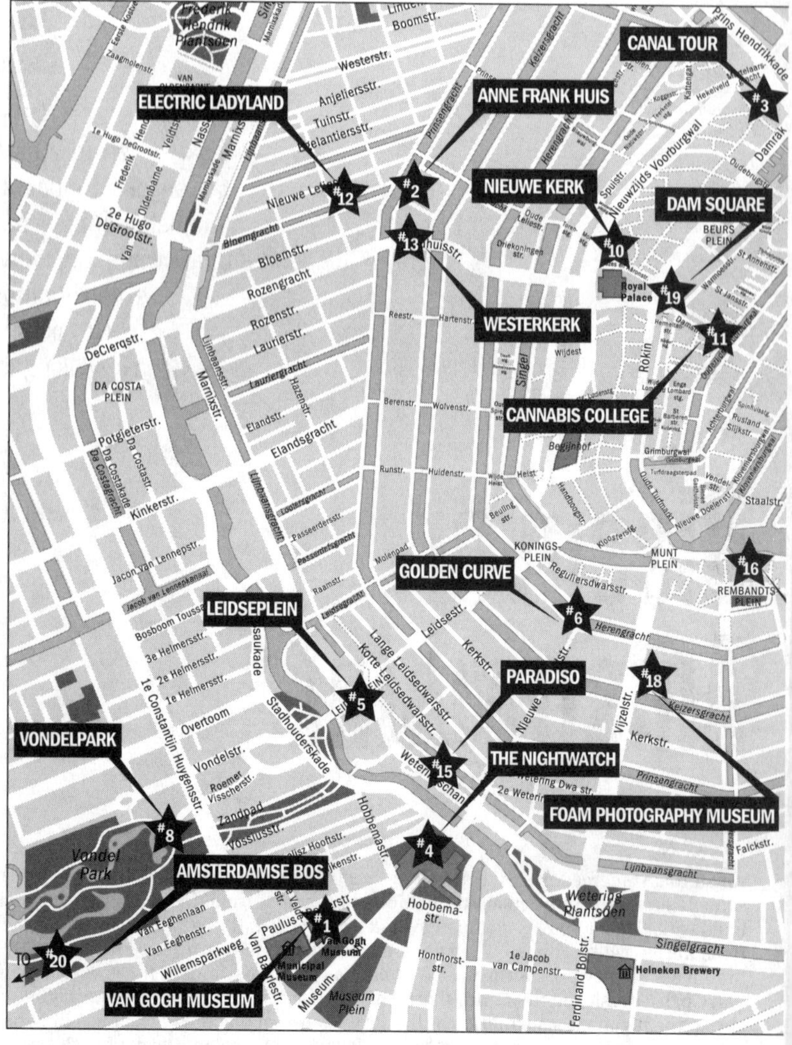

TOP 20 SIGHTS

1. VAN GOGH MUSEUM. This should be your first stop even if you're not a Van Gogh fan. More than 200 works are arranged in chronological order and divided geographically according to where Van Gogh painted (Paris, Arles, Saint-Rémy, and Auvers-sur-Oise). The museum holds *Irises*, *Wheatfield with Crows*, and *Yellow House* as well as a collection of works by the master's contemporaries (see p. 88).

2. ANNE FRANK HUIS. This museum poignantly preserves the memory of Anne Frank. Walk behind the secret, movable bookcase to enter the small rooms that sheltered the Frank family from 1942 to 1944, during the invasion of Nazi Germany (see p. 83).

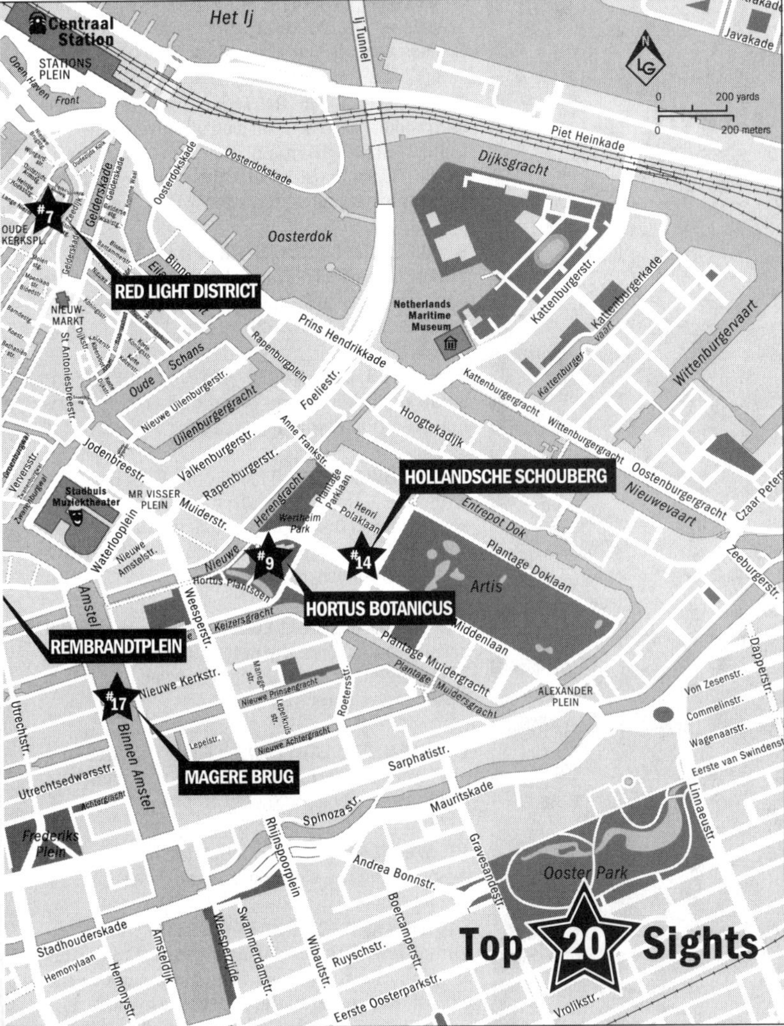

3. TAKE A CANAL TOUR. One of the best ways to see the city is by boat. Open boat tours, like the one offered by Boom! Chicago (see p. 162), are preferable, but even the most tourist-friendly ride will give you a better sense of how the city is put together. For complete listings, see p. 74.

4. THE NIGHT WATCH AND THE MILKMAID. Follow the crowd at the **Rijksmuseum** to the masterpieces by Rembrandt and Vermeer (see p. 91).

5. LEIDSEPLEIN. Night or day, this area is bustling with activity, with locals and tourists alike. Your head will spin with restaurants, bars, and clubs all clamoring for attention (see p. 61, p. 108, and p. 146).

AMSTERDAM BY NUMBERS

Official Age of the City: 698 years old in 2003.

Population: 727,095

Total Area: 212.42 sq. km

Land Area: 158.95 sq. km

Tourists per year: 17,568,000

Cars on Amsterdam's Streets: 234,134

Trams: 260

Canal Houses: 2,500

Bikes on Amsterdam's Streets: 400,000

Bulbflowers in public gardens and parks: 600,000

Canals: 165

Bridges: 1,281

Wooden bridges: 8

Skinny bridges: 1

Chinese temples: 1

Grams of pot you can legally carry: 5g

Rembrandts: 22

*Night Watch*es: 1

Van Goghs: 206

Wax statues at Madame Tussaud: 115

Windmills: 6

Cinemas: 40

6. GOLDEN CURVE. Check out the opulent houses on the stretch of Herengracht between Leidsestraat and Vijzelstraat (see p. 60).

7. RED LIGHT DISTRICT. No trip to Amsterdam is complete without a stroll through the Red Light District. Giggle at the penis fountain in front of Casa Rosso, watch the tourists watching the windows, and watch your wallet (see p. 54).

8. OUTDOOR CONCERT OR MOVIE IN THE VONDELPARK. The only thing better than free concerts and cheap movies is outside free concerts and cheap movies (see p. 64).

9. HORTUS BOTANICUS. One of the oldest medical gardens in the world makes for a relaxing afternoon detour (see p. 68).

10. NIEUWE KERK. The Nieuwe Kerk has risen from the flames time after time to throw its shadow upon **Dam Square.** Duck inside to admire some of the prettiest stained glass in the city or to see its modern art exhibits (see p. 79).

11. CANNABIS COLLEGE. Get the facts straight before you explore the soft drug culture (see p. 78). For general info on smoking, see our **Only in Amsterdam** chapter, p. 119.

12. ELECTRIC LADYLAND. The First Museum of Fluorescent Art. It's better than it sounds, and it sounds pretty good (see p. 87).

13. WESTERKERK. You'll find the best views of the city from the **Westerkerkstoren** (see p. 59).

14. HOLLANDSCHE SCHOUWBERG. This former Jewish theater rivals the Anne Frank Huis as a moving reminder of the Holocaust in the city's Jewish quarter, the Jodenbuurt (see p. 66).

15. PARADISO. No podunk bands play here. Paradiso hosts big names that have included Lenny Kravitz and the Stones (see p. 160).

16. REMBRANDTPLEIN. For the most nightlife in the city, visit the area surrounding this park. Don't forget to glance at the park itself and at the Rembrandt statue within it (see p. 149).

17. MAGERE BRUG. The most famous bridge in the city—the oldest of the city's pedestrian drawbridges and the only one that is hand-operated (see p. 60).

18. FOAM PHOTOGRAPHY MUSEUM. Count on this new museum to have the most contemporary exhibits from both established and up and coming photographers (see p. 86).

19. DAM SQUARE. Check out the national monument in Dam Square, a great place for people-watching and the best meeting point around (see p. 57).

20. AMSTERDAMSE BOS. Go beyond the touristed areas of Amsterdam to its "woods" in the south, full of lush greenery and bike paths (see p. 73).

View from Westerderk Tower

SUGGESTED ITINERARIES

THREE DAYS

DAY ONE: THE MAJOR MUSEUMS

Spend your first morning in the **Museumplein,** exploring the **Rijksmuseum** (p. 91) and the **Van Gogh Museum** (p. 88). Stop into the **Vondelpark** (p. 64) for a picnic lunch. In the afternoon, orient yourself by taking a **boat tour** (p. 74). Spend your first night out at a restaurant and at clubs in the **Leidseplein** (p. 61), dropping by the **Max Euweplein** on your way there.

Lazing About at Vondelpark

DAY TWO: CANAL RING AND NIEUWE ZIJD

If you're an early-riser, check out the **Noordermarkt** (see p. 173) in the Jordaan for organic fruits and vegetables, and walk among the stands of small birds that are also for sale. Then, move to the **Anne Frank Huis** (see p. 83), the most touristed but arguably most important stop in the city. Explore the rest of the Western Canal Ring on our "Authentic, Affordable" walking tour (p. 21). Begin your afternoon at the **Beijnhof** (p. 56), then work your way north to **Dam Square** (p. 57) for the **National Monument** and **Nieuwe Kerk** (p. 79). On your way north, stop into **Beurs van Berlage** (p. 81), the city's old stock exchange. In the early evening, stroll through the **Red Light District** (p. 54)—it can be seedy, but it's a must-see for any visitor. End your evening at one of the many high quality Nieuwe Zijd **coffeeshops** (p. 125).

Magerebrug

LET'S GO PICKS

Easiest place to get hit by a tram: Muntplein.

Best place to check your mate: playing chess at Max Euweplein.

Best obsessive fetish collection: Cat's Cabinet (p. 61).

Best place to cruise that's not a canal: Reguliersdwarsstraat.

Best high-elevation pancakes: Pannenkoekenhuis Upstairs (p. 102).

Most appropriate town in which to play dumb tourist: Zaanse Schans (p. 209).

Grooviest space shakes: Coffeeshop Goa (p. 124).

Most embarrassing museum to attend with your parents: Amsterdam Sex Museum (p. 78).

Friendliest place to smoke up: Yo Yo (p. 134).

Best Dutch brew: Wieckse Witte, a white beer from Maastricht

Best way to break a diet: *stroojpwafels*

DAY THREE: JODENBUURT, THE PLANTAGE, AND REMBRANDTPLEIN

Begin with the **Museum Het Rembrandt** (p. 95) and the **Zuiderkerk** (p. 68). Head south a towards the **Jewish Historical Museum** (p. 94) and the **Portugees-Israelietische Synagoge** (p. 66). To explore greener pastures, visit the **Artis Zoo** (p. 67). In the late afternoon, backtrack over to the northern part of De Pijp to visit the **Heineken Experience** (p. 65). Once you're slightly loaded, ramble on up to **Rembrandtplein** (p. 149) and the hottest streets for clubbing the night away.

FIVE DAYS

DAY FOUR: FLOWERS AND OUDE ZIJD

Get up early for a two-hour excursion to the largest flower auction in the world in **Aalsmeer** (p. 199). On your return to Centraal Station, stroll into the Oude Zijd to visit the **Museum Amstlekring (Our Lord in the Attic)** (p. 79), one of the city's former hidden churches. Have a meal in or just glance at **de Waag** (p. 112), the city's old weighing house on **Nieuwmarkt.** Gape at the lions adorning the **Fo Guang Shan He Hua Temple** (see p. 70), right in the heart of Amsterdam's Chinatown. Head down to Leidseplein and end your evening at **Milkweg (**p. 160**)**, one of the city's hottest clubs.

DAY FIVE: BEYOND THE CENTRUM

In the morning, head to **Westerpark** (p. 63) to hang with the locals, then walk down to the **Oude West,** one of the city's most vibrant and diverse communities. Go shopping there, or grab a bite of African, Indian, or Indonesian food. Hop on the tram or take your **bike** down to the **Amsterdamse Bos** (p. 73), a large park where you can explore to your heart's content. Finish off at the bars in **De Pijp** (p. 154).

SEVEN DAYS

DAY SIX: LOOSE ENDS

Start in the Shipping Quarter, a tiny neighborhood but one filled with some of the city's best shopping, and everybody's favorite coffeeshop, **Barney's**. Now that you know the city well, you're ready to appreciate fully the **Amsterdam Historical Museum** (p. 80). Or explore far away cultures at the **Tropenmuseum** (p. 95). Spend the afternoon at the city's photography centers: **Amsterdams Centrum voor Fotografie** (p. 77), **Foam Photography Museum** (p. 86), and **Huis Marseille** (p. 84). In the evening, visit the **Stadhuis-Muziektheater** (see p. 158) to watch an opera or ballet, or go to the **Concertgebouw** (p. 158) to listen to some first-rate classical music.

DAY SEVEN: GET OUT OF TOWN

Explore **Rotterdam** (p. 230), a city full of modern architecture and modern art, with a young and student-heavy population. Or go to **The Hague** (p. 219), The Netherlands' seat of government, to see the art, the international lawyers, and the **Vredespaleis** (p. 222). If you want to keep traveling, only an hour or so train ride will take you to **De Hoge Veluwe National Park** (p. 244) or to the fascinating caves surrounding **Maastricht** (p. 249).

Portugees-Israelietische Synagogue

AMSTERDAM BY SEASON

FESTIVALS

The **AUB (Amsterdams Uitburo)** provides tickets to and information about most events and festivals (☎900 01 91; www.uitlijn.nl; open daily 9am-9pm). It's an excellent resource, especially in the summer months, when something exciting is going on just about every day in the city.

Lion at National Monument, Dam Square

SPRING

Koninginnedag (Queen's Day; Apr. 30), nominally the celebration of the Beatrix's mum's birthday, turns the city into a huge carnival featuring mountains of food and free-flowing drinks as well as countless outdoor concerts. Also in celebration of Queen's Day is the year's largest flea market, where parrots, skulls, and glue sticks are bought and sold with equal fervor. There is also a **National Museum Weekend** (☎670 11 11), when most museums around The Netherlands are free or discounted. At the **Oosterpark Festival,** two days during the first week in May, the Oosterpark fills with people celebrating international connections over music, food, and games.

SUMMER

The **Holland Festival** (☎530 71 10; www.holndfstvl.nl) in June features more than 30 theater productions from Holland and abroad in a massive celebration of the arts. In 2003, it will take place from June 5-29. Also in June, the **Amster-**

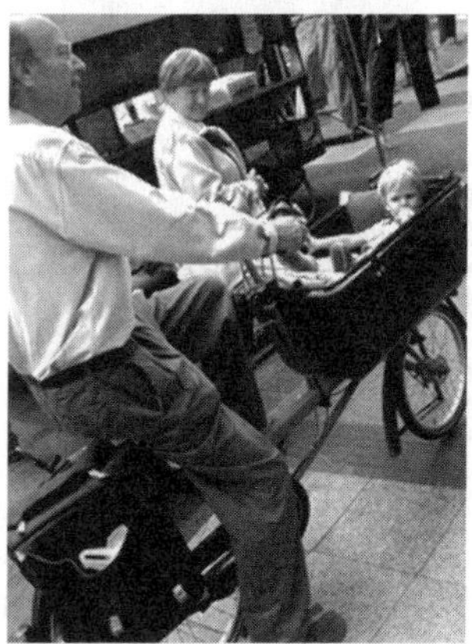

Baby in a Bike Basket

Greenpeace Building

Up by the Port

Stepped Gables

dam Roots Festival (☎531 81 22; www.amsterdamroots.nl) pays tribute to world music and culture in clubs throughout the city, while the **Drum and Rhythm Festival** celebrates, somewhat predictably, both drums and rhythms. The **ITs Festival** (International Theatre school Festival) features performances by students toward the end of June.

July and August see the start of the summer concert series at Amsterdam's Concertgebouw, while the **Grachtenfestival** in August converts the whole of Amsterdam into a venue for over 70 concert performances. **Julidans** (www.julidans.com) brings many international dance acts to Amsterdam, centering on the Stadsschouwburg and Vondelpark theater.

On the first weekend in August, gay pride comes out in street parties along Warmoesstraat, Amstel, Kerkstraat, and Reguliersdwarsstraat, and in the outrageously fun **Gay Pride Boat Parade** (www.amsterdampride.nl), when floats, boats, queens, and queers take over the Prinsengracht. During **Uitmarket** weekend at the end of August (www.uitmarkt.nl), a preview of cultural events means there are free concerts around Dam Square, Leidseplein, and the Museumplein.

There are a number of other festivals that run from June through September, including: the **Dynamo Open Air Festival, Pinkpop** (June), **Oerol** (June), **Mysteryland** (June), **Parkpop** (June), **Dance Valley** (Aug.), **Lowlands** (Aug.), **Awakenings** (Aug.), and **The Netherlands Film Festival** (Sept.).

FALL

On the first Saturday in September, the **Bloemen Corso** (Flower Parade; www.bloemencorsoaalsmeer.nl) runs from Aalsmeer to Amsterdam. Many historical canal houses and windmills open to the public for **National Monument Day** (2nd Sa in Sept.; www.openmonumentendag.nl). Later in the year, the **Cannabis Cup** (Nov., on American Thanksgiving; www.hightimes.com) celebrates the magical mystery weed that brings millions of visitors to Amsterdam every year.

WINTER

The Dutch don't celebrate as much in winter (aside from Christmas and a raging New Year's Eve party), but the upside is that you might get to go **ice-skating** on the canals.

HOLIDAYS

The major holidays in The Netherlands are: **New Year's Day** (Jan. 1); **Good Friday** (Mar. 29); **Easter**

Monday (Mar. 31); **Liberation Day** (May 5); **Ascension Day** (May 9); **Whitsunday and Whitmonday** (June 3-4); **Christmas Day** (Dec. 25); and **Boxing Day** (Dec. 26; called Second Christmas Day in The Netherlands).

THE LAY OF THE LAND AND THE WATER: AN OVERVIEW

Welcome to Amsterdam. The best way to explore the "Venice of the north" is to let the Canals be your guide. In Amsterdam, water runs in concentric circles, radiating from Centraal Station, every visitor's starting point. The **Singel** runs around the **Centrum,** the heart of the Amsterdam of legends. In a space not even a mile in diameter, brothels (the infamous **Red Light District** lies in the Centrum), bars, clubs, and tourists, tourists abound, all with a haze of marijuana smoke over them. The next three canals are the **Herengracht,** the **Keizersgracht,** and the **Prinsengracht.** The land between these three canals is known as the **Canal Ring.** A lively nightlife scene of bars and traditional *bruine cafes* can be found in this area. Farther out lie the more residential neighborhoods of Amsterdam: the **Jordaan** and **the West** (to the west), the **Plantage** and the **Jodenbuurt** to the east, and **De Pijp** to the south.

NEIGHBORHOODS

OUDE ZIJD

One of two wobbly halves of the Centrum, the Oude Zijd (Old Side) is technically the newer side of the city center. There's little question that the Oude Zijd is most famous for its better half (some would say worse), the **Red Light District.** But anyone who comes here only for the legal trappings of the area is missing half the story. While **Warmoesstraat** (incidentally one of the oldest streets in Amsterdam) and **Oudezijds Achtrerburgwal** are wall-to-wall brothels and coffeeshops, the Oude Zijd extends to include the southern end of the **Oudezijds Voorburgwal** and the **Kloveniersburgwal,** both of which are as serene and picturesque as any of Amsterdam's canals, and **Nieuwmarkt,** one of the most pleasant places in Amsterdam to enjoy a sunny afternoon. While a trip through the neon glow of the Red Light District is perhaps mandatory in any Amsterdam excursion, it would be a shame to ignore the hidden architectural gems and small but worthwhile museums that represent the more genteel side of the Oude Zijd. The Oude Zijd also includes **Nieuwmarkt,** which used to be home to one of Amsterdam's largest markets and is now a busy square where locals meet up before heading out to the many coffeeshops, restaurants, and bars in the near vicinity. It's just east of the Red Light District and centers on the **Waag.** Part of Amsterdam's **Chinatown** runs through the Nieuwmarkt area.

RED LIGHT DISTRICT

The Red Light District (bordered by **Warmoesstraat** to the west, **Zeedijk** to the north, **Damstraat** to the south, and **Kloveniersburgwaal** to the east) has existed since the 13th century. It was then that Amsterdam began its life as a seat of maritime trade. And with the inevitable comings and goings of so many lonely (and increasingly wealthy) men, the "world's oldest profession" took its roots in the city. Today, however, the Dutch themselves avoid the area like the plague; it has become overrun with tourists. Sneak a peek at all the tantalizing and titillating thrills that the Red Light District has in store, but be advised that if you decide to eat, shop, or smoke up between Warmoesstraat and Oudezijds Acterburgwal, you'll be paying twice the price for half the value. Bring an open mind, but leave your wallet at home.

NIEUWE ZIJD

The Nieuwe Zijd (New Side) gets its name from the **Nieuwe Kerk,** which lies in the southern part of the neighborhood. This side of the Centrum is technically older than the Oude Zijd, but its church, built in the early 15th century, is younger than the Oude Zijd's Oude Kerk—one of the earliest structures in the city. The Nieuwe Zijd is bordered on the east by Damrak, which turns into Rokin as it crosses **Dam Square**.

The portion of tourist schmaltz fades with each successive street to the west: **Nieuwezijds Voorburgwal,** originally constructed as a bulwark against attack just outside the city center, is now a haven of nightlife; **Spuistraat** has its share of trendy grand cafes; **Kalverstraat** reigns supreme as Amsterdam's premier shopping district; and **Singel,** named after the canal it fronts, is a mixed bag where you'll find hoity-toity restaurants not far from prostitutes beckoning from red-light-lined windows.

SCHEEPVAARTBUURT (SHIPPING QUARTER)

Amsterdam's Shipping Quarter—or **Scheepvaartbuurt,** for those brave enough to attempt the multiple vowels—occupies a narrow spit of land north of the Jordaan and Canal Ring. Centered on the **Haarlemmerstraat,** this increasingly gentrified area has its share of hip restaurants and smokeries, just outside the tourist crush of Nieuwendijk. The neighborhood is well worth the trip for its concentration of some of the best establishments and some of the nicest people you'll meet in the city. If you're here, don't miss the chance to venture just south to **Brouwersgracht,** at the top of the Canal Ring, one of the city's most photogenic canals. At the **Korte Prisengracht, Haarlemmerstraat** becomes **Haarlemmerdijk,** and the district becomes considerably more residential.

CANAL RING

You haven't seen Amsterdam until you've spent some time wandering in the Canal Ring. It's the city's highest rent district and, arguably, its most beautiful. Four main waterways encircle the western and southern sides of the old city like a corset with a little bit of give. Inside the crescent they form is most of the tourist traffic and noise of the city center, while the ring itself is a quieter, more picturesque place. Collectively, **Prinsengracht** (Prince's canal), **Keizersgracht** (Emperor's canal), and **Herengracht** (Gentlemen's canal) are known as the *grachtengordel* (literally "canal girdle"). The Ring is home to some of Amsterdam's most important and beautiful architecture.

This area of Amsterdam was first excavated to build canals in the early 17th century. At that time, the canals ended in squares, with guards who controlled traffic entering the ring. The wealthiest citizens lived here, enjoying the quiet environment and proximity to the city center. Amsterdam's appointed stone mason was Hendrick de Keyser, whose Renaissance style of architecture was the norm. This style incorporated stepped gables into the narrow canal-house design that was dictated by a general dearth of space in The Netherlands. By the middle of the century, however, two younger Dutch architects, Jason van Campen and Philips Vingboons, were rebelling against this style and pushing for a type of "citizen's architecture," one that would replace the Renaissance style—vertical accents and religious overtones included—with a Classicist design.

In this book the Canal Ring is split into two parts—the **Canal Ring West** and the **Central Canal Ring.** The split is at **Leidsegracht,** just northwest of the Leidseplein.

CANAL RING WEST

Unlike some other areas of the city, the Western Canal Ring is much busier in the day than in the night, with nothing particularly crazy in the way of nightlife. Prinsengracht, the busiest of the four canals, tends to pull in more visitors, most likely because of the numerous cafés that attract people wandering up from the **Anne Frank Huis.**

Keeping an eye on your map here is a good idea, as the scenery is similar throughout. One landmark to keep tabs on in the Western Canal Ring is **Westerkerkstoren**, Amsterdam's tallest tower, which sits at the corner of Raadhuisstraat and Prinsengracht, and marks the center of the western part of the ring.

Packing

CENTRAL CANAL RING

The Central Canal Ring is home to a stretch on the Herengracht called the **Golden Bend,** so named because of the wealthiness of the merchants who built these especially wide houses. In the 17th century, citizens had to pay a tax according to the width of their house, and houses could not be more than one plot wide. In order to encourage people to invest in the construction of the Herengracht, the city altered its laws so that a few of the very rich could build houses with expansive fronts.

From June 21-23, the **Amsterdam Canal Garden Foundation** (www.amsterdamsegrachtentuin.nl) opens up about twenty of the private back gardens to the public, and people throughout The Netherlands come to see the tiny hidden treasure of landscape (€10 for a 3-day pass); the rest of the year you can get a taste of Golden Age canal life at **Museum van Loon** or the **Museum Willet Holthuysen.**

The upscale tranquillity of the Central Canal Ring gives way in two squares—the **Leidseplein** and **Rembrandtplein**—that are action-filled centers of nightlife, restaurants, coffeeshops, and bars.

Rent A Boat

LEIDSEPLEIN

The **Leidseplein** offers some of Amsterdam's most densely concentrated—and best—restaurants and nightlife. So named because it once marked the end of the main road from Amsterdam to Leiden, the square punctuates the southern curve of the Canal Ring, just north of Vondelpark and west of the Museumplein. Leidseplein's main space also serves as a gathering point for wandering guitar and accordion musicians and other accomplished street performers.

Currant Boats

from the road

Queen of Hearts?

Researching Dam Square I learned that the crowd is a constant, gathering around whatever attraction pops up. But one buzzing afternoon in June, I came across a different sort of crowd. Although impatient, it was small. A barely noticeable group had formed around the back door of Koninklijk. I learned that a few informed citizens were hoping to catch a glimpse of the Queen.

Two less-than-still guards flanked the exit of the building, while three cops talked on their handsets. They looked more like ski patrol than secret service in their shiny white and orange body suits. At about 2:45pm, once most of the observers had already dispersed, Queen Beatrix emerged from the building, gave an ordinary wave to the devotees, and was whisked off in her souped-up Ford Taurus. The event was over before it began. Within a minute of her exit, all that remained behind the palace were a few dirt-stained pigeons and the alpine policemen. The Netherlands' queen had come and gone, barely disturbing the street's busy routine. It would appear that one of Europe's last remaining monarchs attracts less of a crowd than do the jugglers on the other side of the square.

– Stefan Atkinson

REMBRANDTPLEIN

Rembrandtplein proper consists of a rectangle of grass surrounded by scattered flowerbeds, crisscrossed by pedestrian paths and littered with half-dressed locals lazing about when weather permits. A bronze likeness of the man himself, **Rembrandt van Rijn,** overlooks the scene. It's what surrounds the area that makes it distinctive: right around the square hover all manner of bars and cafés, ranging from mid-level to upscale and all packed with people. The scene is lively but tends to be pricey. Most of the smokehouses in the immediate vicinity of the square are overpriced and overcrowded; to get high in style, walk a block or two to one of the places we've listed (see **Only in Amsterdam,** p. 132). By night, Rembrandtplein competes with Leidseplein for Amsterdam's hottest nightlife, with a particular concentration of gay hotspots. South and west of the square lies **Reguliersdwarsstraat,** often called "the gayest street in Amsterdam." It's always raining men here, though the part most popular with the city's queer community begins west of the intersection with **Vijzelsstraat.** It's home to some of the city's best nightlife (see **Nightlife,** p. 149). **Utrechtsestraat,** which extends due south from Rembrandtplein, bears a concentration of the city's best, and least touristed, restaurants.

THE JORDAAN

If, while wandering through the busy center of Amsterdam you've ever wondered how anyone could actually live in a place so packed with tourists, just head to the Jordaan to find out. It is here that Amsterdammers manage to avoid the hordes of sightseers, relaxing on a front stoop and chatting with neighbors or, in warmer weather, enjoying their dinner *al fresco*. Quiet canals and narrow streets date back to the 17th century when the area began its long stint as a working class neighborhood. Only recently has the region become a preferred perch of Amsterdam's yuppie population, making for an unusual mix of upscale eateries, down-home craft studios, and big cafes that fill up quickly in the evenings. The serene streets and unique architecture make the Jordaan ideal for strolling, especially on weekday mornings, when it's virtually deserted.

To reach this quieter side of Amsterdam, take the #13 or #17 tram from Central Station to Marxinstraat or Westermarkt, from which you can amble past calm canals and buzzing bars at your leisure. Be sure not to miss the less-traveled **Bloemgracht** canal, which is one of the nicest walks in the area, night or day.

WESTERPARK AND THE OUDE WEST

Not as traveled as more central parts of the city, the area north of Vondelpark and west of the outer Singelgracht spans several neighborhoods.

Closest to the center, the **Oud West** (Old West, bounded by Kostverlorenvaart, Hugo de Groot Kade, Vondelpark, and Nassaukade) is a far cry from the neighboring Jordaan. The area has a gritty, urban energy not found in the center of the city. With fewer bars and clubs than the Jordaan, it isn't the best place to wander at night, but during the day it comes alive. A walk down Kinkerstraat, Jan Pieter Heijestraat, or any of the other major streets reveal the dazzling regional diversity to which the area is home; Greek cafes live comfortably alongside Turkish delis and Ethiopian restaurants.

Westerpark is the opposite of its neighbor to the south. Where the Oud West has crowded, tightly-packed streets, Westerpark has winding canals and picturesque greens; where the Oud West bristles with the vibe of an urban city, Westerpark breathes easy with the relaxed attitude of sprawling suburbia. The highlight is, not surprisingly, its eponymous park, a popular place for families that draws big crowds on any sunny day. Take tram #3 to Haarlemmerplein for anything from a brisk ten-minute walk to a leisurely one-hour stroll.

Even further west lie **Bos en Lommer** and **De Baarsjes,** both residential neighborhoods with little to attract even the most curious traveler. **Rembrandtpark,** on the far edge of De Baarsjes, remains an adequate place for jogging and dog-walking.

MUSEUMPLEIN AND VONDELPARK

Outside of the Singelgracht, which encircles the wild, gritty core of the city, Museumplein and Vondelpark occupy a quieter, more gentrified area of town. The debauchery of porn shows and coffeeshops fades into civilized appreciation of art in the city's world-class museums. The three museums are dotted along the Museumplein, an open stretch of lawn that occupies about six square blocks. Behind the modest reflecting pool at one end, the **Rijksmuseum** rises up majestically. The Rijks houses Dutch art, Dutch history, and Dutch applied art (think: furniture) up through the 19th century. The **Stedelijk Museum** displays edgier, frequently abstract modern and contemporary art from the

Bike Riding

Paddleboats

By Boat

Artis Zoo

Bridges at Night

Bloemenmarkt

20th century onwards. Completing the triumvirate is the **Van Gogh Museum,** which memorializes the master who painted sunflowers and cut off his ear. A pleasant, relatively peaceful place to stay, this neighborhood offers Amsterdam's most expensive shopping and the city's classical music retreat, the **Concertgebouw.**

Amsterdammers also flock to the area for the **Vondelpark,** a popular retreat to the land of greenery. Vondelpark lies in the southwestern corner of the city, outside the Canal Ring and just a short walk from the Leidseplein. With meandering walkways and a paved path for bikers and skaters, the park draws large crowds any day of the week and literally packs them in on a nice weekend. Inside the park is the **Openluchttheater,** or open-air theater, where music and dance shows as well as film screenings go on throughout the summer. Finally, the **Filmmuseum** is home to an archive of Dutch cinemas and has screenings of movies old and new daily.

DE PIJP

Just outside the southern stretch of the canal ring, the largely residential De Pijp district teems with cheap, tasty ethnic food and offbeat treasures for the bargain shopper. The neighborhood's main drag, **Ferdinand Bolstraat,** has its share of good eateries, but De Pijp's real gem is the **Albert Cuypmarkt,** where shopkeepers hawk household wares and other sundries to huge crowds every day. The hub of **Albert Cuypstraat,** just west of the market, is packed with low-budget Cambodian, Kurdish, and Surinamese *eethuisjes* (restaurants). **Sarphatipark,** a grassy and befountained plot of parkland, lies in the heart of De Pijp.

JODENBUURT AND THE PLANTAGE

Amsterdam has always been a place of mixed blessings for the Jews, who first arrived in The Netherlands in the early 17th century. In 1579, the Treaty of Utrecht decreed that no one in The Netherlands be persecuted for their religious beliefs. So began the era of Jewish immigration—first from Spain and Portugal and later from Eastern Europe. In time, the area roughly bounded by **Jodenbreestraat, St. Antoniebreestraat,** and **Waterlooplein** gained definition as the **Jewish quarter (Jodenbuurt).** It was full of synagogues, theaters, shops, businesses, schools, and was home to approximately

55,000 Jews. The quarter eventually included wealthier areas like **Nieuwe Prinsengracht, Plantage Middenlaan,** and **Nieuwe Keizersgracht.** When the Germans invaded in 1940, however, that all changed. The Nazis steadily forced the residents of the area into isolation, deportation, and eventually mass extermination. At the end of the war, only 5200 Dutch Jews had survived and the Jodenbuurt, though still existing in name, would never be the same again.

Today, the area is home to a number of excellent museums and monuments commemorating the Jews and members of the Dutch Resistance, but also to sights like **Hollandsche Schouwberg, Stadhuis-Muziektheater, Holland Experience 3D,** and the **Museum Het Rembrandt.** In addition, the neighboring Plantage to the southeast shines with fun escapes (**Artis Zoo** and **NEMO**), interesting museums (**Nationaal Vakbondsmuseum** and **Tropenmuseum**), and pretty stretches of nature **(Hortus Botanicus** and **Wertheim Park).**

Noordermarkt

FredriksPark

Houseboat

To see Amsterdam as locals do, spend a day on **bike.** Amsterdammers bike everywhere, from work in the morning to the bars at night. Make sure to signal and to obey bike traffic lights for your own safety and for the safety of other bikers and pedestrians. Our tour starts and ends at **Frederic Rent a Bike,** Brouwersgracht 78 (☎624 55 09). His is not the only place to rent bikes; see p. 297 for more rental options.

Bike down ***Prinsengracht.*** *Turn left onto* ***Reestraat,*** *which changes to* ***Herenstraat*** *and* ***Gasthuismolensteeg.*** *Turn right onto* ***Singel.*** *Pass one bridge and go right over the next one. Continue for one block.*

1 BEGIJNHOF. This stunning courtyard full of little gardens and surrounded by handsome gabled houses provides a quiet respite from the excesses of the city. Don't miss the Wooden House, Engelsekerk, and Begijnhofkapel (see p. 56).

2 SPUI. Pronounced "spow," this square is home to an art market on Sundays, a book market on Fridays, and is surrounded by bookstores (see p. 58 and p. 172).

3 GOLDEN CURVE. Find your way back to the Canal Ring via Koningsplein, turning left on Herengracht. The stretch of Herengracht between Leidsestraat and Vijzelstraat is known as the Golden Curve or Golden Bend because of its opulent houses. Officials bent the strict house-width rules for wealthy citizens who were willing to invest in the construction of the Herengracht, or gentleman's canal.

4 DE APPEL. After gawking at Amsterdam's mansions, take a detour on Nieuwe Spiegelstraat to De Appel, Nieuwe Spiegelstraat 10. (☎625 56 51), a cutting edge art space that makes even the Stedelijk museum look old-fashioned. (See p. 86).

5 MAGERE BRUG. Continue down Herengracht to Utrechtstraat, turn left on Nieuwe Kerkstraat, and bike over the Magere Brug (skinny bridge), the oldest of the city's pedestrian bridges, and the only one operated by hand (see p. 60).

6 PORTUGEES-ISRAELIETISCHE SYNAGOGE. Once you've gone over the Amstel, turn left and bike along the river. Turn right on Nieuwe Herengracht, then left onto Weesperstraat until you hit the synagoge at Mr. Visserplein 1-3. It is a somber remnant of Amsterdam's once-thriving Jewish community (see p. 66).

7 NIEUWEMARKT. Head up Jodenbreestraat, turn left on Nieuwe Hoofstraat and right on Kloveniersburgwal until you hit Nieuwemarkt. Have a relaxing dinner at In de Waag (see p. 112). Head back to Frederic's via Zeedijk, which turns to Prins Hendrikkade and passes Centraal Station.

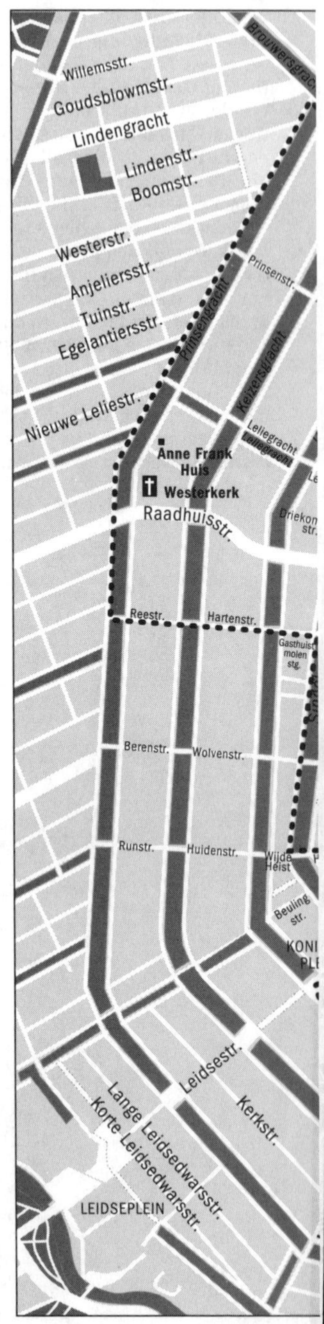

A BIKING TOUR OF THE CITY

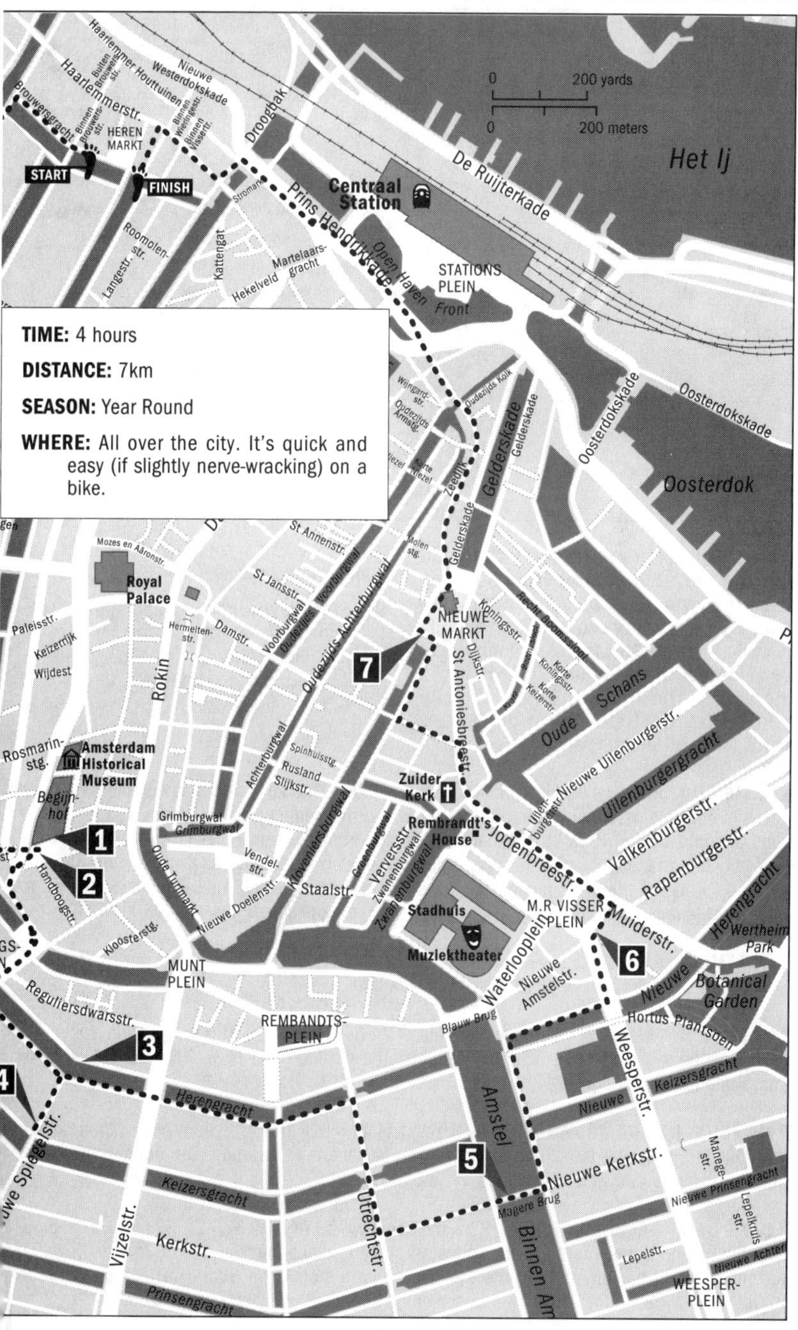

TIME: 4 hours

DISTANCE: 7km

SEASON: Year Round

WHERE: All over the city. It's quick and easy (if slightly nerve-wracking) on a bike.

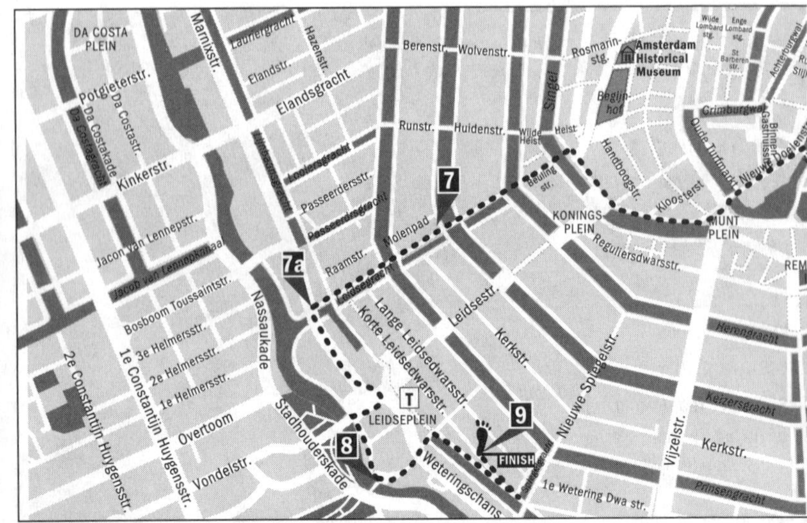

Sex and drugs aren't the only things in Amsterdam, though sometimes it may seem that way. For the gentler sophisticate, the debauchery can wear thin awfully quickly. It is with this traveler in mind that we've designed "The Sophisticated City," a trip around the southern rim of the city center that highlights some of Amsterdam's more refined pleasures.

TIME: An afternoon.

SEASON: Year round, though sunny but crisp fall afternoons are the most sophisticated.

1 ARTIS ZOO. Plantage Kerklaan 38-40 (☎523 36 11). Though a zoo may not seem too genteel, it is one of Amsterdam's greatest treasures and the perfect place to begin. Though it may seem unsophisticated to frolic with camels, Rhesus monkeys and other rare four-legged wonders, the zoo's façade of carelessness hides a darker past. During Nazi occupation the zoo served as a hiding place for persecuted Jews and for young Dutch men who were ordered to serve for Germany. (See p. 67, for more on the zoo during occupation see p. 68.)

2 WERTHELM PARK. Stop here for a moment's reflection by the postcard-worthy fountain, and see the powerful broken glass Auschwitz Memorial.

3 HORTUS BOTANICUS. Plantage Middenlaan 2A (☎625 84 11). This leafy haven away from the city holds a myriad of horticultural delights. The outdoor cafe is also the perfect place to grab a bite to eat. (See p. 68)

4 MUSEUM HET REMBRANDT. Jodenbreestraat 4 (☎520 04 00). Learn about Rembrandt's life in his former residence. While his larger and better-known paintings are not kept here, the museum is home to over 250 etchings. (See p. 95).

5 CAFE DE ENGELBEWAARDER. Kloveniersburgwal 59 (☎625 37 72). By now you're probably thirsty, and there's no more sophisticated place to slake that thirst than Cafe de Engelbewaarder. A great bar any time of the week, but If you stop in on Sunday afternoon between 4:30pm-7pm, you'll be rewarded with a scorching-hot set of live jazz. (See p. 139).

THE SOPHISTICATED CITY

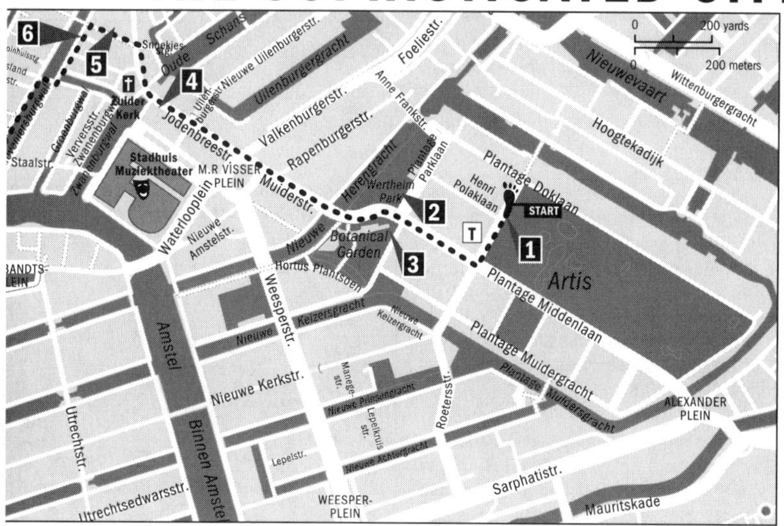

6 THE BOOK EXCHANGE. Kloveniersburgwal 58, (☎626 62 66).Swing by The Book Exchange afterwards and pick up that classic you've always been meaning to read. Owner Barry Klinger founded this haven of English-language literature just south of Nieuwmarkt almost 20 years ago, and ever since it has been growing and amassing a dedicated staff. The selection here is frightfully good for a used bookstore, and for whichever book you're searching, you're likely to find it here; out-of-print gems are tucked onto the shelves; paperbacks are very reasonably priced, or you can swap your old books for theirs. (See p. 169).

7 LEIDSEGRACHT. Stop and relax at the water's edge seats on the Leidsegracht, a less travelled but no less picturesque waterway. At the turn onto Marnixstraat, look up and notice a few lines of **Emily Dickinson** painted on the wall of the building on the corner across the street **(7a).** The poem is untitled, as all sophisticated poems are:

> To make a prairie it takes a clover and one bee,–
> One clover, and a bee,
> And revery.
> The revery alone will do
> If bees are few.

8 MAX EUWEPLEIN. Walk along the boardwalk and stretch your brain at Max Euweplein, where the two-foot high chess pieces are harder to lift, but ensure that you think before you move. (See p. 61 and p. 60).

9 ALTO. Korte Leidsedwarsstraat 115. It's been a long day, and the perfect place to end it is at Alto, where there's no cover and they're cooking jazz every night beginning at 9:45pm to the wee hours of the morning. (See p. 160).

The tour lets off close enough to **Vondelpark** and to the **Museumplein** for you to continue your jaunt there, if you still haven't had your fill of sophisticated sights. Check out what "current" old film is playing at the **Filmmuseum,** (p. 93 and p. 164) or, if it's still early, stop by the **Van Gogh Museum** (p. 88).

A STONER'S TOUR

TIME: Time just doesn't seem the same... this tour could take anywhere from a few hours to a very slow day.

SEASON: 4/20, or any other day of the year.

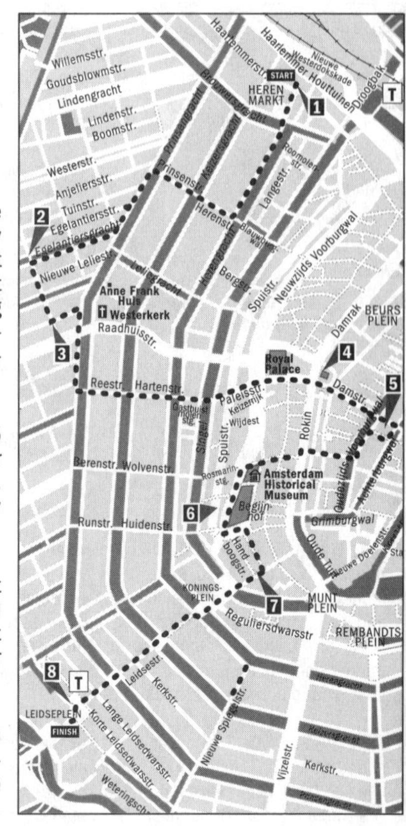

It's tempting for some stoners just to find the coffeeshop nearest Centraal Station and stay there for their whole vacation—but you're not that kind of stoner. You want to explore! But sometimes exploring can be a little confusing when you're, well, stoned. This tour offers a sampling of the city's coffeeshops as well as excellent munchies and psychedelic sights.

1 BARNEY'S. Haarlemmerstraat 102 (☎625 97 61). Wake and bake, sunshine! Start your day with a hearty breakfast and a big fat joint. Huge, greasy breakfasts served with consistently high-quality smokeables (see p. 129).

2 ELECTRIC LADYLAND. 2e Leliedwarsstraat 5 (☎420 37 76). This lesser-known museum will boggle your already-boggled mind. Florescent everyday objects and sculptures from all over the world. (see p. 87).

3 PARADOX. 1e Bloemdwarsstraat 2 (☎623 56 39). Stroll on over to Paradox to smoke a little more or just to chill. This friendly coffeeshop offers the best veggie burgers in the city (see p. 133).

4 DAM SQUARE. Stop by Dam Square, one of the city's most central points, to do some people watching and to admire the national monument (see p. 57).

5 CANNABIS COLLEGE. Oudezijds Achterburgwal 124 (☎423 44 20). Find out everything you've ever wanted to know and more about marijuana and hash. Info on its effects, its medical uses, and on the political side of international drug policy. Best of all, it's free (see p. 78).

6 RISTORANTE CAPRESE. Spuistraat 259-261 (☎620 00 59). Dine in style as you make your way south (see p. 102).

7 DAMPKRING. Handboogstraat 29 (☎638 07 05). One last coffeeshop before you begin your evening. Classy ambiance for a store that's also backpacker friendly (see p. 126).

8 BOOM! CHICAGO. Finish up at Boom! Chicago, the mecca for English-speaking tourists and ex-pats alike. See an improv. show, or if you'd like, plan ahead so you can take one of their open-air boat tours, known unofficially as smokers' tours. Because one good tour deserves another... (see p. 162).

AUTHENTIC, AFFORDABLE AMSTERDAM

TIME: 2-3 hours

SEASON: Year Round

WHERE: Canal Ring West, dipping into The Jordaan and the Nieuwe Zijd.

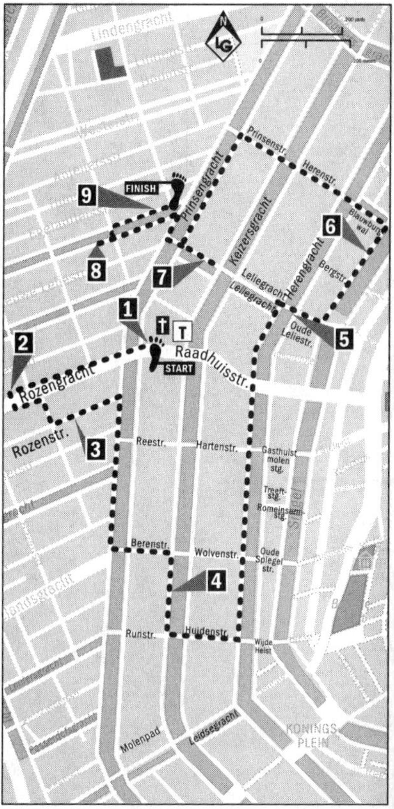

This tour will show you some of the lesser known sights on and around the Western Canal Ring.

1 WESTERKERK. Begin with a sweeping view of the city by climbing the Westetrkerkstoren, Westerkerk's tower (see p. 59).

2 REMBRANDT'S HOUSE. Not to be confused with the Museum Het Rembrandt (see p. 95), Rozengracht 184 is the house where the great artist died penniless. It's marked only by a plaque. On your way there, be sure to window shop along the Rozengracht, a street with boutiques from all over the world.

3 STEDELIJK MUSEUM BUREAU AMSTERDAM. Rozenstraat 59 (☎422 04 71). Not to be confused with the Stedelijk museum itself, this art space, run by the Stedelijk, shows the latest in Dutch art. It's free, so you won't feel bad if the particular exhibit is just too cutting-edge for the man on the street (see p. 88).

4 FELIX MERITIS. Keizersgracht 324 (☎624 93 68). Soak up intellectual headiness at Felix Meritis, the home of the society of arts and sciences in the 18th and early 20th centuries, and the headquarters of the Dutch Communist Party for a few years after World War II. Its canal-side café serves as a forum for impromptu political and intellectual conversations (see p. 59).

5 THEATER INSTITUUT NEDERLAND. Herengracht 168-174 (☎551 33 00). A fascinating museum but, perhaps more interestingly, the city's best 17th-century architectural display. The red "Bartolotti" building on the left was built in 1617 in the Amsterdam Renaissance Style. The grey house on the right was completed in 1638 and was meant to oppose the Renaissance with a new Classicist style, and the city's first neck gable– it's sweeping, rather than stepped (see p. 85).

6 CAPTAIN BANNING COCQ'S HOUSE. Singel 140-142. You may have never heard of Captain Cocq, but if you've been to the Rijksmuseum, you've almost certainly seen him. He's front and center in Rembrandt's *Night Watch.* His opulent home is a stark contrast to that of the painter who immortalized him.

7 GREENPEACE BUILDING. Keizersgracht 174-6. A smashing example of art deco, at the south-eastern-most corner of Leliegracht and Keizersgracht.

8 CLAES CLAESZOON HOFJE. Give your legs a rest at this medieval courtyard, which stands at the corner of Egelantiersgracht and 1e Egelantiersdwarsstraat.

9 SINT ANDRIESHOF. Egelantiersgracht 107-145. One *hofje* is never enough. Step behind the non-descript green door that separates Sint Andrieshof from the street and take a slow stroll around the lush greenery and the quirky architecture of the sloping roofs (see p. 62).

INSIDE:

Once in Amsterdam

WHEN TO GO

AVG TEMP (LOW/HI/MEAN)	JANUARY		APRIL		JULY		OCTOBER	
	°C	°F	°C	°F	°C	°F	°C	°F
	-9/10/2	16/50/36	-2/20/8	28/68/46	6/29/17	43/85/62	0/21/11	32/69/51

Amsterdam's weather is mild and temperate, but unpredictable. Since the area around the city is flat, there is little to prevent winds from blowing in from all directions, sweeping away morning clouds, or bringing in late-afternoon disturbances. Winters in Amsterdam are rainy, so be sure to bring an umbrella or a raincoat. The fog that hangs over the canals on spring and fall mornings, even on sunny days, is particularly romantic. These same canals can become slightly less charming in summer months, though, when they became a breeding ground for mosquitoes.

TRANSPORTATION

BY PLANE

View of Canals and St. Nick's

Red Light District at Night

Clog Boat

Amsterdam's sleek, glassy **Schiphol Airport** (☎800-SCHIPHOL or 72 44 74 65; www.schiphol.nl) serves as a major hub for cheap transatlantic flights. Major carriers include KLM/Northwest (☎800-447-4747; www.nwa.com), Martinair (☎800-627-8462; www.martinairusa.com), Continental, Delta (☎800-241-4141; www.delta-air.com), United ☎800-241-6522; www.ual.com), Air Canada (☎888-247-2262; www.aircanada.ca), and Singapore Airlines (☎800-742-3333; www.singaporeair.com).

Signs (in English and Dutch) direct incoming travelers through the arrivals halls and into the vaulted, glassy expanse of Schiphol Plaza, where tourist services abound. There's a branch of the **VVV** near the entrance to terminal 2 offering reservations, though the few attendants on duty are often quite busy and lines can be long. (open daily 7am-10pm.) You can **exchange cash** at ABN AMRO branches in the arrivals halls or in the lounge areas, or at the 24hr. GWK branch in Schiphol Plaza. For **luggage storage,** head to the lockers throughout the plaza. (Storage €3-8 per 24hr., depending on size; max storage time 7 days; AmEx/DC/MC/V all accepted. If you've misplace your belongings, as so many do in this fine city, there's a **lost-and-found** counter located in the basement between arrivals halls 1 and 2. (☎601 23 49. Open M-F 7:30am-5:30pm, Sa-Su 9am-5pm.) Schiphol Plaza also contains six international **rental car** companies, open daily 7am-11pm, and a bewildering array of shops and restaurants.

The most efficient way to traverse the 18km between Schiphol and central Amsterdam is via **"sneltrein,"** a fast, smooth, light rail connection. Purchase tickets at any of the kiosks that dot both Schiphol Plaza and the arrivals halls (one-way fare to Centraal Station €2,90; 15-20 min.), and board the trains by descending to underground platforms directly below the airport via elevator or escalators located directly in the middle of Schiphol Plaza. You can also buy tickets for destinations around Europe at the rail ticket counters in the center of Schiphol Plaza, or once you arrive at Centraal. For more information about train travel, see below. **Taxis** also make the trek from Schiphol to Amsterdam, or anywhere in The Netherlands. They congregate directly in front of the plaza. For information and reservations call 0800 0900 72 44 74 65 or go to www.schipholtaxi.nl. Fare to Centraal Station costs about €30-35.

BY TRAIN

The hub of rail transport—as well as for trams, buses, and subways—in Amsterdam is **Centraal Station,** Stationsplein 1, at the end of Damrak (international and domestic schedules available at www.ns.nl), a magnificent structure adorned with baroque carvings and ornate gables. The area immediately around Centraal Station buzzes with activity; between the backpack-toting tourists, quietly efficient locals, and assorted beggars, hustlers, buskers and preachers, it's a marvelous spot for people watching. There's a branch of the **VVV** beneath the domed expanse of platform #2 (M-Sa 8am-10pm, Su 9am-5pm), as well as coin-op **lockers** (€2-4, depending on size; 24-hr. max storage time), and a GWK bank with **currency exchange. Taxis** gather just outside the main exit on the Stationsplein.

The national rail company is the efficient **Nederlandse Spoorwegen.** (NS; Netherlands Railways; info ☎0900 92 92, €0,30 per minute; www.ns.nl.) Train service tends to be faster than bus service. *Sneltreins* are the fastest; *stoptreins* make the most stops. One-way tickets are called *enkele reis;* normal round-trip tickets, *retour;* and day return tickets (valid only on day of purchase, but cheaper than normal round-trip tickets), *dagretour.*

Eurail and **InterRail** are valid in The Netherlands. The **Holland Railpass** (US$52-98) is good for three or five travel days in any one-month period. Although available in the US, the Holland Railpass is cheaper in the Netherlands at DER Travel Service or RailEurope. The **Euro Domino** card similarly allows three, five, or ten days' unlimited travel in many European countries. Unfortunately, the Netherlands is not included in this package. **One-day train passes** cost €35,60, which is about the equivalent of the most expensive one-way fare across the country. Finally, the fine for a missing ticket on one of the Netherlands' trains is a whopping €90, so it's not worth it just to hop on a train since they didn't check your tickets on your last trip.

BY TRAM, BUS, AND SUBWAY

The best way to navigate Amsterdam's maze of canals and crooked streets is to use its highly efficient **tram system.** These above-ground streetcars traverse most of the main streets, which have tram stops every several blocks. The currency of trams is the **strippenkart,** a card with anywhere from two to 45 strips. Amster-

from the road

Canal Liberalism

Amsterdam first presented itself to me when I was a schoolgirl in the carefully edited path of the Van Gogh Museum and Anne Frank House. As I grew up, my vision of Amsterdam became shrouded by its reputation for drugs and debauchery; the city's permissiveness made it alluring, but also made it seem sleazy. Yet this year as I lived in Amsterdam I was struck by the serene order of the city. The city had legalized polemical issues like drug legalization, euthanasia and gay marriage issues that other countries fear will unleash chaos and reorganize human existence. Amsterdammers, however, have just accepted these changes with a shrug. At one point as I was biking around the city, I came upon a wedding party on a boat. A small crowd stood on the bridge, blowing bubbles and tossing rice as the boat emerged from under the arch. I was thinking what a rare privilege it was to get to celebrate a wedding on a canal when I saw that the newly married couple were two women. The boat went on its way and once again I was left with a vision of the quiet beauty of Amsterdam's canals, undisturbed by what other cultures are afraid to admit is as normal as blueberry pie.

—Catherine Burch

TASTY TREATS

For all those sweets-lovers out there, Amsterdam will surely not disappoint you. Here's a guide to the delectable candy you can buy during your trip:

Drop: This is *the* candy to have in Amsterdam. A variety of licorice that is unique to this city.

Haagse hopjes: Yummy coffee-flavored caramels that come in a cute tin container.

Stroopwafels: A cookie with two layers of thin waffles filled with a dark sugar syrup.

Pottertjes: A miniature pancake doused with melted butter and topped with powdered sugar.

Limburgase Vlaai (Flan): A pastry alternative, these are made from yeast dough and filled with fruit or creamed rice. The crust is made with a sweet dough rather than the typical short crust pastry.

Boterkoek: A buttery, solid cake normally consumed with a 10:30am coffee.

Suikerbrood: A tasty breakfast bread baked with sugar and sweet spices.

Dutch Chocolate: Amsterdam serves up any kind of chocolate you could possibly want—white, dark, or milk, with or without nuts or fruit.

dam is divided into several zones: Centrum, West, Coentunnel, Oost, Amstelveen, Zuid, and Badhoevedorp. A trip between destinations in the same zone costs two strips. You can buy a one-time strippenkart when boarding any tram (€1,40, good for unlimited trips for one hour), but if you're planning on doing anything besides toking up with the other lemming tourists who never leave the immediate vicinity of the red-light district, it's advisable to buy one of several passes. The basic options are the multiple *strippenkarts*, which allow cheaper transit when you buy strips in bulk (8-*strippenkart* €5,60; 15-*strippenkart* €5,90, seniors and kids €3,70; 45-*strippenkart* €17,40); day passes *(dagkarten)* for unlimited use in any zone (€5,20, seniors and kids €3,60); and unlimited-use passes for one week in the same zone (€20,20, seniors and children €12,80; requires a passport photo and picture ID). You can purchase bulk passes at transit centers, post offices, and some convenience stores.

The same basic system governs **buses,** which travel many of the same routes as trams as well as to more distant locations throughout greater Amsterdam. Bus service also supplements the tram, which stops running at midnight. Fare on night buses, which operate until the trams start up again, is €2, or three strips and a fee of €1,10. The **subway,** officially known as the Metro, but referred to by locals as the underground, can be useful, but only for a few locations. It heads south from Centraal Station and stops at Nieuwmarkt, Waterlooplein, and Weesperplein, and then continues outward to Amsterdam's many surrounding attractions. The zone transit system that governs Amsterdam applies to **long-distance buses** as well. You can use a *strippenkart* to travel throughout the country; the number of strips required depends on the number of zones through which you travel.

Confused? Fear not. For information (including the free and very helpful *Snelwijzer* map and a shorter line than the VVV) and all manner of passes dispensed with friendly zeal, head to the **GVB** (public transport authority), on the Stationsplein across from Centraal Station in the same building as the VVV. (Info ☎09 00 92 92; €0,30 per min.; info line open M-F 6am-midnight, Sa-Su 7am-midnight. Office open M-F 7am-9pm, Sa-Su 8am-9pm) Finally, while the tram and bus operators tend to be lax about checking your tickets, the transit cops are not. If you're caught without a valid pass, you'll be fined €29,10 plus the cost of the original ticket.

BY CAR

The Netherlands has well-maintained roadways and, unlike in the UK, the Dutch drive on the right side of the road. North Americans and Australians need an International Driver's License; if your insurance doesn't cover you abroad, you'll also need a green insurance card. On maps, a green "E" indicates international highways; a red "A," national highways; and small yellow signposts and "N," other main roads. Speed limits are 50km per hr. in towns, 80km outside, and 120km on highways. Fuel comes in two types; some cars use benzene (about €1,40 per liter), while others use gasoline (much less, at €0,50 per liter). The **Royal Dutch Touring Association** (ANWB) offers roadside assistance to members. (☎0800 08 88). For more info, contact the ANWB at Wassenaarseweg 220, 2596 EC The Hague (☎070 314 71 47), or Museumplein 5, 1071 DJ Amsterdam (☎0800 05 03).

Blue Bridge

BY BIKE

The long, flat spaces that connect the cities of the Netherlands, as well as the compact streets that snake through the cities themselves, make cycling an ideal mode of transport. Amsterdam's streets teem with bikes, which most young people and even many older, professional types prefer to cars. The city's streets all have bike paths, which can be easily navigated if you follow some basic rules.

First, observe and follow all street signs and stop lights. Amsterdammers violate these with impunity, thanks to instincts born of years of experience. Because you do not have this experience, if you fail to observe the road rules carefully, you may find yourself in an unexpected meeting with a tram or car. Second, remember the basic rule that you must yield to all traffic coming from the right, whether car or cycle. Third, always stay on the right side of the road. Fourth, be careful of tram tracks. They're just wide enough for bike wheels to become wedged in between; if you do find your bike stuck in them, don't linger while a tram bears down on you, just get away—better to lose your bike than your bike and your life. And five, be sure to signal all turns and stops, ensuring that you don't get rear-ended by an unassuming truckdriver.

Finally, lock your bike. No, wait: always, always lock your bike. Bike theft is rampant in Amsterdam, especially for junkies, who steal and then resell bikes to fund their habits. All rental bikes come with locks and keys; use them even

View from Roof of Metz & Co.

Skating Backwards in Vondelpark

when you stop for a few moments. The majority of thefts take place when riders briefly leave their cycles to snap a photo and fail to lock them while they do so. And keep in mind that most bike insurance does not cover bikes that are stolen with the key left inside; you have to produce the key to avoid getting charged the full amount. Especially if leaving your bike locked for an extended period, ensure that it is placed in a quiet and safe spot, as locks are not entirely effective in deterring bicycle theft.

Bike rental shops abound, but not all are created equal. Your best bet, especially for a longer trip, is **Mac Bike**, with three locations across the city, although you will have to endure the honking sign on the front of every bike (www.macbike.nl; Leidseplein, ☎528 76 88, take tram 1, 2, 5, 6, 7, or 10; Mr. Visserplein, ☎620 09 85, take the metro, any line, from Centraal to Waterlooplein; Centraal Station, 33 Stationsplein, ☎625 38 45; all three open daily 9am-6pm). They rent for €6,50 per day, and an amazing €2,50 for every day past 6. Also offering good deals is **Rent-a-Bike Damstraat**, just off Dam Square, with rentals from €7/day and €31/week (Damstraat 20-22; ☎625 50 29; www.bikes.nl; open daily 9am-6pm). Another good option, although a bit of a hike from the city center, is **Amsterdamse Bos** (Nieuwe Kalfjeslaan 4; ☎643 14 14; www.amsterdamsebos.amsterdam.nl), with €7/day rentals and second-hand bikes on sale from €100. Take the bike for a day around the large green space, or venture to nearby Aalsmeer for a view of flower country. Take bus #172 from Centraal, Dam, Westermarkt, Marnixtraat, Leidseplein, Museumplein, or Stadionplein (45 min., 5 strips from Centraal).

BY THUMB

Hitchhiking can be an effective means of transit, but on the roads out of Amsterdam there is cutthroat competition. Nobody hitchhikes in Amsterdam proper. For more info about hitching, visit www.hitchhikers.org. *Let's Go* does not recommend hitchhiking.

KEEPING IN TOUCH

MAIL

Post offices are generally open M-F 9am-6pm, and some are also open Sa 10am-1:30pm; larger branches may stay open later. Mailing a postcard or letter to anywhere in the EU costs €0,54; to destinations outside Europe, postcards also cost €0,54, letters (up to 20g) €0,75. Mail takes 2-3 days to the UK, 4-6 to North America, 6-8 to Australia and New Zealand, and 8-10 to South Africa. Mark envelopes "air mail," "par avion," or "per luchtpost" or your letter or postcard will never arrive (surface mail and mail by sea take one to four months at best). To send an international letter, there's no need to go to a post office; just drop it into the *overige* slot of a mailbox.

TELEPHONES

Almost every pay phone in the Netherlands requires a "Chipknip" card. You can buy them almost anywhere (hostels, train stations, tobacconists), for as little as €4,54.You insert the card into the phone before you call and then place the call; you can't just enter a calling card number, even if it's 0800. It is possible to use a calling card, you just need to gain access to the phone system via a chipknip card; so if you have a calling card that gives you good rates, just buy ONE chipknip card and you'll never need another. With Chipknip cards, international calls are cheapest at night (8pm-8am). For directory assistance, dial 09 00 80 08; for collect calls, dial 06 04 10. International dial direct numbers include: **AT&T,** ☎0800 022 91 11; **Sprint,** ☎0800 022 91 19; **Australia Direct,** ☎0800 022 20 61; **BT Direct,** ☎0800 022 00 44; **Canada Direct,** ☎0800 022 91 16; **Ireland Direct,** ☎0800 02 20 353; **MCI WorldPhone Direct,** ☎0800 022 91 22; **NZ Direct,** ☎0800 022 44 64; **Telekom South Africa Direct,** ☎0800 022 02 27.

TIME DIFFERENCES

Amsterdam is one hour ahead of Greenwich Mean Time (GMT), and two hours ahead during daylight savings time. Amsterdam is six hours ahead of New York and Toronto, nine hours ahead of Vancouver and San Francisco; at the same time as Johannesburg, Rome, and Paris; two hours behind Moscow, eight behind Tokyo, and nine hours behind Sydney. The Netherlands observes daylight savings time, and fall and spring switch over times vary.

INTERNET

Internet is fairly easy to find in Amsterdam (for listings, see the Service Directory, p. 302), though it may be more difficult to find places to save information to disks or email from them. Also be aware that although Easy Everything is cheap, convenient and has way too many computers for there ever to be a wait, it is not staffed. Watch your belongings and know how to use a computer.

TOURIST, FINANCIAL, AND LOCAL SERVICES

Every town in The Netherlands has a VVV, or Dutch tourist office. While the resources at these offices—brochures, maps, and tickets—can be helpful, the employees rarely are. Be prepared for long lines and possibly poor English speakers. For more specific information on the VVV and other tourist services, see the Service Directory, p. 304.

SAFETY & SECURITY

PERSONAL SAFETY

EXPLORING. To avoid unwanted attention, avoid the typical tourist profile; don't speak English loudly and try to avoid wearing a camera around your neck. Familiarize yourself with your surroundings before setting out, and carry yourself with confidence; if you must check a map on the street, duck into a shop. If you are traveling alone, be sure someone at home knows your itinerary, and never admit that you're traveling alone.

When walking at night, stick to busy, well-lit streets. If you feel uncomfortable, leave as quickly and directly as you can, but don't allow fear of the unknown to turn you into a hermit.

Chinatown Temple

Biking Around Town

Centraal Station

Playground at Artis

Street Basketball

Glasses Shop

DRIVING. If you are using a **car,** learn local driving signals and wear a seatbelt. Children under 40lbs. should ride only in a specially-designed car seat, available for a small fee from most car rental agencies. Study route maps before you hit the road, and if you plan on spending a lot of time on the road, you may want to bring spare parts. If your car breaks down, wait for the police to assist you. For long drives in desolate areas, invest in a cellular phone and a roadside assistance program. Be sure to park your vehicle in a garage or well traveled area, and use a steering wheel locking device in larger cities. **Sleeping in your car** is one of the most dangerous (and often illegal) ways to get your rest.

CON ARTISTS & PICKPOCKETS. The bottom line is **Don't ever let your passport and your bags out of your sight.** Beware of **pickpockets** in Amsterdam crowds, especially in the Red Light District, near Centraal Station and on public transportation.

ETIQUETTE

While Amsterdam is known for its tolerance, it is important to be respectful of Dutch customs and traditions.

SMOKING (TOBACCO)

Typically, restaurants will allow their patrons to smoke cigarettes while dining. Thus, do not expect a smoke-free environment when eating out. Also, like many other European cities, many of the natives smoke. That being said, the anti-smoking campaign is picking up steam due to health concerns. Some employers allow their workers to smoke while working, but increasingly, this trend is becoming less common as companies look to make the workplace a healthy place. Look for designated smoking areas if you are in one of these buildings and the urge to light up hits you.

DRUGS

Yes, marijuana and other soft drugs are tolerated in Amsterdam, but along with experimentation comes the need for responsibility and respect. Just as you wouldn't want to pass out in your parent's living room, be sure to regulate your drug intake so as not to look like a lame tourist. Remember, this is their country, and as a guest, you should be on your best behavior. Refrain from smoking up outside; not only is this an even easier way to pick out a tourist than a camera around one's neck, but it can be seen as offensive. Be sure to ask if it's okay to smoke before lighting up. You may only carry up to 5g. of soft drugs on you at one time. In coffeeshops, drugs may not be advertised in the open, so you will have to ask to see a menu. Also, coffeeshops are legally not allowed to cause a nuisance or disturbance, so if you are being rowdy, you might be asked to leave. For more information see Only in Amsterdam, p. 120.

LOVE FOR HIRE

A walk in the Red Light District will make it abundantly clear that prostitution, which exists in every country the world over, is legal in Amsterdam. All of the prostitutes that you see belong to a union called "The Red Thread" and are tested for HIV and STDs, although testing for these is on a voluntary basis. While it's okay to sneak a quick peak, or even a longer one if you wish, **do not** take photos unless you want to explain yourself to the angriest—and largest—man you'll ever see.

Here are the basic do's and don'ts:

First, be sure to show the women basic respect. Looking is fine, even necessary, but leering and catcalling are absolutely uncalled for. Keep in mind that prostitution is an entirely legal enterprise, and windows are a place of business. Second, show up clean and sober. Prostitutes reserve the right to refuse service to anyone. Third, be sure to be extremely clear and straightforward in your negotiation. Specifically state what you get for the money you're paying—that means which sex acts, in what positions, and especially how much time you have in which to do it. Window prostitutes are self-employed and consequently can set their own prices. Moreover, they aren't required by any means to do anything you want; they must consent to it beforehand. Fourth, don't make trouble. If anyone becomes violent or threatening with a window prostitute, they have access to an emergency button that sets off a loud, noisy alarm. It not only makes an ear-splitting noise, it also summons the police, who invariably side with prostitutes in disputes. If you feel you have a legitimate complaint, head to the **Prostitution Information Center** (see p. 119) and discuss it with them. Fifth, don't ask for a refund if you're not satisfied. All sales are final in this business. Sixth, always practice safe sex. A prostitute should not be expected to, and indeed will not even touch an uncondomed penis.

GENERAL BUSINESS HOURS

Most shops are open M-F 9am-6pm, and generally open late at night on the weekends. During holidays and the tourist season, hours are extended into the night and shops open their doors on Sundays. Post offices close at noon on Saturdays and remain closed on Sundays. Lunch is typically served starting at 11am and ends at 3pm; dinner is served from 5:30pm to 11pm.

GENERAL MANNERS

If you plan to venture out into the streets of Amsterdam, before you brush up on your Dutch, brush up on your manners. Remember to always say "please" and "thank you," and be advised now, this polite exchange could last longer than you are used to. While dining in a restaurant, it is customary to turn one's cell phone off.

TAX AND TIP

The value added tax and service charges are always included in bills for hotels, shopping, taxi fares, and restaurants. If you buy an expensive item like a diamond, you are probably eligible for a tax refund. Keep your receipt and fill out a form at the airport. Tips for services are accepted and appreciated but not necessary.

No server in Amsterdam expects a 15% tip, although it would most likely be appreciated. 10% is more normal and taxi drivers are generally tipped that much as well. Bouncers in Amsterdam clubs are often tipped €1-2 as patrons leave the club.

INSIDE:

Life & Times

Alas, it's not sex, drugs, or rock 'n' roll—the keystones of Dutch history are far less exciting: technology and geography. The Dutch say that though God created the rest of the world, they created The Netherlands. The country is a masterful feat of engineering. Since most of it is below sea level, vigorous pumping and many dikes were used to create dry land, making civilization possible. The first inhabitants of the area lived in **terpen** (mounds) built to keep the sea under control. Once the inhabitants had moulded the land into a livable form, the port city of Amsterdam became of central importance in European trade. Today, Amsterdam's myriad dikes and canals remain a testament to the architectural genius of the Dutch.

AMSTERDAM'S BEGINNINGS

The Romans claimed The Netherlands as part of their empire around 57 BC, colonizing the Celtic **Belgae,** one of the three tribes they found in the area. They ignored the remaining two tribes, the Germanic **Frisians** and **Batavi,** deciding that the mostly marshy area that they inhabited was worthless. The Frisians and Batavi were eventually granted the status of allies with Rome, but these bellicose tribes had difficulty with the idea of foreign rule. However, the deterioration and fall of the Roman Empire soon alleviated the need for an organized struggle. Roman attempts to dam the land or build canals from 12BC-AD 50 were useless, as the area retained the qualities of a marsh. The historian Pliny even went so far as to call their home "wretched" in AD 50.

XXX—NOT AS RACY AS YOU THINK

While some speculate that the triple cross pattern on Amsterdam's shield (and on every *amsterdammertje*—the capped metal poles that separate the streets from the sidewalks) has something to do with the city's liberal attitudes towards sex, the truth is far less sensational. The three crosses represent the crucifixion of Andrew, patron saint of fishermen and fishmongers. Given the role of the sea in the development of Amsterdam's prosperity, the symbol was a fitting choice.

The Romans finally left the area that is the modern-day Netherlands in AD 406 after an invasion by Germanic tribes. Most of the Roman influence was lost—a less complex agrarian society based on small clans replaced the technocracy of the Romans. During the 5th century, the Franks replaced the Romans as the reigning imposters. **Clovis,** king of the Frankish Merovingian tribe, was converted to Christianity; the religion soon permeated the north of Europe. **Saint Willibrod** became the first **bishop of Utrecht** in the beginning of the 8th century. Utrecht was one of the most important Dutch towns in the spread of Christianity (see p. 238). The Frisians killed St. Boniface in 754 in a last feeble attempt to resist conversion, but by that time they had very little power and soon converted.

In 800, Charlemagne's forces took control of Amsterdam and the surrounding area. He saw himself as retaining the legacy of the Roman emperors who had ruled hundreds of years earlier. The empire had no specific capital, so Charlemagne sometimes stayed in The Netherlands at his palace in Nijmengen. Though Charlemagne ruled in name, the country remained more or less under Frankish control until 1519. Even as Charlemagne gained legitimacy when the Pope crowned him the First Holy Roman Emperor, local officials in the Low Countries were much more influential than their distant emperor. Romanesque churches remain in the city, cultural remnants of this window of light in the Dark Ages.

The rule of Louis I after Charlemagne's death saw the decline of the Carolingian empire. The area's newfound independence left it open for the **Vikings** to attack and plunder. Viking danger abated after the 900s; the peace allowed towns in the Low Countries to flourish. Principalities including **Flanders, Hainaut, Brabant, Liège, Utrecht,** and **Groningen** asserted their independence. Their gradual consolidation of power was aided by the entry of the **Burgundian dynasty** into the area. The system of **feudalism** in the Low Countries developed in the 11th century. Caught in the conflict between the French and the English, the **Battle of Bouvines** in 1214 put Flanders firmly under French control.

THE EMERGENCE OF AMSTERDAM

In spite of the slow development of the Low Countries (Belgium, Luxembourg, and The Netherlands), the area that is now Amsterdam was not truly populated until about 1270. In that year, the inhabitants of the mouth of the **Amstel River** built the first dam between the dykes of the preexisting river to keep the sea waters at bay. The name of the city comes directly from the phrase "Dam on the River Amstel." The town, under the control of the province of Holland (the northwest province of today's Netherlands; for more on Holland, see p. 199), grew as maritime trade flourished between northern Europe and Flanders. The earliest document with the name "Amsterdam" on it is a 1275 record that allowed the port of the city to charge a tariff for trade. The city gained its **charter** in 1306. By the end of the 15th century, Amsterdam had become the largest and most important town and port in Holland. For more on the history of the city's slow emergence from the sludge, see p. 39.

THE PROTESTANT REFORMATION AND EIGHTY-YEAR WAR

In the 15th Century, many people in central Europe were unhappy with the excesses of the Catholic Church. When Martin Luther pasted his 95 Theses on the door of a church in Wittenburg, Germany in 1517, his ideas were not new. **Erasmus of Rotterdam,** the humanist scholar, was said to have influenced Luther. While his ideas were not identical to those of Luther, Erasmus was blamed by the Catholics for having influenced him, and by the new Lutherans for not being similar enough to them. His particular dilemma foreshadows the years of uncertainty and religious turmoil that would follow the Reformation in Erasmus's home country, Holland.

While the Protestant Reformation swept the Low Countries, the Spanish took over Amsterdam in 1519. In 1543, Spanish king **Charles V** created the **Political Union of The Netherlands** as part of his mission to conquer the world. This union was composed of present-day Belgium, Luxembourg, and The Netherlands but was not to last. Only a few decades later, it collapsed due to religious differences. **Philip II,** the new king of Catholic Spain, tried to squelch the Protestant Reformation brewing in The Netherlands. The Dutch did not take kindly to this overbearing and meddlesome king and revolted in 1572. While the Dutch provinces varied in the specifics of their religious demands, the **Pacification of Ghent** was signed in 1576, guaranteeing religious freedom and uniting the Low Countries. The city of Amsterdam remained loyal to the Spanish king and hesitated to join the Dutch rebellion led by **William I,** Prince of Orange. In 1578, in a bloodless defeat, the Spanish and many of the members of the Roman Catholic community were

Oldest Wooden Building in Amsterdam

Brown Bar

Chinatown Storefront

The Indonesian Side of the Story...

Sometimes an explanation like "The Dutch colonization of Indonesia contributed to the financial success of the Golden Age" just doesn't do justice to the effects of imperialism.

The Portuguese, who had colonized the country briefly, left Indonesia with some ruins, a few street names, and about five serious Catholics; the Calvinist Dutch, on the other hand, monitored by the **Dutch East India Company,** were more successful (and brutal) colonizers. Military force and exploitative diplomacy gave the Dutch a trade monopoly and funneled all profits away from locals. A "divide and subjugate" strategy created power imbalances among increasingly Dutch-dependent local rulers.

The Dutch East India Company went bankrupt in 1799, but the Dutch, intent on trade, stepped in to pursue what came to be known as the **Dutch East Indies.** The Dutch set up an administration with compliant local rulers as middlemen. The early 20th century saw the creation of the **Ethical Policy,** aimed at improving education and public health and bringing Indonesians closer to European ideals. Indonesians began organizing themselves by religious or ethnic identity and political ideology. Trade

continued next page

deported from Amsterdam. The city returned to the Dutch fold, by then deeply rooted in Protestantism—specifically the strict, ascetic Calvinism. This period was known as the **Alteration.** Any remaining Catholics in Amsterdam were forced to practice in hiding, as their public worship areas were confiscated by the Protestants (see p. 80). On the other hand, the town of Antwerp had fallen to Spain during the war. The resulting Dutch exodus from that town to Amsterdam resulted in a surge in the city's intellectual and cultural energies. The immigration of Jews from Portugal, Germany, and Eastern Europe to this more tolerant city added to Amsterdam's cosmopolitan flavor.

The end of the Eighty-Year War brought with it economic prosperity, taking to heart that old adage, "what doesn't kill you only makes you stronger." In 1579, the **Union of Utrecht** solidified this new state of the **United Provinces of The Netherlands.**

THE GOLDEN AGE (1609-1713)

The seeds of The Netherlands' future commercial dominance were laid around 1600, when three ships set sail from Amsterdam bound for **Indonesia.** Like the first few drops of a massive rainfall, they were but a small harbinger of what was to come. During the first half of the 17th century, while Rembrandt van Rijn was securing the country's place on the artistic map, two newly established commercial trading companies were securing it on the global scale. Because of its fortuitously situated northern ports, The Netherlands were prime to assume the reigns of a quickly expanding global trading enterprise. Both the Verenigde Oostindisch Compagnie (VOC) or **Dutch East India Company,** and the Westindisch Compagnie (WIC) or **West India Company,** founded in 1602 and 1621, respectively, began creating a vast network of Dutch trading posts throughout Southeast Asia, West Africa, and South America.

The VOC was the larger of the two companies and established major trading posts in India, Indonesia, Thailand, China, Sri Lanka, and Bengal. The Dutch became colonizers of Indonesia, which didn't gain its independence until 1949. The WIC did a brisk business in slaves, gold, and ivory off the western coast of Africa, as well as establishing busy ports in Brazil and Surinam, which didn't win independence from the Dutch until 1975. The WIC even had a brief stint beginning in 1626 as the colonizers of **New York** (previously **New Amsterdam**), which Peter Minuit purchased from the Native Americans for 60 guilders. Dutch governor Peter Stuyvesant tried to whip the city's residents into obedient Calvinism until the British took over in 1664. The Dutch preeminence in global trade would last until the end of the 17th century, when both the English and the French wrested control through war.

One of the primary engines behind the expanding success of the Dutch global enterprise was the arms industry. Because of the standardization of the Dutch army during the Eighty Years' War, the need for regular weaponry increased, and, following independence, the rest of Europe sought to obtain these vaunted Dutch arms for themselves. It was these weapons, both in their use and their sale, that made possible The Netherlands' rise to world power.

As a result of this new-found glory, Amsterdam became both the commercial and social capital of Europe. In this age of economic prosperity, aristocrats, merchants, and financiers built homes along the canals and revitalized the city. Its population swelled from 50,000 in 1600 to 200,000 in 1650. Of course, much of this swell was due to increased immigration, from Europe and elsewhere, that further stimulated the already exploding economy. It's a fact that serves as a poignant counterpoint to today's far-right Dutch politicians who are eagerly seeking to stop the influx of immigrants.

ALL GOOD THINGS COME TO AN END

Years of war with Britain were not helpful in keeping the Dutch Golden Age afloat, but perhaps even more detrimental to The Netherlands was peace with it. When the 1688 Glorious Revolution in England dethroned James II, **William III of Orange** (Stadholder of the United Provinces) was asked to take the British throne with his wife, Mary. The Dutch were not opposed to this—the country, and powerful Amsterdam specifically, had become increasingly skeptical about William, who had waged a constant war against France. Now The Netherlands had an ally in England, but the result of the alliance was that England was to focus its naval strengths in the war against France, while The Netherlands focused its land powers. This lead to the neglect of the Dutch navy—the country's strongest asset. With the navy went the Golden Age.
Meanwhile, the differences between Amsterdam's social classes had gradually widened. By the late 18th century, in reaction to the conservatism of the reigning Dutch monarchy (William V took power in 1759), the **Patriot movement** grew in size and influence. The Patriot movement embodied the French Enlightenment ideals that were sweeping across all of Europe at the time

cooperatives and Communist parties became vehicles for political action, but internal conflicts prevented the formation of a united nationalist movement.

The stage was set for the rise of the **Partai Nasional Indonesia (PNI),** a nationalist party founded in 1927 that practiced civil disobedience and was led by charismatic **President Sukarno.** Bahasa Indonesia, the national language, was adopted in 1928 to further an increasing sense of rebellious national unity.

During WWII, Japan defeated the Dutch and invaded Indonesia for its rich oil deposits. Indonesians welcomed the Japanese for liberating them from European control, but soon discovered that incorporation into the **Greater East Asia Co-Prosperity Sphere** was a fate worse than Dutch rule. Power again changed hands as Japan's 3½-year brutal regime ended with their surrender to the Allies in 1945. Eager to take charge before the Dutch returned, Sukarno declared independence several days later. The Dutch had hoped to restore their former colonial empire, but, to their dismay, they found a mobilized and chaotic population willing to fight for the newly declared **Republik Indonesia.** The **Indonesian Revolution** (1945-50) further unified the nation against the Dutch, who for once quietly bowed out. By 1950, the Dutch, embarrassed by international criticism, officially transferred sovereignty to Indonesia.

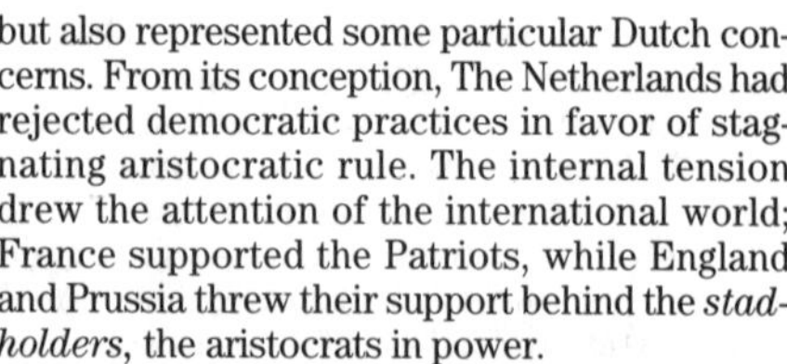

but also represented some particular Dutch concerns. From its conception, The Netherlands had rejected democratic practices in favor of stagnating aristocratic rule. The internal tension drew the attention of the international world; France supported the Patriots, while England and Prussia threw their support behind the *stadholders*, the aristocrats in power.

BATAVIA? WHAT'S THAT?

Fuelled by the momentum of the French Revolution, French forces swept through The Netherlands and brought it under their control by 1795. The territory, then known as the **Batavian Republic,** began the process of political modernization, the democratization for which the Patriots had so long fought. In 1813, after Napoleon's seemingly unending string of military victories finally began to wane, The Netherlands returned to autonomous rule. Ruled by King William I, the Kingdom of The Netherlands was declared in 1814. William sought to maintain control over all of the Low Countries, but Belgium declared its independence in 1830. So great was William's disappointment that he abdicated from the throne soon after Belgian secession. Today, the Dutch government is still a constitutional monarchy, with Queen Beatrix on the throne. For a more personal view of Beatrix, see p. 12.

WORLD WAR TWO

On May 10, 1940, Nazi Germany invaded The Netherlands. The Germans defeated the Dutch forces within a week by bombing much of the country. The Germans occupied the country for most of the war, flooding its delicate lands to make it more difficult for the Allies to invade Germany. Almost as bad as the German occupation was the famine that hit the city late in the war. The Dutch created a clandestine, though largely unsuccessful Resistance movement.

Anne Frank, famous for the diary that she kept during her time in hiding, lived with her family in the "secret annex" of her father's warehouse in Amsterdam. Her diary traces a young girl's experience of persecution. After two years in the annex, the Frank family was found and Anne was taken to the Bergen-Belsen concentration camp, where she died. Her covert existence in a cramped annex illustrates the tragic atrocities of World War II. Now open to the public, the Anne Frank House highlights the inhumanity of World War II and the generosity and courage of some individuals in the Dutch Resistance movement (see p. 83 and p. 82).

KILLING ME SOFTLY...

On April 11, 2001, The Netherlands became the first country in the world to legalize euthanasia. The Dutch Senate voted 46 to 28 in favor of the groundbreaking new law. While assisted suicide has been tolerated in the country for centuries, this newest legislation frees doctors from potential prosecution when they adhere to the government's very strict set of criteria for performing the act.

There is widespread support for the euthanasia law in The Netherlands, though the government has received criticism from both domestic and international anti-euthanasia groups.

Newer, more conservative governments are threatening the law, proving that nothing is sacred as far as liberal policy is concerned.

EMERGING FROM THE MUD

The History of Amsterdam's Canals

One might say that Amsterdam, referred to by some as the "Venice of the North," is absorbed with water. The city, which is almost as renowned for its aimlessly wandering canals as its aimlessly wandering smokers, is laced with waterways that bear constant testimony to the structural history of this waterlogged capital. That history, as well as that structure, has been riddled with floods and defects, as well as engineering marvels that embody humanity's iron (and wooden) grip over nature.

The city's mythology claims that Amsterdam was founded by two fishermen when their boat and their dog ran aground at the mouth of the Amstel river. These two men, who appear alongside their adventurous pup on the city's coat of arms, set about building the dam after which "Amstelredam" (Dam on the river Amstel) was named. Unfortunately for the blossoming city, the dykes that held back the North Sea broke in 1287, and what used to be farmland was drowned in the newly formed saltwater bay, the Zuiderzee (South Sea).

The Dutch started the seemingly desperate and multi-century-long task of reclaiming their land from the ocean. The basic system they worked with has not changed much even as technology has advanced. First, dykes are built up around the land one wishes to reclaim, known as the "polder." The most Dutch of all Dutch symbols—the windmill—is then used to pump out water from these polders. Today, electricity or diesel-driven pumps do the job.

The dry land is flushed with fresh water to remove salinity and ensure its value for crop production. Crisscrossing ditches are dug to drain out water from heavy rain, tides, or sea seepage, and surrounding canals are built to drain excess water to lakes and other areas. The resulting land, the "polderland," is incredibly rich and fertile.

But back to the history: In the 14th century, locks were added to the canals, allowing small vessels to reach the city interior. This, along with Amsterdam's position on the country's main waterways, heightened its position as a leading port city. By the 17th century, after Portugal was annexed by Spain in 1580 and the Dutch East Indies Company was founded, Amsterdam had firmly established itself in international trade and built the ring of canals for which it is now famed.

The port's importance faded away by the 1840s, but the economic downturn was nothing compared to the environmental upheaval to follow. The storms and floods of 1916 were so violent that the Dutch began a major project to reclaim the entire Zuiderzee. From 1927 to 1932, a 30.5km (19-mile) long Barrier Dam, called the Afsluitdijk, was constructed, turning the Zuiderzee into the Ijsselmeer, the freshwater lake on which Amsterdam now sits.

Winning this coastal battle has had its environmental downside as well. Before the Zuiderzee was dammed, the area was a large tidal sink through which water flowing up and down the English Channel and North Sea could drain. Now, without this outlet, the local sea level outside the Ijsselmeer Dam is rising, particularly during high tide. The rising tides put extra stress on the polders and dykes on which the city itself rests. The polders become waterlogged and must be constantly drained, causing them to become dry, compacted, and effectually to sink. The dykes that ring the polders face the danger of collapse due to wear and the stressing pull of the tides. In a country 27% of which is below sea level, none of this can be good news.

Margot Kaminski writes for Lilith Magazine.

in recent news

Shifting Right

Since 1994, Holland's center-left Labor Party has had top perch in the country's coalition government. But in 2002, following the assassination in May of firebrand politico Pim Fortuyn, the Dutch right swept the elections. The Christian Democratic Party–a right-leaning group that led the government from 1977 to 1994 but had fallen out of favor for eight years–stormed in and took first-place in the elections, snaring 43 of Parliament's 150 seats. The Pim Fortuyn List, formerly helmed by its spiritual leader and founder, took second; and the smaller, but still conservative, VVD took third. The three parties form the most conservative government The Netherlands has seen in almost a decade, under new Prime Minister Jan Peter Balkenende.

The hottest issue of debate is unquestionably that of immigration, which is the Dutch link to rising crime rates. Voters have become frustrated with center-left governments that do little to stem the tide of crime; these same voters largely blame high immigration, which comes mainly from the Middle East and North Africa.

Continued next page

Yet Anne Frank and her family's experience was not typical—for the most part the Dutch did not hide their Jews. Latent anti-Semitism, shrouded for years by the tolerance for which the Dutch are so famous, suddenly took hold. Fewer Jews from Amsterdam survived (less than 10%) than in any other Western European city; 70,000 were taken to their deaths. Though many buildings in the Jodenbuurt (Jewish Quarter) survived, the area was left empty as its residents were first isolated and then shipped off to Westerbork (p. 249), a holding camp near Groningen, and then later to Death Camps farther east. Recovery from the war was gradual. The country had to rebuild many of its cities. However, by the 1950s the country, if not all of its citizens, had recovered.

THOSE CRAZY 1960S

Amsterdam was at the forefront of the radical movements that sent the entire world reeling in the 1960s. Public demonstrations kept the streets alive, although the causes—environmental and social—were often not the free-lovin' free-for-all that one would imagine. **Robert Jasper Grootveld,** founder of a movement called "PROVOS" (an abbreviation of *provocatie*, meaning "provocation"), began an anti-smoking campaign in which he spray-painted over cigarette ads with the letter K, for the Dutch word *kanker*, or cancer. His style of protest influenced the anti-war demonstrations in the United States. Some remnants of the Provos movement remain in the Spui (see p. 58). The Provos also disrupted the wedding of Queen Beatrix to ex-nazi Claus van Amsberg in 1966 (see p. 46).

In another frenzy of edgy Dutch radicalism, people fought for the **White Bicycle Plan,** a proposal to put 20,000 bicycles into the city for shared use. While the plan was less than successful (people just took the white bikes and painted them some other color), they did leave a legacy of environmental conscientiousness, and Amsterdam is a city of cyclists.

THE 1970S AND 1980S: HOME SWEET HOME

Housing problems in Amsterdam began after the World War II and continued through the 1970s. The city council's plans to build metro lines involved kicking out residents in the Nieuwmarkt area and moving them to the suburbs. The occupants refused to budge, and police had to resort to tear-gas and brutality finally to remove them. While the metro line was finally constructed in 1980, housing continued to be a problem for the following decade.

The **squatters' movement** (see p. 146) in Amsterdam became a significant political force in the 1980s; during its strongest moments, over 20,000 people occupied buildings without authorization. On April 30, 1980, the day of Queen Beatrix's coronation, squatters organized huge demonstrations against the lucrative spending on royal residences. Once again, violence broke out in the streets of Amsterdam.

Soon the squatters realized that change was better effected through politics. When the 100 squatters living in the old Wyers building learned that their home was to be was to converted into a hotel, they prepared counter-proposals to present to the city council. Though their proposal was unsuccessful, they succeeded in creating a voice against gentrification, and their eventual eviction was without violence.

AMSTERDAM TODAY

The Netherlands suffered the same post-war economic difficulties as the rest of war-torn Europe. The Dutch economy recovered in the 1950s. The 1960s saw tremendous social and cultural upheaval. It was in this decade that Amsterdam and The Netherlands acquired their libertarian reputation. The Dutch tradition of tolerance is upheld today—the use of soft drugs, for example, is tolerated by the Dutch government. Though soft drugs are highly regulated in the attempt to create the safest environment possible, Amsterdam has now become a mecca for soft drug use and experimentation.

Amsterdam and The Netherlands continue to play a disproportionately large role in international politics relative to their geographic size. The Netherlands was an original member of the **European Union (EU),** formed by the Maastricht Treaty signed in 1991. The Netherlands is also the home to the **United Nations' International Court of Justice,** which is in The Hague (see p. 219).

In recent years, The Netherlands has taken on a role of an entirely different stripe: that of international arbiter. The International Court of Justice, housed in the Vredespaleis (Peace Palace) in The Hague, has overseen disputes between sovereign nations since 1946. Its 15 judges are elected to nine-year terms by a special assembly of the United Nations. Its highest profile defendant has undoubtedly been Slobodan Milosovich, former leader of Yugoslavia now on trial for his "ethnic cleansing" of Albanians.

One of the most unique aspects of the country—but one of the least remarked on in the pop-

However, the incoming government's plans range far beyond simply cracking down on immigration policies; many of The Netherlands highly-touted liberal policies are expected to come under stern review. There will be an immediate examination of the recently passed law legalizing euthanasia, and there are also plans to severely cut social welfare spending. Most significant for visitors, however, is that the new government wants to take a hard look at so-called "drug tourism" and explore ways to curb it.

The Netherlands, of course, is not alone in its fast and major shift to the right. Across Europe, especially in France, Italy, and Spain, rising crime and general voter discontent have led to resounding and often surprising victories for conservative (and often extremely conservative) parties and candidates. All this is happening in the context of the further consolidation of the European Union. While the seventeen member nations are attempting to systematize their laws and practices, a minor but nevertheless contentious issue is that of marijuana legalization. As the EU seeks to have a universal law, its many countries will have to come to an agreement on the status of the popular drug, which could have ramifications on Amsterdam's deeply-rooted cannabis culture.

the local story

Gay Amsterdam

Richard Keldoulis, who was born in Australia but moved to Amsterdam 10 years ago, currently helps run Pink Point (see Sights, p. 63).

Q: How do you like the city?
A: It's a great city, very small, very international, it's very liberal of course; being gay is really easy here. It's got all the advantages of a small city and none of the disadvantages; it's not provincial.

Q: Do you think, in general, that the people of Amsterdam are as accepting as the laws? Are people's beliefs a reflection of the legislation?
A: It's probably the best city in the world as far as tolerance is concerned, but it's not perfect. The center of the city is pretty good, but as you go a bit out in the suburbs, and outside of Amsterdam and the big cities, it's less good. Homosexuality is pretty much accepted in a lot of areas. In Australia, you have no idea who's gay or not; here, it's just standard that everyone is out.

Q: What are your thoughts on Pim Fortuyn [an openly gay but extremely conservative politician]?
A: Personally, I hated his politics, and everything he stood for. [*Laughs.*] But he did some good things, and he was gay. He was loved by people who would normally be beating gays up. On the other hand, he brought out a lot of intolerance.

Continued next page

ular press—is its coalition government, in which no one party gains absolute control of the electorate. The makeup of the coalition is determined by which parties fare best in the parliamentary elections; from the most popular party emerges the Prime Minister. In the 1960s, the coalition was led by the Roman Catholic People's Party, which has since faded into obscurity. From 1977-1994, the Christian Democratic Party (CDP) remained in power until it was upset in 1994 by the left-leaning Labor Party. Recent times have seen a move back to the right, and the CDP returned to the top spot following the 2002 elections (see p. 40). This shift to the right was best characterized in that political hand grenade Pim Fortuyn, who died by an assassin's bullet in May 2002.

As for religion, the government of The Netherlands continues its history of tolerance and upholds the doctrine that freedom of religion is a fundamental right. Church and state are separate and individuals have the right to practice as they wish provided their actions do not harm others. The tolerance comes from strange roots, however, as it is the Calvinist attitude, some say, that drives it. Since Calvinists believe in predetermination and in keeping to themselves, historically they don't stick out their necks—either to help people or interfere with their sins. However, the Liberal governments that created the modern Dutch welfare state would disagree with this claim.

PAINTING

The Dutch have a long and varied history in art. Dutch painters are responsible for the departure from the International Gothic Style, the development of the Northern Renaissance, and even the creation of oil painting. In general, Dutch paintings reflect the country's Calvinist tradition. They are characterized by attention to the everyday over religious iconography. Golden Age Dutch paintings are surprisingly small, because they were made for private homes instead of being commissioned by the church.

VAN EYCK

One of the most famous Dutch painters, Johannes van Eyck (1390-1441), is the prime example of how northern European artists differed from their southern counterparts during the Renaissance. He achieved the illusion of nature by paying close attention to details rather than idealizing it as did the southern painters. Toward this end, van Eyck invented **oil painting.** This medium allows the artist more control over the painting and results in a glossy finish. Critics have suggested that he likely used live models, as his paintings depict such sincerity.

The Betrothal of the Arnolfini, van Eyck's most famous painting, from 1434, shows an everyday scene of two people being promised to each other. He was likely present at the actual event and may have served as a sort of notary—the words "Johannes de eyck fuit hic" (Johannes van Eyck was here) appear on the back wall of the painting. This painting is also a precursor to Velazquez's *Las Meninas*, as the mirror in the back of the room shows a reflection of the scene along with the painter, hence beginning the tradition of the "painting of a painting."

Van Eyck departed from the International Gothic style in his attempt to show reality for what it was. Consequently, his figures appear less graceful but more real; he added more observations but also neglected perspective. To see van Eyck paintings, visit the Rijksmuseum (see p. 91).

GOLDEN AGE

The **Golden Age** of the 17th century was one of the most glorious periods in Dutch painting. During the Reformation, people in the North began to question whether painting should continue at all, as Protestants objected to pictures of religious figures or artwork in religious places. As a result, northern painters began to lose their source of income, while the southern painters (still commissioned by the Catholic Church) continued using religious themes. Thus, the Dutch turned to portraiture and painting everyday scenes. As the need for the non-religiously themed paintings diminished, painters soon started painting pieces independently rather than at the discretion of wealthy patrons or the Church, as was the custom.

REMBRANDT

Rembrandt van Rijn, one of the most famous and talented artists in history, is looked upon by the Dutch with a significant amount of pride. Born in 1606 in Leiden, he was part of a new generation of artists that established the **Realist Movement** whereby artists tried to show the world around them as they actually saw it. He enrolled in the University of Leiden but soon discovered his true passion: painting. He left the university for Amsterdam and married a wealthy woman who supported him for much of his life.

He became a portrait painter and quite successful. However, after his wife's death, his popularity plummeted and he found himself in the

Q: Do you feel that tourists who come here are accepting and tolerant of homosexuality?

A: Well, I notice from the kiosk, we get a lot of people walking by and laughing. [But] I always think that tourists are quite open-minded; they're on holiday, they're relaxing, they expect something like this in Amsterdam, so it kind of fits into their picture of how the city is. Even people that you'd imagine would be quite anti-gay, they're usually fine; you know, stumbling into a gay kiosk...it's very funny sometimes, people that don't realize it's gay, and suddenly they realize it's gay, grab the kids and run. [*Laughs.*]

Q: Do you think it's unfair that marijuana, prostitution, and gay marriage are all lumped together when foreigners discuss Amsterdam, even though gay marriage is really a civil rights issue?

A: Yeah, maybe, but it is funny that Holland is so bleeding on all those issues, but we've got a new government coming in anyhow, so it's going to be very conservative here. Whether things will change and turn back, gay marriage won't be, but things like marijuana laws might be. It's been really liberal; Amsterdam has got its own mentality, it's sort of different from the rest of Holland, it's always been very separate and had its own thing.

SOFT DRUGS AND ROCK 'N ROLL

The Changing, Controversial History of Tolerance

Holland is legendary for tolerance of drugs, prostitution, and alternative lifestyles. Prostitution and gay marriage are legal, and although marijuana is not, it is till tolerated in limited quantities (see page p. 120). Some attribute the lax attitude as a historical way of avoiding chaos among the hundreds of territories of which Holland was originally composed. But it was not until 1976, when the Dutch parliament revised the Opium Act and distinguished between hard and soft drugs, that Holland's best-known form of permissiveness came about.

Since The Netherlands began liberalizing drug policy in the mid 1970s, it has become the sweetheart of NORML (the National Organization for the Reform of Marijuana Laws) and legalization movements everywhere. Meanwhile, it has incurred the wrath of drug warriors, most recently Clinton drug czar Barry McCaffrey whose tirade against Dutch drug policy included the false claim that the Dutch murder rate is twice as high as in the United States (it is one-fourth as high).

French President Jacques Chirac joined McCaffrey in the mid-1990s, blaming France's narcotics problems on Dutch drug laws, even though only two percent of marijuana in France originated in The Netherlands. Ironically, Chirac's criticisms came at a time when Dutch authorities were tightening regulations. The attacks shocked many Dutch, who view alcohol as much worse vice. According to a 1999 report from the Dutch Ministry of Health, Welfare, and Sport, "the social and health damage that results from alcohol abuse and alcoholism…is many times greater than the damage resulting from drug abuse."

The Dutch are hardly lax when it comes to hard drugs. Recent surveys show that 7 percent of Amsterdam residents over age 12 have used Ecstasy. Dutch authorities are cracking down hard on production and use of Ecstasy and of other synthetic drugs, just as the U.S. and other countries do. More than 300 seizures were reported in 1998, over thirty production sites were closed, and traffickers were stripped of their financial assets.

Like the U.S., the Dutch are strict on hard drug use, but they wage a different kind of "war on drugs." When it comes to individual users, the Dutch view hard drug use not as criminal behavior, but as a public health problem. To fight and regulate hard drug use, police have cornered the market by regulating coffeeshop sale of marijuana, and municipal authorities embrace "harm reduction" and "demand reduction."

Despite criticism from the U.S., France, and others, many European countries are slowly beginning to move toward the Dutch model of decriminalization. Britain recently announced that it will no longer arrest individual soft-drug users, citing thousands of wasted on-duty hours. While the 1961 Convention on Narcotic Drugs, which classifies pot as a drug "with high abuse potential and no medical value," still prevents nations from formally legalizing marijuana without violating international law, countries like Switzerland who are not signatories are considering moving in that direction. The Swiss States Council (the upper house of parliament) voted to decriminalize pot in 2001. Although the lower house has yet to follow, several Swiss cantons have already decriminalized the drug for anyone over 18. "Coffeeshop" style establishments and the sale of cannabis have begun to proliferate.

Despite these trends, U.S. officials still cling stubbornly to the "gateway theory," remaining adamant that marijuana is intrinsically a dangerous stepping-stone to harder drugs. But statistics from the Dutch Ministry of Health, Welfare, and Sport tell a different story. According to a recent report, 15.6 percent of Dutch citizens 12 and over have tried marijuana compared to 32.9 percent of Americans; likewise, only 2.1 percent have used hard drugs compared to 10 percent of Americans. It appears that the combination of regulated tolerance, hard drug prohibition, and a public health approach to drug abuse is showing some results. More of The Netherlands' neighbors may soon be taking note.

Sasha Polakow-Suransky writes for the American Prospect Magazine.

depths of bankruptcy, which consumed him for the remainder of his life.

While other artists kept extensive records of their work and research, Rembrandt instead painted a series of self-portraits ranging from the time of his youth until right before he died. These serve as an autobiographical account of his life and his development as an artist. As a Realist, he broke free from the dominant practice of idealizing human subjects and did not try to hide his plainness. Sometimes he dressed in elaborate costumes that he bought as antiques. This is hard to tell when looking at his paintings today, as most people are not familiar with 17th-century attire.

In all of his paintings, Rembrandt studied the subject with a high degree of scrutiny and expressed what he saw with honesty. Rembrandt dug deeply into the essence of his subjects, showing us both the good and the bad traits of the person. Upon exposing his subject on his canvas, he declared his paintings done, as they had achieved their purpose.

Critics have always commented on the reality of his paintings; he tended not to paint the famous but rather the common person, often using his Jewish neighbors in the Jodenbuurt as subjects for his paintings.

He is most famous for his *chiaroscuro*, an Italian word for "light and shade." With every angle of light that illuminates his canvas or brush stroke, he reveals to viewers yet another emotion expressed in the face. While he does not use very bright colors—some perhaps would even assert that his paintings are dark—the absence of bright colors adds more depth to paintings and even a degree of mystery. One of his most famous paintings, *The Night Watch* (1642), currently resides in the **Rijksmuseum;** see p. 91. To learn more about Rembrandt's life, visit the Museum het Rembrandt, p. 95.

VERMEER

One of Rembrandt's contemporaries, Johannes Vermeer (1632-1675) is known for painting everyday scenes with a magnificent attention to detail. A slow worker, he studied every angle and curve of his subjects so as to better mirror nature on the canvas. One of his most famous paintings, *The Milkmaid*, shows a woman in a Dutch household performing the simple and ordinary task of pouring milk. What the painting, and most of Vermeer's other paintings, lacks in creativity of subject is more than made up with its honesty.

De Gooyer Windmill in its Urban Setting

Architecture

The Golden Bend

Dutchland?

Ever since World War II, the Dutch have displayed a certain uneasiness when it comes to Germany. You'll never meet a Dutchman happy to hear how much the Dutch language sounds like German. No one wants to have the number one, *een* (ane), pronounced like the German *ein* (eye-n), mainly because the Germans occupied the country throughout World War II, shipping off over 70,000 of the nation's Jews to concentration camps and destroying dikes to flood the land and slow Allied progress. Though relations are friendly now, it took years for war wounds to heal.

The Dutch government demanded German territory as a safety precaution and actually acquired almost 70 sq. km with 10,000 German inhabitants before normalizing the borders in 1963. It was not until 1969 that a German head of state paid an official visit to The Netherlands, laying a wreath at the National Monument on Dam Square and at the Hollandsche Schouwberg in memory of the victims of the Holocaust. Princess Beatrix's decision to marry Claus von Amsberg, a German who had served in the Nazi army during the war, caused a Dutch uproar. But Prince Claus has been a wonderful diplomat, winning the respect of the Dutch along the way. The Netherlands also tasted sweet revenge when they beat West Germany in the semifinals of the European Championship after losing the World Cup to them in 1974.

Vermeer is the master of painting interiors and light. He cuts walls off when they become unnecessary, yet shows them on each side to box in the gently-lit subject. He produced very few paintings, only 33 of which survive (he produced a third as many children). Vermeers in Amsterdam can be found in the **Rijksmuseum** (see p. 91), which holds *The Milkmaid* (1658), *Woman in Blue Reading a Letter* (1664), and *The Little Street* (1658), Vermeer's only street scene.

HALS

Frans Hals (1580-1666) was one of the artists most greatly influenced by the religious turmoil in The Netherlands. He and his family fled from the southern Netherlands to Haarlem to escape religious persecution. Hals carved out a special place for himself in the art world by conveying both the spirit of the situation he painted as well as an intimate portrayal of the subject.

In his *Pieter van den Broecke*, we see how he captured his subject in what appears to be an instantaneous moment, adding a sense of familiarity. While his paintings appear to be done with quick brushwork and in a somewhat haphazard fashion, upon closer reflection one sees the calculated effort Hals made to bring the subject to life. His *The Merry Drinker* (1630) appears in the **Rijksmuseum** and serves as an example of the expressive painting perfected by Hals. Hals and Rembrandt both favored group portraits and shared a painting technique characterized by coarser, "unrefined" brush strokes.

POST-IMPRESSIONISM AND VAN GOGH

A few centuries later, **Vincent Van Gogh** (1853-1890), born in Zundert, created a collection of paintings of an intensely personal style. His **post-Impressionist** work is characterized by bright, often harshly contrasting colors, painted on with thick brush strokes, as witnessed in his *Self-Portrait* and *Starry Night* (both from 1889).

Van Gogh settled in Arles, France, in the last years of his life; he captured the dry, sunny landscape outside and the bright colors of the interiors of Provençal homes in works such as *The Harvest* (1888) and *The Bedroom at Arles* (1888). The mental illness that led him to cut off his own ear is perhaps one of the most famous examples of psychosis; his derangement ultimately resulted in his suicide in 1890. For the most extensive collection of his works, visit the Van Gogh Museum (see p. 88).

PRIMARY COLORS: MONDRIAN'S WORLD

Twentieth-century Dutch painting was dominated by the bright colors of **Piet Mondrian's** works. By the end of his career, Mondrian's style had evolved into one in which forms were reduced to horizontal and vertical elements, exemplified, for example, in *Composition in Red, Black, Blue, Yellow and Grey* (1920).

Mondrian's work and his search for purity of artistic essence was representative of the *De Stijl* ("the style") movement, which not only encompassed painting but also the worlds of sculpture, architecture, and design.

CRAZY MODERN TIMES

What Mondrian contributed in terms of simplicity was countered by **M.C. Escher**'s zany and illusory drawings. Escher drew circular staircases and waterfalls without end and created tessellations that gradually morphed from polygons into living creatures. Art in the post-WWII era was marked by the group of writers and artists who called themselves **COBRA,** after their native towns of Copenhagen, Brussels, and Amsterdam. COBRA member **Karel Appel** painted in a bright, simplistic style similar to that of Joan Miró or Paul Klee.

ARCHITECTURE

All of Amsterdam is an architectural wonder. The complexities of building a city on top of marshland have resulted in a testament to innovative architectural planning and execution. For example, canal houses were built with many large windows to help reduce the weight of the building on top of instable topsoil. Tall, narrow houses were constructed on an angle to allow large pieces of furniture to be hoisted through the windows. The **hooks** that served as pulleys still stick out from just about every canal house.; some are still used. By the middle of the 16th century, a law was passed to limit the angle at that a house could be built to prevent buildings from falling into the streets.

At first glance, all the streets in Amsterdam look alike, just rows upon rows of narrow houses. A closer look reveals architectural elements dating from different epochs. Medieval houses were constructed with timber and clay, but as locals wised up to the dangers of fire, they began to build with brick. The only remaining elements of medieval construction are the timber facades of Begijnhof 34 and Zeedijk 1. The Herengracht has wider houses in the area called

Waterloo with Mozes & Aaronkerk

Carved Doorway

Named Shutters

the local story

An 'Other' Perspective

We interviewed an employee of MarocNet, an Internet shop in the south of De Pijp run by and primarily for) Moroccans in July 2002. He requested that his name not be used.

Q: When did you move to Amsterdam?

A: 13 years ago.

Q: Do you feel you experience any discrimination or exclusion from the Dutch people?

A: Sometimes, but all over the world you see something happen like this. I didn't make [trouble] before with someone but I see it happen. People look with their eyes; you are a foreigner from Morocco, from Turkey.

Q: Do you think there is an element of Dutch culture that is resistant to foreigners?

A: Yeah, of course, it happens all over the world, people put their own people first. Pym Fortuyn said, "our people must be first." They see white as power.

Q: What did you think of Pym Fortuyn?

A: Until 3 months ago, nobody heard about him, nobody talked about him. The publicity made him. Before, I never heard about him. Some people say Pym Fortuyn had a Moroccan boyfriend who didn't want to marry him and it's finished that way. He hated Moroccan people, or all Muslims.

the **Golden Curve**—city officials bent the rules and let wealthy merchants build wider houses to support the construction of the canal.

Like other European artists of the period, Dutch architects drew their inspiration from the Italians during the **Renaissance. Henrick de Keyser** (1565-1621) left the greatest Renaissance mark on the city, designing the **Zuiderkerk,** the **Westerkerk** (see p. 59), the **Noorderkerk,** and the **Bartolotti House,** now the **Theater Instituut Nederland** (see p. 85). His work was characterized by rich ornamentation.

In reaction to the decadence of the Renaissance came the **Classicism** of the 17th-century **Golden Age.** Classical Dutch houses resemble Greek and Roman temples, with columns and decorative scrolls. The clean, crisp Classical austerity was exemplified by the designs of **Adriaan Dortsman** (1625-82), who constructed, among other buildings, the **Museum van Loon** on Keizersgracht (see p. 87). The 18th century heralded an interest in French design and architecture; complicated Rococo decorations adorned houses.

Every visitor to Amsterdam has seen at least one work by 19th-century architect **Pierre Cuypers** (1827-1921). His **Centraal Station** and **Rijksmuseum** demonstrate a fusion of Gothic and Renaissance styles. **Hendrik Petrus Berlage** (1856-1934) was known as the father of modern Dutch architecture. His vision of spartan and utilitarian design frowned upon frivolous ornamentation. For Berlage and his **Amsterdam School,** decoration had to function to support a building and not merely cover up its supports, like in Rococo ornamentation.

Luckily for the city of Amsterdam, members of Berlage's school still preferred some creativity in their individual works. One of the most spectacular works created by **Amsterdam School** members **Piet Kramer** (1881-1961), **Johan van der May** (1878-1949), and **Michel de Klerk** (1884-1923) is the **Scheepvaarthuis** (Shipping House), in which shipping companies could conduct their business. The building's design incorporates the street to resemble a ship's bow (see p. 71).

FILM

The Dutch film industry suffers from a lack of funding and an international Dutch-speaking audience. Despite these constraints, a number of gifted directors have left their marks on the world of cinematography. Prominent Dutch directors include **Marleen Gorris** (1948-), whose *Antonia's Line* (1995) won an Oscar for Best Foreign Film. **Johan van der Keuken** (1938-), known as JVDK to his fans, studied as a photographer and filmmaker in Paris before beginning a long career producing short films devoted to the "perception of reality." **Joris Ivens** (1898-1989) was both a masterful documentary director and an innovative cinematographer. One of Ivens' most notable works is *Rain*, a 15-minute film capturing rainfall in Amsterdam, which took four months to produce.

Rotterdam (see p. 230) is the center of the Dutch film industry, edging out the capital city due to its greater accessibility and rivalling aesthetics. International directors also flock to film in Rotterdam; of most recent interest is *Who am I* (1998), starring **Jackie Chan.** The Netherlands is home to several prominent film festivals, including the International Film Festival in Rotterdam (every January), The Netherlands Film Festival (every September), the Holland Animation Film Festival (November 2002), and the CINEKID—the International Children Film, TV, and New Media Festival Amsterdam (every October).

THEATER

Since the Dutch film industry has been at times threadbare, Dutch actors have turned their efforts toward theater. Dutch theater has consequently seen rich talent throughout the years. A history of outdoor performances greatly benefitted the popularity of Dutch theater. Since the 1960s, avant-garde and experimental theater has flourished in Amsterdam. Today, with over 14,000 theater performances annually in Amsterdam, live drama continues to boom. The scene is characterized by the prominence of many small companies. The **Theater Instituut Nederlands** (p. 85) chronicles the history of Dutch actors and the stage. The **Hollandsche Schouwberg,** on the edge of the Jewish quarter in Amsterdam, was a popular venue for Dutch plays and operettas before World War II (see p. 66).

LITERATURE

In terms of international recognition, Dutch literature faced the same problem as Dutch film or theatre: the language barrier. Fortunately, *Gijsbrecht van Aemstel* (1637) and *Lucifer* (1654), by playwright and Amsterdam native **Joost van den Vondel,** are available in English translation. These plays, both tragedies, figure among the most prominent of the Dutch Renaissance. Perhaps the most brilliant representative of Golden Age literature is **Pieter Corneliszoon Hooft** (1581-1647), now the namesake of Amsterdam's highest-rent shopping street, near the Museumplein. Hooft, a poet and playwright, went to Italy and was strongly influenced by the Renaissance there, bringing the style back to his hometown of Amsterdam.

LGB History: A Time Line

The oldest group for gays and lesbians in Europe, the COC (the full name of which means Dutch Association for the Integration of Homosexuality) has been working for over fifty years to expand the rights of gays and lesbians in The Netherlands. Here's a short history of gay rights in Holland:

1950s- The COC begins to organize small meetings where gays and lesbians first obtain the right to dance together.

January 27, 1971- Repeal of distinction between homosexual and heterosexual legal age of consent.

October 22, 1973- Repeal of homosexuality as grounds for rejection from the military. The move is soon followed by the creation of a subsidy for social inquiry into the causes of discrimination against homosexuals.

1981- Dutch Parliament states that those discriminated against on the basis of homosexuality can be granted political asylum in Holland.

1992- Discrimination against homosexuals on the basis of their sexuality is made illegal.

November 14, 1998- Homosexual parents are granted the right to adopt children.

December 19, 2000- The Netherlands becomes the first country in the world to grant full and legal marriage rights for same-sex couples. The provision went into effect on April 1, 2001.

The **Multatuli Museum** in Amsterdam (see p. 85) celebrates the life and works of **Eduard Douwes Dekker** (1820-1887), who took **Multatuli** (Latin for "I have suffered greatly") as his pen-name. Multatuli wrote during the 19th century and used his experiences in the Dutch East Indies as material for his writing. *Max Havelaar*, his most famous work, is the story of an official's attempts to expose the exploitation of the natives in the Dutch colonies in Indonesia. *Max Havelaar* was a criticism of both Dutch imperialism and of stagnating, self-satisfied Dutch attitudes in The Netherlands. Needless to say, Multatuli's attempts to protect the natives of the Dutch East Indies was not appreciated by colonial authorities.

Twentieth-century Dutch literature is extraordinarily diverse. The atrocity of World War II prompted a surge of literary works, both reflective and accusatory. The most famous is the diary kept by **Anne Frank** as she and her family were in hiding in Amsterdam (see p. 83).

In a completely different vein, one of the best-selling works of Dutch writing in the 20th century is entitled *The Happy Hooker* (1971). Written by **Xaviera Hollander** (1942-), the book chronicles her experiences as a call girl in the United States. Hollander later continued to popularize Dutch writing by putting her skills to use at *Penthouse* magazine. Mainstream modern authors include **Harry Mulisch** (1927-), who wrote *The Assault* (*De Aanslag;* 1982), a story about life in The Netherlands during and shortly after World War II. The story's movie adaptation won an Academy Award for Best Foreign Film in 1987, crowning Mulisch's international reputation. One of Mulisch's more recent works is *Discovery of Heaven* (1992), a reflective theological and philosophical narrative.

MUSIC

Lacking an interesting musical history of its own, Amsterdam's music scene is now a cosmopolitan one. Its colonial past lives on in a new fusion genre called **paramaribop,** which combines Surinamese rhythms with jazz. Paramaribop and Latin music in general are featured at venues all over the city. Amsterdam also throbs all night every night thanks to the myriad of dance clubs and rave parties. The biggest contribution made by Dutch club music is through the genre known as **gabber,** in which the number of beats per minute is unbelievably high, and the music buzzes with the sounds of synthesizers.

Classical music can be heard at the Concertgebouw, which has concerts by its own world-class orchestra, the Concertgebouw Orchestra (see p. 158). The Netherlands Opera performs at the Stadhuis-Muziektheater, called the "Stopera," (see p. 70); big names to look for are **Charlotte Margiono, Jard van Nes,** and **Jan-Ate Stobbe.**

DANCE

Classical ballet and contemporary dance is spearheaded in The Netherlands by the **Dutch National Ballet** and the **Nederlands Dans Theater,** respectively. The Dutch National Ballet performs in the Muziektheater (see p. 70), while the Nederlands Dans Theater uses venues throughout Amsterdam. Even the streets themselves sometime become a stage for dance performances, especially in June during the dance portions of the International Theatre School Festival, when performances are held on Nes, the oldest street in Amsterdam.

SPORTS

FOOTBALL

Football (soccer) is the Dutch national sport. Amsterdam's team—and the nation's best—is **Ajax** (the Amsterdamse Football Club Ajax), which plays out of the **Amsterdam Arena** (see p. 73). Top scorers of Ajax include **Piet van Reenen** and **Johan Cruijff.** The Dutch national team is known as the **Oranje,** arguably one of the better football teams never to win a World Cup. The Oranje fought through to the final matches of two World Cup championships in the 1970s but lost both games. In the United States in 1994 and France in 1998, they were knocked out in the semifinals, finishing both years a respectable fourth worldwide. The Oranje failed to qualify for the 2002 World Cup in Korea and Japan.

After earning the ignominious distinction of the "thirty-third team" for the 2002 World Cup in Korea and Japan—the best of the teams that didn't qualify—the Dutch hope to redeem themselves in Portugal at Euro 2004, which is second only to the World Cup in terms of soccer prestige. Under new head coach **Dick Advocaat,** The Netherlands and the rest of Group 3 (The Netherlands, Belarus, Austria, Czech Republic, and Moldova) play a drawn-out schedule of qualifying matches that lasts from the autumn of 2002 straight through to the end of 2003. Behind the front line of Ruud van Nistelrooy, Jimmy Floyd Hasselbaink, and Patrick Kluivert, the Dutch must withstand a battery of tough European contenders (among them Portugal, Germany, England, and France, who won in the World Cup in 2000) if they are to prove that failure to make the cut in 2002 was a fluke. The Oranje has never won a Cup; the small country's only major football championship came at Euro '88. It should be remembered, however, that not everyone in Amsterdam was abject in 2002. The country's large Turkish and Brazilian populations were jubilant at their respective teams' success—Brazil's dramatic win over Germany in the final was greeted by daylong celebrations in Leidseplein, Dam Square, and the rest of Amsterdam.

Holland's schedule in the qualifying rounds of Euro 2004 is as follows:

September 7, 2002: v. Belarus
October 16, 2002: v. Austria
March 29, 2003: v. Czech Republic
April 2, 2003: v. Moldova
June 7, 2003: v. Belarus
September 6, 2003: v. Austria
September 10, 2003: v. Czech Republic
October 11, 2003: v. Moldova

OTHER SPORTS

When the canals freeze, Amsterdam becomes a **skating** rink for commuters and vacationers alike. Since almost every resident seems to own his own pair of skates, rental skates may be difficult to find. The canal boats chug relentlessly through the ice though, and often it is only the Keizersgracht that is left untouched to skaters' delight. Those in good shape can skate to nearby towns. Every January, when the weather is cold enough, the Elfstedentocht race covers 11 towns and 200km of frozen canals and rivers.

A Dutch creation, **korfball** is a bizarre amalgam of basketball (without backboards) and netball. Invented in 1901 by Amsterdamian schoolteacher **Nico Broekhuysen,** korfball was played on an international level by the 1970s. The **Fédération Internationale de Korfball** has members from over 30 countries, from Armenia to the United States. See http://weezenhof.nl.eu.org/thom/korfbal for a virtual version of the game.

INSIDE:

Sights

OUDE ZIJD

see maps pp. 330-331

If you can see through the thick haze of smoke and neon lights that hangs over the Oude Zijd, there's quite a bit of history to be dug up. Though the University of Amsterdam has claimed many of them, historically important or interesting buildings are littered throughout the southern end of the area. The bulk are closed to the public but still offer a pleasant photo opportunity along the canals of the Oude Zijd. **Oudemanhuispoort** is now a pedestrian walkway between Kloverniersburgwal and Oudezijds Acterburgwal, but it was once an almshouse for elderly men. Interesting more for its history than for its architecture, it nevertheless warrants a peek for the bookmarket to which it is now home (open M-Sa 11am-5pm). There you can find boxes full of paperbacks in a variety of languages for €1, ranging from the esoteric to the banal. Walled in on three sides by the Voorburgwal, Achterburgwal, and Grimburgwal, **Huis aan de Drie Grachten,** which appropriately enough means "House on the Three Canals," Oudezijds Voorburgwal 249, was built in 1609 and today houses a bookshop (open M, W, and F 1-5pm); its primary selling-point is its serendipitous location rather than its unique structure. **Sint Agnietenkapel,** Oudezijds Voorburgwal 231, dates from 1470 and immediately stands out; the courtyard's sheltered brick gate and its promise of quiet can't help but seduce passers-by from the whirlwind of the Oude Zijd. The early architecture and sheer uniqueness of the disproportionately angled housefront are the building's main attractions. In 1660, the brothers Louis and Hendrick Trip commissioned the architectural quirk now called **Trippenhuis,** Kloveneirsburgwal 29, whose coal-black façade appears to belong to a single building but really covers two—one for each of the brothers. (At least it beats drawing a line down the middle of the bedroom.) Also, throw a glance to the other side of the canal, where the one-meter wide **Kleine Trippenhuis,** Kloveniersburgwal 26, still stands. Why so narrow? It was for Mr. Trip's coachman.

If for no other reason, Nieuwmarkt is worth a visit simply to take a look at the **Waag,** Amsterdam's largest surviving medieval building. Dating from the 15th century, the Waag came into existence as one of Amsterdam's fortified city gates (at the time it was known as Sint Antoniespoort and was part of the original city walls). As Amsterdam expanded, it became obsolete as a gate and was converted into a house of public weights and measures. Toward the end of the 17th century, the upstairs part of the central tower was used by the Surgeon's Guild for anatomy lessons. Public dissections were *de rigueur* here; the Surgeon's Guild even went so far as to commission portraits of dissections, of which **Rembrandt's** *The Anatomy Lesson of Dr. Tulp* is a famous example. Following its turn as a weigh house and school of science, the Waag came to house a number of other things, including the Jewish Historical Museum and the Amsterdam Historical Museum. Today, it is home to In de Waag, an outstanding restaurant and café (see p. 112).

MUSEUM IN THIS AREA

Amsterdams Centrum voor Fotografie (Amsterdam Center for Photography), see Museums, p. 77

RED LIGHT DISTRICT

see maps pp. 330-331

Whatever preconceptions you hold, the Red Light District most likely won't live up to many of them and will exceed the rest. It is a heavily touristed area, and for every glowing red window, there is an uninterested family scouring their map, trying to find the way back to Dam Sq. In many ways, the **commodification of sex** dulls its impact—the bark can be much worse than the bite. But it's hard to resist the only-in-Amsterdam allure of the area, and almost everyone seems to come with an open mind and wide eyes.

Since the 13th century, the Red Light District has catered to a busy port city and, more importantly, to the wants and needs of the many sailors coming ashore. Once prostitution had taken root, it wasn't going anywhere, a fact acknowledged by the country's legislators when, in 1911, they cemented one of the cornerstones of Holland's tolerance and made **window prostitution** legal. (Until October, 2000, brothels or other businesses of commercial sex were still banned. Today all are perfectly legal.) Although few tourists will pass through the area without snapping a smiling photo in front of Casa Rosso's giant penis fountain, the best parts of the Red Light District are those at its fringes, where the red glow fades and some of the most historic buildings still stand.

If, however, you have indeed come to revel in all the seediness, there's no better time to appreciate the Red Light District than at night. Though prostitutes work all through the day, it's at night that the streets actually take on a **red radiance,** the sex theaters throw open their doors, and the main streets are so thick with people that you may have to slip out to Damrak for some air. If you're looking to wet your feet in the carnality of the Red Light District but are too tame actually to knock on the door of a window prostitute, there are always **sex shows,** in which actors perform strictly choreographed fantasies on stage; the most famous live sex show takes place at **Casa Rosso,** where €25 will buy you admission.

During the daytime, the Red Light District is comparatively flaccid. Families of tourists parade down **Oudezijds Achterburgwal,** under the impression that if it must be seen, it's better to take the kids in the daylight hours, before things *really* get bad. In general, though, you can get an eyeful no matter the time of day; and even at night, it's not especially dangerous in the area. Men and women alike are content to gawk at the extravagance and shamelessness of it all, and police patrol the area until midnight; they are usually on the scene of any disturbance within a moment or two. Whoever the traveler, no trip to Amsterdam is complete without a visit to its most notorious district—just don't be disappointed if it's not exactly the stuff of your wildest fantasies.

OUDE KERK

Oudekerksplein 23. From Centraal Station, walk down Damrak, take a left at the corner of Oudebrugstg. (right before the Beurs van Berlage), and hang a right on Warmoesstr.; at the next left is the church. ☎ 625 82 84, www.oudekerk.nl. Open M-Sa 11am-5pm, Su 1-5pm. €3,80, students €3.

Reopened to the public in 1999, Oude Kerk may come as a relief, a shelter in the otherwise lurid Red Light District. In fact, the first large covered structure in Amsterdam—which thinks of itself as a "living room"—is more than relief: it's a stunning building with an enormous, yawning interior between whose walls and rafters history breathes. At the head of the church is the massive Vater-Müller organ, which was built in 1724. Oude Kerk also houses the tomb of Rembrandt's wife, Saskia. The 14th-century Gothic church has seen hard times, however, having been stripped of its artwork and religious objects between 1566 and 1578 during the Alteration. Between then and now, the once-mighty Catholic church has served a number of functions, including home for vagrants, theater, market, and a space where fishermen could mend broken sails. Today, though there is still a spare feeling inside the building, the church itself is nevertheless one of the most impressive structures in the city.

SINT NICOLAASKERK

Prins Henrikkade 73. A 2min. walk from Centraal Station; turn left when you exit the Stationplein. ☎ 624 87 49. Open M 1-4pm, Tu, Th, and F 11am-4pm, W noon-4pm, Sa noon-3pm. Su mass at 10:30am. Free.

A burst of color emanates from the stained glass windows over the altar of the otherwise forbidding and grey Sint Nicolaaskerk. Designed by A.C. Bleys and completed in 1887 for the Catholic Church to honor the patron saint of sailors, it replaced a number of Amsterdam's secret churches from the era of the Alteration (see p. 53). Designed in the neo-Baroque style, black marble columns and wooden vaults make the interior grand though heavy. Sa music at 3pm.

Oudemannhuispoort

Trippenhuis

St. Nick's

GET smart

Wow, Spui!

Sundays are different in Amsterdam. The high-paced buzz that reigns supreme temporarily subdues; people rise late, move slowly, and generally mill around. In the **Spui** (pronounced "spow"), a somewhat diminutive square just south of lush Begijnhof and near Muntplein, Sundays have a particularly unique flavor. The normally-crowded square takes on the serenity of an art gallery, presenting the original work of more than 25 Amsterdam artists in what has become well-known in the city as **Artplein.** The exhibition is organized as a single corridor with individual displays neatly aligned on either side. The crowds are never too large, allowing for a level of personal space resembling more closely a gallery than an outdoor market square. The many artists, who are selected through a rigorous application process are happy to answer questions about pieces, which range from photography to sculpture, oil painting to textiles. Often local jewellers and children's artists will join in on the outskirts, adding to the diverse gallery feel. *(Open Su 10am-6pm.)*

MUSEUMS IN THIS AREA

Museum Amstelkring "Ons' Lieve Heer Op Solder" ("Our Lord in the Attic"), see Museums, p. 53.

Cannabis College, see Museums, p. 78.

Hash Marijuana Hemp Museum, see Museums, p. 53.

Amsterdam Erotic Museum, see Museums, p. 53.

Amsterdam Sex Museum, see Museums, p. 53

NIEUWE ZIJD

see maps pp. 330-331

Dam Square has always been a lively center of activity in Amsterdam. On any given summer day, the square is full of jugglers, pickpockets, babies, shoppers, dogs, acrobats, musicians, and street vendors. It is also home to two of the city's most historically significant structures: the **Koninklijk Paleis** and the **Nieuwe Kerk.** In the past, the rather expansive cobblestoned area served a number of different functions. History has seen executions, protests, markets, and celebrations here, as well as the erection and destruction of both the first town hall and the public weights and measures house. Louis Bonaparte, King of The Netherlands until his abdication in 1810, was responsible for razing the weights and measures house because it spoiled his view from the palace. Wide, flat, and rather grand, Dam Sq. traditionally functioned as a symbol of Amsterdam's power in the 17th-century commercial landscape. Visiting the area and its environs can consume the better part of a day, especially if you take the time to drop in at either the **Magna Plaza Shopping Center** (open Su-M 11am-7pm, Tu-Sa 9:30am-9pm), originally constructed in 1899 as a post office, or **De Bijenkorf** ("the beehive"), Holland's swankiest shop for designer goods.

BEGIJNHOF

From Dam, take Nieuwezijds Voorburgwal south 5min. to Spui, then turn left and then left again on Gedempte Begijnensteeg; the gardens will be on your left. Or follow signs to Begijnhof from Spui. No groups, guided tours, bikes, or pets. Begijnhof: Open daily 10am-5pm. Free. Het Houten Huys: ☎623 55 54. Open M-F 10am-4pm. Engelsekerk: Begijnhof 48. ☎624 96 65; www.ercadam.nl. Open for public prayer Su 10:30am. Begijnhofkapel, Begijnhof 30 (☎622 19 18), open M-F 9am-5pm, Sa 9am-7pm, services Sunday at 10am in Dutch and 11:30am in French.

The Nieuwe Zijd's most attractive sight is this stunning courtyard full of little gardens and surrounded by handsome gabled houses that provides a quiet respite from the excesses of the city.

Begijnhof was founded in 1346 as a convent for Beguines, free-thinking religious women who did not take vows but still lived dedicated to religious contemplation, charity, and manual work. Because of major fires in the 15th century, most of the houses date from the 17th and 18th centuries. The oldest house in Amsterdam, the heavily restored **Het Houten Huys (the Wooden House),** is found in this courtyard. Today, Begijnhof is home mostly to observant Catholic women, though the last Beguine died in 1971. While there, be sure to visit the court's two churches. **Engelsekerk** holds one of the city's few all-English services. The building is believed to date from 1392, when it served as Begijnhof's Catholic chapel. In 1607, as a result of the Reformation, the Beguines were forced to turn it over to Amsterdam's English-speaking Presbyterians. It was enlarged in 1665 and restored thirty years ago. Across from Engelsekerk is **Begijnhofkapel,** constructed in 1680 and originally one of Amsterdam's *schuilkerken* or **hidden churches;** see p. 80.

Carved Angel at Nieuwe Kerk

DAM SQUARE AND KONINKLIJK PALACE

From Centraal, take tram #5, 13, 17, or 20 to Dam. Koninklijk Palace (☎620 40 60; www.kon-paleisamsterdam.nl). Square open 24hr. Palace open June-Aug. daily 12:30-5pm, hours variable in winter. ***Admission*** *€4,50, children and seniors €3,60.*

Magna Plaza

Right beside the **Nieuwe Kerk** (see **Museums,** p. 79) and directly on Dam Square is perhaps Amsterdam's most impressive architectural work, **Koninklijk Palace,** completed as the town hall in 1655. Philip Vingboons, a young architect at the time, aimed to replace the entrenched Amsterdam Renaissance style with a more profane Classicist one. (To see the difference, compare this palace to Westerkerk, the church up Raadhuisstraat from the back of Koninklijk, at the Prinsengracht.) Koninklijk did not become a palace until the arrival of finicky Napoleon in 1808, who had it renovated and remodeled to better serve the function of a royal residence. Today, Queen Beatrix still uses the building for official receptions, though she makes her home in The Hague. The palace's indisputable highlight is the beautiful Citizen's Hall, designed to be the universe contained in a single room. Across the large Dam Square is the Dutch **Nationaal Monument,** unveiled on May 4, 1956, to honor Dutch victims of World War II. Inside the 21-meter white stone obelisk is soil from all twelve of Holland's provinces as well as from the Dutch East Indies. Along the back of the monument, you'll find the provinces' crests bor-

Outside the Palace

dered by the years 1940 and 1945. Today, in addition to the purpose it serves as a reminder of Dutch suffering during the war, the monument is one of Amsterdam's central meeting and people-watching spots.

SPUI

Tram #4, 9, 14, 16, 20, 24, or 25 to Spui.

Pronounced "spow," this square is home to an art market on Sundays (see **Wow, Spui!**, p. 56), a book market on Fridays, and is surrounded by bookstores. The Begijnhof is sometimes accessible through an entrance in the north side of the square. Look out for **Het Lievertje** (The Little Urchin), an artful statue by Carel Kneulman that became a symbol for the Provos and was the site of many meetings and riots in the 1960s (see **Life and Times,** p. 40).

MUSEUMS IN THIS AREA

Nieuwe Kerk, see Museums, p. 79.

Amsterdams Historisch Museum (Amsterdam Historical Museum), see Museums, p. 80.

Beurs van Berlage, see Museums, p. 81.

Allard Pierson Museum, see Museums, p. 81.

Madame Tussaud's Wax Museum, see Museums, p. 82.

SCHEEPVAARTBUURT (THE SHIPPING QUARTER)

see map p. 328-329

Situated just north of the Jordaan and west of the center, Amsterdam's **Shipping Quarter** functioned as the conduit for the city's thriving maritime commerce during the 18th and 19th centuries. But when Amsterdam's shipping industry shifted away from the banks of the Ij in the late 1800s, the area was abandoned. The Shipping Quarter underwent various gritty transformations in an attempt to find itself. Until about ten years ago, the quarter housed little more than an assortment of criminals and junkies. But thanks to urban renewal (and an outpouring of investment from the city's coffers), the Scheepvaartbuurt now offers some of the city's best restaurants, coffeehouses, and shopping venues, all without the touristy feel that pervades the areas closer to the center.

The Shipping Quarter begins where Niewendijk intersects with the Singelgracht and the district's main drag—the **Haarlemmerstraat**—begins. The eastern half of the quarter doesn't feel that much different than the city center; it's slightly more residential but packed with restaurants and coffeeshops. This is where urban renewal has worked its magic most effectively. The western half of the quarter, where Haarlemmerstraat becomes **Haarlemmerdijk** across the Korte Prinsengracht (a crucial and confusing fact for navigating local addresses), is significantly more residential. The area's maritime past has largely been forgotten; the only reminders are bronze ship-related monuments—propellers, anchors, and nautical steering wheels—that dot the street corners. Amid the bustle of Haarlemmerstraat and Haarlemmerdijk, it's easy to forget that the Shipping Quarter is bordered on the south by one of Amsterdam's most beautiful canals, the **Brouwersgracht.** It's a great place to chill out, only two blocks and yet a world away in from the Scheepvaartbuurt's frenetic urban pace.

Few sights appear along the Haarlemmerstraat—though the street, with its unparalleled collection of eateries and coffeeshops, is almost a sight in itself. It's worth stopping at the **West Indisch Huis (West Indies House),** Haarlemmerstraat 75, at Herenmarkt; the white, ornately gabled structure dates to 1617. It originally functioned as the headquarters of the Dutch West Indies Company back when the Dutch ranked among the world's most bloodthirsty imperialists. The West Indies House earned its greatest fame as the storage place for Admiral Piet Hein's capture of an enormous amount of silver bullion from the Spanish fleet.

CANAL RING WEST

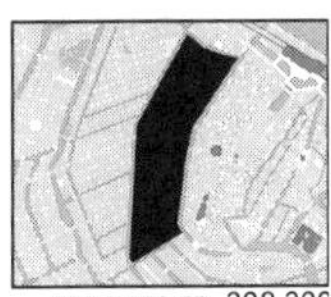

see maps pp. 328-329

There are about 2200 buildings in the canal ring, 1550 of which have been named national monuments, making the neighborhood a sight in itself.

Any visit to the Western Canal Ring must begin at the Westermarkt (Tram #13, 17, or 20 from Centraal), the jumping-off point for all things touristic. The Anne Frank Huis and the Westerkerk with its 85m tower are both just steps away. The Bijbels Museum and the Theater Instituut Nederlands both offer quirky, entertaining collections in magnificent canal house splendor.

Inside the Palace

WESTERKERK

Raadhuisstraat between Keizersgracht and Prinsengracht. Entrance on Prinsengracht. Trams #13, 17, or 20 to Westermarkt. Open Apr.-Sept. M-F 11am-3pm; July-Aug. M-Sa 11am-3pm. Tours of the tower every hr. €3.

This stunning Protestant church was designed by Roman Catholic architect Hendrick de Keyser and completed in 1631. It stands as one of the latest works of Amsterdam Renaissance architecture, built in the final years of that style's great prevalence in the city. The blue and yellow imperial crown of Maximilian, the Hapsburg ruler of the Holy Roman Empire in the late 15th century, rests atop the 85m spire as a reminder of the emperor's importance to the city in its youth. Rembrandt is believed to be buried here, though the exact spot has not been located. In contrast to the decorative exterior, the Protestant church remains properly sober and plain inside. Climb the **Westerkerkstoren** for a great view of the city from the tallest tower in Amsterdam.

Begijnhof

FELIX MERITIS

Keizersgracht 324. (☎624 93 68; balie@felix.meritis.nl; www.felix.meritis.nl)

This imposing structure is more than just a café with outdoor seating, though you wouldn't know it just walking by the place. The building housed the Felix Meritis Society of arts and sciences when it was first built in the late 18th century as a monument to Enlightenment ideals, serving as a cultural center for the city's elite. After World War II, the Dutch Communist Party inhabited the space for a time. Felix Meritis now once again serves as a European center for arts and sciences, hosting cultural events, international

Haarlemerpoort

Check, Checkmate

Of all the peculiar national icons, perhaps none is more so than Max Euwe (1901-1981). Winning the world championship chess title in 1935, Euwe is still the only Dutchman ever to snag that honor. A professor of mathematics, he wrote volumes on chess theory and served as president of the World Chess Federation later in life.

For all his trouble, Euwe can now boast (albeit posthumously) a square that not only bears his name, but pays homage to him and his chosen pastime with an enormous chessboard and two-foot pieces. Visit Max Euweplein, off of Weteringschans between Leidseplein and the Paradiso, for the biggest chess game of your life.

If outside play is not your style, try the **Schaak Cafe,** Bloemgracht 20 (☎622 1801), a basement chess café in the Jordaan with boards on every table and a small but loyal cadre of regulars. Little in the way of fare--beer and coffee both less than €2—but what you'll find is any number of would-be Max Euwes up for a game.

projects, concerts of classical and world music, summer courses (lasting a couple of days and all in English, including intensive Dutch; see www.amsu.edu), and the art cable television station Kunstkanaal. The canalside cafe serves as a forum for impromptu political and intellectual conversations.

INSTITUTE FOR WAR DOCUMENTATION

Herengracht 380. (☎523 38 00; www.oorlogsdoc.knaw.nl.) Open M 1-5pm, Tu-W and F 9am-5pm, Th 9am-9pm.

This ornately decorated stone mansion has intricate carvings and embellishments that set it apart from the usual canal houses. The building proves interesting for its unique history as well as its individual style. Nazis occupied the opulent space during World War II, but the building now houses the *Nederlands Instituut voor Oorlogsdocumentatie*, the Dutch library of war documentation. In addition to a huge collection of Dutch sources and photographs, the library also has books concerning the World War II in English, French, and German.

MUSEUMS IN THIS AREA

Anne Frank Huis, see Museums, p. 83.
Bijbelsmuseum, see Museums, p. 84.
Huis Marseille, see Museums, p. 84.
Theater Instituut Nederland, see museums, p. 85.
Multatuli Museum, see Museums, p. 84.

CENTRAL CANAL RING

see maps pp. 324-325

Two of the city's most famous bridges span the Amstel farther down Amstelstraat from the Rembrandtplein. At Amstelstraat, the **Blauwbrug** (Blue Bridge) stretches across the water. Capped with ornate blue-and-gold crowns, it's one of the city's more spectacular sights. To the right along the Amstel, the **Magere Brug** (Skinny Bridge) sways above the water. Magere Brug is the oldest of the city's pedestrian drawbridges and the only one that is hand-operated. Its original construction in 1670 replaced an even older, skinnier bridge that was built—according to city lore—for two sisters who lived opposite the canal from one another and sought a convenient way to visit.

The Central Canal Ring is home to a stretch on the Herengracht called the **Golden Bend** because of the wealthiness of the merchants who built these especially wide canal houses. In the 17th century, citizens had to pay a tax according to the width of their house, and houses could not be more than one plot wide. In order to encourage people to invest in the construction of the Herengracht, the city altered its laws so that a few of the very rich could build houses with expansive fronts.

The **Cat's Cabinet,** Herengracht 497, is a temple to all things feline, including statuary, portraiture, pop art, and assorted knickknacks. It's housed in the only building on the Golden Bend open to the public. The collection was started by a businessman with an unusually strong attraction to his cat named J. P. Morgan—check out his feline face gracing the dollar bill in the museum. After 18 years of eating, sleeping, and showering with his cat, the man opened the museum in the bottom two floors of his beautiful canal-side mansion when J. P. died in 1990. Cat-lovers will purr at the collection, but it might cause others to take a catnap. (☎626 5378; info@kattenkabinet.nl; www.kattenkabinet.nl. Open M-F 10am-2pm, Sa-Su 1-5pm. €4,50, under 12 €2,50.)

Homomonument

The House with the Heads

MUSEUMS IN THIS AREA

De Appel, see Museums, p. 86.

Foam Photography Museum, see Museums, p. 86.

Museum Willet-Holthuysen, see Museums, p. 86.

Museum van Loon, see Museums, p. 87.

Nationaal Brilmuseum (National Glasses Museum), see Museums, p. 87.

Torture Museum, see Museums, p. 87.

LEIDSEPLEIN

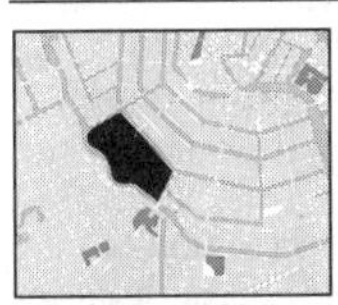

see map p. 325

Just east of Leidseplein along Weteringschans, Greek columns mark the entrance to **Max Euweplein.** Named for the famous Dutch chess player, the square sports an enormous chess board with people-sized pieces (see **Check, Checkmate,** p. 60). One of Amsterdam's more bizarre public spaces, it's notable both for the tiny park across the street (where tons of **bronze iguanas** provide amusement) and the motto inscribed above its pillars, *"Homo sapiens non urinat in ventum"* ("A wise man does not piss into the wind").

Rembrandt Statue

in recent news

A Full Country?

"This is a full country. I think 16 million Dutchmen are about enough." **Pim Fortuyn,** one of the most important Dutch politicians in recent memory, based much of his brief political career on that sentiment before his assassination on May 6, 2002, only nine days before the national election in which his party became the second largest party in power.

Ironically, Fortuyn's assassination had nothing to do with his views on immigration (he was killed by an animal-rights activist), but his legacy will always be tied to that issue. His immense charisma, and the unabashed fashion in which he voiced his anti-immigration and anti-Muslim views, has unleashed a torrent of similar sentiment throughout the country. Both his views and his party, Lijst Pim Fortuyn, are surprisingly popular with the country's young; a shocking amount of anti-immigrant feeling has come out of the woodwork of the under-30 population.

Roughly 10% of the people in The Netherlands are immigrants, although in cities like Rotterdam (where Fortuyn began his political career), it can be as high as 45%.

Continued next page

The Leidseplein proper is less remarkable for its sights than for the myriad restaurants, bars, and coffeeshops that dot its streets.

THE JORDAAN

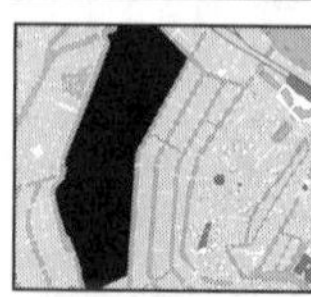

see maps pp. 328-329

The Jordaan, comprising of peaceful residential neighborhoods, is like the eye of the storm in central Amsterdam. Come here to escape the sightseers and grab a beer at a pleasant streetside café. You can find a moment of silence in one of the *hofjes*; before the Alteration (see p. 36), these almshouses were subsidized by the Catholic Church to serve as housing for the poor and the elderly. Step behind the nondescript green door that separates **Sint-Andrieshof** (Egelantiersgracht 107-145; open 9am-6pm; free) from the street and take a slow stroll around the blooming lilacs, the lush greenery, and the quirky architecture of the sloping roofs. Be quiet, though—the courtyard has the hushed solemnity of a church, which probably has less to do with its holy history than the private residences which now enclose it.

HOMOMONUMENT

Take #13, 17, or 20 tram to Westermarkt.

Since 1987, the Homomonument has stood in the center of Amsterdam as a testament to the strength and resilience of the homosexual community. Three pink granite triangles form one large triangle that reaches from the foot of a church to the edge of the canal. The raised triangle points to the **COC** (Dutch Association for the Integration of Homosexuality; see p. 62), one of the oldest gay rights organizations in the world. The ground level triangle points to the **Anne Frank Huis** (see p. 83) and reads *Naar Vriendschap Zulk Een Mateloos Verlangen*, a line from a poem by Jacob Israel de Haan that translates, "such an endless desire for friendship." The triangle with steps into the canal points to the National War Memorial on the Dam, as a reminder that homosexuals were among those sent to concentration camps. The monument serves as a tripartite memorial to men and women persecuted for their homosexuality in the past, a confrontation with continuing discrimination in the present, and an inspiration for the future. On Liberation Day (May 5) and Queen's Day (April 30), come for the massive celebrations on the monument.

PINK POINT

Westermarkt, next to the Homomonument at the corner of Keizersgracht and Raadhuisstraat. www.pinkpoint.org. Open Apr.-Sept. daily noon-6pm.

If the Homomonument serves as a valuable testimony to the ongoing civil rights struggle of homosexuals worldwide, then its neighbor Pink Point stands as a reminder of everything vibrant and fun about gay life in Amsterdam. Since 1998, the kiosk has served as a clearinghouse for information on homosexual happenings. Pick up free listings of gay and lesbian bars, clubs, restaurants, and cultural life. The kiosk also sells a great selection of souvenirs, t-shirts, postcards, and knick-knacks. From June to September, a walking tour on the history of gay life in the city departs every Saturday at 2:30pm (€20). Pink Point is also a good starting place for those attending the gay pride festival held on the first weekend of August. The party lasts all weekend, culminating in a celebration Sunday afternoon at the Stadhuis-Muziektheater.

MUSEUMS IN THIS AREA

Electric Ladyland: First Museum of Fluorescent Art, see Museums, p. 87.

Woonboot Museum, see Museums, p. 88.

Stedelijk Museum Bureau Amsterdam, see Museums, p. 88.

Pianola Museum, see Museums, p. 88.

WESTERPARK

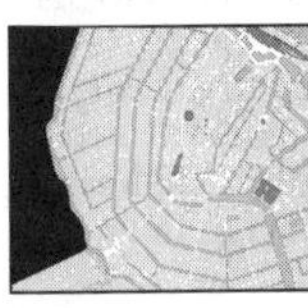

Take tram #3 to Haarlemmerplein.

The Westerpark neighborhood is mostly residential, but its park is worth a visit. The gates—tall wavy blue monstrosities—open onto a wide expanse of green like no other in the city. Banks of thick grass slope into the Haarlemmervaart, which looks more like a river than a canal, and any number of winding dirt paths invite visitors to wander down them. In the center of it all is a large pond, filled with ducks and fish, and the park's sole curiosity: a white, revolving, headless statue. Benches line the pond, and a large playground attracts parents with their children. It's an excellent place to while away an afternoon.

Immigrants in The Netherlands come largely from Surinam and Indonesia, both former colonies, and from North Africa and the Middle East. Many are also European and white, but Fortuyn was more concerned about immigrants from Muslim countries because he saw them as integrating inadequately into the culture.

Immigration to EU countries peaked in the early 1990s, and has declined since; The Netherlands takes in about 40,00 every year—a number Fortuyn and his supporters wanted to see drop to 10,000. The new government, elected in May of 2002, is expected to adopt new measures to speed up the expulsion of immigrants with no express reason to stay.

The political debate takes on a human face when you head to Amsterdam's **Oude West,** or any other heavily immigrant area of the country. The number of languages spoken here (or anywhere in Amsterdam for that matter) would put self-described "diverse" cities such as New York to shame; it would be impossible to imagine the Oude West without its unique juxtaposition of Turkish takeaway restaurants, Middle Eastern bazaars, and North African record shops. It's not hard to see what The Netherlands would lose without its vibrant immigrant population—one that, in large part, defines the experience of the city.

MUSEUMPLEIN AND VONDELPARK

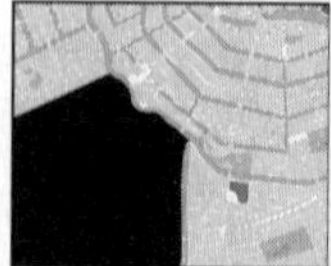
see map p. 334

VONDELPARK

In the southwestern corner of the city, outside the Singelgracht, easily reachable by tram #1, 2, 3, 5, 6, 12, or 20; just a short walk across the canal and to the left from the Leidseplein. www.vondelpark.org

True to it's name as the "People's Park," the Vondelpark is always teeming with Dutch folks looking to spend time outdoors. With meandering walkways and a paved path for bikers and skaters, the park draws large crowds any day of the week and packs them in on a nice weekend. The big corners are popular spots for street performers, making it possible to wander from interpretive dance to juggling to acrobatics to musicians. Rollerbladers line up cones on the weekend by the east entrance and dudes in old-school rollerskates get down, making it feel like *Rollerboogie* when some good tunes blare from the boom box. In the heart of the park lies a special kiddie park with a fountain and a wading pool. Stretching down a while are hexagonal patches of roses, organized by species. Inside the park sits the **Openluchttheater,** or open-air theater, where **free concerts** and dance shows entertain W-Su in the summer. Pick up a monthly program next to the stage or check www.openluchttheater.nl. Every Friday, a **group skate** begins at the Filmmuseum in the Vondelpark. About 350-600 skaters (roller and inline) gather at 8pm for a skate through Amsterdam.

MUSEUMS IN THIS AREA

Van Gogh Museum, see Museums, p. 88.
Stedelijk Museum for Modern and Contemporary Art, see Museums, p. 91.
Rijksmuseum Amsterdam, see Museums, p. 91.
Filmmuseum, see Museums, p. 93.
Concertgebouw, see Arts & Entertainment, p. 158.

DE PIJP

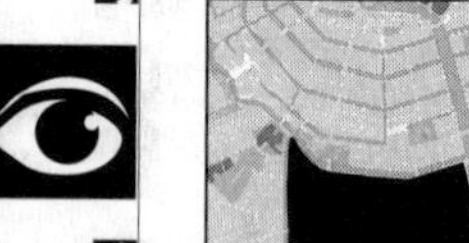
see map p. 326

Named after the long, narrow hallways of row houses that crowd its residential streets supposedly giving it the appearance of being in a pipe, De Pijp stretches south of Singelgracht and is hemmed in by the River Amstel on the east and the Amstel canal and Boerenwetering on the west. Right next to the Museum Quarter but far from its tourist hordes, the district feels gritty and authentic. Originally planned in the late 19th century as a bourgeois suburb, De Pijp has retained its residential character, though it's become decidedly more working class. Today, a mix of immigrants from Surinam, Indonesia, Turkey, Kurdistan, and Morocco call this district home, as reflected in its ethnic markets, restaurants, and shops.

Most of the Pijp is best experienced by wandering around its skinny streets and popping into its cheap, low-end restaurants and shops. The best place to start is amid the crowded, bustling din of the **Albert Cuypmarkt,** a good place to shop and home to some of the best budget-eatery deals in the city (see **Markets,** p. 172). Continue your tour down the district's largest thoroughfare, **Ferdinand Bolstraat,** where a right at the corner of 1e Jan Steenstraat and a two-block stroll will take you to **Sarphatipark,** named for the Doctor Samuel Sarphati, a philanthropist who instituted a series of public works programs in the 19th century. Smack in the center of the Pijp, the Sarphatipark comprises only a few city blocks; it's a pleasant stretch of green criss-crossed by a series of paths and a sinuous little pond. Along the Amstel River lies the strikingly elaborate building of the **Gemeentearchief,** Amsteldijk 67, which houses the city's municipal records as well as showing exhibitions (☎572 02 02; free). The park, and areas to its south, are safe enough by day, but should be approached with caution after dark.

HEINEKEN EXPERIENCE

Stadhouderskade 78, a red brick edifice looming at the corner of Ferdinand Bolstraat. Tram #16, 24, or 25 to Heinekenplein. (☎523 96 66; www.heinekenexperince.com.) Open Tu-Su 10am-6pm; last entry at 5pm. Under 18 must be accompanied by a parent. €7,50, includes 3 free beers or soft drinks.

Busloads of tourists pour in daily to discover that beer is not made in the Heineken Brewery. Plenty is served, however. The factory stopped producing here in 1988 and have turned the place into a tourist amusement park devoted to their green-bottle beer. In the "Experience," visitors guide themselves past holograms, virtual reality machines, and other multimedia treats; there's even a kiosk where you can email a picture of yourself on a Heineken bottle cap to envious friends. Some of the attractions can get a little absurd (e.g., the "bottle ride," designed to replicate the experience of becoming a Heineken beer), but after a few beers you'll go with it and have fun. A visit includes three beers and a souvenir glass, all of which is in itself well worth the price of admission.

JODENBUURT AND THE PLANTAGE

see map p. 327

The Jodenbuurt and Plantage neighborhoods, with their countless green spaces, phenomenal museums and monuments, and host of fun escapes, differ enormously from the vibrant city center, only five minutes away down Oude Hoogstraat. Shrouded in an interesting mixture of deep solemnity and upbeat cultural flair, the Jodenbuurt and Plantage are not to be missed on any sojourn in Amsterdam. The area known as **Mr. Visserplein,** home to the **Portugees-Israelietische Synagoge** (Portuguese Synagogue) and centered around an almost awe-inspiring urban mess of graffiti and abandoned traffic lights, is more gray than green. This area of Amsterdam was home to tens of thousands of Dutch Jews before Nazi occupation in World War II. Indeed, if you pay close enough attention to your surroundings, the area around Mr. Visserplein and Waterlooplein is full of reminders of the Holocaust and the once-thriving Jewish community that it all but erased during World War II.

Blue Teahouse in Vondelpark

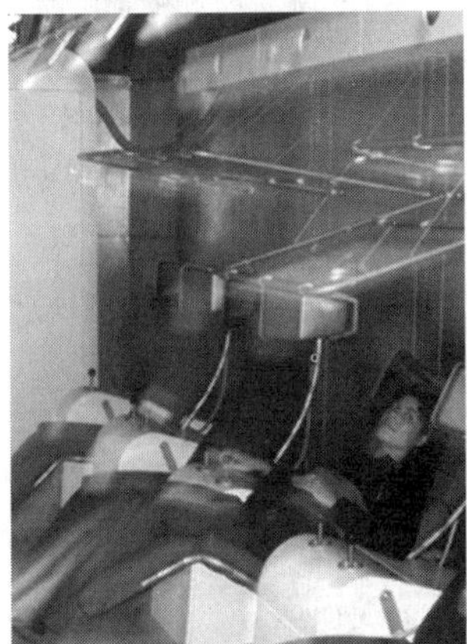
Amusements at the Heineken Experience

Heineken Experience

life*s green

Bean There, Done That

While The Netherlands is universally known for its ability to produce the world's finest tulips, its horticultural flair extends beyond flowers. When the Hortus Botanicus was founded in 1638, it nursed mostly medicinal plants, the kinds regularly used by Dutch apothecaries to concoct cures for the diseases of the day. With the arrival of the Dutch East India Company in the 16th and 17th centuries, however, the botanical gardens came to serve new purposes. On their voyages, merchants smuggled all kinds of things back to The Netherlands, which often included exotic plants. Many of these were placed in the Hortus Botanicus for cultivation and still survive today. Perhaps the most interesting of the specimens is Hortus's very own coffee plant. It was brought to the gardens in 1706 by an East India Company merchant who had smuggled it out of Ethiopia. Not only was it the first coffee plant on European soil, but it also became the forbear of the coffee cultures of Brazil. No small feat for a very small plant.

The area roughly bounded by the **Nieuwe Herengracht, Jodenbreestraat, St. Antoniebreestraat,** and **Waterlooplein** gained definition as the **Jewish Quarter (Jodenbuurt).** Today, the area is home to a number of museums and monuments commemorating the Jews and members of the Dutch Resistance, but also to sights like the **Hollandsche Schouwberg, Stadhuis-Muziektheater,** and the **Rembrandthuis** that reflect the city's deep history and current development. In the **Plantage,** explore **NEMO,** shed a tear at **Shreierstoren,** pet some wildlife at **Artis Zoo,** and unionize at **Nationaal Vakbondsmuseum "De Burcht."**

PORTUGEES-ISRAELIETISCHE SYNAGOGE (THE PORTUGUESE SYNAGOGUE)

Mr. Visserplein 1-3. Take tram #9, 14, or 20 to Waterlooplein. ☎624 53 51; fax 625 46 80; m.dori@esnoga.com; www.esnoga.com. Open Su-F 10am-4pm; Nov.-Mar. Su-Th 10am-4pm., F 10am-3pm. €4,50, children €3,50.

This centuries-old, beautifully maintained Portuguese Synagogue still holds services. The building dates back to 1675 and has remained largely unchanged despite the destructive force of the Nazi occupation during World War II. One of the few tangible remnants of Amsterdam's once-thriving Jewish community, the synagogue features a plain but beautiful *chuppah* (a Jewish wedding canopy) crafted from Brazilian jacaranda wood during the last century. The wooden piles and foundation vaults that support the synagogue can be viewed by boat from the water beneath the synagogue. A video presentation called *Esnoga*, the Portuguese name for the synagogue, gives background on Amsterdam's Jewish community as an introduction to your visit.

HOLLANDSCHE SCHOUWBERG

Plantage Middenlaan 24. Take tram #9, 14, or 20 to Waterlooplein and walk through Mr. Visserplein and southeast on Muiderstraat, which becomes Plantage Middenlaan. ☎626 99 45; fax 624 17 21; info@jhm.nl; www.jhm.nl. Open daily 11am-4pm; closed on Yom Kippur. Free.

This monument, museum, and historic building stands today as one of the region's most inspiring symbols of freedom, a moving testament to Dutch life before, during, and after Hitler. Now housing a memorial "in memory of those who were taken away, 1940-1945," Hollandsche Schouwberg began its life at the end of the 19th century as a theater on the edge of the old Jewish quarter in the Plantage district. Initially called Artis Schouwberg, the theater was a venue for operettas and later, under the name Hollandsche Schouwberg, Dutch language plays and performances. A popular venue for Amsterdam's most prominent citizens, the Schouwberg underwent a terrible metamorphosis under Nazi occupation, transforming from a symbol of entertainment to a symbol of cruelty. In 1941 the Nazi occupants converted the Hollandsche Schouwberg into the Joodsche Schouwberg, the city's sole establishment to which Jewish performers and Jewish patrons were granted access. Not long after that, the building was changed into an assembly point for Dutch Jews who were to be deported to Westerbork, the transit camp to the north (see p. 249). The majority of those in transit there met their end in Auschwitz, Bergen-Belsen, or Sobibor.

In its modern incarnation, the Hollandsche Schouwberg is a monument to the 104,000 Dutch Jews who were deported and exterminated during World War II. When you walk into the memorial room, 6700 surnames (including, of course, Frank) are engraved and illuminated on the wall behind a single, eternally lit flame. A stone monument occupies the space where the theater's stage used to be, and poplar trees grow in the area that was originally the courtyard. Upstairs is an exhibition that details the gradual isolation and ultimate death of the vast majority of Dutch Jews who entered the theater as prisoners. Within walking distance of the monument is the **Auschwitz Nooit Meer (Auschwitz Never Again)** memorial in Wertheim Park.

Synagogue

Brouwerij't Ij

ARTIS ZOO

 *Plantage Kerklaan 38-40. Take tram #9 or 20 to Waterlooplein. Walk southeast through Mr. Visserplein and down Muiderstraat, which becomes Plantage Middenlaan at Nieuwe Herengracht. Two blocks down, turn left on Plantage Kerklaan; it's on your right. ☎523 36 11; info@artis.nl; www.artis.nl. Open daily 9am-5pm. €13,50, ages 4-11 €9,50, seniors over 65 €12.*

Artis is the largest zoo in The Netherlands, as well a zoological museum, a museum of geology, an aquarium, and a planetarium. A day of good weather is enough to make the Artis complex worth a visit, especially for children sick of historical landmarks and their weary parents, and for nature-buffs looking for an escape from the urban rush of the city. During World War II, between 150 and 300 Jews were hidden in the zoo's empty cages (see **Resistance in the Artis Zoo,** p. 68).

Lilypads at Hortus Botanicus

Resistance in the Artis Zoo

Almost every day of the week, the Artis Zoo is packed with happy children and parents, excited about a day out together. But, like many places in the Jodenbuurt and Plantage, Artis's history has a more somber side. During World War II, as the Jewish residents of the Plantage began to experience gradual persecution and isolation by the Nazis, the Dutch Resistance snapped into action. Jews were hidden everywhere in an attempt to avoid deportation to the death camps of the east. Filled with empty cages and empty rooms during the night, Artis seemed the perfect place for people to hide. In fact, during the war some 150 to 300 people hid in Artis. Among the many Jews hiding in animal cages were young men trying to evade their notices of compulsory work in Germany. The museum upstairs at the Hollandsche Schouwberg tells of a woman-in-hiding who used to go to the zoo when she felt unsafe. When the zoo was deserted later in the war, she would sneak into the night house to sęek the company of the monkeys and remain there until it was safe to come out again.

HORTUS BOTANICUS

Plantage Middenlaan 2A. Take tram #7, 9, or 14 to the Waterlooplein/Plantage Parklaan area and follow the signs that point to Hortus Botanicus. The garden's entrance is on Plantage Middenlaan, just southeast of the Nieuwe Herengracht. ☎625 84 11; fax 625 70 06; info@dehortus.nl; www.hortus-botanicus.nl. Open Apr.-Oct. M-F 9am-5pm, Sa-Su 11am-5pm; Dec.-Mar. M-F 9am-4pm, Sa-Su 11am-4pm. Closed Dec. 25 and Jan. 1. Guided tours available Su 2pm for €1 extra. €5, children €2,30.

For those who scoff at the idea of a fascinating afternoon in the company of shrubs and ferns, the Hortus Botanicus will come as a pleasant surprise. With over 6000 species of plants, Hortus (founded in 1638) is one of the oldest gardens of its kind in the world and a modern refuge for a number of plants headed toward extinction. It was originally established as "Hortus Medicus," a medicinal garden for the town's physicians, and many of its more exceptional specimens, including a coffee plant smuggled out of Ethiopia whose clippings spawned the Brazilian coffee empire (see **Bean There, Done That,** p. 66), were gathered during the 17th and 18th centuries by members of the Dutch East India Company. There are a number of simulated ecosystems that guests of the garden can tour, as well as a rock garden, a special area for carnivorous plants, an herb garden, a rosarium, an orchid nursery, three multi-climate greenhouses, and a pond. There is also an educational house, where some truly striking butterflies spend the day fluttering for people with ready cameras. Don't miss Hortus's *Welwitschia mirabilis*, a rare desert plant from Namibia that can live 2000 years and sprouts a grand total of two leaves during that time. In the summer, check out the giant water lily, *Victoria amazonica*.

ZUIDERKERK

Zuiderkerkhof. From Nieuwmarkt, head southwest on Kloveniersburgwal and turn left at Zandstraat; the church will be on your left. zuiderkerk@dro.amsterdam.nl. Tower open for guided tours June-Sept. W-Sa 2, 3, and 4pm. Children under 9 need adult supervision. €3.

Located right in the center of Amsterdam's Nieuwmarkt neighborhood, Zuiderkerk is the Jodenbuurt's most visible landmark. Constructed between 1603 and 1614 under the supervision of architect Hendrick de Keyser, it was the first Protestant church to be built after the Reformation. During and after Holland's Hard Winter of 1944-45, in which temperatures and foodstuffs reached record lows, the building was used as a makeshift morgue. Since 1988, Zuiderkerk has served as the **Municipal Information Center for Phys-**

ical Planning and Housing, which has permanent exhibits on the history and planning of numerous Amsterdam neighborhoods. (☎552 79 87; zuiderkerk@dro.amsterdam.nl. Open M 11am-4pm, Tu-F 9am-4pm, Th 9am-10pm. Free.) The high towers are open during the summer season and boast some of the best views of the city.

NEMO (NEW METROPOLIS)

Oosterdok 2. When you exit Centraal Station, look off to the Oosterdok area on your left for a very large, green building that looks like the hull of a ship emerging out of the water. That is NEMO. Follow the road toward it and walk over the two white bridges until you come to the entrance. ☎0900 919 11 00 (€0,35 per min.); info@e-NEMO.nl; www.e-NEMO.nl. Open Tu-Su 10am-5pm. Closed Dec. 25, Jan. 1, and Apr. 30. €9, students €7, children under 4 free.

When you combine science with the design of super-cool Italian architect Renzo Piano, you're bound to come out with something special and slightly out of the ordinary. This four-story science and creative exploration center, geared toward children ages 6-16, gives visitors the chance to experiment with, poke at, jump on, and learn from exhibits that investigate science and technology. Exhibits are changed regularly to keep up with the evolving technological world. Four levels include exhibits titled "Why the World Works," "Chain Reactions," "Machine Park," and "Bamboo House." For the more mature crowd, there's "Journey through the Mind" and "Super Banker," a simulation game where you invest and gamble money to make it big. Don't miss out on the view from the building; on the eastern side, there is a staircase that traverses the structure's slanted roof.

ARCAM (ARCHITECTURE CENTER AMSTERDAM)

Waterlooplein 213. Take tram #9, 14, or 20 to Waterlooplein. ☎620 48 78; fax 638 55 98. Open Tu-Sa 1-5pm; closed on bank holidays. Free. Wheelchair accessible.

Staffed by professionals with training in design, ARCAM is a fantastic resource for finding out all you could possibly want to know about Amsterdam's vibrant architecture scene. While the center is not really a museum, it hosts a number of changing exhibitions each year that provide guests and residents of the city with some insight into what's behind (and inside) Amsterdam's newest and oldest structures. Arcam will move in spring 2003 to Oosterdok 14, on the northeast corner of the Jodenbuurt area. An extremely detailed architectural map of the city is sold here for €5.

Hortus Botanicus

Scheepvaarthuis Doorway

Schreirstroen

BROUWERIJ 'T IJ

Funenkade 7. Take bus #22 out to the Funenkade stop in front of the windmill. Brouwerij 't Ij is just behind the windmill. ☎622 83 25 or 320 17 86. Open W-Su 3-7:45pm. Free tour F 4pm.

Situated on the body of water known as 't Ij, the sign of the Brouwerij 't Ij is a bright and eye-catching one: an ostrich and its egg in a round seal. The origin of the logo derives from the similarity between the sound of " 't Ij" and the Dutch *de ei*, which means "the egg." Archaic beer bottles now line the walls of this former bathhouse and current bar at the Brouwerij, a no-frills-attached, die-hard brewery for the serious enthusiast. There's plenty of cigarette smoke and lively conversation from merry crowds of locals who routinely pack the bar and large terrace out on the canal. Bring your camera, because after sampling the Brouwerij's nine home brews (six regulars and three seasonal beers for €1,70 each), you're sure to have a foggy memory of this unique brewery.

FO GUANG SHAN HE HUA TEMPLE

Zeedijk 106-118. Just north of the Nieuwmarkt. ☎420 23 57; fax 420 41 00. Open M-Sa noon-5pm, Su 10am-5pm. Free services Su 10:30am are open to the public. 30min. tours by appointment only.

While Amsterdam's Chinatown might be small, the city is home to approximately 20,000 Chinese people, most of whom hail from Hong Kong. On February 2, 2000, Amsterdam's first house of Buddhist worship opened. It is the largest traditional Chinese temple on the European continent, the product of the International Buddhist Progress Society's efforts to introduce more Europeans to Buddhist traditions and values. Its gold and red facade is a wondrous sight.

DE DOKWERKER (THE DOCKWORKER)

Jonas Daniel Meijerplein. Take tram #9, 14, or 20 to Waterlooplein. The statue is across the street, just beside the Portuguese Synagogue.

Unveiled in 1952, this bronze statue just outside the Portuguese Synagogue memorializes the strike held by the dockworkers of Amsterdam in February 1941. The workers were among the first organized groups in Amsterdam to respond to the German occupation, specifically to the arrest of over 400 Jewish men in the area at the order of the German chief of police.

HOLLAND EXPERIENCE 3D

Waterlooplein 17, with an entrance on Jodenbreestraat, as well. Take tram #9, 14, or 20 to Waterlooplein; Holland Experience is adjacent to Het Rembrandthuis. ☎ 422 22 33; fax 422 22 34; info@holland-experience.nl; www.holland-experience.nl. Open daily 10am-6pm; showings on the hour and at 10:30am and 5:30pm. €8, children ages 16 and under and seniors over 65 €6,85, family pass (2 adults and 2 children) €25. Combined ticket with Rembrandthuis €12,50. MC/V.

For a unique and unforgettable Dutch experience, check into this movie/bizarro festival of the senses, which takes viewers on a thirty-minute tour of Holland that includes some rather puzzling shots of aquatic ballet, little girls playing with umbrellas, dykes bursting under the pressure of the sea, and women posing for photographs next to a giant baby made of sand. The moving theater, wind and sound effects, images of modern and traditional Dutch culture, and 80,000 liters of water rushing through the theater make the experience an assault on the senses. Be sure to view the breathtaking aerial photography also on display.

STADHUIS-HET MUZIEKTHEATER

Waterlooplein. Take tram #9 or 20a to Waterlooplein, or take the Metro, any line, from Centraal and get off at the 2nd stop, Waterlooplein. Box office ☎625 54 55; online bookings at www.het-muziektheater.nl. Box office open M-Sa 10am-curtain, Su and holidays 11:30am-curtain; if there is no evening performance, the box office closes at 6pm. AmEx/DC/MC/V.

Nicknamed the "Stopera" by protestors who objected to the demolition of historic buildings in the old Jewish quarter in favor of new buildings, the Muziektheater is home to The Netherlands Opera and the National Ballet and inhabits a large complex on the Amstel with Amsterdam's city hall, or Stadhuis. Productions in 2003 will include Beethoven's *Fidelio*, Puccini's *Madama Butterfly*, Verdi's *Macbeth*, Mozart's *Die Zauberflote*, and Bizet's *Carmen*.

MOZES EN AARON KERK (MOSES AND AARON CHURCH)

Waterlooplein 207. Take sneltram #51 or tram #9, 14, or 20 to Waterlooplein. The large, white church is located where Waterlooplein meets Mr. Visserplein. ☎622 1305; fax 638 63 66.

Now used only for concerts, exhibitions, expositions, and celebrations, Mozes en Aaron Kerk was built in 1841, the sole Christian establishment in the Jewish quarter. Having at one time received visits from Franz Liszt and Camille Saint-Saens, the church has a lively musical past that it has carried into the present with its many musical performances. Call or email for information on upcoming events, or just enjoy this daunting piece of Classical architecture in the heart of Waterlooplein.

WERTHEIM PARK

Plantage Middenlaan, across from Hortus Botanicus. Open daily 8am-sundown.

Home to the **Auschwitz Nooit Meer** (Auschwitz Never Again) monument, this small park on the Nieuwe Herengracht is a great place to stretch out on a sunny day. One of several green spaces in the Plantage, Wertheim Park provides many a contemplative spot for its visitors.

SCHEEPVAARTHUIS (SHIPPING HOUSE)

Prins Henrikkade 108-114, near Centraal Station. ☎625 89 08.

This rather imposing building was constructed in 1916 under the direction of architects Piet Kramer, Johan Melchior van der Mey, and Michel de Kerk. One of the first examples of the Amsterdam School of architecture, it is remarkable for its unique interior, exterior decorations, and especially its multiplicity of sculpted reliefs on the building's façades. Now that it's an office building, its entrance is regulated, but it's worth taking the time to enjoy this unique bit of modern Amsterdam architecture from the outside.

Almost Infinite Canals

Artis Planetarium

Artis Aquarium

GET smart

Dutch Droog Design

Amsterdam has a growing cluster of hip "design" restaurants and even hotels that are slick and sleek. The showroom and center of inspiration for this design is the **Pakhuis,** a 19th-century storehouse for cacao and sugar in the Eastern docklands that was converted into the locus of Dutch furniture design in 1999. In a four-story space that's been made fresh with strategic implementations of steel and glass, the Pakhuis shows the latest wares of 35 different interior and home designers. The Pakhuis indirectly supports **Droog design,** a consortium of young Dutch designs that was started in 1993 by Renny Ramkers and Gijs Bakkers. Droog is the irreverent grandson of De Stijl, continuing in Mondrian and his pals' tradition of minimalism. Characteristic of their cutting-edge creations is a chandelier made of almost 100 bare bulbs hung in an upside down wire bouquet. Droog's spare use of resources and ingenious use of recycled materials seem fitting for a country that so cleverly made land out of water.

The Pakhuis, Oostelijke Handelskade 17, has a chic café overlooking the Ij. Bike east from Centraal Station or take bus #38, 39, or 43 to PTA.

SECOND WORLD WAR NAVAL MONUMENT

The large fountain between NEMO and Scheepvaartmuseum, beside Vereniging Museumhaven.

This magnificent marine monument just east of the displayed boats of the Museumhaven remembers the hundreds of Dutch fighters who died as a result of German U-boats between May, 1940 and May, 1945. The fountain conveys these soldiers' virility and moral fortitude by depicting powerful horses and angels existing happily in the sea.

SCHREIERSTOREN AND VOC CAFE

On Prins Hendrikkade, less than 5min. left from Centraal Station. It is on the far side of the street in the base of a dark, short, stumpy tower. Cafe open Su-Th 9:30am-1:30am and F-Sa until 2:30am; kitchen open 11am-3:30pm. Sandwiches, soups, and salads from €2,50 to €5,50.

Weepy wives, sisters, mothers, and mistresses of sailors bid farewell to their ocean-bound men at this 15th-century tower, which is situated near the Oosterdok, where the Zuider Zee (South Sea) used to meet the shore of The Netherlands. Customers are permitted to climb the two stories to the zenith of this 20-meter tower.

VERENIGING MUSEUMHAVEN AMSTERDAM

On the water between the NEMO and Scheepvaartmuseum. Open daily. Free.

This collection of 18 boats is tucked quietly between NEMO and the Scheepvaartmuseum. While visitors cannot board the vessels, placards explaining the history of each of the late 19th- and early 20th-century ships are posted on the docks.

MUSEUMS IN THE AREA

Joods Historisch Museum (Jewish Historical Museum), see Museums, p. 94.

Verzetsmuseum (Dutch Resistance Museum), see Museums, p. 94.

Museum het Rembrandt, see Museums, p. 95.

Tropenmuseum (Museum of the Tropics), see Museums, p. 95.

Scheepvaartmuseum (Maritime Museum), see Museums, p. 96.

Nationaal Vakbondsmuseum "de Burcht" (National Trade Union Museum "The Fortress"), see Museums, p. 96.

GREATER AMSTERDAM

Sometimes it doesn't hurt to leave the Canal Ring. Here are some major sights that just don't fit on our maps.

AMSTERDAMSE BOS (AMSTERDAM FOREST)

Main entrance at Nieuwe Kalfjeslaan 4. Take bus #172 from Centraal, Dam, Westermarkt, Leidseplein, Museumplein, or Stadionplein to Van Nijenrodeweg, or just ask for Amsterdamse Bos. ☎643 14 14; www.amsterdamsebos.amsterdam.nl.

With 19km of bike trails, countless excellent picnic spots, some weaving waterways, a small petting zoo, and a picturesque pancake house, these woods may well be the city's best-kept secret. The expansive green space at times feels more of a park than of a forest, with several football pitches and roads covering the Amstelveen land. Many a quiet acre exists, however, providing some well-needed repose from the city of red lights. Spend an afternoon, day, or week in the *bos*, which offers **camping** at the southernmost tip of the forest for only €2,80 per night if you bring your own tent (☎641 68 68; camping@dab.amsterdam.nl). **Rental bikes** are available at the main entrance for €3,50 per hr., €5 per 2hr., and €7 per day. Or get your feet wet with 3hr. **canoe, waterbike,** or **electric boat** (2 people in a canoe €8; 2 in a waterbike €8; 5 in an electric boat €22). The forest's most popular attraction is its **petting zoo.** It is located about 3km southwest of the entrance and you can buy a €0,60 milk bottle to feed a thankful goat or sheep. (☎645 50 34; open daily 9am-6pm.) Another fun spot for kids is the **Bosmuseum** at the northwest corner of the *bos*, with interactive nature exhibits, including an underground tunnel that allows visitors to explore life beneath the earth's surface. (☎676 21 52. Open daily 9am-6pm.) **Pannenkoekenboerderij Meerzicht,** Koenenkade 56, sits at the northwestern corner of the forest. It offers both tasty cuisine and titillating views from riverside terraces. Open only for lunch and early dinner, pancakes with traditional (or unusual) ingredients range from €4 to €8, sandwiches from €2 to €3,40. (☎679 27 44; www.boerderijmeerzicht.nl. Open Mar.-Oct. daily 10am-7pm; Nov.-Feb. F-Su 10am-6pm.)

ARENA STADIUM

ArenA Boulevard 1. Metro #54 to ArenA, dir: Gein; 2 zones; 15min. €2,10. Enter on the far side of the stadium, near ingang (gate) F. ☎311 13 36 or 311 14 44 for tickets; www.amsterdamarena.nl; www.ajax.nl. Open daily 10am-5pm, tours every 90min. Guided 1hr. tour of stadium €8; under 12 and over 65 €7; Ajax museum €3,50.

The Dutch passion for football (soccer) rivals any in the world and the state-of-the-art, 52,000-seat stadium built on Amsterdam's outskirts seven years ago is testament to that fact. For a small nation, The Netherlands enjoys a distinguished football history, peaking in the 1970s, when the Dutch invention of the "total football" style earned the nation two second-place finishes in the World Cup. Amsterdam's love for "the beautiful game" focuses, on the local side, on Amsterdamsche Football Club (AFC) Ajax. The team, almost unanimously supported by Amsterdammers, rewards its fans with consistently high-level play, having won both the Dutch Cup and Dutch Championship in 2002. With 40,000 season ticket holders, the stadium's 12,000 remaining tickets (from €15) sell quickly but are available for many matches. Games against hated metropolitan rivals like Feyenoord Rotterdam and FC Utrecht usually sell out. If you do get a ticket, be aware that local hooligans occupy the western goal end of the ArenA, known as F-Side. The tour will take you onto the actual field, home to large concerts, club football matches, and home games of the Amsterdam Admirals, NFL Europe's 6th and final addition in 1996 (games Sa, from €15). The small museum attached to the stadium gives visitors an impassioned look at the town's pride team.

TOURS

Sometimes you just can't do it yourself. Boat tours of the city are a great way to start off any trip to Amsterdam—the city's layout makes much more sense when you view it from the waterways. Bike tours can get you out of the city to see parts of The Netherlands you might never discover by train. And diamond tours are just about the only way visitors can get into a diamond workshop without becoming apprentices.

BOAT TOURS

Amsterdam Canal Cruises, Nicholas Witsenskade 1A (☎626 56 36), boards on the Singel. From Centraal, take tram #16, 24, or 25 and exit at "Ferdinand Bolstraat," then backtrack about 80m to the canal, Singel. 75min. for €8, kids only €3,50. A bit more expensive but perhaps a better choice.

Canal Bike (☎626 55 74, www.canal.nl), at 4 moorings: Rijksmuseum, Leidseplein, Keizergr. at Leidsestraat, and Anne Frank Huis. Not a tour, not a bike, these paddleboats offer a more exercise-intensive experience. Open 10am-10pm, off-season 10am-6:30pm. Printed route guides €2. Required deposit €50. For 1-2 people €7 per hr., for 3+ persons €6.

Canal Bus (☎626 55 74; www.canal.nl), which travels 3 routes with 11 stops (Centraal Station, Rijksmuseum, Leidseplein, Anne Frank Huis, Stadhuis, Westerkerk, Tropenmuseum, NEMO, Scheepvaartmuseum, Artis Zoo, and Rembrandthuis), is worth your while only if you plan on doing heavy sightseeing over a 12hr. period. At €14 for adults and €10 for kids. Your pass is valid until noon the next day and gives you discounts at some museums and restaurants. Runs 10am-6pm.

Lovers, (Prins Hendrikkade 25-27; ☎530 10 90; www.lovers.nl) offers several different options in canal travel. For €8, you can hop on a 1hr. canal cruise (every hour from 10am-5pm) that leaves from the main depot across from Centraal Station. The **Museumboot,** which has pickups every 30-45min. at Centraal, Anne Frank Huis, Rijksmuseum, Bloemenmarkt, Waterlooplein, and the old shipyard, offers a day ticket for €13,50 or €11 after 1pm. For romance, try a candlelight cruise (€23, 9pm daily) or a 3hr. dinner cruise (€65, 7:30pm daily), each of which leaves from outside Centraal.

Wetlands Safari (☎686 34 35; www.wetlandssafari.nl) takes visitors on a different kind of boat tour, allowing tourists to escape urban Amsterdam and explore the beautiful nature and landscape of its surroundings. The 5hr. bus and canoe tour includes a light lunch and more greenery than you can imagine (€30, May 1-Sept. 15 M-F 9:30am from the VVV outside Centraal Station).

BIKE AND BUS TOURS

To rent your own bike, see the **Service Directory,** p. 297.

Lowlands Travel, Korvelplein 176, 5025 JX Tilburg (☎013 468 79 02; info@lowlandstravel.nl; www.lowlandstravel.nl). Tour guide Theo Leerintveld started Lowlands Travel when he decided that travelers interested in seeing The Netherlands' more secret treasures simply weren't being served by the larger tour companies. Now every week Lowlands Travel takes small groups (max. 9 people) on personalized tours of The Netherlands and Belgium in the hope of revealing the places still untouched by souvenir shops and camera-wielding tourists. Several tours are available, including a bike and hike tour, expeditions through northern or southern Holland, and a tour that combines the highlights of The Netherlands and Belgium. All tours include transportation, meals, and accommodations and start at €199.

Mike's Bike Tours, Nieuwezijds 29 (☎622 79 70; mike@bavaria.com; www.mikesbiketours.com), runs very popular tours of the city and surrounding areas led by hilarious, well-informed guides. 3-4hr. tours meet daily at the west entrance of the Rijksmuseum, Stadhouderskade 42. April 1-15 and Sept.-Oct. 12:30pm; May-Aug. 11:30am and 4pm. No reservations necessary. Rain gear provided. Traveler's checks accepted, no credit cards. €20.

Yellow Bike, Nieuwezijds Kolk 29 (☎620 69 40; fax 620 71 40; www.yellowbike.nl), take tram #1, 2, 5, 13, or 17 to Nieuwezijds Kolk or walk a few blocks north from Dam and the street will be on your right. Tour Amsterdam by bike with an English-speaking guide or rent a bike and ride off into the sunset, or even into wine and cheese country. Tours operate Apr. 1-Nov. 1. On special request, group tours can be conducted in German, Dutch, French, or Spanish. Though bike rental is a bit pricey (€8 for 1 day and a credit card imprint or €100 deposit per bike), but the guided tours are a great way to get to know the area and even find some hidden gems. 3hr. city tour departs Su-F at 9:30am and 1pm, Sa 9:30am and 2pm (€17), 6hr. country tour departs daily at 11am (€22,50).

Smallest House in Amsterdam

DIAMOND TOURS

In the late 19th- and early 20th-century, Amsterdam was a major world diamond center, with a massive amount of this precious gem cut and sold in the Waterlooplein and Jodenbuurt area. Today, many of the original manufacturers offer free tours highlighting their process and final result. For those so inclined, the factories are also a great place to purchase the gem, presenting wholesale prices and eliminating the significant tax for tourists. Bring your receipt to the airport for VAT discount.

Paddleboats

Gassan Diamonds, Nieuwe Uilenburgerstraat 173-175 (☎622 53 33; www.gassandiamonds.com), Take the Metro, any line, from Centraal. Exit at Jodenbreestraat and take Uilenburgerstraat east from there. Gassan is large diamond manufacturer on the Uilenburger canal with an impressive showroom and particularly friendly tour guides. Free tours every few minutes. Open daily 9am-5pm.

Stoeltie Diamonds, Wagenstraat 13-17 (☎623 76 01; www.stoeltiediamonds.com), from Rembrandtplein, take Amstelstraat east and turn left on Wagenstraat. Offers comprehensive free tours of their beautiful diamond factory. Open daily 8:30am-5pm.

Amstel Diamonds, Amstel 206-208 (☎623 14 79). Take any subway to Waterlooplein, exit at the Stadhuis/Muziektheater and the factory is on the other side of the Amstel. A small diamond manufacturer that has worked on the river since 1876, it's one of the older locations that's still open. Free guided tours M-Sa 9am-5pm, Su 10am-5pm.

Amsterdam Diamond Center, Rokin 1-5 (☎624 57 87; www.amsterdamdiamondcenter.nl). A certain tourist trap, they do give efficient, interesting tours of their facility on the Dam. Open daily 9:30am-6:30pm.

On the Tour Boat

INSIDE:

Museums

Amsterdam's museums have captured the artsiest, wackiest, and scariest things you've ever seen. Whether you want to admire Rembrandts and Van Goghs, cutting-edge photography, or just to giggle at sex, Amsterdam has a museum for every purpose. The most famous ones are crowded into the Musumplein, but other neighborhoods hide smaller museums, often devoted to specific purposes.

OUDE ZIJD

see maps pp. 330-331

AMSTERDAMS CENTRUM VOOR FOTOGRAFIE (AMSTERDAM CENTER FOR PHOTOGRAPHY)

Bethanienstraat 9, between Kloveniersburgwal and Oudezijds Achterburgwal. Head toward the Flying Dutchman on Oudezijds Achterburgwal; Bethanienstraat will be on the left. (☎622 48 99.) Open W-Sa 1-5pm. Closed July to mid-August. Free.

A brimming forum of the latest work by up-and-coming future photography luminaries, the Centrum voor Fotografie holds six-week-long exhibitions throughout the year (with a mid-summer hiatus). You're likely to find a wide range of quality, but there's always some remarkable and challenging work throughout the three floors. This is where the rising stars of the Dutch photo world get their start (though one exhibition out of every year focuses on an international artist). Darkrooms are available when not being used for lessons (€3,20-9,10 per 2hr.), though membership is required (€9,10 for 2 months).

on the cheap

Save $$$!

Those planning to hit a handful of museums may want to invest in a Museum Jaarkaart (MJK). An especially good deal for younger travelers, the pass (€31,75, under 25 €13,60) entitles the holder to admission at major museums all over The Netherlands, including the Van Gogh Museum, Rijksmuseum, and the Anne Frank Huis. The cards are good for one year, but can be worth it even for those staying a week (combined admission to the Van Gogh Museum and Rijksmuseum is about the price of an under-25 card). Bring a passport photo and buy the MJK card at most of the participating museums. It will save you money, but it may not save you any time; card holders still have to wait in line with everyone else. For more info, check www.museumjaarkaart.nl.

RED LIGHT DISTRICT

see maps pp. 330-331

THE VICES

If it's weed that interests you, far and away your best bet is the staggeringly informative **Cannabis College** (Oudezijds Achterburgwal 124. ☎423 44 20; www.cannabiscollege.com. Open daily 11am-7pm. Free.) For sheer weight of information on everything from the uses of medicinal marijuana to facts about the War on Drugs to the creative applications of industrial hemp, it's ounce-for-ounce the equal of the Hash Museum (see below), and it's free. The staff is incredibly friendly and even more knowledgeable; they are eager to answer any questions you could possibly have. See an artfully designed growroom for a donation of €2,50. You're better off blowing your €5,70 on a bag of grass at one of the many coffeeshops right down the street than dropping it on admission to the **Hash Marijuana Hemp Museum.** Mostly pro-pot leaflets tacked to partitions designed to make a small room seem much larger than it is, the museum's only other attraction is its growroom, which does little more than prove that watching grass grow is indeed as exciting as it sounds. *(Oudezijds Achterburgwal 148. ☎62 35 91; www.sensiseeds.com. Open daily 11am-10pm. €5,70.)*

For a taste of the seaminess that runs down Amsterdam's underbelly in museum form, your best bet is to get your jollies right off the train at the **Amsterdam Sex Museum,** Damrak 18, less than a five-minute walk from Centraal Station. The low admission fee won't leave you feeling burned if you find that walls plastered with pictures of such colorful themes as bestiality and S&M are not your thing. The first of four floors, most of which are fairly uninformative and surprisingly preachy, features some amusing life-size mannequins of pimps, prostitutes, and even one immodest fellow who literally flashes you; at times the experience feels more like a horror museum than an amorous one. Heed, however, the warnings on the way into the gallery of fetishes: it is not for the weak of stomach. *(☎622 83 76. Open daily 10am-11:30pm. €2,50.)* And if you just haven't had enough, you can head over to the **Erotic Museum,** which adds a fifth floor but is otherwise an almost exact replica of the Sex Museum at twice the price (although it does have the distinction of most creative use of fruit with a mannequin). Otherwise, it's the same ol', same ol' about sex through history in all its nutritious and delicious incarnations. If you do decide to take the plunge, be sure to head to the booths on the fourth floor that allow you to listen to phone sex in six different languages. *(Oudezijds Achterburgwal 54, ☎ 624 73 03. Open Su-Th 11am-1am, F-Sa 11am-2am. €5.)*

MUSEUM AMSTELKRING "ONS' LIEVE HEER OP SOLDER" ("OUR LORD IN THE ATTIC")

Oudezijds Voorburgwal 40, at the corner of Oudezijds Armstraat, 5min. from Centraal Station. (☎ 624 66 04; www.museumamstelkring.nl.) Open M-Sa 10am-5pm, Su and holidays 1-5pm. Closed Jan. 1 and Apr. 30. €4,50, students and under 18 €3,40.

It's unfortunate that this hidden church is also one of Amsterdam's best attractions. Most people simply pass Museum Amstelkring by without a second glance. "Ons' Lieve Heer Op Solder" provides a number of pleasant surprises, however, without the mile-long lines at bigger attractions. The last of Amsterdam's secret churches (or the only one that remains in its original state), the museum recalls the time when Amsterdam was officially Protestant and Catholics could not freely practice their religion (see **Shhh... it's a Secret (Church),** p. 80). Today it still hosts occasional services, including Christmas Eve mass. Built in the attics of three adjoining houses on the edge of the Red Light District, the stunning little chapel makes clever use of its clandestine space with a pulpit stored under the altar and galleries suspended from the roof by cast iron rods. There is also an organ tucked into the ceiling, abundant artwork, and a grand collection of silver for the mass. The rooms in the lower levels of the museum are especially interesting as examples of the rigid Dutch Classical school of design, an aesthetic which valued symmetry above all else. One of these rooms, the "Sael," includes a false door just to preserve that symmetry.

NIEUWE ZIJD

see maps pp. 330-331

NIEUWE KERK

Adjacent to Dam Sq., beside Koninklijk Palace. (☎ 638 69 09; www.nieuwekerk.nl.) Open daily 10am-6pm. Organ recitals most Su 8pm, July-Sept. €8, seniors 65+ €7, ages 6-15 €5.

Bijbels Museum

Our Lord in the Attic

Amsterdam History Museum Gallery

SHHH.... IT'S A SECRET (CHURCH)

Today, Dutch society is undoubtedly one of the world's most liberal, but it wasn't always an easy road to its present form. In the 16th century, when Catholicism began toppling in many of European countries, Spain's Hapsburg rulers fought like hell to turn the tide of the Protestant Reformation. Though Amsterdam, Holland's most powerful region, began the war on the side of Spain, it shifted allegiance in 1578, beginning a period called the **Alteration.** During this time, Catholics were not permitted to practice their religion openly and were driven into so-called "secret churches," which took root in private residences and remained imperceptible from the outside. Ons' Lieve Heer Op Solder ("Our Lord in the Attic"), now a museum open to the public, is one such church.

Nieuwe Kerk, the 15th-century church at the heart of the Nieuwe Zijd, is both museum and sight, offering a fascinating escape for any traveler. In early 2003, the originally Catholic church will open its doors to rotating exhibits from the **Stedelijk** collection while that museum is being renovated. Though the Nieuwe Kerk might be massive in scale, some of its greatest pleasures are to be found in its smallest details. Take a moment to stray from the main exhibit to discover the ornate hexagonal pulpit with its intricate carvings (check out the tiny angels sliding down the wooden ropes). Made of mahogany, it was created over a period of 15 years by artist Albert Jansz Vinckenbrinck. Also be sure to tilt your head upwards to glance at another fascinating design feature: winged children who appear to be bearing the weight of the vaulted ceiling. The church, which has been rebuilt several times after fire, is still used for coronations and royal weddings. Queen Wilhelmina was crowned here in 1898, followed by her daughter Juliana in 1948, and granddaughter Beatrix (the reigning monarch) in 1980. As recently as February, 2002, Prince Wilhelm Alexander, the future king of Holland, was married to an Argentine belle in Nieuwe Kerk's hallowed sanctuary.

AMSTERDAMS HISTORISCH MUSEUM (AMSTERDAM HISTORICAL MUSEUM)

Kalverstraat 92, Sint Luciensteeg 27, and Nieuwezijds Voorburgwal 357. Take tram #4, 9, 14, 16, 20a, 24, or 25 to Spui, or 1, 2, or 5 to Nieuwezijds Voorburgwal. (☎523 18 50; www.ahm.nl.) Open M-F 10am-5pm, Sa, Su, and holidays 11am-5pm; closed Apr. 30. ***€6****, ages 6-16 and 65+* ***€4,50****.*

The building itself oozes history; the house, constructed in the 17th century, used to be Amsterdam's city orphanage. This museum, worth visiting after a few days in Amsterdam, is the only one in the city devoted entirely to exploring the city itself. Compelling, colorful, and well-organized exhibits use art (the museum's collection of Renaissance and modern canvases is quite impressive), models, historical artifacts, and audio-visual aids to give the museum's history lesson its context. You will be taken on a tour of Amsterdam's history, beginning on the ground floor with "The Young City, 1350-1550" and continuing through the Reformation, Industrial Revolution, and finishing in "The Modern City, 1850-2000." The section of the museum that features artistic accounts of gory Golden Age anatomy lessons (Rembrandt's among them) is particularly interesting. The space devoted to Amsterdam's maritime history is also fascinating, giving much needed dimension to the stories of exploration and struggle that surround the Dutch East India Company. Be sure to catch one of the Historical Museum's hidden surprises in the passageway between the museum and Begijnhof: an outdoor collection of very large canvases portraying the Amsterdam civic guard. Beyond that passage, the remainder of the museum focuses on Amsterdam's more contemporary history. The collection of visual art is wonderful: photographs and paintings explain to the spectator bit by bit how Amsterdam came to be the city it is today, while contemporary films and displays explore and explain the unconventional Amsterdam of today.

BEURS VAN BERLAGE

Damrak 277. (☎530 41 41; www.beursvanberlage.nl.) Open Tu-Su 11am-5pm. €5, under 18 free.

Architecture buffs will drool over this old stock and commodities exchange, designed by Hendrik van Berlage in 1903. The edifice was influential because of its neo-Romanesque stylings and the techniques it developed to sustain its massive weight in the porous Amsterdam soil. If you look closely in this newly renovated museum, you'll notice double portices, designed by Berlage to support the mass of the building on sinking ground. In 2000, a wide tunnel was built under the structure, continuing the everlasting Dutch battle with land. While the restored interior chambers provide a fascinating look at the workings of the Dutch economy at the turn of the century, the highlight of the museum may well be the vertiginous ascent up a rickety staircase to the top of the clock tower. Those gutsy enough to brave the climb will be rewarded with a sweeping 360° view of the city. The interior space has since been changed from a trading floor into a gallery space featuring rotating exhibits of modern art. The museum also charts Dutch economic history since 1900 but will shift its focus toward the study and exhibition of architectural models, paintings, and photographs, beginning in 2003.

ALLARD PIERSON MUSEUM

Oude Turfmarkt 127. Located across the Amstel from Rokin, less than 5min. from Dam Square. (☎525 25 56; www.uba.uva.nl/apm.) Open Tu-F 10am-5pm, Sa-Su 1-5pm. €4,30, seniors and students €3,20, ages 12-15 €1,40, 4-11 €0,45, under 4 free.

BIZARRE AMSTERDAM

The Van Gogh Museum, the Tropenmuseum, and the Rijksmuseum are obvious must-sees for the museum-goer. But Amsterdam is also host to an eclectic collection of collections. Convince your friends and family that your trip to Amsterdam has been truly educational by sending them a postcard from one of the following (very different) museums:

Nationaal Brilmuseum (National Glasses Museum), in the Rembrandtplein (p. 87).

Amsterdam Sex Museum, in the Oude Zijd (p. 78).

Amsterdam Erotic Museum, in the Oude Zijd (p. 78).

Woonboot Museum, in the Jordaan (p. 88).

Torture Museum, in Nieuwmarkt (p. 87).

Bijbels Museum, in the Canal Ring West (p. 84).

Pianola Museum, in the Jordaan (p. 88).

in recent news

Betrayal Revisited

The fact that nobody ever found the person who betrayed the Frank family to the Nazis has always infuriated readers of Anne's diary. After an extensive search Otto Frank eventually conceded that it would be impossible to find conclusive proof about the person who alerted the Nazis to his family's hiding place.

The main suspects had always been Willem van Maaren—an employee of Frank who was also known as an unsavory character—or their cleaning woman, Lena Hartog.

However, a recent biography of Otto Frank has offered a new suspect and convinced The Netherlands Institute for War Documentation to reopen its investigation about the betrayal. *The Hidden Life of Otto Frank* by Carol Ann Lee proposes that Anton Ahlers not only handed over the family, but blackmailed Otto Frank after the war. Ahlers was a business associate of Frank, but when his own company fell into bankruptcy, Frank was no longer useful. Ahlers, an open anti-Semite, may have told a Nazi friend (who was at the arrest, conveniently enough) about the family. After the diary was published, Ahlers may have blackmailed Otto so that the public wouldn't know that he sold supplies to the Germans at the beginning of the war.

Experience a Classical blast from the ancient past at this comprehensive, well-manicured collection of artifacts from ancient Egypt, Greece, Mesopotamia, Etruria, and Rome. Something out of the ordinary, with vases and statues featuring the city's classiest, albeit 20-millennia-old, full frontal nudes. The museum inhabits the former headquarters of the Dutch central bank, and it shows: the displays often clash with the bright, institutional feel of the place, leaving the visitor with a feeling of real distance from the subject. Thirty-thousand excavated objects—magnificently restored to include even the smallest 10th-century BCE Syrian detail—fill display cases. The museum's mission is to highlight Mediterranean antiquity for scholars and laymen alike, bringing the exhibit to life, ironically enough, with excavated mummies and authentic 10,000-year-old skulls. Special collections include a glass negatives exhibit and a chronological arrangement of plaster casts.

MADAME TUSSAUD'S WAX MUSEUM

Dam 20. Take any tram to Dam Sq.; Madame Tussaud's is on the corner. (☎ 522 10 10; www.madametussauds.com.) Open Sept.-July 14 daily 10am-5:30pm; July 15-Aug. 9:30am-7pm. Closed Apr. 30. €12,50, ages 5-15 €8,50, over 60 €10,50. Discounts for families and groups over 10. €5 brochure is worth it.

The idea of going to see wax sculptures of famous people at an international, Brit-owned chain may seem way too touristy for savvy *Let's Go* readers, but Madame Tussaud's is actually pretty fun. In the spring of 2002, the museum spent over €4 million on renovations, so the wax statues are now presented with sound and motion—you even get to see George W. Bush and Australian superstar Kylie Minogue. Don't miss the great view of Dam Sq. from the round window on the fourth floor either.

The exhibit starts with a Disneyfied version of Dutch history, recreating the fight for independence with the blast of a smoking cannon and then moving into street scenes of the "Golden Age" of the 17th century. It also brings images from Dutch master painters to human scale before moving onto the contemporary political leaders, pop singers, athletes, and movie stars. Camp it up and pose for a cheek-to-cheek picture with your favorite "celebrity." Some of them are obviously fake but chances are you'll be caught off guard at least once.

see maps pp. 328-329

ANNE FRANK HUIS

Prinsengracht 267. Trams #13, 14, 17, or 20 to Westermarkt. (☎556 71 00; www.annefrank.nl.) Open Apr.-Aug. daily 9am-9pm; Sept.-Mar. 9am-7pm. Closed on Yom Kippur. Last admission 30min. before closing. €6,50; ages 10-17 €3 under 10 free.

Anne Frank was a ten-year-old girl when World War II began in 1939. In 1942, when Hitler and the Nazis commenced the deportation of all Jews to ghettoes and concentration camps, Anne's family and four other Dutch Jews hid in the *achterhuis*, or annex, of Otto Frank's warehouse on the Prinsengracht. The eight of them lived in this secret annex for two years, during which time Anne Frank penned her diary, a moving chronicle of life as a Jew in Nazi-occupied Holland. Today, it is one of the most widely read books in the world. It is there that she admitted "it's a wonder that I haven't dropped all my ideals because they seem absurd and impossible to carry out. Yet I keep them, because in spite of everything I still believe that people are really good at heart."

The rooms are no longer furnished, which can sometimes make it difficult to imagine the cramped conditions and lack of privacy that Anne describes. But personal objects in display cases, text panels with excerpts from the diary, and video screens showing the rooms as they once looked all help transport you into Anne's world. The magazine clippings and photos that she used to decorate her room still hang on the wall. Finally, footage of interviews with Otto Frank (Anne's father), Miep Gies (who supplied the family with food and other necessities), and childhood friends of Anne provide further details.

After walking through the house, be sure to check out the state-of-the-art CD-ROM exhibit, which gives the visitor a chance to learn more about the war and navigate through a virtual tour of the house as it looked furnished. Adjacent to that, there's an interactive display that strives to relate the Holocaust to current human rights issues, asking visitors to vote on whether they believe in the freedom of expression or in non-discrimination, assuming of course that the two are mutually exclusive. In the exhibit, visitors watch a film documenting civil rights issues of the past few years, including the Gay Pride

Interactive Exhibit at Anne Frank House

Anne Frank's Posters

Belltower Stairs at Westerkerk

House des Cartes

Just around the corner from the Anne Frank House at 6 Westermarkt (a place to check out if you're in a long line), an inconspicuous plaque above the ground-floor windows marks the spot where Descartes lived in the summer of 1634. The French philosopher, famous for the phrase "I think therefore I am," started the Enlightenment with his rational, skeptical questioning. His recognition of the mind as a separate entity from the universe paved the way for scientific advances in which humans understood themselves as able to master nature. The secular foundation for existence that he propounded was not looked upon favorably by the Catholic church in France, and Descartes fled to the religiously tolerant Amsterdam, where he lived from 1629-1635. The plaque bears a phrase from a letter he wrote to Jean-Louis Guez de Balzac—a French man of letters who studied in Leiden—in 1631 saying, "In which other country can one enjoy such perfect liberty?" The implied answer, of course, is "nowhere."

eruption in Rome in 2000. While the effort at linking the past and present is appreciated, the gawky "Weakest Link" style viewing area diminishes the exhibit's solemnity. While there is an understated panel near the exit that links the Holocaust to present-day genocides in Rwanda and Serbia, there is, unfortunately, no larger exhibit that could truly express Anne Frank's significance today.

The line bending around the corner attests to the popularity of the Anne Frank House. With extended hours in the summer, there is no reason to waste time queued up for admission—the line diminishes considerably after 5pm, which still leaves plenty of time to see everything and even stop at the bookstore or cafe.

BIJBELS MUSEUM

Herengracht 366-368. Tram #1, 2, or 5 to Spui. (☎624 24 36; fax 624 83 55; info@bijbelsmuseum.nl; www.bijbelsmuseum.nl.) Open M-Sa 10am-5pm, Su 1-5pm. €5, children €2,50.

The Bijbels Museum is, essentially, two museums in one. The main focus is the Bible; what began in 1851 as one man's passion for all things biblical has blossomed into a veritable holy land of architectural models and bibliophilia. The museum successfully describes the contents of the Bible and then aims to discern the historical context in which it was written. Highlights include the various models of King Solomon's destroyed Second Temple in Jerusalem, especially the 1989 plexiglass version by Ben Hoezen that contrasts nicely with older, more traditional but equally amazing interpretations. The second part of the museum provides a history of the area. On the bottom floor, the museum switches gears, emphasizing the well-preserved canal houses that have been home to the museum since 1975. Take some time to admire the portraits and ceiling murals in the front rooms, and make sure not to miss the kitchen in the back, one of the best preserved examples from the 17th century. Continue the visit in the two tiny aroma rooms, one with "exalted" fragrances like lotus and myrrh and the other with "everyday" scents from biblical times like fig and pomegranate. The lush garden out back keeps the biblical theme going with date palms and madonna lilies.

HUIS MARSEILLE

Keizergracht 401 (☎531 89 89; www.huis-marseille.nl.) Open Tu-Su 11am-5pm; in summers Tu-W 11am-5pm, Th-Sa 11am-7pm. €2,50, under 12 free.

A must for photography buffs, this museum in a 1665 canal house features rotating exhibits of photography, focusing on the work of a few artists at a time. Exhibits— which change every three months—feature a small number of pieces but are informative and thoughtfully presented in a spacious, beautiful Keizersgracht house.

The museum is also amassing a permanent collection of 20th-century and contemporary works. It includes transcendent pieces by Andreas Gursky and Sam Samore that complement the rotating exhibits.

THEATER INSTITUUT NEDERLAND

Herengracht 168-174. Take any tram to Dam, walk up Raadhuisstraat away from the back of the palace. Turn right at Herengracht. (☎551 33 00; info@tin.nl; www.tin.nl.) Open Tu-F 11am-5pm, Sa-Su 1-5pm. €3,85, students, children, and seniors €1,95.

Housed in five majestic Herengracht canal houses, the Theater Instituut Nederland is a haven of artistic and theatrical expression. The main building of the Instituut is Herengracht 168, which was transformed by Philip Vingboons in 1638 from an alleyway and bakery into a resplendent building with the city's first neck-gable. The museum also extends into the famous Bartolotti house. The buildings now hold a distinctive collection of theater costumes and props, displayed neatly and described by both Dutch and English side panels. Be sure to check out the walls and ceilings of the front reception area; painted by renowned artists Isaac de Moucheron and Jacob de Wit, they tell the legend of Jefta and depict divine figures like Flora, the goddess of the spring. The building also houses a comprehensive library with information and documentation about Dutch theater. In addition, a beautiful, well-lit café dwells in the back with tasty snacks and drinks.

MULTATULI MUSEUM

Korsjespoortsteeg 20. Tram 1, 2, 5, 13 or 17 to Nieuwezijda Kolk, off Herengracht towards the Shipping Quarter. (☎638 19 38; multatulimuseum@wanadoo.nl; www.multatuli-museum.nl/en.) Open Tu 10am-5pm, Sa-Su noon-5pm. Free.

"I am a coffee broker, and I live at No. 37 Lauriergracht, Amsterdam." So begins *Max Havelaar or the Coffee Auctions of the Dutch Trading Company*, just about the only Dutch novel from the 19th century that people still read. Its author, Eduard Douwes Dekker, returned from 20 years in Indonesia disillu-

Heads at the Brilmuseum

Museumplein

Rijksmuseum from across the Canal

sioned by the Dutch government's exploitation of the Javanese and, paradoxically, by his own failure to rise through the ranks of the colonial government. He wavered on whether to express publicly his controversial beliefs. However, in 1860, he wrote this Dutch classic under the pen name Multatuli, Latin for "I have endured much." The novel's anti-colonialist message and fast-paced, witty style made it a classic from the moment it breathed life into the conventional world of mid-19th century Dutch literature.

Today, you can visit a museum dedicated to Dekker's legacy, not on Lauriergracht in the Jordaan but at the author's birthplace in the Western Canal Ring. The Multatuli Museum serves mainly for scholarly research, but the upstairs room does display Multatuli's personal book collection, desk, and the sofa on which he died. A fantastically knowledgeable staff happily recounts the life of Dekker, the most famous author of whom you've never heard.

CENTRAL CANAL RING

see maps pp. 324-325

DE APPEL

Nieuwe Spiegelstraat 10. (☎625 5651; info@deappel.nl; www.deappel.nl.) Open Tu-Su 11am-6pm. €2, students €1.

A cutting-edge art space that makes even the Stedelijk look old-fashioned. De Appel shows contemporary, provocative work—a single artist on the first floor and different exhibits of "cinema, sounds, and synergy" on the second floor. They were the first museum to show video art in The Netherlands, and are now breaking the ground for the newest multimedia installations. Check the web for their Tuesday evening programs (8pm, €2).

FOAM PHOTOGRAPHY MUSEUM

Keizersgracht 609. Tram #16, 24, or 25 to Keisersgracht, between Vijzelstraat and Reguliersgracht. (☎551 6500; info@foam.nl; www.foam.nl.) Open daily 10am-5pm. €3,50, students €2,50.

Opened in June, 2002, Foam showcases appealing photography exhibits that change every few months in a fresh, bright space. The sight is a traditional old canal house but the work inside is young and hip. The museum embraces all kinds of photography, which means its exhibits range from art photography to photojournalism to fashion photography to historical works. The museum recently curated a display of photographs throughout the Vondelpark: they asked professional and amateur photographers to send their most beautiful photos, which were then hung on lampposts. They hope to do more public space exhibits in the future.

MUSEUM WILLET-HOLTHUYSEN

Herengracht 605, between Amstel and Utrechtsestraat. Tram #4, 9, 14, or 20 to Rembrandtplein or Metro to Waterlooplein. (☎523 18 22; www.ahm.nl.) Open M-F 10am-5pm, Sa-Su 11am-5pm. €4, ages 6-16 €2, over 65 €3, under 6 free.

Run by the Amsterdams Historisch Museum, this 17th-century canal house has been preserved as a museum with all its 18th-century furnishings, so you can see how the wealthy in Amsterdam lived over 300 years ago. In 1895, Sandrina Holthuysen donated the family home she shared with her collector husband Abraham Willet. Now, the palatial house with marble and gilt interior stands as a monument to living large. The mansion has been redone in a Baroque, early 18th-century style, with gilt-edged walls, glittering chandeliers, family portraits, Rococo furnishings, and other signs of old-school conspicuous consumption. It holds Abraham's collection of fine porcelain, glassware, and silver. Read the accompanying book to find out the details of life here, such as how water was filtered in the 19th century. The garden out back remains as finely manicured as it was in the Dutch Golden Age.

MUSEUM VAN LOON

Keisersgracht 672, between Vijzelsstraat and Reguliersgracht. Tram #16, 24, or 25 to Keizersgracht. (☎624 52 55; info@museumvanloon.nl; www.museumvanloon.nl.) Open M and F-Su 11am-5pm. €3,50, students and children €2,50.

Built in 1672, Museum Van Loon is a traditional canal side house that showcases family portraits and other artifacts dating to the Golden Age period, bequeathed to the city by the well-to-do Van Loon family. The first occupant of the house was Ferdinand Bol, Rembrandt's most famous pupil. The house is interesting for its preservation of a beautiful, ornate, 18th-century canal house, not just as an art museum. Don't miss the fabulous gilt banister along the central staircase and the gorgeous rose garden out back.

NATIONAAL BRILMUSEUM (NATIONAL GLASSES MUSEUM)

Gasthuismolensteeg 7. Take tram to Dam Sq., walk around the left side of the Palace, turn left, and walk half a block before turning right onto Paleisstraat, which becomes Gasthuismolensteeg. Cross the Singel, and the museum will be in the middle of the next block on your left. (☎421 24 14; brilmuseum.brillenwinkel@worldmail.nl; www.brilmuseumamsterdam.nl.) Open W-F 11:30am-5:30pm, Sa 11:30am-5pm. €4,50, under 12 €2,50; shopping is free.

Located on one of Amsterdam's quieter side streets, it's easy to breeze right by the National Glasses Museum, located in the home of a family that has been collecting specs here for four generations. The four-story building, which dates back to 1620, is stuffed to the gills with glasses—the result of a third-generation optician's 35-year mission to gather and present the world's most fascinating spectacle specimens. While the museum itself doesn't offer much in the way of twists and turns (the exhibits take you through the history of optical science, craftsmanship, and fashion), its novelty alone might make it worth a stop, since you'll probably never spot another place like it. And even if the hefty admission fee is too steep, the shop that occupies the ground floor of the building is definitely worth a peek (sunglasses from €9, most eyewear about €100). Inside you'll find frames from the past century—Schubert's, Buddy Holly's, Dame Edna's—that have not been worn since their famous owners bequeathed them. If you happen to be on the lookout for a pair of unique frames, look no further.

TORTURE MUSEUM

Singel 449. Tram #1, 2, or 5 to Koningsplein; cross the canal and turn right onto Singel. (☎320 66 42.) Open daily 10am-11pm. €5.

About every means of torture imaginable from the Middle Ages is on display at this appropriately dark, claustrophobic museum. Like many of Amsterdam's potentially titillating attractions, it doesn't quite shock as you might expect; the glib explanations of the devices' use and the sight of them sitting so fallow dull the impact of seeing the many racks, guillotines, and thumbscrews. But, if the rest of Amsterdam—the brothels, drugs, and live sex shows—is simply too cheerful for you, this subdued celebration of torture may be just what the executioner ordered.

THE JORDAAN

see maps pp. 328-329

ELECTRIC LADYLAND: THE FIRST MUSEUM OF FLUORESCENT ART

2e Leliedwarsstraat 5 (below the art gallery), off of Prinsengracht between Bloemgracht and Egelantiersgracht. (☎420 37 76; electriclady21@hotmail.com; www.electric-lady-land.com.) Tram #13, 14, 17, or 20, or bus #21, 170, 171, or 172 to Westermarkt. Open Tu-Sa 1-6pm. €5, under 12 free.

From the mines of New Jersey to the heights of the Himalayas, owner Nick Padalino has collected a singularly impressive assortment of fluorescent objects. These include gorgeous rocks that glow green in black light and an array of everyday objects that reveals hidden shades. Even better is Padalino's mind-bending fluorescent sculpture, which he deems "participatory art." Visitors are encouraged to dive into the interactive space and play with the many switches and buttons that turn various lights on and off; try to find the miniature statues and concealed periscopes all about the sculpture. It took him seven years to make, and Padalino—to whom the adjective "knowledgeable" does not do justice—won't hesitate to spend anywhere from an hour to three explaining the science behind the art. The physics is indeed interesting, but the real treat in this basement realm is the truly breathtaking and entirely unique psychedelic sculpture.

WOONBOOTMUSEUM

Prinsengracht opposite #296 facing Elandsgracht (☎427 07 50, info@houseboatmuseum.nl, www.houseboatmuseum.nl.) Open Mar.-Oct. W-Su 11am-5pm; Nov.-Feb. F-Su 11am-5pm. €2,50, under 152cm €2.

Houseboats in Amsterdam began as a way to relieve overcrowding and a severe housing shortage following World War II. Since then, living on the water has become quite popular, with 2500 houseboats now lining the canals. This houseboat lets you see what the floating life might be like, complete with low ceilings, a tiny bathroom, and a slide show about other boats in the area.The museum also includes a limited offering of beverages and a small gift shop.

STEDELIJK MUSEUM BUREAU AMSTERDAM

Rozenstraat 59. (☎422 04 71; fax 626 17 30; mail@smba.nl; www.smba.nl.) Open Tu-Su 11am-5pm. Free.

This adjunct of the Stedelijk devotes itself to exhibiting the newest in Amsterdam art. The 10-12 shows per year range from the rather traditional forms of painting and sculpture to the more outrageous attempts at installation art and performance pieces. Emphasis on contemporary work can be hit or miss, but hey, it's free.

PIANOLA MUSEUM

Westerstraat 106. (☎627 96 24; www.pianola.nl.) Open Su 1-5pm and by appointment during the week. €3,75, children €2,50.

You wouldn't expect to find a pianola museum, well, anywhere, but least of all tucked into the bustling Westerstraat. The museum began as a private collection but now provides a unique glimpse into an otherwise undiscussed niche culture. It houses a towering collection of 15,000 vintage player piano rolls and hosts regular weekend concerts (check website for details). This offbeat museum lets the visitor explore not only the history of the pianola, but the entire scope of the 1920s, when the popularity of this dodo of musical instruments was at its peak. The kind curator may even demonstrate some of the selections on the piano himself.

MUSEUMPLEIN AND VONDELPARK

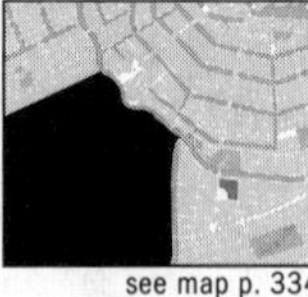
see map p. 334

VAN GOGH MUSEUM

Paulus Potterstraat 7. Tram #2, 5, or 20 to Paulus Potterstraat. Tram #3, 12, or 16 also stop close by at the Museumplein. (☎570 52 52; www.vangoghmuseum.nl.) Open daily 10am-6pm, ticket office and restaurant close at 5:30pm, museum shop closes at 5:45pm. €7, ages 13-17 €2,50, under 12 free. Credit cards accepted with minimum purchase of €25. A desk on the ground floor rents audio guides for €2,50.

With an entirely new wing completed in 1999, the Van Gogh Museum exhibits Vincent's oeuvre and its 19th-century context in a 20th century space. The streamlined 1973 building by Gerrit Rietveld, with stone floors and white walls, is spacious, clean, and bright. It houses the largest collection of paintings and sketches by the sunflower king, as well as a study area devoted to demystifying his tortured genius. A visit here provides not only a detailed vision of Van Gogh's progress from chronicler of Dutch peasantry to *artiste* of Arles, but also a lesson in major artistic movements of the 19th century, including Impressionism, post-Impressionism, Realism, Symbolism, and Salon art.

Museumplein

PRACTICAL INFORMATION

Because everyone wants to the see the real deal of the Van Gogh calendar, poster, or print they have at home, the Van Gogh Museum sports some of the longest lines in town. If you think you'll beat the crowd by showing up a few minutes before the museum opens, you're wrong. On weekends, it even weaves down the stairs and onto the sidewalk before the cash register warms up. If you show up around 10:30am, when the initial line has dissipated, or after 4pm, when people are heading home, you'll encounter the shortest wait

Pick up the audio tour to learn about the artist. You'll hear his name is pronounced "Vahn Hkokh," not "Van Go," and learn about his relationship with his brother Theo, an art dealer who supported him.

Gazing at Van Goghs

ORIENTATION

The museum is relatively small and self-explanatory, making it possible to see it all in one morning or afternoon. The meat of the museum, the **masterpieces** by the star himself, occupy the **first floor**—this is where you should concentrate your time. The collection of his paintings unfolds in chronological order and the beginning, where everyone still has the patience to read all the text panels and labels, creates the worst bottlenecks. These early, less familiar works are dark and focus on Dutch landscape and peasant life. Among them hangs the **The Potato Eaters (1885),** a sober depiction of a struggling peasant family at the dinner table. In 1886, Van Gogh moved to Paris, where he was confronted with modern art for the first time. As a result, his paintings became brighter and more experimental. His love for *japonaiserie* emerged at this time with **The Bridge in the Rain** and **The Courtesan.** In these works, Van Gogh mixed elements of Japanese art and culture with his own distinctive style. The last three phases—Arles, Saint-Remy, and

The New Addition at the Van Gogh Museum

GET smart

Watch It!

People flock to Rembrandt's storied painting of *The Night Watch*, actually entitled *The Militia Company of Frans Banning Cocq*, to see the master's impressive use of light and his ability to capture action. Most don't realize that they're seeing a reduced version of the original. The painting was moved from its original spot in the 1670s, about 30 years after Rembrandt completed it in 1642. When the giant work didn't fit in the new space, someone took the liberty of trimming a considerable chunk off the left side and most of the foreground off the bottom. A shrunken copy of the uncut original hangs beside the group portrait to give the visitor a point of comparison. In 1975, another knife cut into the canvas; this time it belonged to a crazed visitor. He seriously slashed the two figures at the forefront of the picture. Conservationists restored the painting without removing it from the gallery, but the scars can still be seen from just the right angle at the side. Another disturbed person tried to throw acid on the masterpiece in 1990, but the quick reaction of the guards prevented major damage and only the varnish had to be repaired. Ask to see a picture of the painting before it was repaired at the information desk to get a better sense of the damage.

Auvers-sur-Oise—contain some of his most recognizable works. Don't miss the colorful, deceptively simple **The Bedroom** at Arles and studies of **Sunflowers** made for close friend Gauguin.

If following Van Gogh's artistic trajectory piques your interest, head to the **second floor study area,** where you can peruse the many books published about Van Gogh or click on the computer display about his life and work. The floor also holds many smaller paintings not exhibited in the main gallery.

The **third floor** of 19th-century works related to Van Gogh make up an important collection in their own right. Paintings by the Symbolist Redon and the Pointillist Georges Seurat stand out as highlights, as do sculptures by Auguste Rodin.

The recently unveiled **exhibition wing,** designed by Kisho Kurokawa, provides a space for temporary shows on 19th-century art. Architecture buffs come just to see the building, which is designed to surround an outdoor stone floor with a thin stream of water moving over it. The art here is generally excellent.

SPECIAL EXHIBITIONS

2003 celebrates the 150th birthday of Vincent Van Gogh.

AMERICAN BEAUTY (NOV. 11, 2002- JAN. 1, 2003). Painting and sculpture from the Detroit Institute of Arts, 1770-1920, promises some of the best loved American painters such as John Singleton Copley, Mary Cassat, Winslow Homer, and John Singer Sargent.

VINCENT'S CHOICE (FEB. 14, 2003- JUNE 15, 2003). In honor of the birthday, the museum will present around 150 works by artists Van Gogh admired. His taste spans the range from Old Masters such as Rembrandt and Ruisdael to Millet and Delacroix to his friends Toulouse-Lautrec, Bernard, Signac, and Seurat. Curators will mix these inspirational figures in with Van Gogh's own work so their influence can be perceived.

GOGH MODERN (JUNE 27, 2003-OCT. 12,2003). "Vincent van Gogh and contemporary art" will show post-war artists whose art either demonstrates Van Gogh's influence or who follow the ground-breaking master by generally trying to steer art in a new direction.

LA SCALA (NOV. 7, 2003-FEB. 8, 2004). The Opera and the Orient, 1780-1930, will feature costumes, memorabilia, and 200 sketches of the set designs from Milan's world-famous opera. The exhibit will focus on the operas set in faraway lands (*Aida*, *Madame Butterfly*, and *Turnadot*) in order to explore Europe's fascination with Oriental exoticism.

STEDELIJK MUSEUM FOR MODERN AND CONTEMPORARY ART

Paulus Potterstraat 13. Tram #2, 5, or 20 to Paulus Potterstraat. Tram #3, 12, and 16 stop at nearby Museumplein. (☎573 27 45, recorded info 573 29 11; www.stedelijk.nl.) Open daily 11am-5pm. €5, ages 7-16, over 65 and groups over 15 €2,50, under 7 free, families €12,50.

Committed to exhibiting art dating from 1850 and later, the Stedelijk (pronounced "staid-ah-lick") likes to live on the cutting edge. Unfortunately, the museum will close for renovations and expansion on Dec. 31, 2002 and remain closed for three years. During this time, the museum will show some of its collection at the **COBRA** museum and the **Niewe Kerk.** See www.stedelijk.nl for more information.

RIJKSMUSEUM AMSTERDAM

Stadhouderskade 42. Tram #2 or 5 to Paulus Potterstraat or tram #6, 7, or 10 to Spiegelgracht and cross the canal; it's the huge neo-Gothic castle. (☎674 70 00; www.rijksmuseum.nl.) Open daily 10am-5pm. €8,50, under 18 free. Audio guides €3,50, €2,50 for students and under 18. Maps are available at the ticket counters.

In October 2003, the main building of the museum will close for renovations until 2008. The Phillips Wing will remain open to show masterpieces of 17th-century painting.

If you've made it to Amsterdam, it would be sinful to leave without seeing the Rijksmuseum's impressive galleries of works by Rembrandt van Rijn, Johannes Vermeer, Frans Hals, and Jan Steen. Originally opened in 1800, the museum settled into its current monumental quarters, designed by Pierre Cuypers, in 1884. It remains a bastion of traditional art. The Rijks, which means "state" in Dutch, is the national museum of The Netherlands. As such, it houses an encyclopedic collection of top-notch Dutch art and artifacts from the middle ages through the 19th century. It also has a comprehensive exhibit on Dutch history, from a wing on Asiatic art to an immense collection of rich oil paintings. Almost half the museum is devoted to the "applied arts," which means furniture, porcelain, and other decorative objects. There is no way you could take in everything in one visit, so aim to focus your attention on a few works you find appealing.

PRACTICAL INFORMATION. The Rijksmuseum has two different entrances that stand on opposite sides of the wide bicycle underpass that runs through the middle of the building. The east entrance leads directly to the section on Dutch history and to the paintings by Old Dutch Masters, on the second floor, that most come to see. The west entrance gives way to sculpture, applied arts, and the wing of Asiatic art and special exhibits. However, it does not matter which side you enter, as it is easy to cross over from the inside of the building. Just head to the shortest line.

ORIENTATION. You could easily spend an entire visit in the second floor galleries of the Old Dutch Masters, which comprise only about a quarter of the museum. Dutch art is unique because of its focus on the secular and the everyday. You'll find few crucifixions here. In the Golden Age, the free-market nature of art in The Netherlands led to smaller paintings meant for private homes—often interiors and landscapes.

If pressed for time, a good approach is to follow the crowds to Rembrandt's famed militia portrait **The Night Watch.** From there, head back through the Gallery of Honor where you can check out the **pen paintings,** black and white depictions of Dutch sea battles by Willem van de Velde I, as well as the portraits of Dutch notables from the 15th and 16th centuries. In front of the gift shop, take a right and then another right into room 211, where the luminous church interiors of **Pieter Saenredam** hang. Walk through to room 218, where a second essential highlight of the museum resides: the paintings by **Johannes Vermeer.** Only 32 paintings by Vermeer survive; the Rijks possesses four. **The Kitchenmaid,** from 1668, shows a woman in front of an open window pouring a pitcher of milk into a bowl. Despite the motion, the picture retains the tranquillity of a still life. Light glitters on the bread, and the plain back wall is marred with nail marks, creating a sense of space from a flat plane. Vermeer's other works

Stedelijk Museum

Inspecting Rembrandts

Rijksmuseum

in the same room have a similar sense of intimate space and calm control, which make his paintings rare instances of perfection. Similar scenes by **Pieter de Hooch** share the walls. De Hooch influenced Vermeer, but Vermeer focuses his subjects more tightly by concentrating on a smaller portion of the room. He is a master at framing space, and even in his street scene—a rare exterior setting—he places women in doorways. In **The Love Letter,** which also uses a door frame to narrow the viewer's vision, notice the glance of complicity between the two women and the superior stance of the maid over the mistress.

This area of the museum offers even more highlights by other Dutch superstars. Observe the effect of **Frans Hals's** seemingly casual brushstrokes or the turbulent skies in the landscapes by Jacob van Ruisdael. **Hans Bollonger's** vase of vibrant tulips (room 211) was painted two years after the collapse of the tulip market; the insects on the table serve as a reminder of the ephemerality of existence. **Jan Steen's** subversively titled **The Merry Family** depicts a cheerful family boisterously singing and drinking—even the young children have glasses of wine in hand—while a decrepit message in the top right hand corner reads "as the old song is, so will the young pipe play," a subtle moral warning to parents that their children will follow in their footsteps. Room 214 shows Steen's small painting of a woman by her bedside. Scholars have debated whether she is taking off her stocking to go to sleep for the night or putting the stocking on and getting up; see it and decide for yourself. Rooms 225-7 house 19th century Dutch impressionism, which is characterized by more subdued tones than its European counterparts.

The computer facilities behind **The Night Watch,** ARIA (Amsterdam Rijksmuseum InterActive), provide historical information on specific works and allow you to create a personalized map of the museum to help you navigate through its enormous collection.

Back on the ground floor, the **Dutch history** wing traces the nation's past, from the revolt against Philip II of Spain in the 16th century to World War II. With model ships and artifacts culled from shipwrecks, the display details the inextricable relationship of the lowlands and the sea. The exhibit features portraits of political leaders, paintings of early Dutch territory, weapons, and other relics. Ascend to the balcony to learn about the **Dutch East Indies Company (VOC)** from 1602-1800, which became the world's largest trading and transport outfit. The VOC was granted the power to wage war and declare peace, so it carried on governmental affairs in addition to an economic business. The exhibit celebrates the company's administration and material life, revealing little of its effect on the Indians, Indonesians, and Africans it colonized.

Unless you love the beds, chairs, and decorations belonging to the wealthy Dutch of yore, the **applied arts** quarters of the museum, showing ornate home furnishings from the 15th to 18th centuries, can be at the bottom of your list of sights within the Rijks. Highlights include the Delft blue ceramics and the intricate doll house where you can see the minute replica of a canal house interior, including the servant's quarters. It's an example of a **poppenhuis,** huge playthings that belonged to married women and traveled with them as part of their dowry.

The Phillips Wing houses temporary exhibits and several rooms of Asiatic art including artifacts, screen paintings, and statues of Buddha and the Hindu god Shiva.

Joods Historisch Museum

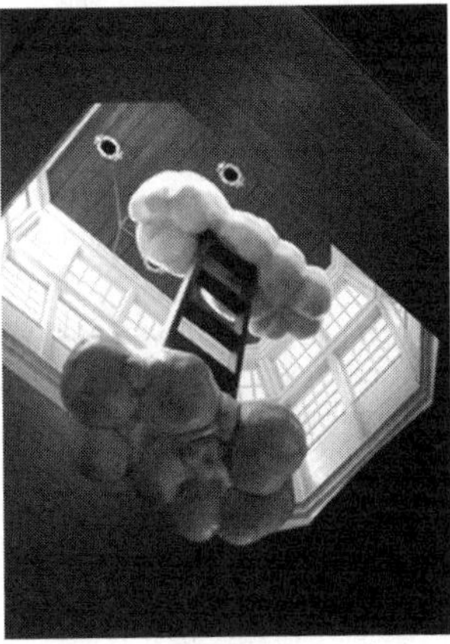

Ladder to Clouds at Joods Historisch Museum

SPECIAL EXHIBITS FOR 2003

The Hare and the Moon: Arita Porcelain from Japan (Oct. 5, 2002 - Jan. 6, 2003)
The Dutch Encounter with Asia (Oct. 10, 2002 - Feb. 9, 2003)
Document The Netherlands: Holidays! (Oct. 26, 2002-Jan. 5, 2003). Photos from Mora Bouchakour.
From Watteau to Ingres (Nov. 2, 2002 - Feb. 2, 2003) 18th century French drawings from the Rijksmuseum.

After October, when the main building of the museum closes for renovation, the Exhibits wing will house the highlights of the permanent collection.

FILMMUSEUM

Vondelpark 3, in the park between the Roemer Visscherstraat and Vondelstraat entrances. (☎589 14 00; www.filmmuseum.nl.)

Although the Filmmuseum is dedicated to the celebration and preservation of film, don't come here expecting to find any regular museum exhibits: most visitors just come to see movies. As the national center for cinematography in The Netherlands, the museum's collection holds 35,000 film titles stretching back to 1898. In addition to screening three films a day (see p. 164), they maintain an information center at 69 Vondelstraat (across the path and to the right when exiting the Filmmuseum), which houses the largest collection of books and periodicals on film in The Netherlands, many of them in English. You can do film research in the non-circulating

NEMO

archives or on the computerized databases; the friendly staff will help you with any request. At the information center, you can also watch videos from the museum's video collection in the library's booths (€12,50, students €4,50), but you'll probably need to reserve ahead of time.

JODENBUURT AND THE PLANTAGE

see map p. 327

JOODS HISTORISCH MUSEUM (JEWISH HISTORICAL MUSEUM)

Jonas Daniel Meijerplein 2-4 at Waterlooplein. Take tram #9, 14, or 20 to Waterlooplein; the museum is near the northwest corner of Mr. Visserplein. (☎626 99 45; info@jhm.nl; www.jhm.nl.) Open daily 11am-5pm; closed on Yom Kippur. €4,54, seniors over 65 and ISIC holders €3, ages 13-18 €2,50, ages 6-12 €1,50.

In the heart of Amsterdam's traditional Jewish neighborhood, the Joods Historisch Museum aims to celebrate Jewish culture and document the religion's cultural legacy through exhibits by Jewish artists and galleries of historically significant Judaica. A truly appealing children's wing joins artwork and curiosities from four centuries of Dutch Jewish life. Additionally, the exhibitions are housed in a building that artfully bridges together four different 17th- and 18th-century synagogues with glass and steel. The historic setting facilitates the visitor's exploration of the history and identity of the Jewish people in The Netherlands and abroad. An architectural marvel, its design also echoes the museum's hope to provide a link from the past to the present for Jews and non-Jews alike. The permanent collection includes old clothing, photographs, religious artifacts, texts, and artwork. Temporary exhibitions change every four months. In 2003, the museum will feature collections that explore, among other things, the works of well-renowned artist **Marc Chagall,** whose breathtaking painting and glasswork made a lasting contribution to modern art and stands as a significant expression of Jewish culture and feeling.

VERZETSMUSEUM (DUTCH RESISTANCE MUSEUM)

Plantage Kerklaan 61. Take tram #9 or 20 to Plantage Kerklaan; #6 or 14 to Plantage Middenlaan/Kerklaan. (☎620 25 35; fax 620 29 60; info@verzetsmuseum.org; www.verzetsmuseum.org.) Open Tu-F 10am-5pm, Sa-M noon-5pm, public holidays noon-5pm; closed Jan. 1, Apr. 30, and Dec. 25. €4,50, ages 7-15 €2,50. Tour of neighborhood available by phone or email appointment (€7,50 per person, groups smaller than 10 €75).

It didn't take the Dutch military very long to fall to the crushing power of the Nazis on May 10, 1940. Despite this, The Netherlands maintained an extraordinarily active resistance throughout the war. The Resistance Museum focuses on the members of this secret army, providing visitors with the details of their lives and struggles. Model streets and a soundtrack of tape-recorded radio reports help to create a full-on sensory experience. On display are photos and letters from those who hid, escaped, or perished before the war's end in 1945. Temporary exhibits examine current forms of resistance in order to acknowledge that the struggle to fight oppression is an ongoing effort. The museum, opened in 1999, is housed in the Plancius Building, originally built in 1876 as the social club for a Jewish choir. The layout of the museum allows visitors to track the occupation and Resistance chronologically, from the German invasion in May, 1940, through liberation, ending with an enlightening exhibit on the postwar Dutch regeneration.

MUSEUM HET REMBRANDT

Jodenbreestraat 4, at the corner of the Oudeschans Canal. Take tram #9, 14, or 20 to Waterlooplein and head northeast across Mr. Visserplein to Jodenbreestraat. (☎ 520 04 00. www.rembrandthuis.nl.) Open M-Sa 10am-5pm, Su 1-5pm. €7, ISIC holders €5, children ages 6-15 €1,50, children under 6 free.

Dutch master Rembrandt van Rijn's house at Waterlooplein, from which he was evicted by tax-hounds in 1658, is now the happy home of the artist's impressive collection of 250 etchings. Travel through all four levels of the beautifully restored house and see the inhumanly claustrophobic box-bed in which Rembrandt slept, tour the studio in which he mentored young and promising painters, and explore the kitchen in which his mistress is said to have assaulted him. In the upstairs studio, Rembrandt produced some of his most important works. On display are some of the artist's tools and plates, and a new wing houses temporary exhibitions. Check the website for the 2003 exhibits. (The art enthusiast should also stop at Rozengracht 184, in the Jordaan, where Rembrandt lived out the remainder of his life.)

Archway in Rembrandthuis

TROPENMUSEUM (MUSEUM OF THE TROPICS)

Tropenmuseum: *Linnaeusstraat 2. Both tram #9 and bus #22 stop right outside the museum; trams #3, 7, 10, and 14 also go to the museum, though not directly from Centraal Station. (☎ 568 82 15; fax 568 83 31; www.tropenmuseum.nl.) Open daily 10am-5pm; Dec. 5, 24, and 31 open 10am-3pm; closed on most bank holidays. €6,80, students and seniors over 65 €4,50, children ages 6-17 €3,40, children under 6 free; family ticket (1-2 adults and max. 4 children) €18,25. Kids won't want to miss the* ***Kindermuseum,*** *in the museum's basement. (☎ 568 83 00; www.kindermuseum.nl.) Ages 6-12 €4,50. Programs in the Kindermuseum are in Dutch only.*

Rembrandthuis

Sponsored by the KIT (Koninklij Instituut voor de Tropen), or Dutch Royal Institute of the Tropics, the Tropenmuseum takes guests on an anthropological tour of Southeast Asia, Oceania, South Asia, West Asia, North Africa, Africa, Latin America, and the Caribbean. The museum is situated in one of Amsterdam's most awe-inspiring buildings. You can enjoy extensive permanent exhibits that explore themes such as man and the environment. Take the elevator up to the second floor and work your way down through this enormous world tour of ancient artifacts and religious pieces. Most of the works on display were obtained

Tropenmuseum

through earlier Dutch colonial expansion, and there is a constant theme of avoiding cross-cultural conflict and bringing about the peaceful melding of different peoples. While the effort at simulation of different cultural atmospheres is commendable, the visitor can't help but feel patronized by the museum's over-simplified packaging of cultures, combining a wide array of peoples into an often-homogeneous whole. However, the documentation of so many diverse cultures is also Tropenmuseum's strongest asset: unlike its neighbors in the Plantage, the exhibits are broad, giving visitors of every interest something to appreciate.

The museum is also home to the celebrated **Kindermuseum (Children's Museum).** Only for children between 6 and 12 and those accompanying them, the Kindermuseum makes a conscious effort to provide something for humans of all ages to enjoy. Permanent exhibitions combine video footage, music, computer technology, and models to create simulations of real environments. Visitors can walk narrow Indian streets, explore the urban Philippines, look in the windows of South American traditional medicine shops, and stroll through a Middle Eastern market. Temporary exhibitions and special events occupy the first floor of the museum and focus, like the permanent collection, on the lives and activities of everyday people living in the tropics and subtropics.

SCHEEPVAARTMUSEUM (MARITIME MUSEUM)

Kattenburgerplein 1. From Centraal Station, follow signs on foot by heading left from the station and passing the large green NEMO after about 10min. It will be on your left. Or take bus #22 or 32 to Scheepvaartmuseum. (☎523 22 22; fax 523 22 13; www.scheepvaartmuseum.nl.) Open Tu-Su 10am-5pm; mid-June to mid-Sept. open daily 10am-5pm; closed Jan. 1, Apr. 30, and Dec. 25. €6, ISIC holders €5,25, ages 6-18 €4, under 6 free, family ticket (max. 2 adults and 3 children) €18.

For lovers of the sea, the vast three-tier Maritime Museum leaves no stone unturned in its exploration of The Netherlands' sea-faring history. The museum is run by the Verenigde Oost-Indische Compagnie (Dutch East India Company), the organization that was in charge of economic expansion in Indonesia during colonialism. Housing 70 real vessels and multiple models, those on display include the spectacular Dutch East Indiaman Den Ary, a model ship that seems to have sailed straight out of the age of pirates and mermaids. The collection of the Maritime Museum, one of the largest in the world, is housed in the 300-year-old National Naval Depot building, formerly used as a warehouse for canons, sails, ropes, ammunition, and other necessities for a day—or year—at sea. Around the many dinghy-sized models, note the beautiful paintings of water scenes and angry-looking Dutch seamen, as well as the beautiful drape displays featuring important figures from Dutch Maritime history. Don't miss the full-size replica of the Dutch East Indiaman "Amsterdam" parked right in front of the museum—as if you could. On weekends at 11am, 1pm, and 3pm, actors re-enact life on-board this ship.

NATIONAAL VAKBONDSMUSEUM "DE BURCHT" (NATIONAL TRADE UNION MUSEUM "THE FORTRESS")

Henri Polaklaan 9. Take tram #9 or 20 to Artis and turn left onto to Henri Polaklaan. (☎624 11 66; fax 623 73 31; www.deburcht-vakbondsmuseum.nl.) Open Tu-F 11am-5pm, Su 1-5pm. €2,30, ages 13-18 and trade unionists worldwide €1,15.

At the beginning of the 20th century, diamonds were one of Amsterdam's major sources of income. The city's industry reached its zenith just before World War I. Jews were especially active in this sector, and the economic success of their neighborhood, the Jodenbuurt, was heavily dependent on the position of diamond workers in the industry. However, in the 1880s and 1890s in The Netherlands and across Europe, workers' rights and conditions were often subordinated to the management's desires for greater gain and profit. Jodenbuurt's Jews felt the pinch so in 1894 **Henri Polak** (1868-1943), a Jewish diamond-cutter living in Amsterdam, founded The

Netherlands' modern trade union movement by calling the first meeting of the ANDB, the Dutch Diamond Workers' Union. The organization consolidated its ranks in 1900, bringing together Jews and Gentiles alike, as well as members from all sectors of the profession. With 10,000 members, it is no surprise that the ANDB was Europe's first union with professionally paid managers and the first union in the world to secure an eight-hour workday for its members. Today, Polak's social crusade and success is documented in the Nationaal Vakbondsmuseum "De Burcht." The building, designed by the famous socialist "community style" artist Hendrik Petrus Berlage, was the original headquarters for the ANDB. Polak wanted it to be a monument for the workers' struggle, and so the design of the building was meant to fit into the populist and socialist underpinnings of trade unionism. Additionally, countless paintings depicting aspects of Dutch social history are on display as part of the museum's permanent collection. When the eight-hour workday was introduced in 1912, socialist painter **Richard Holst** created a triptych for the building's board room showing that the day must be divided into three equal parts: work, relaxation, and sleep. On your way out, notice the gardens in front of many of Henri Polaklaan's residences; at the turn of the century, many of the wealthier Jews running the union moved here and built these homes behind what continue to be Amsterdam's only front yards.

INSIDE:

Food & Drink

Eating in Amsterdam is a culinary adventure. Though Dutch food is common in the city, it's not nearly as exciting, or often as well prepared as some of the selections from the former Dutch empire. Colonial history has brought Surinamese and Indonesian cuisine to Amsterdam, followed closely by near-relatives representing other South American and Asian countries. Indonesian cuisine is probably one of the safest bets for vegetarians and vegans, as traditional Dutch cuisine is hearty, heavy, meaty, and wholesome. Expect a lot of bread and cheese for breakfasts and lunch, and generous portions of meats and fishes for dinner. Popular seafood choices include all sorts of grilled fishes and shellfish, wholesome fish stews, as well as raw herring. To round out a truly authentic Dutch meal, ask (especially in May and June) for white asparagus, which can be a main dish on its own, served with potatoes, ham, and eggs. Early on, the Dutch appropriated dishes from their nearby neighbors, the Swiss, including fondue, a delicious, though not health-conscious option. The Dutch conception of a light snack often includes *tostjes*, piping hot grilled cheese or ham and cheese sandwiches, *broodjes* (sandwiches) *oliebollen* (doughnuts) or *poffertjes* (small pancakes). In short, Amsterdam is not for the dieter.

FOOD BY TYPE

AMERICAN
Dimitri's (106) CRW
Mister Coco's (103) NZ
Old Highlander (102) NZ

BAKERY
Bakkerij Paul Annee (105) CRW

CAFES, EETCAFES, AND SANDWICH SHOPS
Aguada (117) JP
Bar Soup (116) DP
Bolhoed (110) J
Brodje Mokum (111) J
Cafe Vertigo (113) MV
Coffee and Jazz (107) CCR
De Griekse Taverna (113) MV
De Vliegende Schotel (111) J
Eetcafe Tis-Fris (117) JP
En'tre Dok (117) JP
Foodism (102) NZ
Het Blauwe Theehuis (113) MV
Plancius (117) JP
Ruhe Delicatessen (105) CRW
Soup en Zo (117) JP
Tig Barra (112) WO
Theehuis Himalaya (101) OZ
Vennington (106) CRW
Wolvenstraat 23 (104) CRW

CHINESE
Sea Palace (101) OZ
Hoi Tin (101) OZ
Taste of Culture (101) OZ
New Season (101) OZ
Nam Tin (117) JP

DESSERT
Jordino (104) SQ
Peppino Gelateria (115) DP

DUTCH
Cafe de Pels (106) CRW
Cafe Latei (116) JP
Cafe Westers (112) WO
Carousel Pancake House (108) CCR
De Belhamel (108) SQ
De Ondeugd (115) DP
De Smoeshaan (109) LP
De Soepwinkel (115) DP
Granny's (116) DP
Kaartika (106) CRW
Hap-Hum (104) MV
hein (104) CRW
Het Molenpad (106) CRW
In de Waag (112) MV
KinderKookKafe (114) RLD
La Place (102) NZ
Lunchcafe Neilsen (105) CRW

DUTCH (CONT'D.)
Pannenkoekenhuis Upstairs (102) NZ
Spanier en Van Twist (105) CRW

ETHIOPIAN
Abyssinia Afrikaans Eetcafe (111) WO
Axum (106) CCR

FUSION/"GLOBAL"
Restaurant Wanka (111) WO
Harlem: Drinks and Soul Food (103) SQ
Vakzuid (110) Olympic Stadium

INDIAN/PAKISTANI
Balraj (104) SQ
Bombay Inn (109) LP
Curry Garden (110) RP
Dosa (112) WO
Golden Temple (107) CCR

INDONESIAN
Aneka Rasa (101) OZ
Bojo (108) LP
Esoterica (111) WO
Kaartika (106) WO
Padi (103) SQ
Sie Joe (103) NZ

ITALIAN
Abe Veneto (116) JP
L'Angoletto (115) DP
Orvieto (102) NZ
Prego (105) CRW
Ristorante Caprese (102) NZ
Santa Lucia (108) LP

KURDISH
Zagros (114) DP

JAPANESE
Go Sushi (113) MV
Stereo Sushi (102) NZ
Tomo Sushi (110) RP
Wagamama (108) LP
Zento (115) DP

JUICE BARS
Jay's Juice (104) SQ
La Fruteria (103) NZ
Tasty and Healthy (102) NZ

MEXICAN
Rose's Cantina (110) RP
Café Koosje (117) JP

MIDDLE EASTERN
Ben Cohen's Shawarma (111) J
King Solomon's Restaurant (117) JP
Snack Bar Aggie (111) J

SPANISH/PORTUGUESE	
Duende (111)	J
Manzano (111)	J
Mas Tapas (116)	DP
La Sala Comidas Caseras (117)	JP
Tapa Feliz (113)	MV
Toussaint Cafe (111)	WO
SURINAMESE/INDIAN/AFGHAN/PAKISTAN	
Moksi (116)	DP
Usama (103)	NZ
Albina (116)	DP
THAI AND SOUTHEAST ASIAN	
Cambodja City (115)	DP
Khorat Top Thai (113)	MV
NOA (107)	CCR
Rakang (111)	J
Top Thai (105)	CRW
TIBETAN	
Tashi Deleg (107)	CCR
TURKISH	
Eufraat (116)	DP
Kismet (112)	WO
Saray (114)	DP

CCR central canal ring **CRW** canal ring west **DP** de pijp **J** the jordaan **JP** jodenbuurt and the plantage **LP** leidseplein **MV** museumplein and vondelpark **NZ** nieuwe zijd **OZ** oude zijd **RLD** red light district **RP** rembrandtplein **SQ** shipping quarter

OUDE ZIJD

see maps pp. 330-331

It's not that food is hard to find in the Oude Zijd, it's just that you may not want to eat it when you find it. There's no shortage of run-of-the-mill shawerma huts along Warmoesstraat in the Red Light District, but it's not exactly fine dining. Usually, it's not even great budget dining. If you head over to Nieuwmarkt, however, Amsterdam's Chinatown is full of excellent Chinese food in all price ranges.

Aneka Rasa, Warmoesstraat 25-29 (☎626 15 60). A beacon of elegance amidst the seediness of the Red Light District, the Indonesian restaurant will let you and a friend chow down on *rijsttafel* for €15,90-26,80 per person. Other main dishes are available (€11), with plenty of vegetarian plates as well (€8). Open daily 5-10:30pm. AmEx/MC/V. ❹

Theehuis Himalaya, Warmoesstraat 56 (☎626 08 99; www.himalaya.nl), a few blocks south of Centraal. The Himalaya provides a peaceful respite from the lurid grit of Warmoesstraat, where you can sip one of over 40 varieties of tea while overlooking the Damrak. The Buddhist-themed *theehuis* has a book shop and gift shop as well as light, delicious lunches with a good mix of meat and vegetarian options. Tasty *tostis* €3-3,50. Check the bulletin boards for up-to-date info on Zen and New Age happenings throughout the city. Open M 1-6pm, Tu-W and F-Sa 10am-6pm, Th 10am-8:30pm, Su 12:30-5pm. AmEx/MC/V. ❶

New Season, Warmoesstraat 39 (☎625 61 25). No shortage of choices at this all-purpose Malaysian restaurant, whose menu covers a range of dishes, including Cantonese, Szechuan, and Malaysian. Main courses on the enormous menu hover around €7-10, with a vegetarian section of plates for €6. Small, family-style atmosphere in a sit-down restaurant is welcome respite from the hustle and bustle of Warmoesstraat. Open Tu-Su 3-11pm. ❷

Hoi Tin, Zeedijk 122-124 (☎625 64 51). Remarkably authentic dim sum snacks and meals await you at this slightly upscale local favorite in Amsterdam's Chinatown. Meat dishes €9,50-10,50; egg and vegetable dishes €8-14. Seafood can get up to €35. Vegetarian options exist, but you have to scour the menu for them. Open daily 11am-midnight. ❸

Taste of Culture, Zeedijk 109 (☎638 14 66). It's easy to imagine that many an eating contest has been inspired by Taste of Culture's tempting offer: all you can eat for 1hr., only €7,50. Start with the dim sum (appetizers) and then move on to heartier fare; plenty of vegetarian options as well. Open M-W noon-11pm, Th-Su until midnight. Another location at Rokin 152 (☎638 12 49). ❷

Sea Palace, Oosterdokskade 8 (☎626 47 77; www.seapalace.nl). Though the restaurant itself, a gargantuan floating tribute to excess, may be as much an attraction as the food, you will certainly find no shortage of choices. The novel-length menu runs the gamut from Chinese and Cantonese to Indonesian, and 2-4 person dinners run €27-40. Open daily noon-4pm and 6-11pm. AmEx/MC/V. ❺

NIEUWE ZIJD

see maps pp. 330-331

Pannenkoekenhuis Upstairs, Grimburgwal 2 (☎626 56 03). From the Muntplein tram stop, cross the bridge, walk along the Singel, and turn right on Heisteeg, which connects to Grimburgwal, past Spui and Oude Turfmarkt. A tiny nook with some of the best pancakes in the city. Watch your head on the teapot-covered ceiling while waiting for one of the pancake house's 6 tables. The patrons' pleased looks tell you it's worth the wait. Pancakes €4,50-8,50. Try the bacon and pineapple (€7), the more conventional chocolate sauce pancake (€5,15), or take the ultimate lunch-time plunge with the Miranda (pear, egg nog, chocolate sauce, and whipped cream €7,90). Open M-F noon-7pm, Sa noon-6pm, Su noon-5pm. ❶

Stereo Sushi, Jonge Roelensteeg 4 (☎777 30 10), between Kalverstraat and Nieuwezijds Voorburgwal, south of Dam. Step off an obscure alleyway and into one of Amsterdam's strangest and coolest hotspots. Furry walls, trippy fishtank, loungey furniture, and DJs spinning groovy beats nightly transmogrify this Japanese restaurant into a shagadelic dance party that goes into the early hours. Sushi (nigiri €3,50-4; maki €3,50 and €12,50; sashimi €7,50-8,50); and big noodle soups (€10-12). House specialty and a great deal: tasty warm sake (bottle €5). Beer €2; wine €2,50. Open Su and Tu-Th 6pm-1am, F-Sa 6pm-3am. ❸

Ristorante Caprese, Spuistraat 259-261 (☎620 00 59). From Dam, follow Spuistraat south a few blocks. Excellent Italian food prepared in good time and served in the midst of relaxed jazz and comforting candlelight. The prices are a bit higher than elsewhere, but the chef and staff's attention to detail and the restaurant's inexpensive wine (glass of merlot €1,85) make Ristorante Caprese a nice dinner spot. Try the amazing penne arrabbiata €8,50). Open daily 5-10:45pm. ❸

Tasty and Healthy, Korte Lijnbaansteeg 4-6 (☎320 19 34). Between Nieuwezijds Voorburgwal and Spuistraat, north of Dam. Snug spot off a small side street vends fresh fruit juices (€2,50-3,50) and light snacks. Sandwiches €1,60-2,85; baked potatoes with decadent toppings €3,65-4,75. More exotic fruit shakes can make for a meal in themselves; try the energizing "atomic," including dates, organic yogurt, muesli, banana, kiwi, ginseng, mango, bee pollen, and vitamins (€3,40-€4,55). The owner, a nutrition whiz, may recommend some wheatgrass juice for €3, a little cheaper than the city's other "grass" beverages. Open daily 7:30am-7pm. ❶

Old Highlander, St. Jacobstraat 8 (☎420 83 21). From Dam, take Nieuwezijds Voorburgwal northeast about 300m; St. Jacobstraat will be on your right. A wonderfully sedate nook in the middle of chaotic Amsterdam with an indoor waterfall, wooden bridge, and stream. Offers an American menu, serving a healthy breakfast (€8), lunch, and dinner: homemade soups (€3,50), sandwiches (from €5), and salads (€5-8). A perfect place for children tiring of traditional Dutch fare. Will accommodate special health needs. Children's portions and take-out available. Open daily 9am-10pm; kitchen closes at 9pm. ❷

Orvieto, Nieuwendijk 9 (☎626 68 42). Tram 1, 2, 5, 13 and 17 to Niewendijk. Huge portions of Italian fare served by an effusive staff in a convivial setting that's one small step above the basic. Downstairs has small tables ideal for an intimate *conversazione;* upstairs has long tables good for big groups or a festive affair. Specialty pizzas include the rustica (ham, bacon, salami, and mushrooms) and paradiso (chicken, red and green peppers, onion, and mushrooms); both (€9,50). Luscious lasagne alla Roma is *molto bene* (€8,25). Open daily noon-midnight; lunch noon-5pm, dinner 5pm-midnight. MC/V. ❸

Foodism, Oude Leliestraat 8 (☎427 51 03). From Dam, walk up Raadhuisstraat, turn right at Singel, and the restaurant is between Singel and Herengracht on your left. Very cool, very casual, and very tasty. An excellent spot for breakfast, lunch, or dinner. Serves sandwiches (from €5), soups and salads (from €3,50), and pasta dishes (from €8) on one of Amsterdam's nicest side streets. Vegetarian options. Open Su-Th 11am-10pm, F-Sa 11am-11pm. ❷

La Place, Kalverstraat 201 (☎622 01 71). From the Muntplein tram stop, take Kalverstraat northwest; the restaurant is on your right. In the Vroom and Dreesmann department store, with another entrance on Kalverstraat. Sumptuous market-style buffet where you can fill your tray with a do-it-yourself meal. The well-lit and clean dining area is a great place to rest tired feet. Ideal for a quick nutritious lunch in a refreshing, aromatic atmosphere. Bowls of fresh fruit €2,80-3,49; soup €3,79; mains €6-10. Menu and prices change with the season. Open daily 10am-9pm. V. ❷

Mister Coco's, Nieuwendijk 11 (☎623 62 60; www.mrcocos.com). From Centraal, turn right at the main street, left at Martelaarsgracht, and right onto Nieuwendijk. Mr. Coco is the guy on the sign outside—a bald, drunk, ugly clown promising "lousy food and warm beer" to a carnivorous crowd, thankful for his sense of irony. Although certainly a bit of a tourist hangout, Mr. Coco's serves up some of Amsterdam's tastiest ribs (all-you-can-eat €13). Native and tourist alike enjoy large servings and a fun atmosphere at this self-deprecating bar and grill. Two floors get crazy on weekend nights, especially when there's a football game on the big-screen TV. Massive burgers advertised as the "world's biggest" and slathered with toppings €6,30-11. All-day English breakfast €6. Happy hour 5-6pm and 10-11pm: €1,50 off drinks. Open Su-Th 11am-1am, F-Sa 8:30am-3am. AmEx/MC/V. ❸

Sie Joe, Gravenstraat 24 (☎624 18 30; www.siejoe.com). Between Nieuwendijk and Nieuwenzijds Voorburgwal, behind Nieuwe Kerk. Hole-in-the-wall where you can get great Indonesian lunch and early dinner at good prices, especially as compared with nearby Indonesian stops. In this cozy *lunchcafe*, vegetarians can sup upon delectable *gado gado* (mixed vegetables in peanut sauce; €6). The *tjendol* is a delicate mix of soft green noodles, palm sugar, coconut milk, and crushed ice (€3). Lamb and chicken satay €6. Open M-W and F-Sa 11am-7pm, Th 11am-8pm. ❶

Usama, Spuistraat 50 (☎422 64 94), a few blocks from Centraal on Spuistraat. This tiny takeout spot serves up big portions of Surinamese, Pakistani, Indian, and Afghan chow for cheap. The friendly staff encourage patrons to sit together at the 8-person table that consumes a good portion of the shop's floor space. Curry, *roti, nasi,* and more, almost entirely under €9; most dishes around €7. Tasty *tandoori* chicken €8,25. Open daily noon-1am. ❷

La Fruteria, Nieuwezijds Voorburgwal 141 (☎623 29 17), just north of Dam against Nieuwe Kerk. A colorful little store selling fruit shakes and juices made with the freshest produce. Mix and match your own combo of three juiceables. Small €2,40, medium €3, large €3,40. Yogurt with choice of granola mix €2,60-3,50; a host of yummy sandwiches €3-3,60. Open M-Sa 10am-7pm, Su 11am-7pm. ❶

SCHEEPVAARTBUURT (THE SHIPPING QUARTER)

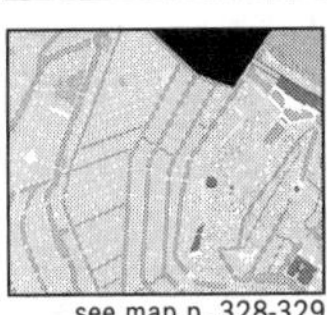

see map p. 328-329

To get to the Scheepvaartbuurt's numerous restaurants and bars from Centraal Station, the closest tram stop, turn right on Prins Hendrikkade, then left and then an immediate right onto Nieuwendijk, which turns into Haarlemmerstraat as it crosses the Singel. Haarlemmerstr. turns into Haarlemmerdijk at Korte Prinsengracht. Alternately, head north the Prinsengracht, which intersects the street two blocks past the Brouwersgracht.

Harlem: Drinks and Soulfood, Haarlemmerstraat 77 (☎330 14 98), at the Herenmarkt. From Centraal Station, turn right. Soul food, couched in Amsterdam's finest nouvelle cuisine, finds a happy home in the Shipping Quarter. Revolving dinner menu boasts about 10 creatively prepared cajun and Caribbean dishes, and there's always a vegetarian option. Lighter lunch includes creamy peanut soup (€3,85), sandwiches (€4-5), as well as unique salad selections such as Marvin's Gay and Franky's Goat to Hollywood (goat cheese, peach, and pine nuts). Dinner €11-16. Inside at the bar, you can relax to cool jazz and chat with the fun and lively folk who pour the drinks; or head outside to the patio for a prime view of busy Haarlemmerstraat. Open M-Th 10am-1am, F-Sa 10am-3am, Su 11am-1am. ❸

Padi, Harlemmerdijk 50 (☎625 12 80). Locals rave about this Indonesian *eethuis*, where a simple, spare interior belies a menu packed with palate-challenging offerings. Appetizers are cheap (*loempia,* spring rolls, only €2), but the best of the bunch is *pangsit goreg* (fresh shrimp in a paper-thin edible wrapper, €4). Entrees like *rendang* or *ikan rica* will fire up your tongue, while *lontong opor* (coconut-simmered chicken, €7,50) will cool it down. Vegetarian

the hidden deal

Hap-Hmm

Tucked into a quiet residential neighborhood in the museum quarter, this is where Dutch people come for dinner when they don't feel like cooking for themselves. **Hap-Hmm,** 1e Helmersstraat 33, has been around since 1935. The same family has been running it for the past 38 years; you can see their family picture on the wall.

Coming to the restaurant with its simple, dated decor and older clientele, you may feel like you're stepping back in time a bit. The food is solidly Dutch, and dinner will cost you about €5 for a choice of dishes (meatballs, pork, tofu) all served with a vegetable of the day and a baked potato (fried potatoes €0,50 extra!). Finish off the old-time Dutch feeling at old-time prices with an apple pie (€1,25).

(☎618 18 84; www.welcome.to/hap-hmm. Open M-F 4:30-10pm.) ❶

options include the *gado gado,* a dinner salad with spicy dressing and hard-boiled egg (€5,25). Open daily 5-10pm. ❷

Jordino, Harlemmerdijk 25 (☎420 32 25). This chocolateria and desserteria serves decadently delectable confections. The ice cream (1 scoop €1; each additional scoop €0,50) is a delight, with seasonal flavors. The real draw is the finely wrought handmade chocolate (100g bag €3,50), each a distinctive experience. Open Su-M 1-8pm, Tu-Sa 10am-8pm. ❶

Balraj, Haarlemmerdijk 28 (☎625 14 28). First-rate Indian chow in an intimate, narrow space that's usually jammed with locals. If you're in the mood for a super-hot delight, try the chicken *madras* (€9,75). The lamb *jai puri* is considerably mellower, though still tasty (€10,75). *Biryani* dishes–both lamb and chicken–are aromatic delights, simmered with cardamom and coconut and served with sides of curd and lentils (€9,75-10,75). Vegetarian dishes are less expensive: *saag paneer* and *alu mattar* each €8,75. Open daily 5-10pm. ❷

Jay's Juice, Haarlemmerstraat 14 (☎623 12 67). Jay himself presides over this diminutive den of fresh juice and good vibes where everything, as Jay says, "comes from the heart." The small interior feels large thanks to colorful murals, and the juice consists only of the freshest ingredients. "Jay's Booster" features tomato, ginger, carrot, and celery; but you can get tempting potions in almost any imaginable admixture of fruit or vegetables. You can add boosters for €0,50, such as ginseng, guarana, or even "hornygoat grass" (10mg of herbal Viagra) if you're in the mood (or would like to be). Homemade vegetarian soups available in winter (€4,75). Buy 10 juices and get 1 free. Juices available in 1/3-liter (€2,30-3,55), half-liter (€3,10-4,60), or full-liter (€5,50-8,20) bottles. Open daily 8am-7pm. ❶

CANAL RING WEST

see maps pp. 328-329

hein, Berenstraat 20 (☎623 10 48). It's a one-woman-show at this refined and relaxed lunchery with an open kitchen. Everything is homemade by Hein herself with the freshest of ingredients. Lunch menu includes crepes and *croques monsieurs.* Snacks and sandwiches_€2-10. Open M and W-Su 9:30am-6pm. Cash or bank cards only. ❶

Wolvenstraat 23, Wolvenstraat 23 (☎320 08 43). Unmarked except by its address, this trendy stop is no ordinary restaurant. A cushioned, lime green lounge area welcomes you at the front and is just about the only constant in the place. In addition to a menu that changes with the seasons, the lunch and dinner selections are entirely different. Lunch here means sandwiches (€2-5,20), salads (€5,65), and omelets (€3-4,30). Dinner, on the other hand, is strictly Chinese cuisine, as two Cantonese chefs take the helm. Between the 2 shifts, slurp down noodle soups (€3,40). The modern mood makes it a popular bar during the weekend. Lunch menu 8am-3:30pm, dinner 6-10:30pm. Open M-Th 8am-1am, F 8am-2am, Sa 9am-2am, Su 10am-1am. Cash or bank cards only. ❷

Bakkerij Paul Annee, Runstraat 25 (☎623 53 22). Super-fresh and super-cheap, this bakery is the hostess with the mostest. The line out the door is a good thing–it gives you more time to choose among the breads packed in the wall of wheat. Don't miss the *appeltas* (€1,10), baked apples with nuts wrapped up in a pastry puff of goodness, the best in the city. ❶

Ruhe Delicatessen, Prinsenstraat 13 (☎626 74 38). A perfect stop for the busy budget traveler. Quality meats, breads, cheese, wine, fruit, and snacks all at very reasonable prices. No tables here, just browse this condensed supermarket or ask the friendly staff to cut you some pieces of salami or brie. Full meal under €5, guaranteed. Open daily noon-10pm. Cash and bank cards accepted. ❶

Prego, Herenstraat 25 (☎638 01 48). If you want great Italian food, save up to visit Prego, between Herengracht and Keizersgracht. Known for its mediterranean specialties (grilled butterfish €20, entrecote €21), this place is a real treat. The friendly waiters rush about the tastefully decorated dining room with starters (from €10), entrees, and desserts (around €8). Serves dinner only and is a well-deserved break from the usual shawerma huts and sandwich shops. Open daily 6-10pm. MC/V. ❺

Lunchcafe Nielson, Berenstraat 19 (☎330 60 06). An extra bright ray of light in an already shining neighborhood. Breakfast and lunch served all day. Dig into french toast or eggs (€4). On the sandwich side, *tostis* start at €2,50 and clubs run to €6,50. Salads from €7,75. Vegetarian friendly. Open Tu-F 8am-5pm, Sa 8am-6pm, Su 9am-5pm; kitchen closes 30min. before restaurant. MC/V. ❶

Spanjer en Van Twist, Leliegracht 60 (☎639 01 09), near the corner of Prinsengracht and Leliegracht. This cafe-restaurant is ideal for a leisurely meal or mid-day drink. For lunch, sandwiches, salads, and pasta run €2,30-7,20. At dinner, starters hover in the same range and the diverse entrees go from €10,80. No reservations. Lunch served until 4pm, dinner 6-11pm. Open daily 10am-1am. ❸

Top Thai, Herenstraat 22 (☎623 46 33; www.topthai.nl), on the Northern end of the Canal Ring, toward the Shipping Quarter. A haven of traditional thai cuisine and atmosphere. Open for dinner only, enjoy phad thai variations from €6 and chicken entrees from €10. Oriental sunshades cover the ceiling, and there are bottles of wine and mineral water at every table. Be sure to take a close look at the altar to

Pannekoekenhuis Upstairs

Spins at Stereo Sushi

Hot Soup

the BIG $plurge

Rijsttafel For Two

Thanks to Dutch colonialism, Amsterdam is blessed with Indonesian and Surinamese galore. Don't leave Amsterdam without trying an Indonesian *rijsttafel* (rice table). A rice table includes up to 25 small bowls of spicy meat, chicken, nuts, pickles, and other various and sundry foods seasoned with thick peanut or coconut milk sauces. It's almost impossible to find this delicacy outside of Amsterdam (except, of course, in Indonesia). **Kaartika,** Overtoom 68, offers the real thing in an elegant atmosphere for a minimum of two people: try the Ramayana (€18,50), the vegetarian Shinta (€18), or the most decadent feast of all, the Mahabarata (€27,50), which includes fried king prawns. If you don't feel like shelling out big bucks, **Bojo** in Leidseplein offers a cheaper (€10,50) though less extensive version of a rijsttafel (p. 108).

(Tram #1, 3, or 6 to Overtoom. ☎618 18 79. Open daily 5-10:30pm.) ❹

Buddha, located above the kitchen's servery. Try the Top Thai Pearls, a sampler of the restaurant's appetizers (€7). Open daily 4:30-10:30pm. MC/V. ❷

Het Molenpad, Prinsengracht 653 (☎625 96 80). The Dutch word, *Gezelligheid,* (coziness) was created to describe places like this. In midsummer, locals fill up the canalside seats out front, and in winter, they gather at the inviting bar of this traditional *bruin cafe.* Usual *eetcafe* offerings (soup €4,50; entrees €8-13,40; dessert €2-5,20) that go perfectly with a *vaasje* of beer (€1,80). Lunch served until 4pm (sandwiches €3-4,35; salad €7). Dutch snacks like *bitterballen* (€3,40) available from 3-10:30pm. Open Su-Th noon-1am, F-Sa noon-2am. Cash and bank cards only. ❷

Cafe De Pels, Huidenstraat 25. A no-frills neighborhood hangout popular with the after-work crowd, especially for drinks, coffee, and sandwiches. Notably, this is the one place that makes good use of the *amsterdammertjes* (3-foot poles that separate the sidewalks from the roads) by putting table tops on them for outdoor seating. Bar snacks and *broodjes* €2-2,60. Same simple menu all day, everyday, excluding Su brunch (11am-2pm), which ranges from €3,75-8,50. Open Su-Th 10am-1am, F-Sa 10am-3am. ❶

Vennington, Prinsenstraat 2 (☎625 93 98). If you hit it at the wrong time, you won't be able to find a table at this popular sandwich shop. But their club sandwich creations (under €6,80) are tasty, and the fruit shakes (under €4) perfectly complement a sunny afternoon. Breakfast (€3,65-9) served until 11am. Open daily 8am-4pm. ❶

Dimitri's, Prinsenstraat 3 (☎627 93 93). It's rare to find a place in Amsterdam that serves all 3 meals, but Dimitri's does, and extremely well, if slowly. Breakfast (8am-noon) sticks to the basics. Lunch (noon-5pm) branches out to solid sandwiches (€4-6) and crostinis (€3,50-4,50) that are just as tasty but not as filling. Dinner (5-10pm) blooms with huge salads, burgers, fajitas (€10), and pasta dishes (most under €11). If you like tuna melts, be sure to try the *crostini tonijn* (€3,90). No reservations. Open daily 8am-10pm. No credit cards. ❷

CENTRAL CANAL RING

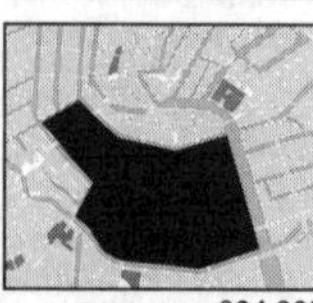

see maps pp. 324-325

Axum, Utrechtsedwarsstraat 85-87 (☎622 83 89). Take tram #4 or 20 to Frederiksplein, go north on Utrechtsestraat for a block, then turn right on Utrechtsedwarsstraat. Homey, family-run eatery serves great traditional Ethiopian fare. No silverware here; feel free to use your hands to scoop up your food with tart *injera.* Ethiopian food will fill you up and make you happy for only about €10. Entrees come steaming in pots of spicy sauce and include sides of lentils, salad, and veggies. Highlights are *yebeg wot* (zesty lamb; €11) and *doro wot* (tangy chicken; €9,75). Plenty of vegetarian options, including the excellent, smooth *shiro wot* (fried chickpeas in Ethiopian herbs; €8,75). Open M-F 5:30-11pm, Sa-Su 11:30. ❷

Coffee and Jazz, Utrechtsestraat 113 (☎624 58 51). Unlikely but appealing fusion of Indonesian and Dutch prevails at this fun *eetcafe*. Juxtaposition of jazz tunes and bamboo furniture. Sweet, fruity *pannenkoeken* (€4,50-7) share the menu with tender lamb and chicken satay (€7-9). At dinner time, only Indonesian food is served: choice of chicken, beef, or lamb with sweet, spicy, or coconut sauce (€10-12). Delectable fruit shakes combine mango, banana, and orange (enough for two; €4,50). Open Tu-F 9:30am-8pm, Sa 10am-4pm. ❷

NOA, Leidsegracht 84 (☎626 08 02; www.withnoa.com), just outside the Leidseplein hype. From Leidesplein, walk past Haagen Dasz down Leisestraat for 2 blocks and take a left onto Prinsengracht. Walk one block, cross the Leidsegracht canal, and take a left down it; NOA will be on your left. Catering to a trendy crowd, NOA fancies itself the hippest lounge around. Its plush sofa seats and sleek decor make this place a futuristic hot spot dotted with updated La-Z-Boys that, while ultra-comfy, make eating at the slightly-too-high tables a bit odd. To be with the hipsters, you're gonna have to pay for it, since the food and drink prices tend to run on the high side: pan-Asian noodle dishes (€15), salads (€13), or dessert of fruit tempura with sorbet and sake. All the fashionable cocktails–*caipirinha*, apple martini, and *mojito* (€7-9). No reservations. AmEx/MC/V. ❹

Golden Temple, Utrechtsestraat 126 (☎626 85 60), between Frederiksplein and Prinsengracht. Take tram #4 to Prinsengracht and walk south for just over 1 block; the Temple will be the 2nd building on your right after you pass Utrechtsedwarsstraat. New Age music and a spartan decor aims for zen-like relaxation. The Temple features food from around the globe, entirely vegetarian, and mostly organic in a plain, calm interior. Even committed carnivores will be satisfied by a filling but not overly rich Indian *thali* or Middle Eastern platter, each of which allow you to mix and match a meal from various regional delicacies (€12). Tart apple crisp makes a great finisher (€3,35). Plenty of vegan options available. Pizzas €6,50-9,50. Open daily 5-9:30pm. AmEx/MC/V. ❸

Tashi Deleg, Utrechtsestraat 65 (☎620 66 24). Tram #4 to Keizersgracht, walk half a block towards Prinsengracht, and it will be on your left. The scent of incense mingles with the smell of savory traditional Tibetan cooking at this mellow *eetcafe*. *Momos* make for a rich appetizer (steamed dumplings with beef; €5,50). Main courses range from the spicy Himalaya

Bon-bons at Jordino

De Vliegende Schotel

Fresh Fish for Sale at Albert Cuyptmarkt

the BIG $plurge

De Belhamel

In its more than hundred-year history, this building in the Shipping Quarter has housed everything from a tea room to a fishery, but today is home to **De Belhamel,** Brouwersgracht 60, one of Amsterdam's ideal places to live it up a little.

Equally suited to a drippingly romantic date and a friendly roundtable among friends, the restaurant also sports an intimate downstairs bar for drinks before or after the meal. And what a meal: the menu dishes up a unique Franco-Dutch cuisine and changes every 3 months, but certain favorites--such as the "beef Belhamel"--are always around. An outside terrace couldn't offer a more picturesque place to enjoy your meal beside the sleepy Brouwersgracht. De Belhamel attracts a crowd diverse in both age and style and a cozy mixture of tourists and locals. Dress is refreshingly casual, but the dining is anything but; nothing but excellent service and amazing dishes here. Appetizers run €8-11, mains around €20, decadent desserts €8,50. Reservations a must; call after 4pm.

(☎622 1095; www.belhamel.nl. Open M-Th 6-10pm, F-Sa 6-10:30pm.) ❺

sha latsa (beef; €11) to *Tse Nezom*, mixed vegetables lightly sauteed with herbs and bamboo (€9,50). If you order the menus for 2 people, you can get a 3-course meal for €18 per person (vegetarian €17 or €20,50 for a more extensive choice) and pack in the most *Deleg* delight for your buck. Set it off with piquant *Tib Chang*, Tibetan rice beer (€1,75), or their speciality, buttered tea. Open Tu-Su 3-11:30pm. V. ❹

Carousel Pancake House, Weteringcircuit (☎625 80 02). Tram #6, 7, 16, 24, or 25 to Westeringcircuit. It all comes full circle at this donut-shaped *eethuis* surrounding a small, old-fashioned immobile carousel, but it still manages to feel like a diner. The place is a somewhat touristy, but the pancakes are excellent. The *pannenkoeken* come in the traditional full-plate size or in little silver dollars *(poffertjes)* with countless varieties of toppings from fruit to bacon and cheese (€3-7,50). Divine apple is liberally dusted with powdered sugar (€4,75). Open daily 10am-9pm. Cash only. ❶

LEIDSEPLEIN

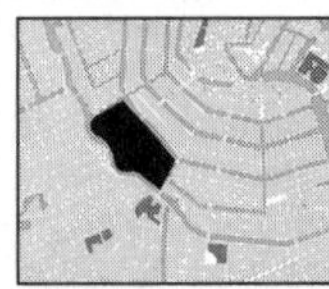

see map p. 325

Bojo, Lange Leidsedwarsstraat 51 (☎622 74 34). From Leidesplein, walk past Haagen Dasz one block, take a right onto Lange Leidsedwarsstraat, and it will be on your left. Bamboo walls and sassy waitstaff predominate at this popular Indonesian joint, but the real star is the Javanese chow for great value. The chef changes the menu frequently, but you can't go wrong with the tender, savory lamb or chicken satay smothered in peanut sauce (€7,50). House fave-rave *Ayam Banjar* features chicken in a sauce that's spicy, sweet, and sour all at the same time (€11). If the choices simply overwhelm you, just grab the mini *rijsttafel* with a sampling of Indonesian specialities piled onto one plate (€9,50). Lychees make for a great dessert (€2). **Bojo Speciaal,** just around the corner to the left on Leidsekruisstraat, offers the same menu, except they serve mixed drinks and offer a fuller *rijsttafel* that comes in separate dishes (€14,50). Open M-Th 4pm-2am, F 4pm-4am, Sa noon-4am, Su noon-2am. ❸

Santa Lucia, Leidsekruisstraat 20-22 (☎623 46 39). Damn fine pizza in a city where a decent slice is hard to come by. Corner location puts you in the middle of the action just off Leidseplein. Vivacious waitstaff exhorts you to eat hot pies bubbling with cheese (tomato and cheese €4) and all types of toppings (mushroom €6,50; pepperoni €7,50). Hot, gooey lasagna €8,50. Open daily noon-11pm. MC/V. ❶

Wagamama, Max Euweplein 10 (☎528 77 78; www.wagamama.com). Loud, crowded Japanese noodle joint devoted to "the way of the noodle." Slick white walls, long wooden tables with benches, and hipster waitstaff. The menu brims with creative entrees: *Yaki Udon* features shiitake mushrooms, egg, leeks, prawns, chicken, red peppers, and Japanese fishcake sauce (€10,40). *Zasai Gohen* combines stir-fried chicken, shiitake mushrooms, and veggies in a spicy sauce atop a bed of white rice. The "positive eating" menu includes a *gyoza* starter, noodle dish and beer or juice (€15, vegetarian €14). Ramen noodle dishes €9-13. Lightening fast service at this chain import from London, especially for Amsterdam's standards. If you're on the go, come recline on the sleek blue lounge up front and sip a fresh juice (carrot, apple, and orange mix €3,50) and watch the action in the Max Euweplein. Open M-Sa noon-11pm, Su noon-10pm. AmEx/DC/MC/V. ❸

De Smoeshaan, Leidsekade 90 (☎625 03 68; post@desmoeshaan.nl; www.desmoeshaan.nl). *Gezellig eetcafe* with real Dutch flavor tucked in just off the main drag. Enjoy a drink (beer €2, wine €2,60-3) or light snack (*tostis* €1,30, *bitterballen* €3) on the patio and watch canal life drift by or in the cosy wooden room under the theater. The kitchen closes at 11pm, after which a bar scene develops, one mellow enough to have a chat with friends or even an intimate *tête-à-tête.* Open Su-Th 11am-1am, F-Sa 11am-3am. AmEx/MC/V. ❶

Bombay Inn, Lange Leidsedwarsstraat 46 (☎624 17 84). From Leidseplein, walk past Haagen Dasz for one block, take a right onto Lange Leidsedwarsstraat, and it's towards the end of the block on the left. Among the constellation of Indian restaurants that dots the Leidseplein, the Inn proffers high-quality fare at excellent value. The choice for budget travelers is clear: just ask for the "tourist menu" and gorge on 3 courses: *papadum* and soup; chicken or lamb curry, mixed rice, and salad; and coffee or dessert (€8,50 or €9,50). Meatless eats such as *alu palaak* and *saag paneer* come cheap as well (*f*8-11/€3-5)–however don't expect any extras, like sauce (€1) or rice (€2,25) unless you're willing to pay. Open daily 3-11pm. AmEx/MC/V. ❷

REMBRANDTPLEIN

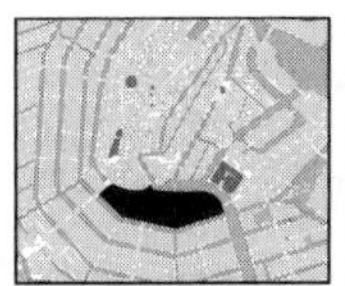

see maps pp. 324-325

Rembrandtplein itself is surrounded by restaurants and pubs, but these tend not to be the best quality and value in the area, although they offer a seat in the center ring and great people watching. **Utrechtsestraat** trundles south of Rembrandtplein from the southeastern corner of the square; here you'll find some of the city's best restaurants and shops, most of which possess a cool, local buzz safely out of the way of the tourist hordes.

Salad at Bolhoed

French Fries with Mayo

Proust

the BIG $plurge

Vakzuid

Though a bit of trek, your efforts will be rewarded. **Vakzuid,** Olympisch Stadion 35, offers tasty Asian fusion treats, is embedded in **Olympisch Stadion,** the bowl-shaped track and field arena built for the 1928 Summer Olympics. Taking up a big chunk of the converted stadium space, Vakzuid boasts a huge restaurant and chill lounge space that opens up into a club at night during weekends. Sparse Zen design blends well with the views of the track and field. Lunch is sandwiches (€4-7,50) and salads (most under €8). For dinner, enjoy appetizers €8,50-13; vegetarian entrees €8; fish and meat dishes €20, and dessert €7. After dinner, visitors often explore the stadium complex, enjoying the numerous Greek statues and other relics of Olympic magic. Su in July and August is a lazy afternoon with barbecues (€8-22,75), dim sum (€5-8,50), and couches outside (3-10pm). Reservations recommended.

(☎570 84 00; www.vakzuid.nl. Tram #6 or 16, or bus #172 to Stadionplein, enter the stadium complex. Nachtbuses #78, 71, 272 and 270 also stop here. Open M-Th 10am-1am, F 10am-3am, Sa 4pm-3am, Su 3-10pm. AmEx/MC/V.) ❺

Rose's Cantina, Reguliersdwarsstraat 40 (☎625 97 97; info@rosescantina.com; www.rosescantina.com). Tram to Koningsplein or Muntplein. Rose's is festive, fun, loud, and a bit hectic. The large 2 fl. space, decorated with the tiles of a Mexican hacienda, is always bustling, making it ideal for group celebrations. There's a quieter garden terrace in back for warmer nights. €13,60 gets you a choice of two: quesadilla, enchilada, burrito, or taco, all served with sides of rice, beans, and guacamole—a filling, but not excessive portion, although you can also get just one (€11,20). Fajitas €16. The margaritas are disappointingly small (€4,60); liter pitchers €28. Open daily 5pm-midnight, later on the weekends. AmEx/MC/V. ❸

Tomo Sushi, Reguliersdwarsstraat 131 (☎528 52 08; www.tomosushi.nl). From Rembrandtplein, walk towards the end with the statue and take the street on the left off the short side of the rectangle. Tomo Sushi will be a quarter of a block down on your right. Hip, slick sushi joint with Jetsons-style furnishings. Style, when it's served with ultra-fresh fish, comes with a price: Sushi and/or *sashimi* combos €15,50-27, most about €22. *Nigiri* €3,60, (the toro and barbecued eel stand out); *maki* cucumber or pickle €3,70; salmon €5. Cleanse your palette with Japanese green tea ice cream (€4). Make a reservation if you want dinner on weekends. Domestic beer €2,80; imported Japanese beer €3,30; warm sake €4,40. Open M-Sa 5pm-midnight. AmEx/MC/V. ❺

Curry Garden, Amstelstraat 26 (☎320 65 51), 2 blocks east of Rembrandtplein. Though it specializes in the spicy, garlicky *Balti* fare, the Garden serves all varieties of Indian food in a clean setting with light wooden tables. Lively weekend crowds attest to the restaurant's reputation for some of the city's best Indian fare. *Balti* dishes €12,50-18; *biryani* dishes €13-18; vegetarian curries €10. Prix-fixe menu €15. Open daily 5-11pm. AmEx/MC/V. ❹

THE JORDAAN

see maps pp. 328-329

After a busy day of sightseeing, you need only stroll down the Prinsengracht, the Rozengracht, or the Elandsgracht to find a place to eat; below, find a few highlights.

Bolhoed, Prinsengracht 60-62 (☎626 18 03), serves up the best in vegetarian and vegan fare, all in a bright, funky setting complete with Sammy the cat. Perfect place to regroup over a cup of tea and one of Bolhoed's delicious desserts (€5). For lunch, try a sandwich, quiche, or bowl of the daily soup, all around €4. Dinner menu always includes a vegan special for €13. Mexican dishes, pasta, and casserole for €12,50-15. Wash it down with fresh juice or organic wine. Imperative to make a reservation for dinner. Cash only. Open daily 4-11:30pm; kitchen closes at 10:45pm. ❸

Manzano, Rozengracht 106 (☎624 57 52, www.manzano.nl). Like stepping into a Picasso painting, this nice retreat from the hectic Rozengracht serves reasonably-priced *tapas* (a wide variety of meat, fish, and vegetable selections). If the candlelit tables and lilting Spanish music don't seduce you, the friendly and helpful staff will. Reservations useful for dinner. Dips and veggie *tapas* from €4-8. Main shes €9-27. Drinks, including margaritas, €5,50-6,50; desserts €5-8. Restaurant open Tu-Su 5:30pm-midnight; shop open noon-10pm. AmEx/MC/V. ❹

Snackbar Aggie, Tweede Goedsbloem Dwarsstraat 25 (☎774 79 61). It's expected that you'll get the munchies once or twice while in Amsterdam, and if you're starving at 2am, there's no better place to go than here. Grab falafel, fries, or an ice-cream cone at this ideal late-night snack joint; nothing's more than around €3. Su-Th 11am-1am, Fr-Sa 11am-3am. ❶

Ben Cohen's Shawarma, Rozengracht 239 (☎627 97 21). Tram #10 to Rozengracht or 3, 14, 17, or 20 to Marnixstraat. Nothing but bare-bones good eating here. Open late and won't break the bank. *Shawarma* €3,50. Open daily, 5pm-3am. ❶

Rakang, Elandsgracht 29 (☎627 50 12 or 620 95 51). If the vivid colors and cheery plates aren't enough to boost your spirits, the emphasis on family-style dining should brighten your mood as the upscale Thai dining lightens your wallet. Appetizers €6-12, salads and soups €8. Prix fixe vegetarian menu €26,50. ❺

Broodje Mokum, Rozengracht 26 (☎623 19 66). Deli-style restaurant great for grabbing a fast sandwich with any number of meats and cheeses. Sandwiches around €2. Open M-F, 6:30am-6pm, Sa 8am-5pm. ❶

Duende, Lindengracht 62 (☎420 66 92; www.cafeduende.nl). Live Flamenco music every Sa at 11pm might be what attracts the well-dressed crowd, or perhaps it's the €4 *tapas*. Larger plates go for €7-10. If you want to escape the crowd and noise, there's a quieter backroom where you and your special someone can make goo-goo eyes at each other. Expect a sentimental candle in a wine bottle at every table. Open Su-F 4pm-1am, Sa 2pm-3am; kitchen M-F 5-11pm, Sa-Su 4-11pm. ❷

De Vliegende Schotel, Nieuwe Leliestraat 162-168 (☎625 20 41; www.vliegendeschotel.com). A vegetarian restaurant as unique as its name, which translates as "flying saucer," this enclave offers a wide selection of heaping dishes for €8-12, with salads and soups €2-5. With walls decorated with children's' drawings, this isn't fine dining, but it's great for a quick lunch or dinner. Open daily 4pm-11:30pm; kitchen closes at 10:45pm. AmEx/MC/V. ❷

WESTERPARK AND THE OUDE WEST

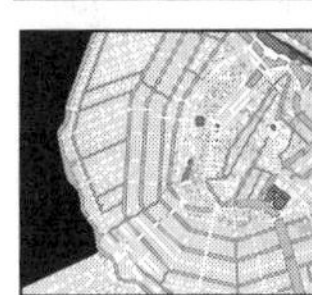

see map p. 335

Restaurant Wanka, Bosboom Toussaintstraat 70 (☎412 61 69). Tram #1 or 6 to 1e Constantijn Huygensstr., or tram #3 or 12 to Overtoom. Walk away from Overtoom 4 blocks on 1e Constantijn Huygensstr., take a right on Bosboom Toussaitnstr.; restaurant is on your left. Self-described "global" cuisine, justifying a menu with both teriyaki shrimp and asparagus and gorgonzola salad. Appetizers from €5-7, entrees €11-16. Always two vegetarian items on the menu. Open Su-Th 6pm-1am, F-Sa 6pm-3am. AmEx/MC/V. ❸

Abyssinia Afrikaans Eet-cafe, Jan Pieter Heijestraat 190 (☎683 07 92). Tram #1 or 6 to Jan Pieter Heijestr. Cross Overtoom away from Vondelpark, the restaurant is on the left side of J.P. Heijest. Ethiopian eatery encourages eating the *injera* (fermented pancake) with your hands but will provide forks on request. Most meals €8-10, including a wide selection of vegetarian options. Reservations suggested. Open daily 5pm-midnight. AmEx/DC/MC/V. ❷

Esoterica, Overtoom 409 (☎689 72 26). Tram #1 or 6 to Overtoomsesluis. Walk three blocks on Overtoom away from the canal; restaurant is on your right on the corner. A quirky enclave specializing in vegetarian and Indonesian cuisine that's worth the walk. If the friendly staff and distinctive menu don't set Esoterica apart, the chess events do. Starters €2,40-5, meals €7,50-8,50. Inexpensive Indonesian rice table (€12,50). Open W-Su 2-10pm. ❷

Toussaint Cafe, Bosboom Toussaintstr. 26 (☎685 07 37). Tram #1 or 6 to 1e Constantijn Huygensstr., or tram #3 or 12 to Overtoom. Walk away from Overtoom 4 blocks on 1e Constantijn Huygensstr., take a right on Bosboom Toussaitnstr., walk 2 blocks and the cafe is on your left on the corner. Small restaurant and bar with sidewalk seating. Popular with the locals. Serves *tapas* all day (combo plate €10,50). Bread and tasty olive oil comes with

the BIG $plurge

In de Waag

The medieval castle at the center of Nieuwmarkt is the only one in Amsterdam where you can get a good bowl of pasta and free internet with any purchase. **In de Waag,** Nieuwmarkt 4, offers food whose higher price actually corresponds to its higher quality. The castle is Amsterdam's oldest building. From 1488, it served as the eastern entrance to the city. Today, you'll find a basic lunch menu (sandwiches and salads €4-5,50) served on the patio in front of the castle. At dinnertime In de Waag ignites its 250 candles and becomes the hippest spot in town. Patrons pack the medieval space and enjoy some of the city's tastiest Italian fare. (leg of lamb €19 and *strangolapretti*, nocci with ricotta and spinach and pepper coulis, €17,50).

In the early 1500s, the building served as the city's primary courthouse for witch trials, condemning hundreds of innocent women to be burned at the stake. Rembrandt is said to have painted **The Anatomy Lesson** in the castle's loft in the 17th century. Today, its structure contributes toward making In de Waag one of the city's most elegantly casual restaurants. *(☎452 77 72; www.indewaag.nl.Open Su-Th 10am-midnight, F-Sa 10am-1am.)* ❹

every hearty meal. Ask about daily specials and quiche. Always vegetarian choices on the menu. Dinner entrees €10-13. Reservations for 3 or more strongly recommended. Open M-Th 10am-midnight, F-Sa 10am-1am. Cash only. ❸

Kismet, 350 Kinkerstraat (☎683 99 75). Tram #7 or 17 to 10 Katestr. Walk two blocks on Kinkerstraat, towards Jan Pieter Huygensstraat; Kismet is on the corner. Small take out place with tasty Turkish treats like grape leaves and baklava. Combo menus €5,50. Open M noon-6pm, Tu-F 9am-6pm, Sa 9am-5pm.❶

Dosa, Overtoom 142 (☎616 48 38). Tram #1 or 6 to 1e Constantijn Huygensstr. Dosa is on the corner of Overtoom and 2e Constantijn Huygensstr. The attractive floral decor and mood lighting provide a pleasant environment in which to enjoy curry, fish, or lamb at this South Indian restaurant. Plenty of vegetarian choices and a surprisingly large variety of *naan* (€1,80-3,65). For dessert, try the Indian rice pudding. Sides hover around €6, while main dishes about €11. Open daily 4pm-midnight. ❸

Tig Barra, Overtoom 31, (☎412 22 10; www.tig-barra.com). Tram #1 or 6 to 1e Constatijn Huygensstr. Walk towards the Singlegr., and Tig Barra is on the right side of the street. The traditional Irish pub food is a heartening break from greasy middle eastern take out. Representing an unexpected side of the Oud West diversity, Tig Barra is through-and-through Irish, from the orange, green, and white flags flying over the door to the constant stream of football matches on the TV. Have a pint of Guiness (€4,30) with Irish fare (€8-11,50). Open M-Th noon-1am, F-Sa 10:30am-1am, Su 10:30am-1am. ❷

Cafe Westers, 1e Constantijn Huygensstraat 35-37 (☎612 16 91). Tram #3 or 12 to Overtoom, walk up 1e Constatijn Huygensstr. towards Lennepkanal; Westers is on your left. Cozy feeling of a *bruine café* in a sizeable restaurant with Dutch menu and a pleasant outdoor terrace. Beer from €1,60. Appetizers and salads €6-8, entrees around €10-11. Vegetarian options available. Dinner daily 5:30-10:30pm. Bar open M-Th 3pm-1am, F 3pm-2am, Sa 11am-2am, Su 11am-1am. Cash only.❷

MUSEUMPLEIN AND VONDELPARK

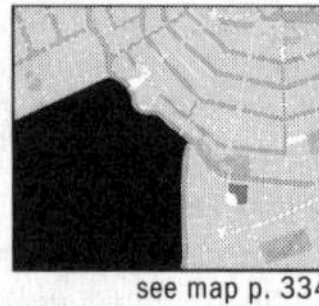
see map p. 334

If you're looking for a quick bite amidst a day of art, the major museums in Museumplein have cafés with unexceptional food. Elsewhere in the neighborhood, food stands offer more basic, equally unexceptional food at slightly cheaper prices (€2-3 for sandwiches and hot dogs). At one end of the Museumplein, on Van Baerlestraat (opposite the Rijksmuseum), is the supermarket **Albert Heijn.** Otherwise, head to one of these options for better food in better style:

Het Blauwe Theehuis (The Blue Teahouse), Vondelpark 5 (☎662 0254; blauwetheehuis@dolfijn.nl; www.blauwetheehuis.nl). In the middle of the park, just north of the Open-Air Theater. Through the trees in the park, you may suddenly glimpse at a 1970s spaceship, full of people having a good time. It's actually the Blue Teahouse, a fabulous café in a round building with wraparound blue terraces. The lunch sandwiches (€4) and evening *tapas* (€3-4) are standard, so come for a drink and chill on the outdoor patio in the warmer months or nestle into the comfortable mothership when it gets colder. DJ F-Sa nights Open Su-Th 9am-1am, F-Sa 9am-3am. ❶

Cafe Vertigo, Vondelpark 3 (☎612 30 21). Adjacent to the Filmmuseum, Vertigo has a wonderful terrace overlooking a duck pond in the park. Great place for a drink after a movie, or during a screening, when the café offers a free drink with admission to the outdoor films shown by the film museum (F €2,50 about 10-10:30pm). Skip the pricier dinner menu in favor of the lunch sandwiches (€3,40 for chicken and avocado or tuna salad or cheese) and tasty pastries (€2). Sept.-Mar. Sa disco nights until 2am. M-Sa lunch until 4pm, Su until 5pm; dinner daily 6-10pm. Open daily 10am-1am. ❶

De Griekse Taverna, Hobbemakade 64-65 (☎671 79 23 www.degrieksetaverna.nl). Take tram #3, 5, 12, or 20 to Museumplein; it's at the corner of Honthorstraat. Excellently prepared Greek food makes this a local favorite. Rustic wooden tables and long vermilion curtains create a comfortable environment. Order starters off a tray for €3 each; "middle dishes" €7-€8 and entrees €12-18. Open Su-Th 5pm-1am, F-Sa 5pm-2am. Cash only. ❸

Khorat Top Thai, 2e Constantijn Huygenstraat 64 (☎683 12 97 www.urbanbite.nl), between Vondelstraat and Overtoom. Tram #1 or 6 to 1e Constantijn Huygenstraat. Reasonably priced Thai food in a family-run restaurant. Chicken entrees €9; pork and beef €10; vegetarian €8; fish €10-16. It's not worth going out of the way, but it provides a good meal off the park or a cheaper option if you're in the neighborhood for dinner. Open daily 4-10pm. Cash only. ❸

Go Sushi, Johannes Verhulststraat 35 (☎471 00 35). Tram #16 to Jacob Olbrecthstraat Tiny place tucked into a quiet neighborhood. 3 pieces of nigiri from €1,20; 3 pieces of maki from €1,80; 4 pieces of inside out roll €4,30. Open M-W noon-7pm, Th-F noon-8pm. ❷

Tapa Feliz, Valeruisstraat 85hs (☎364 12 83). Tram #16 to Emmastraat. Advertising itself as a *tapas* bar and international restaurant, Feliz serves up multicul-

Golden Temple

Bojo

Wagamama

kinderkookkafe

In the heart of the Red Light District, something all too wholesome occurs. The Kinderkookkafe is a restaurant entirely run by children. In this cafe, kids learn how to cook, prepare meals, wait on tables, and then do the dishes. Book well in advance, as seating is very limited for the two days that the restaurant part of the Kinderkookkafe is open to the public. During weekdays, birthday parties and cooking classes for children are held in the building.

Oudezijds Achterburgwal 193. (☎625 32 57; www.dinnersite.nl/kinderkookkafe) Open for dinner Sa 6pm, for high tea Su 5pm. Reservations essential. Dinner €8, ages 5-12 €5. ❷

tural fare in attractive multi-color tiled 2 fl. digs. Sip sangria (half-liter €7,50) and nibble on *tapas* (€2,25-7,25; most €5) throughout the day and well into the night. The warm sandwiches served at lunchtime (€4-6,70) are kinder to the wallet than the dinner entrees, though the paella (€16) is worth a try. Lunch M-F 11:30am-3pm; dinner M-Sa 5:30-10:30pm. Open M-F 11:30am-11pm, Sa 4-11pm. AmEx/MC/V. ❹

DE PIJP

see map p. 326

It's worth walking a few minutes out of the city center to sample the international cuisine that is steamed, sauteed, fried, and served up in De Pijp. Affordable restaurants of all ethnic traditions abound here. On **Albert Cuypstraat**, just west of the market, is a street packed with cheap Surinamese/Chinese/Indonesian combination restaurants that constitute some of the best bargains in city. These restaurants have the decor of a mop closet, so a good strategy is to take a picnic to nearby Saphatipark. On the other hand, De Pijp is increasingly the sight of hip, design restaurants with €20 entrees.

Zagros, Albert Cuypstraat 50 (☎670 04 61). Tram #16, 24 or 25 to Albert Cuyp. Here's your chance to try little-celebrated Kurdish cuisine. The food is influenced by the 5 countries spanned by Kurdistan: Turkey, Iran, Iraq, Syria, and Russia in a plain but appealing candlelit atmosphere. Tart hummus makes a great starter (€2,50). Lamb dominates the menu: grilled lamb chops come with couscous and salad (€11,50); *beste berxe* includes marinated lamb chunks, rice, and salad (€10,50). Veggie options available too; *balcanen sor* blends potatoes, eggplant, and peppers baked in yogurt garlic tomato sauce (€9,50). Try the sticky, sugary baklava if you've still got room left (€3,50). They also have take-out and delivery service, including Italian delicacies. If you come with a group, you can order a belly dancer (€150). Open daily 3pm-midnight. AmEx/MC/V. ❷

Saray, Gerard Doustraat 33 (☎671 92 16). Tram 16, 24, or 25 to Albert Cuyp. Walk back 1 block and turn left onto Gerard Droustraat. Turkish delicacies in a classy, atmospheric setting that's been around for 25 years. *Kofta* is a great starter, combining lentils, onion, and ground beef (€3,40), or you can sample the fried courgette with yogurt and garlic (€3,40). Grilled mains are well within budget range: lamb dishes €9-13,30. Vegetarians can go for the *buglama* (€9,75) or tortellinis with spinach and mushrooms in a creamy sauce (€10,20). Wash it down with *Efes*, the Turkish national beer (€2). Open daily 5-11pm. AmEx/MC/V. ❸

L'Angoletto, Hemonystraat 18 (☎676 41 82). Tram #4 or 9 to Stadhouderskade, walk 2 blocks further down the rail line and take a left for 1block. Sublime Italian pizza and pasta (€5-9) at an old-fashioned family trattoria. Its popularity and tiny size means it fills up quickly so come early or late, or be prepared for a wait. Open Su-F 6-11pm. ❶

De Ondeugd, Ferdinand Bolstraat 13-15 (☎672 06 51; www.ondeugd.nl). "The Naughty One" serves fancy French food in a space that includes a disco-mirror room and a gold room. One of the first restaurants to start the gentrification of De Pijp, with entrees hovering around €20 and appetizers like the lobster coulis €7.50. Open Su-Th 6pm-1am, F-Sa 6pm-3am; kitchen open 6-11pm. AmEx/DC/MC/V. ❹

De Soepwinkel, 1e Sweelinckstraat 19F (☎673 22 93; www.soepwinkel.nl), just off the Albert Cuypmarkt. A hip kitchen that elevates soup-making to a fine art form. The bright, cheery, streamlined decor focuses your attention on their masterpiece soups; six specialities which change every month but always include a vegetarian choice and soup for kids, all served with fresh breads. Summer features lighter fare, such as cold soups; thicker dishes, even stews, predominate when the cold weather arrives. Small €3,50; medium €5,75; large €9. Open M-F 11am-9pm, Sa 11am-6pm. Credit cards accepted. ❶

Cambodja City, Albert Cuypstraat 58-60 (☎671 49 30). Tram #16, 24 or 25 to Albert Cuyp and take a right. Specialties from Thailand, Vietnam, and—you guessed it—Cambodia. What it lacks in atmosphere, it makes up for with great value: the food is good, cheap, and comes in big portions (an excellent choice for take-out to Sarphatipark). Vietnamese noodle soup comes loaded with chicken beef balls and makes for a full meal in itself (€3,75). Thai chicken or lamb curry €7,70; no main dish costs more than €12. The special dinners for 2 people are an incredible deal: 10 choices for €20-32,50. Open Tu-Su 5-10pm. Cash only. ❷

Peppino Gelateria, 1e Sweelinckstraat 16 (☎676 49 10), 1 block off the Albert Cuypmarkt, or tram #4 or 20. Silvano Tofani has been making the best homemade gelato, using only fresh cream and fruit (right before customers' eyes), ever since his father emigrated from Italy. It might be the best ice cream in the city (from €0,75 for one scoop); excellent cappuccino (€1,80). Open April-Oct. daily 10am-11pm. ❶

Zento, Ferdinand Bolstraat 17-19 (☎471 53 16). Tram #16, 24 or 25 to Albert Cuypstraat and walk 2blocks back along the tram line. Amidst the recently hip-ified decor—sleek stools, 70s wood paneling, and the occasional pink pillow—sushi parades by on a conveyor belt that surrounds the bar. Grab whatever strikes your fancy as it passes by and save the plate; the number and color of plates determines the price

Rembrandtplein at Night

Carousel Pancake House

Dining Out

of your bill at the end of your meal. Mobile options include tuna maki (pink; €2,50); california roll (red; €3,50); prawn sushi (orange; €4,50); salmon sashimi (purple; €6,50); and the rare white plate for €8,50. The fusion-tinged ingredients frequently come in more innovative combinations than traditional sushi, such as chicken, avocado and chives (red), grilled vegetable and pesto maki (orange), and asparagus and salmon roe (orange). Trendy sake-based cocktails such as the cosmo sake and caipi sake €5,50, Kirin beer €3,60. Open Tu-W 5-10pm, Th-F 5-11pm, Sa-Su 4-11pm. AmEx/MC/V. ❸

Mas Tapas, Saenredamstraat 37 (☎664 00 66; www.siempre.tapas.com). Tram #16, 24 or 25 to Albert Cuypstraat. Walk 1 block right along Albert Cuyp and then go right for two blocks up Frans Halssta. Attractive neighborhood *tapas* bar has only a few indoor tables; in summer they spill out onto the serene side street. Selection of 12 *tapas* (€2,75 each or 5 for €12,50) include garlicky mushrooms and *ceviche* (marinated fish). Full meals include pinchos morenos (€7,50) and grilled salmon (€12). Spanish San Miguel beer €2. Open daily 4pm-midnight. Cash only. ❸

Bar Soup, Govert Flinckstraat 153 (☎673 00 06). Turn off Albert Cuypmarkt at 1e van de Helststraat, walk one block and turn left. Five homemade soups with surprising and usually very good combinations of ingredients that change daily (vegetarian soups abound) for €3-6,20. Salads €3-€4. Cash only. ❶

Eufraat, 1e van der Heltstraat 72 (☎672 05 79; www.eufraat.com). Specializing in fare from the regions surrounding the Euphrates River (Syria, Turkey, and Iraq), with geographically-themed dishes. Start your feast with a lentil soup (€3) or Assyrian *rissoles* (pancakes stuffed with cheese, lamb, or chicken; €3,60), and then move on to the pastries of broken-wheat stuffed with minced lamb and fried in egg (€9,80) or the leg of lamb, done flavorfully in a garlic tomato sauce with herbs. *Shamirahn* (fried squid) is tender, not chewy (€9,20). Hearty vegetarian stew combines eggplant, mushrooms, tomato, and peppers (€8,30). Wine by the glass from €2. Open daily 5-11pm. AmEx/MC/V. ❷

Moksi, Ferdinand Bolstraat 21 (☎676 82 64). The name of this mellow Surinamese restaurant refers to its signature dish, a mixture of chicken, sausage, beef, and pork in spicy, tangy sauce (€7,50; large €8,40). There are plenty of *roti* and rice dishes as well, including vegetarian options (€5-10). Basic decor. Service can be on the slow side. Open Tu-Sa noon-10pm, Su 4-10pm. Cash only. ❷

Granny's, 1e van der Heltstraat 45 (☎679 44 65). Tram #16, 24 or 25 to Albert Cuyp and walk left for a block down Albert Cuypstraat, then take a right. This "petit grand cafe" is a throwback to the early 1900s, bedecked with tintype photos of guys on big-wheeled bikes and flappers advertising Coca-Cola. Great for families. For a non-Dutch treat, try a big, basic cheeseburger (€3). Great *appelgebak* comes loaded with whipped cream (€2,50). *Pannenkoeken* €3,63-6, *broodjes* €1,60-3. Open 9am-6pm. ❶

Albina, Albert Cuypstraat 69 (☎675 51 35). Tram #16, 24 or 25 to Albert Cuyp and walk right. One of a handful of Surinamese/Chinese/Indonesian restaurants in a row where the food is cheap and you get a lot of it but the decor is nonexistent. *Tjauw minh* (thin noodles that come loaded with veggies and meat) €4,31; *gado gado* (vegetables smothered in peanut sauce) €3,63. Open Tu-Sa 10:30am-10pm, Su noon-10pm. Cash only. ❶

JODENBUURT AND THE PLANTAGE

see map p. 327

Cafe Latei, Zeedijk 143 (☎625 74 85). Sit, read, or chat in this unique cafe-cum-curiosities shop where just about everything is for sale—probably even the plate you're eating off. Though the look of the space changes as items come and go, the feel of it remains something akin to a cluttered, sophisticated kitchen, with classic wall clocks, furniture, plates, postcards, and knick-knacks up for grabs. Grab most of their large sandwiches for under €3, and standard continental breakfast all day for €6,40. Open M-F 8am-5pm, Sa 9am-6pm, Su 11am-6pm. ❶

Abe Veneto, Plantage Kerklaan 2 (☎639 23 64). This quaint Italian eatery plastered with vines and greenery has the food and prices to make any traveler happy. Situated at the corner of Plantage Kerklaan and Plantage Muidergracht with a large selection of pizzas (€4,50-9,50), pastas (€6,50-9,50), and salads (most under €5). Takeout offered, although the comfy atmosphere will make you question the choice. Cash only. ❷

King Solomon Restaurant, Waterlooplein 239 (☎625 58 60). The only kosher restaurant in sight, King Solomon serves it up fresh, with falafel (€7,25), veggie platters (€13,50), and the specialty of any Jewish grandmother, gefilte fish (€6,75). Much more upscale than the shawarma huts in the city and run by a hospitable Orthodox family. In an area famous for its Jewish heritage, enjoy the fare of this pleasant kosher establishment. Open Su-Th noon-10pm, F noon-5pm; in winter Sa from 45min. after sundown until 10pm. ❷

Soup En Zo, Jodenbreestraat 94a (☎422 22 43). Let your nose guide you to the amazing soup at this tiny soupery. Homemade soup and fresh bread make a great lunchtime combo, especially for vegetarians. Several soups and sizes range in price from €2,50 to €5,50, with free bread and fresh soup toppings (coriander, dill, cheese, nuts) to spare. Open M-Sa 11am-8pm, Su 1-7pm. ❶

Plancius, Plantage Kerklaan 61a (☎330 94 69; www.diningcity.nl/plancius), across the street from Artis Zoo. Terrifically chic yet accessible to the whole family, Plancius serves stylish breakfasts, lunches, and dinners for slightly high but still reasonable prices. Sandwiches from €2,60; pasta from €7,50; dinners, like the goat's cheese terrine with aubergine and red pepper caviar, from €15. Open daily 10am-2am; kitchen open 10am-4:30pm and 6-10pm. ❸

Nam Tin, Jodenbreestraat 11 (☎428 85 08), one block up Jodenbreestraat from Mr. Visserpleinan. This enormous and elegant Chinese banquet hall is replete with pink tablecloths, tuxedoed waiters, and Buddhist statues. Cantonese food is Nam Tin's specialty, with dim sum served all day (most dishes under €4) and a large array of noodle soups (around €13). Open M-Sa noon-midnight, Su noon-11:30pm; kitchen open daily noon-10pm. Cash only. ❸

Restaurante La Sala Comidas Caseras, Plantage Kerklaan 41 (☎624 48 46). Spanish and Portuguese food are served at this smallish cafe-restaurant across from the Artis Zoo. Tasty *tapas* (from €3,40) and authentic Spanish entrees (from €16,60). Sip wine on the outside terrace. Open Tu-Su 4pm-midnight. Cash only. ❹

Cafe Koosje, Plantage Middenlaan 37 (☎320 08 17), at the corner of Plantage Middenlaan and Plantage Kerklaan. A convenient place to grab a bite during a busy day or to wind down after a busy day. For lunch, you'll find a selection of *ciabattas* from €3 to €5 and the soup of the day for €4. At dinnertime, there is a more serious menu with a vegetarian enchillada at €9,50 and a decent wine list. ❷

En'tre Dok, Entrepotdok 64 (☎623 23 56). On the Entrepot Dok, the northern edge of the Plantage. Grab a tasty *tapas* dinner at this quick and inexpensive bar/*eetcafe*. Serves up a wide variety of *tapas* (14 choices for €3,50 each), lamb for €13,50, and cheese fondue for two (€20), which you can enjoy either inside or overlooking the canal out front. Open daily 4pm-1am. Cash only. ❸

TisFris, St. Antoniesbreestraat 142 (☎622 04 72). Watch the world go by on this cool cafe's open terrace or through the enormous windows facing Sint Antoniesbreestraat. There's plenty of vegetarian fare, and even a few dishes for the hard-core vegan (tasty avocado, pine nuts, and red onions on a roll €3,80). The crowd is hip, the food is tasty, and the prices reasonable. Open M-Sa 9am-7pm, Su 10am-7pm. ❶

Aguada, Roetersstraat 10 (☎620 37 82). Cheese fondue from €11, salads from €4, and tasty grills all delight at this comfy cafe across the street from the University of Amsterdam. Open M-F 10am-11pm, Sa noon-11pm. Cash only. ❸

BLUEBIRD
AMSTERDAM
BLUEBIRD
AMSTERDAM

INSIDE:

Only in Amsterdam

Amsterdam (and The Netherlands) is unique for its liberal attitude in regards to soft drugs and prostitution—though other countries are beginning to follow suit (see **Soft Drugs and Rock 'N Roll,** p. 44). This chapter outlines the laws and etiquette of the unique Dutch culture, and lists the best coffeeshops and smartshops around.

COMMERCIAL SEX

The "oldest profession" has flourished in Amsterdam since the city's inception around the 13th century. The main center for prostitution has always been in what today is the Red Light District, though it is legal elsewhere in the city as well. The Red Light District originally grew up around modern-day Zeedijk as prostitutes congregated to service sailors who came in and out of port. Window prostitution, which grew out of the practice of prostitutes showing off their goods from the front windows of private houses, was officially legalized in 1911, and in 2000, the law outlawing brothels was taken off the books, making informal streetwalking the only prohibited form of prostitution.

Legal prostitution in Amsterdam comes in three main forms. By far the most visible is **window prostitution,** where scantily-clad women tempt passers-by from small chambers fronted by a plate-glass window. These sex workers are self-employed and rent the windows themselves, and as such each sets her own price. This form of commercial sex gave the Red Light District its name, as lamps both outside and in the windows emit a red light that bathes the whole area by night.

Not surprisingly, then, the most popular spot for window prostitution is the **Red Light District,** particularly between **Zeedijk** and **Warmoesstraat.** There are two more areas, in the **Nieuwe Zijd,** between Spuistraat and Singel, and in **De Pijp** along Ruysdaelkade, where you'll find window prostitution. The latter two tend to be more discreet and more frequented by Dutch men than by tourists.

If you're interested in having sex with a window prostitute, go up to the door and wait for someone inside to open it. You can do pretty much anything you want as long as you clearly negotiate it beforehand. Negotiations occur and money changes hands before any sexual acts take place. Be aware that once your time is up, the hooker will ask you to leave, and there are no refunds (for more etiquette, see **Love for Hire,** p. 31).

Increasingly popular are the recently legalized **brothels,** which come in two main varieties. The term brothel usually refers to an establishment where you enter a bar in which women will make your acquaintance and are available for hour-long sessions. Brothels, also called **sex clubs,** can be pricey. In addition to costly drinks in the bar—women are encouraged by the management to entice patrons into buying bottles of champagne—they charge a cover just to enter the building.

A less expensive and more confidential alternative to the sex club is the variation known as the **private house.** In contrast to brothels, in which you enter a bar with prostitutes and other patrons, in a private house you enter a room and the currently available women walk by for your inspection. Select the one you like (or don't—there's no problem with walking out if none of the prostitutes are to your taste), and rent a room (the cost of which includes the women's services). Most of these establishments are located in Amsterdam's southern districts. **Escort services** are legal in Amsterdam as well. Offering even more discretion than private houses, these services arrange for a call girl to visit you at your home or hotel room.

The best place to go for information about prostitution in Amsterdam is the **Prostitution Information Centre,** Enge Kerksteeg 3, in the Red Light District behind the Oude Kerk. Friendly, helpful staff can answer any question you might have, no matter how much you blush when you ask it. You can also pick up copies of several informative publications: *The Most Frequently Asked Questions about Amsterdam's Red Light District,* a basic guide to the ins and outs of the window prostitution scene (€1,50); *Best Places to Go in Amsterdam,* a single sheet with the PIC's top picks of establishments (€2,50); and the *Pleasure Guide,* a magazine with ads and articles about commercial sex in the city (€2,50). They've also got a great array of handmade souvenirs—fridge magnets and such—as well as a mock-up of the inside of a window brothel. The latter provides an ideal place for taking pictures, which you can't do in actual window-prostitution booths. If you come to poke around, be sure to leave a donation; the PIC is not as yet state-supported and depends on the generosity of visitors to continue its work. (☎420 73 28; pic@pic-amsterdam.com; www.pic-amsterdam.com. Open Tu-W and F-Sa 11:30am-6:30pm.)

Sex shops and **live sex shows** are a related element of the commercial sex industry. The former litter the Red Light District, vending pornos (mags and videos), dildos, lubricants, stimulants, lewd souvenirs, and the like. Porn theaters abound here as well, where an hour of lurid on-screen sex costs less than €10. Sex shops and porn theaters cluster along Reguliersbreestraat, just off Rembrandtplein, as well. Live sex shows are just that. There are quite a few live sex show establishments in the Red Light District, but the most famous (and by some accounts, "classiest") is **Casa Rosso,** right behind the penis fountain, where you can get an eyeful for €25.

COFFEESHOPS

A far cry from your friendly neighborhood Starbucks, the coffee at coffeeshops in the Amsterdam isn't the focal point (in fact, at many you'll find that the coffeemaker is out of order, and few patrons seem to care). Places calling themselves coffeeshops sell pot or hash or will let you buy a drink and smoke your own stuff. Look for the green and white "Coffeeshop BCD" sticker that certifies a coffeeshop's credibility repute. Although Amsterdam is known as the hash capital of the world, **marijuana** is increasingly popular. You can legally purchase up to 5g at a time of marijuana or hash (the previous 30g limit was reduced in response to foreign criticism led by French President Jacques Chirac), although you are permitted to possess up to **1 oz.** (about 28g) at a time. For info on the legal ins and outs, call the **Jellinek clinic** at ☎570 23 55. If your questions pertain only to matters of cannabis or hemp, try the **Cannabis College** (see Museums p. 78).

As with any kind of recreation and experimentation, safety precautions must be taken. **Never buy drugs from street dealers.** Street dealers are mostly strung-out addicts and are often out to mug tourists. Don't get too caught up in Amsterdam's narcotic quirk; use common sense, and remember that any experimentation with drugs can be dangerous. However, if you choose to indulge, you will find that coffeeshops carry a range of products which are described below. Dealers commonly do not get tipped. When you move from one coffeeshop to another, it is courteous to buy a drink in the next coffeeshop even if you already have weed. While it's all right to smoke on the outdoor patio of a coffeeshop, don't go walking down the street smoking a joint like you're James Dean with a cigarette; it's simply not done, especially outside of the Red Light District.

While there are hot spots in Amsterdam that seem to feature as many coffeeshops as restaurants (i.e. Nieuwendijk, Warmoesstraat, and much of the Red Light District), you'll find that the best offerings aren't necessarily concentrated in any particular location. As a general rule, the farther you travel from the touristed spots, the better and cheaper the establishments. When a shop is frequented mainly by Dutch customers, it means they've established a loyal clientele, which in turn means they sell good stuff. Pick up a free copy of the *BCD Official Coffeeshop Guide* for the pot-smoker's map of Amsterdam, or try the *Smoker's Guide* (€3), sold at most coffeeshops. There's nothing wrong with walking in and checking a place out before you settle on smoking there. Peruse the listings below before coffee-shopping and be sure to take your time making your selections. When you enter a shop, ask for the menu. Establishments are not allowed to advertise their products or leave menus on the tables. The quantity of soft drugs in Amsterdam might be unlimited, but your cashflow isn't; taking that extra minute to pick the best spot for what you're after will help to guarantee you get the most bang for your buck. If a friend is tripping, it is important to never leave their side. **Call ☎122** if they need to go to the hospital.

ESSENTIAL INFORMATION

DRUG LAWS

Consistent with its other tolerant attitudes, The Netherlands policy towards **soft drugs** is one of toleration **(not legalization or decriminalization, as many believe).** The definition of soft drugs is determined by what's natural—raw mushrooms and undoctored Marijuana, for example. Laws against **hard drugs** such as cocaine and heroin are strictly enforced, and being caught with them can lead to prison sentences up to 10 years. Don't test the Dutch on this one. With marijuana and hash, it is tolerated to purchase up to 5g during a 24hr. period; and it is acceptable to have up to one ounce (28g) on your person. Any more, and you'll be suspected of **dealing,** which is a crime; only licensed coffeeshops may sell weed. Those under the age of 18 may not purchase weed or even be on the premises of a coffeeshop. Taking drugs outside of the country (including via the post office) is illegal. Drug-sniffing dogs tend to greet any train or plane that comes in from The Netherlands.

HASH. Hash comes in three varieties: black (or Indian), blonde (or Moroccan), and Dutch (also called ice-o-lator hash), all of which can cost from €4 to €30 per gram, though it's the increasingly popular **ice-o-lator hash** that tops out at around €20-30 per g. Typically, the cost of the hash is directly proportional to its quality and strength. Black hash hits harder than blonde, and ice-o-lator can send even the

get smart

In Amsterdam, smart shops have recently risen to the fore, competing with coffeeshops for customers. If you're interested in exploring a smart-drug-created world, you might want to try the following types of natural products. Be advised that most smart shops aren't coffeeshops; they operate much more like pharmacies than bars, so don't plan on whiling away an afternoon at one. And keep in mind that many of these substances have potentially adverse side effects; if combined with other substances, they could cause serious problems.

FOR A SPEEDY HIGH:

Ephedra: Said to speed up your heartbeat and increase alertness. Often consumed in tea-like brews.

Guarana: Supposedly enhances endurance and concentration. Similar effect as caffeine. Guarana is often ground up and added to coffee or cola, to give the drink an added, powerful punch.

Cola Nut: Natives of Brazil chewed this nut to stay awake. Can be an appetite suppressant. Do not combine with ephedra.

FOR RELAXATION:

Skullcap: Smoking skullcap reputedly gives a marijuana-like high.

Valerian: Supposedly produces an effect like Valium; this drug is a powerful muscle relaxant. Helpful for treating insomnia. Do not take in conjunction with other tranquilizing drugs.

most seasoned smoker off his head. What separates hash from weed is that, while weed is the whole plant, hash is the extracted resin crystals, giving a different kind of high.

MARIJUANA. A dried, cured plant also referred to as weed, mary jane, and pot. Different weeds come in and out of favor much like different beers. Any weed with white in its name is guaranteed to be strong, such as white widow, white butterfly, and white ice. Pot in The Netherlands is incredibly strong; today's strains have 4-6% THC content, as opposed to weed two or three decades ago, which might have only 0.4%. As with alcohol, take it easy so you don't pass out. The Dutch tend to mix tobacco with their pot as well, so joints are harsher on your lungs if you're not a cigarette smoker. Pre-rolled joints are always rolled with tobacco; most coffeeshops also offer pure joints at up to twice the cost. Dutch marijuana is the most common and costs anywhere from €3-12 per gram; most coffeeshops sell bags in set amounts (€6, €12, etc.) Staff at coffeeshops are accustomed to explaining the different kinds of pot on the menu to tourists. It is recommended that you buy a gram at a time. Most places will supply rolling papers and filter tips. Europeans smoke joints. When pipes or bongs are provided they are usually for and used by tourists.

SPACECAKES, SPACESHAKES, AND SPACE SWEETS. Cakes and sweets made with hash or weed. The butter used in the cake is hash or weed based. Hash chocolate, popsicles, and bon bons are also available. Because they need to go to your blood, and be digested, they take longer to affect a person, and longer to filter out. They produce a body stone that can take up to an hour or longer to start. Don't go for a second sweet because you don't feel anything immediately.

The amount of pot or hash in baked or frozen goods cannot be regulated (and you don't know what grade of drugs is in them). This makes ingesting this form of cannabis much more dangerous than smoking, where you can control your intake.

SMART SHOPS

Also legal are **smart shops,** which peddle a variety of **"herbal enhancers"** (like ephedra) and **hallucinogens** (like salvia) that walk the line between soft and hard drugs. Some shops are alcohol-free and all have a strict no-hard-drugs policy. All **hard drugs** like heroin, ecstasy, or cocaine are **illegal** and possession is treated as a serious crime. Always remember that all experimentation with drugs is dangerous, and can cause either short or long-term damage.

MAGIC MUSHROOMS. These start to work after 30-60 minutes and you'll feel their affect for four to six hours. As with pot and hash, never look for mushrooms outside of a smart shop and never buy from a street dealer; it's extremely difficult to tell the difference between poisonous mushrooms and hallucinogenic mushrooms. The effect mushrooms, also called 'shrooms, have on you will depend on your mood and the environment in which you take it. Overall, the effect is that you will see reality differently. Colors, forms, shapes, time, and experience seem longer or shorter. Blips will appear on your screen, and you won't be able to see other things. A bad trip will most likely come about if you mix hallucinogens, such as 'shrooms, with alcohol. If you have been drinking before taking shrooms, drink a Coke to get some sugar in your system. Try to avoid eating before taking shrooms, as doing so will likely dull your high or could intensify nausea; save the food for until after your trip is over. Often people become panicky and have a faster heartbeat with 'shrooms. It should take up to eight hours for the effects to go away. Additionally, people often take too many 'shrooms because they don't realize that it takes half an hour for them to kick in. If you are having a bad trip, don't be ashamed to tell someone, because you won't be arrested in Amsterdam for using. It is not a crime here, and they've seen it all before.

SHOPS BY NEIGHBORHOOD

OUDE ZIJD AND RED LIGHT DISTRICT

see maps pp. 330-331

Despite the proliferation of coffeeshops in the area, for a quality smoke, you're better off looking outside the Red Light District. Because of the heavy tourist traffic, shops don't have to rely on repeat business and as a consequent customer satisfaction isn't a priority. In short, they can sell you lousy weed and get away with it. The most telling fact: Dutch people don't buy their weed in the Red Light District. However, a couple worthwhile places do exist.

Cannabis College's Grow Room

Space Smoothies

Super Skunky

the local story

Pot Quiz:

Mark has owned The Rookies coffeeshop in Leidseplein for over 10 years. He's a "second-generation cannabis retailer" and on the board of two cannabis unions.

Q: What do you like about working in a coffeeshop?

A: It's not aggressive, it's a very tolerant atmosphere and people from all over the world come in.

Q: What do you think it is about Dutch culture that makes cannabis permissible here and nowhere else?

A: Well, it started because they needed to separate the soft and hard drugs markets. If a young person wants to get high, then he goes to a coffeeshop and he doesn't get involved with other stuff. In other countries, the same person who sells cannabis will sell ecstasy, pills, cocaine, and other drugs. The coffeeshops are very clean; there are no hard drugs here. Coffeeshops are still here because it's really working. Neighboring countries are beginning to follow our system. The Christian Democrats Party wants to get rid of everything, but it's unrealistic to think you can get rid of drugs in general; there's always going to be people who use them. It's better to leave it in the open instead of shoving it under the carpet, because then if it's still in the open you have more social control on it.

Cont. next page.

Hill Street Blues, Warmoesstraat 52, (☎638 79 22). Rock 'n' roll vibe permeates this coffeeshop and bar. Don't let the loud music that wafts into the street drive you away, though; it's an extremely laid-back vibe inside. And even if you don't want to smoke (weed and hash €4,50-11,50 per g.), you won't be able to resist the incredibly cheap beer (€2,80 for a pint; €2,10 during happy hour 6-9pm). The bar hosts a pool competition every other Su; €5 entrance fee. Open 9am-1am, F-Sa 9am-3am.

Rusland, Ruslandstraat 16 (☎627 94 68). From Muntplein, head down Nieuwe Doelenstraat, then down Kloveniersburgwal; Rusland will be on your left. One of Amsterdam's oldest coffeeshops, Rusland is an intimate, comfy nook with an extensive menu, a huge selection of tea, and killer vitamin shakes. If you like the handblown lamps on the walls, go downstairs and check out the selection of handblown pipes, where pillowed benches provide a comfy place for an afternoon smoke. Rolled joints €2,30; hash and grass available in €12 quantities. Open Su-Th 10am-midnight, Fr-Sa 10am-1am.

The Greenhouse Effect, Warmoesstraat 53 (☎623 74 62: www.the-greenhouse-effect.com). Also a hotel and bar, you could arrive and never leave this all-purpose establishment and still experience most of the Red Light District's thrills. In fact, the coffeeshop also happens to be one of the area's most pleasant, a low-key place where you can either smoke or just buy your stuff and head to the bar next door for Happy Hour (8-10pm; pints €2,30) and watch the game. Open Su-Th 9am-1am, F-Sa 9am-3am

Funny People Coffeeshop, Nieuwebrugsteeg 24 (☎623 86 63; www.funnypeople.nl). Friendly, laid-back coffeeshop offers the perfect place for a wake 'n' bake with its early opening time and large windows through which the sun rolls in. Grass €3-6,50/g; hash €3,50-7 per g. Rolled joints €3 (pure joints for €6). Open M-Sa 8am-8pm, Su 9am-8pm.

Cafe del Mondo, Nieuwmarkt 28 (☎624 13 73; www.cafedelmondo.nl). Across the street from de Waag. Big stereo system, outside terrace, and convenient location make this bar and coffeeshop one of the nicest spots along Nieuwmarkt. Serves alcohol as well as weed, including the "screaming orgasm" cocktail (€5,25). Pre-rolled joints €3,50. Open Su-Th 9am-1am, F-Sa 9am-3am.

Coffeeshop Goa, Kloveniersburgwal 42. Great tunes and famous spacecake (€4) make Goa a nice place to relax. Head for the sunlit terrace beside a pleasant canal, or try the intimate, smoky tables indoors. Also has some of the cheapest pure joints in town (€4,60). Open daily 9am-midnight.

SMART SHOP

Conscious Dreams Kokopelli, Warmoesstraat 12 (☎421 70 00). From Centraal Station, turn right at the main street, left at Martelaarsgracht, and right on Nieuwendijk. This smart shop is perhaps the best place to begin your psychedelic survey. Books, lava lamps, and a knowledgeable staff that includes a neurophysician and biologist will coat your trip: magic 'shrooms, oxygen drinks, vitamins, and herbs. Plus, Internet access (€1 for 15 min.) and DJs spinning tunes F-Su 5-10pm give you many reasons to relax in the chill space overlooking the canal. Smoke a joint, sample an energy drink, or begin your trip in a fun, safe place. Herbal X €3-14. Mushrooms €12 for happy/funny effect, €18 for real trippy. If you want the most powerful trip of all, ask about saliva (.5g costs €14-41, depending on strength), but discuss it with the staff first. Open daily 11am-10pm.

NIEUWE ZIJD

see maps pp. 330-331

In Amsterdam's **Nieuwe Zijd,** you'll find a landfill of coffeeshops, many of which should have died in the early 90s and are barely preferable to smoking alone in your hotel room. The following are a good number of gems.

Grey Area, Oude Leliestraat 2 (☎420 43 01; www.greyarea.nl). From Dam, follow Raadhuisstraat to Singel, turn right and then left on Oude Leliestraat. Where coffeeshop owners themselves go for the best. One of the only owner-operated spots left in the city, the petite shop plastered with images of American pop culture has received 13 "High Times" Cannabis Cups since 1996. No wonder Amsterdammers flock here, whether looking for the light "bubble gum" weed or the more ponderous "grey mist" (€7.50 for 1g). The yankee expat behind the counter will be happy to lend one of the coffeeshop's classy glass bongs. Amsterdam's cheapest pure marijuana joints (€3,50) and juice (€1.50) also available. Open Tu-Su noon-8pm.

Kadinsky, Rosmarijnsteeg 9 (☎624 70 23), a few blocks north of the intersection of Spui and Nieuwezijds Voorburgwal, between the 2 streets. Stylish joint hidden away off an alley near Spui and one of the city's most comfortable, friendly, and hip stoneries. Grandiose fresh flower bouquet greets you upon entrance and window-side bar opens onto the street for indoor/outdoor chillage on sunny days. Great weekly deals on house weed and hashish (from €5 per g) plus, 20% off all drugs every 8th day (call ahead if it excites you that much). Mixed joints €3,70; pure €4. 20min. free Internet with purchase. Trippy pinball machine €0,50 per play. Open daily 10am-1am.

Q: When the laws on marijuana were first relaxed in the early 1970s, did anyone protest?

A: Of course; it's only 10% of the Dutch population that smokes. Even now if you want to open a coffeeshop a lot of people are against it. It's still somehow a conservative country.

Q: 10%?

A: More youngsters smoke in England than in The Netherlands. Maybe 1.5% of users have a problem with cannabis but with alcohol it's as high as 20%. A lot of people are pointing at the 1.5%—I think it's ridiculous.

Q: Since cannabis isn't legal here, just tolerated, how socially accepted is it? Would employers ever hesitate to hire someone who had worked in a coffeeshop?

A: Not really, it depends on the person. I had a manager who worked here four years and is now a policeman.

Q: How do you think membership in the EU will affect the status of coffeeshops?

A: It's a minor thing, I think. They just made a law that allows a French policeman to arrest someone here if he committed a felony. But there are two exceptions that they can't hurt somebody: one is for coffeeshops selling soft drugs and the other is euthanasia. Only France and Sweden are giving us problems about it, France especially. But their alcoholism rate is so high; it's really ridiculous that they're complaining about the drug issue. They complain that drugs come from Holland, but so many drugs come from Morocco. And if it comes from Morocco, then it has to come through France.

Rolling One

Abraxas

Good Times at Abraxas

Abraxas, J. Roelensteeg 12-14 (☎625 57 63; www.abraxas.tv), Between Nieuwezijds Voorburgwal and Kalverstraat just south of Dam. One of the swankiest coffeeshops in Amsterdam, with three floors of bright, mellow chillspace. Serves the full palette of hash and weed products plus juice and sodas in a totally casual, no-pressure atmosphere. On weekends (Th-Sa nights), a get high to the beat of a DJ playing mellow lounge tunes and plenty of jazz for the 18 to 35-year-old clientele. If you've got nothing planned for a few hours, take on any-flavored spaceshakes (€5,70). 12min. free Internet access with a drink, €5 per hour after that. Open daily 10am-1am. No cover.

La Canna, Nieuwendijk 121-125 (☎428 44 82; www.lacanna.nl). Whatever your trip is, this party multiplex a few blocks from Centraal has what you need. Follow Damrak straight out from the station, turn right on Karnemelsteeg and then left on Nieuwendijk. This coffeeshop/smartshop/bar/restaurant/hostel (see p. 183) is the largest cannabis house in Amsterdam and ranges over 3 floors of action. First floor houses a bar with restaurant (beer €2,25; snacks €3-5); DJs spin creative house mixes Th-Sa. Second floor has a coffeehouse (minimum buy 50 and features pool tables (€1 per game). On the third, there's more pool and another bar. If the scene starts to run you down, pep up with the house-brew energy drink (€3). Smart shop on the ground floor vends magic mushrooms (€10-17,50 depending on intensity) and smart drugs (€5-25); knowledgeable staff dispenses detailed information about the various products. Open Su-Th 10am-1am, F-Sa 10am-3am.

Dutch Flowers, Singel 387 (☎624 76 24). From Muntplein, take the Singel past 2 bridges and it'll be on your right. Huge menu and widely regarded as offering some of the best stuff in the city, evidenced by the nearly continuous line at the chest-high cannabis-bar at the front. Winner of the coveted "High life" prize for best hash in Amsterdam's annual Cannabis Cup. With crooked paintings on the inside walls, outside seating on the beautiful Singel canal, and beer (€1,60). Loose weed from €4,50. Open Su-Th 10am-1am, F-Sa 10am-2am.

Dampkring, Handboogstraat 29 (☎638 07 05; www.dampkring.nl). From Muntplein, take Singel to Heiligweg, turn right and it is near the corner of Heiligweg and Handboogstraat. While ambient lighting and a posh design lend a classy air to Dampkring, it is inviting enough for even the stinkiest backpacker to feel at ease. Extremely detailed cannabis menu with 10 choices of pre-rolled joints from €2,80-5,70. Same owner as De Tweede Kamer (below), with the same excellent value and strong soft drugs. Open M-Th 10am-1am, F-Sa 10am-2am, Su 11am-1am.

Cafe de Kuil, Oudebrugsteeg 27 (☎623 48 48; www.cannabis-cafe.com). From Centraal, take Damrak straight out and turn right at Oudebrugsteeg. Though it's only a few blocks from Centraal Station, this coffeehouse provides a mellow escape from the intensity of the city center. Classic rock vibe draws an older crown that appreciates Hendrix, Beatles, and house fave Zappa. Beer €1,70-3,20; martini only €2. And, as the sign outside demonstrates, it's always 4:20, with hash and pot, sold in increments of 1-5 g, ranging from €5,50-8,50 and €25-40. Also, examine your purchase with the house microscope, through which you can look at the important THC content of the goods. Standard joints €3,20; pot-only joint €4,60. Pool €1 per game. Open Su-Th noon-1am, F-Sa noon-3am.

Softland, Spuistraat 222 (☎420 97 99). From Dam, walk a few blocks south on Spuistraat. The winner of 3 Cannabis Cup prizes (People's Cup 3rd prize, Best Weed 2nd prize, Best Hash 3rd prize), Softland serves up very tasty space cakes (€5), hemp tea (€3,50), milkshakes, coffee, munchies, and, of course, joints (€3-4), hash, and weed. Its slightly Martian decor—bright but sparsely placed lights, and comfy couches—make it a bit of a trippy spot to chill out away from the more upscale cafes on Spuistraat. Internet €2 for 45min. Open daily 11am-1am.

De Tweede Kamer (The Second Room), Heisteeg 6 (☎422 22 36; www.channels.nl/amsterdam/twkamer.html). Head north along Nieuwezijds Voorburgwal from Spui for a block, then turn left onto the dinky alleyway that is Heisteeg. This *gezellig* (cozy) smokery just underwent a major remodeling, hanging elegant burgundy drapes and maintaining the atmosphere for which it has become known. Also known around town for its very high quality cannabis—some say Amsterdam's best. The sister store of Dampkring with a slightly larger selection will tickle the fancy of any marauding puffer. Strongest hash, "Sherazade," ice-o-lated cannabis from Afghanistan and grown in Morocco, sells at €20 per g. For bud, sample "Kalimist" (€8,20 per g). Even the cheapest choices (€7,50 per g of hash and €5 per g of pot) kick well. Open M-Sa 10am-1am, Su 11am-1am.

Wolke Wietje, Kolksteeg 1a (☎462 93 25), from Dam take Nieuwezijds Voorburgwal north to Nieuwezijds Kolk, turn left, and the coffeeshop is on your right near Nieuwendijk. A small cafe with an interesting and comfy ambience that offers hash (from €6 per g), black hash (from €7.50 per g), pure joints (€5,75), weed (from €10 per g), space cake, cookies, *tostis*, and other munchies. Relax amidst the glow of the exotic fish tank and candles. Open daily 7am-1am.

Coffeeshop Any Day, Korte Kolksteeg 5 (☎420 86 98). Take Spuistraat a few blocks north from Dam and you'll find the store on your right at Korte Kolksteeg. It might be tiny (15 seats), but a sizable selection, low prices (hash €5-16, marijuana €5-8,50), and friendly staff are ready to help you, um, any day.

Dutch Flowers

Wolke Wietje

Magic Valley

the local story

American Tale

Jon is the co-owner of Grey Area, the only coffeeshop in Amsterdam owned and run by an American ex-pat.

Q: Where are you from?
A: Rhode Island, the biggest little state in the U.S.

Q: What brought you to Amsterdam?
A: We became aware of the opportunity to open a coffeeshop in Holland in 1992. We were impressed by the Dutch tolerant attitude and so jumped at the opportunity.

Q: How did the shop come about?
A: The shop had been a coffeeshop before we took over in 1994, but had been closed. There's a place to live above the shop, so we crashed above and worked below. The shop became a vehicle for realizing our dreams of selling cannabis in a tolerant atmosphere. In 1996, coffeeshop permits were issued, and we became the proud owners of an official license to sell cannabis.

Q: What sets your shop apart from the others?
A: Our philosophy is simply to have a good time and provide top-quality products. We work with a cottage industry styled supply line, where we have small growers, who can focus on quality, who supply us exclusively with their special strains. We also view our shop as a meeting point.

Coffee and fruit drinks €1,50-3. Known around town for both its pure pot joints (skunk €4,10; haze €6,80). Don't miss out on de verdamper, an impressive vaporizer that looks like a middle school science project with a somewhat less virtuous purpose. Open daily 10am-midnight.

SMART SHOPS

The Magic Mushroom, Spuistraat 249 (☎427 57 65), 5min. south of Dam. At this museum of a smartshop, procure all the mushrooms, herbal XTC, energy and smart drinks, smart drugs, and stoner art you've been dreaming of. Halogen-lit display cases present merchandise and offer informative insight into the world of hallucinogens and smart drugs. There's even a chill-out corner with pillows and candles where you can try your newly bought merchandise and check your email (€2 for 20min.). Open daily 11am-10pm.

The Essential Seeds Company Art and Smart Shop, Nieuwezijds Voorburgwal/Hekelveld 2 (☎622 10 33; info@seedsexpress.nl; www.seedsexpress.nl). From Centraal, turn right, and then left at Martelaarsgracht; the shop is on your right just after the street becomes Nieuwezijds Voorburgwal. A smart shop that boasts 45 different kinds of seeds, 7 varieties of shrooms, and a complete selection of smart products. Knowledgeable staff welcomes both novices and experts. Be sure to check out the collection of colored glass pipes and bongs that comprise the trippy art collection. Open daily 9am-9pm.

Magic Valley, Spuistraat 60 (☎320 30 01), just few blocks north of Dam Sq. Magic mushrooms, hemp seeds, herbal XTC, energizers, and sex stimulants in a small shop that looks like it was molded from magic plaster. Expert trippers, try their Hawaiian shrooms, Copeladia (€16). And hey, show this book and the owner will hook you up with a free Energizer energy drink or 10% off all magical fungi. Open daily 11am-10pm. AmEx/MC/V.

SCHEEPVAARTBUURT (THE SHIPPING QUARTER)

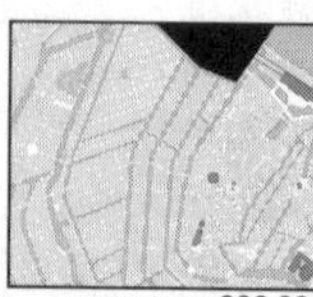
see map p. 328-329

The two-block stretch of Haarlemmerstraat just over the Haarlemmersluis and the section of Singel on either side of the bridge houses the vast majority of the Shipping Quarter's coffeeshops. Though some are just smaller branches of larger chains—such as the **Rokery,** at Singel 10, and **Bulldog,** at Singel 12—some possess a more distinctive flavor.

Barney's Coffeeshop, Haarlemmerstraat 102 (☎625 97 61; www.barneys-amsterdam.com). Popular spot known for its friendly staff and amazing breakfast. Ideal for early-morning munchies, options include the Irish breakfast (bacon, sausage, egg, beans, mushrooms, tomatoes, and toast; €9,50) and rib-eye (bacon, egg, beans, toast, and big-ass steak; €12,80), as well as a vegetarian option (€9,30). Locals praise the consistently high quality of smokeable goods. Both pot and hash are sold in increments of 1-5g; pot ranges from €6-11 for 1g; hash ranges from €5,50-11,50, with the popular but incredibly potent "helter skelter" variety going for €25 per g. Rolled joints also available (€3,50-5). If you need a drink, you can conveniently roll down to Barney's recently opened **Brasserie** next door, which features much of the same menu and friendly people. Both open daily 7am-8pm.

Blue Velvet, Haarlemmerstraat 64 (☎627 73 29). White and ice-blue environs feel as cool as they look. The snow white cat on the premises attests to the quality of the goods available–she spends most of her time passed out on the bar. Beer €1,80; mixed drinks €4-5. Pre-rolled joints €3-4; hash and weed sold in €12 bags–visitors rate the ice as especially good. Internet kiosks in the back €1 for 15min. Open daily 11am-midnight.

Pablow Picasso, Haarlemmerstraat 6 (☎638 8079). The room is a bit crowded and the environment isn't as personal as some of the joints down the street, but Pablow Picasso–whose reverence for the painter apparently stops short of spelling his name correctly–does offer a real blunt of a deal: buy €11 worth of hash between 8am-noon and get a free breakfast. It's not quite the feast that Barney's serves up, but hey–it's free. Open daily 8am-8pm.

Pink Floyd, Harlemmerstraat 44 (www.pinkfloyd.nl). Cramped atmosphere, but cartoon murals indoors featuring Floyd, the porcine mascot, will certainly amuse even the hardest-hearted of stoners. Staff willing to counsel in the basics of pot and hashery. Great hash, including the tightly rolled "temple" ball; for marijuana, or opt for the stronger "ice" variety which costs a pretty penny but hits like a brick (€15,90 for 1g). "Super" joints also available (€3,25; three for €9). And if you want the mellow in your soul without the smoke in your lungs, opt for grass tea (€3,20) or the special cake (€3,60). Open daily 8:30am-8pm.

CANAL RING WEST

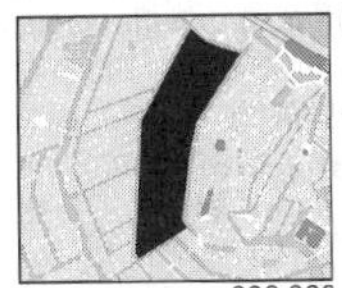

see maps pp. 328-329

Siberie, Brouwersgracht 11 (☎623 59 09; info@siberie.nl; www.siberie.nl) just past the intersection at Singel. Unassumingly tucked into the top corner of the Canal Ring, this pleasant coffeeshop exudes a warm,

Breaking Off a Chunk of Sweet Tooth

Space Smoothies at Greenhouse Effect

The Noon Revellers

life's green

And the winner is...

Every year, on American Thanksgiving (the 4th Thursday of November), Amsterdam plays host to the **Cannabis Cup,** the largest marijuana tasting festival in the world. It's held at Miklweg (p. 160). Cannabis Cup winners from 2001 listed in *Let's Go: Amsterdam* are below. For more information on next year's Cannabis Cup, visit www.420tours.com.

SWEET TOOTH from Barneys, p. 129. (first place), **HELTER SKELTER** 3rd place for hash.

BLUEBERRY from The Noon, p. 130. (second place)

CRYSTAL CLEAR from Katsu (first place for hash), and **SUPER SAGE** (press cup for weed) p. 134.

GREY MIST from Grey Area (2nd place for hash) p. 125.

friendly vibe. Wide selection of weed and hash from around the world, including when available ice-o-lator hash for about €13,50 per g. Get high enough and you might think the *Little Shop of Horrors*-esque light fixtures are fixing to eat you. Snacks (tosti €1,60) and Internet (€1,15 per 30min.) also available. Open Su-Th 11am-11pm, F-Sa 11am-midnight.

Extreme Amsterdam, Huidenstraat 13 (☎773 56 98; www.coffeeshopXtreme.com). Between Herengracht and Keizersgracht and below street level, this gem of a coffeeshop offers free Internet access to its patrons. Good quality weed and hash evidenced by large number of Dutch customers. Good selection in all sizes and prices (rolled joints €2,80-4,50) as well as a very friendly staff, able to answer your questions and join you in your indulgence. Selection of florescent bongs compliments the colorful decor. Open daily 10am-1am.

Amnesia, Herengracht 133 (☎638 30 03), at the corner of Herengracht and Bergstraat. Quiet spot with nice canal views and a jazzy red interior. Usual menu sold in €4,50 and €11,50 amounts. Weed joints €3. Space cake for €3,50. Open Su-F 11am-11pm, Sa 11am-midnight.

CENTRAL CANAL RING

see maps pp. 324-325

The Noon, Zieseniskade 22 (www.thenoon.net). From Leidseplein, head east on Kl. Gartmanpints, then cross to the south side of Lijnbaansgracht and continue for about a block. Great atmosphere near the buzz of Leidseplein but immune to the tourist hordes. Buddha mural, embroidered velvet pillows, and writhing wooden statues of dragons on the bar aim for the ambience of an Asian temple. Customers can also sit in the boat out front, and on rare occasions they'll even take it for a ride. Weed and hash ranges from the standard to the extremely powerful; the Blue Berry bud recently won the Cannabis Cup (1g for €7, 5g for €23). White Melon (1g for €6, 2.5g for €11) and the Noon Blueberry Ice hash (1g for €26) also come highly recommended. Intense pot-only joints of blueberry €7. Open daily 9am-1am.

Stix, Utrechtsetraat 21 (www.stix.nl). From the side of Rembrandtplein across from the statue, walk down Utrechtsetraat for a block and Stix will be just past the Herengracht on your left. Locals chill to cool jazz in this tiny, stylish, sophisticated coffeeshop with clean, smooth wooden tables and navy blue seats. Big picture windows and high ceilings provide a light, airy feel and the staff is happy to let you inspect samples of their high-quality all organic smokeables. Glass bongs quite cheap (from €7,50 to €28). The house blends of weed, Royal Stix, and Shiva or the homemade Gunpowder, which is pure THC, pack the strongest kick. Sold in 1g increments for €5,50-8; buy 5g and get 10% off. Pre-rolled joints €3,50-4. Open daily 11am-1am.

Coffeeshop Little, Vijzelstraat 47 (☎420 13 86). Take tram #16, 24, or 25 to Weteringcircuit and backtrack a half-block; it'll be on the right. Descend the yellow-tiled stairs to this mellow coffeeshop that feels like a home living room. True to its name, this coffeeshop is as *gezellig* (cozy) as they come, with a chess table and cushy couches for enjoying your high. Good deals on hash and weed (€6-7 per g; joint €2,80). Open Su-Th 10am-midnight, F-Sa 10am-1am.

Tops, Prinsengracht 480 (☎638 41 08). Young, student-oriented crowd grooves to the beat of American pop and rap at this fun, canalside coffeehouse. 8 Internet terminals feature super-fast DSL connections (€1,60 for 20min.). Weed sold in €6, €12 or €23 bags, which gets you up to 4.3g of bud. Drinks too: Beer €1,60, in a bottle, €2,80 or mixed drinks from €3. Open Su-Th 10pm-1am, F-Sa 10pm-3am.

Global Chillage, Kerkstraat 51 (☎777 99 77; www.globalchillage.org), between Leidsestraat and Nieuwe Spiegelstraat. Tram #1, 2, or 5 to Prinsengracht, then walk back along tram line for 1 block, take a right onto Kerkstraat, and it will be on your left. A mural of mythical creatures, bright purple and red booths, and an artificial tree in the wall whose leaves overhang the ceiling (surrounded by large artificial butterflies) give the feeling that you've entered the world of *The Hobbit*. Fantasy furnishings and mellow ambient trance music provides good environment to get high or to trip. Standard array of pot and hash available in €6 and €12 bags, which gets you respectively, 0.8-1.1g and 1.7-2.2g. Joints with 0.25g of weed €4; the organic, pot-only "Surprise" spliff packs in all different weed varieties (€12 for 3g of weed). Open daily 10am-midnight.

SMART SHOPS

Dreamlounge Smartshop, Kerkstraat 93 (☎626 69 07; info@dreamlounge.nl; www.consciousdreams.nl). Dreamy chill space facilitates some good trippin'. Mushrooms €11,50 or €16; herbal ecstasy €11,50 for 2 doses. Staff has personal knowledge to guide your experience. Affiliated with Conscious Dreams Kokopelli (see p. 125). Internet access €1,20 for 15min., €4,80 every hr. Open M-W 11am-7pm, Th-Sa 11am-8pm, Su noon-5pm. AmEx/MC/V.

Seeds of Passion, Utrechtsestraat 26 (☎625 11 00; www.seedsofpassion.nl). Oh, how does your garden grow? An upscale store selling cannabis seeds from all over the world including many specialty kinds (€12-125 for 10 seeds); they also provide books and other helpful information. A huge specialty selection

The Noon

Barney's Coffeeshop

Barney's Breakfast n Bong

life's green

Hash Screening

If you're going to be spending time in coffeeshops, you can impress your friends (and save money) by being able to tell the difference between good and bad quality hash. To conduct your test, place a small quantity of hash on a flat, non-flammable surface. Take a lighter, and move the flame lightly over the hash for a few moments. If the hash catches on fire on the first few attempts, you're looking at a quality smoke. If after some effort you still can't get the little lump to catch on, you've probably wasted your money on bad hash. Allow the hash to burn for a second or two and then blow it out. The smoke emitted by the hash should be white or bluish-grey, and its smell should be thick and sweet. Beware of unpleasant odors—they can signal the presence of contaminants in your stash. Once you've blown the test sample out, look for a ring of oil around the hash. The lighter the oil is in color, the better quality the hash. Also, check the color of the ash; overly dark ash can indicate poor quality.

If you don't have the time to mess with a lighter, just check the general consistency of the hash by crumbling it between your fingers. If it's hard, odorless, or nasty smelling, look elsewhere for better stuff.

of seeds makes this the place to go if you're in this particular market; just keep it in the country. Open M-Sa 11am-6pm.

LEIDSEPLEIN

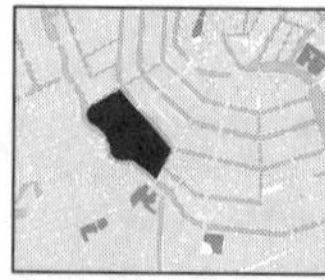

see map p. 325

The Rookies, Korte Leidsedwarsstraat 145-147 (☎639 09 78). Facing Haagen Dazs, take a right and it'll be 2 blocks down on your left. A hustling, bustling, rustling diverse crowd of locals and travelers alike pack into this lively coffeehouse even on weeknights. One of the few remaining places outside of the Red Light District that serves both liquor and marijuana. All bags, such as the potent house specialty "Rookie Skunk," sold in €12 increments. Pre-rolled joint €3, pot-only joint €5 or you can borrow a bong. Shoot a rack of pool for €1. Beer €1,60. Open Su-Th 10am-1am, F-Sa 10am-3am. Cash only.

SMART SHOP

Tatanka, Korte Leidsedwarstraat 151A (☎771 69 16). Facing Haagen Dazs, take a right and it'll be 2 blocks down on your left (right next to The Rookies). Gorgeous 2-story feels as much like a museum as a smartshop. Range of goods includes variety of 'shrooms (Mexican and Thai €12, "the philosopher" €15) and smart drugs, as well as sterling silver and turquoise jewelry. Chill-out room upstairs to start your trip. Staff can tune you into whatever hallucinogen intrigues you. Buy 4 packs of mushrooms, get 1 free. Open 11am-10pm. Cash only.

REMBRANDTPLEIN

see maps pp. 324-325

The Other Side, Reguliersdwarsstraat 6 (☎421 10 14; www.theotherside.nl). Tram #1, 2, or 5 to Koningsplein. Friendly, active coffeeshop popular with the gay scene. Look for highlighted weed and hash on the menu; it's the best stuff. Bags sold in increments of €11,50, €23, and €46; discounts make it cheaper to buy in bulk. Open daily 11am-1am.

Free I, Reguliersdwarsstraat 70 (☎622 77 27). Tram #1, 2, or 5 to Koningsplein. Decor of a beach mural atop bamboo walls doesn't quite add up to a great atmosphere. Knowledgeable staff can help with recommendations for beginning or expert smokers. Try the "Power Haze" grass (€9,50 per g, €42,75 per 5g) or the "Spice Ice" hash, the strongest you can smoke, for a serious high; Afghan (€13) hash makes for a less intense experience. Open daily 9am-1am.

The Saint, Reguliersteeg 1 (☎638 90 49), on an alley off Reguliersbreegstraat. Dank, dim, intimate den pulses with a mellow vibe. Middle Eastern wall decorations surround a handful of stools and tables; in summer, there are some tables in the alley near the Singel. There's also a bar where you can sip fresh fruit juice and fruit shakes that combine mango, orange, honey, and pineapple with hash (€5; without hash €3,50). All weed and hash sold in €13 bags, which gets you 1.4-3.2g. Open daily 9:30am-1am; in summer 8:00am-1am.

THE JORDAAN

see maps pp. 328-329

Paradox, 1e Bloemdwarsstraat 2 (☎623 56 39; www.paradoxamsterdam.demon.nl). The owners match the feel of this place: colorful, free, and ready to have a good time. Weed and hash €5-24. More than just munchies: Grab the best veggie burger you've ever had for €4,10 or a big yogurt shake for €3,50. Open daily 10am-8pm, kitchen closes at 4pm.

La Tertulia, Prinsengracht 312 (www.coffeeshopamsterdam.com). Whether it's the Brazilian lounge music piping over the stereo or the kitschy decor, complete with tropical plants and koi pond, there's something distinctive about La Tertulia. Come for a late-morning bite; they offer an assortment of tostis (under €2,50.) Weed brownies €4; rolled joints €2.

Spirit Coffeeshop, Westerstraat 121 (☎625 46 50; www.coffeeshop-spirit.com). Open later than most coffeeshops, Spirit boasts a unique array of activities for the discriminating stoner, including pool, arcade games, and foosball. All beverages €1,50; grass will run you €6 or €12 a bag, amounts vary based on quality. Open daily 1pm-1am.

Black Star Coffeeshop, Rozengracht 1a (☎626 9469; fax 423 3822; etwi@euronet.nl). A different blend of coffeeshop, this distinctive number features heavy jazz and reggae on the stereo and bags of grass for €10 (1.5-3 grams, depending on the type). Internet access available (€1 per 15 or 20 min.).

WESTERPARK AND THE OUDE WEST

see map p. 335

Kashmir Lounge, Jan Pieter Heijestr. 85-87 (☎683 22 68). Tram #1 or 6 to Jan Pieter Heijestr., walk away from Overtoom up J.P. Heijestr., cross Lennepkanal, and Kashmir is on your right. From the dark interior, lit mysteriously by candlelight, to the intricate orna-

Rookies

BlueBird

BlueBird Bi-Level

mentation on every wall to the large pillow corner, it's the perfect place to sit back and toke up. Located in the diverse and lively Oud West, Kashmir attracts a crowd of every stripe. Hash €6,80-8 per g. Marijuana €4,50-6. Rolled joints €2,30-4,55. Open M-Th 10am-1am, F-Sa 10am-3am, Su 11am-1am.

The Top, Gilles van Ledenberchstr. 135 (☎686 51 44). Tram #3 to Hugo de Grootpl., then walk away from the Nassaukade for 2 blocks; The Top is on the corner. Small neighborhood place with a psychedelic interior, a big table for reading the paper, and a corner for reclining. Grass €3-7 for 1g. Hash €3-10. Prerolled €3-4. Open M-F 10am-midnight, Sa noon-midnight, Su 1pm-12am.

Sativa, Kinkerstr. 12B (☎412 40 03). Tram #7 or 17 to Kinkerstr.; Sativa is half a block from the Naussakade on the left. 2-floor establishment serving up the standard assortment of weed and hash in an soothing, casual atmosphere. Marijuana €6 for 1g, hash from €8-13 for 1g. Prerolled joints €2,30-3,40. Open M-F 9am-1am, Sa-Su noon-1am.

MUSEUMPLEIN AND VONDELPARK

see map p. 334

tWEEDy, Vondelstraat 104 (☎618 03 44), on the corner of Vondelstraat and 2e Constantijn Huygenstraat. A low-key coffeeshop with a pool table known for its friendly, knowledgeable staff. Park side location makes it a great place for grabbing a J before taking a nature walk. The excellent, oily hashish Malana Cream is a specialty. €7,50–€15 gets you from 1.2-2.26g for white widow to the stronger power plant weed. Open daily 11am-midnight.

DE PIJP

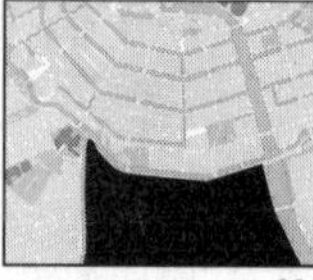
see map p. 326

Yo Yo, 2e van der Heijdenstraat 79 (☎664 71 73). Tram #3, 4 or 20 to Van Wou/Ceintuurbaan. A light, bright space decorated with fresh sunflowers that doubles as an art gallery; it will dispel any fears that coffeeshops are dens of the underworld. Run by a mother, famous for its apple pies (€1,50 per slice), it's one of the few coffeeshops where non-smokers will come just to have a cup of coffee. F night they cook a big dinner (€5); tostis, soup and, (normal) brownies served the rest of the time. All weed is organic and sold in bags for €5 or €10, with a monthly special for €3,50. Open daily noon-8pm.

Katsu, 1e van der Helststraat 70 (www.katsu.nl). Probably the most popular coffeeshop in de Pijp, a neighborhood joint with a pleasantly beat-up feel that's loud, lively, and packed every day with locals of all ages. Its "Crystal Clear" water hash won the Cannabis Cup 2001 (€12per .5g). All marijuana and hash sold in €12 increments, which gets you 1-3.8g of weed or .5-3.4g of hash. A vaporizer is available for use. Open Su-Th 11am-11pm, F-Sa 11am-midnight.

Bom Shankar Chaishop, Albert Cuypstraat 17 (☎673 08 95). Great local spot with a friendly, open vibe. South Asian motif prevails, with cool mural of Goa Beach and delicious house specialty, spicy chai (€1,35). Smokeable selection includes many varieties of Moroccan hash and weed (€7,26-12,22 per gram). Discount available for bulk purchases. Good customers can use the music studio with bongo drums and computers in the back. Also, check out the pretty "Rio Grande" bathrooms. Chess tournaments too; check with store for times. Open daily 10am-10pm.

Media, Gerard Doustraat 83-85 (☎664 58 89). Loud, soulful music and a fun-loving, raucous crowd of locals populate this coffeeshop. Popular with supporters of the famed AFC Ajax football club, hence it's populated by a tougher, but still very friendly, crowd. You can also get your own game on at their pool table or dart board. Pot sold in increments of €5,75 and €11,50, which gets you between .7-1g or 1.6-2.2g of pot, and .7-1.5g or 1.8-3.3g of hash. Joints €2,80-3,40. Free fruit plate. Open daily 10am-1am.

JODENBUURT AND THE PLANTAGE

see map p. 327

Bluebird, Sint Antoniebreestraat 71 (☎622 52 32; www.coffeeshop-bluebird.com). Two stories of azure chill-space include a big overstuffed leather couch for a communal vibe as well as quieter alcoves for a thoughtful smoke. Vast menu presented in two thick scrapbooks that include real samples of each variety of hash and marijuana for inspection; one of the best selections in the city. Sample the high-quality house blend (1.4g for €12) or try the ice-o-lator hash (0.5g for €12). Tasty fresh juices come in a rainbow of fruit flavors (€1,40-2). Open daily 9:30am-1am.

Het Ballonnetje, Roetersstraat 12 (☎622 80 27). Take tram #6, 7, 10, or 20 to Weesperplein; Het Ballonnetje is across the street from the University of Amsterdam. With 35 kinds of tea (€1,20), soup, cookies, and plenty of other homemade goodies, this coffeeshop is a pleasant stop not only for smokers, but also for those just looking for a bite to eat and a place to rest. Terrariums, houseplants, and a healthy mix of students and locals make the shop a welcome respite from the more commercial coffeeshops in the city.

De Overkant, Nieuwe Herengracht 71 (☎620 65 77), is just the place to settle in for a midday smoke among a friendly, non-tourist crowd. Order from an animated, informative menu with weekly specials. The large storefront windows allow a pensive and drug-induced view of the canal. Joints €2,80. Open M-Sa 10am-midnight, Su noon-midnight

Smoesie, Waterlooplein 361 (☎422 00 61; www.smoesie.com), is a hip little coffeeshop with a young crowd. The purple solarium at the front invites the weary traveler, who can grab a beer for €1,70 and joints for €2,80 in this cozy smokery. Open Su-Th 10am-1am, F-Sa 10am-2am.

BLITZ

INSIDE:

Nightlife

Amsterdam's reputation as a capital of libertinism may be most famously embodied by its coffeeshops, but its nightlife provides ample opportunity to do (or be) anything (or anyone) you want. Clubs cater to gay and straight, scenesters and dancers alike, while bars alternate between classic, old-Amsterdam *bruine cafes* (brown cafes—whose ceilings are weathered and brown from years of tobacco smoke) and their modern counterpart, the fancily named **grand cafe.** Step out into Amsterdam after dark and you'll probably acquire first-hand knowledge about why it's said that the best visit to this city is one that you can't remember.

Though Amsterdam boasts a world-class nightclub scene, it is one that is refreshingly focused on dancing and having a good time rather than posing and outglamming the other clubsters. That said, you'll find a few long lines and discerning bouncers at the most popular establishments, which cluster near **Rembrandtplein** and lie along **Reguliersdwarsstraat.** To increase your chances of admission, try one or all of the following: be neatly dressed (lose the baseball cap that says "Fighting Cocks," sporto); be sober in mind and behavior (bouncers revel in throwing out swaying drunks on their rear); and be female (or in the presence of same-sex clubs, seek to achieve gender balance). If you want to return to a club, it's very wise to **tip the bouncer** as you leave to assure his grace upon your next visit. Even if you're leaving town forever, it's customary—and expected—to tip him €1-2 anyway. Lines are short, even nonexistent, before midnight, so showing up early can help you get in. Keep in mind, though, that this works well only because people don't show up at clubs until about midnight or 1am. Before then, locals pack into bars to pre-party.

LGB ▼ AMSTERDAM

Gay Proud

The gay scene in Amsterdam is one of the largest and most accessible in Europe—perhaps even in the Western world. Rainbow flags fly proudly here and the city entertains a very active gay **nightlife** scene with dozens of **clubs** and **bars** reserved solely for gay and lesbian customers. **Reguliersdwarsstraat,** lined with bars, clubs, and cafes, is Amsterdam's gay center, though there's still plenty open to the straight set. While gay culture in Amsterdam is by no means restricted to sexual entertainment, the city's **leather scene** is particularly prominent, and there are a variety of **sex shows** to sample from. For those who wish to sweat out their stay in Amsterdam, **saunas** specifically for the gay set are located throughout the city. Though there's plenty to rave about, it should be noted that Amsterdam's gay scene has one sizable downside: it's somewhat male-centric. The number of places and activities geared toward lesbians, though of high quality, is small.

The best source for getting the latest scoop on hip Amsterdam nightlife is *Shark* (www.underwateramsterdam.com), a free biweekly publication that covers weekly dance clubs, live music, and assorted alternative events. It has an excellent section on gay and lesbian nightlife, too, as well as notes on independent film and cool bars and restaurants.

GAY AND LESBIAN NIGHTLIFE

Amsterdam's gay nightlife scene rivals that of Paris and Berlin as Europe's best. **Reguliersdwarsstraat** reigns as the undisputed king (or queen?) of the gay party scene. Its clubs tend to be large, upbeat, cruisey, and not just a little showy. For something more intense, try **Warmoesstraat,** where you'll find smaller, darker clubs that feature more in the way of rubber and leather, as well as the occasional darkroom for the truly intrepid. There are fewer options in the way of clubs that cater specifically to lesbians, but those that do are popular and fun, with decidedly less attitude than their gay male counterparts. Many gay clubs have lesbian-themed nights, too. The existence of a distinctive gay and lesbian nightlife scene shouldn't at all be taken to suggest that clubs are either/or. On the contrary, most clubs—gay and straight—welcome all sorts, and most ostensibly straight clubs draw a fair number of gay patrons, particularly on Eurohouse or techno nights. For gay and lesbian events, the best publication is the monthly *Gay and Night*, which has information on gay life in the city (mostly in Dutch, but some in English) as well as info on upcoming festivals, parties, and events, and ads for singles and escorts.

BEER AND SPIRITS

Amsterdam is a drinker's paradise, especially if your drink is **beer.** In addition to its native brews—the familiar Amstel, Grolsch, and Heineken, as well as the more exotic De Konninck and Wieckse Witte—you'll also find bars vending a panoply of Belgian Trappist ales and hearty German lagers. Best of all, you can buy suds for relatively cheaply. A small glass (*fluitje*, about 220 cL) of native brew—Heineken, Amstel, or Grolsch—runs about €1,60-2, and you can get a larger size *vaasjes*, about 250 cL, for €1,90-3,50. Pints, generally consumed only by American and British ex-pats and tourists, cost €3-5. The Belgian Trappist ales—such as Vos, Duvel, and Palm—tend to be pricier (€2,70-4,50 for a *vaasje*-sized glass), but they pack a headier kick due to their high alcohol content.

A glass of Dutch spirits, including the beloved local gin, *jenever*, will usually cost about €1,80-2,20, while other hard liquor runs €2,20-3,50. When the Dutch drink the hard stuff, they drink it straight. If you want a mixed drink, add the cost of a tonic or soda (usually €1,20-2,50) to the cost of the spirits. Can't decide? Ask the bartender for a *kopstoot* (kop-stout; meaning "head-butt"), which is a *fluitje* of local beer and a shot of *jenever*.

ESSENTIAL INFORMATION

LIQUOR LAWS

For those looking to party with alcohol, it is important to know the laws so that you can plan accordingly. Those 16 and older can buy beer or wine, while those 18 and older can purchase liquor. You may buy alcoholic beverages pretty much everywhere, from such obvious places as clubs or bars to less obvious places like the supermarket (where they can only sell beer, wine, and other drinks with an alcohol content of up to 13%). As always, try to keep track of your alcohol intake. Driving while under the influence of alcohol is against the law, and this extends to the control of cars and of bikes.

TYPES OF BARS

Dutch bars come in two varieties: *Bruine cafes* (brown cafés) are the traditional wooden pubs, some of which are up to 300 years old. They cater largely to locals and derive their name from the tone of their interiors. Most have brown walls—in the older ones, stained by tobacco smoke, but in more recent incarnations, just made that way. They usually epitomize *gezellig* (coziness), tending to the small, and have walls jammed and ceilings hung with old-style beer ads and other random detritus. Grand cafes, on the other hand, are a modern riposte to their brown counterparts. As sleek and airy as the *bruine cafes* are cozy and dim, grand cafes cater to a younger, hipper, more international set, often with fashionable terraces outside for the see-and-be-seen scene.

Whether brown or grand, though, Dutch bar life has a distinctly mellow tenor. Locals tend to claim a table for hours at a time while nursing a single drink (foreigners constantly remark that while the Dutch drink frequently, they never seem to drink much). That said, however, you will find your share of lively, drunken haunts where there's plenty of company to get ploughed with, though more often than not the biggest drinkers are tourists.

The line between bar and cafe blurs here, too. Most bars serve food, and just about all restaurants and cafes serve alcohol. In many cases, bar-cafes are just that: cafes by day where people eat and chill, which morph into drink-intensive bar scenes by night, usually around 9-10pm.

Drink prices at bars and even at more upscale clubs tend to be fairly constant within the range we've given. There's still the matter of **tipping**, though. A gratuity of about 10% is customary in both bars and clubs, and the easiest and most common way to tip is by rounding up to the nearest euro.

If **live music** is your thing, head to Leidseplein, home to the city's most famous and popular venues. Be warned, though, that due to Byzantine regulations, some of them, including the Melkweg and Paradiso, charge a membership fee to patrons. The fee lasts for the duration of the month in which you purchase it and will put you out an additional €2,50 to the ticket price. See **Live Music** listings, p. 159.

NIGHTLIFE BY NEIGHBORHOOD

OUDE ZIJD

Café de Engelbewaarder, Kloveniersburgwal 59 (☎625 37 72). A great atmosphere any time of the week but comes alive Su 4:40pm-7pm for a set of superb live jazz. Maes beer on tap €1,70. Big, welcoming room and exceptionally friendly bartenders round out the experi-

Nachtcafes

Even in Amsterdam, all good things must end. In fact, the city heavily regulates bar closing times, limiting hours of operation for bars to 1am Sunday through Thursday and 3am Friday and Saturday. But if you've just got to keep the party going, fear not; just head to one of Amsterdam's **nachtcafes (night bars),** bars that have a special license to stay open an hour or two later than their standard counterparts. One of the most famous is **San Francisco,** Zeedijk 40-42, where a edgy crowd of hard drinkers piles in when the rest of the Red Light District has gone to sleep (open Su-Th midnight-4am, F-Sa midnight-5am). There's also quite a concentration of night bars in **De Pijp.** There, you can get your late-night drink on at **De Klikspaan,** Ferdinand Bolstraat 40; **'t Masker,** Van Woustraat 106; and **Alemii,** Ceintuurbaan 420. They're all open Su-Th 8pm-3am, F-Sa 8pm-4am.

Nachtcafes are all about drinking, so you won't find anything elaborate in the way of atmosphere. In fact, most have to adhere to a subdued aesthetic motif per local regulations. Getting a late-night bar license requires maintaining an unobtrusive exterior and interior (both are usually black and dim), and the music stays low in order not to disturb sleeping neighbors. Drink prices to be on the steep side, too—a *fluitje* runs about €2,40 and pints cost €4,50. The whole affair can have a vaguely illicit, speakeasy feel, especially because you have to ring a bell to gain admittance.

see maps pp. 330-331

ence. Open M-Th noon-1am, F-Sa noon-3am, Su 2pm-1am. Kitchen open 5:30-10pm.

Café De Jaren, Nieuwe Doelenstraat 20-22 (☎625 57 71; www.cafe-de-jaren.nl). From Muntplein, cross the Amstel and proceed straight ahead for half a block; the Jaren will be on your right. Sweet relief on a hot day, this fabulous cafe's air of sophistication doesn't quite go with its budget-friendly prices. Gaze at sweeping views of the Amstel through vaulted plate-glass windows or, better, from the Jaren's waterfront deck. It's as authentic a slice of Amsterdam cafe society as you're likely to find, and a bona fide student haunt, too, thanks to the University of Amsterdam's location right across the street. Soups and salads €3,40-6; sandwiches €2,50-4,50. Full hot meals hover around €11. Beer in the bottle or from the tap €1,70-3,10. Open Su-Th 10am-1am, F-Sa 10am-2am; kitchen open Su-Th till 11pm, F-Sa till midnight; dinner served 5:30-10:30pm.

Wijnand Fockink, 31 Pijlsteeg (☎639 26 95), on an alleyway just off Dam Sq. Perhaps the most unique bar you'll visit in Amsterdam, the place is over 100-years old and looks it: dusty and creaky floors, antique decor, and no chairs. The hook: a largely untouristed sight where they've been brewing the best *fockink* liquor in the city for 400 years. Try a glass of the potent stuff for only €2; there's also a *slijterij* where you can bring bottles home to show your friends what *fockink* in Amsterdam is all about (bottles €19). Open daily 3-9pm.

Casablanca, Zeedijk 24-26 (☎625 56 85; www.casablanca-amsterdam.nl), between Oudezijds Kolk and Vredenburgersteeg. Casablanca has been around since 1946 and, though its heyday as *the* jazz bar in Amsterdam has faded, it's still one of the best spots to hear live jazz acts in the city. Jazz acts play only Su-W nights; from Th-Sa you'll find DJ-hosted dance parties with the occasional karaoke performance. Dim and smoky, the Casablanca retains a moody feel and is still quite popular with locals. Check the website to see what acts are coming up. No cover. Open Su-Th 8pm-3am, F-Sa 8pm-4am.

Lokaal 't Loosje, Nieuwmarkt 32-34 (☎627 26 35). Classic *bruine cafe* beloved by locals for its mellow come-as-you-are vibe and its classic art deco wall tile decor. Frequented mainly by a 20-something-and-older crowd, it's one of the better places to sit outside and watch the buzz of the Nieuwmarkt ebb and flow. A glass of beer runs an average €1,70. Open Su-Th 9:30am-1am, F-Sa 9:30am-3am.

Durty Nelly's Pub, Warmoesstraat 115-117 (☎638 01 25). From Centraal Station, go south on Damrak, turn right on Brugsteeg, and then right on Warmoesstraat; Nelly's is 2 blocks on the left. Down-home Irish pub on the edge of the Red Light District where Celtic barkeeps know how to draw a mean pint of Guinness (€4,50; other beer €1,80-4). Good quality pub grub; grab a lighter meal (baked potato loaded with your choice of toppings €4-5) or heartier fare for €10-12. Vegetarian dishes run €8,75. Superpowered A/C and big-screen TV with the latest sporting events make Nelly's a great place to beat the heat on hot summer days. Open Su-Th 9am-1am (until 4am for hostel guests, see p. 179); F-Sa 9am-3am (until 5am for hostel guests); kitchen open noon-10pm.

Lime, Zeedijk 104 (☎639 30 20), just north of Nieuwmarkt. Ultimate lounge with all the accoutrements of the space-age bachelor pad. A disco ball casts swatches of light on pleather seats with faux-chromium armrests and conceptual wall hangings. Popular with the pre-club crowd, though refreshingly low on attitude. Su cocktail evenings are inviting with reduced-price cocktails and a DJ spinning from 5pm-1am. Beer €1,80; bottles of Bacardi Breezers and imported brews €3,85. Open M-Th 5pm-1am, F-Sa 5pm-3am, Su 5pm-2am.

Cafe Heffer, Oudebrugsteeg 7 (☎428 44 90), at Beursstraat. Situated in the former house of the city tax collector, the Heffer blends the traditional Dutch *bruine cafe* motif with modern touches. High ceilings, ample light, and a quiet, sprawling patio on the edge of the Red Light District offer an oasis from the ebb and flow of the pushers, pimps, and prostitutes. The beer is a bit pricey (€2,10 a glass; €4,60 for a pint), but the cafe's pleasant atmosphere makes it a stylish place to hang out. Open Su-Th 10am-1am, F-Sa 10am-3am; kitchen closes at 6pm.

Cock & Feathers, Zeedijk 23-25, (☎624 31 41). Mood lighting and a low-key environment make this gay bar the perfect pre-club spot to hit for a drink or a quick bite. Music plays and the disco revolves, but the atmosphere is much more "sit and talk" than "get up and dance." Inexpensive food, with main dishes as low as €5, and the standard assortment of alcoholic beverages at the usual prices. Open Su and Tu-Th 5pm-1am, F-Sa 5pm-3am; kitchen open 6pm-10pm.

Stablemaster, Warmoesstraat 23 (☎625 01 48). This hard-core leather bar is strewn with gay erotica and famed for its "JO parties," for which patrons strip down to the buck and let it all hang out (from 9pm every night of business). Any form of sex goes as long as it's safe; condoms are provided free of charge, men only. Cover €6; 1-drink min. Beer €2,50; mixed drinks €4. Open Su-M and Th 5pm-1am and F-Sa 5pm-3am.

Getto, Warmoestr. 51 (☎421 51 51, www.getto.nl). In the heart of the Red-Light District, this bar and cafe is beloved for its kicky cocktail menu (try the "getto blast," a potent combination of rum, vodka, kahlua, orange juice, and pineapple juice for €6) and its hip, loungey decor. Primarily a gay and lesbian establishment, but everyone feels welcome here. 2-for-1 cocktail Happy Hour daily 5pm-7pm. Tarot card readings on Su nights. Open Tu-Th 4pm-1am, F-Sa 4pm-2am, Su 4pm-midnight.

Café de Hoogte, Nieuwe Hoogstraat 2A (☎626 06 04). From Nieuwmarkt, head down the left side of Kloveniersburgwaal and turn left onto Nieuwe Hogstr., which will be the 1st street on your left. Bar caters mainly to tourists, but who wouldn't love the rock bottom price for a pint of beer (€3)? Upbeat rock music and a quiet environment, but little that stands out from the crowd of *bruine cafes*. Internet, €1,40 per 20min. Light sandwiches €1,60-3,10. Open M-F 10am-1am, Sa 10am-3am, Su noon-1am.

Cafe de Stevens, Geldersekade 123, (☎620 69 70). Just off Nieuwmarkt. If you're put off by the unmitigated pretension of neighbor Cafe Cube, head to the welcomingly understated Stevens, a great place to read the newspaper in the afternoon or enjoy an after-dinner *apertif* while listening to the low-key mix on the stereo. Or just have one of the cheaper pints of Heineken you'll find (€3,20). Warm snacks and *broodjes* served M-F noon-2pm, Sa-Su noon-4pm. Open Su-Th 11:30am-1am, F-Sa 11:30am-3am.

CLUBS

Cockring, Warmoestr. 90 (☎623 96 04, www.clubcockring.com). From Centraal Station, head down Damrak, then left on Brugsteeg and right on Warmoesstraat; Cockring will be 2 blocks down on the right–just look for the giant cockring on the sign. Cockring is something between a sex club and a disco; you can come to dance or get lucky. DJs spin nightly for a youngish crowd of studly men who readily doff clothing as things heat up. Dark room in the back where anything goes. Disco M-Tu, Th-Su techno/trance; Th and Su strippers of reported international repute. Men only. No cover, except for special parties, when it runs around €5. Open Su-Th 11pm-4am, F-Sa 11pm-5am.

out & about

Jenever- Proost!

There's more to Dutch drinking than Heineken and Amstel. Not for the faint of heart or weak of stomach, *jenever* is Dutch gin, distilled from juniper berries. Originally valued for supposed medicinal properties, the Dutch now down the oily drink without regard to any sort of health benefits (or dangers). There are two types of *jenever, jonge* (young), and *oude* (old). The names are misleading, however, because they have nothing to do with the age of the actual drink. *Oude jenever* is light yellow and has a stronger taste than than the *jonge*, which is clear and more similar to the gin most people are familiar with. The Dutch sip shots of gin, or drink it with black currant flavoring.

NIEUWE ZIJD

see maps pp. 330-331

BARS

Absinthe, Nieuwezijds Voorburgwal 171 (☎320 67 80), just south of Dam. Recently remodeled and reborn, Absinthe draws a young, hip crowd with a loungey, mellow vibe. Lively bar that fills with the purple light of several discoballs. Don't leave without some of the fluorescent-green house drink (a variant called "smart absinthe" with 10% wormwood, €10). Buzzing bar with a few quiet corners for intimate chats. Trancey music sets a good tone, and it's soft enough to speak without shouting. Open Su-Th 8pm-3am, F-Sa 8pm-4am.

The Tara, Rokin 85-89 (☎421 26 54; www.thetara.com), a few blocks south of Dam. Vast Irish-themed watering hole with a maze-like interior featuring plenty of cozy, candlelit corners. Good for any group, big or small, with an excellent selection of draft beer. Slightly older crowd gets raucous on weekend nights, although there is a good mix of young and old, foreign and domestic. Three bars where they know how to pull a real pint of Guiness. DJs and/or bands usually appear F-Sa—call ahead or check the website for details. Beer €2; pints €3,80. Open Su-Th 11am-1am, F-Sa 11am-3am.

NL Lounge, Nieuwezijds Voorburgwal 169 (☎622 75 10), just south of Dam, on the same side of the street. Far too cool for an outside sign, the trendy NL is the unmarked destination where slick, chic, sophisticated Amsterdam insiders of all persuasions come to mingle. Get lost in the stiff drinks (€6) and intense red theme. No cover, but get there early (before midnight) on weekend nights unless you're willing to wait in line. Open Su-Th 10pm-3am, F-Sa 10pm-4am.

Harry's Bar, Spuistraat 285 (☎624 43 84), a few blocks south of Dam. Conspicuously consume cocktails and cigars with a well-dressed, mixed crowd at this decadent den. Comfy leather chairs, hardwood floors, pristine paintings, delicate wine-vessels, and 3 stories to enjoy a smoke (cubans €3,90-28,40) and a dry martini (€8) in style. Try the Bellini (peach schnapps and champagne, €6,75). Beer €2-5,50. Open Su-Th 5pm-1am, F-Sa 5pm-3am.

Gullem, Raamsteg 4 (☎330 28 90), between Spuistraat and Singel, a few blocks south of Dam. Mecca for beer aficionados, Gullem has a menu of brews that spans 2 walls and includes over 200 varieties, mostly Belgian but with Dutch, Czech, and German options as well (€2,20-€7,70). The house brew on tap is Holland's delicious Leeuw (*fluitjes* €1,80, pints €3,60). If you're really thirsty, spring for the McChouffe (€8), which comes in a huge (0.75L) tankard. The atmosphere is young, fun, and convivial. Patient bartenders can help you navigate the massive menu of suds. Open Su-Th 8pm-1am, F-Sa 8pm-2am.

Why Not, Nieuwezijds Voorburgwal 28. From Centraal, turn right at the main street then left at Martelaarsgracht; it becomes Nieuwezijds Voorburgwal. Downstairs, the Why Not is a popular gay bar with a highly cruisey vibe. It's well-decorated and cozy, populated with men of all ages. Upstairs, the **Blue Boy** is a steamy sex club, with nightly live sex shows (€23, starting at 11pm) as well as escorts available. Drinks on the pricey side (beer €3,20; *jenever* €4). Happy Hour 4-6pm has 2-for-1 drinks. Open Su-Th noon-1am, F-Sa noon-2am.

Seymour Likely Lounge, Nieuwezijds Voorburgwal 250 (☎627 14 27), 5min. south of Dam. Popular spot to go out before clubs and after other places close down. Trendy decor mixes and matches flowery wallpaper, bizarre elf statues, and a big aquarium. Music played quietly enough that you can talk without yelling. Nightly from 11pm, DJs spin and drinkers dance. Beer €2, mixed drinks €5. Open Su-Th 10pm-3am, F-Sa 10pm-4am.

Blarney Stone, Nieuwendijk 29 (☎623 38 30). From Centraal, turn right on the main street, left on Martelaarsgracht, and right on Nieuwendijk. Honest-to-goodness Irish pub where you can get the real deal: drafts of Guinness, Kilkenny, and Strongbow. Big-screen TV features all major soccer and rugby matches. Grab a pint on the tasteful patio. Tasty English breakfast all night (includes eggs, bacon, and toast; €4,50). Glass of beer €2; pint €4. Happy Hour 9-10pm: everything half-price. Open Su-Th 10pm-1am, F-Sa 10pm-3am, earlier for big Irish and British sporting events.

Belgique, Gravenstraat 2 (☎625 19 74; belgique@xs4all.nl), behind Nieuwe Kerk and between Niewendijk and Nieuwezijds Voorburgwal. If you're ready to graduate from keg swill to the real stuff, step up to this bar that specializes in over 50 varieties of high-quality (and high-alcohol) Belgian brew. House specialties–8 on tap and many more in bottles–include La Trappe and la Chouffe, fresh from the asceticism of a Trappist monastery and ready to fuel debauchery in Amsterdam (€1,80-5). Open Su-Th 3pm-midnight, F-Sa noon-3am.

Bep, Nieuwezijds Voorburgwal 260 (☎626 56 49). Created in the image of the space-age bachelor pad, with fake stone walls and a glittery disco ball. Tiny, but popular with the pre-club crowd, it gets very crowded on weekend nights when the mass of sharply done-up hipsters spills out onto the front patio. Both lunch (*broodjes* and soup €4) and dinner (range of curries €11-15,50) are on the pricier side, as you're paying for the funky setting. Beer €1,80; spirits €3,40-4,80; *mojito* €5. Open Su-Th noon-1am, F-Sa noon-3am; kitchen closes 10pm.

Café 't Smalle

Lux

Narcoleptic Cat at Sound Garden

Boys' Nights Out

Amsterdam sports a wall-to-wall range of gay nightlife to rival any city in the world. Here's an agenda that will keep you busy every night of the week. **Monday:** Hang out at the safe-sex parties at the Stable Master (p. 141). **Tuesday:** Belt out a ballad at the drag-queen-hosted karaoke night at Lellebel (p. 150). **Wednesday:** Dress sexy for upbeat DJ-hosted dance action at Life, Club More's new men's evening (p. 153). **Thursday:** Drop into Cockring for dancing and live sex shows (p. 141). **Friday:** Cruise and groove to old-school dance tracks at Exit (p. 151). **Saturday:** Try the massive commercial, leather-flavored dance party at iT (p. 151); **Sunday:** Unwind at the Tea Dance at the Back Door, with free food, cigs, and joints (p. 151).

Vrankvijk, Spuistraat 216, 3 blocks north of the Spui; just look for the building splattered with wild murals. Booming punk music and incredibly cheap drinks (*fluitje* €1; bottle of Gulpener €1,50; glass of Chouffe €1,50) in a long-standing, well-known squat with no visible tourists (see **Squat Culture,** p. 146). Leave your bourgeois accoutrements at home when you come here, as the crowd consists largely of mohawked, leather-jacketed folks who still seem pissed about the death of Sid Vicious. Sprawl out beneath the political-poster-plastered walls and drink up; a percentage of the money for the drinks goes to support progressive causes–and body piercings. Ring bell to be let in. Open M-W 9pm-1am, Th 9:30pm-1am, F-Sa 10pm-3am; Su open when they want until 1am.

CLUBS

Meander, Voetboogstraat 3b (☎625 84 30; www.cafemeander.com). From Muntplein, take the Singel to Heiligweg, turn right, and then left at Voetboogstraat. Live bands jam at this bar-cafe populated by crowds of youthful hipsters. There are shows nightly, ranging from jazz to funk to soul to blues to R&B to salsa to DJ-hosted dance sessions (monthly schedule posted on website). Dim, smoky atmosphere, constant din, and dense crowds make for a raucous, high-energy good time. Cover from €5. Open Su-Th 9pm-3am, F-Sa 9pm-4am.

Dansen Bij Jansen, Handboogstraat 11-13 (☎620 17 79; www.dansenbijansen.nl), near Konigsplein. *The* student dance club in Amsterdam, as popular with locals from the nearby University of Amsterdam as the backpacking set. Each night features a different DJ with a distinctive style–mainly House and dance-intensive breakbeats with the occasional disco theme night. Dionysian dance frenzy dominates the downstairs, a more relaxed bar upstairs. Emphasis is on drinking and dancing; there's not a shred of snooty clubster attitude, though you have to show a student ID to enter or be accompanied by a student. Open Su-Th 11pm-4am, F-Sa 11pm-5am.

Item, Nieuwezijds Voorburgwal 163-165, just south of Dam. Young, trendy, and tourist oriented. In an area with few late-night discos, Item stands out, offering a standard dance floor topped by an upstairs lounge. Tu reggae night, W drum and bass, Th House, F Progressive and trance. Sa "Protocol" features House and funky techno (girls get in free Sa before midnight). Dance enough and you'll want to get under the chill waterfall tucked neatly behind the bar. Cover €10-15. Open Su-Th 11pm-4am, F-Sa 11pm-5am.

SCHEEPVAARTBUURT (THE SHIPPING QUARTER)

BARS

see map p. 328-329

Cafe de Wilde Zee, Haarlemmerstraat 32 (☎624 64 06). A sophisticated slice above the rest, Wilde Zee offers an hip, yet intimate, environment in which to enjoy a civilized glass of wine (€2,60-3) or one of their reasonably priced sandwiches (€2,60-3,30). Stylistically engaging furniture and selection of curious art adorning the walls add to the bar's singular ambiance. A selection of Dutch beers rounds out the options (€2-3). Open M-Tu 11am-8pm, W-Su 11am-1am.

Dulac, Harlemmerstraat 118 (☎624 42 65). Dulac's interior and exterior have a moody, baroque feel, and a hip mix of locals and out-of-towners come here for both the wide selection of drinks and extensive dinner fare. Beer runs €3,85 per pint; cocktails and mixed drinks are a little pricey at €7. For a delicious dinner, try a variety of *tapas* (each for €3-5,30). For a livelier time, show up F-Sa 11pm-3am for "Latin Club," featuring various latin and salsa DJs (no cover). Open Su-Th 4pm-1am, F-Sa 4pm-3am.

De Blauwe Druife (The Blue Grape), Harlemmerstraat 91 (☎626 98 97), at Binnen Bowers Straat. Walk into old-school Amsterdam at this brown cafe, popular with locals since its inception in 1733. Its interior bears marks of its age; its dark, brooding, and packed with trinkets that clutter the walls and hang from the ceiling. The patio outside is popular on pleasant days. Snacks are within budget: *broodjes* €2, *bitterballen* €4. Beer on tap runs €1,70 per a glass. Open Su-Th noon-1am, F-Sa noon-3am.

CANAL RING WEST

see maps pp. 328-329

Bar 8, Berenstraat 8 (☎624 42 92). No *bruine cafe gezelligheid* (atmosphere) here. It's unadulterated trendiness dressed in white at this new bar that serves a hip, if touristy, crowd. There's a different cocktail featured every week, and the place doesn't fill up until midnight when the young, often English-speaking crowd from surrounding hotels down beer (€3) and cocktails (€9). Open Tu-Th 6pm-1am, F-Sa 6pm-3am.

Cafe Kalkhoven, Prinsengracht 283 (☎624 86 49). The old wooden barrels behind the bar, chandeliers extending from dark-painted ceilings, food choices of *tostis* or *appeltas* (ham and cheese or apple strudel,

LGB AMSTERDAM

Girls' Nights Out

Though fewer gay establishments in Amsterdam cater to women, there are still some lesbian parties.

Monday: Drink up at mixed queer night, "Blue Monday," at Vrankvrijk (p. 144).

Tuesday-Wednesday: Join the good times and mellow vibe at Vive la Vie (p. 150).

Thursday: Disco with bisexual and lesbian women at You II (p. 151).

Friday: Head upstairs at the Havana where DJs spin dance tracks for ladies only.

Saturday: COC hosts a woman's cafe, "Just Girlz," with themed evenings, video screenings, and other activities (p. 63).

This whirlwind schedule proves that dykes in The Netherlands aren't just for holding back water.

in recent news

Squat Culture

What began as a radical movement to protest the housing shortage that was being exacerbated by speculative landowners has settled into a quieter counterculture throughout The Netherlands. Any building not put to use for a year and a day can be legally squatted by anyone who furnishes the place with a mattress, chair, and table and announces his or her intent to inhabit. Squats became hippie communes of sorts, housing people who like to live at the fringe of society. The practice was allowed to deter real estate investors from buying buildings, sitting on them without using them, and then selling them at a profit a few years later. The last mayor of Amsterdam, Schelto Patyn, set to work cleaning the place up and eradicating many of the squats.

A handful of large squats still exist in Amsterdam and its environs (like Vrankvijk, p. 144), but the communities and their members, a wonderful mix of artists, punks, and expats, lead a precarious existence, never sure when the authorities will tell them to move on.

One of the most vibrant squats resides in the old **Film Academie,** Overtoom 301, called **De Peper** (☎779 49 12; www.ot301@squat.net).

cont. next page

both €1,80), and Heineken flowing freely for €4 per pint all have a markedly Dutch flavor. Settle down for a drink in the back area, where there is a candle at every table. Despite their otherwise authentic atmosphere, the owner is heard to say over the sounds of U2, "we *don't* play Dutch music." Open daily 11am-1am.

CENTRAL CANAL RING

see maps pp. 324-325

Mankind, Weteringstraat 60 (☎638 47 55; www.mankind.nl). Tram #6, 7, or 10 to Speigelgracht or tram #16, 24, or 25 to Westeringcircuit. From Leidesplein, facing the Marriott, walk left down Kl. Gartmanplants for 2 blocks (the street becomes the Lijnbaansgracht). Mellow neighborhood bar with loyal local following. 2 outdoor porches: one with views of the Rijksmuseum and the other situated along the sparkling Lijnbaansgracht. Mixed crowd, but gay-owned and gay-friendly. Standard array of snacks (*tostis* €2; *bitterballen* €3; cheap, tasty *dagschotel* €8,10). Open daily noon-midnight. Cash only.

LEIDSEPLEIN

see map p. 325

Lux, Marnixstraat 403 (☎422 14 12). More a lounge than a bar, Lux has a distinctive retro design that sets it apart from its peers. There's not much dancing, but the candles, wave lamps, and DJ spinning W-Su will all get you pumped to go hit the clubs later on. Beer €2; hard liquor €4. Open Su-Th 8pm-3am, F-Sa 8pm-4am. Cash only.

Bourbon Street Jazz & Blues Club, Leidsekruisstr. 6-8 (☎623 34 40; www.bourbonstreet.nl). Take the tram to Leidseplein, head north on Leidsestraat, go east on Lange Leidsedwarsstraat, and then turn north on Leidsekruisstraat. Blues, soul, funk, and rock bands keep the crowds heavy every night. Mostly smaller bands play this intimate venue, although in the past they have drawn the Stones and Sting. M and Tu free jam sessions while the weekends are typically more about rock. You won't find schedules in local papers; instead, call or check the web or the sheet posted in the front window to find out what's on. Beer €2,50, pints €5. Cover Su and Th €3, F-Sa; free if you enter 10-10:30pm. Open Su-Th 10pm-4am, F-Sa 10pm-5am.

Paradiso, Weteringschans 6-8 (☎626 45 21; www.paradiso.nl). When big-name rock, punk, new-wave, hip-hop, and reggae bands come to Amsterdam, they almost invariably play here in this former church that has converted into a temple to rock 'n' roll. Grace the place where Lenny Kravitz got his big break, and the Stones taped their latest live album. Upstairs there's also a smaller stage where up-and-coming talents are showcased. Tickets range from €5-25; additional *de rigueur* monthly membership fee €2,50. Sa night the cool kids come here for the nightclub "Paradisco" (€5, plus membership fee) and there are other occasional clubnights as well.

Melkweg, Lijnbaansgracht 234a (☎624 17 77; www.melweg.nl), off Leidseplein. Take tram #1, 2, 5, 6, 7, 10, or 20 to Leidesplen and then turn down the smaller sidestreet to the left of the grand Staddshouwberg theater. Legendary nightspot in an old mil factory (whose name means "Milky Way") where live bands, theater, films, dance shows, an art gallery (free W-Su 2-8pm), tea room cafe, and discoteque make for sensory overload. Concert tickets from €9,50-22 in addition to a €2,50 monthly membership fee. Th Latin music €750. Sa house and trance midnight-5am; cover €950. Box office open M-F 1-5pm, Sa-Su 4-6pm; until 7:30pm on show days.

Bamboo Bar, Lange Leidsedwarsstraat 64 (☎624 39 93; www.bamboobar.com). *Noir* decorations, disco ball, and slick hardwood bar share space with tribal masks and tiki torches in a jungle motif that barely manages to feel classy as well as hokey. Beer (€2) or vast menu of cocktails (€4-7,50, most €6,30) includes the down-home Alabama Slamma' (€4,50) and killa Long Island Iced Tea (€7,20). Shooters like the "Slippery Nipple" €3,20. Open Su-Th 8pm-3am, F-Sa 8pm-4am. Cash only.

Cafe de Koe, Marnixstraat 381 (☎625 44 82). A relaxed crowd, rock music, and slightly haphazard decor make this restaurant and bar a happening spot. Occasional live music on Su afternoons Sept.-June and a music trivia "pop quiz" the last Su of the month. Nicer for a sit-down dinner than most bars, try the daily special €8; or choose from the wide variety of meat, fish, veggie, and pasta dishes (€8-12). Cafe open daily 4pm-1am, Sa 4pm-3am; kitchen open 6-10:30pm. AmEx/MC/V.

Alto, Korte Leidsedwarsstraat 115, in Leidesplein. Take a right in front of Haagen Dazs; it will be 1 block down on your left. Hepcats left over from the 50s mingle with young aficionados at this busy nightspot where the vibe is cool but the jazz is hot. Show up early to get a table up front, though you can hear (if not see too clearly) the act from the bar away from the stage. Free nightly jazz: Su-Th 9:45pm-2am, F-Sa until 3am. Open Su-Th until 3am, F-Sa until 4am. Cash Only.

Weber, Marnixstraat 397 (☎622 99 10), between Leidseplein and Leidsegracht. All the style and sophistication of Amsterdam's edgiest bars with none of the

Take tram #1 or 6 to Jan Pieter Heijestraat, cross the street, and look for the big door with the bulletin board to the left. De Peper actually recently negotiated with the local government and now legally rents while maintaining the spirit of a squat. It holds social and political workshops and has a theater for drama, dance, and concerts. Three nights a week (usually Tu, Fri, and Su), they screen movies not shown in the mainstream theatres and hosts a vegan cafe at evenings around 7pm.

Be sure to call ahead so they can cook enough food; same-night reservations are accepted from 4pm. Artists and performers are welcome at the bar/café Th from 10pm (free). Opens at 6pm Tu, F, and Su, while dinner (€5) is available from 7-8:30pm.

For more information on squats in The Netherlands and around the world, check www.squat.net. *Shark* also has a good section of listings on squat events in the Amsterdam area, so be sure to pick up the latest copy of the bi-weekly pamphlet at bars or restaurants.

Making Out at Mazzo

Club More

Korsakof

attendant attitude. Friendly, come-as-you-are bar hosts crowds that include pre-club drinkers and grizzled locals alike. Decor teems with stylish eclectica. Though velvet curtains, felt-patterned wallpaper, and the occasional Buddha statue may seem incongruous, it all comes together quite nicely. Downstairs grotto provides a *gezellig* spot for chilling and conversations. Open Su-Th 8pm-3am, F-Sa 8pm-4am. Cash only.

Aroma, Leidsestraat 96 (☎624 29 41; service@cafe-aroma.nl; www.cafe-aroma.nl). From Leidesplein, walk past the Haagen Dazs down Leidsestraat; it's 1 block down on the left-hand corner. This den of haute couture beckons just north of Leidseplein. The interior space feels like the set of *2001: A Space Odyssey,* with white walls, and scoop-style plastic chairs; it glows with warm orange light. International entrees €7-16. DJs spin cutting-edge lounge, funk, world music, or garage (depending on the night) to a super-hip crowd. Small beer €1,85, large €3,75. Melon, mango, and kiwi shakes €4,25. Open Su-Th 9am-1am, F-Sa 9am-3am.

Kamer 401, Marnixstraat 401(☎320 45 80), between Leidsegracht and Leidseplein. Gorgeous bar-restaurant right around the corner from the Leidseplein scene. Done up stylishly in chrome and glass with a shiny zinc bar, the Kamer has an international menu that changes weekly but always has 6 or so excellent options (main courses about €15, soups €4,50). Before 10pm, it's more of a restaurant; after, it's more of a bar. *Fluitje* of Dommelsch €2; Corona, Asahi, or Hoegaarden €3-3,50; spirits €3,80. Open Su-Th 4pm-1am, F-Sa 4pm-3am; kitchen closes at 10:30pm.

Pirates, Korte Leidsedwarsstraat 129 (☎639 05 23; www.cafepirates.nl). Hokey bar where the bartenders dress in pirate shirts and serve cheap drinks to the very young crowd. If you come on the right night (usually F-Sa), it can be fun to drink! drink! drink! (beer €2,20; shots €2,80) and dance to DJs spinning pop tunes. Many a drunken sailor has fallen prey to the demon rum here (the party rages pretty hard).Women drink for half-price on Th. Open W-Su 9pm-3am, Th-Sa 9pm-4am.

CLUB

De Beetles, Lange Leidsedwarsstraat 81 (☎625 95 88; www.beetles.nl). Not to be confused with the British fab four, there's an ideal mix of cool and crazy at this hip Leidseplein drink house. Eclectic house tunes nightly; Su reggae and Th goa trance; special guest DJs drop in F-Sa, with a serious dance scene. Beer and soda €2, hard liquor €3,50-5. F-Sa 9pm-12:30am 6 beers for €2. Open Su-Th 9pm-4am, F-Sa 9pm-5am. Cash only.

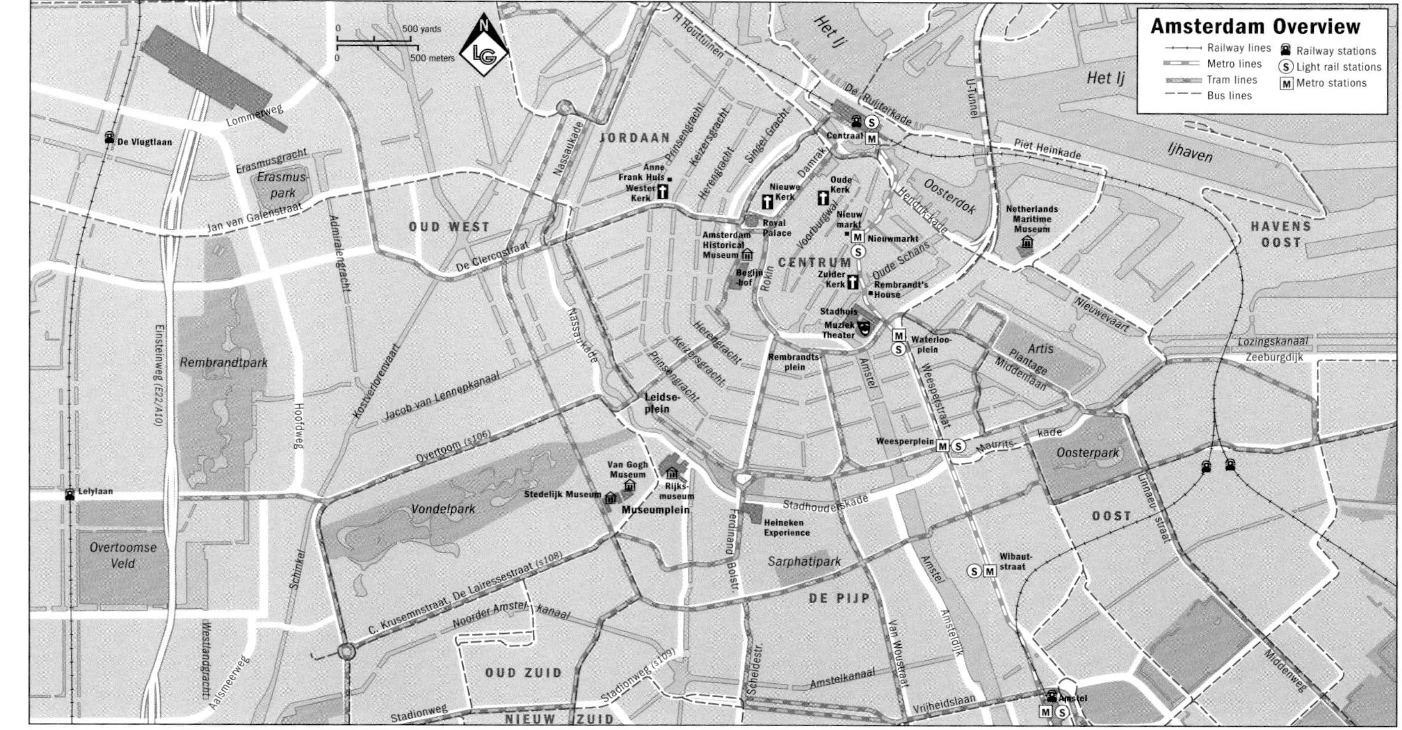

Amsterdam Overview
Railway lines
Metro lines
Tram lines
Bus lines
Railway stations
Light rail stations
Metro stations
0
500 yards
0
500 meters
N
LG
Het Ij
Het Ij
Ijhaven
JORDAAN
OUD WEST
CENTRUM
HAVENS OOST
OOST
DE PIJP
OUD ZUID
NIEUW ZUID
De Vlugtlaan
Lelylaan
Amstel
Centraal
Lommerweg
Erasmusgracht
Erasmus-park
Jan van Galenstraat
Admiralengracht
De Clercqstraat
Einsteinweg (E22/A10)
Rembrandtpark
Hoofdweg
Kostverlorenvaart
Jacob van Lennepkanaal
Overtoom (s106)
Vondelpark
Overtoomse Veld
Schinkel
Westlandgracht
Aalsmeerweg
C. Krusemnstraat, De Lairessestraat (s108)
Noorder Amstel- kanaal
Stadionweg
Stadionweg (s109)
Nassaukade
Nassaukade
H Houttuinen
Prinsengracht
Keizersgracht
Herengracht
Singel Gracht
Anne Frank Huis
Wester Kerk
Nieuwe Kerk
Royal Palace
Amsterdam Historical Museum
Begijn -hof
Damrak
Oude Kerk
Voorburgwal
Nieuw markt
Nieuwmarkt
Zuider Kerk
Rembrandt's House
Oude Schans
Rokin
Stadhuis Muziek Theater
Waterloo-plein
Rembrandts-plein
Amstel
Leidse-plein
Van Gogh Museum
Stedelijk Museum
Rijks-museum
Museumplein
De Ruijterkade
U-Tunnel
Piet Heinkade
Oosterdok
Hendrikkade
Netherlands Maritime Museum
Nieuwevaart
Lozingskanaal
Zeeburgdijk
Artis Plantage Middenlaan
Weesperstraat
Weesperplein
Maurits-kade
Oosterpark
Linnaeu- straat
Stadhouderskade
Ferdinand Bolstr.
Heineken Experience
Sarphatipark
Wibaut-straat
Amstel
Amsteldijk
Van Woustraat
Scheldestr.
Amstelkanaal
Vrijheidslaan
Middenweg

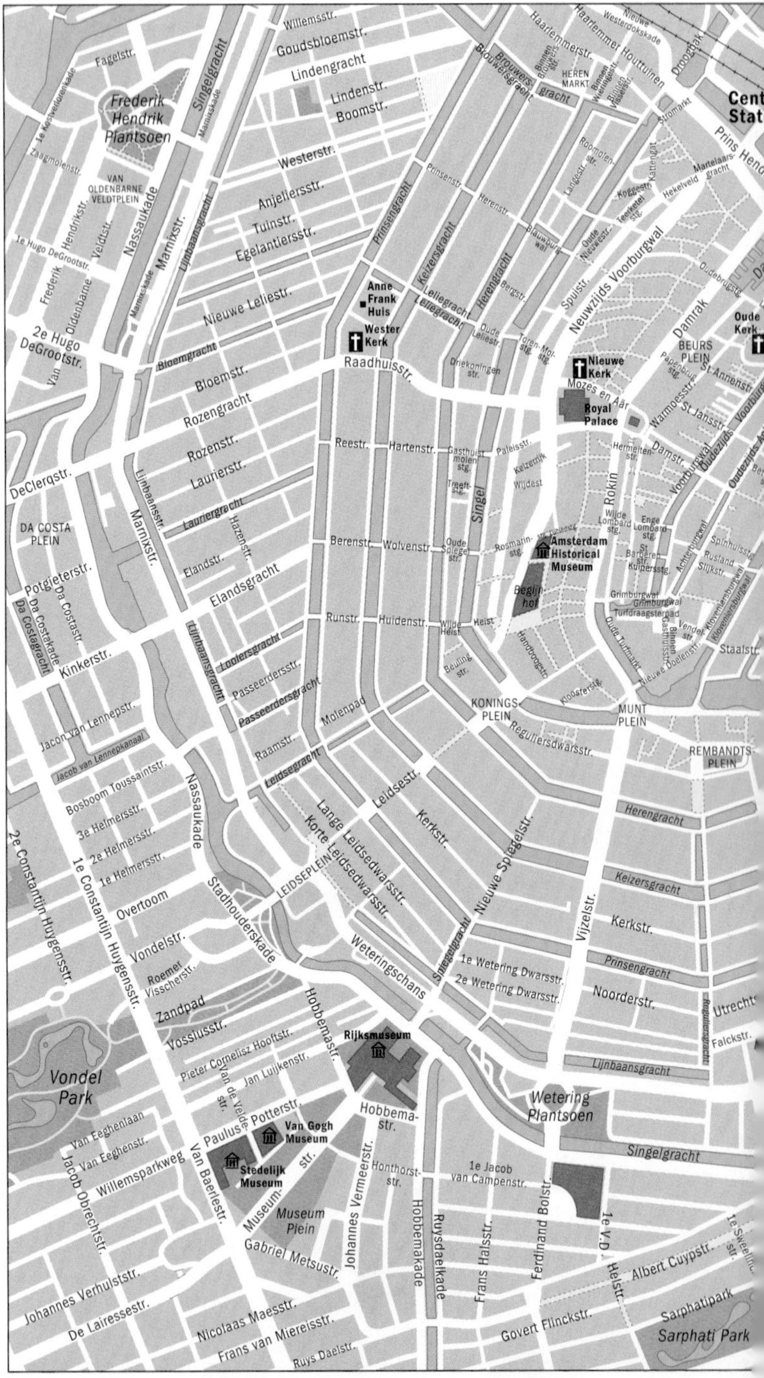

Willemsstr.
Goudsbloemstr.
Lindengracht
Lindenstr.
Boomstr.
Westerstr.
Anjeliersstr.
Tuinstr.
Egelantiersstr.
Nieuwe Leliestr.
Bloemgracht
Bloemstr.
Rozengracht
Rozenstr.
Lauriersstr.
Lauriergracht
Elandstr.
Elandsgracht
Hazenstr.
Looiersgracht
Passeerderstr.
Passeerdersgracht
Raamstr.
Leidsegracht
Fagelstr.
Frederik Hendrik Plantsoen
1e Kostverlorenkade
Zaagmolenstr.
VAN OLDENBARNEVELDTPLEIN
Nassaukade
Marnixstr.
Marnixkade
Singelgracht
Lijnbaansgracht
1e Hugo DeGrootstr.
Hendrikstr.
Frederik
Oldenbarne
Veldtstr.
2e Hugo DeGrootstr.
Van
DeClerqstr.
DA COSTA PLEIN
Lijnbaansstr.
Potgieterstr.
Da Costastr.
Da Costakade
Da Costagracht
Kinkerstr.
Jacob van Lennepstr.
Jacob van Lennepkanaal
Bosboom Toussaintstr.
3e Helmersstr.
2e Helmersstr.
1e Helmersstr.
Overtoom
Vondelstr.
Roemer Visscherstr.
Zandpad
Vossiusstr.
2e Constantijn Huygensstr.
1e Constantijn Huygensstr.
Vondel Park
Stadhouderskade
LEIDSEPLEIN
Pieter Cornelisz Hooftstr.
Jan Luijkenstr.
Van de Veldestr.
Paulus Potterstr.
Van Eeghenlaan
Van Eeghenstr.
Jacob Obrechtstr.
Willemsparkweg
Van Baerlestr.
Stedelijk Museum
Van Gogh Museum
Museumstr.
Museum Plein
Gabriel Metsustr.
Johannes Verhulststr.
De Lairessestr.
Nicolaas Maesstr.
Frans van Mierisstr.
Ruys Daelstr.
Johannes Vermeerstr.
Hobbemastr.
Hobbemakade
Honthorststr.
Rijksmuseum
Ruysdaelkade
Frans Halsstr.
1e Jacob van Campenstr.
Ferdinand Bolstr.
1e V.D. Helstr.
Albert Cuypstr.
Govert Flinckstr.
Sarphatipark
Sarphati Park
1e Sweelinckstr.
Wetering Plantsoen
Singelgracht
Lijnbaansgracht
Weteringschans
1e Wetering Dwarsstr.
2e Wetering Dwarsstr.
Spiegelgracht
Nieuwe Spiegelstr.
Lange Leidsedwarsstr.
Korte Leidsedwarsstr.
Leidsestr.
Kerkstr.
Molenpad
Runstr.
Huidenstr.
Berenstr.
Wolvenstr.
Reestr.
Hartenstr.
Raadhuisstr.
Anne Frank Huis
Wester Kerk
Prinsengracht
Keizersgracht
Herengracht
Singel
Prinsenstr.
Herenstr.
Leliegracht
Bergstr.
Oude Leliestr.
Driekoningenstr.
Torensteeg
Molsteeg
Gasthuismolensteeg
Paleisstr.
Keizerrijk
Wijdesteeg
Trefftsteeg
Oude Spiegelstr.
Rosmarijnsteeg
Amsterdam Historical Museum
Begijnhof
Wijde Heisteeg
Heisteeg
Beulingstr.
Handboogstr.
KONINGSPLEIN
Reguliersdwarsstr.
Kloosterstg.
MUNT PLEIN
REMBANDTSPLEIN
Herengracht
Keizersgracht
Kerkstr.
Prinsengracht
Noorderstr.
Vijzelstr.
Reguliersgracht
Utrechtsestr.
Falckstr.
Rokin
Wijde Lombardsteeg
Enge Lombardsteeg
St Barberenstr.
Kuipersstg.
Grimburgwal
Turfdraagsterpad
Oude Turfmarkt
Binnen Gasthuisstr.
Vendelstr.
Nieuwe Doelenstr.
Staalstr.
Kloveniersburgwal
Achterburgwal
Spinhuissteeg
Rusland
Slijkstr.
Hermelyensteeg
Damstr.
Voorburgwal
Oudezijds Voorburgwal
Oudezijds Achterburgwal
Nieuwe Kerk
Mozes en Aär
Royal Palace
Warmoesstr.
St Jansstr.
St Annenstr.
Papenbrugsteeg
BEURS PLEIN
Damrak
Oude Kerk
Oudebrugsteeg
Nieuwezijds Voorburgwal
Spuistr.
Blauwburgwal
Oude Nieuwestr.
Langestr.
Roomolenstr.
Koggestr.
Teerketelsteeg
Kattengat
Hekelveld
Martelaarsgracht
Prins Hendrik
Stromarkt
Brouwersgracht
Brouwersgracht
HEREN MARKT
Binnen Brouwersstr.
Binnen Wieringerstr.
Binnen Vissersstr.
Haarlemmerstr.
Haarlemmer Houttuinen
Nieuwe Westerdokskade
Droogbak
Central Station

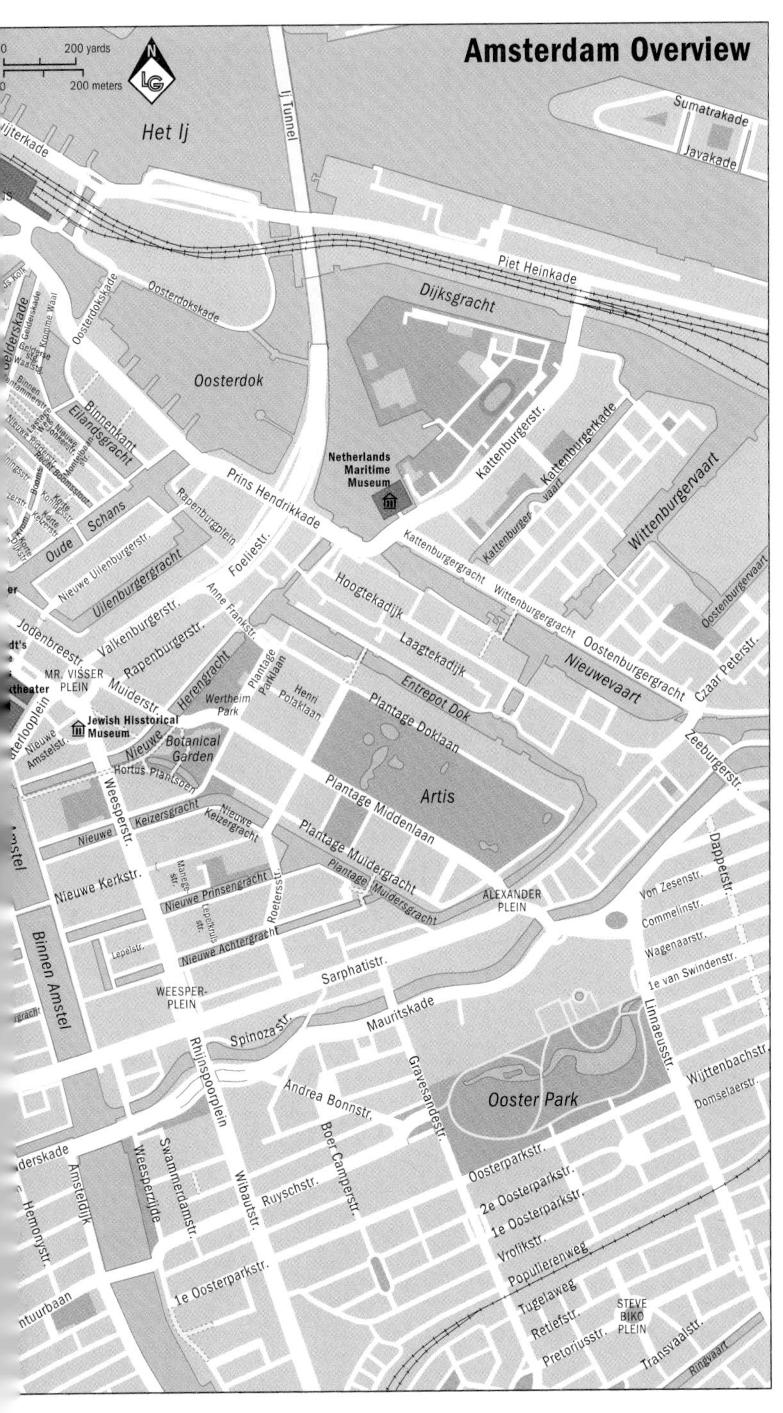
Amsterdam Overview
0
200 yards
200 meters
Het Ij
Ij Tunnel
Sumatrakade
Javakade
Piet Heinkade
Dijksgracht
Oosterdokskade
Oosterdok
Netherlands Maritime Museum
Kattenburgerstr.
Kattenburgerkade
Wittenburgervaart
Prins Hendrikkade
Rapenburgplein
Binnenkant
Eilandsgracht
Schans
Oude
Nieuwe Uilenburgerstr.
Uilenburgergracht
Foeliestr.
Kattenburgergracht
Wittenburgergracht
Oostenburgervaart
Oostenburgergracht
Nieuwevaart
Czaar Peterstr.
Hoogtekadijk
Laagtekadijk
Entrepot Dok
Anne Frankstr.
Valkenburgerstr.
Rapenburgerstr.
Jodenbreestr.
MR. VISSER PLEIN
Muiderstr.
Herengracht
Plantage Parklaan
Henri Polaklaan
Wertheim Park
Jewish Hisstorical Museum
Nieuwe
Botanical Garden
Hortus Plantsoen
Plantage Doklaan
Artis
Zeeburgerstr.
Plantage Middenlaan
Plantage Muidergracht
Weesperstr.
Nieuwe Keizersgracht
Nieuwe Kerkstr.
Nieuwe Prinsengracht
Roetersstr.
ALEXANDER PLEIN
Dapperstr.
Von Zesenstr.
Commelinstr.
Wagenaarstr.
1e van Swindenstr.
Nieuwe Achtergracht
Binnen Amstel
WEESPER-PLEIN
Sarphatistr.
Mauritskade
Spinozastr.
Rhijnspoorplein
Gravesandestr.
Linnaeusstr.
Wijttenbachstr.
Domselaerstr.
Andrea Bonnstr.
Boerhaavestr.
Ooster Park
Amsteldijk
Weesperzijde
Swammerdamstr.
Wibautstr.
Ruyschstr.
Oosterparkstr.
2e Oosterparkstr.
1e Oosterparkstr.
Vrolikstr.
Populierenweg
Tugelaweg
Retiefstr.
Pretoriusstr.
STEVE BIKO PLEIN
Transvaalstr.
Ringvaart
Hemonystr.
1e Oosterparkstr.

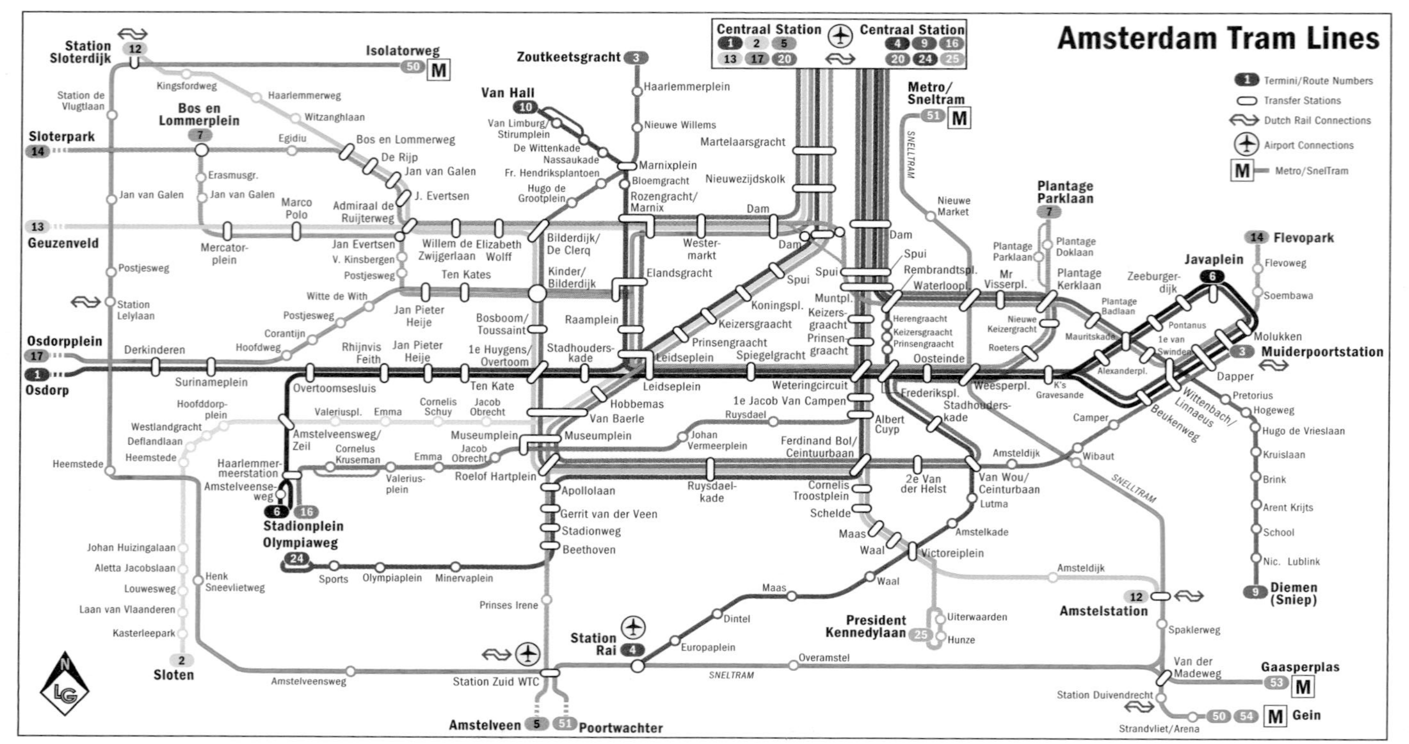

Amsterdam Tram Lines
Termini/Route Numbers
Transfer Stations
Dutch Rail Connections
Airport Connections
Metro/SnelTram
Centraal Station 1 2 5 13 17 20
Centraal Station 4 9 16 20 24 25
Metro/Sneltram 51
Station Sloterdijk 12
Isolatorweg 50
Zoutkeetsgracht 3
Van Hall 10
Bos en Lommerplein 7
Sloterpark 14
Geuzenveld 13
Osdorpplein 17
Osdorp 1
Stadionplein 6 16
Olympiaweg 24
Sloten 2
Station Rai 4
Amstelveen 5
Poortwachter 51
President Kennedylaan 25
Amstelstation 12
Gaasperplas 53
Gein 50 54
Diemen (Sniep) 9
Muiderpoortstation 3
Javaplein 6
Flevopark 14
Plantage Parklaan 7
Station de Vlugtlaan
Kingsfordweg
Haarlemmerweg
Witzanghlaan
Egidiu
Bos en Lommerweg
De Rijp
Jan van Galen
J. Evertsen
Erasmusgr.
Marco Polo
Admiraal de Ruijterweg
Mercator-plein
Jan Evertsen
V. Kinsbergen
Postjesweg
Willem de Zwijgerlaan
Elizabeth Wolff
Ten Kates
Witte de With
Corantijn
Hoofdweg
Station Lelylaan
Derkinderen
Surinameplein
Rhijnvis Feith
Jan Pieter Heije
1e Huygens/Overtoom
Bosboom/Toussaint
Overtoomsesluis
Ten Kate
Hoofddorp-plein
Westlandgracht
Deflandlaan
Heemstede
Valeriuspl.
Emma
Cornelis Schuy
Jacob Obrecht
Amstelveensweg/Zeil
Cornelus Kruseman
Valerius-plein
Haarlemmer-meerstation
Amstelveense-weg
Roelof Hartplein
Museumplein
Van Baerle
Hobbemas
Haarlemmerplein
Nieuwe Willems
Van Limburg/Stirumplein
De Wittenkade
Nassaukade
Fr. Hendriksplantoen
Hugo de Grootplein
Marnixplein
Bloemgracht
Rozengracht/Marnix
Martelaarsgracht
Nieuwezijdskolk
Dam
Bilderdijk/De Clerq
Kinder/Bilderdijk
Wester-markt
Elandsgracht
Raamplein
Stadhouders-kade
Leidseplein
Spui
Koningspl.
Keizersgracht
Prinsengracht
Spiegelgracht
Muntpl.
Keizers-graacht
Prinsen-graacht
Rembrandtspl.
Waterloopl.
Herengraacht
Keizersgraacht
Prinsengraacht
Weteringcircuit
1e Jacob Van Campen
Ruysdael
Johan Vermeerplein
Albert Cuyp
Ferdinand Bol/Ceintuurbaan
Frederikspl.
Stadhouders-kade
Oosteinde
Weesperpl.
Ruysdael-kade
Cornelis Troostplein
Schelde
Maas
Waal
Victoreiplein
2e Van der Helst
Van Wou/Ceinturbaan
Lutma
Amstelkade
Amsteldijk
Apollolaan
Gerrit van der Veen
Stadionweg
Beethoven
Sports
Olympiaplein
Minervaplein
Prinses Irene
Station Zuid WTC
Amstelveensweg
Johan Huizingalaan
Aletta Jacobslaan
Louwesweg
Laan van Vlaanderen
Kasterleepark
Henk Sneevlietweg
Europaplein
Dintel
Overamstel
SNELTRAM
Uiterwaarden
Hunze
Nieuwe Market
Mr Visserpl.
Plantage Parklaan
Plantage Doklaan
Plantage Kerklaan
Nieuwe Keizergracht
Roeters
Plantage Badlaan
Mauritskade
Zeeburger-dijk
Pontanus
1e van Swinden
Alexanderpl.
K's Gravesande
Flevoweg
Soembawa
Molukken
Dapper
Wittenbach/Linnaeus
Beukenweg
Pretorius
Hogeweg
Hugo de Vrieslaan
Kruislaan
Brink
Arent Krijts
School
Nic. Lublink
Camper
Wibaut
Spaklerweg
Van der Madeweg
Station Duivendrecht
Strandvliet/Arena
LG

REMBRANDTPLEIN

see maps pp. 324-325

BARS

Arc Bar, Reguliersdwarsstraat 44 (☎689 70 70; www.bararc.com). Just opened in June 2002, Arc is the hippest place around providing a cutting-edge space for you to sip your chic cocktails in (martinis €6,50; caipirinha, margarita, mojito, or Long Island iced tea €7,50). Lounge in a beige leather chair while you watch discreet projections of clouds and other phenomena on the wall. On the weekends, the black table tops in the front are mechanically lowered to become a platform for dancing, while Su cools down with jazz. Open daily 10am-1am, F-Sa 10am-3am.

M Bar, Reguliersdwarsstraat 13-15, just off Leidsestraat. Tram #1, 2, or 5 to Koningsplein. Sleek, slick, slippery minimalist bar, located on a famously gay street but drawing a mainly straight crowd. Chill on the high-backed blue velvet couches or the tiny stools, or simply pose against the red light stripes that glow against the back wall. DJs spin house, club, and techno Th-Su. Beer €2, bottles €4,40; wine €2,75; mixed drinks €6. Open W-Th and Su 6pm-3am, F-Sa 6pm-4am. Cash only.

Montmartre, Halvemaarsteg 17 (☎620 76 22). Rococo interior bedecked with flowers and rich draperies houses some of the wildest parties in Amsterdam for men and men who love men (women are welcome too). Very cute bartenders serve 2-for-1 beers during daily Happy Hour 6-8pm. Voted best gay bar in Amsterdam by local gay mag *Gay Krant* 5 years running, (although last year it was nudged into second place); and best gay bar in Benelux for 2002. The party rages hardest Tu, Th, Sa-Su. Open Su-Th 5pm-1am, F-Sa 54pm-3am. Cash only.

La Esquina, Reguliersdwarsstraat 55 (☎627 54 58). Too sexy!!! Hot waitstaff serves sangria (pitchers €13,50) to a sharply-dressed gay and straight crowd. Italian food and 24 varieties of *tapas* include garlic shrimp or chicken (€5) and squid in vinaigrette (€5). Wild weekend fiestas span 2 fl. and spill out onto the outdoor patio. F-Sa features DJ-hosted retro 70s party (11pm). Open daily noon-1am, later on weekends. AmEx/V.

Cafe April, Regulierdwarsstraat 37 (☎625 9572; www.april-exit.com). Tram #1, 2, or 5 to Koningsplein. Popular gay bar that's laid-back by day, increasingly active and cruisey as the night wears on. It's the sister establishment to popular gay nightspot Exit (p. 151). Clusters of marble tables spill onto the sidewalk up front, while in back there's a rotating bar

Ministry

Sunday Nights at Backdoor

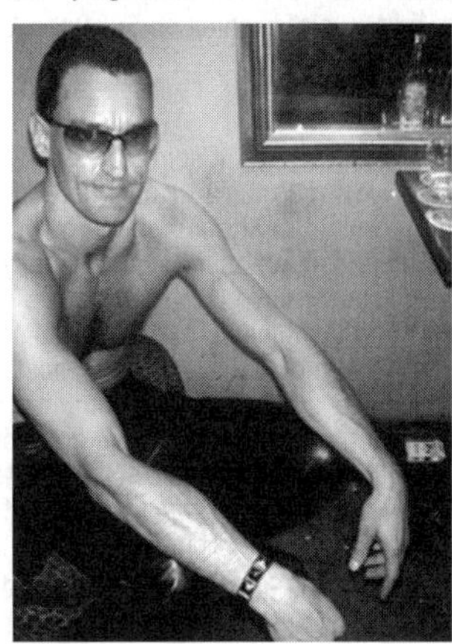
Exit, No Shirts Allowed

and a third bar room that is set to open this year. Siren lights embedded on the ceiling sound off to the *Price is Right* jingle at odd intervals on F-Sa nights, signaling 2-for-1 drinks and a mad rush of manhood to the bar. Happy Hour 2-for-1 drinks Su 6-8pm, M-Th 6-7pm. Open Su-Th 2pm-1am, F-Sa 2pm-3am. Cash only.

Vive La Vie, Amstelstraat 7 (☎624 01 14; www.vivelavie.net), just east of Rembrandtplein. Fun, friendly lesbian bar where the emphasis is on good times, good folks, and good drinking, all without a shred of attitude. Small, lively, and packed on weekends. No dance floor, but that doesn't stop the ladies—and a few select male friends—from grooving to feel-good pop anthems. Biggest nights are Th-Sa; Su is mellower. Open Su-Th 3pm-1am, F-Sa 3pm-3am. Cash only.

Cafe Menschen, Amstelstraat 202 (☎627 87 27), at Amstelstraat. Cornerside bar has great views of the picturesque Blauwbrug and, best of all, pours glasses of Dommelsch beer for a mere €1 (albeit they're on the small side). Locals and tourists both take advantage of the cheap booze, but only true regulars get their names on little plaques along the bar next to their favorite stool. *Tostis* €1,50; *broodjes* €1,30. Open M-Th 1pm-1am, F-Sa 11-2am.

Soho, Reguliersdwarsstraat 36 (☎616 12 13). Tram #1, 2, or 5 to Koningsplein. Looks like an old boys' club, but in fact all kinds of boys crowd into this bustling, predominately gay bar. Leather wallpaper and bookshelves with dusty tomes line the walls, elegant staircases snake between the 2 floors, and an impressive 2-story mirror reflects all the action. Traditional accoutrements don't match the crowd, though, which is young, cruisey, and a little preppy. Well-situated in the thick of Reguliersdwarsstraat, making it ideal for pre-club drinking. DJ nightly. Open Su-Th 8pm-3am, F-Sa 8pm-4am. Cash only.

Mr. Coco's, Thorbeckeplein 8-12 (☎627 24 23; clowns@mrcocos.com; www.mrcocos.com). Tram #4, 5, 9, or 20 to Rembrandtplein. Same hideously ugly clown mascot as the Nieuwendijk location, but with more local students and fewer tourists. W, F, and Sa the cavernous bar becomes a serious party with loud rock music and a young, hard-drinkin', sexy-dancin' crowd. On "Wacky Wednesday," €20,67 gets you all the ribs you can eat and all the beer you can drink. If you really want to get your drink on, go for the "meter wave," a powerful vodka and citrus concoction that comes in a meter-long glass and packs a 7-shot punch (€12). 2-for-1 drinks during Happy Hour (daily 5-6pm, F also noon-3pm). Open W 5pm-1am, Th noon-1am, F-Sa noon-3am. Credit cards for food only.

Lellebel, Utrechtsestraat 4 (☎427 51 39; www.lellebel.nl). Just off the southeast corner of Rembrantplein. Friendly, local crowd comes to this campy, vampy gay bar run by a cadre of outrageous drag queens. Your hostesses Sylvia and Patricia tend bar almost every night for their fun-loving, low-key crowd of admirers. Women welcome. Fabulous theme nights include: karaoke on Tu; open podium on F where guests can strut their stuff and there's a prize for the winner; big, popular drag show featuring queens from all over Amsterdam (Sa); DJ-hosted "world music" evening on Su. Open M-Th 9pm-3am, F-Sa 8pm-4am, Su 8pm-3am.

CLUBS

Escape, Rembrandtplein 11 (☎622 11 11; www.escape.com). Party people pour into this massive venue for a night at one of Amsterdam's hottest clubs. It features 2 floors with 6 bars (including a champagne bar staffed by particularly beautiful girls), a chillout space upstairs, and an enormous, sensually-charged dance floor down, where dressed-to-the-nines scenesters groove to house, trance, disco, and dance classics. Sa is Chemistry, hugely popular and fashionable night when famed DJ Marcella spins trance and house (€14; the same renowned model-turned-DJ also hosts a smaller party, "Rush" on Th, €10). Su is Impact, featuring heavy house and deep trance (€13,50). F continually changing theme nights keep the crowd entertained (€15); the first Friday of every month is the gay party "Salvation." Lines grow long, and hulky bouncers scan the crowd for miscreants; be sober, well-dressed, and female to increase your chances of entry. Beer €2,30, mixed drinks €6-7. Open Th-Su 11pm-4am, F-Sa 11pm-5am.

The Ministry, Reguliersdwarsstraat 12 (☎ 623 39 81; www.ministry.nl). The very popular Ministry is upscale enough to be classy and hip, but without any attitude or exclusivity; it's all about getting your groove on to some seriously good tunes. Theme nights change constantly;

young, well-dressed crowd gets down to live music, dance classics, R&B, UK garage, 2-step, hip-hop, and old-school disco (check website for latest schedule). More of a straight club for the area, but it doesn't seem to matter too much; all are welcome. M open live jam session gets packed, so come early (€7). Cover €5-12; look for fliers for free admittance. Open Su-Th 11pm-4am, F-Sa 11pm-5am.

The Back Door, Amstelstraat 32 (☎620 23 33; www.backdoor.nl), 1 block east of Rembrandtplein, away from the statue. Just emerging from a recent makeover, the Door provides 2 different dens—a red-walled, smoky dance area and a chatty, upbeat bar—and several different theme club nights. W is Heat, a gay party with harder house music (€5), Th is Latin and Salsa, F and Sa DJs spin house and R&B classics for a mixed crowd (about €10), and Su is Tea Dance, a packed and popular gay party that features free food, joints, and cigarettes, all in a sleek red and black setting (€10). Downstairs cocktail cafe (open W-Th and Su 6pm-1am, F-Sa 6pm-3am); if you show your receipt at the club, you may get in for half the cover charge. Open W-Su in summer 10pm-4am; in winter 9pm-3am.

Exit, Reguliersdwarsstraat 42 (☎625 87 88; www.april-exit.com), just west of the intersection with Vijzelstraat Tram to Rembrandtplein or Koningsplein and walk along Reguliersdwarsstraat. Men! Men! Men! Enter Exit to find one of the most popular gay discos in The Netherlands. Downstairs bar plays popular dance classics; upstairs is a DJ-driven high-energy techno party where a young, good-looking crowd sheds its inhibitions—and sometimes its clothes—to get funky. Balcony overlooks dance floor to facilitate cruising. In the back, there's a darkroom where you'll just have to find out what awaits you. Mostly men, though female friends often appear. Cover €7 F-Sa, €3 Th and Su. Open Su-Th midnight-4am, F-Sa midnight-5am. Cash only.

You II, Amstel 178 (☎421 09 00; www.youll.nl). From Rembrandtplein, head east down Amstelstr., then turn left at Bakkerstraat and then right when you come to the river; it's 1½ blocks up on the left. Amsterdam's best and most popular lesbian nightclub has a circular bar in front opening into a small but crowded dance floor in back, where mirrors under archways give the illusion of more space. F men only, Sa women only; Th and Su are mixed, but straight men are allowed only when accompanied by a female friend. Fun theme nights prevail. Cover only Sa €7. Beer €2,50, liquor €4. Open Th and Su 10pm-4am, F-Sa 10pm-5am. Cash only.

The iT, Amstelstraat 24 (☎625 01 11; www.it.nl), 1 block east of Rembrandtplein (in the opposite direction of the statue). Break out your best black leather ensemble for this famed discotheque specializing in

Lux DJ

Tinfoil Man at Exit

Dancing in the Cage at Beetles

house and trance. Dry ice adds smoky intrigue to the packed dance floor, and platforms rise above it for elevated vamping. Small chill-out bar ideal for chatting up that special person. F is mixed, but Sa it's a gay-men-only, not-for-the-faint-of-heart "Gay Gangbang" party. Drinks €3-8. Cover €9,50 for non-members, €7 for members; year-long membership €24. Dress well to get in. Open F-Sa 11pm-5am. Cash only.

K2 Apres-Ski Lounge, Paardenstraat 13-15 (☎627 27 10; www.apres-skilounge.nl). From Rembrandtplein, walk east down Amstelstraat and take a left onto Paardenstraat; K2 is on your right. Done up like a ski chalet, the K2 packs in young Dutch folks intent on dancing and drinking, and they do plenty of both. The front room is adorned like the interior of a log cabin with antlers, while another nook has photos of Sherpas and the bar in the back aims to remind you of your childhood in Austria with skies and sleds. The nonstop music—hosted by "Ski-Jays"—is loud and upbeat, and the vibe is attitude-free, cruisey, mainly straight, low on personal space, but most of all, uninhibited and fun. On occasion, the Ski-Jay will turn on the snow machine. No cover, but you've got to pay the wardrobe folks €1 per item you check. Draft beer €2; bottles €4; Red Bull and vodka €6. Cash only.

THE JORDAAN

see maps pp. 328-329

BARS

Café 't Smalle, Egelantiersgracht 12 (☎623 96 17), at the corner of Prinsengracht and Egelantiersgracht. A bar rich with its own history, 't Smalle was founded in 1780 as the tasting room of a neighboring distillery. A good place to go in the afternoon as well as the evening, and rightfully one of the most popular cafes in the west, 't Smalle has canal-side seats in the summer and a warm, old-fashioned interior. Famous pea soup (€4) served in winter. Open Su-Th 10am-1am, F-Sa 10am-2am.

Sound Garden, Marnixstraat 164-166 (☎620 28 53). Tram #10 13, 17, or 20 to Marnixstraat. Amsterdam's true rock 'n' roll dive. Diverse in age and style, patrons at Sound Garden share one thing in common: a love of beer. Try the house brew—Flater's Kater, a Dutch expression meaning "hangover," which boasts an impressive 9.5% alcohol content (€2,90). Inside are listings of the latest music happenings in and around town; if music's not your thing, head outside to the gorgeous terrace that sits on the canal. Open M-Th 1pm-1am, F 1pm-3am, Sa 3pm-3am, Su 3pm-1am.

Proust, Noordermarkt 3 (☎623 91 45). If you want the party, this is where it's at. Before swinging by one of the late-night clubs, come to Proust for a pre-party drink. Wedged between the Prinsengracht and the Noorderkerk, this neighborhood bistro attracts an uber-hip crowd that inevitably spills out onto the terrace it shares with neighboring bar, **Finch.** Mostly groups of pulsating mixed European singles, speaking Dutch, German and French. It's almost indistinguishable from **Finch,** but Proust does boast a more accessible bar, louder music, and more literary namesake. Lunch sandwiches €4,50; salads €7,50. Dinner entrees start at €9 with plenty of veggie options like lasagna, burritos, and pasta. Open daily 11am-1am, F-Sa 11am-2am. Lunch served until 5pm, dinner 6-10pm.

Maloe Melo, Lijnbaansgracht 163 (☎420 45 92; bluescafe@maloemelo.com; www.maloemelo.com), in the Jordaan. Maloe Melo is the best deal in the Jordaan for a night out: the beer is cheap and the bands are free. Both local and visiting amateur groups play on W, F, and Sa; mostly blues, rock, and alternative country. Stop in and you might catch an act before its big break. Regular jam sessions other nights of the week. Check website for line-up details. No cover. Music in the back room from 10:30pm. Open Su-Th 9pm-3am, F-Sa 9pm-4am.

Wil's Cafe, Prinsengracht 126 (☎020 320 2753). On a nice day, try the outside tables or come inside for the funky candles, beat-up sofa, and homey interior that set Wil's apart from its neighbors on the Prinsengracht. Get a *ciabatta* as a light meal (€3-4) with your glass of Grolsch (€1,70), and come for the live blues on Sunday and Monday (3-6pm). In the evening, Wil's becomes a hip place for young and old. Open Su-Th 10am-1am, F-Sa 10am-3am; kitchen open 6-10pm.

Cafe Thijssen, Lindengracht 2 (☎623 89 94; www.cafe-thijssen.nl), at the corner of Brouwersgracht. After a dinner in one of Lindengracht's many candlelit bistros, come here for a glass of beer (€1,70-3) in a relaxed atmosphere. Not as crowded as **Proust** or **Finch,** but just as lively, it's a nice spot for an early evening drink, especially at one of the many outdoor tables. Open M-Th 8pm-1am, F 8pm-3am, Sa 7:30pm-3am, Su 9pm-1am.

Saarein II, Elandstraat 119 (☎623 49 01). Tram #7, 10, 17, or 20 to Elandsgracht, on corner of Elandstraat and Hazenstraat. Under new management for the past five years, what was the hottest lesbian bar in the Jordaan has only gotten better. Full bar (beers €2), a small menu (offerings include pizza and ravioli dishes €6-9), and a pool table all attract a mixed crowd, though weekends are still mostly women. Open Su-Th 5pm-1am, F-Sa 5pm-2am; kitchen open 6-9:30pm.

Cafe P96, Prinsengracht 96 (☎622 18 64). When you're not ready for the night to end just yet, go to P96 for the full bar and the pub snacks. Open Su-Th 8pm-3am, F-Sa 8pm-4am.

Café de Tuin, Tweede Tuindwarsstraat 13 (☎624 45 59). Another favorite spot in the Jordaan. Beer starts at €1,70 in this traditional *bruin café*. Open M-Th 10am-1am, F-Sa 10am-2am, Su 11am-1am.

CLUBS

On warm summer nights in the Jordaan, clubs don't really start swinging 'till midnight or one in the morning.

Mazzo, Rozengracht 114 (☎626 75 00; info@mazzo.nl; www.mazzo.nl). Even the bouncers are nice here! The usual black walls, colored spotlights, and pumping music are complemented by a large bar in the back with lots of room to rest between dances; some couples here, but plenty of well-dressed singles if you're looking for love. Beer €1,85, mixed drinks €5. Techno on Th, drum and bass every F, techhouse on Sa; check website for changing events on W and Su. Cover W, Th, and Su €5-10; Fr €8-10; Sa €10. Open W, Th, Su 11pm-4am, F-Sa 11pm-5am.

Club More, Rozengracht 133 (☎528 74 59; www.expectmore.nl). For some people, the strobe lights, mind-bending techno, and a huge video display might induce a headache, but those with higher tolerance will be rewarded with great music and an uninhibited crowd that tends to be half local and half tourist. Revolving cast of DJs spin techno, club house, and funk groove Th-Sa nights. Cover €10-12. Open Th-F 11pm-4am, Sa 11pm-5am, Su 4pm-12am.

Korsakoff, Lijnbaansgracht 161 (☎625 78 504). Here, it's all about finding a way to get your groove on to heavy industrial music while dressed in leather and

Dancer at Korsakof

Late night Snack at Café de Jaren

Lellebel

chains, which is surprisingly easy and fun once you get into it. Korsakoff draws a lively crowd that's diverse both in age and temperament; while many in the crowd sport multiple facial piercings, it's not a requirement to join the party. Open Su-Th 10pm-3am, F-Sa 10pm-4am.

WESTERPARK AND OUDE WEST

see map p. 335

CLUB

West Pacific, Polonceaukade 3 (☎488 77 78), at the Westergasfabriekterrein. Out past the Westerpark, the West Pacific's location away from the city center assures a less touristy crowd; this is where "real" Amsterdammers head to party. The scene is young and dance-oriented, particularly on weekends. DJ-driven house music dominates in 2 big rooms (each with its own bar) packed with a crowd that's beautiful but unassuming; even if the usual pretension of the club scene isn't your thing, you won't feel uncomfortable here. Small cover charge. Open Su-Th noon-1am, F-Sa noon-3am; music starts at 11pm.

DE PIJP

see map p. 326

BARS

De Vrolijke Drinker, Frans Halstraat 66a (☎771 43 16). An elegant neighborhood bar on the corner of a quiet street that plays mellow jazz and provides excellent, friendly service. Small beer €1,70, wine €2,50, and a complete bar of Johnnie Walker €3,40-€11. Open M-F 4pm-1am, F-Sa 4pm-3am. Cash.

Kingfisher, Ferdinand Bolstraat 24 (☎671 23 95). Hipsters and yuppies alike congregate in this bar, which is cool without being trendy and comfortable without being just another *bruine cafe*. Low-priced beer selections from around the world include Japanese Kirin, Indian Cobra and, of course, Kingfisher (€1,60 on tap, €3 in a bottle. Great food, too. Club sandwiches €4. *Dagschotel* €11 (vegetarian option always available). *Jenever* €1,50, cocktails €4,20. Frozen fruit smoothies €3. Open Su-Th 11am-1pm, F and Sa 11am-3pm.

De Engel (The Angel), Albert Cuypstraat 182 (☎675 0544). Look for the high gold angel on the roof. Thought drinking was sinful? The Angel, a bar in the cavernous space of a converted church, innocently seduces you with its cherubic decor and fabulous retro chandeliers. Beer from the €1,80 Heinekein to €4,60 for the premiere Belgian La Chouffe. On the balcony, diners are served (€20). Open M-F 10am-1am, Sa-Su 10am-2am.

O'Donnell's, Ferdinand Bolstraat 5 (☎676 77 86). Though the prices are somewhat on the high end of the budget range, this Irish pub has a friendly buzz and authentic atmosphere, with wood paneling and Guinness ads throughout (pints €4,50). British and Irish sports matches screened here, too. Serves breakfast (€9), lunch (about €4,50), and dinner (€12). Open daily 11am-2am; kitchen open daily 11:30am-10pm. AmEx/MC.

De Duvel (The Devil), 1e van der Helstraat 59-61 (☎675 75 17; www.duvel.nl), 1½ blocks south off the Albert Cuypmarkt. A yuppie bar with the prices to prove it and some red decor thrown in incidentally–it is however a cozy place to drink. Beer €1,90; bar snacks €2,50-5,80; lunch €5 and dinner from €13,60 for a spinach ricotta with cannelloni to €18,50 for grilled tournedos in a madeira sauce. Open Su-M 4pm-2am, Tu-Sa 6pm-2am; kitchen closes at 11pm. MC/V.

Cafe Berkhout, Stadhouderskade 77 (☎662 96 39), at Ferdinand Bolstraat, across from the Heineken Brewery. Casual, breezy *eetcafe* jammed with locals. Games–chess and Scrabble–available for free at the bar to while away the time. Cheap drinks: vaasje €1,80; pint €3,80; martini €2,30. Also good Dutch snacks (*bitterballe* 3,90; chicken sate with salad €8; Hamburger "Berkhout" with bacon, cheese, egg, and tomato; *broodjes* €2,30) and *dagmenu* (full, filling meal €11-13). Open M-Th 7am-1am, F 7am-2am, Sa 9am-2am, Su 10am-1am. AmEx/MC/V.

De Badcuyp, 1e Sweelinckstraat 10 (☎675 96 69; info@badcuyp.demon.nl; www.badcuyp.demon.nl), on Albert Cuyp Straat, in De Pijp. A vibrant, gritty venue for world music in an immigrant neighborhood. Tu 9pm-midnight blues and world (free), W salsa dance (€2,50), Su jazz. The last Su of every month is a groovin African dance party (€2,50). Also houses a cafe with €10,50 dinners.

JODENBUURT AND THE PLANTAGE

see map p. 327

BAR

Maximiliaan, Kloveniersburgwal 6-8 (626 62 80; info@maximiliaan.nl; www.maximiliaan.nl). A beautiful wooden brewhouse just south of Nieuwmarkt. Some items on the menu are pricey, making meals here somewhat out of the range of the budget traveler, but it's worth stopping in for the fabulous brews, five of which are made on the premises. Alcohol content can get to a heady 7%. And if you want to see the suds develop from start to finish, make an appointment to take a spin through the on-site brewing facilities (minimum 10 people, €6 per person). Open Tu-Th and Su 3pm-1am, F-Sa 3pm-3am.

CLUB

Arena, Gravesandestraat 51-53 (☎850 24 00; www.arena.nl), in the Oost. Take night bus #76 or 77, or tram #9 to Tropenmuseum; turn right on Mauritskade and then left on Gravesandestr. Former chapel throws great parties. Every Friday and Saturday at 11pm (cover €10-15), dance to an eclectic mix in large party spaces. The crowd is young, down-to-earth, and keeps it rockin' until the early hours. Perhaps a bit touristy, with the pricey Hotel Arena next-door, but the colorful wall lights and fluorescent wall fixtures help maintain a very chill atmosphere. Open F-Sa 11pm-4am, Su 6pm-3am.

CONCERT-GEBOUW

1 JULI
T/M
31 AUG

ROBECO Z MER CONCERTE

INSIDE:

Arts & Entertainment

Amsterdam in the summer is like a new-sprung love affair: often alluring, sometimes confusing, but always deliciously entertaining. Throughout the year the city is a whirlwind of artistic activity, providing venues for hundreds of plays, concerts, festivals, and fairs. With so many opportunities and so little time to explore them, the average traveler might feel overwhelmed by the city's frenetic entertainment scene. To thwart such confusion, the **Amsterdams Uit Buro (AUB),** Leidseplein 26, is stuffed with fliers, pamphlets, and guides to help you sift through what's being offered at any given time. The AUB also sells tickets and makes reservations for just about any cultural event in the city. Pick up the free monthly *UITKRANT* at any AUB office for a breakdown of what's on. (☎621 13 11; www.uitlijn.nl. Open F-W 10am-6pm, Th 10am-9pm.) The **VVV's** theater desk, Stationsplein 10, can also make reservations for cultural events. (Open M-Sa 10am-5pm.) The monthly *Day by Day*, available from the tourist office, also provides comprehensive cultural listings. If you're still thirsty for more, the mini-magazine *Boom!*, free at restaurants and cafes around the city, is chock full of tourist info. If you're looking for a slightly edgier guide to entertainment in Amsterdam, consider picking up a *Shark* (available online at www.underwateramsterdam.com; print versions are available at the AUB and assorted restaurants, bars, and shops throughout the city), which provides comprehensive listings for clubs, squats, music, film, and gay events.

CLASSICAL MUSIC, OPERA, AND DANCE

Amsterdam is world-renowned for its innovative classical performing arts scenes. In 1986, the city invested in the construction of the prestigious **Stadhuis-Muziektheater** complex, which now houses both the **National Ballet** (www.het-nationale-ballet.nl)and the **Netherlands Opera** (www.dno.nl) in addition to regularly featuring the **Netherlands Philharmonic Orchestra,** www.orkest.nl). At the Museumplein, the **Concertgebouw** also attracts top-notch performers and is home to one of the world's finest classical orchestras. Tickets for many of these events are available through the AUB. (☎0900 01 91; www.aub.nl. Box office next to the Stadsschouwburg in Leidesplein. Open daily 10am-6pm.)

Churches throughout the city also host regular organ, choral, and chamber music concerts (tickets usually from about €2,50). An international center for **contemporary music,** the famous **IJsbreker** theater features dozens of superior contemporary artists who breathe life into the works of folks like Schönberg, Crumb, and Arvo Pärt every year. Amsterdam's rock, pop, world music, and jazz music scene is similarly vital, with hundreds of bubbling hot venues scattered throughout the city.

VENUES AND COMPANIES

Concertgebouw, Concertgebouwplein 2-6 (☎671 83 45; www.concertegebouw.nl), across Paulus Potterstraat from the open expanse of the **Museumplein.** Take tram #2, 3, 5, 12, or 16 to Museumplein. The concert hall for one of the world's finest orchestras, the not-so-creatively named Royal Concertgebouw Orchestra. Programs are often star-studded and occasionally include jazz, world, folk, and contemporary performances. Stop by the hall to get a program of concerts, some of which cost as little as €7. Su morning concerts with guided tours before the performance are a cheaper option. Sept.-June, those under 27 can get last minute tickets for anything that isn't sold out for €7. Free lunchtime concert W 12:30pm, no tickets necessary. Ticket office open daily 10am-7pm.

Stadhuis-Muziektheater, Waterlooplein (☎625 54 55; www.hetmuziektheater.nl) in **Jodenbuurt,** also known as the Stopera, is the gargantuan home to the Dutch National Ballet and the Netherlands Opera. Tickets can be obtained through either the Muziektheater box office or through the AUB (see p. 157). Box office open M-Sa 10am-curtain up, Su and holidays 11:30am-curtain up. Opera tickets start at €22; ballet tickets from €11. For ballet only, student rush tickets are available 30min. before the show for €6.

Bimhuis, Oude Schaans 73-77 (☎623 13 61; bimhuis@bimhuis.nl; www.bimhuis.nl), in the **Jodenbuurt.** Metro: Nieuwmarkt or tram to Waterlooplein. Amsterdam's premier venue for jazz and improv. music for over 20 years, Bimhuis features the famous, the obscure, and the local legend. The performers, who hail from Europe, the Americas, Asia, and Africa, are united in their devotion to the unscripted melody.Beyond the bar, the stage is surrounded by benches and a ring of cafe tables. Tickets run €10-15, students and seniors €2 less. Free Tu jam session at 10.

Beurs van Berlage Theater, Damrak 213 (☎627 04 66;www.beursvanberlage.nl), in the **Oude Zijd.** This monumental building, the former stock exchange, is now home to the Netherlands Philharmonic Orchestra and the Netherlands Chamber Orchestra. It has 3 grand concert halls and a museum with art exhibits (€5). You can arrange tours of the building (☎620 81 82). Concerts €8-20, student and senior discounts, depending on the show.

Koninklijk Carré Theater, Amstel 115-125 (☎622 52 25; kassa@theatercarre.nl; www.carretheater.nl) in the **Jodenbuurt.** Tram #6,7, 10 or Metro: Weesperplein. Grand, old-fashioned theater with red velvet opened in 1888 showing old-time amusements such as cabaret, the circus, and musical theater (*Jesus Christ Superstar* coming Apr. 15-20, 2003). Other offerings from touring companies such as Irish dance, lesser-known pop groups, Chinese acrobatic troupes and Israeli percussion ensembles. Tickets €10-50, students can get €5 tickets on the day of the performance.

IJsbreker, Weesperzijde 23 (☎668 18 05; www.ysbreker.nl; post@ysbreker.nl). Tram #6, 7, 10, 20 or bus 56 to Weesperplein or tram #3 to Ruyschstraat; it's just south of the Jodenbuurt. A world-renowned center for new music, showcasing both local and international talent. Experimental and avant-garde programs, as well as a chamber music series. €6-16, students and seniors €2 less. MC/V.

Marionette Theater, Nieuwe Jonkerstraat 8 (☎620 80 27; www.marionettentheater.nl; info@marionettentheater.nl). In an intimate, charming space on a quiet street in the **Oude Zijd,** the Marionette Theater performs a full program of Mozart and Offenbach operas entirely with–you guessed it–marionettes. Performances are twice a month, tickets available through phone, web or AUB. €10, students and seniors €7, kids €3,50.

Tropeninstituut Theater, Linnaeusstraat 2 (☎568 85 00; www.kit.nl/tropenmuseum), in the **Plantage.** Take tram #6, 9, or 10. Features non-western performing arts, from Ghanan dance to Latin American balladeers to Surinamese theater. Box office open M-Sa noon-4pm and 1hr. before performance (or make reservations by phone, or online with a surcharge).

Conservatorium van Amsterdam, Van Baerlestraat (5277550; www.cva.ahk.nl; info@cva.ahk.nl) in the **Museumplein.** Tram #2, 3, 5, 12, or 16. The conservatory of Amsterdam, so the student performances of jazz, classical and the occasional opera are free.

Churches. While almost all of Amsterdam's churches host concert programs, the **Oude Kerk** (☎625 82 84, p. 55) and **Engelse Kerk** (p. 56) all have regular summertime programs that feature some wonderful chamber, choral, organ, and early music.

LIVE MUSIC

In addition to the below venues, you can also catch the occasional live jazz performance at **Elsa's Jazz Cafe,** Middenweg 73 (☎668 50 10), in the East, and **Toomler's** on Friday nights (see p. 162). World music can sometimes be found at the **Melkweg** (see p. 163), **Carre Theater** (see p. 158), or the **Tropeninstitut** (see p. 159).

ROCK AND POP

Bourbon Street Jazz & Blues Club, Leidsekruisstr. 6-8 (☎623 34 40; www.bourbonstreet.nl). Take the tram to Leidseplein, head north on Leidsestraat, go east on Lange Leidsedwarsstraat, and then turn north on Leidsekruisstraat. Blues, soul, funk, and rock bands keep the crowds heavy every night. Mostly smaller bands play this intimate venue, although in the past they have drawn the Stones and Sting. M and Tu free jam sessions while the weekends are typically more about rock. You won't find schedules in local papers; instead, call or check the web or the sheet posted in the front window to find out what's

Melkweg Façade

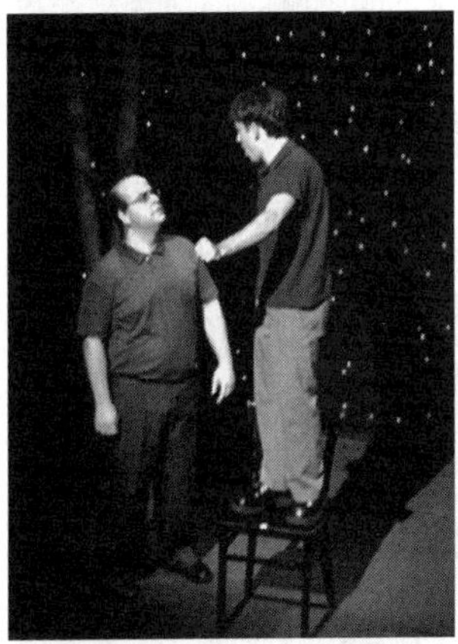
Boom Chicago

Tuschinski Theater

Truth is Stranger than "Fiction"

Amsterdam plays a seminal role in that touchstone of modern American pop culture, the Quentin Tarantino film *Pulp Fiction.* One of the movie's first scenes is with Vincent Vega regaling Jules Winfield about the "little differences" that make Amsterdam special. Among them:

Bars in movies. As Vincent reports, in Amsterdam you can go into a movie theater and get a beer—"I mean, a real glass of beer." This is true enough. To drink up and see a fine film, head to the movies (see p. 163).

Hash bar policy. "It breaks down like this," Vincent reports. "It's legal to buy it, it's legal to own it, and, if you're the proprietor of a hash bar, it's legal to sell it." Well, partly right, Mr. Vega. It's illegal to buy, sell, or carry over 5g of hash or marijuana. Vincent goes on to say, "It's legal to carry it, which doesn't really matter 'cause—get a load of this—if the cops stop you, it's illegal for them to search you. Searching you is a right that the cops in Amsterdam don't have." As for this point, well, if you're caught, you're probably screwed, so play by the rules.

Continued next page.

on. Beer €2,50, pints €5. Cover Su and Th €3, F-Sa; free if you enter 10-10:30pm. Open Su-Th 10pm-4am, F-Sa 10pm-5am.

Maloe Melo, Lijnbaansgracht 163 (☎420 45 92; bluescafe@maloemelo.com; www.maloemelo.com), in the Jordaan. Maloe Melo is the best deal in the Jordaan for a night out: the beer is cheap and the bands are free. Both local and visiting amateur groups play on W, F, and Sa; mostly blues, rock, and alternative country. Stop in and you might catch an act before its big break. Regular jam sessions other nights of the week. Check website for line-up details. No cover. Music in the back room from 10:30pm. Open Su-Th 9pm-3am, F-Sa 9pm-4am.

Melkweg, Lijnbaansgracht 234a (☎624 17 77; www.melweg.nl), off Leidseplein. Take tram #1, 2, 5, 6, 7, 10, or 20 to Leidesplen and then turn down the smaller sidestreet to the left of the grand Staddshouwberg theater. Legendary nightspot in an old mil factory (whose name means "Milky Way") where live bands, theater, films, dance shows, an art gallery (free W-Su 2-8pm), tea room cafe, and discoteque make for sensory overload. Concert tickets from €9,50-22 in addition to a €2,50 monthly membership fee. Th Latin music €750. Sa house and trance midnight-5am; cover €950. Box office open M-F 1-5pm, Sa-Su 4-6pm; until 7:30pm on show days.

Paradiso, Weteringschans 6-8 (☎626 45 21; www.paradiso.nl). When big-name rock, punk, new-wave, hip-hop, and reggae bands come to Amsterdam, they almost invariably play here in this former church that has converted into a temple to rock 'n' roll. Grace the place where Lenny Kravitz got his big break, and the Stones taped their latest live album. Upstairs there's also a smaller stage where up-and-coming talents are showcased. Tickets range from €5-25; additional *de rigueur* monthly membership fee €2,50. Sa night the cool kids come here for the nightclub "Paradisco" (€5, plus membership fee) and there are other occasional clubnights as well.

JAZZ, CONTEMPORARY, AND WORLD MUSIC

Alto, Korte Leidsedwarsstraat 115, in Leidesplein. Take a right in front of Haagen Dazs; it will be 1 block down on your left. Hepcats left over from the 50s mingle with young aficionados at this busy nightspot where the vibe is cool but the jazz is hot. Show up early to get a table up front, though you can hear (if not see too clearly) the act from the bar away from the stage. Free nightly jazz: Su-Th 9:45pm-2am, F-Sa until 3am. Open Su-Th until 3am, F-Sa until 4am. Cash Only.

Casablanca, Zeedijk 24-26 (☎625 56 85; www.casablanca-amsterdam.nl), between Oudezijds

Kolk and Vredenburgersteeg. Casablanca has been around since 1946 and, though its heyday as *the* jazz bar in Amsterdam has faded, it's still one of the best spots to hear live jazz acts in the city. Jazz acts play only Su-W nights; from Th-Sa you'll find DJ-hosted dance parties with the occasional karaoke performance. Dim and smoky, the Casablanca retains a moody feel and is still quite popular with locals. Check the website to see what acts are coming up. No cover. Open Su-Th 8pm-3am, F-Sa 8pm-4am.

Cristofori, Prisengracht 581-3 (☎626 84 85; www.cristofori.nl).Take tram #1, 2, or 5 to Prisengracht. Su night jazz and other contemporary and chamber music in an old canal house.

De Badcuyp, 1e Sweelinckstraat 10 (☎675 96 69; info@badcuyp.demon.nl; www.badcuyp.demon.nl), on Albert Cuyp Straat, in De Pijp. A vibrant, gritty venue for world music in an immigrant neighborhood. Tu 9pm-midnight blues and world (free), W salsa dance (€2,50), Su jazz. The last Su of every month is a groovin African dance party (€2,50). Also houses a cafe with €10,50 dinners.

Meander, Voetboogstraat 3b (☎625 84 30; www.cafemeander.com). From Muntplein, take the Singel to Heiligweg, turn right, and then left at Voetboogstraat. Live bands jam at this bar-cafe populated by crowds of youthful hipsters. There are shows nightly, ranging from jazz to funk to soul to blues to R&B to salsa to DJ-hosted dance sessions (monthly schedule posted on website). Dim, smokey atmosphere, constant din, and dense crowds make for a raucous, high-energy good time. Cover from €5. Open Su-Th 9pm-3am, F-Sa 9pm-4am.

Panama, Oostelijke Handelskade 4 (☎311 86 86; www.panama.nl), in the Eastern docklands. From Centraal Station, take bus #32 or 39. The abandoned warehouse location means they lure you to their opulent playland for whole night: a theater and nightclub that usually attracts a crowd in their 30s and 40s. The live music is mostly Latin, with some jazz and Caribbean; much is accompanied by dance (€5-20). "Twilight Zone" Sa 10:30-11pm. The last Su of every month is a gay night, "Club BPM," with a special performance at 10:00pm. (€15 before 9:30pm, €20 after). Cover Th €6, F-Sa €12.

Pompoen, Spuistraat 2 (☎521 30 00; www.pompoen.nl; info@pompoen.nl). Take tram #1, 2, 5, 13, 17, or 20 to Martelaarsgracht, the first stop after Centraal. Each week the brassy, upscale Pompoen books a very good jazz act (Tu-W free, Th-Sa €5). M is given over to "new jazz" which means funk, big band, poetry or Latin is on stage (€3-6). The restaurant serves a good 3-course dinner for €15; if you eat there, no cover is charged for the music. Open Su-Th 8pm-3am, F-Sa 8pm-4am.

Truth is Stranger than "Fiction," continued.

Dutch fetish for mayo on fries. As Vincent says, "they drown 'em in that shit." True enough: if you get French fries in a Dutch eatery, they will probably come slathered in, or at least with an ample side of, mayo.

Though Americans may cringe, as did Jules, it's really not such a bad custom. You can get the mayo flavored with curry spices or spicy Japanese "samurai" tincture, and once your taste adjusts, you may find it quite delicious. For a go, head for any of the countless fry-sellers that populate Amsterdam. If you're in the area, grab some fried potato lovin' at **Snack-bar Eucalyptus ❶,** Nieuwe Vijzelstraat 3, just across from the Weteringcircuit stop on tram lines #16, 24, or 25.

As you can see, Vincent Vega's take on Amsterdam is mostly right, so don't knock foreign-seeming local customs. As Vincent admonished Jules, "You'd dig it the most!"

THEATER

If it's live theater you're after, the AUB is your best resource, hands down. Year-round (but especially in the summer), the city is bursting with opportunities to see live theater, both Dutch and international. There are many different varieties of theater in the city, including **cabarets, musicals, stand-up comedy** (often in English) **spoken dramas,** and **dance.** Ticket prices vary widely; cheaper tickets are usually €11-23 and more expensive ones €23-46.

COMEDY

Boom! chicago, Leidseplein 12 (☎423 01 01; www.boomchicago.nl). Trams #1, 2, 5, 6, 7, 10, or 20 to **Leidseplein.** You don't have to travel to Amsterdam to find funny Americans. But you can. 2003 is this troupe's ten year anniversary performing sketch and improvisational comedy at the theatre on the Leidseplein. These expats promise a wry look at life on the continent that makes fun of people on both sides of the Atlantic. Show starts at 8:15pm Su-F, Sa at 7:30pm and 10:45pm. Heineken Late Nite is a 90min. all improv show on F at 11:30pm. Dinner is served–rib roast €17,50, tuna €14,75, starters €10, dessert of apple pie or brownie €6,75–but you can get better value elsewhere. The restaurant and theater open at 6:30pm (6pm on Sa) and it's a good idea to arrive early since seating is not reserved. Bring in a copy of *Boom!*, for a €2 discount on tickets 6pm Su-Th. VIP tickets (Su-Th €29; Fri and Sa €31,50) for the include the best tables covered with (gasp!) tablecloths. Otherwise, tickets Su-Th €16; F-Sa €18,50; Heineken Late Nite €10. Credit cards accepted.

Boom Chicago also organizes **boat trips** in small, open boats through the non-profit organization Sint Nicolaas Boat Stichting (€10). They are arranged at irregular times, so call ahead or drop by Boom Chicago.

Comedy Cafe, Max Euweplein 43-45 (☎638 39 71; www.comedycafe.nl). Take the tram to Leidseplein. A rotating line-up of comics from around the world, some in English and some in Dutch; call or check the web (Th-F 9pm, Sa 9 and 11:30pm; €12). W open-mic night, with a typically unpredictable bag of performances (9pm; no cover). "Off Your Head" delivers wacky improv comedy in English (Tu and Su 9pm; €9). Three-course dinner (€31) in their restaurant beforehand that includes a ticket to the show; reservation usually necessary.

Toomler, Breitnerstraat 2 (☎670 7400; www.toomler.nl), next to the Hilton Amsterdam. Take tram #16 to Cornelius Schutstraat and walk left across the canal for 3 blocks; or, take bus #15, 145, 170, or 197. They host Comedy Train International, an all-out laugh-riot in English (Sa 7pm and more frequently during the summer festival). Features other nights include live music and more comedy, although it's frequently in Dutch (€2-5).

LIVE THEATER VENUES

Stadsschouwburg, Leidseplein 26 (☎624 23 11; www.stadsschouwburgamsterdam.nl). The main theater for plays in Amsterdam. Home of the Netherlands Dance Theater, it also features modern dance and opera. July Dance Festival (www.julidans.com). Tickets €10-19.

Bellevue Theater/Nieuwe de la Mar, Leidsekade 90 (☎530 53 01; www.theaterbellevue.nl or www.nieuwedelamartheater.nl). Take tram #1, 2, 5, 6, 7, 10, or 20 to Leidseplein. A complex with three stages for popular theater, musicals, modern dance, cabaret. The Nieuwe de la Mar, which merged with Bellevue fifteen years ago, runs more experimental theater out of the same box office and complex. Most shows in Dutch, but check the current offerings. Box office open daily 11am-6pm.

Pompoen Theater, Spuistraat 2 (☎521 30 00; www.pompoen.nl), in the Nieuwe Zijd. Very diverse program ranges from stand-up comedy to Shakespearean monologues to children's plays. There's also a computer-generated film about the city's history, *The Miracle of Amsterdam* (every hr. 11am-5pm).

Koninklijk Theater Carré, Amstel 115-125 (☎622 61 77; www.theatercarre.nl), in the Jodenbuurt. Dutch productions of theatrical favorites like *Cats*, *42nd Street*, and *Riverdance*. Ticket office open M-Sa 10am-7pm, Su 1-7pm.

De Kleine Komedie, Amstel 56-58 (☎624 05 34; kleinkom@xs4all.nl). Take tram #4, 5, 9, or 20 to Rembrandtplein. The premiere spot for cabaret in the Netherlands as well as a full program of musical theater and spoken drama at one of the oldest theaters in Amsterdam.

Badhuis-Theater de Bochel, Andreas Bonnstraat 28 (☎668 51 02), in the East. Take tram #3. An irregular schedule of various off-beat productions (experimental theater, children's workshops, dance parties) in this bathouse-turned-theater.

Melkweg, Lijnbaansgracht 234a (☎624 17 77; www.melkweg.nl). Along with the cinema, club, and art gallery, the Melkweg is a popular venue for touring theater groups. See p. 160.

De Balie, Kleine-Gartmanplansoen 10 (☎553 51 00; www.balie.nl), just off of Leidseplein. De Balie is a center for film, photography, theater, and new media. Interesting contemporary theater is almost a guarantee. Check with the box office for info on whether a film is subtitled in English. Also plays host to dramatic productions and new media.

Amsterdamse Bos Openluchttheater, Amsterdamse Bos 1 (☎640 92 52; www.bostheater.nl). Serious plays (usually in Dutch) for the summertime in this outdoor amphitheater.

Felix Meritis, Keizersgracht 324 (☎624 93 68; balie@felix.meritis.nl; www.felix.meritis.nl), hosts concerts of classical and world music. See p. 59.

Vondelpark Openluchttheater (☎673 14 99; www.openluchtheater.nl), in the center of the park. Free summer (May-Aug.) outdoor theater as well as music, dance, and kids shows.

Marionette Theater, see Venues and Companies, p. 159.

Casablanca, (☎625 56 85; www.casablanca.nl) A small variety theater and circus with an old-time feel (e5). Children's magician Su afternoon. Old-world dinner about €17.

FILM

The Dutch love movies, and in Amsterdam you can find everything from the tackiest American blockbuster to the most obscure indie flick. The city is distinctive for its preponderance of cinemas showing independent films and for the **Filmmuseum,** a national cinematic library.Since the Dutch tend to appreciate movies for their artistic qualities, they are rarely dubbed into the Netherlandish tongue. With the exception of cartoons, people prefer subtitles. Bearing this in mind, you must remember that if you're planning to view a non-English film, it will be shown in its original language with Dutch subtitles. Some theaters may offer English subtitles for foreign films, but you should check with the box office first or else look for an "EO" or "Engels Ondertitled" sign. Most movies are released in the Netherlands a few months after their debut, although big box office hits will sometimes get to the Dutch screen right away. Check out www.movieguide.nl for listings or stop by any movie theater and pick up a copy of *Film Agenda*, a free guide to what's playing during a given week throughout the city. At the AUB, the *Film Krant* provides comprehensive listings and is an especially good resource for retrospectives and art house films. The best site for film news is www.filmfocus.nl, which has showtimes as well as critical reviews and festival information.

The French company **Pathé** owns four of the bigger cinema houses in the city—The City, Calypso, Pathe de Munt, and the historic Tuschinski—information for all these is at www.pathe.nl. Pathé tends to show mainstream films although there are independent flicks in the lot as well. Prices for all four cinemas: M-Th €7,20, F-Sun €7,80; students €6,10, €7,80; kids under 11 €6,10, €7,80; 65 and over €6,10, €6,70. €1,60 cheaper for any showing before 6pm and only €4,00 for any show before noon. Pick up the program for all at any one of them.

Although you may be going to see an American film, their are still cultural differences at the movie theater: in Amsterdam, people do not eat while watching films and many theaters do not serve popcorn; instead the Dutch like to bring a drink in with them. In *Pulp Fiction*, Vincent tells Jules that one of the coolest things about Amsterdam is that you can go into a movie theater and order a beer. Well, here you are, so go to the movies and get your glass of beer.

Filmmuseum, Vondelpark 3, between Roemer Visscherstraat and Vondelstraat entrances. (☎589 14 00; info@filmmuseum.nl; www.filmmuseum.nl). A stately house with at least three daily screenings, many of them older classics or organized around a special theme like the works of Fellini. In 2003, a program of films about and from the Dutch East Indies will be presented. €6,25, students €3,75. F night they have an outdoor screening for €2,50, which also gets you a free drink at the next door Cafe Vertigo (see p. 113).

The Movies, Harlemmerstraat 159 (☎624 57 90; www.themovies.nl), in the **Shipping Quarter.** Bus 18 or 22, or Tram #3 to Haarlemmer Sq. The Movies is the city's oldest movie theater, and has been restored to its original classic Art Deco style. The fare is more independent although not too far out there. Sa "seize the night" series plays favorites anywhere from 2 to 40 years ago. In the adjacent restaurant and bar, the savory *dagschotels* tend to be dear (about €17), but budget travelers can afford the appetizers (€7,50), light snacks, and drinks. There is a 4-course menu, including the price of a ticket for €27, an elegant dinner-and-a-movie package. Movie only €7,50, students €6,50. Credit cards in restaurant only.

Kriterion Theater and Cafe, Roetersstraat 170 (☎623 17 08; fax 625 14 79; info@kriterion.nl; www.kriterion.nl), in **Jodenbuurt.** Take tram #6, 7, 10, or 20 to Weesperplein. Run by a student collective from nearby University of Amsterdam, Kriterion is an art house movie theater with the potential to satisfy just about everyone, regardless of age or taste. The cafe is not just an adjunct to the theater; it's a cool, laid-back place where students come for discussions over cigarettes while jazz plays in the background. Independent and studio films run daily, and children's movies are also shown regularly. Cafe open Su-Th 11am-1am, F-Sa 12:30pm-3am. €6,20, weekends €6,60; students and seniors €5,00, weekends €5, 40.

Smart Project Space, 1e Constantijn Huygenstraat 20 (☎427 5951; info@smartprojectspace.net), in the **Oude West.** No popcorn sold here–this place is about showing art. Taken over by squatters to be used for art space, this house shows independent films, with a special focus on Latin American cinema. They also have changing exhibits of art and a hip restaurant and bar in front. €5,50, students and seniors €4,50.

Tuschinski Cinema, Reguliersbreestraat 26-28 (☎626 26 33), between Rembrandtplein and Muntplein. Step from the gaudy world of the **Rembrandtplein's** porno shops and fast food stands into an oasis of old-world elegance. This ornate movie theater from 1921, is one of Europe's first experiments in Art Deco. Although a group of drunk Nazis once got out of hand and started a fire in its cabaret, the theater miraculously survived WWII and has remained in operation for over 75 years. Guided tours July-Aug. Su-M 10:30am. A ticket to a screening of one of their Hollywood features allows you to explore on your own; theater 1 is the main stage and has private boxes. It tends to show a commercial hit while the other screens are devoted to artsy shows. Tuschinski is a Pathé cinema so see above for more information.

De Belie, Kleine-Gartmanplansoen 10 (☎553 51 00; www.balie.nl). Just off of **Leidseplein.** An intellectual center in a former courthouse, De Balie offers film (€5), theater (€8), new media, political debates, and lectures (€8). Films are generally on non-commercial theme topics such as contemporary life in China. Café (food €3-8) with changing art displays and free internet (you're expected to buy a drink). Pick up a program in the lobby or check the website for more information on events.

Het Ketelhuis, Haarlemmerweg 8-10 (☎684 00 90; www.ketelhuis.nl), west of the **Shipping Quarter.** Take tram #10 to Van Limburg Stirumplein. A living room for Dutch cinema in an abandoned warehouse. While the majority of Amsterdam's cinemas show mostly foreign films, Het Ketelhuis, located in the Westergasfabrik complex, is dedicated to the promotion of Dutch film. Films very rarely in English. €6, 90, students €5,70.

Rialto, Ceintuurbaan 338 (☎675 39 94; www.rialtofilm.nl) in **De Pijp**. Take tram #3, 20, 24, or 25 to Ferdinand Bol/Ceintuurbaan. Wonderful art house cinema in a newly renovated complex showing a wide variety of international movies on 2 screens. Interesting retrospectives and series; documentaries Th at 8pm. €6,50, €7,50 on weekends, €1 less for students and seniors.

Cinecenter, Lijnbaansgracht 236 (☎623 66 15; www.cinecenter.nl), just off **Leidesplein.** Not catering to the masses, the Cinecenter runs medium-artsy films, many of which are foreign. €6,50 weekdays, €7,50 weekends; students and seniors €5,50, €6,50 weekends.

De Tropeninstituut Theater, Linnaeusstraat 2 (☎568 85 00; www.kit.nl/tropenmuseum), in the **Plantage.** Take tram #6, 9, or 10. Rare gems from all over the world. This theater, connected to the Tropenmuseum (see p. 95), is especially notable for its unique international series and retrospectives. Check for English subtitles ahead of time.

SPORTS AND OTHER ENTERTAINMENT

Bungy Jump Holland, Westerdoksdijk 44 (☎419 60 05; www.bungy.nl). Fall from a crane 75m above the Ij canal. You get to choose whether you end up wet or dry. 1st jump €50, 2nd €40; duo jump €100.

Deco Sauna, Herengracht 117 (☎330 35 65; www.saunadeco.nl). Pamper yourself amidst fabulous '20s art deco style with massage, Shiatsu, or reflexology. (€27 for 25min., €44 for 55min.) Also offers facials, manicures, and special "beauty days" from €100.

Holland Casino Amsterdam, Max Euweplein 62 (☎521 11 11; www.hollandcasino.nl). Head through Max Euweplein's columns and past a lovely curved fountain to the mammoth temple to Mammon. The largest and ritziest of the Netherlands's national gaming houses, the casino proffers all kinds of ways to lose money—slots, blackjack, baccarat, and wily one-armed bandits. You need to be 18 to enter, but even if you're 81, the doormen will send you away unless you can provide proof of age in the form of a government-issued ID. Open daily 1pm-3am. €3,50 entry fee. Min. wager at tables €2, for slots €0,50.

Klimmuur Centruum, De Ruyterkade 160 (☎427 57 77), about a 10min walk to the right of Centraal Station; it's the enormous corrugated tilting block. An incredible indoor wall climbing facility. Open M-F 5-10pm, Sa-Su 10am-10pm.

Knijn Bowling, Scheldeplein 3 (☎664 22 11; www.knijnbowling.nl) in the South. Tram 4. The Dutch aren't famous for bowling but Knijn makes a noble try. Prices are for groups of up to 6 people M-F 10am-5pm €14,50, M-Su 5pm-1am and Sa noon-5pm €19,50. F and Sa night with Twilight Zone (F 11pm-12:30am, Sa 11:30pm-1am) €9,50 per person. "Su Barbecue" (€30) has western bowling with a DJ from 4:30-5:30pm followed by an enormous Southern/Tex-Mex feast.

Snooker & Poolclub Oud-West, Overtoom 209 (☎618 80 19). Tram 1 or 6 to Constantijn Huygenstra. (the next stop after Leidseplein) and continue walking down Overtoom; it will be on your left. Full-size snooker in a converted church with pool tables on the balcony and 2 dart lanes. Full bar. Use of table for 1hr. costs €6 before 2pm, €7,50 after. Open Su-Th noon-1am F-Sa noon-2am. Reservations recommended for F-Sa.

INSIDE:

Shopping

Amsterdam is brimming with funky little boutiques selling all kinds of quirky and well-designed goods. The little passageways that cross the three central canals in between Raadhuisstraat and Leidsegracht, famously known as the "Nine Streets," are strewn with fun designs, as are the similarly charming little streets in the **Jordaan.** The other streets rife with goodies are: **Utrechtestraat,** south of Rembrandtplein; **Niewe Hoogstraat,** in the Jodenbuurt; and **Haarlemmerstraat,** in the Shipping Quarter. In addition, **Kalverstraat and Niewendijk** is a very popular commercial strip that gets packed on the weekends and is thankfully pedestrian-only.

The cheapest goods in the city can be found in **De Pijp,** which is packed with bargain finds from all over the world as well as the bounteous **Albert Cuyp market.** In fact, you can get almost anything for a good price at Amsterdam's many outdoor **markets.** The most expensive shopping, on P.C. Hoofstraat, is full of international designers and, in comparison to the rest of Amsterdam, is actually pretty sterile and boring.

ANTIQUES AND FLEA MARKETS

Horeca Antiek Garage, Westerstraat 10-12 (☎423 32 10; www.horeca-antiek.com). The owner of this cute shop claims he got the idea to combine an espresso bar with an antique store. Nestled in the Jordaan, the store is stocked to the brim with furniture and curiosities; if you have room to bring home something strange, here's where to find it. Discover anything from an old Dutch movie poster or beer stein to a pith helmet, or choose from the staggering number of mannequin torsos. Customers line up and eye the wares as they order at the counter. Open M 9am-5pm, Tu-Sa 11am-5pm.

A DARKER SHADE OF PURPLE

Tulip growers have managed to create every imaginable strain of tulip, from smooth-edged to fringed, single-hued to multi-colored. Hybridizers have not succeeded in what seems to be a simple task: the creation of a black tulip. Scientists have come close, growing tulips that are darker and darker shades of purple, but have not achieved an absolute shade of black. The difficulty of this quest has sparked the romantic imaginations of artists and writers—Alexandre Dumas, author of *The Count of Monte Cristo*, wrote a short, melodramatic story—creatively named *The Black Tulip* (1850)—in which a mysterious black tulip was the center of intrigue.

It is actually impossible for any living organism, tulips included, to be black, as black is the absence of all color. But if you insist on having something in your garden that is as black (or purple) as midnight, try tulip strains "Burgundy," "Black Diamond," or "Black Parrot." Try the **Bloemenmarkt** (see p. 172) to sate your tulipmania.

Nic Nic, Gasthuismolensteeg 5 (☎622 85 23). Nearly everyone who passes the exceptionally cluttered window of Nic Nic just *has* to go inside and take a peek. The offerings in the antique and curiosities shop are simply too cool to pass by. Everything from art deco furniture to '50s dishware to dolls to knick-knacks are on sale for very reasonable prices. This is the kind of place that asks people to dig just a little deeper for that one incredible thing that they never knew they couldn't live without. Open M-Th noon-6pm, F-Sa 10am-5pm.

Santa Jet, Albert Cuypstraat 69 (☎675 51 35). Folk art and artifacts from Latin America, including bags, clothing, mirrors, and many iterations of the Virgin Mary. Open Tu-Sa 10:30am-10pm, Su noon-10pm.

See also **Markets,** p. 172.

BODY PIERCING

Body Manipulations (☎420 80 85; piercing@bodymadam.demon.nl; www.bodym-europe.com), on Oude Hoogstraat in the Oude Zijd. Very helpful staff will assist you in all your desires to be punctured and adorned at this careful, hygienic establishment. Most body piercing €27,50, ear €5, nose €16, plus the price of the jewelry (€3,50-31). 5% off if you show this book and 10% off for a repeat piercing. Women and gay friendly. No appointment required. Open M-W and F-Sa 11am-6pm, Th 11am-8pm.

BOOKS ETC.

A Space Oddity, Prinsengracht 204 (☎427 40 36). Storeowner Jeff Bas has assembled an impressive assortment of sci-fi and comic book paraphenalia, from old action figures to movie promos. The young at heart will find old and rare toy incarnations of their favorite movies and comic books, from *Star Wars* to *Spider-Man*. Some as cheap as €10, others as expensive as you can imagine. Open M 1-5:30pm, Tu-F 11am-5:30pm, Sa 1-5pm. V.

American Book Center, Kalverstraat 185 (☎625 55 37; www.abc.nl), discounts 10% for students and teachers. Open M-W and F-Sa 10am-8pm, Th 10am-10pm, Su 11am-6:30pm.

Arcitectura and Natura, Leliegracht 22 (☎623 61 86; www.archined.nl/architectura), in the Canal Ring West. Can't read Dutch? Well, it doesn't matter, because it's the pictures that make these coffee table books extraordinary. Enough of them are in English, anyway. Heavy and beautiful, the tomes here tend to be expensive. Open M noon-6:30pm, Tu-Sa 9am-6pm. V/MC/AmEx.

Athenaeum Boekhandel, Spui 14-16 (☎622 62 48; www.athenaeum.nl), at the bottom of the Nieuwe Zijd in the Spui. Everything from your most obscure literary needs to cultural criticism and philosophy to beautiful art coffeetable books; most are in English. Also maintains a newsstand with a very extensive selection of American and British magazines. Open M 11am-6pm, Tu-W and F-Sa 9:30am-6pm, Th 9:30am-9pm, Su noon-5:30pm. AmEX/MC/V.

The Book Exchange, Kloveniersburgwal 58 (☎626 62 66), between the Oude Zijd and the Jodenbuurt, deals in used texts and has a friendly, tasteful, knowledgeable staff. Frightfully good selection of used English-language books, from the basic fiction and nonfiction to the more esoteric. Any book you could want to pass the time at the many canal-side cafes, all reasonably priced (paperbacks €3-11). You can also drop in to sell those old paperbacks; true to its name, the Exchange offers a more favorable deal if you're willing to trade. Open M-F 10am-6pm, Sa 10am-5:30pm, Su 11:30am-4pm.

English Bookshop, Lauriergracht 71 (☎626 42 30), in the Jordaan. Renovated and reopened in July 2002, it now offers coffee and tea to sip while you browse its strong selection of books and American magazines. Open Tu-Su 10am-6pm.

Waterstone's, Kalverstraat 152 (☎638 38 21), carries a wide selection. Open Su-M 11am-6pm, Tu-W 9am-6pm, Th 9am-9pm, F 9am-7pm, Sa 10am-7pm.

CLOTHING

Betsy Palmer Shoes, Van Woustraat 46 (☎470 97 95; info@betsypalmer.com; www.betsypalmer.com), in De Pijp, or Rokin 9-15 (☎422 10 40), in the Nieuwe Zijd. Although these chic women's shoes are priced on the high side, the store has frequent sales. Open daily 10am-6pm.

Biba, Nieuwe Hoogstraat 26 (☎330 57 21; fax 330 57 22). Many items here cost a pretty penny, but the collection of classic and ultra-modern jewelry make it worth a stop for the design-conscious. Open M 1-6pm, Tu-Sa 11am-6pm, Su 1pm-5pm. AmEx/MC/V.

De Hoed Van Tijn, Nieuwe Hoogstraat 15 (☎623 27 59). Fedora, berets, pork pie tophats, and every other manner of head ornament are here, and all range in price from €20 and €30 to €100 and €200. However, if you're hunting for a stylish chapeau, there's no better place to look. Open M noon-6pm, Tu-F 11am-6pm, Sa 11am-5pm.

Episode, Waterlooplein 1 (☎320 30 00). A great selection of secondhand clothing at reasonable prices awaits your discovery at this shop off to the side of the great Waterlooplein flea market. Open M-Sa 9:30am-6pm.

H&M, Kalverstraat 125-9 (☎624 06 24), in the Nieuwe Zijd. This Swedish chain (official name: Hennes & Mauritz) made it big by selling trendy clothing for surprisingly low prices. Open M noon-6pm, Tu-W and F-Su 10am-6pm, Th 10am-9pm. V/MC/AmEx.

Hippie Chicks at Waterloo

Spui Book Market

Store Interior

Itchy Bitchy, Van Woustraat 185 (☎664 57 12), in De Pijp. Get your Eurotrash on! Edgy, stylish women's wear for clubs all over the continent. All of the clothes are new, and many of the items are designed and made in-house. Open M 1-6pm, Tu-W and F-Su 10am-6pm, Th 10am-9pm.

Laundry Industry, Spui 1 (☎420 25 54), in the Nieuwe Zijd. The Dutch are proud to call this respected international brand their own. Prices for the "clean" suits and semi-casual men's and women's wear on middle to high range. Open daily 11am-6pm. V/MC/AmEx.

Little Miss Strange, Jan Pieter Heijestraat 117. Second-hand clothes shop specializing in hand-me-downs from the 50s, 60s, and 70s. Pick through the many tightly-packed racks of styles imported from America. Open W-F 1pm-6pm, Sa 1pm-5pm.

Megazino, Rozengracht 207-213 (☎330 10 31; megazino@hotmail.com; www.megazinobv.com), in the Jordaan. A designer outlet with name brands for reduced prices. They get their items—sometimes a season or two behind—directly from the factory. Open Su-M noon-6pm, Tu-Sa 10am-6m. AmEx/MC/V.

Puck, Nieuwe Hoogstraat 1a (☎625 42 01). Classic secondhand items in excellent condition are found in this bright and airy corner shop in the Jodenbuurt. Best of al!, items (which include dresses, suits, hats, accessories, linens, Japanese and Korean kimonos, and children's apparel) come without the musty smell that characterizes many vintage goods. Open M-F 11am-6pm, Sa 11am-5pm.

DEPARTMENT STORES

De Bijenkorf, Dam 1 (☎621 80 80). Amsterdam's best-known department store. Books, clothes, home goods—standard (but stylish) department store stock.

Hema, Nieuwendijk 174 (☎638 99 63). Compared to De Bijenkorf, Hema is a more affordable department store carrying many of the same items.

Magna Plaza, Nieuwezijds Voorburgwal 182 (☎626 91 99). Not so much a department store, but rather a shopping center with high-end fashion boutiques.

GALLERIES

Packed with right around 140 galleries, it seems Amsterdam is selling art everywhere you turn. Moreover, the galleries offer great places to see art for free. Many of the galleries are concentrated on **Spiegelstraat/Nieuwe Spiegelstraat,** the "driveway" to the Rijksmuseum.

E.H. Ariens Kappers, 32 Nieuwe Speigelstraat (☎623 53 56), in the Central Canal Ring. Top-class woodblock prints and drawings by Old Dutch masters and Japanese artists like Hiroshige. Open Mar-Oct Tu-Sa 11am-6pm.

Frozen Fountain, Prisengracht 629 (☎622 93 75), in the Central Canal Ring. Colorful, cutting-edge furniture and home design, usually by young Dutch designers. Open M 1-6pm, Tu-F 10am-6pm, Sa 10am-5pm.

Loerakker, Keizergracht 380 (☎622 17 32; www.come.to/loerakkergalerie), in the Canal Ring West. Shows the often beautiful painting and photography of young Dutch artists. Open W-Sa 1-5:30pm.

Mendo, Berenstraat 11 (☎612 12 16; contact@mendo.nl; www.mendo.nl), in the Canal Ring West. Come just to see the cool things they display: painting, sculpture, and photography in addition to a provocative collection of art books. Open W-F 11am-6pm Sa-Su noon-5pm. Credit cards accepted.

Amsterdam Smallest Gallery, Westermarkt 60 (☎622 37 56; www.smallestgallery.com). Built into the northern side of Westerkerk church in the Canal Ring West, right beside Anne Frank Huis, this tiny art gallery displays the work of Sonja, an Amsterdam-based artist whose colorful depictions of Amsterdam life give the shop an attractive glow. With originals from €30, and postcard-sized miniatures at €8 each, go home with both a painting in your pocket, along with some extra cash. Open Sept-May M-T 11am-5pm, June-Aug daily except W 10am-6pm. AmEx/MC/V.

GIFTS

Amsterdam, especially the Canal Ring West, abounds with one-of-a-kind boutiques.

Abracadabra, Sarphati Park 24 (☎676 66 83), in De Pijp. Abracadabra stocks glitttery delights at very low prices: jewelry, lanterns, picture frames, pillows, incense, and other baubles, mostly imported from India. Remarkable for the great bargains on jewelry, where necklaces and earrings can cost €5. V/MC.

Beadies, Huidenstraat 6 (☎428 51 61; www.beadies.com). Find all the ingredients to make your own jewelry. Put it together yourself or have beadies' pros do it for you. Bracelets and necklaces from €5 (depending on the cost of materials). Open M 1-6pm, Tu-Sa 10:30am-6pm, Th 10:30am-9pm.

Cine Qua Non, Staalstraat 14 (☎625 55 88). Find posters, books, and related ephemera from movies both classic and camp at this small shop devoted to the by-products of the film industry. Features posters of *Apocalypse Now* next to postcards of such favorites as the seminal *Bat Attack*. Open Tu-Sa 1-6pm.

Cortina Paper, Reestraat 22 (☎623 66 76), in the Canal Ring West. Elegant stationary, specialty notebooks, and photo albums as well as gorgeous selection of wrapping paper. Open M 1-6pm, Tu-Sa 11am-6pm. V/MC/AmEx.

De Kinderfeestwinkel, 1e van der Helststraat 15 (☎672 22 15), in De Pijp. A fantastical "fairy" shop packed with all sorts of playful, glittery goodies, toys, party decorations, and children's costumes, all arranged by color. Open Tu-Sa 10am-6pm, M 1-6pm.

De Witte Tanden Winkel, Runstraat 5 (☎623 34 43). Hop aboard the ferris wheel of dental hygiene! Good for a laugh, the White Tooth Shop is also the place to go for good ol' American toothpaste. Novelty brushes €2-14. Open M 1-6pm, Tu-F 10am-6pm, Sa 10am-5pm.

In Oprichting, Herenstraat 38 (☎639 28 52). When it's time to go gift-shopping for those relatives and friends who would not be content with a commemorative cheese clog, come here for the sheep-shaped nightlight that your sister has always wanted. Nice selection of puzzles, housewares, and toys for all ages. Open M noon-6pm, Tu-sA 11am-5pm.

Kitsch Kitchen, 1e Bloemdwarsstraat 21-23 (☎428 49 69). A walk into the Jordaan will bring you to an explosion of color in the form of offbeat tupperware and other home furnishings. Perfect place to stock up on kooky gifts. Open M-Sa 10am-6pm.

La Savonnerie, Prinsengracht 294 (☎428 11 39; www.savonnerie.nl). Beautiful, handmade soaps in many colors and scents (€1 and up). Open Tu-F 10am-6pm, Sa 10am-5pm.

ROB, Warmoestraat 32 (☎625 46 86). Anything you want in rubber and leather, from the standard (jackets) to the vaguely provocative (tight pants) to the fetishly outrageous (masks and restraints). Bring the whole family! Open M-F noon-7pm, Sa 1am-6pm, Su 1-6pm.

Condomerie het Gulden Vlies, Warmoestraat 141 (☎627 41 74). Bring home a taste of Amsterdam's sexy (or, more accurately, sexual) side. Condoms available in all shapes, sizes, and flavors. Express your Dutch pride and invest in a football package–one condom bedecked with a soccer ball and 11 bright orange condoms to support the national team. Open M-Sa 11am-6pm.

Hera Kaarsen, Overtoom 402, (☎616 28 86; www.herakaarsen.nl). If you've ever wanted a candle in the shape of a grapefruit, then you've come to the right place. Stocks a staggering variety of colorful and curious home-made candles, from around €14. Also has a selection of lamps and other assorted knick-knacks. Open Tu-F 11am-6pm, Sa 11am-5pm.

HOME GOODS AND FURNITURE

De Emaillekeizer, 1e Sweelinckstraat 15 (☎664 18 47; www.emaillekeizer.nl; emaillekeizer@zonnet.nl), a block and a half off the Albert Cuypmarket in De Pijp. Selling bright baskets, colorful woven deck chairs, a handsome beaded door divider, and other knicknacks primarily from Ghana. Incredibly cheap dishware and teapots. If you're in town for a little while and realize you might like a plate, mug, or teapot, this is the place to go. Open M 1-6pm, Tu-Sa 11am-6pm.

Gallerie Casbah, 1e Van Der Helstraat (☎671 04 74), in De Pijp. Beautifully ornate imports from Morocco. Mostly serious pieces such as tiled fountains, 1m vases and rugs although there are also some wonderful plates and book bindings. Open daily 11am-6pm. Cash.

Maranon Hangmatten, Singel 488-90 (☎622 82 61; www.maranon.net), in the Central Canal Ring. Right off the flower market, this is the best temporary refuge in the city. Come in for a rest to "test" the colorful, comfortable hammocks hanging from the ceiling. Open M-Sa 9am-6pm, Su 10am-5:30pm. V/MC/AmEx.

The Purple Onion, Haarlemmerdijk 139 (☎427 37 50), in the Shipping Quarter. Step into this incense-filled shop to a world of eclectic goods imported from India. The owners, a Dutch anthropologist and an Indian scientist, select items using natural materials, such as wooden sculptures and handmade bedspreads. Open Tu-Sa 11:30am-6pm. V/MC.

INTERNATIONAL STORES

Dun Yong, Stormsteeg 9 (☎622 17 63; info@dunyong.com; www.dunyong.com), on the corner of Gelderskade. A world of Chinese kitsch and culture awaits at this 5-floor shop bursting with foodstuffs, paper fans, mini ceramic Buddhas, decorations, and just about anything else you can imagine. Open M-Sa 9am-6pm, Su noon-6pm.

Japanese Winkeltje, NZ Voorburgwal 177 (☎627 95 23; japans@planet.nl; www.japanesewinkeltje.nl), in the Nieuwe Zijd. Sushi plates, kimonos, art, sandals, mats, books, postcards, and specialty food from the Eastern island. The Japanese cultural center next door offers classes in language, calligraphy, and cooking as well as booking trips to Japan. Open Su-M 1-6pm, Tu-Sa 9:30am-6pm. V/MC/AmEx.

Morning Glory-yocha, Van Woustraat 48 (☎471 14 00; info@yocha.nl), in De Pijp. Predominantly pastel collection of stationary, bags, and toys with the Japanese cartoon characters from Sanrio and Morning Glory–we're talking Hello Kitty, Babu, and Bleur Bear. Open M noon-6pm, Tu-Su 10am-6pm.

Tibet Winkel, Spuistraat 185a (☎420 54 38; www.tibetwinkel.nl). The proceeds from the goods in this store (music, books, incense, and other knickknacks from Tibet) help fund the Tibet Support Group, which works to support the Tibetan people in their struggle for self-determination (for more info, see www.xs4all.nl/~tibetsg). Open M 1-6pm, Tu-Su 10am-6pm.

MARKETS

Each year on April 30, all of Amsterdam is transformed into a giant flea market in honor of Queen's Day (see p. 7). But you can enjoy bargain-hunting and treasure-shopping in Amsterdam's markets more than once a year.

Albert Cuypmarkt, on Albert Cuypstraat, between Van Woustraat and Ferdinand Bolstraat, in De Pijp. The city's–and the country's–largest market, it stretches more than a 1/2-mile down Albert Cuypstraat. There's little you can't find here, whether you're interested in freshly caught herring, schmaltzy souvenirs, underwear galore, or even erotic chocolates. Check out the restaurants along Albert Cuypstraat behind the stalls for great deals on cheap, tasty fare from around the world. Open **M-Sa** 9am-4pm

Bloemenmarkt, on the Singel canal. Pick up bulbs at this floating market. Open **daily** 8am-8pm.

Dappermarkt, on Dapperstraat. If you're looking to get a glimpse of Amsterdam's Middle Eastern and North African communities in action, stop by the Dappermarkt and sort through piles of useful, useless, and staggeringly cheap stuff. Offering everything from pharmaceuticals and stockings to fresh fruit and peanuts; it's worth the trek if you're on the hunt for a bargain. Open **M-Sa** 9am-4pm.

Nieuwmarkt hosts a Boerenmarkt (organic food market) every **Sa** from 9am-5pm, as well as an antiques market every **Su** from 9am-5pm (May-Sept.). Those interested in market shopping should also check out the

Noordermarkt in the Jordaan (**M** 9am-1pm) for home goods, clothes, trinkets, and organic produce (fruits and vegetables' market Sa 9am-4pm).

Spui, where on **Su,** local and international artists present their oils, etchings, sculptures, and jewelry, turning the bustling square into an outdoor gallery (open Mar.-Dec. 10am-6pm). **F** the area transforms yet again, into a book market that occasionally yields rare editions and 17th-century Dutch romances (open 10am-6pm).

Waterlooplein has an open air market **daily**. Tapestries, used clothing, and traditional Dutch art are all on sale in this large market beside the Stadhuis-Muziektheater (daily 9am-5pm).

MUSIC

Africa & World Music Record Shop, Kinkerstraat 294, (☎412 17 76). Tram #7 or 17 to Ten Katestr. A unique look into the diverse musical styles of North Africa, from Fela Kuti to the wildest extensions of world beat. The shop carries a wide selection of world music. Open M 1-7pm, Tu-W and F-Sa 11am-7pm, Th 11am-9pm, Su noon-7pm. AmEx/MC/V.

Back Beat Records, Egelantierstraat 19 (☎627 16 57; backbeat@xs4all.nl). In the Jordaan, tightly packed collection of jazz, soul, funk, blues, and R&B. Most prices are a bit steep, but there are some bargains to be found. New CD's as well as new and used vinyl. Open M-Sa 11am-6pm.

Concerto, Utrechtsestraat 52-60 (☎623 52 28; info@concerto.nu), in the Central Canal Ring. Around since 1955 and arguably the best music store in Amsterdam, Concerto sells a broad selection of CDs from five adjoining houses: second hand, dance, pop, jazz/world, and classical. Records downstairs. Listening station where they'll play anything. Open M-W and F-Sa 10am-6pm, Th 10am-9pm, Su noon-6pm. V/MC/AmEx.

Dance Tracks, Nieuwe Nieuwstraat 69 (☎639 08 53). This record/CD shop advertises as "strictly dance music," and that's exactly what it means. Expect to find all sorts of cuts in the dance genre—bootlegs, rare records, and tons of hip-hop and house music. Open M 1-7pm, Tu-W and F-Sa 11am-7pm, Th 11am-9pm, Su 1-6pm. Credit cards accepted.

De Plaatboef, Rozengracht 40 (☎422 87 77; www.plaatboef.com), in the Jordaan. Big selection of new and used CDs (around €11). Credit cards accepted for purchases over €40. Open M noon-6pm, Tu-Sa 10am-6pm.

Roots Music, Jonge Roelensteeg 6 (☎620 44 70). If you're want reggae, Latin, or African beats, look no further than this mousehole-sized music shop. Roots houses a great selection of vinyl, 7-inches, and CDs at very affordable prices. Open Su-M 12:30-6pm, Tu-W and F-Sa 10:30am-6pm, Th 10:30am-9pm.

Soul Food, Nieuwe Nieuwstraat 27c. Specializes in dance music, both CD and vinyl. Wide selection of new and old cuts from Europe, the US, and abroad. Open M 1-9pm, Tu-W and F-Sa 11am-7pm, Th 11am-9pm, Su 1-7pm.

Schot CD Shop, van Baerlestraat 5 (☎662 37 59), between P.C. Hooftstraaat and Vossiusstraat. From the Museumplein, walk away from the Rijksmuseum and take your first right on van Baerlestraat; it will be 2 blocks down on the right. Diverse selection of music, with everything from world music to classical, opera, New Age, jazz, soul, and a larger selection of pop. Prices vary widely, but there are many special deals. Outside are some good jazz, classical, and world music as well as corny '70s hits (€4,60, 3 for €12,00). Open daily 10:30am-7pm. Credit cards accepted.

Wenterwereld Records, 13a 1e Bloemwarsstraat (☎622 23 30). If you've ever wanted to round out the "Nederpop" section of your record collection, this is the place to do it. A wonderful assortment of used and new records (€8,50-17,50); most are Dutch, and many of the American records are quite obscure. Also has an impressive collection of old comic books for sale, most in Dutch. An in-store turntable lets you listen before you buy. Open M-Sa, noon-5:30pm. No credit cards.

SMOKING ACCESSORIES

The Head Man, 1e Sweelinckstraat 7 (☎670 78 26). Full-service head shop in de Pijp with knowledgeable and helpful staff vending all manner of smoking devices: chillums, pipes, bongs, and more. Designs range from small and efficient to elaborate and gorgeous. Ask about the vaporizers—a new, increasingly popular way to take pot or hash (€45-273). Also a huge selection of stonerwear from the world's hemp-producing regions, including t-shirts (€4,50-6,80) and many different styles of rasta hats (€11,30-22,70). Open M-Sa 1-6pm.

TOYS AND ENTERTAINMENT

Juggle Store, Staalstraat 3 (☎420 19 80; shop@juggle-store.com; www.juggle-store.com). *The* store for absolutely all of your juggling needs. The expert staff has selected the best juggling products on the market (as well as crafted some great in-shop ones, as well). A free split-second juggling lesson is available on request. Open Tu-Sa noon-5pm

De Beestenwinkel, Staalstraat 11 (☎623 18 05), in the Jodenbuurt. This corner shop specializes in cool animal toys of every sort. But be warned: there's an especially cuddly collection of plush animals that you won't be able to resist. Open M noon-6pm, Tu-Sa 10am-6pm, Su noon-5pm.

Okado, 1e Sweelinckstraat 18 (☎664 59 78), in De Pijp. All manner of spirited knickknacks, including chess sets, toys, dolls, puppets, ceramics, and woodworks. All the goods in the store are designed or constructed by mentally handicapped folks, in conjunction with the Dutch charitable foundation AGO. Crafts range from cheap and inexpensive to elaborate and mid-range. Open M 1-5pm, Tu-Sa 10:30am-5pm.

VINTAGE CLOTHING

Laura Dols, Wolvenstraat 6-7 (☎624 99 66), in the Canal Ring West. Two shops across the street from one another vend fanciful men's and women's clothing, such as tutus and cowboy shirts. Open M-Sa 11am-6pm, Th 11am-9pm, Su 2-6pm. Credit cards accepted.

Ree-member, Ree-Straat 26-w (☎622 13 29), in the Canal Ring West. Well-chosen display of beautiful vintage clothes and '60s standards, like Lacoste polo shirts. Also sells shoes and bags. Great selection of coats. Open daily 11am-6pm. Credit cards accepted.

Wini, Haarlemmerstraat 29 (☎427 93 93), in the Shipping Quarter. Young hipsters (men and women) shop here for their cool, stylish clothing. Wini also offers a great selection of bags and shoes. Open daily 11am-6pm.

Zipper, Huidenstraat 7 (☎623 73 02), in the Canal Ring West, or Nieuwe Hoogstraat 8 (☎627 03 53), in the Jodenbuurt. Most renowned for their vast collection of vintage jeans, Zipper also stocks a sizable collection of young, '70s leaning (Adidas, cutout T-shirts, big belts) clothing for hipsters to fill the gaps in their wardrobes. Open M-Sa 11am-6pm, Th 11am-9pm, Su 1-5pm. Credit cards accepted.

SHOPPING BY LOCATION

OUDE ZIJD

Episode (169)	clothes
Oudemanhuispoort (168)	books
Body Manipulations (168)	body piercing
The Book Exchange (169)	books

NIEUWE ZIJD

Soul Food (173)	music
Dance Tracks (173)	music
Roots Music (173)	music
Hema (170)	department store
Magna Plaza (170)	department store
Athenaeum Boekhandel (168)	books
H&M (169)	clothes
Laundry Industry (170)	clothes
Japanese Winkeltje (172)	international
Tibet Winkel (172)	international
American Book Center (168)	books
Waterstone's (169)	books

CANAL RING WEST

Beadies (171)	gifts
Cine Qua Non (171)	gifts
Condomerie het Gulden Vlies (171)	gifts
In Oprichting (171)	gifts
Nic Nic (168)	antiques
ROB (171)	gifts
La Savonnerie (171)	gifts
De Witte Tanden Winkel (171)	gifts
Arcitectura and Natura (168)	books
Loerakker (170)	gallery
Mendo (170)	gallery
Amsterdam Smallest Gallery (170)	gallery
Cortina Paper (171)	gifts
Laura Dols (174)	vintage clothes
Ree-member (174)	vintage clothes
Zipper (174)	vintage clothes

CENTRAL CANAL RING

E.H. Ariens Kappers (170)	gallery
Frozen Fountain (170)	gallery
Maranon Hangmatten (172)	home goods
Concerto (173)	music

THE JORDAAN

Horeca Antiek Garage (167)	antiques
Back Beat Records (173)	music
A Space Oddity (168)	books
Wenterwereld Records (173)	music
Kitsch Kitchen (171)	gifts
English Bookshop (169)	books
Megazino (170)	clothes
De Plaatboef (173)	music

WESTERPARK AND OUDE WEST

Afric and World Music Shop (173)	music
Hera Kaarsen (171)	gifts
Little Miss Strange (170)	clothes

DE PIJP

De Beestenwinkel (174)	toys
The Head Man (174)	smoking
Okado (174)	toys
Santa Jet (168)	antiques
Itchy Bitchy (170)	clothes
Abracadabra (171)	gifts
De Kinderfeestwinkel (171)	gifts
De Emallekeizer (171)	home goods
Gallerie Casbah (172)	home goods
Morning Glory-yocha (172)	international
Betsy Palmer Shoes (169)	clothes

NIEUWMARKT

Biba (169)	clothes
De Hoed Van Tijn (169)	clothes
De Bijenkorf (170)	department store
Dun Yong (171)	international
Juggle Store (174)	toys

JODENBUURT AND THE PLANTAGE

Puck (170)	clothes
Zipper (174)	vintage clothes

SHIPPING QUARTER

The Purple Onion (172)	home goods
Wini (174)	vintage clothes

INSIDE:

Accommodations

Many of the accommodations in these listings are converted canal houses or equally old buildings, most of which have amazingly steep staircases. Unless otherwise indicated, these places do not have elevators, which means that you will likely have to lug your baggage up at least two imposing flights of stairs. That mammoth suitcase with wheels won't seem so convenient when you have to drag it up to the fourth floor. So, when packing, consider a backpack or two smaller pieces of luggage instead. Some of the shared bathrooms have antechambers so you can get dressed fresh from the shower. Shower shoes are also a good idea, and some who are squeamish about covering their bodies may also want to pack a big towel.

High season is usually considered the summer months and the few days before Christmas until New Year's Day.

Many of the smaller hotels in Amsterdam only accept credit cards with a hefty surcharge—between 4 and 6½%. This is not because the establishments are trying to cheat their customers or even because they are afraid that you'll cancel the charge. Credit companies make it difficult for accepting credit cards to be worth the while of small establishments, so they charge the same amount that the company charges them. We try to list all the hotels with surcharges, but even ones without extra charges will have incentives like free breakfast for customers to pay in cash.

For each neighborhood, hostels are listed first, and then hotels and inns. Some hotels are listed as hostels because they provide dorm-style accommodations.

UNDER €15 PER PERSON

Anna Youth Hostel (182)	NZ
Bob's Youth Hostel (182)	NZ
Budget Hotel Tamara (183)	NZ
The Shelter Jordan (190)	J
The Shelter (179)	RLD

UNDER €25 PER PERSON

City Hostel Stadsdoelen (179)	OZ
De Witte Tulip Hostel (180)	RLD
Nell's Inn Hostel (179)	OZ
Euphemia Budget Hotel (188)	CCR
Flying Pig Downtown (182)	NZ
Flying Pig Palace (193)	MV
Hans Brinker (189)	LP
Hotel Brian (184)	NZ
Hostel Cosmos (183)	NZ
International Budget Hostel (189)	LP
La Canna (183)	NZ
Tourist Inn (183)	NZ
Young Budget Hotel Kabul (180)	RLD

UNDER €40 PER PERSON

ANCO Hotel and Bar (182)	RLD
Bicycle Hotel (194)	DP
Budget Hotel Weber (189)	LP
Frisco Inn (179)	OZ
Hotel ABBA (192)	WO
Hotel Aspen (188)	CRW
Hotel Belga (187)	CRW
Hotel Brouwer (184)	CRW
Hotel Clemens (187)	CRW
Hotel de Lantaerne (189)	LP
Hotel Groenendael (184)	NZ
Hotel Heart of Amsterdam (181)	RLD
Hotel Hegra (188)	CRW
Hotel My Home (186)	SQ
Hotel Pax (187)	CRW
Hotel P.C. Hooft (194)	MV
Hotel Pension Kitty (195)	JP
Hotel Princess (192)	WO
Hotel Titus (190)	LP
Hotel van Onna (191)	J
Hotel Wynnobel (194)	MV
NJHC City Hostel Vondelpark (192)	MV
Old Nickel (181)	RLD
Old Quarter (180)	RLD
Radion Inn Youth Hostel (188)	CCR
Ramenas Hotel (186)	SQ
Westertoren Hotel (187)	CRW
Westropa Hotel (191)	WO

UNDER €50 PER PERSON

Belfort Hotel (192)	WO
De Oranje Tulip (184)	NZ
Frederic's Rent a Bike (186)	SQ
The Greenhouse Effect Hotel (181)	RLD
Hemp Hotel (187)	CCR
Hotel Asterisk (188)	CCR
Hotel Barbacan (195)	JP
Hotel Bema (193)	MV
Hotel The Crown (181)	RLD
Hotel Crystal (192)	WO
Hotel de la Haye (190)	LP
Hotel De Stadhouder (194)	DP
Hotel Jupiter (192)	WO
Hotel Mevlana (185)	NZ
Hotel Museumzicht (194)	MV
Hotel Royal Taste (181)	RLD
International Student Center (187)	CRW
Quentin Hotel (189)	LP

OVER €50 PER PERSON

Apple Inn Hotel (194)	MV
City Hotel (190)	RP
The Golden Bear (188)	CCR
Hotel Acacia (191)	J
Hotel Bellington (193)	MV
Hotel La Boheme (190)	LP
Hotel Continental (185)	NZ
Hotel de Filosoof (186)	WO
Hotel Europa 92 (193)	MV
Hotel Fantasia (195)	JP
Hotel Hoksbergen (185)	CRW
Hotel International (182)	RLD
Hotel Kap (188)	CCR
Hotel Monopole (190)	RP
Hotel Nova (185)	NZ
Hotel Rokin (184)	NZ
Hotel Sander (194)	MV
Hotel Singel (185)	CRW
Hotel Winston (180)	RLD
Hotel Vijaya (181)	RLD
Nadia Hotel (187)	CRW
Stablemaster Hotel (182)	OZ
Wiechmann Hotel (187)	CRW

NEIGHBORHOOD LEGEND

OZ=Oude Zijd RLD=Red Light District
NZ=Nieuwe Zijd
CCR=Canal Ring CRW=Canal Ring West
RP=Rembrandtplein LP=Leidseplein
MV=Museumplein&Vondelpark DP=De Pijp
SQ=Shipping Quarter J=Jordaan
WO=Westerpark&Oude West
JP =Jodenbuurt and the Plantage

OUDE ZIJD

see maps pp. 330-331

HOSTELS

City Hostel Stadsdoelen, Kloveniersburgwal 97 (☎624 68 32; www.hostelbooking.com; www.njhc.org). Take tram #4, 9, 16, 20, 24, or 25 to Muntplein. From Muntplein, proceed down Nieuwe Doelenstraat (which is just off of Muntplein); Kloveniersburgwal will be on your right over the bridge. Located in a quieter corner of central Amsterdam, the slightly smaller sister to the Vondelpark hostel sleeps 170 and provides clean, drug-free lodgings for very reasonable prices. Accommodations are very plain, but get the job done. Breakfast, lockers, and linen included. Reception 7am-1am. Internet (€1/12min.) and kitchen facilities. Pool table and bar (happy hour 9-10pm, when beer is €1/glass). Bike rental for €5.70/day. Book through website. Steep locker deposit of €20. 8-20 bed dorms for €20,65 per person; €2,50 discount with HI membership. MC/V. ❶

Nelly's Hostel, Warmoesstraat 115/117 (☎638 01 25; nellys@xs4all.nl). From Centraal Station, go south on Damrak, turn right on Brugsteeg, and then right on Warmoesstraat; Nelly's is 2 blocks on the left. Cozy hostel above an Irish pub (see p. 179) sleeps 46 in clean, mixed-sex, dorm-style accommodations. Guests get to drink after hours in the bar. Breakfast and linens included. Locker deposit €10. Reception 24hr.Dorms €20 from Su-Th, €25 F-Sa. Cash only. ❶

HOTEL

Frisco Inn, Beursstraat 5 (☎620 16 10). From Centraal Station, go south on Damrak, then left at Brugsteeg, and take the next right onto Beursstraat; it's the 2nd building on your left. On one of the quietest streets in the Oude Zijd, this small, centrally-located hotel behind the Beurs van Berlage rents 28 beds in solid, dependable rooms. Downstairs bar sells beer (€1,80) to guests only. All rooms renovated at the end of 2002 and now include bathroom and TV.Smoking allowed provided you open the windows. 24hr. reception. No curfew. Doubles, triples, a quads available, €30-35 per person. ❷

1001 Nights at Greenhouse Effect

Greenhouse Effect Jungle Book Room

Old Nickel

RED LIGHT DISTRICT

see maps pp. 330-331

HOSTEL

The Shelter, Barndesteeg 21 (☎625 32 30; city@shelter.nl; www.shelter.nl), off the Nieuwmarkt (Metro: Nieuwmarkt). Finding virtue amid the red

the BIG $plurge

hotel winston

Warmoesstraat 125 From Centraal Station, go down Damrak 2 blocks, then left on Brugsteeg and right when you hit Warmoesstr.; the Winston will be 2 blocks down on the left. (☎623 13 80; fax 639 23 08; winston@winston.nl; www.winston.nl).

The reasonably-priced rooms keep this hotel from being a real "splurge"—the indulgence is to be surrounded by art even while you sleep. Winston features designer digs devoted to a theme of contemporary art. Murals splash across the halls and rooms double as installations by local artists (though the particularly creatively decorated ones cost about €3-12 more). Slick staff can fill you in on the best of nearby nightlife, though you might just want to chill in the stylish, minimalist bar (for guests only, open 9am-3am), or the hotel's **Club Winston,** both of which are located on the premises. Book well in advance, especially if you're intent on a themed room. Breakfast included. Singles €57-61 (about €8 more for a private bathroom); doubles €71-80 (about €10 more for private bathroom). ❸

lights, travelers find incredibly clean rooms and a friendly staff at this hostel. Religious slogans abound, but like its cohort in the Jordaan, everyone is made to feel welcome; the cozy courtyard provides an oasis from the surrounding debauchery. Breakfast included. No drugs; smoking permitted only in hallways. Locker deposit €5. Linens included, towels available to rent, €1. Curfew Su-Th midnight, F-Sa 1am. Dorms €13-16,50 per person, depending on season. MC/V with 5% surcharge. ❶

Young Budget Hotel Kabul, Warmoesstraat 38-42 (☎623 7158 or 623 7059; fax 620 08 69; kabulhotel@hotmail.com), just down Warmoesstraat and about 5min. from Centraal Station. The usual hostel experience awaits at the inexplicably named Kabul, where 4-16 person dorms have comfortable enough beds in carpeted, relatively spacious rooms. Breakfast and sheets included. Internet downstairs, €1 for 17 min. No curfew. Max. stay 1 week. €5 key deposit. €21-29 per person, depending on day of the week and season. V/MC/Amex. ❶

De Witte Tulp Hostel, Warmoesstraat 87 (☎625 59 74; fax 422 0885). All are welcome at the Amsterdam Visitors Club, where you'll find low-key, basic budget digs in a sociable, youthful environment. Downstairs pub serves drinks (beer €4,50 a pint) and snacks, and hotel guests receive a 10% discount and 1/2 off breakfast. No smoking in rooms. Sheets included. Rooms available include singles and up to 10-person dorm rooms; €20-35 per person (€15 for a dorm in the low season). AmEx/MC/V. ❶

HOTELS

The Red Light District isn't wanting for hotels, but be advised that accommodations here aren't any cheaper than the rest of the city, are usually booked solid during the summer months, and while it may initially seem like a good idea to shack up across the street from a brothel, after a while the proximity to the pulsing heart of the Red Light District may become a little too close for comfort.

Old Quarter, Warmoesstraat 20-22 (☎626 64 29; info@oldquarter.a2000.nl). Walking away from the Station, make a left onto Prins Hendrikskade, and bear right at Nieuwbrigstg. Warmoesstr. is the first right. The smaller rooms here aren't bad, and the nicest are extremely good for the money. All rooms are quite modern and include TV and phone; some have a strikingly good view of the canal. Downstairs *bruine cafe* makes a great place to watch the latest football match (kitchen open 12pm-10pm). Also swing by for the Th night jazz jam sessions, and rock and funk acts on F and Sa. 24-hr. reception. Breakfast included. Singles from €35; doubles from €60. Elevator makes hotel wheelchair accessible. ❷

The Greenhouse Effect Hotel, Warmoesstraat 55 (☎624 49 74; fax 427 79 06; www.the-greenhouse-effect.com). Reasonably priced theme rooms (including the ubiquitous Arabian Nights) await you. Located 5min. from Centraal Station. Hotel guests are treated to an all-day Happy Hour at the friendly downstairs bar, pints of beer €2,30. Look at the website for discounts. Singles €50 (€60 with bathroom); doubles with bath €85; triples with bath €100; apartments to 2-4 people from €110-155. AmEx/MC/V. ❸

Hotel Royal Taste, Oudezijds Achterburgwal 47 (☎623 24 78; fax 623 44 37; www.hotelroyaltaste.com). Smack in the middle of the Red Light District, Royal Taste provides clean, comfortable accommodations at reasonable prices. The bar downstairs features a big-screen TV for special events. Rooms with bath, fridge, and television. Breakfast included. Single €45; double, triples, quads all €40 per person. AmEx/MC/V. ❷

Hotel The Crown, Oudezijds Voorburgwal 21 (☎626 96 64; info@hotelthecrown.com; www.hotelthecrown.com). This British-owned hotel provides clean, handsome digs located in the picturesque end of the Red Light District. Bar open until 5am, with pool table and dart board (beer €3,50/pint). Self-described as "smoker-friendly." Rooms from single to 6-person, with shower but hall toilet, €50 per person (a few rooms have hall showers and are slightly less expensive). Credit card required for reservation confirmation, but pay with cash only. ❷

Old Nickel, Nieuwebrugsteeg 11 (☎624 19 12). From Centraal, turn left onto Prins Hendrikskade and then bear right onto Nieuwebrugstg. In a quiet corner of the Red Light District, this hotel with a downstairs bar offers a peaceful and inexpensive place to spend the night. Shared facilities are very high-end. Breakfast included. Singles, doubles, triples, and quads, all from €35 per person. AmEx/MC/V. ❷

Hotel Vijaya, Oudezijds Voorburgwal 44 (☎626 94 06 or 638 01 02; fax 620 52 77; www.hotelvijaya.com, info@hotelvijaya.com). Very clean and extremely adequate rooms on the fringe of the pulsing Red Light District. Breakfast is included. Neighboring restaurant specializes in tandoori cuisine. Rooms come with TV and telephone reception (to place outgoing calls you have to use the phone downstairs); all with private bathroom. Singles €70, doubles €92, triples €125, quads €150; all about €10 cheaper in the off-season.❹

Hotel Heart of Amsterdam, Oudezijds Achterburgwal 118-120 (☎624 88 79; fax 638 94 97; www.hotelheartofamsterdam.nl). Clean rooms with television, toilet, shower, phone, and safe, all on one of the busiest strips in the Red Light District. Breakfast included. 28 rooms, from singles to 8-person suites, from €31-50 per person. AmEx/MC/V. ❷

Conveniently Located

Boat Where the Cat People Live

Antique Canalhouse

LGB ▼
AMSTERDAM

Hotels for Men

ANCO Hotel and Bar, Oudezijds Voorburgwal 55 (☎624 11 26; fax 620 52 65; info@ancohotel.com), in the Red Light District. This male-only hotel offers plenty of amenities (including rooms with canal views, 24hr. access, and free cable TV) and is a brisk 5min. walk from the leather district. A downstairs bar offers a good springboard to a wild evening of clubbing (open 9am-10pm). Breakfast is included. 3- to 4-person dorms €34-40; singles €52-55; doubles €75-80, with private bathroom and minibar €110-135. ❷

Stablemaster Hotel, Warmoesstraat 23 (☎625 01 48, fax 624 87 47; a.g.jones@speed.a2000.nl, in the Oude Zijd. Situated above a hard-core leather bar of the same name (see p. 141), the rooms in this gay hotel include radio, fridge, phone, and lots of magazines about the local queer scene. Well-kept hall baths and good security. Be prepared to shell out €50 for the key deposit. Men only. Singles €60; doubles €95; triples €115. Apartments for long-term rental €135 per night; women allowed.). ❸

Hotel Internationaal, Warmoesstraat 1-3 (☎624 55 20; www.hotelinternationaal.com, info@hotelinternationaal.com). Same directions as Hotel Old Quarter. Smoke-filled downstairs bar dating from the 1700s has its charm; rooms themselves are small but very clean. Breakfast available for €5. Twin €75 (double with private bathroom €92,50); triple with shared facilities €100. ❹

NIEUWE ZIJD

see maps pp. 330-331

HOSTELS

While some of these accommodations call themselves inns or hotels, all have dorm-style rooms available for guests.

Anna Youth Hostel, Spuistraat 6 (see sidebar, p. 184). ❶

Flying Pig Downtown, Nieuwendijk 100 (☎420 68 22; downtown@flyingpig.nl; www.flyingpig.nl). From the main entrance of Centraal Station, walk towards Damrak. Pass the Victoria Hotel and take the first alley on your right. At the end of that alley, you'll find Nieuwendijk. Helpful and professional staff as well as a knockout location make the Flying Pig Downtown a perennial favorite among backpackers. The hostel caters to a younger crowd, mostly 18- to 35-years-old. Dorms are spacious, and there is also a monster chill-out space/bar in the front end of the building where you can curl up and read, smoke, or watch the parade go by on the busy avenue outside; the bar is open until 4am M-F (5am on weekends). Free Internet. Sheets provided. Key deposit, which includes a locker, €10. Breakfast included; there is also a kitchen in which you can make your own meals. 4- to 6-bed dorms €25; 8- to 10-bed dorms €22; 16- to 22-bed dorms €19; singles and twins €72. ISIC cardholders receive a free beer at the bar in summer and a 5% discount in winter. AmEx/MC/V. ❶

Bob's Youth Hostel, Nieuwezijds Voorburgwal 92 (☎623 00 63), from Centraal Station, turn right on the main street and left at Martelaarsgracht, continuing as it becomes Nieuwezijds Voorburgwal. Well-known by European backpackers, Bob's provides the bare necessities to its guests, no frills attached. The hostel's young clientele relax in the underground reception area, the only place where drugs are permitted. With giant dorm rooms, this is a good spot for lone travelers looking to make friends with fellow wanderers. Breakfast included. Lockers and luggage storage available free of charge. Linens provided, but bring a towel. Key deposit is €10 for a room key, €10 extra for a locker key. 2-night min. stay on weekends, 7-day max. stay. Reception 8am-3am. No lockout or curfew. No reservations, so arrive before 10am to stand a chance of getting a room. Dorms €17; doubles €70, additional person €10. ❶

La Canna, Nieuwendijk 121-125 (☎428 44 82; www.lacanna.nl). From Centraal, take the main street to the right, head left on Martelaarsgracht and then right on Nieuwendijk. This centrally located party multiplex (see **Only In Amsterdam,** p. 126) also rents rooms, convenient for those looking for less distance to cover on that long stumble home at the end of the night; a good place to crash if you're just looking for a clean bed to sleep in at night. Check-in is in the smartshop. Free lockers (bring your own lock). No curfew. 24hr. security. Coed dorms €18; singles with continental breakfast €53, with English breakfast €57; with bath €63, €67; doubles €71, €79; triples €109, €121; quads €132, €148; larger room €162 and €178 for 4 and €5 per each additional person above that. ❶

Tourist Inn, Spuistraat 52 (☎421 58 41; fax 427 09 00; sales@tourist-in.nl; www.tourist-inn.nl). From Centraal, turn right at the main street, left at Martelaarsgracht. A couple blocks ahead, keep right onto Spuistraat. A great value for backpackers and small families, the inn is exceptionally clean, friendly, and comfortable. Breakfast included. Lockers €30 deposit plus €1,20 per day. Laundry facilities around the corner; linens and a towel are included. Reception 24hr. No lockout or curfew. Walk-ins are welcome, but reservations are strongly advised, particularly in the summer season. Prices vary by season. Dorms €25-35; doubles €65-95; triples €75-120; quads €100-140; quints €125-160; six-person room €150-180. AmEx/MC/V. ❶

Hostel Cosmos, Nieuwe Nieuwestraat 17 (☎625 24 38; www.hostelcosmos.com; info@hostelcosmos.com), between Nieuwendijk and Nieuwezijds Voorburgwal, a few blocks north of Dam Sq. This well-located hostel offers 30 beds in 6 rooms. The recently renovated 1st and 2nd floors will please any weary traveler, with their clean and comfy hallways and rooms. All rooms have TV with VCR. Reception 24hr. Online reservations. Prices vary by season. Dorms €22-31; doubles €70-84; quads €112-140; 6- or 8-person room €176-208. Cash only. ❷

Budget Hotel Tamara, Nieuwezijds Voorburgwal 144 (☎624 24 84). Friendly Irish staff welcomes backpackers to Amsterdam in true budget style, with respect to both the cost and the lodgings. Diminutive rooms get the job done—they're clean and sanitary, but some are rundown with writing on the walls. Guests get a free drink at the Blarney Stone Pub (see **Nightlife,** p. 179). No breakfast but free tea and coffee in the morning. Reception 24hr. Internet access €2,50 for 30min. Dorms €17,50, €25 on weekends; singles €35, €40; doubles €50, €60; triples €75, €90; quads €80, €120. Cash only. ❶

Steep Staircase Within

Homey Jordaan

Kitchen Window

the hidden deal

Anna Youth Hostel

This hostel caters to the quiet, independent traveler. Unlike many of the city's crowded hostels, there are no drugs permitted. The spacious dorms, pristine decor, and relaxing atmosphere are what make **Anna Youth Hostel** Spuistraat 6, by far the most beautiful hostel in the city. The quiet ambiance is surprising given the hostel's central location in the Nieuwe Zijd. Even more surprising are the prices–some of the lowest around for dorms. Walk-ins welcome, though reservations are recommended. 2-night min. stay on weekends.

(☎620 11 55. Reception 8am-1pm, 5pm through the night. Towel, linens, and safe all provided. Dorms €16-17; doubles with bath €75 during the week, €80 during the weekend. Cash only. Closed Jan. and Feb.) ❶

HOTELS

Hotel Brouwer, Singel 83 (☎624 63 58; fax 520 62 64; akita@hotelbrouwer.nl; www.hotelbrouwer.nl). From Centraal Station, cross the water, turn right onto Prins Hendrikkade and left onto Singel. Small hotel run by the same family for 3 generations. Eight gorgeously restored rooms, each with private bathroom, canal view, and named for a Dutch painter. Choose from Vermeer, Van Gogh, Mondrian, and Escher, among others. Breakfast included. No smoking in the rooms. Tiny elevator. Singles €45; doubles €80; doubles for single use (or vice versa) €65. Cash only. ❷

De Oranje Tulp, Damrak 32 (☎428 16 18; fax 428 60 44; reservations@oranje-tulp-hotel.a200.nl; http://people.a2000.nl/oranje00). Located 3min. from Centraal, down the main street heading straight out of the station and hidden above a restaurant. Great location and super value for slick, well-appointed rooms, all of which include phone and TV, some of which look onto the Damrak action. Clean and modern throughout. Guests get special deal on dinner in downstairs restaurant. Online reservations accepted. Breakfast included. Singles €45-60; doubles €75-110; triples €80-110; quads €80-120; quints €80-140. AmEx/DC/MC/V. ❷

Hotel Groenendael, Nieuwendijk 15 (☎624 48 22; HotelGroenendael@europe.com; www.hotelgroenendael.com). Turn right on the main street out of the station, then go left at Martelaarsgracht and then right on Nieuwendijk. Friendly, mellow hotel located right by Centraal Station; one of the best deals in the city. Rooms are well-lit and decorated with bright, cheerful colors; some have balconies. Plenty of clean bathrooms and showers, mostly located off shared hallways. Breakfast included (8:30-10am); served in a lounge decorated with international knickknacks. Free lockers. Key deposit €5. Singles €32; doubles €50, with shower €55; triples €75. Cash only. ❷

Hotel Rokin, Rokin 73 (☎626 74 56; reception@rokinhotel.com; www.rokinhotel.com). A tad upscale, but well worth the extra cash. Well-located just a few blocks south from Dam Sq. in a house that conspicuously leans forward over the street. Clean, classy digs include TV and VCR as well as continental breakfast. Despite budget rates, the place upholds a comfortable and even elegant ambience throughout. Prices vary by season. Singles €50-60; doubles €60-75; triples €110-145; quads €140-185. 6-person rooms €195-255 per night. AmEx/MC/V. ❸

Hotel Brian, Singel 69 (☎624 46 61). From Centraal Station, turn right at the Victoria Hotel, then turn left onto Singel. Basic communal digs in a friendly, very low-key atmosphere with a liberal drug policy. The rooms are clean with an effort made at decoration. Picturesque canalside locations put you near the action in Nieuwendijk, the Shipping Quarter, and

Spui. Breakfast included. Key deposit €10. Reception 8am-11pm. Bed in a 2-, 3-, or 4-person room €27. ❶

Hotel Nova, Nieuwezijds Voorburgwal 276 (☎623 00 66; novahotel@wxs.nl; www.bookings.nl/hotels/nova). Make sure to get good directions to your room at reception for this 60-room labyrinth. However once you finally get there, you'll be quite pleased. Exceptionally large, clean accommodations a stone's throw from the city center await, with a full plate of amenities: all rooms come with bathroom, TV, phone, and refrigerator. Breakfast included. Singles €100, €75 in the low season; doubles €140, €93; triples €170, €113; quads €198, €140. AmEx/MC/V. ❺

Hotel Continental, Damrak 40-41 (☎622 33 63; info@hotelcontinental.nl; www.hotelcontinental.nl). Damrak location puts you right near the action, 2min. straight ahead from Centraal Station. More upscale than the standard budget accommodation, with small but comfy rooms, each with TV and phone. Continental breakfast served 7:30-10am, €5. Reception 24hr. Singles weekday €65, weekend €80; doubles €90, €115, with bath €105, €135. AmEx/MC/V with 5% surcharge. ❸

Hotel Hoksbergen, Singel 301 (☎626 60 43; fax 638 34 79; info@hotelhoksbergen.nl; www.hotelhoksbergen.nl). Tram 1, 2, or 5 to Spui. On the east side of the Singel canal, between Rosmarijnsteeg and Paleisstraat. This quaint, 300-year-old canal house offers its patrons a shower, toilet, phone, and television in every room. And it's clean. Singles €76-90; doubles €90-104; triples €104-130; apartments (4-6 persons) €150-200. AmEx/MC/V. ❹

Hotel Singel, Singel 15 (☎626 31 08; fax 620 37 77) A classy, simple, self-advertised 3-star hotel, this canal house on the Singel includes breakfast with a smile and perhaps a waft of tobacco smoke. The pleasant rooms and clean design help make it a decent value. Singles €90; doubles €135; triples €165. AmEx/D/MC/V. ❹

Hotel Mevlana, Nieuwezijds Voorburgwal 160 (☎627 93 61; fax 627 21 15), a few blocks north of Dam. Perhaps not the most luxurious accommodation around, but with phones in every room and reasonable prices in this central location. Above a good Indonesian eatery. Singles €45, weekends €50; doubles €70, €80; triples €105, €120. Cash only. ❷

SCHEEPVAARTBUURT (THE SHIPPING QUARTER)

see map p. 328-329

Northwest of the center of Amsterdam, the Shipping Quarter is less touristy than most of the other neighborhoods. Nevertheless, budget options for accommodations are available.

Hotel Suite Home

Porthole Windows

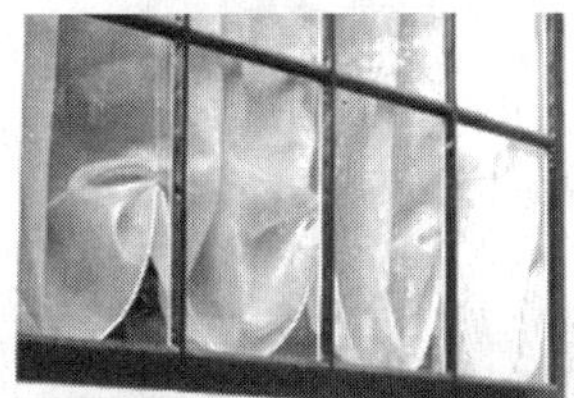

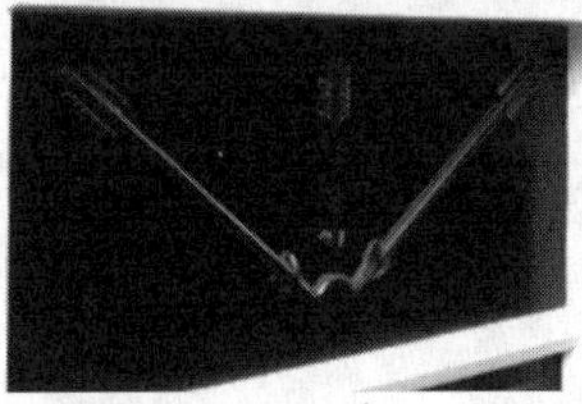
Ironwork Arrow

the BIG $plurge

Hotel de Filosoof

By far the best hotel in the Oud West, the small, creative **Hotel de Filosoof** would surely cost €50 more if it were closer to the center of the city. Wittgenstein, Spinoza, Aristotle—whether you've read their works or just like to name-drop, you'll feel the presence of the great philosophers of the world here. The 38 rooms each have a philosophical or "cultural" theme. Stay in a room devoted to the Greek classics or try Eastern philosophy in the "zen" room.

All rooms with bath, phone, and TV. Breakfast included. Bar in lobby. Reception 24hr. Call 2-3 weeks in advance for July and Aug.

(Anna Vondelstraat 6. Tram #1 or 6 to Jan Pieter Heijestr.; walk along Overtoom toward Leidsepl., then turn right. ☎683 30 13; fax 685 37 50; reservations@hotelfilosoof.nl; www.hotelfilosoof.nl. Singles €108-112; doubles €135; triples €170; slightly less expensive in the off season. AmEx/MC/V. ❹*)*

HOTELS

Ramenas Hotel, Haarlemmerdijk 61 (☎624 69 60 30; fax 420 22 61; www.amsterdamhotels.com). Walk from Centraal Station along Nieuwendijk as it turns into Haarlemmerstraat and then Haarlemmerdijk. Above an above-average cafe marked by its plush green, velvet upholstery, the Ramenas rents ascetic rooms, but they get the job done. It's far from luxurious, but the hall bathrooms are exceptionally clean and the rooms are plenty comfortable. Breakfast included. Doubles, triples, and quints €27,50 per person; with private bathroom €34. Cash only. ❶

Frederic Rent a Bike, Brouwersgracht 78 (☎624 55 09; www.frederic.nl). In addition to bikes, Frederic also rents rooms, some of which you'll find in the back of his rental shop, while the rest are located throughout the city in varying locations and in all different price ranges, from budget digs to penthouse luxury. The Brouwersgracht location, for example, includes a single and 2 doubles, 1 with a shared bath, 1 with a private bath, each named after a different painter (Chagall, Picasso, or Matisse). Amenities vary with the rooms—some have free wet bar, drinks, rolling papers, and games—which are all clean and creatively decorated. Visit Frederic's website for virtual tours of the accommodations, reservations, and tons of information and links about Amsterdam. Because of the wide variety of rooms, prices vary. Singles €50-60; doubles €60-70; apartments available for short-term stays as well. Cash only, but credit card required for reservation. ❸

Hotel My Home, Harlemmerstraat 82 (☎624 23 20; fax 427 94 52; info@hotelmyhome.a2000.nl; www.amsterdambudgethotel.com). From Centraal Station, head south on Nieuwezijds Voorburgwal, turn right on Nieuwendijk, and continue across the Singelgracht; it will be 1 block on your left. Safe and basically clean budget digs in a low-frill environment. Hall bathrooms are clean and relatively larger. Free continental breakfast includes all the coffee you can chug to jump-start your day. Friendly, relaxed staff can provide the inside scoop on the city scene. Sheets and towels provided. No curfew. Online reservations available. 4- to 5-person dorms €25; doubles €57, €63 with shower; triples and quads €28 per person. AmEx/MC/V. ❶

CANAL RING WEST

see maps pp. 328-329

The atmosphere in the Canal Ring West reflects its geographic placement in the city. Accommodations in the area strike a balance between residential and legendary Amsterdam, both in terms of their surroundings and their decorations.

Hotel Clemens, Raadhuisstraat 39 (☎624 60 89; fax 626 96 58; info@clemenshotel.nl; www.clemenshotel.nl). Tram 13, 17, or 20 to Westermarkt. A true gem with elegant deluxe and budget rooms, each of which have been recently renovated in a different color scheme. Phone, fridge, TV, Internet connection, safe, and hairdryer in all rooms. Deluxe rooms have more space and private bath. Breakfast €7. Key deposit €20. Book well in advance. Min. stay of 3 nights during weekend. Rental laptops at reception. Singles €55; budget doubles €70-75; deluxe €110; budget triples with bath and toilet €125; deluxe €150. Cash only for budget rooms; cash or credit for deluxe rooms. ❷

Wiechmann Hotel, Prinsengracht 328-332 (☎626 33 21; fax 626 89 62; info@hotelwiechmann.nl; www.hotelwiechmann.nl). Tram #1, 2, or 5 to Prinsengracht; turn right and walk along the left side of the canal. Three restored canal houses run by an easygoing couple. Sizeable rooms, many with canal views. Breakfast included. Key deposit €20. Min. stay 2 nights on weekends. All rooms with bath. Single €70-90; double with bathtub €125-135; triples and quads €170-230. MC/V accepted for deluxe rooms only. ❸

Westertoren Hotel, Raadhuisstraat 35b (☎624 46 39). Tram #13, 17, or 20 to Westermarkt. Perfect for groups, as this hotel has a few rooms that sleep up to 6 persons. Clean rooms and friendly staff. Not all rooms have shower and toilet. Breakfast included. Tea and coffee in room. 3 night min. weekend stay. Rooms in summer €40-50; in winter €30-45. Credit cards accepted; pay on arrival. ❷

Hotel Belga, Hartenstraat 8 (☎624 90 80; fax 623 68 62; hotelbelga@zonnet.nl; reserve through www.hotelnet.nl). Tram #1, 2, or 5 to Dam. Walk away from the palace on Raadhuisstraat. Turn left at Herengracht and take the 1st right on Hartenstraat. Rooms are sunny if bland, all with TV, phone, and safe. Most rooms with shower and toilet. Breakfast included. 2-night min. stay during summer weekends. Singles €41-57; doubles €62-84 with bath €77,50-118; triples €95-140,50; quads €134-188,50; quints €147-204. MC/V. ❷

Hotel Pax, Raadhuisstraat 37 (☎624 97 35). Tram #13, 17, or 20 to Westermarkt. A smidgen less inviting than its neighbors on Raahuisstraat, with creaky floors and dark, mirrored walls. Budget hotel with cot beds and shared facilities. Run by 2 friendly brothers. Each room has sink and TV. Singles in June-Aug €40, in Sept-May €25; doubles €60,32; triples €69,55; quads €80,69. Credit cards accepted with 3.5% surcharge. ❷

the hidden deal

Hemp Hotel and Cafe

The **Hemp Hotel** ❸, Frederiksplein 15, has only 5 rooms, but they're all lovingly done up with colorful, elaborate decor to celebrate all 5 of the world's major hemp-producing regions: India, Tibet, Afghanistan, Morocco and the Caribbean. Almost everything is made of hemp—the bedclothes, the curtains, and even the soap. Friendly staff has made a career out of publicizing the useful side of hemp. Clean hall baths, and all rooms have TV, and 2 have a balcony. Single €50, doubles €70, or €65 with shared shower.

The **Hemp Bar** is downstairs from the hotel is a quiet, mellow spot popular with English-speaking expats. You can imbibe all manner of booze, but hemp beer is the house speciality (€2 other beers €1,70-2,50, juice €1,40). Be warned, however; hemp brew won't get you high, because it has no THC. However, if you want to smoke cannabis or hash, you're welcome and they provide pipes and bongs for use, though they don't sell it. It's also open a few hours later than most Dutch bars, and is ideal for a mellow nightcap. Open Su-Th 4pm-3am, F-Sa 4pm-4am. V.

Hotel Hegra, Herengracht 269 (☎623 78 77; fax 623 81 59). From Centraal Station, tram #1, 2 or 5 to the Dam. Follow Raadhuisstraat away from the back of the palace. Cross the first canal (Singel) and turn left. Go right on Romeinsarmsteeg and then right at Herengracht. Small family hotel on a lovely canal. Basic rooms, most with shower and no toilet. Breakfast included. Singles €40; doubles €60, with shower €75, with bath €60. Credit cards accepted. ❷

Hotel Aspen, Raadhuisstraat 31 (☎626 67 14; fax 620 08 66; hotelaspen@planet.nl; www.hotelaspen.nl). Tram #13, 17, or 20 to Westermarkt. Friendly staff and spartan lodgings. All rooms have shower and toilet, except for the singles and 1 small double. No breakfast. Reserve through email to ensure availability. Singles €35; doubles €44-65; triples €75-80; quads €92. Cash only. ❷

CENTRAL CANAL RING

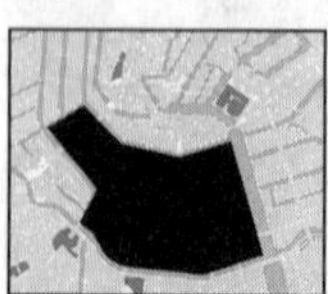

see maps pp. 324-325

HOTELS

Hemp Hotel, Frederiksplein 15 (☎625 44 25; www.hemp-hotel.com; mila@hemp-hotel.com). See sidebar, p. 187.

Euphemia Budget Hotel, Fokke Simonszstraat 1-9 (☎622 90 45; info@euphemiahotel.nl; www.euphemiahotel.com), 10min. from Rembrandtplein or Leidseplein. Take tram #16, 24, or 25 to Weteringcircuit, backtrack on Vijzelstraat for about 200m, and turn right on Fokke Simonszstraat. Welcoming, well-priced, quiet budget digs housed in a former monastery. Rooms are basic but clean and bright, and recent renovations lend a colorful feel throughout. Gay friendly. Excellent breakfast €5. Internet use €1. Reception 8am-11pm. Doubles, triples, or mixed dorms of 4 people €23-55 per person depending on season, availability, and type of accommodation. Discounts for reservations made on their website. AmEx/MC/V with 5% surcharge. ❶

The Golden Bear, Kerkstraat 37 (☎624 47 85; fax 627 01 64; www.goldenbear.nl; hotel@goldenbear.nl). Take tram #1, 2 or 5 to Prinsengracht, backtrack one block to Kerkstraat and turn left. Opened in 1948, the Golden Bear, in the Leidseplein, may be the oldest openly gay hotel in the world. It's certainly the oldest one in Amsterdam. Mainly male couples frequent the digs, though lesbians are welcome as well. All rooms include phone, safe, and color cable TV (some include VCRs as well). Breakfast included, and served until luxuriously late (8:30am-noon) Basic single from €50, basic double from €61 (with bath, €102,27). ❸

Hotel Kap, Den Texstraat 5b (☎624 59 08; fax 627 12 89; info@kaphotel.nl; www.kaphotel.nl). Tram #16, 24, or 25 to Weteringcircuit. Go left down Weteringschans, then right at 2e Weteringplantsoen, and left at Den Texstraat. Hotel Kap will be on your left. Very personable staff rents clean, comfortable rooms on a quiet, residential street. Breakfast served in lovely lounge, with garden at the back (8-10:30am). Reception 8am-10:30pm. Check-out 11am. TV. Depending on space and facilities, singles €57; double €86-109, triples €109-118, quad €136 AmEx/MC/V with 5% surcharge. ❸

Hotel Asterisk, Den Texstraat 14-16 (☎626 23 96 or 624 17 68; fax 638 27 90; hotelasterisk@chello.nl; www.asteriskhotel.nl). Tram #16, 24, or 25 to Weteringcircuit, turn left at the roundabout, and then proceed to Den Texstraat where the hotel will be on the right. Attractive, quiet hotel with a sense of peace and order. 40 clean, bright rooms include cable TV, phone, and safe. Helpful, personable staff can provide all manner of insight on activities in and around Amsterdam. Elevator in main building. Singles €44, with shower or toilet €48, with both €84; doubles €65, with facilities from €115-125; triples €130-136; quads €150. MC/V with 4% surcharge; free breakfast for those who pay in cash. ❷

Radion Inn Youth Hostel, Utrechtsedwarsstraat 79 (☎625 03 45; fax 330 54 47; utd79@hotmail.com; www.radioinn.nl). Take tram #4 and exit at Prinsengracht; walk south along Utrechtsestraat for a block and turn left on Utrechtsedwarsstraat; the hotel will be the 3rd building on your left. Somewhere between a 70s garage sale and a budget hotel. Housed in an old radio store, the homey lobby is filled with the defunct gadgets and 2 cats. No two of the 8 rooms are the same; fake-fur stoles, defunct computers strewn with graffiti, and disassembled mannequins lend an artsy, retro feel. TV and sink in each room, but all rooms have hall toilet and shower, which are adequately clean. Kitchen available for use 24hr. Singles in high season €45, in low season €35; doubles €58, €52; triples €69, 60. Cash only. ❷

LEIDSEPLEIN

see map p. 325

HOSTEL

International Budget Hostel, Leidsegracht 76-1 (☎624 27 84; fax 626 18 39; info@internationalbudgethostel.com; www.internationalbudgethostel.com). Tram #1, 2, or 5 to Prinsengracht, turn right and walk along Prinsengracht to Leidsegracht. Pretty second floor flower-box exterior gives way to cramped rooms with spare white walls and wooden ceiling beams inside. Sister hostel of Euphemia Hotel (see p. 188) has 12 quads and 2 twins near the Leidseplein; some rooms have lovely canal views. Breakfast €2-4. Min. 2-night stay on summer weekends. Beds in a quad €24-27 per person depending on season. Credit cards with 5% surcharge. ❶

Hans Brinker Hotel, Kerkstraat 136 (☎622 06 87; www.hansbrinker.com; fax 638 20 66). Take tram #1, 2, or 5 from Centraal Station, get off at Kerkstraat, and it's 1 block down on the left. Really like a hostel with cheap, bunk bed rooms and self-service sheets. This huge hotel has spartan, clean rooms, all with baths. Bar (for guests only) serves really cheap drinks (pint €2,75; pitcher €10; vodka and Red Bull €6 will get you going; Happy Hour 5-6pm gets you 2 for 1 beer, wine or soft drink; open 5pm-3am). All-you-can-eat breakfast buffet included (7:30-10am). Key deposit €5; safe €0,50. Reception 24hr. No visitors. 6-12 person dorms (single-sex and mixed) €21; singles €52; doubles €58-75; triples €90, quads €96; quints €120. AmEx/MC/V. ❶

HOTELS

Quentin Hotel, Leidsekade 89 (☎626 21 87; fax 622 01 21). The Quentin proves that you don't have to sacrifice style to get budget accommodations; these digs are jazzy and hip, in a great canalside setting. Hallway walls are plastered with vintage music posters, and each room bears its own distinctive motif and has cable TV. Continental breakfast served but not included in room price. Recent renovations have given a crisp, modern feeling and most rooms private facilities: singles €35, with facilities €75; doubles €90; triples €133, AmEx/MC/V, with 5% surcharge. ❷

Hotel de Lantaerne, Leidsekade 111 (☎623 22 21; reservations@hotellantaerne.com; www.hotellan-

Watching the Hollyhocks Grow

The Famous American Hotel

Spacious Accommodations

taerne.com). Lovely accommodations located in two converted houses along the Leidsegracht, and right by Leidseplein. TV, phone, and hairdryer in the stylish rooms with Roman numeral print bedspreads. Breakfast included. Singles €65, with bath €75; doubles €80, €110; triples €105, €140. Studio with kitchenette for 3 €150; for 4 €170. Credit cards with 5% surcharge. ❷

Hotel de la Haye, Leidsegracht 114 (☎624 40 44; fax 638 52 54; info@hoteldelhaye.com; www.hoteldelahaye.com). Tram #1, 2, or 5 to Leidseplein. Walk up Marnixstraat 1 block and turn right. Conveniently located hotel combines the noise of the Leidseplein and the serenity of a canal view. Breakfast included in pretty canal view room with fresh flowers. Sink in each room. Pay on arrival. Reception 8am-10pm, no curfew. Singles in high season €59, in low season €35; basic doubles €82, €65; doubles with bath €95, €75; triples €130, €100; quads €168, €120; quint with balcony and canal view €185, €150. Additional low season weekend charge of about €5 per person. ❸

Hotel Titus, Leidsekade 74 (☎626 57 58; info@hoteltitus.nl; www.hoteltitus.nl). Tram #1, 2, or 5 to Leidesplein. Walk past the theater on your right, take a right onto Manixstraat, and then left onto Leidsekade. Bare in an almost chic, minimalist sort of way, the Titus' rooms come equipped with TV and phones, and are sparklingly clean throughout. Cushy lounge where (included) breakfast is served every morning. Reception 8am-midnight. Singles €40-60, doubles €80-120, triples €120-160, quads €140-180. Credit cards accepted with 5% surcharge. ❸

Hotel La Boheme, Marnixstraat 415 (624 28 28; email hotel@boheme.A2000.nl; www.hotelbooker.com/amsterdam/laboheme.html). Tram #1, 2, or 5 to Leidesplein and take a right after the theater onto Marnixstraat. Clean, professional hotel with chic café and bar; all rooms have phone and TV. Breakfast included. Reception 8am-11pm. Singles with shared facilities €55; doubles with facilities €105 in high season, €95 in low season; triples with facilities €140, 130; look for specials on the internet. Credit cards accepted. ❸

REMBRANDTPLEIN

see maps pp. 324-325

Accommodations in this neighborhood cater to those who want to party all night long and then collapse in bed without worrying about a long commute back to a suburban hotel.

City Hotel, Utrechtsestraat 2 (☎627 23 23; www.city-hotel.nl). On the south side of Rembrandtplein. Classy accommodations above a pub right on the Rembrandtplein. Many rooms have great views of the square, and the ones on higher floors overlook the city skyline. Rooms, hall baths, and showers all immaculately kept. TV and breakfast included. Reception 10am-6pm. Doubles in high season €90, in low season €80; doubles with facilities €100, €90; triples €105, €135; quads €180, €140; quints €225, €175; six €270, €210. AmEx/DC/MC/V. ❹

Hotel Monopole, Amstel 60 (☎624 62 71; fax 624 58 97; arad@monopole.demon.nl; www.monopole.demon.nl). Tram #4 or 9 to Rembrandtplein. From Rembrandtplein, go north on Halvemaanstraat, then head right when you hit the river. Lovely setting right by the Amstel offsets adequate but livable rooms (not all rooms have views–ask ahead!). Just around the corner from lots of major Rembrandtplein nightclubs. Breakfast included. Singles €85; doubles €95, with facilities €125; triples €160; quads €200; quints €260. MC/V with a 5% surcharge. ❹

THE JORDAAN

see maps pp. 328-329

Lodgings in the Jordaan afford peace and quiet a comfortable distance from the frenzied city center.

HOSTEL

The Shelter Jordan, Bloemstraat 179 (☎624 47 17; fax 627 61 37; reservation@jordan.shelter.nl; www.shelter.nl). Tram #13 or 17 to

Marnixstraat; follow Lijnbaansgracht (off Rozengracht) for 50m, turn right on Bloemstraat and the shelter is on your right. Find this well-maintained hostel and its English-speaking, amazingly friendly staff in a quiet corner of the Jordaan. Its cafe is a pleasant retreat from the busier watering holes on the Prinsengracht and is open until midnight; Internet access (20min. for €0,50), and even a piano. Breakfast included. Dinner €5, lunch €2-3. Christian-themed, including nightly Bible study groups, but everyone is made to feel more than welcome. Lockers with €5 key deposit and free storage for larger bags. Curfew 2am. Single-sex dorms. No smoking, no alcohol. Age limit 35. Be sure to arrive by 11am to get a room; during peak season it can get busy. Sept.-May dorms €14 per night; June €15; July-Aug. €16,50. Cash only. ❶

HOTELS

Hotel van Onna, Bloemgracht 104 (☎626 58 01; www.netcentrum.com/onna). Tram #13 or 17 from Centraal Station to Westermarkt, also close to the Bloemgracht stop on tram #10. No televisions and no smoking means visitors get a peaceful night's rest on the nicest canal in the Jordaan. The small but very comfortable rooms all have private bathrooms, and the gentle owner will help you with all your needs. Breakfast included in the superlative dining room. Reception 8am-11pm. Rooms for 1-4 people €40 per person. Cash only. ❷

Hotel Acacia, Lindengracht 251 (☎622 14 60; fax 638 07 48; acacia.nl@wxs.nl). From Centraal Station take bus #18 to Willemstraat. Tram #3 to Bloemgracht is also close. If watching the houseboats peacefully rocking along the canals of the Jordaan isn't quite good enough for you, why not try living in one? Acacia has 2 houseboats with rooms for 2-4 people available. All rooms come with private bath and include breakfast. Studios and houseboats include small kitchenette. Singles, €65; doubles €80; triples €99; quads €120; quints €130. Studios: doubles €90; triples €105. Houseboats: doubles €95-110; triples €115; quads €130. MC/V with 5% surcharge. ❸

WESTERPARK AND OUDE WEST

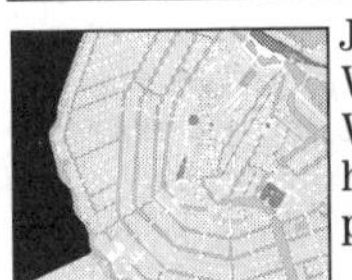

see map p. 335

Just outside the Jordaan, the Westerpark and the Oude West is a residential area with hotels that run around €50 per night.

Westropa Hotel, Nassaukade 387-390 (☎683 49 35; fax 618 45 08; htl@westropa.demon.nl; www.westropa.demon.nl). Tram #1 to Stadhouderskade, which becomes Nas-

Little Door with Roses

Frisbee Players in Vondelpark

Kitty Climbing the Wall

saukade at the Overtoom intersection; Westropa is just around the corner on the left. Great value for a 3-star, 70-room hotel, Westropa caters to the quieter traveler. Large lobby with bar open until midnight. All rooms with bath, phone, TV, and safe. Breakfast buffet included. Reception 24hr. Singles €85; doubles €140; triples €166; in low season €63, €100, and €120, respectively. AmEx/D/MC/V. ❸

Hotel Crystal, 2e Helmersstraat 6 (☎618 05 21; fax 618 05 61). Tram #1 to intersection of Overtoom and Nassaukade, walk 2 blocks up Nassaukade away from Leidsepl. and turn left. The 17-room family hotel lies within short walking distance of Leidsepl., Museumpl, and Vondelpark. The rooms aren't palatial, but they're clean and very comfortable, especially those with private bathrooms. The hall bathrooms are well maintained as well. Breakfast included. Pay in cash upon arrival, credit card guarantee required. Singles in summer €50, in low season €3; bunked single €60, €54; double €68, €64; twin with bath €102, €73; triple with bath €125, €95; spacious quad with bath €147, €113. ❷

Hotel Jupiter, 2e Helmersstraat 14 (☎618 71 32; fax 616 88 38). Same directions as Hotel Crystal. You pay for location (short walk to Leidseplein, Museumplein, and Vondel Park) rather than decor or a polite staff. Phone and TV in each room. Breakfast included. Cash only but credit card reservation required. Singles €40, with bath €46; doubles €75, €100; triples with bath €135; quads with bath €150. Low season: singles with bath €43; doubles €88; triples €115; quads €129. ❷

Hotel Abba, Overtoom 122 (☎618 30 58; fax 685 34 77). Tram #1 or 6 to 1e Constantijn Huygensstr, Abba is across the street. Overtoom can get noisy and crowded, but this budget hotel is nevertheless attractive for its proximity to Leidseplein and the museums. Breakfast included. Pay in cash upon arrival, but credit card reservation required. Single €37,50, with bath €55; twin €60, €80; triple €90, €100; rooms for 4 or 5 people €35 per person. ❷

Belfort Hotel, Surinamplein 53 (☎617 43 33; info@hotel-belfort.nl; www.belforthotel.nl). Tram #1 or 17 from Centraal Station to Surinamplein Although this hotel is convenient to nothing in the city, the high-rise design of this 25-room hotel makes it easy to find from the tram stop. Cleanliness and amenities (every room has private toilet and shower, breakfast included, phone, TV, plus in-house restaurant and bar) make up for bland character and location far from city center. Reception 24hr. Credit card guarantee required. Singles in summer €70, off season €65; doubles €90, €80; triples €115, €95; quads €150, €135. AmEx/MC/V. ❸

Hotel Princess, Overtoom 80 (☎612 29 47; fax 616 04 09). Tram #1 or 6 to Constantijn Huygensstraat. Think of this place as Hotel Crystal's pricier sister. All rooms one each floor share a toilet and shower. Rooms overlooking noisy Overtoom have tiny balconies. Breakfast included. Cash payment on arrival. Singles in summer €43, off season €36; doubles €70, €62; triples €90, €80; quads €110; €100. ❷

MUSEUMPLEIN & VONDELPARK

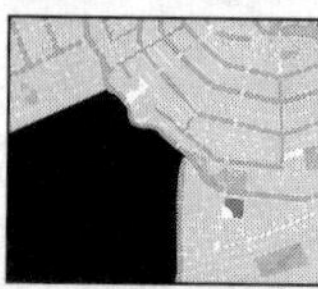

see map p. 334

The neighborhood around the Museumplein and the Vondelpark is quiet and peaceful, but still very close to the central canal ring, and just across the river from the nightlife hotspot of Leidesplein. There are a handful of pricier hotels along Vondelstraat, most of which rent double rooms starting at €115-per night.

HOSTELS

NJHC City Hostel Vondelpark (HI), Zandpad 5 (☎589 89 96; www.njhc.org/vondelpark), bordering Vondelpark. Take tram #1, 2, or 5 to Leidseplein, walk to the Marriott and take a left. Walk a block and turn right onto Zanpad right before the park. The Hostel will be down at the end on the right. A palatial hostel with exceptionally clean rooms. Option of 10-20 person single sex dormitory rooms or smaller, mixed rooms all with bath, which makes the hostel a good option for families. With a lobby lounge, bar with terrace on the park, TV/rec room and smoking room (the rest of the hostel is non-smoking), NJHC takes care of all your needs. Breakfast and sheets included. Lockers in the lobby €2,50, or bring a padlock for room lockers. Reception 7:30am-midnight. Bike rental €5,50 per day. Internet access €5 per hr. This hostel fills up quickly, so it's important to make a reservation. Assure a spot by paying before with credit card at www.hostelbooking.com or reserve a more tentative place by phone or the hostel's website. 12-14 person dorm €21 high season, €19 low season; bed in 6-8 bedroom €23, €21.50; doubles €71, €53,30; quads €108, €96. IYHF members €2,50 less. ❶

The Flying Pig Palace, Vossiusstraat 46-47 (☎400 41 87; palace@flyingpig.nl, www.flyingpig.nl). Take tram #1, 2, or 5 from Centraal Station to Leidsepl., walk to the Marriott and turn left. Go past the entrance to the park and then take the first right onto Vossuistraat. The palace is down a long block on your left. Not the cleanest hostel, but this place is fun and friendly for the backpacker. The cosy bar with rugs and pillows at one end is a laid-back place for young travellers to come together. All rooms mixed gender. Breakfast included. Key deposit €10. Reception 8am-9pm. Sheets free, towels €0.70. Free Internet. Kitchen. All Flying Pig hostels are for travelers aged 18-35. Stop by at 8am or call at 8:30am to reserve a room for the same night or make reservations via Internet and pay 10% deposit ahead of time. The Flying Pig is in the unique position of having queen sized bunk beds in some of their dorms (sleeps 2 for the price of 1.5 people, starting at €27). Dorms €18-23 per person in high season, €16-€21 low season. Doubles €58, €54, with bath €62, €58. If you are staying a while, ask about the option of doing work in exchange for rent. AmEx/MC/V. ❶

HOTELS

Hotel Bema, Concertgebouw 19b (☎679 13 96; www.bemahotel.com; postbus@hotelbema.demon.nl). Tram #16 to Museumplein; when facing the Concertgebouw, take a left, cross the street, it's on the left-hand street that curves around. Charming 7 room hotel with a little more style than the rest. Free breakfast delivered to the room. Reception 8am-midnight. Singles €45-55, doubles €55-70 (with shower €70-75; with bath €75-85), triples €85 (with shower €95), quad with shower €115. Credit cards accepted, 5% surcharge. ❷

Hotel Bellington, P.C Hoftstraat 78-80 (☎671 64 78; fax 671 86 37; www.hotel-bellington.com). From Schiphol Airport, ride bus #197 to Hobbemasstraat or take tram #2 or 5 to same stop. Backtrack along the tram line toward the park and take a left on to P.C. Hoftstraat. A well groomed hotel on one of Amsterdam's ritziest streets. Phone and TV in room. Breakfast included. Reception 8am-11pm. Doubles €95, triples €125, quad €145. AmEx/MC/V. ❹

Hotel Europa 92, 1e Constantijn Huygenstraat 103-105, between. Vondelstraat and Overtoom (☎618 88 08; fax 683 64 05; info@europa92.nl;

Ivied Stairs

Houseboat Living

Finding a Green Spot

www.europa92.nl). Tram #1, 6 to 1e Constantijn Huygenstraat Converted from 2 adjacent houses into 1 labyrinthine hotel. Offers clean, professional rooms and a pretty garden terrace. Every room has phone, TV, and private bath with hairdryer. It's fully modernized like a larger hotel, but is smaller so has a personalized character. Breakfast included and served in an attractive room. Tiny elevator means you only need to carry your luggage for no more than half a flight of stairs. Singles in high season €90, in low season €65; doubles €125, €100; triples €150, €115; quads €170, €135. Credit cards add 4% surcharge. ❹

Hotel Wynnobel, Vossiusstraat 9 (☎662 22 98). Follow directions to the Flying Pig Palace and you will come to it first on Vossuistraat. Managed by a stalwart Frenchman, Hotel Wynnobel possesses both the charms and the set-backs of being old-fashioned. It has the cosy feel of a home and a small garden in the back. Nothing here is mechanized–that means no phones, no TV, no website, and no credit cards. All 11 rooms share facilities on each floor. Singles €35, doubles €60-70 (the smaller and higher up the room is, the cheaper), triples €90, quads €120, quints €150, for six €170. ❷

Hotel Museumzicht, Jan Luykenstraat 22 (☎671 52 24; fax 671 35 97). Directly from Schiphol ride bus #197 to Hobbemasstraat. From Centraal Station, take tram #2 or 5 to same stop. Small house with old-fashioned personality. Some rooms have views of the Rijksmuseum. Comfortable lounge and a little dog running around make it feel homey. Breakfast included. Single €45; double €75 (with bath €95); triple €95. Credit cards accepted with 5% surcharge. ❷

Hotel P.C. Hooft, P.C. Hooftstraat 63 (☎662 71 07; fax 675 89 61). Tram #2 or 5, get off at the Rijksmuseum. Standing with your back to the museum, walk to the right for 2 blocks and then take a left onto P.C. Hoofstraat, it will be on the left. Tidy, underwhelming rooms, but they come at tidy prices. Breakfast included. All 16 rooms have sink and TV. Some available with shower for €10 extra. All toilets shared. Single €40, double €60, triple €80, quad €100. V/MC. ❷

Apple Inn Hotel, Koninginneweg 93 (☎662 78 94; www.apple-inn.nl). Tram #2 to Emmastraat and walk 200m further in the direction of the tram. Further isolated than the other hotels in the area, the Apple Inn will put you in a peaceful, residential neighborhood of the city. Clean rooms with bath, TV, phone, and hairdryer. Breakfast included. Singles in high season €90, in low season €50-60; doubles €120-130, €90-100, triples €140-150, €120-130, quads €180-190, 165. Credit cards accepted. ❷

Hotel Sander, 69 Jacob Obrechtstraat (☎662 75 74; fax 679 6067; htlsandr@xs4all.nl; www.xs4all.nl/~htlsandr). Tram #16 to Jacob Obrechtstraat Modernized hotel on a quiet street; each room has phone, TV, bath and safe (€2,50 a night). Elevator. Breakfast included. 24 hr. bar in lobby. Singles in high season €105, in low season €98, doubles €125, 116, triples €165, 115, quads €215, 205. AmEx/MC/V

DE PIJP

see map p. 326

De Pijp has affordable hotels and hostels; Amsterdam's walkability and public transport make the neighborhood an essential consideration for the budget traveler.

Bicycle Hotel, Van Ostadestraat 123 (☎679 34 52; info@bicyclehotel.com; www.bicyclehotel.com). From Centraal Station, take tram #24 or 25 and get off at the ninth stop "Ceintuurbaan," continue south along Ferdinand Bolstraat for 1 block, then turn left on Van Ostadestraat; the Hotel will be half a block down on the left. Clean digs and spotless bathrooms. A bicycle-friendly hotel with a bike garage and maps of recommended bike trips outside Amsterdam. They also rent bikes (€5 per day), and the cycling motif prevails throughout hotel decor. All rooms have TV and breakfast is included. Doubles €68-70, with bath €99; triples €90, €120; quads with bath €130. Cash only. ❸

Hotel De Stadhouder, Stadhouderskade 76 (☎671 84 28; fax 664 74 10), at Ferdinand Bolstraat. From Centraal Station, take tram #16, 24, or 25, and exit at Ferdinand Bolstraat;

it's just across from the Heineken Brewery. 20 well-kept rooms, all with TVs and daily linen/towel service, some with patios or delicious canal views. Elevator. Breakfast included. Singles €45-70; doubles €59-89; triples €95-135; quads €110-140. AmEx/MC/V. ❸

JODENBUURT AND THE PLANTAGE

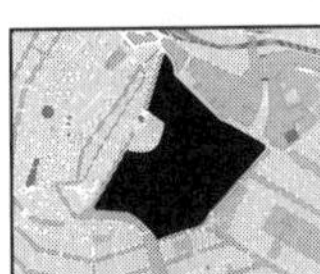

see map p. 327

HOTELS

Hotel Pension Kitty, Plantage Middenlaan 40 (☎622 68 19). Take tram #9 or 14 to Plantage Kerklaan. From there, take Plantage Middenlaan southeast and the unmarked Hotel Pension Kitty should be on your right. Under the watchful eye of its charismatic 80-year-old proprietress, Hotel Pension Kitty provides for a peaceful respite from the city. Located just a few blocks from the zoo, Hortus Botanicus, and the Jewish Museum, this hotel is 4 floors of grandmotherly warmth. The environment at Kitty is laid-back and comforting, but the staff asks that guests try their best to maintain the quiet atmosphere. Some rooms have private toilets. No children. Singles €50; doubles €60-70. ❷

Hotel Fantasia, Nieuwe Keizersgracht 16 (☎623 82 59; fax 622 39 13; info@fantasia-hotel.com; www.fantasia-hotel.com). Take tram #9, 14, or 20 to Waterlooplein and turn left on Nieuwe Keizersgracht. A clean, friendly, family-owned establishment in an 18th-century house on a quiet canal in the center of Amsterdam. Facilities include radios, telephones, safe, and coffee- and tea-makers. Most rooms with bath. Breakfast included. Singles €50-58; doubles €75-85; triples €105; quads €125. Closed Dec. 16-26 and Jan. 6-Feb. 21. ❸

Hotel Barbacan, Plantage Muidergracht 89 (☎623 62 41; info@barbacan.nl; www.barbacan.nl). Take tram #9 or 14 to Plantage Kerklaan and then take Plantage Muidergracht southeast; the hotel will be on your left. Shag carpets, soft duvets, and included breakfast show that comfort comes first at this quiet hotel. Singles (depending on season) €40-45; doubles €63-72, with bath €88-98; triples €86-95, €111-121; quads with bath €131-149. AmEx/MC/V with 5% surcharge. ❷

INSIDE:

Daytripping

With all the fantastical tripping you can do in Amsterdam, you may wonder why you would ever want to leave the city. The answer is clear: for the cheese, the clogs, the windmills, and all the idyllic (yes, even *quaint)* Dutch charm that you can stomach. A 20-minute ride out of town will take you to all the tulips you've seen in the travel brochures. A slightly longer jaunt brings you to Leiden, a bustling university town; to Rotterdam, a city with a cosmopolitan flavor; or even to Brussels, to satisfy the international jetsetter in you. This guide covers most of The Netherlands, all of which is easily accessible by train, or even bike, from Amsterdam. Biking through the low countries can be especially rewarding—because the country is mostly below sea level, there are few hills. Spring—when fields of tulips create a sea of colors along the roads, is an ideal time to see the country.

The towns and cities in this chapter are listed in order of their approximate distance from Amsterdam, by route, so that it's easy to hop from one town to another. Leiden, The Hague, and Rotterdam are all on the same train line, for example. The closer and smaller ones are an easy two-hour excursion, while larger and more distant areas like Maastricht or the Wadden Islands are better seen over a couple of days.

DESTINATION	TRANSPORTATION TIME	COST
Haarlem	20min.	€2,90
Zandvoort-aan-zee	10min. from Haarlem	8 strips or €2,75
Bloemendaal-aan-zee	25min.	€8,96
Zaanse Schans	20min.	€2,25
Leiden	20min.	€5,40
Noordwijk	10min. from Leiden	5 strips or €3,40
Lisse	20min. from Leiden	€
Utrecht	30min.	€4,50
The Hague	50min.	€8
Rotterdam	1hr.	€10
Gouda	15min. from Rotterdam	€3
Delft	1hr.	€8,90
Arnhem	80min.	€4,50
De Hoge Veluwe National Park	25min. from Arnhem	€
Wadden Islands	Nearest 2hr.; farthest 3hr. 15min.	€16,80; €33
Groningen	2½hr.	€23,80
Maastricht	2½hr.	€23,80
Brussels	2½hr.	€32,50

TULIP COUNTRY

AALSMEER

BLOEMENVEILING AALSMEER (FLOWER AUCTION)

Legmeerdijk 313. Take bus #172 (45min., every 15min., 5 strips). For the best action, arrive early; buses leave Amsterdam and Haarlem starting at 6:10am. ☎0297 39 21 85; info@vba.nl; www.vba-aalsmeer.nl. Open M-F 7:30-11am. €4, ages 6-11 €2, groups over 15 €3 per person.

Easily accessible by bus (or even bike) from Amsterdam and Haarlem, the easygoing, old-fashioned flower town of Aalsmeer is home to the world's largest flower auction. With an impressive trading floor, on which the world price of flowers is heavily determined, the Bloemenveiling Aalsmeer is the largest trade building in the world (with 878,000 square meters of floor space) and serves as an enjoyable, and unforgettable, Amsterdam excursion.

HISTORISCHE TUIN

Uiterweg 32. From the center of town, turn right along Stationsweg and left on Uiterweg. ☎0297 32 25 62; www.htaalsmeer.org. Open Mar.-Sept. Tu-Th 10am-4:40pm, F-Su 1:30-4:30pm. €3, under 12 €1,50.

These unique historical gardens are worth a visit for the flower-minded. They celebrate Holland's botanical history by presenting exhibits on traditional farm life and by nursing several centuries-old plants. Look for special flower sales in the spring.

While in Aalsmeer you may also want to take a ride with **Westeinder Rondvaart.** They run a quaint, open-air vessel that traverses the picturesque lakes west of the city center. (☎0297 34 15 82; info@westeinderrondvaart.nl; www.westeinder-rondvaart.nl. Operates May-Oct. Tu-W and F-Sa 1:30, 2:45, and 4pm, Su 2:30pm. €6, under 12 €3.)

> **ESSENTIAL INFORMATION**
>
> **HOLLAND VS. THE NETHERLANDS**
>
> Holland. We've all heard of it. Some of us were even taught in high school that the country has two names—Holland and The Netherlands. And for those who live in America and Great Britain, it's true; the names are easily interchangeable in everyday language.
>
> But there is a difference. The country's official name is The Netherlands, leaving the elusive question: what is Holland?
>
> Holland is a province in The Netherlands that includes Amsterdam. To say that Amsterdam is in Holland is true, though to be perfectly accurate, it is in North Holland. North Holland and South Holland are the two most populous of the nation's 12 provinces. They include The Hague, Rotterdam, Haarlem, and Leiden. The word Holland comes from *"houtland,"* or wooded land, while the term Netherlands comes from *nederland,* literally low country.

LISSE

KEUKENHOF GARDENS

Take bus #50 or 51 toward Lisse from the Leiden train station (5 strips). It should be marked Keukenhof and make no other stops. ☎0252 46 55 55; info@keukenhof.nl; www.keukenhof.nl. Open Mar. 21-May 18, daily 8am-7:30pm; tickets on sale until 6pm. €11, children ages 4-11 €5,50. Open also for a few days in mid-Oct. for the sale of bulbs; check web site for more information.

The unquestionable highlight of the comfortable town of **Lisse** are the breathtaking Keukenhof Gardens, which in late spring become a kaleidoscope of color as over five million bulbs explode into life. Lisse can be reached by bike or bus from either Haarlem or Leiden Centraal. The gardens are impeccably kept, with fountains, a windmill, and even a petting zoo among the flowers that keep visitors occupied. Make sure to visit all three greenhouses, one of which contains the winners from a

national tulip contest. From the gardens, where all species of tulip are showcased for close examination, take in views of the area's surrounding **tulip fields.** The long strips of color in the landscape are the pride of the Dutch and are visited each year by hundreds of thousands of tourists from The Netherlands and all over Europe.

OTHER SIGHTS

ZWARTE (BLACK) TULIP MUSEUM. Details the history and science of "bulbiculture," or tulip raising, through videos, photos, artifacts, and a comprehensive botanical library. The quest for the black tulip is ongoing, though some say it is futile, since the color does not exist naturally. (☎025 241 79 00; museum.dezwartetulip@12move.nl. Open Tu-Su 1-5pm. €3, children and seniors €2.)

DEVER HOUSE. Built in the 14th century and older than any structure standing in Amsterdam, this tower-house was built by Renier Dever, an influential vassal of early Holland. The ancient building has been a museum since 1978. (☎0252 41 14 30. Open Tu-Su 2-5pm. Free.)

HAARLEM ☎023

Haarlem's narrow cobblestone streets, calm canals, and fields of tulips and daffodils make for a great escape from the urban frenzy of Amsterdam. Most visitors come to Haarlem to take in its many artistic and historical sights—the city is littered with Renaissance façades, idyllic *hofjes* (elderly women's almshouses), medieval architecture, and is home to the renowned Frans Hals Museum. Haarlem was the cultural center of 16th- and 17th-century Holland and, as a city, is older than Amsterdam. But there's more than antiquated charm here—Haarlem bustles with a mellow energy befitting a mid-sized urban center (pop. 160,000; The Netherlands's 12th-largest city). With coffeeshops, a buzzing nightlife, and the most restaurants per capita of any Dutch city, there's plenty to do here after nightfall.

In August the town hosts a four-day jazz festival (☎527 3347; www.haarlemjazz.nl). There's a culinary festival in Grote Markt August 1-4.

PRACTICAL INFORMATION

Reach Haarlem from Amsterdam either by train from Centraal Station (20min., €2,90 one way) or by bus #80 from Marnixstraat near Leidseplein (2 per hr., 2 strips). Just outside the train station in Haarlem, buses depart from the VVV on the Stationsplein and travel all over Noord-Holland. An information center provides schedules and sells *strippenkarten.* (Open M-F 7am-6pm, Sa-Su 9:45am-5:45pm.) The VVV **tourist office,** Stationsplein 1, just to your right when you walk out of the train station, sells maps (€2) and finds private rooms (from €18,50 for a €5 fee. (☎090 06 16 16 00; info@vvvzk.nl; www.vvvzk.nl. Open M-F 9:30am-5:30pm, Sa 10am-4pm; off-season Sa 10am-2pm.) Another source of information is the commercial web site www.haarlemonline.nl.

ACCOMMODATIONS

Joops Intercity Apartments, Oude Groenmarkt 20 (☎532 20 08; joops@easynet.nl). Walk to Grote Markt and take a right; Oude Groenmarkt runs along the right hand side of the giant church. Centrally located. Bright, clean, spacious rooms and apartments with big windows. Reception 7:30am-9pm. Optional continental breakfast €9,50. Rooms with shower and toilet down the hall: singles €28-40; doubles €55. Studios with shower, toilet, and kitchenette: small single or double €65; large single or double €75; triple €95; quad €115. Extra large with balcony: 1 or 2 people €100; triple or quad with 2 bedrooms €120. Large apartment with living room, kitchen, and bath: €107 for 2, €20 extra per person up to 10 persons. AmEx/MC/V. ❶

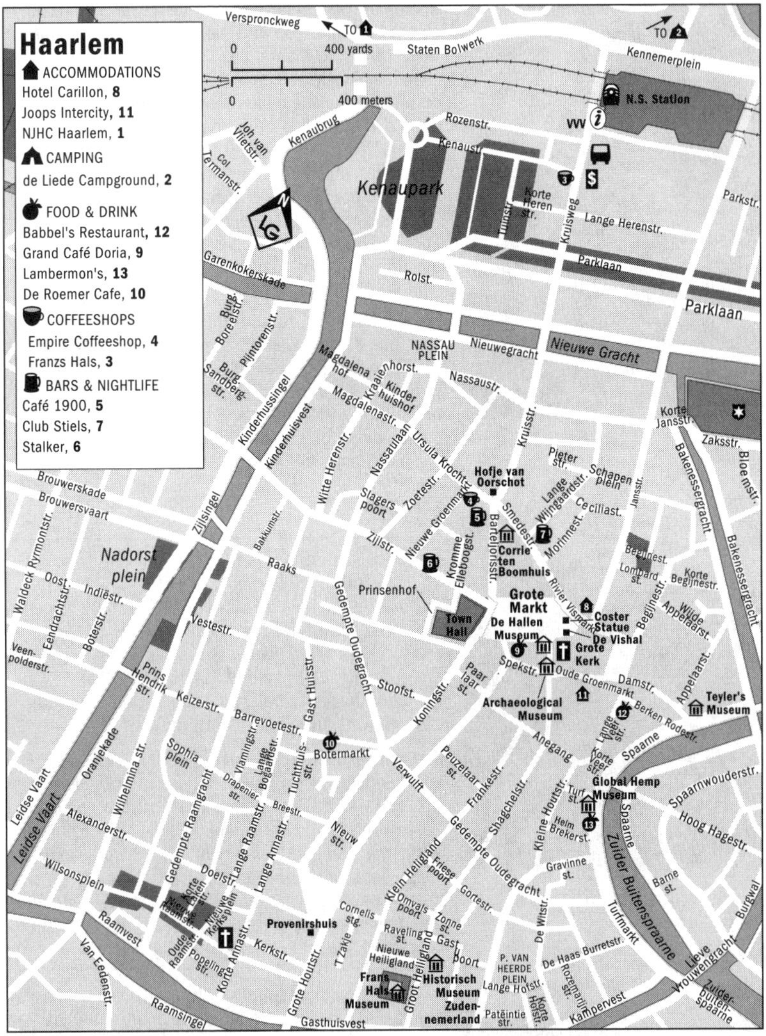

Haarlem

ACCOMMODATIONS
Hotel Carillon, **8**
Joops Intercity, **11**
NJHC Haarlem, **1**

CAMPING
de Liede Campground, **2**

FOOD & DRINK
Babbel's Restaurant, **12**
Grand Café Doria, **9**
Lambermon's, **13**
De Roemer Cafe, **10**

COFFEESHOPS
Empire Coffeeshop, **4**
Franzs Hals, **3**

BARS & NIGHTLIFE
Café 1900, **5**
Club Stiels, **7**
Stalker, **6**

Hotel Carillon, Grote Markt 27 (☎531 05 91; info@hotelcarillon.com; www.hotelcarillon.com). Ideally located right on the town square, to the left of the Grote Kerk. Basic rooms make up in cleanliness what they lack in space. Despite their diminutive size, many include TV and phone. The rooms lie above a classy restaurant/bar with a great outdoor patio (beer from €1,70). Breakfast included. Reception and bar 7:30am-midnight. Singles €28,30, with facilities €55; doubles €55, €71; triples €92; quads €99. MC/V. ❷

NJHC-Hostel Haarlem (HI), Jan Gijzenpad 3 (☎537 37 93; www.njhc.org/haarlem). The best place to stay in Haarlem is just out of the city center. It lies 3km from Haarlem's train station, surrounded by a wooded park and situated on the banks of a placid canal. Take bus #2 (dir: Haarlem-Noord; every 10min. until 6pm, then every 15min. until 12:30am); after that, take a cab from Haarlem station (about €12) and get off at Jeugdherberg; the driver will tell you where it is. Packed with amenities, the hostel is great for travelers visiting Haarlem.

Cheese

Windmill

Wooden Bridge

Rooms are spare but cheery, bright, and impeccably clean. Staff runs fun and friendly pub, "The Shuffle," where, if you're man enough, you can order the 2.5L "boot" (deposit of 1 shoe required). The party spills onto the canalside patio on summer nights, where an open fire doubles as a barbecue. Bike rental €6,80 per day (passport or €150 deposit required). Sheets included; sleeping bags not allowed. Breakfast included; box lunches €4,15; 3-course dinner €8,70. Key deposit €10 or passport. Beds in 2- to 8-person dorms in high season €22-24.50, in low season €19-22. €2,50 less per person per night with HI membership. AmEx/MC/V. ❶

De Liede Campground, Lie Oever 68 (☎535 86 66). Take bus #2 (dir: Zuiderpolder) and tell the bus driver where you're going; he will direct you on the 10min. walk from the bus stop. On a swimmable canal with a restaurant, pool table, and tennis table. €2,75 per person plus €0,70 tax and €2,75 per tent, €2,75 per car. Cash only. ❶

FOOD

Haarlem smugly calls itself the "most delicious city in Holland." The slogan refers to the city's restaurants, which abound but tend to be expensive. The unofficial restaurant row, with the nicest series of restaurants, is Lange Veerstraat. For cheaper meals, try cafés in the **Grote Markt** or in the **Botermarkt,** which have the added advantage of outdoor patios in a stunning setting.

Lambermon's, Spaarne 69 (☎542 78 04; info@lambermons.nl; www.lambermons.nl). From the Grote Markt, take a right and another right on to Lange Veerstraat. Take one of the little streets on your left to the river and then a right; it's 2 blocks down. A lavish treat for the foodie in you, Lambermon's is the best in haute cuisine that Haarlem has to offer. The menu changes nightly and consists of 10 delectable courses (€7 each); most people have about 4 or 5. The first 8 are usually exquisitely prepared fish and meat (although vegetarian alternatives are always available), and the feast always finishes with a cheese and then dessert. Wines (€3,50-4,50 a glass) are selected to complement each dish although a full wine menu is also always available. The warmly lit atmosphere is chic but relaxed, and the kitchen is open for all to see. The first course is served at 6:30pm and each subsequent one at 30min. intervals,. Reservations necessary. AmEx/MC/V. ❺

Grand Café Doria, Grote Houtstraat 1a (☎531 33 35; www.doria.nl), right in the Grote Markt, to the right of the Grote Kerk. Looks like a standard Dutch café but specializes in Italian fare including pizza margherita (€6) and pasta bolognese (€8,50). Its outdoor patio serves as a fabulous place to chill by day and turns into a lively bar scene by night. Open M-W 11am-7:30pm, Th 11am-9pm, F 11am-midnight, Sa 1-11pm. ❷

Babbel's, Lange Veerstraat 23 (☎542 35 78). Walk behind the Grote Kerk and take a right onto Lange Veerstraat. Babbel's serves very good traditional (mostly) meat dishes—all entrees come with salad, french fries, and vegetables—in an elegant dark wood setting with slightly lower prices than the other upscale restaurants that surround them. Try the carpaccio with fresh Parmesan (€7,50) for a starter and the turkey fillet (€14,50) or steak frites (€13) for a main meal. You might even get to sit in the special toy closet. Open daily 5:30-9:30pm. Cash only. ❷

De Roemer Cafe, Botermarkt 17 (☎532 52 76). A typical Dutch café on the Botermarkt, with a large selection of specialty beer (€1,70-8,40). The outstanding offering of the house is the *gambas piri piri* (€10,20), a very spicy shrimp dish. Or you can just go for a nice mozzarella, tomato, and pesto *tosti* for €2,60. Open M-Th 9am-1pm, F-Sa 9am-2pm, Su noon-1am. Cash only. ❷

Canals

Kass

Speeltoren

SIGHTS

The action centers on the **Grote Markt,** Haarlem's vital, vibrant main square since the town's founding in 1245. To get there from the train station, head south along Kruisweg, which becomes Kruisstraat when it crosses the Nieuwe Gracht. Continue south when Kruisstraat becomes Barteljorisstraat, and you're there. Just north of the *kerk* beckons the 15-ft. high statue of **Laurens Coster** (see **Coster's Last Stand,** p. 204).

FRANS HALS MUSEUM

Groot Heiligland 62. From Grote Markt in front of the church, take a right on to Warmoestraat and go 3½ blocks down.☎511 57 75; franshalsmuseum@haarlem.nl; www.franshalsmuseum.com. Open Tu-Sa 11am-5pm, Su noon-5pm. €5,40, seniors and groups €4, under 19 free. Wheelchair accessible. The museum also has a nice café.

This wonderful museum houses a collection of Golden Age paintings by several masters, including the dramatic Haarlem landscapes by Jacob van Ruisdael, serene churches by Pieter Saerendam, and eleven works by Haarlem resident Frans Hals himself. Hals's portraits of bourgeois merchants have a breezy casual brushstroke that was considered sloppy in his own day but is now understood to have been an initial move toward Impressionism. He arranged his group subjects of militia companies with greater motion and freedom than other portraitists of his time, who favored stodgy, rigid poses. In **The Officers of the Civic Guard of St. George,** see if you can spot a self-portrait of the artist among the militia company (upper left).

COSTER'S LAST STAND

Some locals insist that Laurens Coster (1370-1440), Haarlem's most famous citizen after Frans Hals, invented printing in 1423, 13 years before Johannes Gutenberg. As the story goes, Coster was carving a letter out of tree bark when he dropped it into some mud and was struck with the inspiration for the basic notion behind the printing press. Little evidence supports the claim, and few historians buy it, but many Haarlemmers continue to believe in the legend.

The statue at the northeast corner of the Grote Markt commemorates Coster, who presides heroically over the square, his right hand raised, holding the letter "A" that (according to local legend, at least) gave rise to the popularization of the printed word.

The museum building itself, a square shell surrounding a courtyard, was built in 1608 as a home for old men and in 1810 became an orphanage. In 1913, it was converted into a museum but the dining room was preserved; check out the wooden rafters with the faces of old men carved into them.

GROTE KERK (ST. BAVO'S)

Grote Markt. ☎532 43 99 or 553 20 40; info@bavo.nl; www.bavo.nl. Open M-Sa 10am-4pm. Guided tours and by appointment. €1,50, children €1. Free organ concerts (www.organfestival.nl) Tu at 8:15pm and Th at 3pm.

The church's breathtaking inner space glows with light from enormous stained glass windows and houses the mammoth, floor-to-ceiling Müller organ which Handel and a 10-year-old Mozart once played. Dating from around 1313 (although it was rebuilt many times over the years), the church has many wonderful nooks and artifacts to explore including Haarlem's oldest safe, an iron cage with hundreds of keys, a modern sculpture commemorating the resistance, a Christening chapel with a gate attached by children's hands, a cannon ball in the wall to remember the Spanish siege of 1572-3, black marks on the pillar in the brewers' guild showing the heights of a giant and a dwarf, and model ships which valorize Holland's initial victory over the city in 1219. On the oak pulpit and its handrails, Satan and his snakes flee from the Gospel and baptismal waters. Marble figures of women in front of the organ symbolize Poetry and Music dedicating their work to Piety and so receiving Eternal Value (the angel over their heads). To the right of the organ you'll find one of the cathedral's strangest features, the gated "Dog Whipper's Chapel," from which an attendant would emerge to remove troublesome hounds from the church. This is the church that Pieter Saenredam painted so beautifully; he is buried here along with the landscapist Jacob van Ruisdael and Frans Hals (look for the lantern in the choir cage). If you get tired, the section in memoriam of the Brewers' guild even hosts a little café.

CORRIE TEN BOOMHUIS

Barteljorisstraat 19, 2min. from the Grote Markt, on the street that leads to the train station. ☎531 08 23; info@corrietenboom.com; www.corrietenboom.com. Open Tu-Sa 10am-4pm. You must go on a guided tour but the times vary; call to find out or check the clock outside. Free, but donations accepted.

Corrie ten Boom and her family were pillars in the Dutch Resistance and organized the protection of many Jews, as well as other persecuted Dutch, during World War II. This house, despite its public location on a main thoroughfare, was a kind of headquarters of the Resistance. It is estimated that Corrie saved the lives of over 800 people, mostly by arranging to have them hidden. She kept only the most dangerous ones—those who looked the most "Jewish," and an asthmatic woman because her breathing was loud. When she was found out, Corrie was sent to a concentration camp and managed to emerge with an even stronger faith in God. She became an evangelist and won global renown for her message of forgiveness, writing a book called *The Hiding Place*, which was also turned into a film. The house is a wonderful way to hear her very moving story. Most extraordinary is the actual hiding place, a narrow space behind a brick wall in which six fugitives hid from the Gestapo for three days until they could escape, even though they had no food, water, or facilities.

TEYLERS MUSEUM

Spaarne 16. From the Grote Markt, walk behind the church to Damstraat and then take a left at the river. ☎ 531 90 10; teyler@euronet.nl; www.teylersmuseum.nl. Open Tu-Su 10am-5pm, Su noon-5pm. €4,50, children ages 5-18 €1, groups over 20 €3,40. Wheelchair accessible.

Opened in 1784 by the wealthy silk merchant Pieter Teyler, this is the oldest museum in The Netherlands, and with its antiquated displays of scientific curiosities, it does seem to belong to the centuries of yore. The collection of fossils, dinosaur bones, old coins, and obsolete "instruments" (such as the largest electrostatic generator ever built) are still displayed as they were in the past, while a more recent addition to the museum shows a charming collection of 19th-century paintings. The beautiful Classical domed building is a sight in its own right; be sure to look up when you go in.

DE HALLEN MUSEUM (VLEESHAL & VERWEYHAL)

Grote Market 16, just to the right of the Grote Kerk. ☎ 511 57 75; www.franshalsmuseum.com. Open M-Sa 11am-5pm, Su 1-5pm. €4, under 19 free.

Now owned by the Frans Hals museum, Haarlem's collection of modern art is housed in the 17th-century Dutch Renaissance *vleeshal* (an indoor meat market created at the beginning of the 17th century for sanitation purposes). A reminder of its old use can be seen in the ox and sheep's heads that adorn the outside of the building. The museum shows changing exhibits of modern art that are generally good, and houses a large collection of work by the 20th-century artist Kees Verwey, for whom the adjoining hall is named. Check out the roof terrace for a cool view over Haarlem.

HISTORISCH MUSEUM ZUD-ENNEMERLAND

Groot Heiligland 47, across from the Frans Hals Museum. ☎ 542 24 27. English cards to translate the wall writings are available. Open Tu-Sa noon-5pm, Su 1-5pm. €1, under 19 free.

This small, user-friendly museum works hard to present Haarlem's history engagingly. A ten-minute TV-style film narrated by the alleged father of printing Laurens Coster (see Coster's Last Stand, p. 204) plays in English. The museum also offers interactive video displays (Dutch only) and a timeline illustrated with various artifacts. In spring 2003, they will have an exhibit on the contributions of immigrants to The Netherlands throughout the ages.

GLOBAL HEMP MUSEUM

Spaarne 94. ☎ 534 99 39; www.globalhempmuseum.com. Open daily 11am-8pm, Su noon-8pm. €2,50.

Thought the cannabis plant could only be used to get high? This museum will turn those silly assumptions of yours right around. It's dedicated to showing the many uses of hemp, from hemp denim to hemp make-up and even a hemp snowboard. On display are several flowering plants and a recreation of the Mellow Yellow, the first coffeeshop

Grote St. Nicolaaskerk

Yard Clad with Clogs

Edam

ever opened (in Amsterdam in 1973). Up front, a store proffers hemp products and bongs, although they don't sell anything with THC.

DE VISHAL

To the left of the Grote Kerk. www.devishal.nl. Open M-Sa 11am-5pm, Su 1-5pm. Free.

A gallery space showing changing exhibits of the latest in multi-media art: painting, photography, sculpture, or fashion in the 17th-century fish market.

OTHER SIGHTS

The city has 19 **hofjes,** or almshouses, which have provided free housing for older women for five centuries and continue to do so today. Many of the *hofjes* surround beautiful garden courtyards, and about nine of them allow visitors to stroll in to take a look. Check out the **Hofje van Oorschot,** where Kruisstraat becomes Barteljorisstraat. This most famous of Haarlem's *hofjes* features a gorgeous courtyard with lavender and roses punctuated by a statue of Eve. Tourists are welcome to wander through. (Open daily 10am-5pm.) Another ancient *hofje* (though less spectacular to look at) is the **Provenrshuis.**

At the west end of the Grote Markt looms the glorious medieval (Town Hall), originally the hunting lodge of the Count of Holland. It was built from the 14th through 17th centuries, reflected in its mélange of spires and statues of varying architectural styles.

Underneath the De Hallen Museum to the right of the Grote Kerk is the **Archeologisch Museum.** (☎531 31 35; open W-Su 1-5pm; free). The **Theo Swagemakers Museum,** Stoofsteeg 6, has a collection of the artist's drawings and paintings (☎532 77 61; open Th-Su 1-5pm; €3). Upstairs from the Historisch Museum is the **Spaarnestad Fotoarchief,** a free photo gallery with changing exhibits. (☎518 51 52; www.spaarnefoto.nl. Open Tu-Sa 12-5pm, Su 1-5pm.) To the left of the Teylers museum is the 1598 **Waag** (weighhouse), which was formerly used during trade on the Spaarne River. Across the Spaarne looms the **Amsterdamse Poort,** built around 1400, the last segment of the city's fortification still standing from when a defensive wall encircled the whole town (cross the bridge to the left of the Teyler's museum, take a left on Spaarne and then turn on to Oostvest). The **Niewe Kerk** (no entrance) was built in 1649 by Jacob van Compen, who also designed the Royal Palace.

COFFEESHOPS

Hash and marijuana are as accepted here as in the big city. Haarlem's best coffeehouse is **Empire Coffeeshop,** Krocht 8, just off Barteljorisstraat, which has a pool table (€1), foosball (€0,50), and Internet (although expensive at €1 for 15min). Weed and hash are €6-12 for 0.8-3g. (☎531 44 53; www.theempireshop.com. Open daily 10am-midnight.) One wonders whether Golden Age artist Frans Hals would have been proud or prostrate to know about his namesake, the **Coffeehouse Frans Hals,** Kruisweg 46, right across from the train station. Connoisseur counter dispenses advice and vends weed, hash chocolate bars, and lollipops. (1g €6-10, chocolate €7, lolly €3,40). (☎531 77 70. Open Su-Th and Su 9am-1am, F-Sa 9am-2am.)

NIGHTLIFE

Haarlem's nightlife doesn't rock as hard as Amsterdam's, but the upside is that bars and clubs are more accessible and less crowded. In summer, you may also want to consider taking a bus to nearby Bloemendaal-aan-Zee for dinner, drinks, and parties on the beach (see p. 208).

Cafe Stiels, Smedestraat 21 (☎531 69 40; www.stels.nl), just northwest of the city center, is a stylish, candlelit drinking den that grows more active as the night progresses. Su-Th live bands play covers, soul, R&B, and acid jazz, while F-Sa 20-somethings boogie to DJs spinning dance classics and disco. No cover. Open Su-Th 6pm-2am, F-Sa 6pm-4am.

Cafe 1900, Barteljorisstraat 10 (☎531 82 83), just northwest of the Grote Markt, serves a light lunch throughout the day (salads and sandwiches about €5) and morphs into a chill bar with dance space. Free live music Su. M brings a singer (small cover) and Th-Sa a DJ hosts a pop music dance party (no cover). Open M-Th 9am-12:30am, F-Sa 9am-1am, Su 11am-1am.

Stalker, Kromme Elleboogsteeg 20 (☎531 46 52; www.clubstalker.nl). The only "real" club in Haarlem, where the locals keep the party going until dawn and the DJs play all different styles of house beats. Out-of-towners should show up early to assure admittance. Open Th-F and Su midnight-5am, Sa 11pm-5am.

NEAR HAARLEM

ZANDVOORT-AAN-ZEE

From Amsterdam, buses leave from the station at Marnixstraat and Elandsgracht every 30min. (1hr., 8 strips). From Haarlem, you can take a train (10min., round-trip €2,75).

Just seven miles from Haarlem, the seaside town of Zandvoort draws gaggles of sun-starved Netherlanders to its miles of sandy beaches during summer. To find the shore from the train station, follow the signs to the Raadhuis, and from there head west along Kerkstraat until you fall into the ocean. The water is generally too cold for swimming, although it becomes most appealing in August (20° C), and brave souls take the plunge year round. Though you can stake out a spot on the sand for free, most locals enjoy the beach in one of several "beach clubs" that consist of wooden pavilions along the shore (summer only) with enclosed restaurants, outdoor patios, and stretches of sand with chaise lounges for sunbathing. They all have different themes, but admission is free as long as you're buying drinks or food. If you're in a friskier mood, head to one of the several nudist beach clubs on the "Naaktstrand," about 20min. south of the main beach.

The VVV tourist office, Schoolplein 1, is just east of the town square off Louisdavidstraat and about eight minutes from the beach and the station. Signs from the station lead the way. (☎571 79 47; info@vvvzk.nl; www.vvvzk.nl. Hours vary according to season; generally open M-Sa 9am-5pm.) The cheapest Hotel in Zandvort, the **Hotel Noordzee ❸,** Hogeweg 15, has cheerful rooms just 100m from the beach. (Breakfast included. Rooms have TV and hall shower and toilet. ☎571 31 27; www.hotel-nor-

Delicious Meal

Frans Haals Museum

Secret Passageways

dzee.nl; Doubles begin at €47-60, depending on season). Otherwise, you can book inexpensive bed and breakfast rooms through the VVV, with an additional 10% fee (these are in private residences and usually don't like smokers).

Rent bikes at **Rent a Bike Centre,** Passage 20. (☎571 33 43. Basic bikes €6 per day, 3-speed bike €7 per day.) North of Zandvoort, to the right of Bloemendaal, lies the **Zuid-Kennemerland National Park** (visitors center ☎527 18 71), where you can ride lovely bike trails through the dunes (stay on marked trails since it is a nature sanctuary). A little closer to Zandvoort, just north of the town, lies the **Kraansvlak Dune Reserve,** also very pleasant for a walk or bike ride. (☎0900 796 47 36; www.pwn.nl. Open M-Sa 9am-6pm, Su 10am-6pm. MC/V.) There is also a free **circus,** Gasthuispein 5 (☎23 571 86 86; www.circuszandvoort.nl) with games and a movie theater. Zandvoort's **restaurants** tend toward the expensive, true to beach resort style, but enough of them line the streets radiating from the **Raadhuisplein** that you can find some budget deals. On sunny days, the best choice might be one of the many **food trucks** that park along the strand, vending seafood (cooked or raw) fresh from the Atlantic (meals €3,50-6,50). Kerkstraat and Haltestraat in particular are packed with eateries, most of which feature chill outdoor patios and many of which develop lively bar scenes by night. **Grand Cafe 25,** Kerkstraat 25, features a classy bar and comfy, multi-colored linen chairs ideal for lounging and enjoying a drink. (☎571 35 10. Open 11am-3am, later on weekends) off Kerkstraat, to the right when walking toward the beach is **Yanks,** Dorpsplein 2, the rowdy, over-the-top cowboy-themed bar and coffeeshop. (☎571 94 55; www.yanks.nl. Open daily 9am-3am in summer, 10am-3am).

BLOEMENDAAL-AAN-ZEE

A 30min. walk to the right of Zandvoort Beach. Or take bus #81 from Haarlem or Zandvoort.

In recent years, Bloemendaal has been transformed from a quiet, family beach town into the site of the best beach parties in Holland. **Woodstock 69** (☎573 21 52; www.woodstock69.nl) started holding "Beach Bop" parties on Sunday night. The parties were so successful that thousands of people from Amsterdam and other countries started to pour in to rage on the beach, making Bloemendaal a pocket of hipness on the coast. Other clubs sprang up to support the revelers, but the magnitude of the parties became too much for tiny Bloemendaal to handle, so the authorities have now limited the **Beach Bop** to the last Sunday of every month (see www.beachbop.info), although lower-profile parties go on other nights of the week, too. The clubs are open only in summer months, generally April to September. Woodstock '69 is the pot of gold at the end of the rainbow, a backpacker's paradise with couches and bongos on the beach, bedlounges at the bar, and a restaurant serving tasty international food—all in colorful, comfortable hippie style. **Republic ❸** (☎573 07 30), brings urban hipness to the beach with sleek modern Indonesian/Japanese design and fusion gourmet cuisine; watch the chic eat their tempura barefoot. In between them, **De Zomer ❷** (☎571 80 08; www.dezomer.nl), serving €10 small packages of Chinese food on Saturdays, and **Solaris** (☎573 21 55; www.strandclubsolaris.nl), are two other younger clubs that help support the DJ concert series **Paradiso-aan-Zee** (www.paradisoaanzee.nl). Bloemendaal also boasts the **Kopje van Bloemendaal,** the highest sand dune in The Netherlands.

Haarlem GroteMarkt

Hofje van Staats

Organ in the Grotekerk

ZAANSE SCHANS ☎075

Unleash your inner tourist for a day at the delightful Zaanse Schans, a 17th-century town on the River Zaan only 20 minutes from Amsterdam. Feel free to fumble around with an oversized map and wear a fannypack because, with its cheese farm, wooden shoe workshop, and working windmills, that's precisely what Zaanse Schans is for. In the 1950s, people in Zaan region were concerned that industrialization was quietly destroying their historic landmarks, so they transported the landmarks on barges and trucks (they were wooden and therefore light) to this pretty plot of land. Ducks paddle happily around the canals next to the tourists while sheep and cows graze on fields down the street. While walking around Zaanse Schans with the numerous tourist groups, it may feel like a museum village, but in fact a handful of people now live and work here (about 40 in 25 houses). For that Golden Age feel you've been searching for, Zaanse Schans is perfect.

Most attractions in the town are open daily in the summer 10am-5pm, but only on weekends in winter. Zaanse Schans is best suited to be a true one-day trip, but if you like it so much you want to stay on the VVV center can direct you to accommodations.

PRACTICAL INFORMATION

From Amsterdam, take the *stoptrein* heading to Alkmaar and get off at Koog Zandijk (20 min; €2,25 one way). From there, follow the signs to

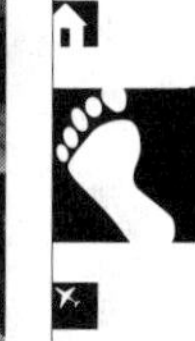

Teller's Museum

Enjoying Boat Life

Haarlem's Old Hospital

Zaanse Schans, a 12min. walk across a bridge. Zaanse Schans has an **information center,** Schansend 1 (☎616 82 18; www.zaanseschans.nl; info@zaanseschans.nl). Open daily 8:30am-5pm; in summer 8:30am-5:30pm.

SIGHTS

The best way to see picturesque Zaanse Schans is just to wander around, popping into whatever place interests you. The highlight of the attractions are the **working windmills,** some of last remaining ones in the world. You can see the wheels inside grinding with their strange power and then head up to the deck for a nice view of the area. The town has eight windmills in all; two regularly allow visitors. The lovely **De Kat Windmill** has been grinding plants into artists' pigments since 1782. (☎621 04 77. Open Apr.-Oct. daily 9am-5pm; Nov.-Mar. Sa-Su 9am-5pm. €2, ages 6-12 €1, groups of 10 €1,50.) The **De Zoeker windmill** is the oldest oil mill in the world; it works by a deafening banging beam. (☎62 79 42. Open Mar.-Oct. daily 9:30am-4:30pm. €2.)

Other highlights include **Cheesefarm Catharina Hoeve,** which offers free bite-sized samples of its homemade wares as well as a free tour of its workshop. (☎621 58 20. Open daily 8am-6pm.) Watch craftsmen mold blocks of wood into comfy clogs at **Klompenmakerij de Zaanse Schans** (☎617 71 21). There's also a charming display that unravels the mystery of the wooden shoe's prominence in Dutch history.

See where the ubiquitous Albert Heijn supermarket craze started at the man's original old shop, now a museum the **Albert Heijn Museumwinkel**. Next door you can stop by the **Museum van het Nederlandse Uurwerk (Museum of the Dutch Clock),** Kalverringdijk 3, to sneak a peek at the oldest working pendulum clock in the world, as well as a number of other fascinating timepieces. (☎617 97 69. Open Apr.-Oct. 31 daily 10am-5pm. €2,30.) Other attractions include the pint-sized **Museum Het Noorderhuis,** a restored home that features original costumes from the Zaan region in two reconstructed rooms. (☎617 32 37. Open Mar.-June and Sept.-Oct. Tu-Su 10am-5pm; July-Aug. daily 10am-5pm; Nov.-Feb. Sa-Su 10am-5pm. €1, seniors and children ages 4-11 €0,50. At the **Hut van de Kapitein,** boats are still repaired and built once a week; the rest of the time it's just a store selling nautical clothing and trinkets (open Mar.-Dec. daily 10am-5pm). If travel by water is your thing, consider cruising around Zaanse Schans with **Rederij de Schans.** (☎614 67 62. Hourly departures Apr.-Sept. daily 11am-4pm. €5.)

NOORDWIJK ☎071

Beautiful white-sand beaches are about an hour from Amsterdam in the town of Noordwijk. While the stunning hamlet on the coast of Holland has always been a favorite resort for Dutch and German tourists, international travelers are only beginning to discover its wonders. Outdoor activities abound, and visitors can sample from a number of exciting offerings: horseback riding through the dunes, surfing through the brisk seacoast water, or tossing frisbees around on over 13km of sparkling white sand.

TRANSPORTATION

To get to Noordwijk, take a train from Centraal Station to Leiden Centraal Station. Outside the station in Leiden is a terminal where you can catch a bus to Noordwijk for 5 strips or €3,40. The Flying Pig also runs a shuttle bus (€2 each way) that leaves from their downtown hostel in Amsterdam daily in summer at 8pm and from the Vondelpark hostel at 8:30pm (☎071 36 22 533; reservations necessary) and leaves from Noordwijk to Amsterdam at 7:00pm.

ORIENTATION AND PRACTICAL INFORMATION

Get off the bus when you see the beach, at the second to last stop, or if you go to the last stop, the beach will just be a four-minute walk past the VVV. At the **VVV Noordwijk,** De Grent 8 (☎361 93 21; info@vvv.noordwijk.nl; www.vvvnoordwijk.nl), you can pick up a free map. Koningen Wilhemina Blvd. is the street that runs parallel to the beach along the center of town, while the next one in is conveniently named Parallel Boulevard.Wilhemina turns inward and becomes De Grent at the police station on the beach while Kon. Astrid Blvd. continues along down the coast.

Noordwijk-aan-Zee is easily walkable, although renting a bike is a great way to take in the nearby dune trails or to leave the crowds behind on the beach. Bike rental is available at **Mooijekind,** Schoolstraat 68, starting at €6 a day. (☎361 28 26. Open daily 8:30am-6pm.)

ACCOMMODATIONS

Flying Pig Beach Hostel, Parallel Blvd. 208 (☎362 25 33; fax 362 25 53; beachhostel@flyingpig.nl; www.flyingpig.nl). From Leiden, take bus #40

Hofje Doorway

Courtyard of Frans Haals Museum

Haarlem's Gravenstenenbrug

Dutch Architecture

Special Flower Candles

Carved Hound Detail in the Grotekerk

or 42 for 20min. to "Vuurtorenplein," face south and the Pig will be 100m on your left side. Located in the center of town, 2min. from the beach. The Beach Hostel is a rare find among budget accommodations, offering excellent service, plus bright, clean, nicely decorated lodgings. Every night, staff members prepare home-cooked meals for guests (€6); regular volleyball games at sunset take everyone to the beach across the street. The sun-drenched chill-spot at the front of the hostel is an ideal place to curl up, nap, and forget the hustle and bustle of Amsterdam. A full range of activities is offered through the Pig, including the Kite Surfing Experience (€20); rental of surfboards, in-line skates, and mountain bikes; and horseback riding. Breakfast included. Kitchen facilities. Free Internet. Key deposit €10. Reception 9am-midnight. Dorms (14-bed) €14 or queen size bed for 2 in dorm €21; 7-bed dorm €17,50; 4-bed dorm €20,50; doubles €25,50 per person, with bath €31 per person. Open Mar.-Oct. ❶

NJHC-Herberg De Duinark (HI), Langevelderlaan 45 (☎0252 37 29 20; www.njhc.org/noordwijk). Take bus #57 and walk 30min. following the signs to Sancta Maria or you can call a bus (☎023 515 53 17). The sizable hostel is especially geared towards groups, though the facilities serve individual travelers as well. Canoe, scooter, mountain bike, and power kite rentals are available, only 10-15min. from the beach. Bring a towel as rentals are not available. Reception 8am-midnight. Check in before 6pm. Members €18,80; nonmembers €21,30. AmEx/MC/V. ❶

Op Hoop van Zegen Camping, Westeinde 76 (☎237 54 91; http://members.lycos.nl/ophoopvanzegen). Campsite in the woods with a heated facility building, 2.5km from the beach. €17.50. ❶

FOOD

Hoofdstraat, a two-minute walk from the Flying Pig Beach Hostel, is lined with small shops and restaurants. For cafes and bars, try **Koningin Wilhelmina Boulevard,** where most of the establishments have terraces which overlook the North Sea.

Chicoleo, Koningin Wilhelmina Blvd. 7b (☎361 21 21; www.chicoleo.nl). This colorful Mexican restaurant and Argentinian steakhouse is a local favorite in Noordwijk. Stop in on the weekend and catch live musical acts (F-Su 7pm) that will surely add some spice to your salsa. Full veggie menu. Lunch €5; dinner entrees from €11,25-€20. Take-out available. Open daily noon-midnight. AmEx/MC/V. ❹

Harbour Lights, Koningin Wilhelmina Blvd. 9 (☎361 77 05). Have a beer and play some darts at this intimate seaside pub. The bar and café attracts locals and tourists of all ages, many of whom know that it's one of the few places in town that'll serve up a pint of

Guinness (€4). Domestic beers (10 on tap and several more in bottles) will cost you slightly less. *Dagschotel* (daily special) €8, dinners about €10. Open daily noon-2am. ❷

Vivaldis, Koningin Wilhelmina Blvd. 17 (☎361 67 04). Choose from the 50 homemade flavors (hazelnut to pear), grab a big old cone and stuff it with Vivaldis's superb ice cream. Cones €0,70-2,30. Open in summer daily noon-midnight. ❶

Restaurant de Filosoof, de Grent 4 (☎364 67 01; www.defilosoof.nl), right next to the VVV. A bit more expensive but good food in a cheerful, upscale setting. Start with the shrimp salad with mango and pineapple (€8,50) and move onto a chicken curry (€13,50), or go for the "surf and turf" (€19) and have it all. Credit cards accepted. ❹

OUTDOOR ACTIVITIES

Visitors come to Noordwijk for the beach, but that doesn't mean they just laze under the sun. The waves are good for surfing about a week out of every month—and you can rent boards, wetsuits and anything else you need. One popular activity is **kitesurfing,** which involves surfing on a board while attached to a kite that catches the wind high above you; lessons are necessary for novices. **Beach Break,** Bomstraat 13, will take care of all your water sporting needs. Surf lessons run two hours and cost €35; surfboard rental is €10 per hour; wetsuits are €5 per hour. Other rentals also available. A beginning kite surfing class is €95, while a private lesson runs €130 and rental of a complete set for your own use is €40. They also sell bathing suits, sarongs, towels, sunglasses, and other beach goodies. Walk up from the beach at the police station, go down Hoofdstraat and turn left on Bomstraat. (☎407 70 55; www.beachbreak.nl. Open M 1-6pm, Tu-W and F 10am-6pm, Th 10am-9pm, Sa 10am-5pm; Su 1-5pm.)

When you start to tire of the water, there are sunset **horseback rides** on the beach at **Barnhoeve,** Schoolstraat 71 (☎361 21 95; €13,50 per hour). Or check out the **Space Expo,** Keperlaan 3, a permanent space exhibition that attracts thousands of space fanatics each year. The Space Expo is the visitors center of the ESTEC, the largest branch of the European Space Agency. (☎364 64 89; fax 364 64 5; www.space-expo.nl. Open Tu-Su 10am-5pm. €6,80, ages 4-12 €4.55). Across from the VVV is the **'t Negentiende Hole** ("the nineteenth hole") **mini-golf,** which the Dutch tactfully call Midget Golf. (☎361 88 59. Open daily 10am-midnight; in winter Sa-Su only. €3, children €1.)

LEIDEN ☎071

Home to one of the oldest and most prestigious universities in Europe, Leiden brims with bookstores, bicycles, windmills, gated gardens, antique churches, hidden walkways, and some truly outstanding museums. Leiden has historically been The Netherlands' primary textile producer and today stands as one of Europe's intellectual centers; many of the city's buildings are painted with famous excerpts from Shakespeare, Verlaine, and Basho. Rembrandt's birthplace and the site of some of Europe's first **tulips,** The Netherlands' third-largest city offers visitors a picture-perfect gateway to flower country and a rewarding look into Dutch and world history.

TRANSPORTATION

Trains haul into Leiden's slick, white-and-glass Centraal Station from Amsterdam (20min., every 30min. until 2:45am, €5,40) and The Hague (20min., every 30min. until 3:15am, €4,20). Be careful as you're exiting the station—there are two exits. The exit down near train platforms 1 and 2 leads to the city center, while the other exit leads only to the excellent Museum Naturalis (see p. 216). Buses to Noordwijk (see p. 211), Flower Country (see p. 199), and other nearby destinations depart from berths located outside and just to the right of the station's main entrance.

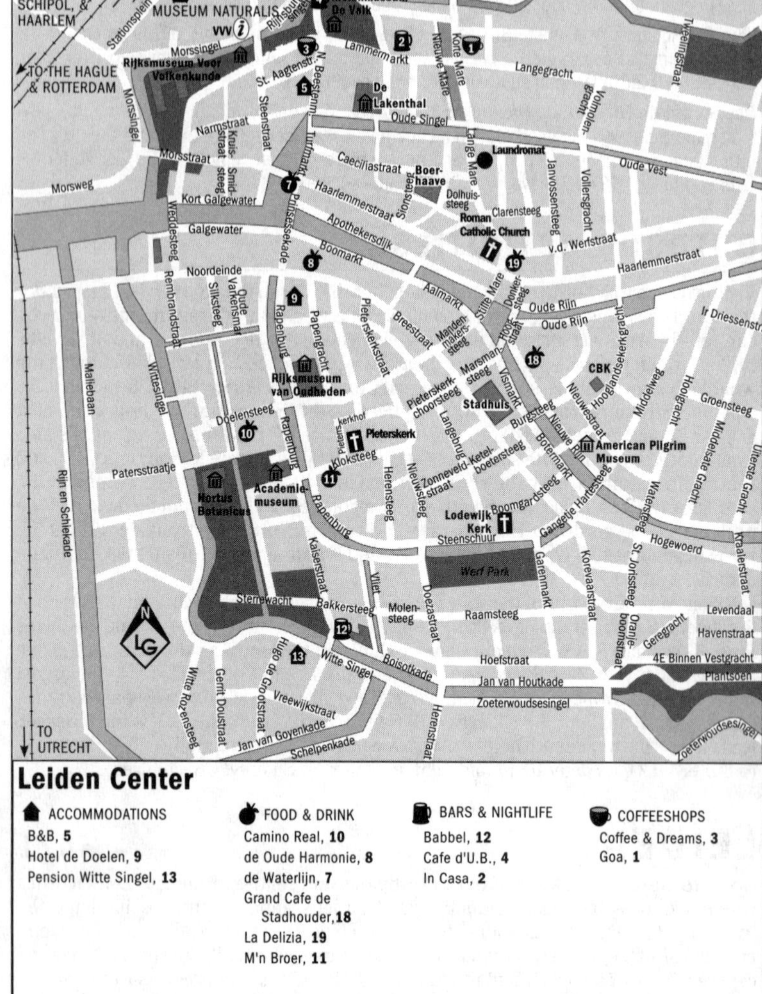

ORIENTATION AND PRACTICAL INFORMATION

The city of Leiden (population 120,000) is about 40km southwest of Amsterdam, near the North Sea and on the way to the Hague. The old city center lies southeast of Leiden Centraal, and the interesting areas are roughly enclosed within the **Morssingel** canal in the north, the **Witte Singel** in the west and south, and the **Herengracht** in the east. The small city center can be explored in several hours and has no shortage of picturesque canals, awesome sights, informative museums, and tasty restaurants.

The **VVV,** Stationsweg 2d, is less than a five-minute walk from the train station (from the south exit, take Steenstraat south and its blue-and-white signs will be up on your left) and sells maps (from €1,15) and walking tour brochures (€2), and can help find **hotel rooms** (fee €2,50 for one person, €2 for each additional person), although you can easily find them yourself. (☎090 02 22 23 33; fax 516 12 27; www.leiden.nl. Open M-F 10am-6:30pm, Sa 10am-4:30pm; Apr.-May and July-Aug. also open Su 11am-3pm.)

ACCOMMODATIONS

Hotel Pension Witte Singel, Witte Singel 80 (☎512 45 92; fax 514 28 90; wvandriel@pensione-ws.demon.nl). Take bus #43 to Merenwijk and tell the driver your destination (15min. walk from Leiden Centraal). Work your way south on the street that changes from Turfmarkt to Prinsessekade to Rapenburg to Kaiserstraat until Witte Singel; the hotel is across the water on your right. Owner is friendly and lobby area is elegant. Immaculate rooms overlook gorgeous gardens and canals. Singles from €31; doubles from €46,50). ❷

Hotel de Doelen, Rapenburg 2 (☎512 05 27; fax 512 84 53; www.dedoelen.com). From the south exit of the station, take Steenstraat to Morsstraat, turn left, cross the canal and follow it right. More centrally located and classier than the Pension Witte Singel, with the prices to prove it. Breakfast €7. Every room comes with shower, toilet, TV, and phone. Singles €65-68; doubles €85-120. AmEx/MC/V. ❸

B&B, Beestenmarkt 14 (☎514 66 30). From the south exit of the station take Steenstraat and it's on your left, 400m ahead on the same strip as the mighty McDonald's. Above a café with very cozy (though perhaps on weekends, less than quiet) rooms. Breakfast included. Shower and TV in every room. Shared toilets. Singles €60; doubles €80; triples €100; quads €120. Cash only. ❸

FOOD

Leiden abounds with restaurants of all types. The Super de Boer supermarket is opposite the train station at Stationsweg 40. (Open M-F 7am-9pm, Sa 9am-8pm, Su noon-7pm.)

de Oude Harmonie, Breestraat 16 (☎512 21 53), just off Rapenburg. Locals and students pack into this popular *eetcafe*, where candlelight and stained glass set the mood, especially on weekend nights. Lunch features *broodjes* under €3 and omelettes from €3,70 to €4,30. Dinner means tasty international entrees at good prices (€5,70-12,95). Lunch daily 1-3pm; dinner 5-9pm. Open Su 3pm-1am, M-Th noon-1am, F-Sa from noon until whenever the management feels like wrapping up. ❷

La Delizia, Lange Mare 112 (☎514 35 79). Follow Apothekersdijk east. At the fork in the canal keep right and it's just ahead on the left side of the canal. A perfect place to refuel, with an all-day menu, friendly service, and even friendlier prices. Italian-themed sandwiches €2,75-4,50; soups €3-4; salads €5-6.

Panorama

North Sea Jazz Festival

Fountain Outside Buitenof

Good-sized pizza and pasta dishes (€5,50-8,50). The restaurant doubles as an ice-cream parlor, with 12 flavors and a good selection of sundaes (try the Natuurijs Coupe—strawberry, blueberry, and banana ice cream mixed with orange juice and whipped cream €6,10). Open Tu-Sa 11am-10pm, Su 3:30-10pm. Cash only. ❶

de Waterlijn, Prinsessekade 5 (☎512 12 79). From the station, take Steenstraat south to Morsstraat and cross the canal on your left, then turn right; it's on your right. Sitting entirely on a canal is a bright little café and eatery with sandwiches for €2,50 and the house specialty, the french kiss (baguette with melted brie and tomatoes) for a measly €3,60. If the weather is nice, enjoy your meal on the wicker-chaired patio above the canal. Cash only. ❶

Camino Real, Doelensteeg 8 (☎514 90 69), off an alley between the Hortus and the Rijksmuseum van Oudheden. Just about the only thing Mexican about the former taco joint is the nachos and guacamole appetizer (€3,20). Lunch dishes (such as the pain fez, Turkish bread stuffed with mincemeat), fall well within budget range at €4,75 and are served from a sleek, chrome bar. Dinnertime appetizers make for a light but delicious meal (sashimi salad €8,65). Or just drop in for a drink. Open M-F 11am-2am, Sa noon-1am, Su 4pm-midnight. ❷

Grandcafe de Stadhouder, Nieuwe Rijn 13 (☎514 92 75), is a delightful restaurant with a floating patio on the canal out front. On uglier days, the colorful indoor lounge with sphere-shaped chandeliers is especially inviting. For lunch (11am-4pm) ingest sandwiches, *tostis*, omelettes, soup, or pancakes, almost all under €5. Dinner is pricier (3-course dinner menus from €21). Open daily 11am-12:30am; kitchen closes at 10pm. AmEx/MC/V. ❺

M'n Broer, Kloksteeg 7 (☎512 50 24), just off Rapenburg, across from the Hortus Botanicus. This dark dinner spot is French-inspired and will delight you with both its prices and its flavors. Grab a vegetarian entree for €9-9,50, a daily fish specialty, or enjoy most rich desserts for under €4,50. Open daily 5pm-midnight. ❷

SIGHTS

Leiden teems with museums, three of which are must-sees. Make sure you have a Museum Jahrkaart (MJK) to get into them for free (see p. 78).

MUSEUM NATURALIS

Darwinweg. From the north exit of Leiden Centraal (near platform 9), you will see the blue and yellow Leiden University Medical Center. Facing the building, turn right and cut between it and the new-age parking complex on its right (follow the signs to "Naturalis"). ☎568 76 00; www.naturalis.nl. Open Sept.-June Tu-Su 10am-6pm; July-Aug. daily 10am-6pm. €6, ages 4-12, €3,50.

Museum Naturalis, The Netherlands' national museum of natural history, is a spacious, modern, and beautifully displayed exhibition, exploring the history of the earth and its inhabitants. An absolute must-see for nature-lovers, the museum, with its eye candy exhibitions, has English and Dutch panels, providing visitors with scientific and anthropological explanations of the natural world—fossils, minerals, animals, evolution, and even astronomy. Even those who don't normally enjoy museums will appreciate the awe-inspiring dinosaur exhibit and the hands-on, diverse exhibitions, designed to appeal to audiences of all ages. The museum is only a five-minute walk from the trains, so you can get from Amsterdam to Naturalis in under an hour.

RIJKSMUSEUM VOOR VOLKENKUNDE (NATIONAL MUSEUM OF ETHNOLOGY)

Steenstraat 1, just over the canal from the VVV. ☎516 88 00; www.rmv.nl. Open Tu-Su 10am-5pm. €6,50, children ages 4-12 €3,50.

One of the world's oldest and best anthropological museums. On display in the regal and grandiose complex are totems and togs, swords and statues, and masks and mukluks from all over the world, with a particularly good selection of cultural artifacts from the Dutch East Indies. Recent renovations lend technological sophistication to the exhibits; interactive touch screens offer thoughtful explanations in English as well as Dutch, and guides (sometimes decked out in traditional dress) give illuminating presentations on the international collection, which explores the ethnicities and cultures of every continent but Europe.

RIJKSMUSEUM VAN OUDHEDEN (NATIONAL MUSEUM OF ANTIQUITIES)

Rapenburg 28, across the footbridge from the main gate to the Hortus Botanicus. ☎ 516 31 63; www.rmo.nl. Open Tu-F 10am-5pm, Sa-Su noon-5pm. €6,50, ages 6-18 €3,50.

This branch of the Rijksmuseum harbors the restored Egyptian Temple of Taffeh, a gift removed from the reservoir basin of the Aswan Dam. The excellent collection also features mummies and sarcophagi from North Africa and Europe during the Classical period. Don't miss the outstanding collection of artifacts from The Netherlands during the Roman Empire, but feel free to skip the medieval collection. Also included in the price of admission is the **Nationaal Penningkabinet,** The Netherlands' National Coin Cabinet, with several old, new, odd, and unreleased Dutch coins. The enormous museum offers a free English pocket guide for Dutch-impaired visitors.

OTHER MUSEUMS

If you're able to tear yourself away from the three museums listed above, visit Leiden's smaller museums, which also merit a peek. Scale steep staircases to inspect the innards of a functioning windmill from 1743 at the **Molenmuseum "De Valk,"** 2e Binnenvestgracht 1. On the ground floor of the windmill, the living quarters have been preserved as they were in its latest miller's day, with paintings and photographs depicting life at the end of the 19th century. (Open Tu-Sa 10am-5pm, Su 1-5pm. €2,50.) The **Museum De Lakenhal,** Oude Singel 32, exhibits works by Rembrandt and Jan Steen in an old canal house setting. Included in the museum are ever-changing contemporary photography exhibits and Dutch- and English-language displays on the history of Leiden and its important 700-year textile industry. (☎ 516 53 60. Open Tu-Sa 10am-5pm, Su noon-5pm. €4.) After the Pilgrims' departure from England but before their voyage to America, they found refuge in Leiden and a handful of other Dutch towns. Relive this period at the small but rich **American Pilgrim Museum,** Beschuitsteeg 9, housed in two rooms of Leiden's oldest house, built in 1371. (☎ 512 24 13. Open W-Sa 1-5pm. Extensive guided tour €2.)

OTHER SIGHTS

Leiden's appeal extends beyond its museums. The city's lovely canals are lined with covered bridges, cafés and bars, and stretches of parks. By far, the most impressive of Leiden's gardens is **Hortus Botanicus,** Rapenburg 73, sharing a main gate with the Academy building and **Universiteit Leiden's** 400-year-old possession. Hortus is the site of Western Europe's first tulips and happens to be The Netherlands' oldest botanical garden. Originally founded as a center for medical research and botanical instruction, the gardens house a wonderful reconstruction of the Clusius garden (open only on weekdays), the 18th-century orangery with tub plants and rare 200-year-old trees; they also allow visitors to peruse the tropical greenhouses with first-class plant collections. Its grassy knolls alongside the delectable **Witte Singel** canal make it an ideal picnic spot, too. (☎ 527 72 49; www.hortusleiden.nl. Guided tours available by appointment. Open Mar.-Nov. daily 10am-6pm; Nov.-Feb. Su-F 10am-4pm. €4, children 4-12 €2.) While in the area, be sure to take in the newly renovated **Pieterskerk,** Kloksteeg 16, the 500-year-old Gothic church home to the graves of Dutch painter Jan Steen and renowned pilgrim John Robinson. (☎ 512 43 19. Open daily 1:30pm-4pm. Free.) Facing the church, look to your left and you'll see the characteristic red-and-white geometrically patterned shutters of Leiden's university buildings. This one is called **Het Gravensteen** and is a former prison with a continued interest in jurisprudence—today it houses Universiteit Leiden's law faculty. From there, backtrack

Architectural Madness!

Ascend the escalators at the **Blaak** metro station in Rotterdam and you may think you've stumbled into Wonderland. Crazy, disproportioned yellow houses lean intently toward you, as if listening to your conversation. Beside these intrusive buildings stands a structure that looks more like a spaceship than anything else. A look back at the metro station reveals an aluminum discus looming over the escalators. Yet, this corner of Rotterdam, drunk as it is with its own architectural idiosyncrasy, isn't the exception but the rule.

After the German bombing that razed the city at the beginning of World War II, Rotterdam was put in the unenviable position of having to rebuild almost everything. A battery of experimental architects took to the task, and the results, if a bit mixed, are always interesting. Any trip to Rotterdam should include an up-close glimpse of its most recognizable structural curiosity, the **Erasmus Bridge,** whose striking white allure and strange arrangement of support cables make it look like a swan trailing its tailfeathers.

Rotterdam's architectural singularity doesn't end with its monumental public structures; it extends to nearly every office building, bank, and shopping center. Though the most famous buildings are, indeed, impressive, a truly complete architectural tour of Rotterdam mustn't overlook its smaller, but no less distinctive, creations.

toward Hortus and turn left on Rapenburg. Follow the canal a few blocks as it curves; on your right will be the welcoming, lush **Werfpark.** This green space, with a small cafe at its northwest edge, was the site of a gunpowder storage facility that exploded in 1807, destroying the surrounding city blocks. Miraculously, the **St. Lodewijk Church,** across the canal from the eastern side of the park, survived almost entirely unscathed. Ironically, this explosion site is one of the quietest areas in the city, good for reading a book or taking an afternoon nap.

NIGHTLIFE & COFFEESHOPS

While this city is, by all accounts, a university town, most students party at private fraternity-style events and hit up the discos and bars later at night. If you're generally looking to bar- or club-hop, head to the upper stretch of Nieuwe Beestenmarkt, just south of the windmill, which you'll find packed with bustling bars, clubs, and coffeeshops.

In Casa, Lammermarkt 100 (☎514 49 79). From Leiden Centraal, take Steenstraat past the VVV to 2e Binnenvestgracht, where you should turn left and then right on Lammermarkt; the late-night bender is on your left. In Casa is Leiden's self-named *studentendiscotheek*, with dance parties Th-Su evenings. Specializes in mainstream hip-hop. Get your dance on late into the night with the student-heavy crowd. Open Th 10pm-3:30am, F 11pm-3:30am, Sa 10pm-4am, Su 5-9pm. Cover €10.

Cafe d'U.B., Nieuwe Beestenmarkt 4 (☎512 04 55). A good pregame spot in the area. From the trains, take Steenstraat south, turn left at 2e Binnenvestgracht, continue around the corner and it's across the street on your left. It has beer for €1,50, mixed drinks for €4,50, and a projection screen showing movies or sports, so you might want to just skip the dancing. Like many other bars in Leiden, it is open on Saturday nights until 2am, at which point it shuts its doors but continues the party until the numbers thin.

Coffee and Dreams (☎512 22 92), at the corner of 2e Binnenvestgracht and Nieuwebeestenmarkt. Serves alcohol as well as pot and hash, and has an edgier vibe. While, by law, soft drugs can be sold only until 10pm, the bar keeps a-rockin' on Th-Sa until 2am. Joints €2,50-3,70; beers €1,70; mixed drinks €4,50. Pot and hashbar open daily 4-10pm; bar open Su-W until 1am.

Babbels (☎514 00 02), along the Witte Singel where Kaiserstraat becomes Boisotkade– about 15min. south by foot from the train station. University students congregate and imbibe here. Excellent selection of beer (€1,75-3,30). Open daily 3:30pm-midnight.

Goa, Korte Mare 8 (☎522 64 76; www.goacoffeeshop.nl), is an elegant little coffeeshop 10min. from Leiden Centraal. Take Steenstraat south and turn left at Beestenmarkt and follow the canal, Oude Singel, a few block to Korte Mare, on your left. With a pool table, beautiful wooden tables and chairs, and Primera (moroccan hash) at €9 per gram, you can puff down in style. Open daily 4-10pm.

THE HAGUE (DEN HAAG) ☎070

In many senses, The Hague is the all-business older brother to Amsterdam's wild and crazy younger sibling; there are precious few coffeeshops amidst The Hague's intimidating collection of historically significant buildings and monuments. Nevertheless, it is a city that lives a double life. Willem II moved his royal residence to The Hague in 1248, so there's no shortage of history here. But it has also become a modern, bustling metropolis, and a multitude of designer stores have sprung up among the palaces, embassies, and museums. After all, the countless diplomats need somewhere to shop. But somehow, the past and present have found a way to cohabitate comfortably in the city, and it's the visitor that profits, for in The Hague one finds all the pleasures of a city rich with history without foregoing the trappings of modern existence.

Joker's Doorway

Passage

The Hague Grotekerk

TRANSPORTATION

Trains roll in from Amsterdam (50min., €8 one way) and Rotterdam (25min., €3,40) to both of The Hague's major stations, **Centraal Station** and **Holland Spoor.** Centraal Station is right on the eastern edge of The Hague's downtown; Holland Spoor lies a few kilometers south of the city center but is convenient to the NJHC youth hostel. Trams #1, 9, and 12 connect the two stations.

PRACTICAL INFORMATION

The **VVV tourist office,** Kon. Julianapl. 30, is just outside the north entrance to Centraal Station, next to the Hotel Sofitel. They book rooms for a €1,75 fee and sell highly detailed maps of the city center (€2). They've even got an interactive hotel booking computer that is available 24hr. if you arrive after the VVV shuts its doors. (☎0900 340 35 05; www.denhaag.com. Open M and Sa 10am-5pm. Tu-F 9am-5:30pm, Su 11am-5pm.) **Net-cafe,** Van Mannankade 2, right next to Holland Spoor, has over 20 terminals that cater to all your surfing needs. (☎388 64 05 €1 for 15 min.

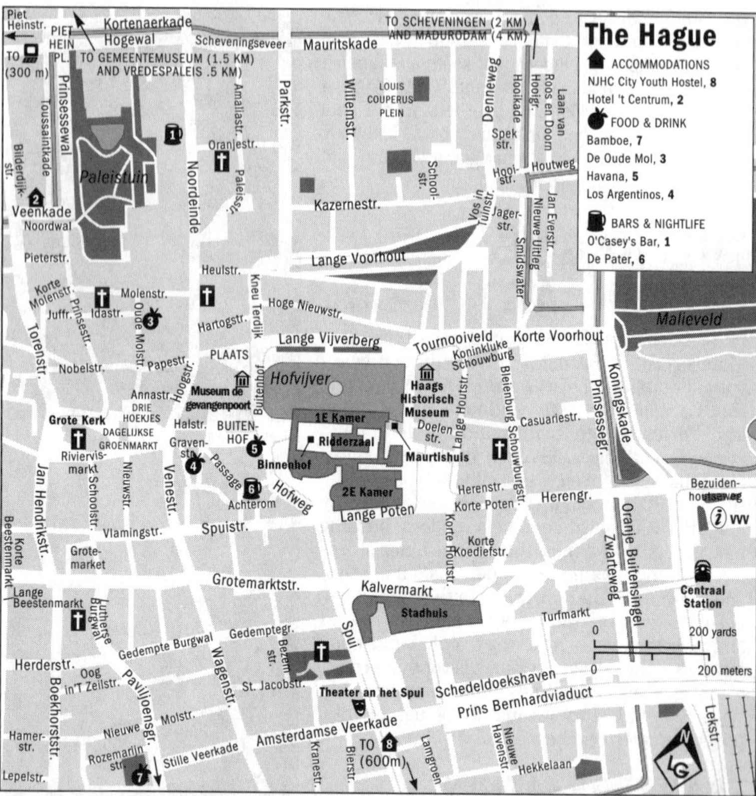

Open daily noon-midnight.). **Post Office,** Kerkplein 6, next to Grote Kerk. (Open M 11am-5pm, Tu-Sa 9am-5pm.) **American Book Ctr.,** Lange Poten 23, offers a wide selection of English-language books and magazines. (☎364 27 42;, www.abc.nl. Open M 11am-7pm, Tu-W and F 10am-7pm, Th 10am-9pm, Sa 10am-6pm, Su noon-6pm.

ACCOMMODATIONS

Let's Go does not recommend staying in one of the budget hotels lining Stationsweg, as they are unfriendly and not the best deal for the rooms. Instead try:

NJHC City Hostel, Scheepmakerstraat 27 (☎315 78 88; www.njhc.org/denhaag). Turn right from Holland Spoor, follow the tram tracks, turn right at the big intersection, and Scheepmakerstraat is 3min. ahead, on your right. From Centraal Station, take tram #1 (dir: Delft), 9 (dir: Vrederust), or 12 (dir: Duindrop) to Rijswijkseplein (2 strips); cross to the left in front of the tram, cross the big intersection, and Scheepmakerstraat is straight ahead. A huge, modern hostel that feels more like a hotel, NJHC features private baths and a helpful, friendly staff that knows anything you could want to know about Den Haag. Buffet breakfast and sheets included. Locker rental €2 for 24hr. 8-person dorms €23 per bed, €20,50 for HI members. Singles €47; doubles €61; triples €77,50; all prices lower during the off-season. 4-, 5- and 6-person rooms available for HI members only. Downstairs is **Brasserie Backpackers,** a huge in-house restaurant and bar that serves lunch and dinner (beer €1,70; main dishes from €8). Open daily until 1am. ❶

Hotel 't Centrum, Veenkade 5-6 (☎346 36 57). A nice place to stay in a quiet corner of The Hague. Nevertheless an easy walk to the city center. Includes breakfast in a pleasant downstairs dining area. Single €40, with bath €65; doubles with bath €75. ❷

FOOD AND DRINK

Restaurants in The Hague run the gamut from humble to sumptuous. For the former, head to the **Lange** and **Korte Poten,** two streets that run behind the Binnenhof and brim with takeaway joints where you can grab a quick falafel, shawarma, or doner kebob. For the latter, check out the grand cafes that crowd the squares on either side of the Binnenhof. For an afternoon bite, cruise by Spuiplein, where you can eat lunch at one of several cafes beside inground fountains that spit ten feet high and a strange assortment of modern art creations that line the pedestrian walkway.

Havana, Buitenhof 19 (☎356 29 00). Tram #3 or 10 to Buitenhof. This bar and restaurant specializes in Cuban fare and has a sprawling outdoor terrace where you can booze and schmooze with Dutch politicos and The Hague's beautiful people. Beer €1,70; entrees €11-13. Open daily 10:30am-1am. ❸

Cafe de Oude Mol, Oude Molstraat 61 (☎345 16 23). Tram #3 to Grote Halstraat, walk through the pavilion to your right, where you'll hit Oude Molstraat; follow for 2 blocks and the restaurant is on the right. At Oude Mol, you'll find a cramped but hip environment with both a small outdoor patio and an impossibly steep and winding staircase straight out of an Escher painting. But if the waitresses can make the trek with full trays of food, so can you, and it's well worth it for the blizzard of mouthwatering *tapas* available, all from €3-5. Open Su-W 5pm-1am, Th-Sa 5pm-2am. Live music M. ❷

Bamboe, Zuidwal 8a (☎427 86 71). Tram #16 or 17 to Spui; cross the street and walk along the canal on Bierkade, which turns into Zuidwal after 2 blocks. Small neighborhood restaurant and bar offers a large selection of Indonesian cuisine; the pleasant location along the canal and especially friendly staff make it worth the trip from the city center. Starters €2-4, main courses €6-12; an Indonesian *rijstaffel*, though, costs €16-20 per person. Plenty of vegetarian options. Open daily noon-1am; kitchen open 5-10pm. ❹

Los Argentinos, Kettingstraat 14 (☎346 85 23), just off the Buitenhof. Tram #10 to Granvenstraat. There's no shortage of Argentinian restaurants in the area, and this meathouse has one of the best deals in town. For €9,50 they serve a cut of real South American beef, fries, and unlimited access to the salad bar. Open daily 3-11pm. AmEx/MC/V. ❷

Knights Hall

Peace Palace

Mauritshuis

SIGHTS

The Hague has served as the seat of Dutch government for 800 years, and has of late become a focal point for international criminal justice. Government buffs will drool at the sightseeing prospects.

PEACE PALACE (HET VREDESPALEIS)

Carnegieplein 2. 3min. on tram #7 or 8 north of the Binnenhof. ☎302 41 37 or 302 42 42; peacepal@planet.nl or carnegie@carnegie-stichting.nl; www.vredespaleis.nl. Tours M-F 10, 11am, 2, and 3pm. Book in advance through tourist office, by emailing, or by calling directly. Admission €3,50, children under 13 €2.30. No tours when the court is in session.

The opulent home of the International Court of Justice and the Permanent Court of Arbitration was donated by Andrew Carnegie in 1913. It has served as the site of international arbitrations, peace-treaty negotiations, and war crimes trials since then. The tour focuses more on the building's objects (donated from each country participating) and artwork than the workings of the courts, but the objects are magnificent, and the tour is the only option for visitors who want to get past the gates. The building is surrounded by impeccably kept grounds and gardens that are closed to the public.

MAURITSHUIS

Korte Vijverberg 8. Just outside the north entrance of the Binnenhof. ☎302 34 35; communicatie@mauritshuis.nl; www.mauritshuis.nl. Open Tu-Sa 10am-5pm, Su 11am-5pm. €7, children under 18 free.

Of the 32 Vermeer paintings in existence, three are housed at the Mauritshuis, including his Mona Lisa, *Girl with a Pearl Earring*, and one of his only two landscapes, *View of Delft*. The museum also has major works by Rembrandt, van der Weyden, and Jan Steen. For a museum with such a breathtaking collection of Dutch artwork, the Mauritshuis is exceptionally manageable and won't steal more than two hours of an afternoon.

BINNENHOF AND RIDDERZAAL

The most central point in the city, accessible by trams #1, 2, 3, 6, 7, 8, 9, 16, and 17. ☎364 61 44 . Open M-Sa 10am-4pm; last tour leaves at 3:45pm. Entrance to courtyard free; tours €5.

Beside the Hofvijver, the giant reflecting pool with its own fountain and island is the "home of Dutch democracy," the Binnenhof (literally inner courtyard) Parliament building. Built in the 13th century, it has a long history as home to many of The Netherlands' most prominent historical figures and events. Show up at **Binnenhof 8a** (tucked behind Ridderzaal, in the center of the courtyard) for a guided tour, which covers both Ridderzaal (Hall of Knights) and either the first or second chamber of Binnenhof. Because Dutch democracy needs its quiet, the chambers are closed when Parliament is in session. The tour is in Dutch, though an English translation is provided on paper. Even if politics isn't your thing, be sure to see the courtyard, one of The Hague's most photogenic sights.

GEMEENTEMUSEUM

Stadhouderslaan 41. From Holland Spoor, take tram #10; from Centraal Station, hop on bus #4; both stop right in front of the museum complex. ☎338 11 11; www.gemeentemuseum.nl. Open Tu-Su 11am-5pm, €6,80; free with MJK. Wheelchair accessible.

For fans of minimal ism, there's no better place to head than The Hague's Gemeentemuseum, which boasts an entire floor dedicated to De Stijl, including a large selection of one of its major devotees, **Piet Mondriaan.** Don't be put off by the museum's garish yellow exterior; it was, in fact, the work of famous Dutch architect H.P. Berlage. The interior is a different matter, however, with well-designed rooms and an excess of white space surrounding each work that both highlights the art and draws attention to the structure of the building itself. In addition to the enormous collection of minimalism and, of all things, glasswork, Gemeentemuseum has some wonderful work by Jozef Israels and other members of the Hague School, a late 19th-century artistic movement, as well as works by Francis Bacon and the German Expressionists that shouldn't be missed.

Gemeentemuseum

MADURODAM

George Maduroplein 1. Take tram #1 or 9 (dir: Scheveningen) to Madurodam, or bus #10. ☎416 24 00; info@madurodam.nl; www.madurodam.nl. Open Sept.-Feb. daily 9am-6pm; Mar.-June 9am-8pm; July-Aug. 9am-10pm. €10, children ages 4-11 €7.50.

Think of it as Holland-in-a-box. It's surprising just how much time you can spend wandering among the staggeringly detailed miniature recreations (the scale is 1:25) of almost all of The Netherlands; working trains, boats, drawbridges, windmills, ferries, and even waterskiers are in constant motion throughout Madurodam's vast expanse. For some, the obvious response to such an attraction is, "Why see Holland in miniature when you can see it for real?" Certainly, it isn't for everyone, but the attraction is surprisingly satisfying, as each step through the park reveals a new detail.

The Hague

HAAGS HISTORISCH MUSEUM

Korte Vijverberg 7. Across the street from Mauritshuis outside the north entrance to the Binnenhof. ☎364 69 40; info@haagshistorischmuseum.nl; www.haagshistorischmuseum.nl. Open Tu-F 11am-5pm, Sa-Su noon-5pm. €3,60, children under 18 free.

Less a collection of artifacts than an exploration of history through paintings, The Hague's historical museum features some worthwhile exhibits, including one on the country's most famous ruler, Willem of Orange. A first-floor emphasis on contemporary art gives the impression that The Hague is still making history today.

GROTE KERK

Kerkplein. ☎302 86 30. Only open during public events; check entrance or call for information.

It's too bad that the church isn't open more regularly, but it's still quite a sight from the outside. Built in the 15th century, it remains one of The Hague's most impressive sights, even if it now has to tower over the myriad department stores that play at its feet.

Paleistuin Park in the Hague

MUSEUM DE GEVANGENPOORT

Buitenhof 33. Just across the street from the Hofvijer. ☎346 0861; info@gevangenpoort.nl; www.gevangenpoort.nl. Dutch tour comes with English print translation. Open Tu-F 11am-5pm, Sa-Su 1-5pm (last tour leaves at 4pm). Tours in English July-Aug. daily 2pm. Tours €3,60, children €2,70.

Today, the prisons in Holland are quite nice, but it was not always that way. The one-hour tour through this old prison gate takes you through dark cells and torture rooms. The tour shows the vast disparity between the treatment of common prisoners, who were penned into damp underground rooms, and rich ones, who received their own private rooms complete with fireplaces. Children will either be impressed or frightened by the array of torture instruments.

NIGHTLIFE

Most of the nightlife in The Hague centers around bar-cafes where folks drink and chill, and the party stays low-key. For dance craziness, you're better off prowling Scheveningen's Strandweg (p. 224). Nevertheless, there are some bars well worth visiting.

O'Casey's Bar, Noordeinde 140 (☎363 06 98; ocaseys@hotmail.com; www.ocaseys.net.) The best pint of Guinness in the city (€4). Its splendorous *biergarten* is regally situated just behind the back wall of the Dutch Queen's palace. More to the point, it's got some of the cheapest eats in town: M-F 5-8pm, you can get a full plate of food for €5, and F 8-10pm, cocktails are €5. Irish drinking songs pump on the stereo. Open Su-Th noon-1am, F-Sa noon-2am; kitchen closes at 9:30pm.

De Pater (The Priest), Achterom 8 (☎345 08 52), is pious in name only. The beer's pricey at over €2, but it's still one of The Hague's best music bars. De Pater features international sets including salsa, Latin beats, and jazz for a young, lively crowd. Shows start at 10:30pm; call ahead for schedules. Open Tu-Sa 10pm-2am, Su 5pm-2am.

ENTERTAINMENT

Theater aan het Spui, Spui 187 (☎346 52 72; www.theateraanhetspui.nl). Tram #16 or 17 to Spui. Experimental theater, indie music, and modern dance all find a home at the Spui Theater, with its funky stage design and overall hip approach to entertainment. Though some plays are in Dutch, there are regular concerts featuring the latest cutting-edge sound. Closed from the end of June to Aug.; check website for latest offerings.

North Sea Jazz Festival (www.northseajazz.nl). Brings the absolute best names in jazz together in one place for 3 days in mid-July every year. The festival takes place in Scheveningen by the sea.

Parkpop (☎523 90 64; www.parkpop.nl). Hosts what The Netherlands hails as the largest free public pop concert in the world. Held on 3 big stages in the Zuiderpark during late June every year.

NEAR THE HAGUE

SCHEVENINGEN

Scheveningen is where all those diplomats who constantly carouse within the walled-in streets of The Hague come to let their hair down. Located in the northernmost part of the city, right up against the North Sea, the town is little more than a long strip of shore packed end to end with bars and nightclubs. On a sunny day, it's a great place to come spend a few hours at the beach, but Scheveningen's real fame is in its nightlife, when the dozens of bars fill up with tourists and locals alike.

PRACTICAL INFORMATION

The **Hague VVV** sells cycling maps, but routes and nearby towns are also clearly marked along paths. The Scheveningen branch of the **VVV,** Gevers Deynootweg

1134, has info on rooms. (☎09 00 340 35 05. €0,40 per min. Open M 11am-6pm, Tu-F 9:30am-6pm, Sa 10am-5pm, Su 1-5pm.) **Trams** #1, 8, and 9 make the trek to Scheveningen from The Hague, though well-marked paths provide a great hike or **bike ride** (rent from Holland Spoor or Centraal Station, less than €4 per day), which you can then extend into a shoreline cycle trek.

ACCOMMODATIONS

Accommodations in a beach resort like Scheveningen don't come cheap, but there are some noteworthy exceptions. You can also try prowling Gevers Deynootweg, where most of the hotels are located.

Hotel Hage, Seinpostduin 22-23 (☎351 46 96; fax 358 58 51). Tram #8 to Gevers Deynootweg, cross the street toward the sea and Seinpostduin is just ahead on your left; walk up it and the hotel is on the right. A comfortable place to stay and one of the better deals in town, just a hop from the beach. Singles €49; doubles €88; triples €110. ❸

Camping Duinhorst, Buurtweg 135 (☎324 22 70; www.duinhorst.nl), in the nearby town of Wassenar. Take bus #43 from Centraal Station. Open Apr.-Oct. €3,75 per person; €2,25 per tent. ❶

FOOD AND DRINK

Eating in Scheveningen is best done at any of the fresh fish vendors that roll up to the Strandweg and sell *broodjes* (around €4) and meals of cod and calamari, perch, and pike (plates of fish and burgers €3-5). The restaurants along the Strand tend to double as bars and triple as dance clubs, and every one has a particularly garish theme, from the South Seas, to giant gorillas, to crazy pianos. Dinner isn't cheap along the Strand, with main dishes running anywhere from €10 to €20.

SIGHTS

The **Strandweg** stretches along the beach, scattered with outdoor terraces and a few carnivalesque attractions. The beach itself is dotted with beach clubs that serve food and have space where you can recline with a beer and catch some rays. The prefabricated huts change yearly, but the best ones tend to cluster at the less crowded northern end of the strand (look for the big steel obelisk).

BEELDEN AAN ZEE. More an experience than a museum, it's the unique design of Beelden aan Zee that's most captivating: the rooms are both indoors and outdoors, and weave seamlessly in and out of one another, guiding visitors as they wind among the many strange statues—some harrowing, some beautiful. The dunes of the beach press right against the window of the museum, and from the roof you can look out over the sea. While Scheveningen is nicest on a sunny day, Beelden aan Zee's powerful artwork is best appreciated on an appropriately gray day to capture the mood; but, no matter what the weather, it is one of the most engaging museums you'll find anywhere. (*Harteveltstraat 1. Take tram #1 or 9 to Circustheater, follow Badhuisweg to Gevers Deynootweg, turn left until Harteveltstraat comes up on the right. ☎358 58 57; www.beeldenaanzee.nl. Open Tu-Su 11am-5pm. €5, students €2,50.)*

SEA LIFE SCHEVININGEN. Ideal for kids, this aquarium packs eels, rays, tropical fish, and even some small sharks into a variety of uniquely designed displays. However, while it's big on design (including one room, not for the claustrophobic, in which you walk through a tube inside the tank), it's somewhat slight on content. There just aren't that many fish, and while children will no doubt delight at the undersea wonders, unless you're an aquarium buff you may find yourself with a sore spot in your wallet. (*Standweg 13. Right on the beach. ☎354 21 00; www.sealife.nl. Open daily 10am-7pm. Admission €9, kids €6. Visa.)*

SCHEVENINGEN PIER. Dead in the center of the strand, the pier dates back 100 years, but recent renovations have erased the ravages of time. The walkway extends several hundred meters out above the ocean, and houses music festivals and art shows throughout the year. (*☎306 55 00; info@pier.nl; www.pier.nl. Check website for schedules. Entrance to pier €1).*

DELFT

☎015

The lillied canals and stone footbridges that still line the streets of Delft are the very ones along which renowned painter Johannes Vermeer once walked as he contemplated his masterpieces. **Vermeer** (1632-1675) is a local hero here. He was born and raised in Delft and is buried in the town's Oude Kerk. It was he who most timelessly memorialized the beauty of the town in his famous *View of Delft*. In fact, Delft's colorful markets and lovely canal houses attracted numerous celebrated painters during the Golden Age, among them **Jan Steen, Carel Fabritius, Pieter de Hoogh,** and **Willem van Aelst.** Over the centuries, the city also held court as a commercial center, one of the six seats of the Dutch East India Company, and home of the blue and white ceramic work known as Delftware.

Delft's history is a dramatic one, replete with glorious highs and disastrous lows. It is believed that the city began its life in 1070, developing out of a community that surrounded Duke Godfrey of Lorraine's castle. In 1436, the town's Nieuwe Delf and Oude Delf became a unified entity. As the city's commercial sector developed, some 200 breweries came into operation along the canals; the production of butter, cloth, and woven carpets added to the town's prosperity. In 1536, Delft met with its first catastrophe: an immense fire that consumed two-thirds of the city's buildings. The plague followed in the next year. While fires and wars would continue to damage the community over the coming centuries, the arrival of **Willem of Orange** in 1583 restored some glory to Delft. In 1568, Willem led the resistance against enemy forces in the war against Spain from the city. In 1584, Willem was shot dead in Delft by an assassin. The arrival of the Golden Age in the 17th century couldn't have come too soon for Delft, which experienced magnificent growth in trade, the arts, and the sciences.

Today, Delft's population has grown to about 95,000 people, including 13,000 students. The city is a center for science and technology in The Netherlands but still maintains its timeless character. Six hundred national monuments, museums, and three working **Delftware factories** make the town a popular destination for tourists. Thursdays and Saturdays, when townspeople flood to the bustling marketplace, are the best days to visit.

PRACTICAL INFORMATION

The easiest way into Delft is the 15-minute ride on **tram** #1 from The Hague (2 strips) to Delft station. **Trains** also arrive from Amsterdam (1hr., one-way €8,90).

The **VVV tourist office,** Markt 85, has hiking and cycling maps and books rooms (€1,75 plus 10% deposit). From the station, cross the bridge, turn left, turn right at the first light, and follow signs to the Markt. (☎213 01 00; www.vvvdelft.nl. Open M-Sa 9am-5:30pm; Apr.-Sept. also Su 11am-3pm.) Thursday is generally **market day** (open 9am-5pm) on the Markt. There is also a flower and plant market held at the same time on Hippolytusbuurt. On Saturday, there is a general market on the Brabantse Turfmarkt from 9am to 5pm. If you want to take a water bike along the canals of Delft, try **Rondvaart Delft,** Koornmarkt 113. (☎212 63 85. Open Mar.-Oct. daily 10am-6pm. €8,50, plus a €15 deposit.) **Maps of walking routes** are available at the VVV shop and provide structured tours of the city. Some route titles include "Following in the footsteps of Johannes Vermeer" and "Famous Delft painters, writers, and scientists."

ACCOMMODATIONS

There are some exceptions, but most digs in quaint Delft don't come cheap.

Herberg de Emauspoort, Vrouwenregt 9-11 (☎219 02 19; emauspoort@emauspoort.nl; www.emauspoort.nl). In this old Dutch-style hotel, the atmosphere is casual and service is excellent. From April to October, two authentic gypsy caravans are available for rent to visitors at no extra cost, but book in advance because they are popular. All rooms include bath, TV, and phone. The complimentary breakfast comprises selections from the hotel's own confectionary. Doubles from €82,50; triples €115; quads €140. ❹

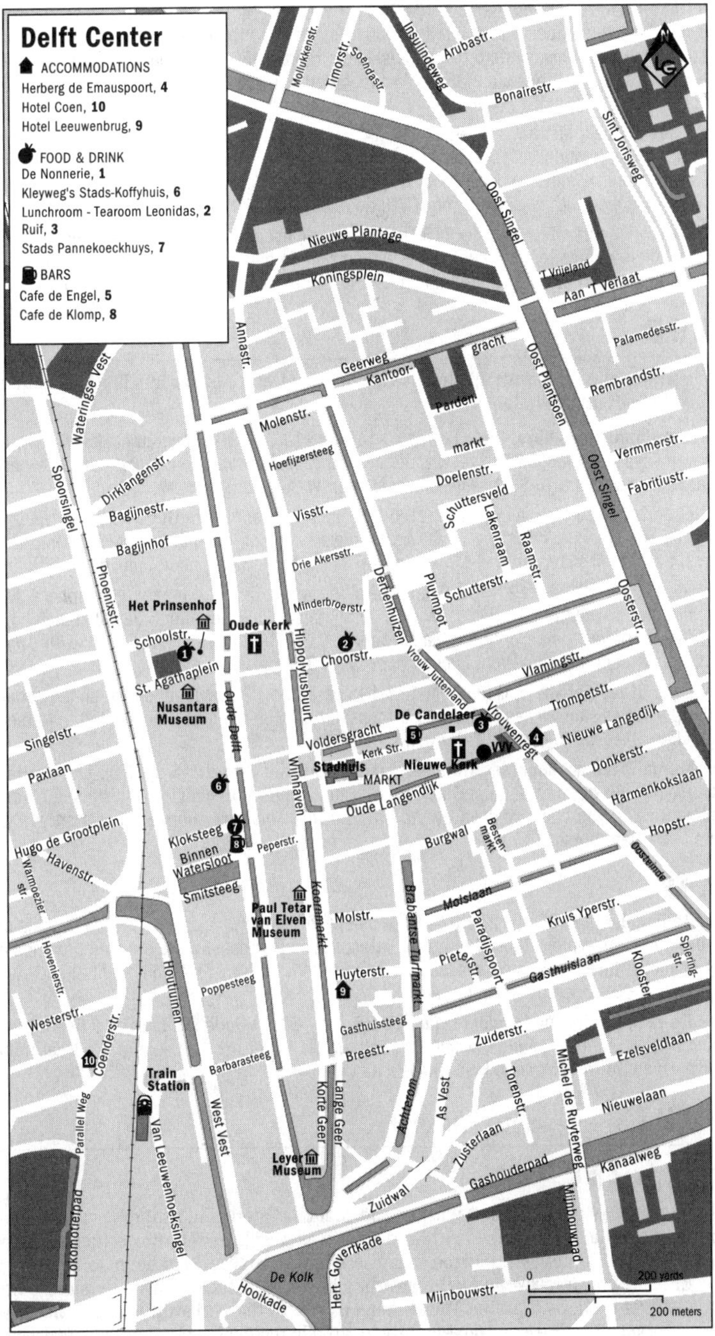

Delft Center

ACCOMMODATIONS
Herberg de Emauspoort, **4**
Hotel Coen, **10**
Hotel Leeuwenbrug, **9**

FOOD & DRINK
De Nonnerie, **1**
Kleyweg's Stads-Koffyhuis, **6**
Lunchroom - Tearoom Leonidas, **2**
Ruif, **3**
Stads Pannekoeckhuys, **7**

BARS
Cafe de Engel, **5**
Cafe de Klomp, **8**

Het Prinsenhof
Oude Kerk
Nusantara Museum
De Candelaer
Stadhuis
Nieuwe Kerk
VVV
MARKT
Paul Tetar van Elven Museum
Leyer Museum
Train Station
De Kolk

Molukkenstr. Timorstr. Soendastr. Insulindeweg Arubastr. Bonairestr. Sint Jorisweg Oost Singel Nieuwe Plantage Koningsplein 'T Vrijeland Aan 'T Verlaat Palamedesstr. Annastr. Geerweg Kantoor- gracht Paarden- markt Rembrandtstr. Oost Plantsoen Wateringse Vest Molenstr. Hoefijzersteeg Vermmerstr. Doelenstr. Fabritiustr. Spoorsingel Dirklangenstr. Bagijnestr. Visstr. Schuttersveld Lakenraam Bagijnhof Raamstr. Drie Akersstr. Phoenixstr. Dertienhuizen Pluympot Schutterstr. Oosterstr. Minderbroerstr. Schoolstr. Hippolytusbuurt Choorstr. Vrouw Juttenland Vlamingstr. St. Agathaplein Oude Delft Trompetstr. Vrouwenregt Singelstr. Voldersgracht Kerk Str. Nieuwe Langedijk Donkerstr. Paxlaan Wijnhaven Harmenkokslaan Oude Langendijk Burgwal Beesten- markt Hopstr. Hugo de Grootplein Kloksteeg Binnen Watersloot Peperstr. Oosteinde Havenstr. Warmoezierstr. Smitsteeg Brabantse Turfmarkt Molslaan Koornmarkt Paradijspoort Kruis Yperstr. Molstr. Pieterstr. Spieringstr. Hovenierstr. Houttuinen Poppesteeg Huyterstr. Gasthuislaan Klooster Westerstr. Gasthuissteeg Zuiderstr. Coenderstr. Breestr. Barbarasteeg Ezelsveldlaan Torenstr. Michel de Ruyterweg Parallel Weg Van Leeuwenhoeksingel West Vest Korte Geer Lange Geer Achterom As Vest Nieuwelaan Zusterlaan Kanaalweg Gashouderpad Zuidwal Mijnbouwpad Lokomotiefpad Hert. Govertkade Hooikade Mijnbouwstr.

0 200 yards
0 200 meters

Hotel Leeuwenbrug, Koornmarkt 16 (☎214 77 41; sales@leeuwenbrug.nl; www.leeuwenbrug.nl). From the station, cross three canals, turn left, and the hotel is on the right. A little steep in price but offers comfortable, sophisticated rooms, all with shower (you can pay more for a bathtub or a "deluxe" suite). Breakfast included. Singles from €72; doubles from €87, extra bed €16. AmEx/MC/V. ❹

Hotel Coen, Coenderstraat 47 (☎214 59 14; info@Hotelcoen.nl; www.hotelcoen.nl). Right behind the train station. A family hotel with all the comforts, including bathroom, TV, phone, and even a sauna, although breakfast isn't included. And if you can't get enough Delftware, the baths are tiled with it. Singles from €70; doubles from €90; quad €125. AmEx/MC/V. ❸

Delftse Hout Recreation Area (☎213 00 40; info-delftsehout@tours.nl; www.tours.nl/delftsehout) offers **campsites** and cabins. Reception May to mid-Sept. 9am-10pm; mid-Sept. to Apr. 9am-6pm. Linens not included. Pitch €22 for 2 people; camping hut for 4 €30. ❷

FOOD

While a good meal can turn up almost anywhere in Delft, restaurants line **Volderstraat** and **Oude Delft** in particular.

Stads Pannekoeckhuys, Oude Delft 113-115 (☎213 01 930). Giant pancakes filled with sweet or savory fillings (€4-9). Warm waitstaff and casual environment round out the experience. Open Apr.-Sept. Tu-Su 11am-9pm; Nov.-Mar. W-Su 11am-9pm. ❶

De Nonnerie, St. Agathaplein (☎212 18 60), across the canal from Oude Kerk and through the gate. The stunning courtyard of St. Agathaplein is reason enough to visit; food is just a bonus. Sandwiches start around €3. Open Tu-F 11am-5pm, Sa-Su noon-5pm. ❶

Ruif, Kerkstraat 22-24 (☎214 22 06; info@ruif.nl; www.ruif.nl). A moody atmosphere, full bar, and diverse menu make this canal-side restaurant a good bet after a day of church-hopping. Plenty of vegetarian options. Main courses €11-14, starters €4-6. Open Su-Th 3pm-1am, F 3pm-2am, Sa 1pm-2am; kitchen open 5:30-9:30pm. ❸

Kleyweg's Stads-Koffyhuis, Oude Delft 133-135 (☎212 46 25). With a terrace on the canal, Kleyweg's serves sandwiches (€3,65-4,50) considered to be the best *broodjes* in The Netherlands. Pancakes €7-8. Open M-F 9am-7pm, Sa 9am-8pm. ❶

Lunchroom-Tearoom Chocolaterie Leonidas, Choorstraat 24 (☎215 78 21), just off Hippolytusbuurt. Sit down for a quiet Dutch meal or treat yourself to high tea. If it's just the bonbons you want, you can buy them by the boxful at the adjoining shop. Entrees start at €4. Open M-Sa 9am-5pm. ❶

BARS

Cafe de Engel, Markt 66a (☎213 57 08). A big, warm, friendly place to spend an evening or an afternoon; large projection TV plays the latest sports broadcast while the stereo pumps a diverse mix of tunes. Fill up on snacks (€2-5) and *tostis* (€2-3,85), if you're not already full on beer (€1,60). Open daily 10am-1am.

Cafe De Klomp, Binnenwatersloot 5 (☎212 38 10), just off Oude Delft. Enjoy a beer at the oldest pub in The Netherlands, which has celebrated more than 350 birthdays. Beer from €1,60. Open Su-Th 4pm-1am, F-Sa 4pm-2am.

SIGHTS

DELFTWARE

Very few visitors come to Delft without the slightest interest in its famous namesake porcelain product. The blue-on-white design was developed in the 16th century to compete with the newly imported Chinese counterpart, and it's been sought after ever since. If your interest in Delftware runs beyond the tacky, cheap versions sold in the souvenir shops that line Markt, head to where the real stuff is made. **De Candelaer,** Kerkstraat 13a-14, is conveniently located in the center of town. Inside, watch

Delftware made from scratch. Each piece comes with a certificate of authenticity. (☎213 18 48; www.candelaer.nl. Open daily 9am-6pm. Demonstrations free. Shop accepts AmEx/MC/V and will ship to the US.) If your thirst for Delftware still isn't slaked, head to the outskirts of town to see how the bigger factories do it. Try **De Delftse Pauw,** Delftweg 133, which can be reached by tram #1, stop to Vrijenbanselaan. (☎212 47 43; info@delftsepauw.com; www.delftsepauw.com. Open Apr.-Oct. daily 9am-4:30pm; Nov.-Mar. M-F 9am-4:40pm, Sa-Su 11am-1pm. Demonstrations free.)

NUSANTARA MUSEUM

St. Agathaplein 4, off Oude Delft. ☎260 23 75. Open Tu-Sa 10am-5pm, Su 1-5pm. €2,50.

Unlike anything else in Delft, the Nusantara houses a stunning collection of unique ethnographic objects from the former Dutch colonies in an ingenious layout that carries you through the museum. Cultures such as the Sumatra and Java are represented in masks, drums, and statues.

NIEUWE KERK

On the central Markt. ☎212 30 25. Church open Apr.-Oct. M-Sa 9am-6pm; Nov.-Mar. M-F 11am-4pm, Sa 11am-5pm. €2. Tower closes 1hr. earlier, and can be climbed for an additional €1,60.

Built in 1381, the Nieuwe Kerk hosts the mausoleum of Dutch liberator Willem of Orange. The mausoleum, flanked by a statue of his dog, was repaired in 2000. But the real attraction of this newer of the two churches is its tower, which you can ascend, as caretakers of the 48-bell carillon have for six centuries, for a view of old Delft. The church still hosts regular Sunday services, which are open to the public.

OUDE KERK

Heilige Geestkerkhof 25. Across the canal from St. Agathaplein. ☎212 30 15. Open M-Sa 9am-6pm; Nov.-Mar. M-F 11am-4pm, Sa 11am-5pm. Tours every hr. €2.

The Oude Kerk, a Dutch Reformed church, is also worth a stop. Founded around 1200, the church is home to the memorial stones of such celebrities as **Piet Heyn** and scientist **Antoni van Leeuwenhoek.** The tower is about 75m high and leans a staggering 2m out of line.

OTHER SIGHTS

Opposite the Oude Kerk is **Sint Agathaplein,** and through the gate the **Waalse Kerk (Walloon Church),** in use as a French church since 1584. Built as a

William of Orange's Tomb, Delft

Delft House

Delftware Painter

15th-century nun's cloister, **Het Prinsenhof,** Sint Agathaplein 1, off Oude Singel, was Willem's abode until a fanatic French Catholic hired by Spain's Phillip II assassinated him in 1584. Today, it houses paintings, tapestries, and pottery. Don't miss the bullet holes that remain in the wall from the Prince's murder. (☎260 23 58. Open Tu-Sa 10am-5pm, Su 1-5pm. €3,40.) The **Legermuseum** (Military Museum), Korte Geer 1, features an extensive display on the history of the Dutch military and the House of Orange. Original costumes, weapons, armor, and paintings are on display, though with opportunities to dress up and play knight, it's somewhat geared toward kids. (☎215 05 00; www.armymuseum.nl. Open M-F 10am-5pm, Sa-Su noon-5pm. €4,40.) The **Paul Tetar van Elven Museum,** Koornmarkt 67, was the home of Paul Tetar van Elven (1823-1896). Magnificent period rooms, curiosities, paintings, drawings, and furniture are on display for visitors. (☎212 42 06. Open Apr. 21-Oct. 28 Tu-Su 1-5pm. €2).

ROTTERDAM ☎010

The second-largest city in The Netherlands and the busiest port city in the world, Rotterdam is the very definition of a bustling metropolis. An arsenal of razor-sharp skyscrapers glitters against the seacoast sky as businessmen duck in and out of revolving doors. Busy people hop on and off trams with feverish frequency and delighted shoppers with bags stuffed full rest their feet at street-side cafes. Rotterdam is full of ships, trains, and planes coming and going in a constant continental exchange, humming with activity even after the sun sets over the skyline. A modern kind of town, the greater part of the city lacks the quaint, classic feel that characterizes much of The Netherlands. After Rotterdam was bombed in 1940, not many of the city's modern structures, let alone those from the Golden Age, remained. Experimental architects replaced the rubble with striking (some say strikingly ugly) buildings, creating an urban, industrial conglomerate. Artsy and innovative, yet desolate and almost decrepit in its hyper-modernity, the Rotterdam that arose from the ashes—rife with museums, parks, and ground-breaking architecture—is today one of the centers of cultural activity in Europe.

PRACTICAL INFORMATION

Tourist office: VVV, Coolsingel 67 (☎0900 403 40 65), opposite the *Stadhuis,* books rooms for a €1,60 fee. Detailed maps of the city available for €3,85. Open M-Th 9:30am-6pm, F 9:30am-9pm, Sa 9:30am-5pm.

Banks: Most open M-F 9am-4pm. In Centraal Station, there is an **exchange office** open M-Sa 7:30am-10pm and Su 9am-10pm.

Chamber of Commerce: Beursplein 37 (☎405 77 77).

Groceries: Find your essentials and groceries at **Spar,** Witte de Withstraat 36, next to the Home Hotel. Follow Coolsingel down from Weena (the major street that runs in front of Centraal), pass Westblaak, and Witte de Withstraat is the next street on the right. Open M-F 8:30am-7pm, Sa 8:30am-5pm.

Emergency: ☎476 87 50. **Police:** Doelwater 5 (☎274 99 11).

Laundry: West Wasserette, Nieuwe Binnenweg 251b (☎425 93 74).

Post Office: Coolsingel 42 (☎233 02 55). **Postal code:** 3016 CM.

ACCOMMODATIONS

NJHC City-Hostel Rotterdam (HI), Rochussenstaat 107-109 (☎436 57 63). Take the metro to Dijkzigt; at the top of the metro escalator, exit onto Rochussentraat and turn left. Or take tram #4 to Mathenesserlaan. A comfy place to spend the night. Breakfast and linens included. Reception 7am-midnight, but no curfew. Laundry available. Internet €7 per hr. Bike rental €5,70 per day. Dorms €22,50; singles €30,75; doubles €52; triples €74,50. Cheaper during the low season and for HI members. ❶

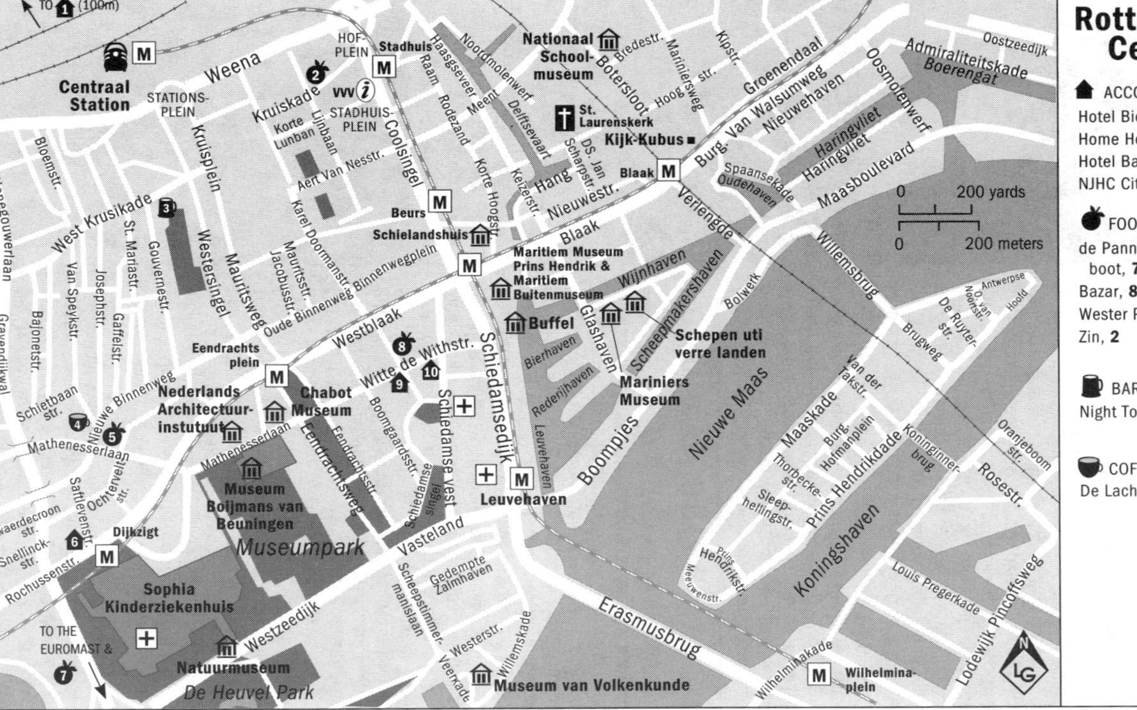

Rotterdam Center

ACCOMMODATIONS

Hotel Bienvenue, **1**
Home Hotel, **9**
Hotel Bazar, **10**
NJHC City Hostel, **6**

FOOD & DRINK

de Pannenkoeken-boot, **7**
Bazar, **8**
Wester Paviljoen, **5**
Zin, **2**

BARS

Night Town, **3**

COFFEESHOPS

De Lachende Paus, **4**

Award Winning Sandwich in Delft

Stads-Koffyhuis

Delft Canal

Hotel Bienvenue, Spoorsingel 24 (☎466 93 94). Exit through the back of the station, walk straight along the canal for 5min., and it's on the right. Walk out the front doors of Centraal Station and you've stepped into the thick of one of the busiest cities in the world. Walk out the back, and it's an entirely different story: nothing but peaceful, grass-lined canals. This is where you'll find Bienvenue, for the quietest night you can spend in Rotterdam. Reception M-F 7:30am-9pm, Sa-Su 8am-9pm. Breakfast included. Singles with hall bath €43; doubles with bath €70; triples with bath €90; quad, shower included, toilet in hall €115. AmEx/MC/V with 5.5% surcharge. ❷

Hotel Bazar, Witte de Withstraat 16 (☎206 51 51; fax 206 51 59). Turn onto Schilderstraat from Schiedamse Dijk and follow the street until it turns into Witte de Withstraat. If you've gotten tired of Europe, you can escape to the Middle East or South America in one of Bazar's 18 comfortable themed rooms. All include bath, TV, and minibar, as well as breakfast. Singles €65; doubles €75. ❸

Home Hotel, Witte de Withstraat 38 (☎414 21 50; fax 414 16 90). Follow directions to Hotel Bazar. Home Hotel rents a variety of rooms all along Witte de Withstraat, as well as on some nearby streets. Handsome rooms include bath, kitchen, and telephone. Singles €60; doubles €70. Special rates on a sliding scale for longer stays. AmEx/MC/V. ❸

FOOD AND DRINK

In general, to find food on the cheap, you need only head to Witte de Withstraat for Chinese and shawarma, where you can easily grab a meal for under €5. Or, try **Lijbaan** for its array of pubs, bars, and all their accompanying culinary charm. A few places are worth singling out, however.

Bazar, Witte de Withstraat 16 (☎206 51 51), on the 1st fl. of the hotel by the same name. Here you'll find a unique blend of world cuisines, especially concentrated on flavors from the Middle East and North Africa. The results of such cultural experimentation are often delicious, and you can dine for under €10. The atmosphere is festive but casual and attracts a crowd of the young and the young at heart; overall, a great place to eat after a long day of architectural appreciation. Open M-Th 8am-1am, F 8am-2am, Sa 10am-2am, Su 10am-1am. ❷

De Pannenkoekenboot Rotterdam, Parkhaven (☎436 72 95; www.pannenkoekenboot.nl), across from the Euromast. A unique culinary experience that offers an unlimited pancake buffet afloat in the harbor. Buffet Sa-Su 1:30, 3, 4:30, and 6pm; W and F 4:30 and 6pm. €12, children €7. Harbor sightseeing Pancake Cruise Sa 8-11pm, Sa 8-11pm. Adults €21, children €15. ❸

Wester Paviljoen, Mathenesserlaan 155 (☎436 26 45), just off Rochussenstraat. A hip place to enjoy a drink and read the newspaper, or just have dinner (main dishes €10-13; salads €7,50; sandwiches €3-5; beer €1,80). Wide, comfortable room and an incredibly friendly staff make this a great place to unwind. Open M-Th 8pm-1am, F 8pm-2am, Sa 9am-2am, Su 9am-1am; kitchen closes at 11pm. ❸

Zin, Lijbaan 40 (☎281 09 10; www.zin-reizenen-spijzen.nl), just off Weena. If you're not afraid to show just how cool you are, then come mingle with Rotterdam's scenemakers over *tapas* (€4-9) and cocktails (€5-6). A world-conscious menu, with culinary curiosities from Japan to Italy, has main courses from €12 and *broodjes* from €4. Open Su-Th noon-midnight, F-Sa noon-2am; kitchen closes at 10:30pm. Visa. ❸

Cube Houses, Rotterdam

SIGHTS

NEDERLANDS ARCHITECTUURINSTITUUT

Museumpark 25. Tram #5 to Museumpark. ☎440 12 00; info@nai.nl; www.nai.nl. Open Tu-Sa 10am-5pm, Su 11am-5pm. Library and reading room open Tu-Sa 10am-5pm. €5, ages 4-16 €3.

The museum's approach is a bit in-your-face, but then again, the architecture of Rotterdam is a bit in-your-face, too. At times, the exhibits can be heavy on style and light on substance, but it doesn't detract from the overall rewards of a visit to this unique institution, over which architecture students will no doubt fawn. The Architectuurinstituut itself is one of Rotterdam's primary architectural attractions, and innovative interior design enhances the exhibits. The building also houses a library and archives with one of the largest architectural collections in the world, both of which are open to the public.

Euromast & TunnelMarker Building

MUSEUM BOIJMANS VAN BEUNINGEN

Museumpark 18-20. Tram #5 or M: Endrachtspl.; across the street from the architecture institute. ☎441 95 37; http://boijmans.kennisnet.nl. Open Tu-Sa 10am-5pm, Su 11am-5pm. €6, under 18 free.

A permanent collection of primarily Dutch art from 1750 to 1930 with especially good *fin-de-siecle* pieces and consistently impressive rotating shows in a huge exhibition space make this one of Rotterdam's primary attractions. Although modest in size, the collection nevertheless features Bruegel's **The Tower of Babel,** and works by Rembrandt, van Gogh, and Rubens, as well as works by more modern talents such as Rubinstein, Rothko, and Magritte.

Museumpark

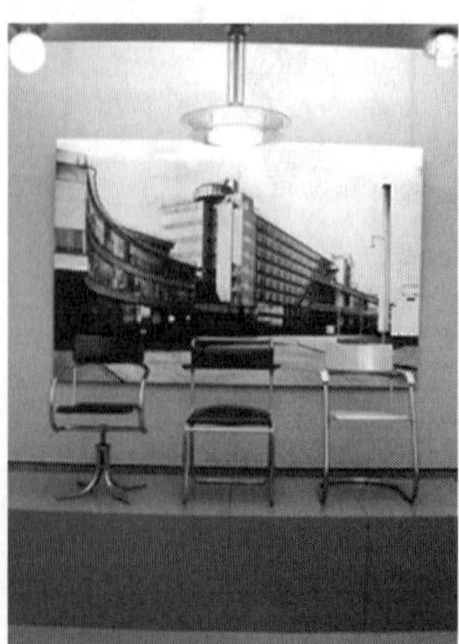
Museum Boijmans van Beuningen

Museumpark

Netherlands Architecture Institute

ST. LAURENSKERK

Grote Kerkplein 15. M: Blaak. ☎ 413 14 94; info@laurenskerk.nl. Open Tu-Sa 10am-4pm. Services on Su. Free.

Though it was bombed and almost completely destroyed on May 14, 1940, the Grote, or St. Laurenskerk, has been restored to its medieval splendor and is without question one of the most remarkable buildings in the country. While there are no eye-dazzling stained-glass windows or stunning sculptures to be seen here, the church's three organs make it worth the visit. The great red and gold organ at the back of the church is the largest mechanical organ in Europe. In the summer, the church holds organ concerts at 4pm on Saturdays (€5); check with the church for more complete concert listings. There is also a permanent exhibition that commemorates the bombing of Rotterdam with video footage and photographs.

EUROMAST

Parkhaven 20. Tram #8 to Euromast. ☎ 436 48 11; www.euromast.nl. Open Apr.-Sept. daily 10am-7pm; Oct.-Mar. 10am-5pm. Space Tower has same hours except Jan.-Feb. when it is open Sa-Su only. €7,50.

The tallest structure in The Netherlands, this popular site is the best way to take in a breathtaking view of Rotterdam's skyline. Ride 100m up in a high-speed elevator to gaze on the city from the original viewing deck or restaurant. Or, if you're more daring, take a space-age trip up the Space Tower in a revolving capsule, a section added ten years after the Euromast's original construction in 1960 that extended the tower another 85m.

MUSEUMPARK

Take tram #5. Free.

Of the many parks in The Netherlands, few are as enjoyable as the Museumpark. Conceived by the Office for Metropolitan Architecture in Rotterdam, the Museumpark seamlessly integrates art and urban landscape architecture. The park features a number of sculptures, mosaics, and monuments, designed by some of the world's foremost artists and architects, interwoven among serene fountains and hedgerows. Also worth a trip is the nearby **De Heuvel Park,** just across the street toward the Euromast. It's nearly three times the size of Museumpark and has rolling expanses of grass to kick off your shoes and run around in, and there are any number of places to while away an afternoon—shaded benches, weeping willows, and winding streams all entice, while musicians play and ice-cream vendors peddle frozen treats.

KIJK-KUBUS (CUBE HOUSES)

Overblaak 70. Take tram #1 or the metro to Blaak, turn left, and look up. ☎414 22 85; www.cubehouse.nl. Open Mar.-Dec. daily 11am-5pm; Jan.-Feb. F-Su 11am-5pm. €1,75, children €1.25.

For a dramatic example of Rotterdam's eccentric designs (heavily influenced by the de Stijl school), check out architect Piet Blom's Kijk-Kubus housing complex. Built in 1982, the yellow, cube-shaped houses are mounted on tall concrete columns and oriented at a bizarre angle. Though they have been inhabited for the last 20 years, a "show cube" fitted with custom cube house furniture is open to the public, so you can see what it would be like to live in such a strange home.

View of one of Rotterdam's Modern Bridge

MARITIEM MUSEUM

Leeuvehaven 1. A 5min. walk from Coolsingel. ☎413 26 80; www.maritiemmuseum.nl. Open Tu-Sa 10am-5pm, Su 11am-5pm; July-Aug. also M 10am-5pm. €3,50. Wheelchair accessible.

Water is the lifeblood and the curse of The Netherlands, but there is no city for which it's more important than Rotterdam. Through interactive multimedia displays, exhibits that show what it's like to be inside a ship, and hundreds of model ships constructed with amazing detail, the museum basks in the city's history as the busiest port in the world. A stop aboard the *De Buffel*, a restored 19th-century turret ship, is included with admission. Make sure to swing by the **Zadkine Monument,** to the left of the museum. Known as the Monument for the Destroyed City and erected only 11 years after the bombing, it powerfully depicts a man with a hole in his heart writhing in agony.

Oude Binnenweg

OTHER MUSEUMS

Explore Rotterdam's history and contrast before and after the 1940 bombing at the **Schielandshuis** (Historical Museum), Korte Hoogestraat 31. To get there from Church Plein, turn right on Westblaak, and Korte Hoogestraat is on the left.(☎217 67 67; www.hmr.rotterdam.nl. Open Tu-F 10am-5pm, Sa-Su 11am-5pm. €2,70.) Visitors can walk through six reconstructed classrooms, including a medieval cathedral school, to explore the history of Dutch primary education at the **Nationaal Schoolmuseum,** Nieuwmarkt 1. Take the metro to Blaak or tram #1. (☎404 54 25; info@schoolmuseum.nl; www.schoolmuseum.nl. Open Tu-Sa 10am-5pm, Su 1-5pm. €2,50.) The **Oorlogversetzmuseum Rotterdam** (Rotterdam War Resistance Museum), Veerlaan 82-92, looks at the history of

Shopping in Rotterdam

the Resistance movement in Rotterdam during World War II. (☎484 89 31; ovmrotterdam@hetnet.nl. Open Tu-F 10am-4pm, Su noon-4pm. €1,20.) The giant whale skeleton in the front lobby may be the most impressive thing about the **Natuurmuseum,** Westzeedijk 345, which also sports a varied collection of birds, butterflies, and fish—all stuffed, of course. It's in the southwest corner of Museumpark, near the Euromast. Take tram #5 to Museumpark. (☎436 42 22; www.nmr.nl. Open Tu-Sa 10am-5pm, Su 11am-5pm. €3.)

NIGHTLIFE

For coffeeshop-hopping, try **Oude Binnenweg** and **Nieuwe Binnenweg,** both of which offer a variety of shops and bars.

Lachende Paus (The Laughing Pope), Nieuwe Binnenweg 139a (☎436 21 11). A smartshop with everything you might need to get your feet off the ground. Especially friendly staff and a very Zen atmosphere, with little Buddhist and Hindu statues everywhere. Open daily 10am-midnight.

Night Town, West Kruiskade 26-28 (☎436 12 10; www.nighttown.nl). An all-purpose hotspot for nocturnal fun; bands M-Th, dancing F-Sa. Cover for dancing €8, bands run €11-25. Check website for lineup. Open F-Su 11pm-5am.

SHOPPING

A truly modern metropolis, Rotterdam is the place to go for designer goods of all sorts. Clothes, furniture, housewares—the city has it all stocked, stacked, and ready for gift wrapping. Some of Rotterdam's best shopping can be done in the **Koopgoot** (Shopping Drain). Designed by architect P.B. de Bruijn, the Shopping Drain is an underground complex that houses shops, restaurants, and entertainment facilities. In the same area, you'll also find big-name department store **De Bijenkorf.** (Underneath Coolsingel. M: Beurs.) **Nieuwe Binnenweg** and **Oude Binnenweg,** two streets in the center of the city, also feature some great shops. (Take tram #4 or 5 to Endrachtsplein.) In the shadow of the cube houses is where you'll find the **City Centre Market,** the biggest market in The Netherlands. Endless rows of stalls sell fresh fish, fruit, gourmet pastries, socks, antiques, handbags, books, and anything else you never knew you needed. (M: Blaak. Open Tu and Sa-Su 9am-5pm; occasionally F nights.)

FESTIVALS

Rotterdam is well known throughout Europe for the great selection of cultural and athletic activities it hosts during the year. Toward the end of January, the **Rotterdam International Film Festival** (☎890 90 90) provides a venue for hundreds of non-commercial films, special programs, and retrospectives. The **ABN AMRO World Tennis Tournament** (☎090 02 35) attracts thousands of spectators and top tennis talent in February. In May, the **Dunya Festival** (☎233 09 10) features music, poetry, and storytelling from around the world, as well as a special program specifically for younger patrons. **Bang the Drum** (June) turns Rotterdam's Afrikaanderplein into the site of a massive music and dance extravaganza as over a thousand *djembe* players gather together in a celebration of African music. Also in June, **Poetry International** (☎28 22 27 77; www.poetry.nl) invites dozens of poets from all over the world to read their works in Rotterdam. A book market, interviews, lectures, discussions, and more are included in the gathering. Later in the month, **De Parade** (☎03 34 65 45 77) marches into Rotterdam, bringing with it theater, music, and a variety of other amusements for young and old. June is polished off by the **Festival of Architecture** (☎436 99 09), when remarkably designed buildings all over the city open to the public. In July, both the **Metropolis Pop Festival** (☎282 19 15) and **Zomerpodium** (☎425 32 92) attract a host of musical acts to the city. If you haven't had enough entertainment by then, the **Solero Zomercarnaval** (☎414 17 72), with its brass bands, DJs, parties, and climactic Battle of the Drums, should do the job. The carnival also features a Caribbean street parade and market. Things begin to quiet down in July with **Kolkkonsert** (☎090 04 03 40 65), a festival geared toward classical music lovers. The **Chinese Cultural Festival** in July finishes off the month with dragon and lion dances, music, fireworks, and much more. In August, **Mr Zap Pleinbioscoop** (☎425 32 92) projects feature films from a variety of different genres onto the largest screen in Europe. Things heat up again in November with **DEAF (Dutch Electronic Art Festival),** where artists explore the changing face of art in the computer age.

NEAR ROTTERDAM

GOUDA ☎018

*Trains roll into town from Rotterdam (15min., one-way €3) and Amsterdam (1hr., €8). From the station, cross the bridge over the canal, walk straight on Kleiweg, which turns into Hoogstraat and leads to the Markt and the **VVV tourist office** (☎0900 468 32 888; fax 258 32 10; vvv.gouda@12move.nl; www.vvvgouda.nl). Open M-Sa 9am-5pm; in summer also Su noon-3pm.*

Gouda (HOW-da) is the quintessential Dutch town, with canals, a windmill, and its well-known cheese. A regional **cheese market** is held weekly in summer (Th 10am-12:30pm). The market features a number of tourist treats, among them cheese-making demonstrations and free samples presented by Gouda's tasty cheese-maidens. If you've ever had a burning desire to know your own weight in cheese, head to **Kaaswaag Gouda (Weigh House Gouda),** Markt 35-36, in the central Markt area. They helpfully provide this as well as other information about Gouda's mainstay: cheese. The Kaaswaag features a permanent exhibition about Gouda and its cheese trade. (☎252 99 96. Open Apr.-Oct. Tu-W 1-5pm, Th 10am-5pm, F-Su 1-5pm. Entrance is free during the cheese market.) Those with less interest in cheese can try **De Vlaam,** Markt 69, tucked in among the many bars and *pannenkoekens*, a bakery famous for its take on *sirupwafels*, the delicious Dutch treat. (€6 for a whole tin). (☎251 33 59. Open M-W and F 8:30am-6pm, Th 8:30am-9pm, Sa 8am-5pm.) The gargantuan, late Gothic **Sint Janskerk** has managed to maintain its collection of 16th-century stained-glass windows, despite attacks by both lightning and Reformation iconoclasts. (Open Mar.-Oct. M-Sa 9am-5pm; Nov.-Feb. M-Sa 10am-4pm. €1,90.) The **Goudse Pottenbakkerij "Adrie Moerings,"** Peperstraat 76, has produced the famous Gouda clay smoking pipes since the 17th century. (☎201 28 42. Open M-F 9am-5pm, Sa 11am-5pm. Free.) Around the corner on Oosthaven, the **Museum het Catharina Gasthuis,** Achter de Kerk 14, houses a wonderful collection of everything from Flemish art and early surgical instruments to period furniture, dolls, and weaponry in a former chapel and adjoining torture chamber. (☎01 82 58 84 40. Open M-Sa 10am-5pm, Su noon-5pm. €6,50.)

Lion Bridge in Rotterdam

Crazy Architecture in Rotterdam

Modern Buildings in Rotterdam

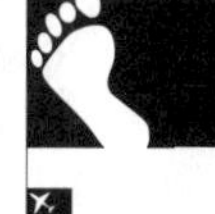

UTRECHT

☎030

With tree-lined canals, a Gothic cathedral, numerous museums and galleries, stretches of green, a crazy nightlife, and a prestigious university, Utrecht (pop. 250,000) offers plenty to the visitor with varied interests. The city is situated roughly 20 miles southeast of Amsterdam, in the center of The Netherlands. With a more spacious layout, many more parks, fewer tourists, and a smaller population than Amsterdam, Utrecht is a perfect break from the hectic buzz of the nation's capital. Even the canals are different, lying below street level against underground cellars. Once the Christian capital of the Low Countries, Utrecht's cross of Protestant churches (the only such cross in Europe) cuts a swath of religious atmosphere through the city. The main canal, Oudegracht, bends so all the stone could be delivered for ongoing church construction in the area. These days, more than 50,000 students create a stronger presence than do the bishops.

TRANSPORTATION

Take the **train** from Amsterdam (30min., 3-6 per hr., €4,50 one way). When you arrive, you'll be in a building connected to The Netherlands' largest shopping mall, the **Hoog Catharijne.** It's easiest to follow the signs through the mall to the Vredenburg (music hall), near the center of the city. Turn left out of the mall and go until Lange Viestraat, then turn right and walk a block into the city's center. Oudegracht, Utrecht's main canal, will cross beneath you.

PRACTICAL INFORMATION

The **VVV** office sits at Vinkenbrugstraat 19. Pick up a map of the city and a complete listing of museums and sights for €2. Head East on Lange Viestraat from Oudegracht and at the end of the first block, turn right into a large square and keep right. It's at the southwest corner of the square. (☎0900 128 87 32, €0,50/min; info@vvvutrecht.nl; www.12utrecht.nl. Open M-W, and F 9:30am-6:30pm, Th 9:30am-9pm, Sa 9:30am-5pm, Su 10am-2pm).

Shuttevaer, Bemuurde Weerd O.Z. 17, offers canal tours, which leave from the corner of Oude Gracht and Lange Viestraat every hour on the hour. (☎272 01 11; www.schuttevaer.com. Open 11am-6pm. €6; children under 12 €4,50). Stop by **Ron-Dom,** Domplein 9, the cultural history visitor's center, to get good information on the churches and museums of Utrecht.

The pulsing center of Utrecht is known as the **Museumkwartier,** and lies a five-minute walk from Utrecht Centraal's Vredenburg exit. Generally speaking, the Museumkwartier is the area bound north and south by Oudegracht and Nieuwegracht. The main east-west thoroughfare is Vredenburg/Lange Viestraat/Potterstraat (the name changes as you walk from Centraal to Oudesgracht). Here, you'll find countless churches, museums, fashionable shops, restaurants, art galleries, and a number of theaters and coffeeshops.

ACCOMMODATIONS

B&B Utrecht City Centre, Lucasbolwerk 4 (☎0650 434 884; www.hostelutrecht.nl), near the corner of Lucasbolwerk and Nobelstraat, a 5min. walk to the center of Utrecht. If at Utrecht Centraal, give the number a call and they may pick you up. This hostel, a gorgeous spot in the middle of the city, operates under a unique set of ideals. For a blanket fee of €16, you get a dorm bed, 24hr. free breakfast, use of the kitchen, sauna, piano, guitars, didgeridoo, and home video system (with hundreds of DVDs to chose from). Free Internet. With no max. stay and €5 per day bike rental, you just might decide to move in. The owner employs only a cleaning lady and runs this hotel through her cell phone, thus saving money and allowing for such great amenities. Feels more like a home than a hostel. Reserve by phone or online. Dorms €16; singles €55; doubles €65; triples €85, quads €100. MC/V. ❶

NJHC Ridderhofstad Rhijnauwen, Rhijnauwenselaan 14, Bunnik (☎656 12 77; fax 657 10 65; www.njhc.org/bunnik). Take bus #40, 41, or 43 from Centraal Station (10-15min., €2,10 each way) and ask tell the driver to let you off at Bunnik. From the stop, cross the street, backtrack, turn right on Rhijnauwen, and it's just over 0.5km down the road. While not convenient for exploring Utrecht (the last bus leaves Utrecht Centraal at 12:50am), the hostel's pastoral setting provides the perfect place to recharge after a busy day (or many of them). Rent a bike and take time to explore the fort and numerous paths behind the hostel. The hostel's small bar has all the warm feeling and cold beer of a *bruine café*. (Open 10am-midnight.) Lunch and dinner served (€6,50 and €8,70, respectively) and lunchbags are available (€4,15). Dorms €19,75, weekends €21; €2 less off-season. Doubles €50; triples €62-€75; quads €76-93; quints €95-115. Credit cards accepted. ❶

B&B Utrecht, Egelantierstraat 25 (☎0650 434 884; www.hotelinfo.nl). Take bus #3 to Watertoren (€1). Cross the street and head to Anemoonstraat. Go 2 blocks to the end and turn left. The street turns into Elegantierstraat and the hostel is on your left (if you're at Utrecht Centraal, call them and you might get a free ride). Run by the same woman as the B&B Utrecht City Centre, this hostel is further from the city center and has a more traditional hostel feel. 24hr. breakfast, free Internet, and free lunchbags. Dorm beds €12; singles €40, doubles €45, triples from €70, and quads from €85. MC/V. ❶

FOOD AND DRINK

For cheap eating in Utrecht, try any of the restaurants that line **Nobelstraat** (Lange Viestraat becomes Nobelstraat East of the Museumkwartier). Or, try one of the many restaurants lining the **Oudegracht**.

Het Nachtrestaurant, Oudegracht 158 (☎230 20 36), a *tapas* "night restaurant" popular for a tasty meal or drinks. Enter on the canal for Mediterranean *tapas* (€2,50-6,50) and sangria (€3,10 per glass). Sit among a very hip crowd, either by the canal or in the cozy lounge area. Open M-Sa 6pm-late, Su 3pm-late. Mastercard. ❸

Toque Toque, Oudegracht 138 (☎231 87 87; www.toque.nl). Upscale restaurant with 9-page wine list, large salads under €12,50, and homemade, fresh pastas between €10,50 and €15. Deep red walls, an aluminum bar, and seats outside overlooking the canal add to the ambience. Very cool hangout at the heart of the city for drinks (pints, €2; house wines €3 a glass) or tasty international entrees. Open daily 11am-midnight; kitchen open 11am-3pm and 6-10pm. AmEx/MC/V. ❹

Van Eycks and more Van Eycks

Netherlands Architecture Institute

World's Largest Port

Venezia, Oudegracht 105, is Utrecht's most popular ice cream shop. With sundaes from €2 and heaping 3-scoop cones for €2,70, you should join the throngs of ice cream eaters that line the city's streets. Open daily 11am-11pm. Cash only. ❶

SIGHTS

DOMKERK AND DOMTOREN

Achter de Dom 1. From Oudegracht and Lange Viestraat with Centraal behind you, turn right onto Oudegracht. ***Domkerk:*** *☎231 04 03. Open M-Sa 10am-5pm, Su 2-4pm. Free.* ***Domtoren:*** *Open Sept.-June; daily tours every hr. 10am-4pm; July-Aug. tours every 30min. 10am-4:30pm. Tickets for tours sold at RonDom. Tours €6, children €3,60.*

Any perusal of Utrecht's sights must begin at the awe-inspiring Domkerk, begun in 1254 and finished 250 years later. After the two curves it's on the left. Initially a Roman Catholic cathedral, the Domkerk has held Protestant services since 1580. Originally attached to the cathedral but freestanding since a tornado blew away the nave in 1674, the Domtoren is the highest tower in The Netherlands. Its peak holds 60,000kg of bronze bells, which ring on Sundays and holidays. Climb the 465 steps to take in views of Amersfoort and Amsterdam. On clear days, Rotterdam and The Hague are also visible.

MUSEUM CATHARIJNECONVENT

Lange Nieuwstraat 38. ☎231 72 96; www.catharijneconvent.nl. Open Tu-F 10am-5pm, Sa-Su 11am-5pm. €6, family ticket €15.

This gothic convent-turned-museum focuses on the history of Christianity in The Netherlands through works of art. Once the Christian capital of the Low Countries, Utrecht explodes with relics from its past. The museum holds many traditional Catholic relics, but also art that was critical of the Catholic religion, including a dual portrait of the Devil and the Pope and a painting of a nun and monk making love. The museum's medieval collection is especially impressive, including 15th-century manuscripts and miniatures.

OTHER SIGHTS

The Museum Quarter contains the core of Utrecht's extended family of museums. Close to the Museum Van Speelklok to Pierement is the beautiful **Aboriginal Art Museum,** Oude Gracht 176, 1½ blocks down Oudegracht from Domtoren. Its exhibits on ceremonial art from Australian Aborigines, though presented in Dutch, are accessible to any audience (☎238 01 00. Open Tu-F 10am-5pm, Sa-Su 11am-5pm. €7, under 12 €5). Don't miss the **Waterleidingmuseum (Waterworks Museum),** Lauwerhof 29, situated in a water tower on the North side of Lange Viestraat. Here, you'll find four floors of Netherlands water history from former employees of the Water Company. The colorful 39-meter water tower from 1895 is worth the five-minute walk from the Museumkwartier (☎248 72 11. Open Tu-Sa 1:30-5pm. €2).

Venture farther into the quarter by heading South on Lange Nieuwstraat, the street running parallel to and between Oudegracht and Nieuwegracht. Continue down Lange Nieuwstraat from Museum Catharijneconvent to the end and turn right to **Centraal Museum,** Nicolaaskerkhof 10, to see the largest collection of works by de Stijl designer Gerrit Reitveld. (☎236 23 62. Open Tu-Su 11am-5pm. €8, under 13 free.) And finally, for astronomy buffs, the **Observatory Sonnenborgh Museum,** The Netherlands' oldest observatory, has telescopes and a large collection of antique scientific instruments. (☎230 28 18; www.sonnenborgh.nl. Hours depend on the cosmos; call or check the web.)

NIGHTLIFE

Utrecht is, among many other things, a college town. Home to The Netherlands' largest university, Universiteit Utrecht, the city's nightlife thrives seven days a week. Pick up a copy of *UiLoper* at bars or restaurants to scout the bar and cultural scene.

Woolloo Moolloo, Janskerkhof 14, is where the party's at. Student ID is required for entry into the large dance hall, which hosts DJs every night of the week. Open W-Sa 11pm-4am and later. Cover €5-20.

't Oude Pothuys, Oudegracht 279 (☎231 89 70), take Oudegracht south from the main strip. A large underground bar with live music nightly, one of the city's busiest nightspots. Enjoy €1,70 beers in a chill atmosphere with a good mix of young and old. Open daily 10pm-3am.

De Winkel van Sinkel, Oude Gracht 158 (☎230 30 30). A popular grandcafe in an old canalside warehouse. The complex is open late every night, with discos Sa. Open Su-F 11am-2am, Sa 11am-5am.

Stadskasteel Oudaen, Oudegracht 99 (☎231 18 64; www.oudaen.nl), with its majestic feel, classed-up crowd, and slick staff, is dressed to impress every night of the week. The food is on the pricey side, so enjoy the good selection of home-brews from their brewery (€1,90). Open daily 11am-2am.

ACU Politiek Cultureel Centrum, Voorstraat 71 (☎231 45 90). Head east on Lange Viestraat from Oudegracht and turn left onto Voorstraat). A legalized squat with a crowded bar open every night and discos on F-Sa till 4am. Also hosts live music, political events, and offers a €5 veggie dinner M-Th, 6-7:30pm. Open Su-Th 6pm-1am, F-Sa 6pm-4am.

ARNHEM ☎026

Nearly continuous parks run along the perimeter of this small city. Arnhem is a good one-night stop on the Neder Rijn (Lower Rhine), especially on the way to De Hoge Veluwe National Park. A sleepy city (pop. 140,000) that somehow wakes up in the evening, this capital of the province of Gelderland is home to several good restaurants and nighteries.

TRANSPORTATION

Trains pull in daily from Amsterdam's Centraal Station (80min.; €11,80 one way) in roughly 15 minute intervals. Apeldoorn and, preferably, Arnhem (both 15km from the park) are good bases for exploration of De Hoge Veluwe. From the **Arnhem** train station, take bus #107 to the park's northwestern Otterlo entrance. (Every half-hour from 6:44-10:14am and 2:44-6:14pm, and otherwise, every hour between 6:44am-11:14pm. 25 min., €4,20 or 6 strips.)

ORIENTATION AND PRACTICAL INFORMATION

The city center of Arnhem lies south of the main street, Jansbudensingel, which runs east-west at the exit of the train station. The next five blocks are for pedestrians only, and on the southeast corner (farthest corner from trains) of the center is **Eusebiuskerk**, the 15th-century church destroyed in the 1944 Battle of Arnhem and restored thereafter.

To get to the **VVV,** Willemsplein 8, exit the train station, turn left, continue down the street for one block, and you'll see the blue flag on your left. Provides free maps of the town. (☎0900 202 40 75, €0,50/min.; info@vvvarnhem.nl; www.vvvarnhem.nl. Open M 11am-5:30pm, Tu-F 9am-5:30pm, Sa 10am-4pm.)

ACCOMMODATIONS

NJHC Herberg Alteveer (HI), Diepenbrocklaan 27, (☎442 01 14; arnhem@njhc.org) Take bus #3 from the station (10min., €2,10 return) to the Rijnstate Hospital stop. From the bus stop, turn right as you face the hospital (Ziekenhuis Rijnstate), cross the street at the intersection and turn left on Cattepoelseweg. Then, about 150m ahead, turn right up the brick steps, at the top, turn right. The hostel will be straight ahead. Breakfast and linen included. Offers standard but clean and friendly accommodations in a woodsy setting. There's a bar and reading room that serves cheap beer (pints €1,25). Laundry wash, €3,25; dry, €1,75. Key deposit €5. Reception 8am-11pm. No curfew. Depending on season, dorms €20,75-22,10; singles €30; doubles €50,60-53,30; triples €69,10-73,15; quads €87,55-92,95; quints €109,45-116,20; non-members add €2,50. ❶

Felix Reijmers, Boaterdijk 23 (☎443 66 06). From the station, take the main street left, and then hang a right at Nieuweplein. Following South toward the Rhine, and it's on your right along the river. This 5-room "boatel" sits on the Neder Rijn. All rooms have bath and brilliant riverside views. Singles €38,50; doubles €57,50. Cash only. ❷

FOOD AND DRINK

Pizzeria Pinoccio, Korenmarkt 25b (☎443 22 08), offers good prices, a great location, and even better food in the heart of the city. It has tables out and inside, and offers a wide selection of generously-sized pizzas-for-one (€5,60-11; adventurers, try the "surprise pizza" for €11), reasonably priced meat entrees (rack of ribs for €12), and pasta. Open M-W 5-9:30pm, Th-F 5-10pm, Sa-Su 4–10pm. Cash only. ❸

Proef Lokaal de Waag, Markt 38 (☎370 59 60) at Walburgstraat, just south of Eusebiuskerk, on the southeast end of the city. A gorgeous restaurant built in a restored mansion from 1761. For lunch, soups €4,10, sandwiches around €8. For dinner, veggie lasagne (€13,90) and a well-priced, well-portioned rack of lamb (€18,30). Open M-Th 10:30-midnight, F 9am-1am, Sa 10:30am-2am, Su, 11:30am-midnight. MC/V. ❹

Pasam, Varkensstraat 33 (☎446 07 58). From the train station, turn left on the main street and right at Nieuweplein. Left on Rijnstraat and then a quick left puts Varkensstraat up on your right. Shoarma combo €6,20, veggie *broodjes* €3,50 and less. Open daily 1pm-5am. ❶

SIGHTS

In September 1944, the Nazis bombed the town in what has become known as the Battle of Arnhem. Arnhem, like many Dutch cities, had to be completely rebuilt after the war. The town's most conspicuous sight is **Eusebiuskerk,** Kerkplein 1. From the train station, walk out to the main street, turn left and after one block turn right, following Nieuweplein three blocks to Oeverstraat, where you go left; the church is up that street about 400 meters. Here, the grand church, restored in the neo-Gothic style soon after its 15th-century tower crashed to the ground in battle, towers over a frighteningly empty square. Today, it is again the base for **Eusebiustoren,** the 93-meter tower whose 53-bell carillon is the largest in Western Europe. During restoration, a glass elevator was installed to take visitors up to the beautiful views (☎443 50 68. Open Tu-Sa 10am-5pm, Su noon-5pm. Elevator €2,50; under 14 €2). The large gray building behind the church is Arnhem's city hall, **Stadhuis,** built in 1964. Between the church and hall and against Walburgstraat, you'll find **Duivelshuis,** Koningstraat 1. This mansion with deformed, distorted faces and animal-like human statues carved into its sides was built in 1545. Untouched by the bombings, it was ironically owned by a successful Dutch warmongerer who sculpted the images to protest the town hall's illegalization of gold-coated front steps. Across Walburgstraat is the courthouse, **Paleis van Justitie,** Walburgerstraat 2-4, and behind it, the Gelderland capital building, **Huis der Provincie,** Markt 11. Behind the government buildings you might smell the **Neder Rijn,** or Lower Rhine, running west-northwest across the South of the city.

NIGHTLIFE

Luther Danscafe, Korenmarkt 26 (☎442 81 07). 20-somethings crowd all 3 floors, drinking on the 1st, chilling on the 2nd, and grooving to R&B and dance classics on the 3rd. Club dress code. Beer €2, most mixed drinks €4. Open Th-Sa 6pm-2am; in summer W 1pm-1am, Th-F 1pm-2am, Su 1pm-1am.

Speak Easy, Varkensstraat (☎443 07 58) is a chill coffeeshop. Fom the station take the main street left, go right at Nieuweplein, left at Rijnstraat, and a quick left up to Varkensstraat on your right. Joints from €2.50; free coffee or tea with purchase. Open M-T 9am-11pm, W-Su 9am-midnight.

Le Grand Cafe, Korenmarkt 16 (☎442 62 81). The decor rather awkwardly mixes and matches moose heads, palm trees, and fake Greek statuary, but the atmosphere is low-key and the food is tasty. *Tostis* €2,50, full meals €4,65-6,25, beer €2. Open Su-W 10am-1am, Th-Sa 10am-2am.

Small Town Cart

Cheese Sellers

NEAR ARNHEM

NATIONAAL PARK VELUWEZOOM ☎026

A short bus trip from Arnhem (#43b from the train station and ask the driver to let you off at Groenenstraat; 20 min.; 4 strips), this pine forest nature preserve has a multiplicity of bike and footpaths. They're great for picnics on a sunny-day. (Park VVV ☎495 30 50; www.natuurmonumenten.nl. €2,75, children €1,60). Within the park, you'll also find **Kasteel Rosendael,** a furnished 18th-century castle with an 800-year-old tower. Its well-maintained living spaces and gallery of shells are worth a peak. (☎364 46 45. Open Tu-Su 10am-5pm. €3,60, children €1,60.)

APELDOORN ☎055

While not a magnificent town in itself, Apeldoorn (pop. 153,000), 25km North of Arnhem, is another good jumping-off place for **De Hoge Veluwe.** The **VVV tourist office,** Stationstraat 72, five minutes straight ahead from the station, sells bike maps for €4,20. (☎0 900 168 16 36, €0,45/min.; open M-F 9am-5:30pm, Sa 9am-5pm.) The town is home to the magnificent **Museum Paleis Het Loo,** a 17th-century palace that was home to the many King Willems of Orange. It's built on a sizeable plot of land, so the pristine gardens, full of Neoclassical sculptures, fountains and a colonnade have been precisely and symmetrically trimmed for almost 350 years. From the station, take bus #1, 102, or 104

Traditional Architecture

Dutch Tiles

Market

Horse Country

(20min., 2 strips) to get to the museum. (☎577 24 00; www.paleishetloo.nl Open Tu-Su 10am-5pm. Guided tours in English by appointment only. €9, under 18, €3.). Also nearby is **Apenheul,** or "apes' refuge," an interactive zoo in Berg & Bos nature preserve, with 30 different species of ape. Grab bus #2 or 3 (10 min., 2 strips). Gorillas, orangutans, and bonobos live on large islands throughout the park, while smaller apes dwell in the area around the many walking paths. You're more likely to get pickpocketed here than in Amsterdam Centraal—special monkey-proof money belts are provided by the park. (☎357 57 57; www.apenheul.nl. Open daily Apr.-May 9:30am-6pm; June-Aug. 9:30am-6pm; Sept.-Oct 9:30am-5pm. €12; under 10, €10.)

DE HOGE VELUWE NATIONAL PARK

☎**0318**

De Hoge Veluwe is a far cry from Amsterdam, both in terms of landscape and location. The 13,565 acre nature preserve is The Netherlands' largest and contains wooded areas, moors, grass plains, and sand dunes. Over 42km of bikepaths and 1,000 white bikes available **free of charge** at five convenient spots in the park make exploring the varying (though flat) scenery a true treat. The handful of lakes and countless places to pull over make the park ideal for picnicking. Venture to the southern end of the park to watch the wildlife. Early morning and late afternoon are the best times to catch a glimpse of the deer, wild boars, and numerous birds that inhabit the park.

TRANSPORTATION & PRACTICAL INFORMATION

From the **Arnhem** train station, take bus #107 to the park's northwestern Otterlo entrance, (every half-hour from 6:44am-10:14am and 2:44pm-6:14pm, otherwise, hourly between 6:44am-11:14pm. 25 min., €4,20 or 6 strips). From **Apeldoorn,** take bus #110 to the Hoenderloo entrance of the park or farther in at the museum. (Every hr. from the Apeldoorn station, last bus leaves the park at 5:45pm. 25 min., €4,20 or 6 strips.) In both cases, if you get off the bus inside the park you'll have to buy your park ticket from the driver, which is often easier.

Begin by picking up a map (€2) at **De Hoge Veluwe Visitor Center,** known as the **Bezoekerscentrum.** (☎59 16 27; www.hogeveluwe.nl).

The park is open Nov.-Mar. 9am-5:30pm, Apr. 8am-8pm, May and Aug. 8am-9pm, June-July 8am-10pm, Sept. 9am-8pm, Oct. 9am-7pm. €5; ages 6-12 €2,50; May-Sept. 50% discount after 5pm.

CAMPING

Camping is available at a campground right by the Hoenderloo entrance. (☎055 378 22 32. Open Apr.-Oct. €3,50 per person, ages 6-12 €1,75; electricity €2.)

FOOD

The most economical and enjoyable way to refuel during a day in the park is with a picnic lunch. There are, however, two restaurants within the park. **De Koperen Kop ❸,** a self-service restaurant at the center of the park and next to the Visitor Center and Museonder, offers a special (€11,25) for every season. The more upscale **Rijzenburg ❺,** has a three-course menu from €21,30. **Monsieur Jacques ❶,** located inside the Kröller-Müller Museum, is a less expensive option. It sells sandwiches and drinks at only slightly inflated prices, and the outdoor terrace makes it worth a stop. A kiosk next to De Koperen Kop sells ice cream and cold drinks in the warmer months.

SIGHTS

Tucked deep within the park, the **Kröller-Müller Museum** is a true gem. Surprisingly, the large complex houses several Van Gogh paintings as well as early studies by Mondrian, Pointillist masterpieces by Seurat and Signac, and modernist works by Picasso, Leger, and Brancusi. The magnificent sculpture garden provides plenty of opportunity to roam on foot and take in the 3D works by Dubuffet, Oldenburg, and Rodin, among others. (☎59 12 41; www.kmm.nl; Open Tu-Su 10am-5pm; sculpture garden closes at 4:30pm. €5, ages 6-12 €2,75.) A few kilometers north lies the **St. Hubertus Hunting Lodge.** Designed by Berlage, the castle is open daily for free guided tours. There is also a suggested walk circling the lodge that rambles past a meditation garden, peat bog, watermill, and sheep meadow, all in 2.6km. Spots for the lodge tours are limited and fill up especially fast in summer. Reserve early on the day of the tour at the visitors center. Also check out the visually inventive **Museonder,** an underground museum in the visitor center that teaches travelers about the flora, fauna, and ecosystem of the park. (Open daily 10am-5pm. Free with park ticket.)

GRONINGEN ☎050

With 35,000 students and the nightlife to prove it, Groningen ranks as perhaps the most happening city in the northern region of The Netherlands. While only a fifth of the city's population (175,000) attends Rijksuniversiteit Groningen or the Hanzehogeschool (Institute for Higher Professional Education), the old center is vibrant all night long, attesting to the dominance of the city's youthful inhabitants. Even without cars, which are outlawed from a handful of the most central streets, Gronin buzzes with people on bicycles and blades.

Heavily bombed in World War II, Groningen rebuilt itself completely. Yet unlike some other Dutch cities, Groningen managed to keep some if its old-world feel along side its bland '50s architecture. Some beautiful older buildings remain, including Martinitoren, Stadhuis, the University, and Prinsenhoftuin.

ORIENTATION AND PRACTICAL INFORMATION

Getting to Groningen, particularly from Amsterdam, is not always an easy task. The **train** from Amsterdam takes about 2.5 hours (€23,80 one way). The way it works is that you can either take the train straight to Groningen, or you can take the train to another city (often Amersfoot), where you switch trains and continue to Groningen. Depending on when you decide to leave for the north, the train you take from Amsterdam Centraal will be one of this variety. When you buy your ticket in Amsterdam (or Groningen, on return), ask the attendant if the next train requires a switch in another city. Once you get to the transfer, you will only have to cross the platform and board the opposite train *only in the section of that train that has a sign listing your final destination.* Again, it's best to check with the conductor as even the Dutch seem to get confused in this situation.

The old center is no bigger than a square kilometer, and is easily walkable. It's bordered by public transit in the south and canals in the east, north, and west. The center is a ten-minute walk from the train station: go out to the main street, turn right and cross the second bridge on your left. Once you've crossed, follow Herestraat until its end, Groningen's historic **Grote Markt.** At night, the place to be is east of Grote Markt—look for Poelerstraat on the southeast corner of the square.

The **VVV office,** Grote Markt 25, is in the far corner of the Grote Markt next to the unmistakable Martinitoren. They offer guided walking tours in July and August. Reserve in advance. (☎0900 202 30 50; www.vvvgroningen.nl. Open M-W 9am-6pm, Th 9am-8pm, Fri 9am-6pm, Sa 10am-5pm, only Jul.-Aug. Su 11am-3pm; walking tours Su 1-3pm, M 2:30-4:30pm. €3,50, under 12 €2,25.)

ACCOMMODATIONS

Hotel Friesland, Kleine Pelsterstraat 4 (☎312 13 07). It's a 5-10min. walk from the train station: cross the canal at the Groninger Museum (on your right as you exit the station) and walk up Ubbo Emmiusstraat, turn right on Gedempte Zuiderdiep, left on Pelsterstraat, and right onto Kleine Pelsterstraat. You'll enjoy friendly service, bright bedrooms with high ceilings, and impeccably clean shared bathrooms. Breakfast included. Singles €23,50; doubles €43,50; triples €60; quads €80. Credit cards accepted. ❶

Simplon Jongerenhotel, Boterdiep 73-2 (☎313 52 21; fax 360 31 39; simplon-jongerenhotel@xs4all.nl; www.xs4all.nl/~simplon). From the train station, take bus #1 in the direction of Korrewegwijk and get off at the Boterdiep stop; the hostel is the white building through the yellow and black striped entranceway. A 10min. walk from the center of Groningen, the Simplon pulls in a young and fun crowd with its clean accommodations at rock-bottom prices. Breakfast €3.40. Free lockers. Linens €2.50 for guests staying in the dorms, included in price of private rooms. Lockout noon-3pm. Bed in one of the 5 dorms, (4 mixed, 1 females only) €11; singles in high season €28, in low season €25; doubles €41,30, €38,50; triples €59, €55,60; quads €76, €71,45. ❶

Martini Budget Hotel, Gedempte Zuiderdiep 8 (☎312 99 19; www.martinihotel.nl). From the station, cross the canal at the Groninger Museum and follow that street a few blocks to Gedempte Zuiderdiep. Turn right and it'll be on your right. About halfway between the train station and Grote Markt, this large, new hotel is a great value with comfy rooms and clean showers and bathrooms. Breakfast €7,50. TV in every room. Singles €30, with bath €45; doubles €37,50, €65; triples €45, €72,50; quads €85; quints €90. MC/V. ❷

FOOD AND DRINK

Satehuis, Herestraat 111 (☎311 28 65). Enjoy the Indonesian-style *satay* in the small world of bamboo and rattan. Meals, 6 sticks of *satay* served with rice and sides, from €6,10-10,40. Special movie deal buys a meal, drink, and ticket to the cinema across the street for €14. ❷

Eetcafe De 1e Kamer, Peperstraat 9 (☎318 17 21). This classy stop serves up some of the cheapest eats in town. From Grote Markt, take Poelestraat from the southeastern corner of the square and turn right up at Peperstraat. Fill up on the daily special for just €5,80 or choose between peppersteak, schnitzel, or vegetarian stew (under €7,20). After the kitchen closes grab a beer (€2) and chat. Open daily 5pm-6am; kitchen closes at 9:30pm. ❷

SIGHTS

GRONINGER MUSEUM

Sits in the middle of the canal in front of and to the right of the train station. Walk across the blue pedestrian bridge. ☎366 65 55; www.groninger-museum.nl. Open Sept.-June Tu-Su 10am-5pm; July-Aug. M 1-5pm, Tu-Su 10am-5pm. €6, seniors over 65 €5, ages 5-15 €3.

The Groninger Museum, housed in a multicolored, almost entropic building, exhibits both modern art, traditional paintings, and ancient artifacts. Built by Italian architects, with five pavilions and a cafe, its steel-trimmed galleries create a futuristic laboratory atmosphere for its exhibits. It's a museum defined by risk, both architecturally and artistically, yet its archaeology and history exhibits (featuring crafts from the empire, 16th-century Chinese sculpture, and 18th-century Dutch china) are reminiscent of the Rijksmuseum. The only way they push the envelope is in the way the works are shown: between rainbow tiled walls and ethereal curtain compartmentalizers. The museum shows traditional Dutch paintings, including some Rembrant sketches and a Van Gogh, but its changing and contemporary exhibits are much more interesting.

Delftware Factory

NOORDELIJK SCHEEPVAART & NEIMEYER TABAKSMUSEUM (SHIPPING AND TOBACCO MUSEUM)

Brugstraat 24-26. Head up Ubbo Emmiusstraat and continue, as it becomes Folkingestraat, until Vismarkt. Turn left on the second street leaving Vismarkt from the west; after 2 blocks, that street becomes Brugstraat. ☎312 22 02. Open Tu-Sa 10am-5pm, Su 1-5pm. €2,75, children ages 7-14 and seniors over 65 €1,40, children under 7 free.

With two fascinating museums in one, and a diminutive tariff, the Noordelijk is an easy and fun stop for an hour. While the Scheepvaart focuses on the history of Dutch trade from the middle ages, the Tabaksmuseum celebrates the important commercial and political history of the tobacco trade, and displays fabulous ivory and crystal pipes. The museum even charts the current anti-smoking campaign as one of many deterrents, through history, to the trade and possession of the luxury good.

Delft House on the Canal

MARTINITOREN

On the northeast corner of Grote Markt. Buy tickets at the VVV (across the street) or at the tower's first floor when VVV is not open. Open Apr.-Oct. daily 11am-5pm; Nov.-Mar. noon-4pm. €2.20, children under 12 €1.20.

The **Martinitoren** offers the best view of the city. Standing at 97 meters, it miraculously survived the war untouched, unlike its neighbors on the north side of Grote Markt and those across, on the Zuid Zijd, which suffered total destruction. The new buildings, with the none-too-exciting architectural style of the 1950s, pale in comparison to those that survived the fighting.

Delft Market

OTHER SIGHTS

While in the area of the Martinitoren, look to the west side of the square and you'll see **Stadhuis,** the Groningen city hall. The Stadhuis prevails over the **Grote Markt,** which becomes a real marketplace every Tuesday and Saturday. Facing the Stadhuis, turn left and then right onto the street that heads out of the square. In a few blocks, it becomes Brugstraat; right before the first canal, turn left onto Kleineder A. There, take in the opaque glass **urinoir** designed by Rem Koolhaas so men can pee publicly in style. Backtrack along the same canal past Brugstraat and take it easy at **Noorderplantseon,** a rolling, fountained park that hosts the annual **Noorderzon (Northern Sun) Festival** of art in late August and sits on the northwestern corner of the city (follow the canal north of Brugstraat and turn left across the last canal before the curve to the right, and then turn right into the park). Or, head north of Brugstraat and turn right onto Turftorenstraat, take the curve right, and at the street, turn left and then right onto **Academieplein,** which harbors the academic buildings of **Rijksuniversiteit Groningen,** the 35,000-student university that provides the city's boisterous nightlife. As you walk up the street, on your left is **Academiebegouw,** the administrative center, and on your right, the university's main library. Continue on Academie Plein until Oude Boteringestraat to see one of the oldest stone houses in the city (#24), the house with the 13 temples (#23), the former District Court (#36-38), and the one-time residence of the Queen's Commissioner (#44). Keep walking toward bigger numbers until you hit the canal, referred to in Groningen as *diep* rather than *gracht.* A ten-minute stroll to your right, along the canal, will bring you to the **Prinsenhoftuin,** Turfsingel 43, a tremendous flower garden with walking paths and an overwhelming aroma. Escape the city's mundane postwar urbanity in these **Princes' Court Gardens,** originally designed in 1625 with a rose garden and covered paths. When in bloom, the fragrant roses make it impossible not to linger, especially when the **Theeschenkerij Tea Hut** inside the garden makes it so tempting to order a cup of tea (€0,80) and lounge in the sun or under one of the charming canopied underpasses. On your way out, take the advice of the Latin inscription on the sundial above the entrance to heart: "The past is nothing, the future uncertain, the present unstable; ensure that you do not lose this time, which is yours alone." (☎318 38 10. Open Apr.-Oct. 15 10am-sundown.) Continue along the canal; turn right onto Turfstraat and left onto Singelstraat, and you'll find yourself imposed upon by the **Prinsenhof (Princes' Court),** which once served as a cloisters but now serves as the home of the local radio and TV station.

OTHER MUSEUMS

The **Natuurmuseum,** Praediniussingel 59, displays aspects of natural history and offers a special garden walk. Facing the Stadhuis in Grote Markt, turn left and then right on the street out of the square, continuing until the canal, turning left on Kleine der A, and following it down to signs that say Museumbrug; it's on your left. The museum is three floors of nature-lover's paradise, with restored beehives and birdnests, and a good collection of life-size wildlife models. (☎367 61 70; groningen@natuurmuseum.org; www.natuurmuseum.org. Open Tu-F 10am-5pm, Sa-Su 1-5pm. €2,80, under 13 €1,75). The **Volkenkundig,** or Ethnographic Museum, 't Jatstraat 104, is also worth a visit. A university run museum devoted to the study of ethnography, or issues related to ethnicity and culture, and more specifically, the religious and pragmatic art of the South Pacific, Asia, Africa, and North and South America. (☎363 57 91; volkkmus@theol.rug.nl. Open Tu-F 10am-4pm, Sa-Su 1-5pm. Free.)

NIGHTLIFE AND COFFEESHOPS

The best bet for a night on the town lies just off the southeastern corner of Grote Markt on Poelestraat and Peperstraat. The bars and restaurants on these two streets are literally packed shoulder-to-shoulder and offer good prices and a buzzing atmosphere to the mainly student crowd. The students boast that the bars close only when the people stop drinking, usually around four in the morning on the weekends.

Jazzcafe de Spieghel, Peperstraat 11 (☎312 63 00). The intimate, candle-lit place houses 2 floors of live jazz, funk, or blues every night at 11 or later. Pick up a free copy of *UlLoper* from the VVV to find out what's on. Tokers welcome. Wine €2 per glass. Open daily 8pm-4am.

Tramps, Peperstraat 10 (☎318 54 36), is a hotspot late at night. Beers €1,70 and a special sweet, green shooter called *Boswandeling* (4 for €6,60). Enjoy the politically-themed decor and requests from the bar's 300-CD collection. Open Su-W until 4am, Th-Sa until; 5am.

Cafe de Vlaamsche Reus, Poelestraat 15 (☎314 83 13). A young crowd keeps things lively. A beer here will run under €1,80. To sit outside, try the megabar overlooking the Grote Markt known familiarly as the Zuid Zijd (South Side). Open daily from 9pm.

COFFEESHOPS

Groningen's streets are lined with a total of 14 coffeeshops, almost all of which offer better prices than those in Amsterdam. These two have a cool, comfortable ambience.

The Glory, Steentilstraat 3 (☎312 57 42), is a super-chill spot open later at night with a small projection screen, a vague green, Bob Marley theme, and theater-style seats at small tables. Spacecake or joints €2,50; bud and hash in €5 and €15 increments. Open M-W noon-1am, Th-F noon-2am, Sa 10am-3am.

De Vliegende Hollander, Gedempte Zuiderdiep 63 (www.de-vliegende-hollander.nl). Dutch for "the flying Hollander." Select your goodies from a touch computer screen in €5 and €15 packets. "Top 44" and "K2" are particularly kind (0,8 g for €6).

NEAR GRONINGEN

KAMP WESTERBORK ☎0593

Oosthalen 8. Take a train from Groningen to Beilin (€6,10) and then a €3,50 trein-taxi to the Herinneringscentrum at Westerbork. ☎59 26 00; www.kampwesterbork.nl. Open Feb.-June and Sept.-Dec. M-F 10am-5pm, Sa-Su 1-5pm; July-Aug. M-F 10am-5pm, Sa-Su 11am-5pm. Guided tours available mid-June to mid-Sept. (daily 2pm). €3,85, children ages 8-18 €2.

Built by the Nazis in 1939 as a detainment camp for Jews in the north of The Netherlands, Kamp Westerbork held 100,000 Dutch Jews before sending them east to the concentration camps, from 1942 until liberation. The transport camp was the last stop on Dutch land for virtually all of the country's Jews, including the Frank family in 1944. The **Herinneringscentrum** runs a museum that documents life inside the camp through movies and photos. Ask at reception to borrow the English guidebook.

About 2.6km from Herinneringscentrum is the actually camp, accessible by Westerbork shuttle from 11am-5pm (round-trip €1,75). On the drive, look for five stone coffins on your right, one for each of the five concentration camps to which Jews were sent from here. On one side of the coffin is the number sent and on the other is the number exterminated. The exhibits and displays are in Dutch, but a 700-meter walk to the far end of the camp (watchtower and barbed wire), will give you some idea of life inside Westerbork. After World War II, the site was used as a refugee camp for 12,500 Moluccans. A small population inhabiting the eastern tip of Indonesia, Moluccans joined the drive for Indonesian independence but found the Dutch government unsympathetic to their nationalist causes. They remained an independent community within The Netherlands by living in Westerbork with the hope that they would return home *en masse*. The Moluccans ultimately integrated into the Dutch population.

MAASTRICHT ☎043

Maastricht, one of the oldest cities in The Netherlands, is in a little pocket of land that juts down into territory surrounded by Belgium and Germany. Its strategic location has made it a hotbed of military conquest throughout history. Romans originally settled the town as a stop on their way to Cologne at the crossing of the River Maas

(Maastricht means "Maas crossing."). Although its defensive walls went up in 1229, the town was captured by the Spanish in 1579 and then by the French in 1673. In 1814, it joined the Kingdom of The Netherlands and then resisted siege by the Belgians. After being occupied by the Germans during WWII, Maastricht was one of the first towns to be liberated. This past of international convergence gives Maastricht resonance as the sight of the 1991 treaty that established the **European Union.** Today, too, the city's attractions are mainly historical—the pleasant Old World feel of its cobblestone streets, the ancient churches of The Netherlands, and its astounding, vast subterranean defense system, **The Caves of Mount St. Pieter.** Medieval architecture mingles with the young student population and modern commercialism to produce a serene yet active town (pop. 125,000) known for its appealing quality of life.

ORIENTATION & PRACTICAL INFORMATION

Maastricht is bisected by the River Maas, and the old town (with most of the sights) lies on the western side of the river, across from the train station. The heart of the town is the **Vrithof,** a large square flanked by two churches, although the Markt and the Onze Lieve Vrouwe Plein are also organizing open squares.

Trains (2½hr., €23,80 one way) leave from Centraal Station in Amsterdam every half-hour at 27 and 57 minutes after the hour. You can also arrive by plane; KLM (www.klm-excel.com) flies from Amsterdam, London, and Munich. Direct trains from Maastricht to Amsterdam leave every hour at 29 minutes past the hour.

Pick up a map (€1) of the city center at the VVV Kleine Straat 1. It's a pleasant 15-minute walk from the station. Go straight on Stationstraat, cross the bridge, and walk straight for another block. When you hit a wall, take a right, and the VVV tourist office will be one block down on your right. (☎325 21 21; www.vvvmaastricht.nl. Open Nov.-Apr. M-F 9am-6pm, Sa 9am-5pm; May-Oct. M-Sa 9am-6pm, Su 11am-3pm.)

Maastricht is small enough that you can **walk** everywhere in the town; even the Caves of St. Pieter, which lie on the outskirts, are only a 20-minute walk. If you are going farther, Maastricht has a **bus** system; the information is available at a booth outside the train station. You can get **taxis** at the Vrithof, Market and Central Street; sometimes it is cheaper to pick one up at these stops rather than hailing one on the street.

Internet Access: **Cafe de Unit** (open M-Sa noon-7pm; €1,50 for 30min.) on Leliestraat (with your back to the Vrithof walk onto Paleistraat and take a right onto the first street, a narrow alley).

ACCOMMODATIONS

The VVV can book rooms in private bed and breakfasts for low prices (doubles €32-60); many of them are near the center of town but rent only one or two rooms.

Botel, Maasboulevard 95 (☎321 90 23; fax 325 79 98). From the train, walk across the bridge and take a left. Walk down the river until you hit it. A hotel on a moored boat with tiny cabin rooms and a cosy deckroom lounge; the best budget digs in the center of town. 24hr. reception. If you rent a room without bath, the nearest one may be on a different floor. Breakfast €4. Singles €27, with shower and toilet €30; doubles €41, €43; triples €60; quads €80; quint €95; six €114. Cash only. ❶

Le Virage, Cortenstraat 2-2b (☎321 66 08; fax 321 4890; www.levirage.nl). When facing the Onze Vrouwe church, it's on the right hand back corner of the square. 4 spacious suites with bedroom, living room, kitchenette, and bathroom above a café. Breakfast €9. Double apartments €90; triples €112; quads €136. ❹

City-Hostel de Dousberg (HI), Dousbergweg 4 (☎346 67 77; fax 346 6755; www.dousberg.nl). From Centraal Station, take bus #11 to the Dousberg stop (2 strips) and cross the street. Buses run every 30min. until 6pm. After 6pm, take bus #33 (every hr. until midnight), on weekends take bus #8 or 18. HI abode offering low prices in an inconvenient location. With well-kept rooms off cinder block hallways, indoor and outdoor pools, and tennis courts (€20 per hr.; bring your own racquet), you may feel like you're back in high school. Breakfast included with HI membership. Lockout 10:30am-3pm. Curfew 1am. All rooms have shower and toilet. Dorm bed in single sex room (10-14 beds) €19,75; triples €74,35; quads €92; quints €110, six €173; non-members pay €2,50 extra. Credit cards accepted. ❶

FOOD AND DRINK

The best areas for cafés are around the **Onze Lieve Vrouwe Plein,** the **Markt,** the **Vrithof** (especially), and **Platielstraaat** along to St. Amorsplein. Maastricht is also known for its collection of more luxurious (and expensive) French-influenced restaurants.

De Blindgenger, Koestraat 3 (☎325 06 19), right off the Onze Lieve Vrouwe Plein in the far right-hand corner from the church. A warm, red cafe filled with art and antique mirrors make this a good environment to fill up on a tasty *dagschotel* (special) (€8) or other classic favorites like chicken satay with peanut sauce. Open daily 11am-11pm. ❷

Chalet Bergrust, Luikerweg 71 (☎325 54 21), just next to the Grotten Noord Caves of St. Pieter. A good, low-priced Dutch café on perhaps the only hilltop in The Netherlands. Beautiful view over the town. Lunch options run about €4. Open daily in summer and holiday season 10am-10pm; in winter W and F-Su 11am-6pm. ❶

L'Hermitage, St. Bernadusstraat 20 (☎325 17 77), off the southeast corner of the Onze Lieve Vrouwe Plein. A friendly Mexican café that's a favorite with students and locals (cajun *quesadillas* €9, spare ribs €13). French dishes round out the cuisine. Open daily 5:30-11pm. ❸

SIGHTS

CAVES OF MOUNT SAINT PIETER

*☎325 21 21; fax 321 78 78. There are two entrances to the vast system of caves; the **Zonneberg Caves,** Slavante 1, give a tour in English July-Aug. daily at 2:45pm. Otherwise the tours are in Dutch, but you may be able to get an English translation depending on your guide. The tour times change throughout the year so it's best to call ahead. The Zonneberg tour focuses more on WWII history while the **Grotten Noord** concentrates on the defense of local farmers over the ages. The Grotten caves, Luikerweg 71, can be reached by a 20min. walk following the signs to Grotten Noord or by bus every 30min. The Zonnenberg caves are farther away and are best reached by boat. €3, children under 12 €2. A combination boat trip and visit to the Zonneberg Caves (3hr. total) costs €8,75, children €5,50.*

The caves of Mount St. Pieter are an enormous underground labyrinth that was used as a defensive hide-away during the many sieges on Maastricht. The Romans initially built a tunnel through the "marl" (limestone), and over the centuries the Dutch expanded the complex until it consisted of over 20,000 vast passages capable of sheltering 40,000 people. They were instrumental in defeating the Belgians during sieges and in sheltering people during World War II. This history has left its mark on the walls in the form of inscriptions by soldiers and generations of inhabitants. Bring your coat as the caves can get chilly.

BONNEFANTENMUSEUM

Ave. Ceramique 250. Walk down the river on the side of the train station for 10min.; it's the huge building that looks like a metal rocket ship. ☎329 01 90; info@bonnefanten.nl; www.bonnefanten.nl. Open Tu-Su 11am-5pm. €7, students, seniors, and groups over 10 €6, children under 13 free.

In a 1995 landmark rocketship of a building by Italian architect Aldo Rossi, the Bonnefanten houses a marvelous collection of both traditional and contemporary art in spacious galleries that have a hip edge to them. Their "Old Master painting and Sculpture" collection concentrates on Southern Netherlandish and Flemish art and includes works by Pieter Brueghel the Younger. The museum is not afraid to be playful. It has a yellow cylinder stretching between floors so that viewers can watch other museum-goers circling a sculpture by Luciano Fabro. Other highlights include Edward Muybridge's *Animals in Motion* series of animals and naked humans. The contemporary floor of the museum strives to be on the vanguard of the art world and includes such works as Suchan Kinoshita's wood closet containing suspended hourglasses. In the courtyard outside are enormous designs from industrial materials by Sol Le Witt and Richard Serra.

BASILICA OF ST. SERVATIUS

The huge church on the Vrithof. The entrance is to the right on Keizer Karelplein. www.servatius.nl. You can buy an identification leaflet on the different nooks and statues of the church at the information desk for €0,50. Open daily 10am-5pm; July-Aug. 10am-6pm. €2, seniors €1,50, children €0,50.

This beautiful church, a central Maastricht landmark, fuses cultural, architectural and ecclesiastical history. It is the only church in The Netherlands to be built over the grave of a saint: St. Servatius (d. 384) was the first Bishop of The Netherlands. The original church was built over his tomb c. 570, and the remains have been excavated and are on display in an underground chamber. Of the spectacular building that stands today, the inner Romanesque part was constructed in the 11th century, while the outer Gothic structure was constructed in the 14th and 15th centuries. At the early entrance to the right off the back, there is a tiled labyrinth on the floor; see if you can get from "one of the four corners of the earth" (Rome, Constantinople, Colon, or Achen) to the "celestial city" of Jerusalem. (Hint: you must go by St. Servatius). The church surrounds a lovely inner lavender **courtyard** where the huge old bell from 1515, affectionately known as the Granmeer ("grandmother") sits. On your way into the church, you will pass its treasury, which contains a golden chest with part of St. Servaas' skeleton, as well as a silver arm with the arm bone of the apostle Thomas.

ONZE LIEVE VROUWE BASILIEK (BASILICA OF OUR DEAR LADY)

Follow signs to the Onze Lieve Vrouwe Plein. ☎325 18 51. Open Easter-Oct. M-Sa 11am-5pm, Su 1-5pm. Free. There is also a room with ecclesiastical relics (€1,60, children €0,45), but it's not really worth it.

A medieval basilica in honor of Mary, with an dark, dank feel punctuated by beautiful colored stained glass; parts of the cruciform church date to the 11th century. Mary is here affectionately termed "Star of the Sea," because she is said to have miraculously saved the lives of sailors at sea during a storm around 1700. See the hundreds of votive candles now placed around her statue in prayer to her miracle-working power.

NATUURHISTORISCH MUSEUM

De Bosquetplein 6-7. ☎350 54 90; www.nhmmaastricht.nl. Open M-F 10am-5pm, Sa-Su 2-5pm. €3, children ages 6-12 €2, children under 6 free.

This museum features the remains of a newly discovered ancient species, the Montasaurus dinosaur, and giant turtles found fossilized in the sandstone of the St. Pietersberg caves. The rest of the museum follows geological developments from the beginning of time to the contemporary flora and fauna of Southern Limburg. In the back there are child-friendly exhibits of fish tanks and a modest botanical garden. The museum is curated in Dutch, but there are follow-along booklets available in English.

OTHER SIGHTS

St. Jan's Church, a Gothic structure to the left of the St. Servatuis Basilica, has been a Protestant church since 1632 and has a beautiful view of the city from its high tower. (Open Mar.-Sept. M-Sa 11am-4pm. Church free; tower €1,15.). On the outskirts of the old centrum lies the **Helpoort,** Sint Bernardusstraat 1, the only city gate from 1229 still standing. Walk along the Onze Lieve Vrouwe rampart (the canons are on display for tourists only; they would have been pointing outwards from the walls during a real attack) and learn all about the history of the fortified city from the knowledgeable staff. (Open mid-Apr. to Oct. 1:30-4:30pm. Free.) More military sights are at the high pentagonal **Fort St. Pieter,** Luikerweg 80 (across from the Grotten Noord; €3), which provided protection for the city from 1702. To continue the historical extravaganza, visit the **Derlon Museum Cellar.** Part of a Roman cobblestone road and other objects from the 2nd, 3rd, and 4th centuries were discovered during construction of the new Derlon Hotel. (The basement is open Su noon-4pm. Free.) You can also take **boat trips** through the Rederij Stiphout (☎351 53 00; info@stiphout.nl; www.stiphout.nl) from €5,50 for a basic tour on the River Maas to €43,50 for a candlelight cruise.

NIGHTLIFE AND COFFEESHOPS

Marijuana is not accepted here with the same breezy liberality of Amsterdam, so, although coffeeshops exist, they tend to be more discreet. One of the best coffeeshops in The Netherlands is Maastricht's **Tea Room Heaven 69,** Brusselsestraat 146. Behind the window blinds is a friendly two-tiered complex with plants, pool table, fountain and, best of all, a full kitchen serving lunch and dinner for when the munchies strike (☎325 34 29; www.heaven69.nl. Open daily 9am-midnight.)

The nightlife in Maastricht is really about pubbing. Serving over 100 different beers, **Falstaff,** Amorsplein 6, has the best selection in town. Lots of specialty Belgian brews on tap (€2,60) and plenty more options in the fridge keep students and beer connoisseurs alike happy. (☎321 72 38; www.cafe-falstaff.com. Open Su-Th 11am-2am, F-Sa 11am-3am.) Students stay out late to drink at **Metamorfoos,** Kleine Gracht 40-42, a café-brasserie. (Happy Hour 1-2am with 2 for 1 drinks, meat and chips special €5,75. ☎321 27 14. Open M-F noon-5am, Sa-Su 3pm-5am.) Closer to the river, **de Kadans,** Kesselkade 62, serves brasserie food (prix-fixe menu €14,18) and pumps house music Th-Sa downstairs at the **K-Club.** (☎326 17 00. Brasserie open M-W 11am-midnight, Th-Sa 11am-5am, Su noon-1am; kitchen closes at 10pm. Sa cover €3,50. Club open Th-Sa 11pm-5am.) For more dancing, try **Night Live,** Kesselkade 43, where loud music and a young crowd make this converted church jam. The entrance is to the right of the church down at the end of the alley. (Open Th-Sa 11-6am. Su salsa. Cover €3,40-6.) For other entertainment, check out the listings in the free weekly *Uit in Maastricht.*

WADDEN ISLANDS (WADDENEILANDEN)

Tucked away off the northwestern coast of The Netherlands and inauspiciously named (*wadden* means "mud flat"), the Wadden Islands are an unassuming vacation destination. The Dutch wouldn't have it any other way, happy to keep these idyllic islands to themselves. Even when Netherlanders flock here during the summer, the islands still feel sleepy and isolated. Largely deserted bike paths wind through vast, flat stretches of grazing land and lead to some of Europe's most pristine nature reserves. The islands also offer excellent beaches: long, sandy strands where the sun-warmed shallows of the Waddenzee make for relatively temperate swimming. Though transit to the Waddens can tax the wallet of the budget traveler, abundant campsites and plenty of good youth hostels render a trip to these resplendent islands affordable.

ORIENTATION. The islands arch clockwise around the northwestern coast of The Netherlands. Texel (see p. 254), closest to Amsterdam, is the largest and most populous; Terschelling (see p. 256), the middle child of the five, bustles with nightlife and brims with nature preserves; while on Ameland (see p. 257), it's possible to bike for miles without seeing another soul. The second and fifth islands, tiny Vlieland and far-flung Schiermonnikoog, fill out the archipelago.

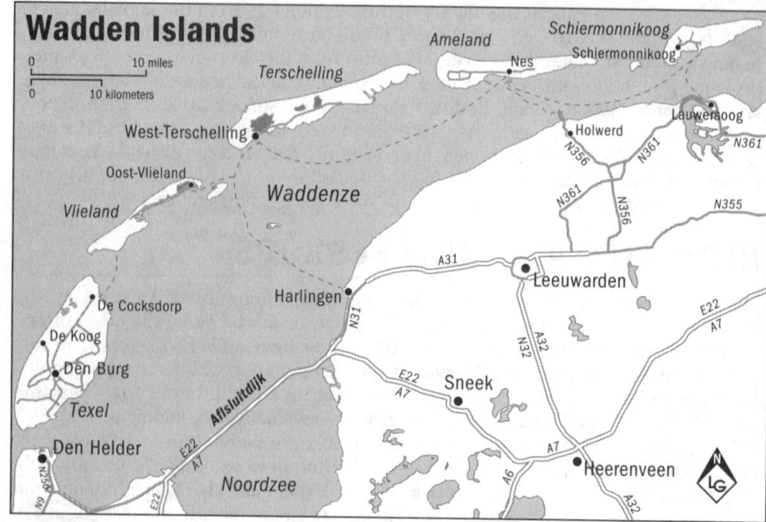

TEXEL

☎0222

Texel, because of its proximity to Amsterdam and the less-than-daunting twenty minutes it takes the ferry to cross the Waddenzee, is the most touristed of the islands. While its four siblings are certainly quieter by degrees as they arch farther northward, Texel is no less charming for its relative popularity. And there's no better way to appreciate its stunning yet serene natural beauty than by navigating the bike trails that transect the island.

TRANSPORTATION AND PRACTICAL INFORMATION

To reach **Texel,** take the train from Amsterdam to **Den Helder** (90min., €10,80 one way), then grab bus #33 right next to the train station (two strips); it will drop you off at the docks, from which a **ferry** will take you to 't Hoorntje, the southernmost town on Texel (☎36 99 61; 20min., every hr. 6:30am-9:30pm, round-trip €4). **Buses** depart from the ferry dock to various locales throughout the island, though the best way to travel is to rent a **bike** from **Verhuurbedrijf Heijne,** opposite the ferry dock. (From €4,50 per day. Open Apr.-Oct. daily 9am-8pm; Nov.-Mar. 9am-6pm.) If you prefer public transportation, purchase a **Texel Ticket,** which allows unlimited one-day travel on the island's bus system (runs mid-June to mid-Sept.; €3,50). The **VVV tourist office,** Emmaln 66, is located just outside Den Burg, about 300m south of the main bus stop; look for the blue signs. (☎31 47 41; info@texel.net; www.texel.net. Open M-Th 9am-6pm, F 9am-9pm, Sa 9am-5:30pm; July-Aug. also Su 10am-1:30pm.)

FOOD AND DRINK

The island's two major villages are the central **Den Burg** and the beachfront **De Koog.** The pub **De 12 Balcken Tavern ❸,** Weverstraat 20, in Den Burg, serves truly heavenly spare ribs, marinated, grilled, and served with salad and a heaping bowl of french fries (one serving costs €12 and feeds 2). You can also get a shot of *'t Jutterje,* the island's popular liquorice-flavored schnapps, blended from herbs and wheat, for €2. (☎31 26 81. Open M-Sa 10am-2am, Su 5pm-2am; lunch served 1-5pm, dinner 6-10pm.) **Pizzeria Venezia ❷,** Kogerstraat 7, in Den Burg, offers a solid pizza in a homey setting with long wooden tables and candlelight; the real star, though, is the calzone, literally as big as your head (€8,75-10,75). Delicious, velvety soups make great starters (€3). Plenty of vegetarian options available. (☎31 25 70. Pizzas €5-9,50 Open Apr.-Oct. daily noon-11pm; Nov.-May 4-11pm. MC.) Your best bet for eating in De Koog is to stroll the main drag, Dorpstraat, where vendors hawk *loempia,* fresh fruit, and *appeltaart* (all €2-5). All manner of bars, shoarma huts, and *pannekoekens* are within reach. The

Albert Heijn **supermarket,** Waalderstraat 48, in Den Burg, is the best place for campers to grab food and sundries. (Open M-Th and Sa 8am-8pm, F 8am-9pm.) In De Koog, you can also head to **Super de Boer,** Nikadel (Open M-h and Sa 8am-6pm, F 8am-8pm).

ACCOMMODATIONS

Texel's youth hostel is easily accessible via bus #29 from the ferry (4 strips); tell the bus driver your destination. Called **Panorama (HI) ❶,** Schansweg 7, it's snuggled amid lovely but fragrant sheep pastures 7km from the dock at 't Horntje and 3km from Den Burg's center. Friendly bar has Textel's own brew on tap, Texels Wit (€2). (☎31 54 41. Bikes from €4 per day. Breakfast and sheets included. Reception 8:30am-10:30pm. Dorms €15,90-18,95; €2,50 more for non-members. The diminutive **Hotel de Merel ❷,** Warmoestraat 22, offers ten lovely rooms right in the center of Den Burg. From the bus stop in Den Burg Square, turn left on Elemert and left again on Warmoestraat (☎31 31 32. Breakfast included. Reception 8am-10pm. Singles €47, with bath €50; doubles €64, €70. Off-season €4-12 less, with discounts for longer stays.) **Campgrounds** provide a cheap accommodation option (€2,50-5 per person; around €7 per tent) and allow you to get close to the nature scene; most sites cluster south of De Koog, but there are campgrounds right behind De Koog's main strand, as well as more secluded ones near De Cocksdorp; the tourist office can arrange reservations.

MUSEUMS

A trip around Texel's 54km perimeter will fill an entire day, taking you to the island's best sights. Though the VVV boasts that Texel features five museums, only two are truly worth the money. **EcoMare Museum and Aquarium,** Ruijslaan 92, about 2km south of De Koog, just off the Ruijslaan bike path, features an aquarium as well as exhibits on Texel's ecology. The museum's real stars, though, are its playful *zeehonden* (seals). EcoMare serves as a home to representatives of each of the several species that thrive in the waters of the North Sea, and the most lively (though crowded) times to visit are during the feeding hours (11am and 3pm). The staff can also arrange tours of the surrounding **nature reserves,** each of which focus on specific features of the ecology, such as native birds and tidepool life. For information on tours of reserves, call or check the board at the museum. (☎31 77 41; infobalie@ecomare.nl; www.ecomare.nl. €7, under 13 €3,50. Open daily 9am-5pm.)

On the other side of the island in the quaint burg of **Oudeschild,** a working windmill marks the site of the **Maritime and Beachcomber's Museum** (Maritiem en Jutters Museum), Barentzstraat 21, a monument to the sea and all that's in it. Displays include a creepy selection of relics scavenged from shipwrecks, and a vast assemblage of washed-ashore detritus, astonishing in its volume and variety, and impressively artful in its presentation. The highlight is an exhibit in which you step inside an imagined recreation of a sunken ship, creaky deck and underwater noises included. (☎31 49 56; www.texelsmaritiem.nl. Open Tu-Sa 10am-5pm; July-Aug. M-Sa 10am-5pm. €4,10)

BEACHES

Texel's greatest treasures lie outdoors. Its bike paths carve along the shoreline and through its pristine nature reserves, past some of the best **beaches** in The Netherlands. Texel's stretch of sand runs largely uninterrupted up the western coast and is divided into strands, called *paals,* which run in ascending numerical order from south to north. The most popular strands lie near De Koog, especially Paal 20. Just west of town, you'll find all manner of beach clubs and lots of folks sunning and splashing. There are miles of shoreline, and it becomes progressively less populated as you travel north and south of paal 20; 12, 13, and 15 are especially nice. All the beaches are open to the public, and the water becomes friendly to swimmers when it warms in July and August. At the northern and southern tips of the islands, **nude beaches** beckon the uninhibited; you can bare it all near paal 9 (2km southwest of Den Hoorn) or paal 27 (5km west of De Cocksdorp).

NIGHTLIFE

After sun sets on the beaches of Texel, the young and sunburned head to shoreside De Koog for its sprightly nightlife. By day, **Le Berry,** Dorpstraat 3, has a welcoming, smoky pub atmosphere, but at night the locals let their hair down and dance to the groove. A slightly more mature and sophisticated, but no less lively, crowd than at other nearby establishments. (☎31 71 14; www.leberry.nl. Open noon-3am, doors close at 2am. Dancing from 11pm, **Cafe Sam-Sam,** Dorpstraat 146, always knows how to have a good time. Catering to a crowd that's young but mostly post-pubescent, the Sam hosts nightly dancing to all manner of DJ-driven beats, usually kicking off around 9pm and going until 3am (or whenever the crowd dissipates), including campy '70s parties every Thursday during summer. (☎31 75 90; www.samsam-texel.nl. Beer €1,50; mixed drinks €4,50.) Den Burg possesses something of a scene, too, with nightclubs and bars clustering just off the town square along Kantoorstraat. **De Pilaar,** Kantoorstraat 5, draws a hip crowd with occasional live music (whoever the discriminating owners feel like hiring, running the gamut from country and blues to rock and soul, and a wide selection of Belgian and locally-brewed beer. (☎31 40 75. Open daily 8pm-3am; no entry after 2am.) Next door, **Question Plaza,** Kantoorstraat 1, may indeed raise queries regarding the tact of its faux-piazza interior decor, but the frisky, very youthful crowd is usually too busy drinking and dancing to house, techno, and dance classics to notice. (☎31 01 55; www.questionplaza.nl. Cover €6. Open daily 9pm-3am; no entry after 2am.)

TERSCHELLING ☎0562

With 80% of the island covered by a European Nature Reserve, **Terschelling** (pop. 4500) offers secluded beaches that stretch around the western tip and across the northern coast of the long, narrow island. A remote attraction to say the least, Terschelling is nevertheless more than worth visiting, as it offers trails through green pastures spotted with cows and horses, and at the same time seemingly endless beaches buttressed by a rollicking sea. Don't miss the view from the western tip of the island; at the ferry landing, turn left and walk till you can walk no farther--at the statue of the sailor is an unparalleled view of infinite blue waves, lilting sailboats, and sandy stretches. To explore the rest of the island's striking scenery, rent a **bike** from **Tijs Knop,** Torenstraat 10-12, one block up from the pier. (☎44 20 52. Bikes start at €4,50 per day, €20 per week.) The hills of Terschelling make for great **mountain biking** as well. **JOBA Sports** (☎44 93 24) runs rugged off-road tours through the nature reserve (€27). Get up close and personal with the seals of the Waddenzee with **Stella Maris Zeehonden Expedities.** (☎44 40 85. Tours last around 2½hr.; departure times depend on weather and season. Call ahead to reserve a spot.) Both tours can also be booked at the VVV (see below).

TRANSPORTATION AND PRACTICAL INFORMATION

Take a train from Amsterdam directly to **Harlingen Haven,** which drops you right at the ferry landing (3hrs., €25,10). **Ferries** (☎051 749 15 00, or for 24hr. recorded info, 0900 363 57 36, €0,10 per min.; www.rederij-doeksen.nl) depart for **Terschelling** (1-2hr., 3-5 per day, €17,63 one way). The VVV **tourist office,** W. Barentzkade 19, sits opposite the ferry landing. (☎44 30 00; vvvter@euronet.nl. Open M-Sa 9:30am-5:30pm.)

ACCOMMODATIONS

The **Terschelling Hostel (HI) ❶,** Van Heusdenweg 39, is located on the waterfront, just out of town. With your back to the harbor, take a right, walk along the pier, continue 1.5km on the bike path to Midland, and it's on the left, when the paved road curves away from the ocean. The bar and many of the guest rooms feature sweeping ocean views, and the kitchen serves up a great *dagschotel* for €8,70. Recent renovations have made most of the dorms into smaller, two-to-six-person rooms, but some bunk-style accommodations remain. (☎44 23 38; www.njhc.org/terschelling. Breakfast included. Sheets included; towels €3. Laundry €7. Reception 9am-10pm. Bed in 6-person room €18, off-season €15; €2,50 more for non-HI members) Campgrounds abound on Terschelling, especially along the Midslander Hoofdweg on the south-west coast. With a nice location and every amenity a camper could want (showers, toilets, laundry, and even a small grocery store with rock-bottom prices), **Camping Cupido ❶,** Hee 8, is one of the best bets. Located about 3km east of Terschelling West; turn left at the second blue "Hee" sign. Reception 9am-7pm. (☎44 22 19. €3 per person; €2,75 for a big tent, €2 for a small one.)

FOOD

As slick as it looks, **Zeezicht ❸**, Wm. Barentszkade 20, offers a pleasant, relaxed atmosphere for a great dinner with a sweeping view of the ocean. The main courses are on the pricier side (€12-16,50), but come in enormous portions with sides of potatoes and salad, guaranteed to satisfy even the heartiest appetites. Next to the VVV, across from the ferry landing. (☎244 22 68. Open daily 10am-midnight; kitchen closes at 9:30pm. AmEx/MC/V.) **De Dis ❶**, Boomstraat 17, proffers freshly-made sandwiches and salads, ideal for taking on a hike or for a beach picnic (☎44 31 83. *Broodjes* €2,30-5,50; Greek, potato, and other pre-made salads €1,40-1,80 per 100g. Open M-F 9am-6pm, Sa-Su 9am-5pm.). Campers can pick up groceries and other supplies at **Supermarkt Spanjer,** Boomstraat 13. (Open M-F 8am-8pm, Sa 8am-5pm.)

MUSEUMS

Although it's a bit far from town, the **Wrakkenmuseum,** Formerum Zuid 13, is well worth the 8km bike ride from West Terschelling. The museum is essentially just a collection of salvaged junk, but in its own quirky, back-country way, it achieves a sense of grandeur. Plus, in the newly annexed cafe, you can even get a bite for your trouble (*tostis* €2,50; hamburger special €3,50). The ride out to the museum is half the fun—it's got some of the nicest scenery on the island. Follow the bike path to Formerum; once in Formerum, take a left at the small statue of Rembrandt—the museum is about five minutes ahead on the left. (☎44 93 95. Open 10am-8pm, until 11pm in the summer. €2.) Closer to the main drag is the **Zeeaquarium and Natuurmuseum,** Burgemeester Reedekerstraat 11, which is a cut above the average taxidermist's. Though the signage is all in Dutch and you'll miss a lot of the information if you can't read it, most of the exhibits speak quite well for themselves, and, hey, fish are always cool. (☎44 23 90. Open M-F 9am-5pm, Sa-Su 2-5pm; in winter open daily 2-5pm. €4.) West Terschelling's historical museum, **'t Behouden Huys,** Commandeurstraat 30, offers a small but interesting collection of historical ephemera and detailed ship miniatures. For the Dutch-impaired, most of the story, however interesting, falls on blind eyes. (☎44 23 89. Open M-F 10am-5pm, Sa 1pm-5pm; Jun.-Sept., also Su 1pm-5pm. €3.)

NIGHTLIFE

Young people flood Terschelling during the summer, accounting for the island's surprisingly active **nightlife. Cafe De Zeevaart,** Torenstraat 22, possesses an old-salt, seaside-grog-house feel. (☎44 26 77. Plate of *bitterballen* €4,50. Open daily 10am-2am.). A younger crowd packs the sweaty dance floor at **Braskoer,** Torenstraat 32. (☎44 21 97. Wieckse Witte €2,50, Bacardi Breezer €4,50. Cover €5. Open daily 10am-2am; dancing from 9pm.)

AMELAND ☎0519

If Siberia sounds like it's too populous for you, give Ameland a try. The fourth of the Wadden Islands, it has the size and beauty of Terschelling with the remoteness of Vlieland. **Bike paths** criss-cross the island's isolated stretches, and a trip down any will reveal stunning beaches and rolling slopes of pastureland, the equal of any of its Wadden neighbors. Of the island's four villages, the largest and busiest (used in the most relative of senses) is **Nes,** where the ferry drops its passengers. The youth hostel is 9km to the west, in **Hollum.** With so few people, though, Ameland is the ideal place to get away from it all; and the best way to appreciate it is on the bike path. Be warned, however, that this far from The Netherlands' central cities, the English becomes much scarcer; although, for many, that will be one of the island's primary attractions.

TRANSPORTATION AND PRACTICAL INFORMATION

Ameland isn't the easiest of the islands to get to, but once you're there you'll be glad you made the trek. Inter-island journeys are nearly impossible; the ferry from Terschelling, when it runs, does so extremely infrequently. Whether coming from Amsterdam or Terschelling, you'll need to pass through **Leeuwarden** (from Amsterdam, €23, 2½hr.). From the Leeuwarden station, take Bus #66 to Ameland (9 strips), which drops you at the **ferry** landing in Holwerd; a ticket across the Waddenzee costs €10 and the trip takes 45min., dropping you in central Nes. To reach the **VVV tourist**

office, Postbus 14, walk straight from the ferry landing and it's on the right at the intersection. (☎54 65 46; www.ameland.nl. Open M-F 9am-12:30pm and 1:30pm-6pm; Sa 10am-3:30pm.) **Internet** access is available on two consoles at **Ameland Taxi,** Torenstraat 20, in Nes. (€1 for 15min.) To rent a bicycle, head to the island's popular chain, **Nobel's,** Standweg 3 in Nes. (☎55 42 78. Bikes €4-8 per day, €14-27 per week. Open daily 8:30am-6pm.) The youth hostel (see below) also rents bikes.

ACCOMMODATIONS

Ameland's **NJHC Hostel Ameland (HI) ❶,** Oranjeweg 59, is in the western town of Hollum; to get there, at the ferry landing simply jump on the bus headed for "Jeugherberg Vuurtoren"—it drops you right at the hostel (4 strips), and leaves right after the ferry arrives. The hostel and in-house bar are both extremely welcoming and friendly, and, in keeping with the feel of the island as a whole, usually pretty quiet. (☎53 53; www.njhc.org/ameland. Bed in a 4-person dorm €16,90-20,70, depending on season; €2,50 more for non-HI members. Sheets and breakfast included. Bike rental €4,50 per day.) In Nes, closer to the ferry and the livelier side of the island (if there is such a thing), is **Hotel de Helmen ❹,** J. Hofkerweg 1, which offers luxury bungalows as well as more basic double rooms. (☎54 20 02; info@hotel-hofker.nl; www.hotel-hofker.nl. 2-person studio €70; 5-person bungalows €345-620 per week, €15 cleaning fee.)

FOOD

In general, to find food, bars, or anything resembling nightlife, head to Nes. Operating under the maxim that when you're the only game in town you're by default the best, **Azie ❸,** Torenstraat 13, has the ambiguous distinction of being the only Chinese restaurant on the island. But it does offer a wide and varied menu, with main dishes €7,50-16 and 2-person sampler meals €27,50. (☎54 25 85. Open daily 11:30am-10:30pm.) In Hollum, head straight for **Cantina Dolores ❸,** Yme Dunweg 1, which serves up surprisingly convincing Tex-Mex fare with a pleasant soundtrack of authentic Mexican blues and salsa. (☎55 45 20. Starters €3-5; large main plates hover around €12. Open daily 4pm-12am; kitchen open until 10pm.) For groceries, hit up **C1000** in Nes, Torenstraat 9. (Open M-F 8am-8pm, Sa 8am-6pm.)

BRUSSELS ☎02

PHONE CODES | **Belgium Country code:** 32. **International dialing prefix:** 00.

Despite the city's instant association with NATO and the European Union, the diplomats have always been outshone by the two boy heroes that Brussels loves best: Tintin and the Mannekin Pis. In the late 1920s, cartoonist Hergé created a comic strip hero, Tintin, who righted international wrongs with his dog Snowy long before Brussels became the capital of the EU. The museums of Brussels are rich with collections of Flemish masters, modern art, and antique sculptures, but you don't need to go inside for a visual feast—the outside of the town itself is an Art nouveau marvel. Don't let its international flavor dissuade you from a visit—Brussels is but a short, if slow, train ride from Amsterdam.

TRANSPORTATION

Trains: Info ☎555 25 55. All international trains stop at **Gare du Midi/Zuid;** most also stop at **Gare Centrale** (near the Grand-Place) or **Gare du Nord** (near the Botanical Gardens). To: **Amsterdam** (2½hr., €32,50, under 26 €15,90).

Public Transportation: Runs daily 6am-midnight. 1hr. tickets €1,40 valid on **buses,** the **Métro (M),** and **trams.** Day pass €3,60, 5-trip pass €6,20, 10-trip pass €9. Information at

Société des Transports Intercommunaux Bruxellois (STIB), Gare du Midi. Schedule info (☎515 20 00; www.stib.irisnet.be. Open M-F 7:30am-5pm, 1st and last Su of each month 8am-2pm. Also at the Porte de Namur and Rogier Métro stops. Open M-F 8:30am-5:15pm.

ORIENTATION AND PRACTICAL INFORMATION

Most major attractions are clustered between the **Bourse** (Stock Market) to the west, the **Parc de Bruxelles** to the east, and the **Grand-Place.** Two **Métro** lines circle the city and efficient trams run north to south. A **tourist passport** *(Carte d'un Jour;* €7,45 at the TIB and bookshops) includes two days of public transit, a map, and reduced museum prices.

Tourist Offices: National, 63 r. du Marché aux Herbes (☎504 03 90; fax 504 02 70; info@opt.be; www.belgium-tourism.net), 1 block from the Grand-Place. Books rooms all over Belgium and gives out the free weekly *What's On.* Open Sept.-June M-F 9am-6pm, Sa 9am-1pm and 2-6pm; July-Aug. M-F 9am-7pm, Sa-Su 9am-1pm and 2-7pm. **Brussels International-Tourism and Congress (TIB);** ☎513 89 40; www.tib.be), on the Grand-Place, in the Town Hall, offers bus tours (3hr.; €19,90, students €17.) Open daily 9am-6pm; Nov.-Mar. 10am-2pm.

Embassies: Australia, 6-8 r. Guimard, 1040 (☎231 05 00; fax 230 68 02); **Canada,** 2 av. Tervueren, 1040 (☎741 06 11; fax 448 00 00); **Ireland,** 89/93 r. Froissart, 1040 (☎230 53 37; fax 230 53 12); **New Zealand,** 47 bd. du Régent, 1000 (☎513 48 56); **South Africa,** 26 r. de la Loi (☎285 44 02), generally open M-F 9am-5pm; **UK,** 85 r. Arlon (☎287 62 11; fax 287 63 55); **US,** 27 bd. du Régent, 1000 (☎508 21 11; fax 511 96 52; www.usinfo.be), open M-F 9am-noon.

Gay and Lesbian Services: Call ☎733 10 24 for info on local events. Staffed Tu 8-10pm, W 8-11pm, F 8-11pm.

Laundromat: Salon Lavoir, 62 r. Blaes, around the corner from the Jeugdherberg Brueghel. M: Gare Centrale. Wash and dry €3,25. Open daily 7am-10pm.

Emergencies: Ambulance or **first aid,** ☎100. **Police,** ☎101.

Medical Assistance: Free Clinic, 154a chaussée de Wavre (☎512 13 14). Misleading name–you'll have to pay. Open M-F 9am-6pm. **Medical Services,** 24hr. ☎479 18 18.

Internet Access: easyEverything (www.easyeverything.com) 9-13 de Brouckère. Around €1,25 per 66min., depending on time of day.

Post Office: (☎226 21 11) pl. de la Monnaie, Centre Monnaie, 2nd fl. M: de Brouckère. Open M-F 8am-7pm, Sa 9:30am-3pm.

ACCOMMODATIONS

Accommodations in Brussels can be difficult to find, especially on weekends in June and July. In general, hotels and hostels are well-kept and centrally located. Staffs will call each other if prospective guests arrive and they are booked.

Hotel Des Eperonniers, 1 r. des Eperonniers (☎513 53 66). Follow r. Inf. Isabelle from Central Station into Place Agora. Great location close to the Grand Place and well-kept rooms. Breakfast €3,75. Reception 7am-12pm. Singles €25-42; doubles €42-47. ❶

Hôtel Pacific, 57 r. Antoine Dansaert (☎511 84 59). M: Bourse; follow the street directly in front of the Bourse, which becomes Dansaert after the intersection; it's on the right. Excellent location and basic rooms. Breakfast included. Showers €5. Reception 7am-midnight. Curfew midnight. Singles €30; doubles €50; triples €70. ❷

Sleep Well, 23 r. du Damier (☎218 50 50; info@sleepwell.be, www.sleepwell.be), near Gare du Nord. M: Rogier. Exit onto r. Jardin Botanique, face the pyramid and go right; take the 1st right on r. des Cendres, then at the intersection go slightly to the right and continue onto r. de Damier. Breakfast included. Internet access. Curfew 3am. Lockout 10am-4pm. Dorms €16; singles €23,50; doubles €36. Reduced price after 1st night. ❶

IN THE CITY

International Man of Mystery

Tintin (pronounced "tan-tan") is the greatest comic-strip hero in the French-speaking world. From Nice to Quebec City, the journalist remains perpetually young to fans who play the hardest of hard-ball at auctions for Tintin memorabilia. His creator, Georges Rémi (whose pen-name "Hergé," are his initials pronounced backwards) sent him to the Kremlin, Shanghai, the Congo, outer space, and the wilderness of...Chicago. Countless dissertations and novels have been written about Tintin's possible androgyny; many also say that Indiana Jones was Tintin grown into a man. But Tintin is more than your average cartoon joe: when former French president Charles de Gaulle was asked whom he feared the most, he replied, "Tintin is my only international competitor."

Auberge de Jeunesse "Jacques Brel" (HI), 30 r. de la Sablonnière (☎218 01 87), on pl. des Barricades. M: Botanique. From the Métro, walk down Rue Royale away from the domed building at the end of the street, with the botanical gardens to your right, and take the 1st left onto Sablonnière. Spacious rooms. Breakfast included. Sheets €3,25. Reception 8am-1am. Dorms €12,50; singles €22,50; doubles €35; triples €43,50. Membership required. ❶

Jeugdherberg Bruegel (HI), 2 r. de Saint Esprit (☎511 04 36; jeugdherberg.bruegel@ping.be). From the back exit of Gare Centrale, go right on bd. de l'Empereur, and turn left onto r. de Saint Esprit. Breakfast and sheets included. Reception 7am-1am. Lockout 10am-2pm. Curfew 1am. Dorms €12,50; singles €22,50; doubles €35. Non-members add €2,50. ❶

FOOD AND DRINK

Cheap restaurants cluster around the **Grand-Place.** Shellfish and speciality *paella* are served up on **rue des Bouchers,** just north of Grand-Place. The small restaurants on **quai aux Briques,** in the Ste-Catherine area behind pl. St-Gery, serve cheaper seafood to a more local clientele. Just south of Grand-Place, the **rue du Marché-aux-Fromages** has cheap Middle Eastern food. **Belgaufras,** a hot waffel vendor, is everywhere (€1,40). The two-level **Super GB** grocery store, on the corner of r. du March-aux Poulets and r. des Halles (M: Bourse), is open M-Sa 9am-8pm and F 9am-9pm.

Chez Léon, r. des Bouchers 18 (☎511 14 15). Open for over a century. Serves famed seafood popular with locals and tourists alike. Mussels and chips €15-22. Open daily noon-11pm. ❺

Zebra, St-Gèry 33-35. This inexpensive but chic café is centrally located and serves light, tasty sandwiches and pastas (€2-6). Open daily 10am-1am. ❶

Arcadi Cafe, r. d'Arenberg 1b (511 33 34). Huge selection of quiche, sandwiches, and pastries (€3-6). Lots of vegetarian choices. Open daily 7:30am-11pm. ❶

Le Perroquet, r. Watteau 31 (512 99 22). Sit down for lunch, an afternoon beer, or a late-night pastry. Lively from open to close. Loads of salads and sandwiches from €5. Open daily noon-1am. ❶

Hemispheres, r. de l'Ecuver 65 (☎513 93 70). Libyan, Turkish, Chinese, and Indian cuisine convene at this summit of great Eastern platters. Vegetarian meals €7-10. Open M-F noon-3pm and 6:30-10:30pm, Sa 6:30pm-midnight. ❷

Ultième Hallutinatie, Rue Royale 316. Housed in a splendid stained glass Art Nouveau house and gar-

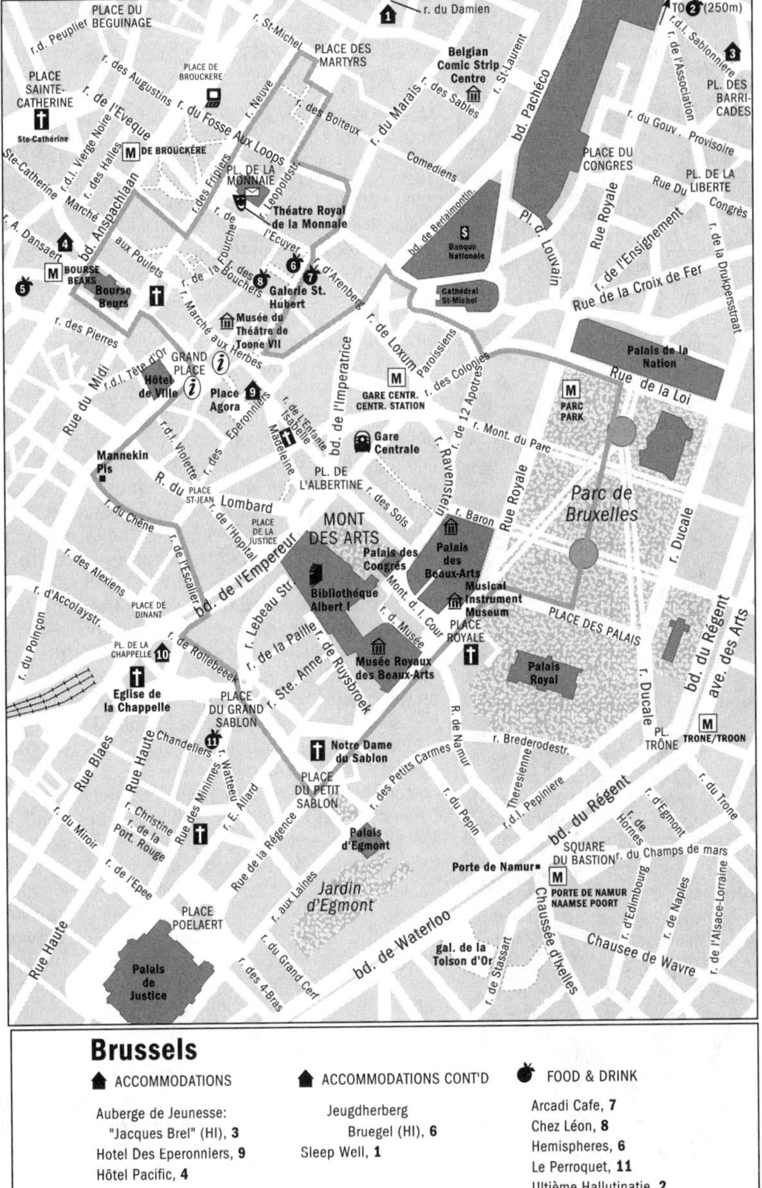

Brussels

ACCOMMODATIONS	ACCOMMODATIONS CONT'D	FOOD & DRINK
Auberge de Jeunesse: "Jacques Brel" (HI), **3**	Jeugdherberg Bruegel (HI), **6**	Arcadi Cafe, **7**
Hotel Des Eperonniers, **9**	Sleep Well, **1**	Chez Léon, **8**
Hôtel Pacific, **4**		Hemispheres, **6**
		Le Perroquet, **11**
		Ultième Hallutinatie, **2**

den. Restaurant in the front and a tavern with an outdoor patio in back. Salads, pastas, and omelettes in the tavern from €6,20. Open M-F 11-2:30pm and 7:30-10:30pm, Sa 4-10:30pm. Closed Saturday midday and Sunday. ❷

from the road

Mexican Hospitality

Amsterdam, where I spent most of my time as a researcher, is crawling with cultural predicaments for the American abroad. No matter how liberating the narcotic and sexual abandon might be, as a traveler unused to over-the-counter marijuana and to the concept of the prostitute as legitimate businesswoman, I could not help but feel somewhat out of sorts.

Nevertheless, these and the many other quirks of Amsterdam were overcome easily enough, and I managed to navigate the city with a certain, tentative ease; mostly, I have to admit, because of the fact that the English language works as *lingua franca*, which means that to a man every Amsterdammer speaks it fluidly and naturally.

In Ameland, the situation is different. The fourth of the Wadden Islands, it's most helpful to think of it as Nebraska with beaches. The few Dutch on the island who do speak English handle it at a high school level. And, so, at the Mexican restaurant that I visited for dinner it wasn't the food that proved problematic—it was only the simple act of ordering it that tripped me up.

continued next page

SIGHTS

MUSÉES ROYAUX DES BEAUX ARTS

R. de la Régence 3. M: Parc or port de Namur, a block south of the Parc. (☎508 32 11; info@fine-arts-museum.be). Open Tu-Su 10am-5pm. 15th- to 16th- and 19th-century rooms and Gallery of Sculptures close noon-1pm; 17th- to 18th- and 20th-century rooms close 1-2pm. €5, students €3,50. 1st W of each month free 1-5pm.

Houses both the **Musée d'Art Ancien** and the **Musée d'Art Moderne,** as well as a sculpture gallery and temporary exhibitions. The *blue* and *brown* sections of the museum make up the Musée d'Art Ancien, which houses a huge collection by the Flemish masters. The 15th- to 16th-century *blue* section features Bruegel's depiction of daily Flemish life along with scenes by the Dutch painter Jan Steen that portray debauchery amidst robes and religious rites. The highlight of the section is Bruegel the Elder's **Landscape with the Fall of Icarus**. The painting, celebrated in W. H. Auden's poem "Musee des Beaux Arts" has a barely discernible Icarus figure. The focus on the work is on the Flemish landscape—in the foreground a farmer plows the land in his clogs, while merchant ships go on their way in the back. The 17th- to 18th-century *brown* section showcases the impressive Salle de Rubens. Across the main entrance hall, the *yellow* and *green* sections make up the Musée d'Art Moderne. The 19th-century *yellow* section shows Dutch and Flemish Impressionists alongside paintings by Seurat and Gauguin, portraits by Van Gogh and Gericault, a large Ensor collection, and works by neo-classicists Ingres, Delacroix, and David, including David's **Death of Marat.** Finally, the 20th-century *green* section, located deep in the basement, offers works by Miró, Picasso, and Brussels-based Magritte, plus a collection of the latest, cutting-edge works. No matter what your artistic tastes, the panoramic view of Brussels' cityscape from the fourth floor of the 19th century wing is worth the admission fee—you can see all the way to the Atomium and beyond.

GRAND-PLACE

Light & sound show Apr.-Aug. and Dec. daily ~10 or 11pm.

One look and you'll understand why Victor Hugo called the gold-trimmed **Grand-Place** "the most beautiful square in the world" after he lived at #26 Grand Place in 1852. Built in the 15th century and ravaged by French troops in 1695, the square was restored to its original splendor in only five years. A daily flower market and feverish tourist activity add color. At night 800 multi-colored floodlights illuminate the **Town Hall** on the Grand Place, accompanied by loud classical music. While there, check out the **Mannekin Pis,** two blocks behind

Town Hall on the corner of r. de l'Etuve and r. du Chêne. It's Brussels' most giggled-at sight, a statue of an impudent boy (with an apparently gargantuan bladder) steadily urinating. One story goes that a 17th-century mayor promised to build a statue in the position that his lost son was found; another says it commemorates a boy who ingeniously defused a bomb. Locals have created hundreds of outfits for him, competitively dressing him with the ritual coats of their region, each with a little hole for his you-know-what.

MUSÉE DE CINQUANTENAIRE (MUSÉES ROYAUX D'ART ET D'HISTOIRE)

10 parc du Cinquantenaire. M: Mérode. From the station, walk straight through the arch, turn left, go past the doors that appear to be the entrance, and turn left again for the real entrance. (☎741 72 11.) Open Tu-Su 10am-5pm. €4, students €3.

The enormous museum covers a wide variety of periods and parts—Roman torsos without heads, Syrian heads without torsos, and Egyptian caskets with feet. The eerily illuminated "Salle au Tresor" is one the museum's main attractions.

BELGIAN COMIC STRIP CENTRE

20 r. des Sables. M: Rogier. From the Gare Centrale, take bd. de l'Impératrice until it becomes bd. de Berlaimont, and turn left onto r. des Sables. (☎219 19 80.) Open Tu-Su 10am-6pm. €6,20

This museum in the "Comic Strip Capital of the World" pays homage to *les bandes dessineés* with hundreds of Belgian comics on display. The **museum library** features a reproduction of Tintin's rocket ship and works by over 700 artists. It is located in a renovated Art Nouveau textile warehouse designed by Horta. For Tintin souvenirs, check out the museum store or the Tintin Boutique near the Grand-Place.

OTHER SIGHTS

Museum of the City of Brussels (Maison de Roi), across from the Town Hall on the Grand-Place. The museum also explains the history of Brussels. (Open Tu-F 10am-5pm, Sa-Su 10am-1pm. €2,50, students €2) In the glorious arcade, **Galerie St. Hubert,** one block behind the Grand-Place, you can window-shop for everything from square umbrellas to marzipan frogs. Built over six centuries, the magnificent **Cathédral Saint Michel** is an excellent example of the Gothic style and mixes in a little Romanesque and modern architecture for good measure. (Pl. St-Gudule, just north of Gare Centrale. Open M-F 7am-7pm, Sa-Su 8:30am-7pm. Free.) The enormous 20th-century master architect Baron Victor Horta's graceful home, today the **Musée Horta,** is a skillful application of his Art Nouveau style to a domestic setting. (25 r. Américaine.

To the waitress' credit, she did her best to interpret the menu for me in English; I couldn't help but appreciate the irony that, though I was in her country, *she* was struggling to speak *my* language. Finally completing my order, as she left I said the one Dutch expression I'd managed to learn with authority: "Dank u wel," which means, of course, "Thank you."

"A spliff," she replied. Somewhat taken aback, I said, "No, thank you." I hadn't realized they sold those at this restaurant. "A spliff," she repeated, though this time it sounded more like "ass pleats," a condition with which I was unfamiliar but sincerely hoped to never run afoul of. Finally, to my idiotic grin, she smiled warmly back and walked off to file my order with the cook.

During our exchange, the man at the table across from mine had been laughing to himself, as I imagine I would have been in his place. But, kind soul that he was, he leaned towards me with the smirk the Dutch reserve for the most hopeless of American intruders, and said in a low voice, "*Alstublieft*—it means 'you're welcome.'" I had just encountered my first real cultural divide during my time in this small and unpredictable country. Flushed at just how thoroughly I had both misheard and misinterpreted the waitress, and grateful for the man's enlightenment, I could only stammer in reply, "Oh—thank you."

It occurs to me now that he was either not quick enough or, more likely, too kind to make the obvious reply.

—Ian MacKenzie

LOVE YOU
XXX

INSIDE:

Planning Your Trip

DOCUMENTS & FORMALITIES

EMBASSIES AND CONSULATES

For foreign consular services in Amsterdam, check the **Service Directory** (see p. 297).

DUTCH EMBASSIES

Australia, 120 Empire Circuit, Yarralumla Canberra, ACT 2600 (☎02 62 7331 11; fax 62 73 3206; www.netherlandsembassy.org.au).

Canada, 350 Albert St., Ste. 2020, Ottawa, ON K1R 1A4 (☎613-237-5030; fax 237-6471; www.netherlandsembassy.ca).

Ireland, 160 Merrion Rd., Dublin 4 (☎01 269 3444; fax 283 9690; www.netherlandsembassy.ie).

New Zealand, P.O. Box 840, at Ballance and Featherston St., Wellington (☎04 471 6390; fax 04 471 2923: http://netherlandsembassy.co.nz).

South Africa, 825 Arcadia St., Pretoria, P.O. Box 117, Pretoria (☎012 344 3910; fax 343 9950; www.dutchembassy.co.za).

United Kingdom, 38 Hyde Park Gate, London SW7 5DP (☎020 75 90 32 00; fax 72 25 09 47; www.netherlands-embassy.org.uk).

United States, 4200 Linnean Ave., NW, Washington, D.C. 20008 (☎202-244-5300; fax 362-3430; www.netherlands-embassy.org).

ONE EUROPE

The idea of European unity has come a long way since 1958, when the European Economic Community (EEC) was created in order to promote solidarity and cooperation. Since then, the EEC has become the European Union (EU), with political, legal, and economic institutions spanning 15 member states: Austria, Belgium, Denmark, Finland, France, Germany, Greece, Ireland, Italy, Luxembourg, The Netherlands, Portugal, Spain, Sweden, and the UK.

What does this have to do with the average non-EU tourist? In 1999, the EU established **freedom of movement** across 14 European countries–the entire EU minus Ireland and the UK, plus Iceland and Norway. This means that border controls between participating countries have been abolished, and visa policies harmonized. While you're still required to carry a passport (or government-issued ID card for EU citizens) when crossing an internal border, once you've been admitted into one country, you're free to travel to all participating states. Britain and Ireland have also formed a **common travel area,** abolishing passport controls between the UK and the Republic of Ireland. This means that the only times you'll see a border guard within the EU are traveling between the British Isles and the Continent.

Also see **The Euro** (p. 267) and European Customs and EU customs regulations (p. 268)

DUTCH CONSULATES

Australia, Level 19, Bondi Junction Plaza, 500 Oxford St., Bondi Junction NSW 2022 (☎02 93 87 6644; fax 93 87 3962; www.netherlandsconsulate.org.au.).

Canada, Ste. 821-475 Howe St., Vancouver, BC, V6C 2B3 (☎604-684-6448; fax 684-3549; www.netherlands-consulate.org).

New Zealand, P.O. Box 3816, L. J. Hooker Building, 1st fl., 57 Symonds St., Auckland (☎09 3795 3 99; fax 3795 807).

South Africa, 100 Strand St., Cape Town 8000; P.O. Box 346, Cape Town 8001 (☎021 421 5660; fax 418 2690; www.dutch-consulate.co.za).

United Kingdom, Thistle Court 1/2 Thistle St., Edinburgh, EH2 1DD (☎0131 220 3226); 18 Carden Pl., Aberdeen AB 10 1UQ (☎1224 561616); Office 8A, 29-33 Lordswood Rd., Harborne, Birmingham B17 9RA (☎121 428 4386); 3 Anndandale Terr., Dalnottar Ave., Old Kilpatrick, Glasgow G60 5DJ (☎1389 875744).

United States, One Rockefeller Plaza, 11th fl., New York, NY 10020 (☎212-246-1429; fax 333-3603; www.cgny.org); 11766 Wilshire Blvd., Ste. 1150, Los Angeles, CA 90025 (☎310-268-1598; fax 312-0989; www.ncla.org); 2200 Post Oak Blvd., Ste. 610, Houston, TX 77056-4783 (☎713-622-8000; fax 622-3581; www.cghouston.org); 303 E. Wacker Dr., Ste. 2600, Chicago, IL 60601 (☎312-856-0110; fax 856-9218; www.cgchicago.org).

TOURIST OFFICES

The Netherlands Board of Tourism, Vlietweg 50, 2266 KA, Leidschendam, (☎070 370 57 05; fax 320 16 54; www.visitholland.com). Also has a very helpful and comprehensive website that offers a variety of services including news updates, hotel reservations, and information on Dutch art and culture. The office also offers free information over the phone from various countries. From the US and Canada call 1-888-GOHOLLAND (☎888-464-6552)

VVV, Stationsplein. 10 (☎0900 400 40 40. €0,55 per min., available M-F 9am-5pm). When exiting Centraal Station, the office is across the tram tracks to the left. Once there, if you make it through the hefty lines, you can get help with hostel/hotel reservations (€3 per person). You can also buy tickets for museums, canal boat tours, and the Circle Tram 20. Open daily 9am-5pm. Expect a long wait here and at the other offices at platform #2 inside **Centraal Station,** (open M-Sa 8am-8pm, Su 9am-5pm); **Leidsepl. 1,** around the corner on Leidsestraat. (open M-Th 9am-6pm, F-Sa 9am-7pm, Su 9am-5pm); **Stationplein,** Argonautenstr. 98. (Open M-F 9:30am-5:30pm, Sa 10am-4pm.).

For tour information, see the **Service Directory,** p. 297.

PASSPORTS

REQUIREMENTS. Citizens of Australia, Canada, Ireland, New Zealand, South Africa, the UK, and the US need valid passports to enter The Netherlands and to re-enter their home countries. The Netherlands does not allow entrance if the holder's passport expires in under six months; returning home with an expired passport is illegal, and may result in a fine.

NEW PASSPORTS. Citizens of Australia, Canada, Ireland, New Zealand, the United Kingdom, and the United States can apply for a passport at any post office, passport office, or court of law. Citizens of South Africa can apply for a passport at any office of Foreign Affairs. Any new passport or renewal applications must be filed well in advance of the departure date, although most passport offices offer rush services for a very steep fee.

PASSPORT MAINTENANCE. Be sure to photocopy the page of your passport with your photo, as well as your visas, traveler's check serial numbers, and any other important documents. Carry one set of copies in a safe place, apart from the originals, and leave another set at home. Consulates also recommend that you carry an expired passport or an official copy of your birth certificate in a part of your baggage separate from other documents.

If you lose your passport, immediately notify the local police and the nearest embassy or consulate of your home government. To expedite its replacement, you will need to know all information previously recorded and show ID and proof of citizenship. In some cases, a replacement may take weeks to process, and it may be valid only for a limited time. Any visas stamped in your old passport will be irretrievably lost. In an emergency, ask for immediate temporary traveling papers that will permit you to re-enter your home country.

VISAS & WORK PERMITS

VISAS. As of August 2002, citizens of Australia, Canada, Ireland, New Zealand, the UK, and the US need only a passport to stay in The Netherlands for up to 90 days. Those seeking an extended stay, employment, or student status should obtain a visa and a residence permit. Citizens of **South Africa** need a visa to enter The Netherlands; contact the nearest Netherlands Consulate (see consulates, previous page). Be sure to double-check on entrance requirements at the nearest embassy or consulate (listed under **Embassies & Consulates Abroad,** on p. 265)

THE EURO

The official currency of 12 members of the European Union—Austria, Belgium, Finland, France, Germany, Greece, Ireland, Italy, Luxembourg, The Netherlands, Portugal, and Spain—is now the euro.

The currency has some important—and positive—consequences for travelers hitting more than one euro-zone country. For one thing, moneychangers across the euro-zone are obliged to exchange money at the official, fixed rate (see below), and at no commission (though they may still charge a small service fee). Second, euro-denominated travelers cheques allow you to pay for goods and services across the euro-zone, again at the official rate and commission-free.

At the time of printing, 1€=US$0.94=CAD$1.43=AUD$1.64 etc. For more info, check a currency converter (such as www.xe.com or www.europa.eu.int.)

CUSTOMS IN THE EU

As well as freedom of movement of people within the EU (see p. 266), travelers in the countries that are members of the EU (Austria, Belgium, Denmark, Finland, France, Germany, Greece, Ireland, Italy, Luxembourg, The Netherlands, Portugal, Spain, Sweden, and the UK) can also take advantage of the freedom of movement of goods. This means that there are no customs controls at internal EU borders (i.e., you can take the blue customs channel at the airport), and travelers are free to transport whatever legal substances they like as long as it is for their own personal (non-commercial) use—up to 800 cigarettes, 10L of spirits, 90L of wine (60L of sparkling wine), and 110L of beer. You should also be aware that duty-free was abolished on June 30, 1999 for travel between EU member states; however, travelers between the EU and the rest of the world still get a duty-free allowance when passing through customs.

for up-to-date info before departure. US citizens can also consult www.pueblo.gsa.gov/cic_text/travel/foreign/foreignentryreqs.html.

WORK PERMITS. Admission as a visitor does not include the right to work, which is authorized only by a work permit. Entering The Netherlands to study also requires a special visa. For more information, see **Alternatives to Tourism**.

IDENTIFICATION

When you travel, always carry two or more forms of identification on your person, including at least one photo ID; a passport combined with a driver's license or birth certificate is usually adequate. Never carry all your forms of ID together, split them up in case of theft or loss, and keep photocopies of them in your luggage and at home.

TEACHER, STUDENT & YOUTH IDENTIFICATION. The **International Student Identity Card (ISIC),** the most widely accepted form of student ID, provides discounts on sights, accommodations, food, and transport; access to a 24-hour emergency helpline (in North America call ☎877-370-ISIC; elsewhere call US collect ☎+1 715-345-0505); and insurance benefits for US cardholders. For example, The Flying Pig hostels offer discounts or free drinks with the cards depending on the season, and some canal boat tours also offer discounts. The ISIC is preferable to an institution-specific card (such as a university ID) because it is more likely to be recognized and honored abroad. Applicants must be degree-seeking students of a secondary or post-secondary school and must be of at least 12 years of age. Because of the proliferation of fake ISICs, some services (particularly airlines) require additional proof of student identity, such as a school ID or a letter attesting to your student status, signed by your registrar and stamped with your school seal.

The **International Teacher Identity Card (ITIC)** offers teachers the same insurance coverage as well as similar but limited discounts. For travelers who are 25 years old or under but are not students, the **International Youth Travel Card** also offers many of the same benefits as the ISIC.

Each of these identity cards costs US$22 or equivalent. ISIC and ITIC cards are valid for roughly one and a half academic years; IYTC cards are valid for one year from the date of issue. Many student travel agencies issue the cards, including STA Travel in Australia and New Zealand; Travel CUTS in Canada; usit in the Republic of Ireland and Northern Ireland; SASTS in South Africa; Campus Travel and STA Travel in the UK; and STA Travel in the US. For a listing of issuing agencies, or for more information, contact the **International Student Travel Confederation (ISTC),** Herengracht 479, 1017 BS Amsterdam, Netherlands (☎+31 20 421 28 00; fax 421 28 10; istcinfo@istc.org; www.istc.org).

CUSTOMS

Upon entering The Netherlands, you must declare certain items from abroad and pay a duty on the value of those articles if they exceed the allowance established by The Netherlands customs service. Note that goods and gifts purchased at **duty-free** shops abroad are not exempt from duty or sales tax; "duty-free" merely means that you need not pay a tax in the country of purchase. Duty-free allowances were abolished for travel between EU member states on July 1, 1999, but still exist for those arriving from outside the EU. Upon returning home, you must similarly declare all articles acquired abroad and pay a duty on the value of articles in excess of your home country's allowance. In order to expedite your return, make a list of any valuables brought from home and register them with customs before traveling abroad, and be sure to keep receipts for all goods acquired abroad.

MONEY

CURRENCY & EXCHANGE

The currency chart below is based on August 2002 exchange rates between local currency and Australian dollars (AUS$), Canadian dollars (CDN$), Irish pounds (IR£), New Zealand dollars (NZ$), South African Rand (ZAR), British pounds (UK£), and US dollars (US$). Check the currency converter on financial websites such as www.bloomburg.com and www.xe.com, or a major newspaper for the latest exchange rates.

EUROS (EUR€)		
	AUS$ = 0.61EUR€	EUR€ = 1.65AUS$
	CDN$ = 0.69EUR€	EUR€ = 1.45CDN$
	IR£ = 1.27EUR€	EUR€ = 0.79IR£
	NZ$ = 0.52EUR€	EUR€ = 1.93NZ$
	ZAR = 0.11EUR€	EUR€ = 9.25ZAR
	US$ = 1.06EUR€	EUR€ = 0.94US$
	UK£ = 1.54EUR€	EUR€ =0.65UK£

As a general rule, it's cheaper to convert money in The Netherlands than at home. However, you should bring enough foreign currency to last for the first 24 to 72 hours of a trip to avoid being penniless should you arrive after bank hours or on a holiday. Travelers from the US can get foreign currency from the comfort of home: **International Currency Express** (☎888-278-6628) deliver foreign currency or traveler's checks second-day (US$12) at competitive exchange rates.

When changing money, go to banks that have at most a 5% margin between their buy and sell prices. Since you lose money with every transaction, **convert large sums** (unless the Euro is depreciating rapidly), **but no more than you'll need.**

If you use traveler's checks or bills, carry some in small denominations (the equivalent of US$50 or less) for times when you are forced to exchange money at disadvantageous rates, but bring a range of denominations since charges may be levied per check cashed. Store your money in a variety of forms; ideally, at any given time you will be carrying some cash, some traveler's checks, and an ATM and/or credit card.

TRAVELER'S CHECKS

Traveler's checks are one of the safest and least troublesome means of carrying funds. American Express and Visa are the most widely recognized brands. Many banks and agencies sell them for a small commission. Check issuers provide

PIN & ATMS

To use a cash or credit card to withdraw money from a cash machine (ATM) in Europe, you must have a four-digit **Personal Identification Number (PIN).** If your PIN is longer than four digits, ask your bank whether you can just use the first four, or whether you'll need a new one. **Credit cards** don't usually come with PINs, so if you intend to hit up ATMs in Europe with a credit card to get cash advances, call your credit card company before leaving to request one.

People with alphabetic, rather than numerical, PINs may also be thrown off by the lack of letters on European cash machines. The following handy chart gives the corresponding numbers to use: 1=QZ; 2=ABC; 3=DEF; 4=GHI; 5=JKL; 6=MNO; 7=PRS; 8=TUV; and 9=WXY. Note that if you mistakenly punch the wrong code into the machine three times, it will swallow your card for good.

refunds if the checks are lost or stolen, and many provide additional services, such as toll-free refund hotlines abroad, emergency message services, and stolen credit card assistance. They are readily accepted in Amsterdam, but less welcome than cash. Ask about toll-free refund hotlines and the location of refund centers when purchasing checks, and always carry emergency cash.

American Express: Checks available with commission at select banks and all AmEx offices. US residents can also purchase checks by phone (☎888-887-8986) or online (www.aexp.com). AAA offers commission-free checks to its members. Checks available in US, Australian, British, Canadian, Japanese, and Euro currencies. *Cheques for Two* can be signed by either of 2 people traveling together. For purchase locations or more information contact AmEx's service centers: In the US and Canada ☎800-221-7282; in the UK ☎0800 521 313; in Australia ☎800 25 19 02; in New Zealand 0800 441 068; elsewhere US collect ☎+1 801-964-6665.

Visa: Checks available (generally with commission) at banks worldwide. For the location of the nearest office, call Visa's service centers: In the US ☎800-227-6811; in the UK ☎0800 89 50 78; elsewhere UK collect ☎+44 020 7937 8091. Checks available in US, British, Canadian, Japanese, and Euro currencies.

Travelex/Thomas Cook. In the US and Canada ☎800-287-7362; in the UK ☎0800 62 21 01; elsewhere UK collect ☎+44 1733 31 89 50.

CREDIT, DEBIT, AND ATM CARDS

Where they are accepted, credit cards often offer superior exchange rates—up to 5% better than the retail rate used by banks and other currency exchange establishments. Credit cards may also offer services such as insurance or emergency help, and are sometimes required to reserve hotel rooms or rental cars. Although credit cards are widely accepted in Amsterdam, many budget hotels require a stay of several nights or charge a surcharge if you want to use your credit card to pay your bill. It is advisable to make your reservation with a credit card but then to pay in cash. **MasterCard** (sometimes called EuroCard or Access in Europe) and **Visa** are the most welcomed; **American Express** cards work at some ATMs and at AmEx offices and major airports.

ATM machines are widespread in Amsterdam and The Netherlands. Depending on the system that your home bank uses, you can most likely access your personal bank account from abroad. ATMs get the same wholesale exchange rate as credit cards, but there is often a limit on the amount of money you can withdraw per day (around US$500), and unfortunately computer networks sometimes fail. There is typically also a surcharge of US$1-5 per withdrawal from your home bank.

The two major international money networks are **Cirrus** (to locate ATMs US ☎800-424-7787 or www.mastercard.com) and **Visa/PLUS** (to locate ATMs US ☎800-843-7587 or www.visa.com).

GETTING MONEY FROM HOME

If you run out of money while traveling, the easiest and cheapest solution is to have someone back home make a deposit to your credit card or cash (ATM) card. Failing that, consider one of the following options.

WIRING MONEY. It is possible to arrange a **bank money transfer**, which means asking a bank back home to wire money to a bank in Amsterdam. This is the cheapest way to transfer cash, but it's also the slowest, usually taking several days or more. Note that some banks may only release your funds in local currency, potentially sticking you with a poor exchange rate; inquire about this in advance. Money transfer services like **Western Union** are faster and more convenient than bank transfers—but also much pricier. Western Union has many locations worldwide. To find one, visit www.westernunion.com, or call in the US ☎800-325-6000, in Canada ☎800-235-0000, in the UK ☎0800 83 38 33, in Australia ☎800 501 500, in New Zealand ☎800 27 0000, in South Africa ☎0860 100031, or in Amsterdam, at Central Station ☎627 27 31. Money transfer services are also available at **American Express** and **Thomas Cook** offices.

US STATE DEPARTMENT (US CITIZENS ONLY). In dire emergencies only, the US State Department will forward money within hours to the nearest consular office, which will then disburse it according to instructions for a US$15 fee. If you wish to use this service, you must contact the Overseas Citizens Service division of the US State Department (☎202-647-5225; nights, Sundays, and holidays ☎202-647-4000).

> **ESSENTIAL INFORMATION**
>
> ## PACKING
>
> Pack lightly: set out everything you think you'll need, then pack half of it and twice the money. For a longer stay, you might prefer a **suitcase** to a conspicuous backpack. Bring a **daypack** for carrying things around. Keep money, passport, and other valuables with you in a neck pouch or money belt. Bring a combination lock for your bag or for hostel lockers.
>
> **CURRENT & ADAPTERS**
>
> In Amsterdam, electric current is 220 volts AC, enough to fry any 110V North American appliance. North Americans should buy an adapter (which changes the shape of the plug) and a converter (which changes the voltage; US$20). Don't make the mistake of using only an adapter (unless instructions explicitly state otherwise). New Zealanders and South Africans (who both use 220V at home) as well as Australians (who use 240/250V) won't need a converter but will need an adapter for anything electrical. Check http://kropla.com/electric.htm.

COSTS

The cost of your trip will vary considerably, depending on where you go, how you travel, and where you stay. The single biggest cost of your trip will probably be your round-trip (return) airfare to Amsterdam (see Getting to Amsterdam: By Plane, p. 274). If you plan to travel throughout Europe, a railpass (or bus pass) may be another major pre-departure expense (see Getting to Amsterdam: By Train, p. 277). Before you go, spend some time calculating a reasonable per-day budget that will meet your needs.

STAYING ON A BUDGET. To give you a general idea, a bare-bones day in Amsterdam (camping or sleeping in hostels/guesthouses, buying food at supermarkets) would cost about US$30-35; a slightly more comfortable day (sleeping in hostels/guesthouses and the occasional budget hotel, eating one meal a day at a restaurant, going out at night) would run US$50-60; and for a luxurious day, the sky's the limit. It is recommended that you keep the amount of cash on your person to about $35 because pick-pocketing in Amsterdam is well-practiced. Also, don't forget to factor in emergency reserve funds (at least US$200) when planning how much money you'll need.

TIPS FOR SAVING MONEY. Considering that saving just a few dollars a day over the course of your trip might pay for days or weeks of additional travel, the art of penny-pinching is well worth learning. Learn to take advantage of freebies: for example, museums will typically be free once a week or once a month, and in the summer there are often free open-air concerts and/or cultural events.

HEALTH

Common sense is the simplest prescription for good health while you travel. For a basic **first-aid kit,** pack: bandages, pain reliever, antibiotic cream, a thermometer, tweezers, moleskin, decongestant, motion-sickness remedy, diarrhea or upset-stomach medication (Pepto Bismol or Imodium), an antihistamine, sunscreen, insect repellent, burn ointment, and a syringe for emergencies (get an explanatory letter from your doctor).

In your **passport,** write the names of any people you wish to be contacted in case of a medical emergency, and also list any allergies or medical conditions of which you would want doctors to be aware. Matching a prescription to a foreign equivalent is not always easy or legal. Carry up-to-date, legible prescriptions or a statement from your doctor stating the medication's trade name, manufacturer, chemical name, and dosage. While traveling, be sure to keep all medication with you in your carry-on luggage.

IMMUNIZATIONS

Travelers over two years old should be sure that the following vaccines are up to date: MMR (for measles, mumps, and rubella); DTaP or Td (for diptheria, tetanus, and pertussis), OPV (for polio), HbCV (for haemophilus influenza B), and HBV (for hepatitis B). For recommendations on immunizations and prophylaxis, consult the CDC (see below) in the US or the equivalent in your home country, and check with a doctor for guidance.

AIDS, HIV, & STDS

For detailed information on **Acquired Immune Deficiency Syndrome (AIDS)** in Amsterdam and The Netherlands, call the **US Centers for Disease Control's** 24-hour hotline at (☎800-342-2437), or contact the **Joint United Nations Programme on HIV/AIDS (UNAIDS),** 20, ave. Appia, CH-1211 Geneva 27, Switzerland (☎+41 22 791 3666; fax 22 791 4187). **Sexually transmitted diseases** (STDs) such as gonorrhea, chlamydia, genital warts, syphilis, and herpes are easier to catch than HIV and can be just as deadly. **Hepatitis** B and C can also be transmitted sexually. Though condoms may protect you from some STDs, oral or even tactile contact can lead to transmission. If you think you may have contracted an STD, see a doctor immediately.

MEDICAL ASSISTANCE ON THE ROAD

There is little medical risk to traveling through The Netherlands, but you may want to take out travel insurance just in case. Citizens of the EU and Australia benefit from reciprocal health arrangements with The Netherlands, and should check at home to find out which medical and dental services are covered and how.

If you are concerned about obtaining medical assistance while traveling, you may wish to employ special support services. The MedPass from GlobalCare, Inc., 2001 Westside Pkwy., #120, Alpharetta, GA 30004, USA (☎800-860-1111; fax 770-677-0455; www.globalems.com), provides 24-hour international medical assistance, support, and medical evacuation resources. The **International Association for Medical Assis-**

tance to Travelers (**IAMAT;** US ☎716-754-4883, Canada ☎416-652-0137, New Zealand ☎03 352 20 53; www.sentex.net/~iamat) has free membership, lists English-speaking doctors worldwide, and offers detailed info on immunization requirements and sanitation. If your regular **insurance** policy does not cover travel abroad, you may wish to purchase additional coverage.

Those with medical conditions (such as diabetes, allergies to antibiotics, epilepsy, heart conditions) may want to obtain a **Medic Alert** membership (first year US$35, annually thereafter US$20), which includes a stainless steel ID tag, among other benefits, like a 24-hour collect-call number. Contact the Medic Alert Foundation, 2323 Colorado Ave, Turlock, CA 95382, USA (☎888-633-4298, outside US ☎209-668-3333; www.medicalert.org).

ESSENTIAL INFORMATION

TRAVEL ADVISORIES.

The following government offices provide travel information and advisories by telephone, by fax, or via the web:

Australian Department of Foreign Affairs and Trade: ☎1300 555135; faxback service 02 6261 1299; www.dfat.gov.au.

Canadian Department of Foreign Affairs and International Trade (DFAIT): In Canada and the US call ☎800-267-6788, elsewhere call ☎+1 613-944-6788; www.dfait-maeci.gc.ca. Call for their free booklet, *Bon Voyage...But.*

New Zealand Ministry of Foreign Affairs: ☎04 494 8500; fax 494 8506; www.mft.govt.nz/trav.html.

United Kingdom Foreign and Commonwealth Office: ☎020 7008 0232; fax 7008 0155; www.fco.gov.uk.

US Department of State: ☎202-647-5225, faxback service 202-647-3000; http://travel.state.gov. For *A Safe Trip Abroad*, call 202-512-1800.

INSURANCE

Travel insurance generally covers four basic areas: medical/health problems, property loss, trip cancellation/interruption, and emergency evacuation. Although your regular insurance policies may well extend to travel-related accidents, you may consider purchasing travel insurance if the cost of potential trip cancellation or medical evacuation is greater than you can absorb. Prices for travel insurance purchased separately generally run about US$50 per week for full coverage, while trip cancellation/interruption may be purchased separately at a rate of about US$5.50 per US$100 of coverage.

Medical insurance (especially university policies) often covers costs incurred abroad; check with your provider. **US Medicare** does not cover foreign travel. **Canadians** are protected by their home province's health insurance plan for up to 90 days after leaving the country; check with the provincial Ministry of Health or Health Plan Headquarters for details. **Australians** traveling in The Netherlands are entitled to many of the services that they would receive at home as part of the Reciprocal Health Care Agreement. **Homeowners' insurance** (or your family's coverage) often covers theft during travel and loss of travel documents (passport, plane ticket, railpass, etc.) up to US$500.

ISIC and **ITIC** provide basic insurance benefits, including US$100 per day of in-hospital sickness for up to 60 days, US$3000 of accident-related medical reimbursement, and US$25,000 for emergency medical transport. Cardholders have access to a toll-free 24hr. helpline for medical, legal, and financial emergencies overseas (US and Canada ☎877-370-4742, elsewhere US collect ☎+1 715-345-0505). **American Express** (US ☎800-528-4800) grants most cardholders automatic car rental insurance (collision and theft, but not liability) and ground travel accident coverage of US$100,000 on flight purchases made with the card.

KEEPING IN TOUCH

For more on communications services, see **Once in Amsterdam,** p. 23.

BY MAIL

Post offices are generally open Monday through Friday 9am-6pm, and some are also open Saturday 10am-1:30pm; larger branches may stay open later. Main post offices in Amsterdam are located at Singel 250, at the corner of Radhuisstraat (M-W and F 9am-6pm, Th 9am-9pm, Sa 10am-1:30pm); Oosterdokskade 5, just east of Centraal Station (M-F 9am-6pm, Sa 9am-noon); St. Antoniebreestraat 16, near Niewmarkt; and Waterlooplein 2, in the Stadhuis. Mailing a postcard or letter to anywhere in the EU costs €0,54; to destinations outside Europe, postcards also cost €0,54, letters (up to 20g) €0,75. Mail takes 2-3 days to the UK, 4-6 to North America, 6-8 to Australia and New Zealand, and 8-10 to South Africa. Mark envelopes "air mail," "par avion," or "per luchtpost" or your letter or postcard will never arrive (surface mail and mail by sea take one to four months at best). To send an international letter, there's no need to go to a post office; just drop it into the overige slot of a mailbox.

Airmail letters under 1oz. between North America and Amsterdam take 4-7 days and cost US$0.80 or CDN$1.25. Letters up to 20g take 2-3 days from the UK and cost UK£0.68 UK Swiftair delivers letters a day faster for UK£2.85 more. Allow at least 5-6 days from Australia or New Zealand (postage NZ$1.80-6/AUS$1.50 for letters up to 50g). Check mail rates online at: Australia (www.auspost.com.au/pac); Canada (http://www.canadapost.ca/personal/rates/default-e.asp); Ireland (www.anpost.ie); NZ (www.nzpost.co.nz/nzpost/inrates); UK (www.royalmail.com); US (http://ircalc.usps.gov). Amsterdam encompasses several postal districts; to get exact postal codes, surf over to www.postcode.nl.

Federal Express (Australia ☎13 26 10; US and Canada ☎800-247-4747; New Zealand ☎0800 73 33 39; UK ☎0800 12 38 00) handles express mail services from most home countries to Amsterdam; for example, they can get a letter from New York to Amsterdam in two days for US$28.70.

BY PHONE

Remember before you call that Amsterdam is one hour ahead of Greenwich Mean Time. To place a call to Amsterdam: first, dial the **international dialing prefix** (if calling from Australia, dial 0011; Canada or the US, 011; the Republic of Ireland, New Zealand, or the UK, 00; South Africa, 09); second, dial the **country code** for The Netherlands, 31; third, dial the **city code** for Amsterdam, 20; and last, dial the **local number.** For information on calling home from Amsterdam, please see Once In.

GETTING THERE

BY PLANE

When it comes to airfare, a little effort can save you a bundle. If your plans are flexible enough to deal with the restrictions, courier fares are the cheapest. Tickets bought from consolidators and standby seating are also good deals, but last-minute specials, airfare wars, and charter flights often beat these fares. The key is to hunt around, to be flexible, and to ask persistently about discounts. Students, seniors, and those under 26 should never pay full price for a ticket. For **Budget and Student Travel Agencies,** see **Service Directory,** p. 304.

AIRFARES

Airfares to Amsterdam peak from June to September; holidays are also expensive. Midweek (M-Th morning) round-trip flights run US$40-50 cheaper than weekend flights, but they are generally more crowded and less likely to permit frequent-flier upgrades. Traveling with an "open return" ticket can be pricier than fixing a return date when buying the ticket. Round-trip flights are by far the cheapest; "open-jaw"

(arriving in and departing from different cities, e.g. Amsterdam-Paris and Rome-Amsterdam) tickets tend to be pricier.

Budget fares for round-trip flights to Amsterdam from the US or Canadian east coast cost US$500-700, US$300-500 in the off season (roughly Oct.-June); from the US or Canadian west coast US$850-950/US$550-700; from the UK, UK£50-70; from Australia, AUS$1700-2000. Full price fairs from airlines will tend to be much more expensive.

Carriers to Amsterdam's **Schipol Airport** include KLM/Northwest (☎800-447-4747; www.nwa.com), Martinair (☎800-627-8462; www.martinairusa.com), Continental, Delta (☎800-241-4141; www.delta-air.com), United (☎800-241-6522; www.ual.com), and Singapore Airlines (☎800-742-3333; www.singaporeair.com).

ESSENTIAL INFORMATION

INTERNET FLIGHT PLANNING

The Internet is one of the best places to look for travel bargains. Many airline sites offer last-minute deals. Make sure the sites are secure before handing over credit card info. For travel to Amsterdam, try www.klm.nl, www.singaporeair.com, and www.quickairways.nl.

Other sites do the legwork and **compile deals** for you: Surf to www.bestfares.com or www.travelzoo.com.

For **student quotes,** try: www.sta-travel.com or www.studentuniverse.com.

For **full travel services,** visit: msn.expedia.com or www.travelocity.com.

Priceline (www.priceline.com) allows you to specify a price, and obligates you to buy any ticket that meets it.

Skyauction (www.skyauction.com) bidding on both last-minute and advance-purchase tickets.

BY TRAIN

Eurostar, Eurostar House, Waterloo Station, **London** SE1 8SE (UK☎08705 186 186; US☎800-387-6782; elsewhere call UK +44 1233 61 75 75; www.eurostar.com, www.raileurope.com) runs a frequent train service between London and the continent. Ten to 28 trains per day run to Paris (3hr., 2nd class, US$120-250), Brussels (4hr., 2nd class, US$120-250), and Eurodisney. Routes include stops at Ashford in England, and Calais and Lille in France. Book at major rail stations in the UK, at the office above, by phone, or on the web. From Brussels, trains run frequently to Amsterdam (2½hr., €44, under 26 €20).

BY BOAT

The following fares listed are **one-way** for **adult foot passengers** unless otherwise noted. Though standard return fares are in most cases simply twice the one-way fare, **fixed-period returns** (usually within five days) are almost invariably cheaper. Ferries run **year-round** unless otherwise noted. **Bikes** usually cost a few pounds extra. For a **camper/trailer** supplement, you will have to add anywhere from UK£20-140 to the "with car" fare. If more than one price is quoted, the quote in British pounds is valid for departures from the UK, etc. A directory of ferries in this region can be found at www.seaview.co.uk/ferries.html. Ferries traverse the North Sea, connecting **England** to The Netherlands. Boats arrive in **Hook of Holland** (3¾-8½hr.), near Delft and The Hague, from **Harwich,** northeast of London; in **Rotterdam** from **Hull** (13½hr.), near York; and in **Amsterdam** from **Newcastle-upon-Tyne** (14hr.).

DFDS Seaways: UK ☎08705 33 30 00, US ☎800-533-3755; www.scansea.com. **Newcastle** to **Amsterdam** (14hr.). Single cabins from US$236, cheaper rates for 2-, 3-, or 4-berth rooms.

P&O North Sea Ferries: UK ☎0870 129 6002; Neth ☎181 255 555 www.ponsf.com. Daily ferries from **Hull** to **Rotterdam, Netherlands** (13½hr.). UK£38-99, students UK£24-31, cars UK£63-78. Online bookings.

BY CAR

INTERNATIONAL DRIVING PERMIT (IDP). If you plan to drive a car while in Amsterdam, you must be over 18 and it is highly recommended that you have an International Driving Permit (IDP). In the event that you're in a situation (e.g. an accident or stranded in a small town) where the police do not know English, information on the IDP is printed in ten languages.

Your IDP, valid for one year, must be issued in your own country before you depart. An application for an IDP usually needs to include one or two photos, a current local license, an additional form of identification, and a fee.

CAR INSURANCE. Most credit cards cover standard insurance. If you rent, lease, or borrow a car, you will need a **green card,** or **International Insurance Certificate,** to certify that you have liability insurance and that it applies abroad. Green cards can be obtained at car rental agencies, car dealers (for those leasing cars), some travel agents, and some border crossings. Rental agencies may require you to purchase theft insurance in countries that they consider to have a high risk of auto theft.

SPECIFIC CONCERNS

WOMEN TRAVELERS

Women exploring on their own inevitably face some additional safety concerns, but it's easy to be adventurous without taking undue risks. If you are concerned, consider staying in hostels that offer single rooms that lock from the inside or in religious organizations with rooms for women only. Communal showers in some hostels are safer than others; check them before settling in. Stick to centrally located accommodations and avoid solitary late-night treks or metro rides.

Always carry extra money for a phone call, bus, or taxi. **Hitchhiking** is never safe for lone women, or even for two women traveling together. Choose train compartments occupied by women or couples; ask the conductor to put together a women-only compartment if there isn't one. Look as if you know where you're going and approach older women or couples for directions if you're lost or uncomfortable.

Generally, the less you look like a tourist, the better off you'll be. Wearing a conspicuous **wedding band** may help prevent unwanted overtures. Some travelers report that carrying pictures of or talking about a "husband" or "children" is extremely useful to help document marriage status.

Your best answer to verbal harassment is no answer at all; feigning deafness, sitting motionless, and staring straight ahead at nothing in particular will do a world of good that reactions usually don't achieve. The extremely persistent can sometimes be dissuaded by a firm, loud, and very public "Go away!" (or "ga weg!" in Dutch). Don't hesitate to seek out a police officer or a passerby if you are being harassed. Memorize the emergency numbers in places you visit, and consider carrying a whistle or airhorn on your keychain. A self-defense course will not only prepare you for a potential attack, but will also raise your level of awareness of your surroundings as well as your confidence.

TRAVELING ALONE

There are many benefits to traveling alone, including independence and greater interaction with locals. On the other hand, any solo traveler is a more vulnerable target of harassment and street theft. As a lone traveler, try not to stand out as a tourist, look confident, and be especially careful in deserted or very crowded areas. If questioned, never admit that you are traveling alone. Maintain regular contact with someone at home who knows your itinerary. For more tips, pick up *Traveling Solo* by Eleanor Berman (Globe Pequot Press, US$17) or subscribe to **Connecting: Solo Travel**

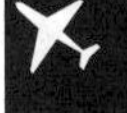

Network, 689 Park Rd., Unit 6, Gibsons, BC V0N 1V7, Canada (☎604-886-9099; www.cstn.org; membership US$35). **Travel Companion Exchange,** P.O. Box 833, Amityville, NY 11701, USA (☎631-454-0880, or in the US ☎800-392-1256; www.whytravelalone.com; US$48), will link solo travelers with companions with similar travel habits and interests.

OLDER TRAVELERS

Senior citizens are eligible for a wide range of discounts on transportation, museums, movies, theaters, concerts, restaurants, and accommodations. If you don't see a senior citizen price listed, ask, and you may be delightfully surprised. The books *No Problem! Worldwise Tips for Mature Adventurers*, by Janice Kenyon (Orca Book Publishers; US$16) and *Unbelievably Good Deals and Great Adventures That You Absolutely Can't Get Unless You're Over 50*, by Joan Rattner Heilman (NTC/Contemporary Publishing; US$13) are both excellent resources. For more information, contact one of the following organizations:

Elderhostel, 11 Ave. de Lafayette, Boston, MA 02111 (☎877-426-8056; www.elderhostel.org). Organizes 1- to 4-week "educational adventures" in The Netherlands on varied subjects for those 55+.

The Mature Traveler, P.O. Box 15791, Sacramento, CA 95852 (☎800-460-6676). Deals, discounts, and travel packages for the 50+ traveler. Subscription$30.

BISEXUAL, GAY, & LESBIAN TRAVELERS

In Amsterdam, anything goes. Amsterdam has the most tolerant laws for homosexuals in the world--it became the first country to legalize gay marriage in 2000. Listed below are contact organizations, mail-order bookstores, and publishers that offer materials addressing some specific concerns. **Out and About** (www.planetout.com) offers a bi-weekly newsletter addressing travel concerns and a comprehensive site addressing gay travel concerns. Sidebars throughout this guide will highlight accommodations, entertainment, and nightlife of particular gay-friendly interest.

GAY/LESBIAN RESOURCES

The monthly ***Culture and Camp*** provides info on gay venues and events. The ***Gay Krant*** and the fortnightly ***Shark*** also provide excellent and thorough listings of what's going down in queer Amsterdam.

COC, Rozenstraat 14 (☎626 30 87; www.cocamsterdam.nl), exists as a social network and information center. Maps designed specifically for the gay traveler available in the lobby. Office open M-Tu and Th-F 10am-5pm, W 10am-8pm. The cafe on the ground floor turns into a multicultural discotheque on F and Sa nights. Cafe open Th 8pm-12am, F 8pm-10pm; disco F-Sa 10pm-4am (Sa is women-only). For more on the COC, see p. 63.

Vrolijk, Paleisstraat 135 (☎623 51 42; vrolijk@xs4all.nl; www.vrolijk.nu), claims to be the largest gay and lesbian bookstore in Europe. With an excellent selection of literature and periodicals, it's an ideal place to stop in for tips on what's hot and what's not in gay Amsterdam; shop online for books as well. Open M 11am-6pm, Tu-W 10am-6pm, Th 10am-9pm, F 10am-6pm, Sa 10am-5pm.

Gay and Lesbian Switchboard (☎623 65 65) is available to answer questions, suggest events, or listen to personal problems. All switchboard volunteers speak English and some speak other languages. Phone staffed daily 10am-10pm.

Gay Krant Reisservice, Kloveniersburgwal 40 (☎421 00 00; reis@gaykrant.nl; www.gaykrant.nl/reis). A travel service devoted exclusively to gay and lesbian travelers. Also features an impressive display of magazines and newspapers for gay travelers. Newsletters available. Open M 2-6pm, Tu-F 10am-6pm, Sa 10am-4pm.

SAD/Schorerfoundation, P.C. Hoofstraat 5 (☎662 42 06). A counseling center for gay men and women. Open M-Th 10am-5pm.

Xantippe Unlimited, Prinsengracht 290 (☎623 58 54; xantippe@xs4all.nl; www.dds.nl/~xantippe). General bookstore, but with a specialization in women's and lesbian issues. Open M 1-7pm, Tu-F 10am-7pm, Sa 10am-6pm, Su noon-5pm.

FURTHER READING

The monthly ***Culture and Camp*** (ƒ5/€2,27) provides info on gay venues and events. The ***Gay Krant*** (ƒ5/€2,27) and the fortnightly ***Shark*** also provide excellent and thorough listings of what's going down in queer Amsterdam. The following books are also helpful resources:

Spartacus International Gay Guide 2001-2002. Bruno Gmunder Verlag (US$33).

Damron Amsterdam Guide, Damron Men's Guide, Damron's Accommodations, and *The Women's Traveller.* Damron Travel Guides (US$10-19). For more info, call ☎800-462-6654 or visit www.damron.com.

Ferrari Guides' Gay Travel A to Z, Ferrari Guides' Men's Travel in Your Pocket, and *Ferrari Guides' Inn Places.* Ferrari Publications (US$16-20). Purchase the guides online at www.ferrariguides.com.

The Gay Vacation Guide: The Best Trips and How to Plan Them, Mark Chesnut. Citadel Press (US$15).

Dykes below sealevel: Gids voor lesbisch Nederland. Amsterdam: Xantippe Unlimited, 2000.

TRAVELERS WITH DISABILITIES

Those with disabilities should inform airlines and hotels of their disabilities when making reservations; some time may be needed to prepare special accommodations. Call ahead to restaurants, museums, and other facilities to find out about the existence of ramps, the widths of doors, the dimensions of elevators, etc.

Amsterdam is a particularly difficult city to navigate from a wheelchair. This otherwise tolerant and accommodating city has not yet made significant efforts for handicapped travelers. The streets are narrow, the trams have steps up and narrow doors, and only the better hotels have street-level entrances and elevators. Places that are wheelchair accessible have been awarded an **International Accessibility Symbol** (IAS). Call the NIZW (☎+31 0 30 230 66 03) or the Afdeling Gehandicaptenvoorlichting (☎+31 070 314 14 200) for more information. Unless it is indicated otherwise, readers should assume that all listings in this book are not wheelchair accessible. **Guide dog owners** should inquire as to the quarantine policies of each destination country. At the very least, they will need to provide a certificate of immunization against rabies.

Rail is probably the most convenient form of travel for disabled travelers in Europe: many stations have ramps, and some trains have wheelchair lifts, special seating areas, and specially equipped toilets. All Eurostar, some InterCity (IC), and some EuroCity (EC) trains are wheelchair-accessible and CityNightLine trains, French TGV (high speed), and Conrail trains feature special compartments. Most trains in The Netherlands are wheelchair-accessible.

For those who wish to rent cars, some major **car rental** agencies (Hertz, Avis, and National) offer hand-controlled vehicles.

AccessWise, Jachthoornlaan 1a, Arnhem (☎26 370 61 61; fax 26 377 67 53; info@accesswise.org; www.accesswise.org). Information for travelers with disabilities on traveling in The Netherlands and from The Netherlands through Europe. Currently the website is only in Dutch, but call and they'll speak English.

Beumar de Jong, Haarlemmermeerstraat 49-51 (☎+31 020 615 71 88). To rent wheelchairs for your stay in Amsterdam; located in the Shipping Quarter. Call in advance. €20 per week, €200 deposit.

Mobility International Nederland, Heidestein 7 (☎+31 034 352 17 95; bijning@worldonline.nl). Gives advice on suitable accommodations for disabled.

Stichting Recreatie Gehandicapten, (☎+31 023 536 84 09). Organizes trips for disabled people in Amsterdam and the rest of Europe.

Nederlands Asthma Fonds, (☎31 033 434 12 12). Has information on hotels and other accommodations that are suitable for asthma, bronchitis, or emphysema.

USEFUL ORGANIZATIONS

Mobility International USA (MIUSA), P.O. Box 10767, Eugene, OR 97440 (☎541-343-1284, voice and TDD; www.miusa.org). Sells *A World of Options: A Guide to International Educational Exchange, Community Service, and Travel for Persons with Disabilities* (US$35).

Society for the Advancement of Travel for the Handicapped (SATH), 347 Fifth Ave., #610, New York, NY 10016 (☎212-447-7284; www.sath.org). An advocacy group that publishes free online travel information and the travel magazine *OPEN WORLD* (US$18, free for members). Annual membership US$45, students and seniors US$30.

TOUR AGENCIES

Directions Unlimited, 123 Green Ln., Bedford Hills, NY 10507 (☎800-533-5343). Books individual and group vacations for the physically disabled; not an info service.

MINORITY TRAVELERS

Amsterdam is an integrated, multicultural city. Surinamese, Indonesian, Moroccan, Turkish, African, and Antillean immigrants have made their homes in Amsterdam, serving as a lasting reminder of Amsterdam's colonial history. But while Amsterdam has a reputation for tolerance, it also has a surprising reputation for racism. The country, like many European countries today, is in the process of making tougher penalties for illegal immigrants—most of whom are minorities. This should not discourage non-caucasian travelers from visiting the city—most Amsterdammers are very tolerant and welcoming. But minority travelers should be aware that their presence might possibly elicit a different reaction than those of their non-minority friends. While nobody is exempt from random acts of racially prejudiced violence, in general, Amsterdam is a safe place to visit.

TRAVELERS WITH CHILDREN

Family vacations often require that you slow your pace, and always require that you plan ahead. When deciding where to stay, remember the special needs of young children; if you pick a small hotel, call ahead and make sure it's child-friendly. If you rent a car, make sure the rental company provides a car seat for younger children.

Amsterdam is a great city to visit with children. With lively streets and winding canals, there is always something to see or do. In nice weather, families head to the city's numerous parks, such as the Vondelpark, Sarphartipark, or the Plantage, home also to the Artis Zoo. Museums, tourist attractions, accommodations, and restaurants often offer discounts for children. Children under two generally fly for 10% of the adult airfare on international flights (this does not necessarily include a seat). International fares are usually discounted 25% for children from two to 11.

Look for the **Kids in the City** sidebars in this book for kid-oriented sights and activities. For more information, consult one of the following books:

Backpacking with Babies and Small Children, Goldie Silverman. Wilderness Press (US$10).

Take Your Kids to Europe, Cynthia W. Harriman. Cardogan Books (US$18).

How to take Great Trips with Your Kids, Sanford and Jane Portnoy. Harvard Common Press (US $10).

Have Kid, Will Travel: 101 Survival Strategies for Vacationing With Babies and Young Children, Claire and Lucille Tristram. Andrews McMeel Publishing (US$9).

Adventuring with Children: An Inspirational Guide to World Travel and the Outdoors, Nan Jeffrey. Avalon House Publishing (US$15).

Trouble Free Travel with Children, Vicki Lansky. Book Peddlers (US$9).

DIETARY CONCERNS

While traditional Dutch food is hearty and heavy, based on fish and meats, vegetarians traveling through The Netherlands should not have any problems as there will be suitable selections in most restaurants. Our restaurant listings often make note of vegetarian and vegan options where available. Die-hard meat-eaters will find themselves in paradise, as Argentinian and other South American steakhouses abound. But Amsterdam also boasts the best Indonesian cuisine outside of Indonesia, a legacy from Dutch colonial days. Indonesian food includes numerous vegetarian possibilities. And despite the Dutch reputation for eating beef and raw fish, they also early on adopted the Swiss tradition of fondue—a less healthy vegetarian option. The **North American Vegetarian Society,** P.O. Box 72, Dolgeville, NY 13329 (☎518-568-7970; www.navs-online.org), publishes information about vegetarian travel, including *Transformative Adventures, a Guide to Vacations and Retreats* (US$15).

Travelers who keep kosher should contact synagogues in larger cities for information on kosher restaurants. Your own synagogue or college Hillel should have access to lists of Jewish institutions across the nation. If you are strict in your observance, you may have to prepare your own food on the road. A good resource is the *Jewish Travel Guide*, by Michael Zaidner (Vallentine Mitchell, US$17).

For more information, visit your local bookstore, health food store, or library, and consult *The Vegetarian Traveler: Where to Stay if You're Vegetarian*, by Jed and Susan Civic (Larson Publications, US$16) and *Europe on 10 Salads a Day*, by Greg and Mary Jane Edwards (Mustang Publishing, US$10).

OTHER RESOURCES

Let's Go tries to cover all aspects of budget travel, but we can't put *everything* in our guides. Listed below are books and websites that can serve as jumping off points for your own research.

USEFUL PUBLICATIONS

Ethnic Amsterdam: A complete guide to the city's faces, places, and cultures. Uitgeverij Vassalucci 2001. ISBN 90 5000 308 7. €13,50.

Smokers Guide to Amsterdam. Available in Amsterdam. See www.smokersguide.com

WORLD WIDE WEB

Almost every aspect of budget travel is accessible via the Web. Within 10min. at the keyboard, you can make a reservation at a hostel, get advice on travel hotspots from other travelers who have just returned from Amsterdam, or find out exactly how much a train from Amsterdam to Gouda costs.

Listed here are some budget travel sites to start off your surfing; other relevant web sites are listed throughout the book. Because website turnover is high, use search engines (such as www.google.com) to strike out on your own.

OUR PERSONAL FAVORITE...

WWW.LETSGO.COM Our newly designed website now features the full online content of all of our guides. In addition, trial versions of all nine City Guides are available for download on Palm OS™ PDAs. Our website also contains our newsletter, links for photos and streaming video, online ordering of our titles, info about our books, and a travel forum buzzing with stories and tips.

THE ART OF BUDGET TRAVEL

How to See the World: www.artoftravel.com. A compendium of great travel tips, from cheap flights to self defense to interacting with local culture.

Rec. Travel Library: www.travel-library.com. A fantastic set of links for general information and personal travelogues.

Lycos: cityguide.lycos.com. General introductions to cities and regions throughout The Netherlands, accompanied by links to applicable histories, news, and local tourism sites.

Backpacker's Ultimate Guide: www.bugeurope.com. Tips on packing, transportation, and where to go. Also tons of country-specific travel information. **Backpack Europe:** www.backpackeurope.com. Helpful tips, a bulletin board, and links.

Euro Cheapo: http://www.eurocheapo.com/amsterdam/Amsterdam. Sights, accommodations and coffeeshops with reader reviews.

INFORMATION ON AMSTERDAM

City of Amsterdam Online: www.amsterdam.nl/e_index.html. Maintained by the city, the site contains news from local government and links to sports and entertainment.

Amsterdam - The Channels: www.channels.nl. Virtual tour of Amsterdam, tourist and transportation information, and some hotel listings and reviews.

Visit Amsterdam: www.holland.com. Maintained by The Netherlands Board of Tourism, this is a comprehensive site with information on planning your trip and attractions in the city. **The Netherlands Rail Planner:** http://www.ns.nl/domestic/index.cgi. Input your destination, date, and time of your desired travel and you will get a detailed train schedule. Prices only available for trips within The Netherlands.

INSIDE:

Alternatives to Tourism

Consume enough Dutch chocolate and beer or stroll along enough canals and it won't be long before you'll want to stay forever in Amsterdam. Vacationing in Amsterdam for a few days or weeks should certainly be a memorable experience, but if you are looking for a more rewarding and complete way to see the city, you may want to consider alternatives to tourism. Working, studying, volunteering, or some combination thereof for an extended period of time can be a great way to better experience and understand life in Amsterdam and in The Netherlands. This chapter outlines some of the different ways to get to know the city more thoroughly, whether you want to pay your way through, study, or just get the personal satisfaction that comes from volunteering. This chapter will help you find a way to relocate to Amsterdam for a summer, a year, or a lifetime. It will make all your Dutch dreams come true.

VISAS AND PERMITS

The Dutch Ministry of Justice's Immigration and Naturalization Service runs a helpful website at ***www.immigratiedienst.nl.*** *The full online version (in English and Dutch) will be operational as of December 2002, but at the time of this book's printing it already contained a pulldown menu in which you can enter your nationality, length of stay, and reason for stay in The Netherlands, and receive information on visa and permit requirements specific to your situation.*

If you're a citizen of Australia, Canada, Ireland, New Zealand, the UK, the US, or any EU nation, you need only a valid passport to enter and stay in The Netherlands for up to three months on vacation; no entry visa is required. South African citizens need an entry visa just to enter The Netherlands, even for a vacation of less than three months. If you're planning to stay in The Netherlands for more than three months, though, or intend to work or study for any length of time, you'll need some kind of visa or permit (unless you're an citizen of the EU, in most cases), details of which are outlined below.

Note that citizens of any nation other than Australia, Canada, New Zealand, the US, the EU, Norway, Iceland, Switzerland, Liechtenstein, Monaco, or Japan do require an MVV (see **South Africa,** below) for any stay over three months. The aforementioned nations are also the only ones whose citizens do not require an entry visa for tourist stays of less than three months.

RESIDENCE PERMITS

If you plan to stay in Amsterdam or The Netherlands for longer than three months for any reason, you need to apply for a **residence permit** *(Verblijfsvergunning)* from the Dutch consulate or embassy in your country (see **Service Directory,** p. 299) or from the Aliens Police in The Netherlands. Permits can also be issued to those who enter the country as tourists and then decide that they wish to remain (except South African citizens). Residence permits are valid for one year but can be renewed. According to Dutch law, foreigners must carry their passports or an ID card at all times. In Amsterdam, you can apply for a residence permit at the **Aliens Police Office** (☎559 91 11), Bijlmerdreef 90, 1102 CS, Amsterdam Zuidoost. The cost of applying ranges from €22,69-56,72. EU and EEA citizens receive residence permits easily; citizens of other nations will have to demonstrate that they have a realistic prospect of a job or that they will be studying.

WORK PERMITS

Non-EU citizens wishing to work in The Netherlands require a **work permit.** Employers should contact the Ministry of Social Affairs (Gewestelijk Arbeidsbureau) in The Hague through the District Labor Bureau; it is the employer who must make an application on behalf of the employee 30 days before the beginning of work. There are District Labor Bureau offices in most major Dutch cities. Work permits will usually be issued only to persons with special skills, as the employer must reasonably demonstrate that no EU citizen is qualified for the job. If you plan to work for more than three months, which means you need a residence permit, you should apply for the residence permit first (through a Dutch embassy or consulate or through the Aliens Police in The Netherlands) and then have your employer apply for your work permit once the residence permit process is underway.

STUDENT VISAS

Study of more than three months' duration for non-EU citizens requires a **student visa,** to be procured at least two months in advance; the program in question should provide all the necessary—and abundant—paperwork. A residence permit for study (not for paid employment) is also required, under which you may work no more than 10 hours per week or perform seasonal work in June, July, and August. Study of less than three months' duration does not require a student visa.

NATIONALITY-SPECIFIC REQUIREMENTS

EU/EEA

Citizens of the European Union, including Ireland and the UK, as well as citizens of the European Economic Area (that is, Norway and Iceland), do not need student visas or work permits to study or work in The Netherlands. Nor do they officially need residence permits, even for stays of more than three months. However, getting a residence permit even if you are an EU citizen makes sense, as bureaucratic hassles ensue if you don't have one. Even if you are not an EU citizen, you may be able to claim EU work and study status if your parents were born in an EU country.

AUSTRALIA, CANADA, NEW ZEALAND, AND THE US

Australian, Canadian, New Zealand, and US citizens need a work permit to work in The Netherlands. For stays of under three months, no residence permit is required; for stays over three months, a residence permit for paid employment is required. These can be obtained at Dutch embassies or consulates abroad or at the Aliens Police Office in The Netherlands. A student visa is needed for study over three months; it should be procured through the educational institution. If study is over three months, a residence permit for study is also required.

Australian, Canadian, and New Zealand citizens between the ages of 18 and 30 can apply to take part in the Working Holiday Scheme, which allows you to work in The Netherlands for one year. Applications can be made at Dutch embassies and consulates.

For US college students, recent graduates, and young adults, the simplest way to get legal permission to work in The Netherlands is through Council Exchanges Work Abroad Programs. Fees range from US$300-425. Council Exchanges can help obtain a three- to six-month work permit/visa and also provide assistance finding jobs and housing.

SOUTH AFRICA

For stays of under three months, South African citizens require an entry visa, plus a work permit if working. South Africans need a residence permit plus a **Machtiging tot Voorlopig Verblijf,** an authorization for temporary stay (MVV), for any stay over three months in The Netherlands, including stays for study or work. (The student visa or work permit is also required.) Applications for an MVV can be made to the Dutch consulate or embassy in South Africa, or the applicant's sponsor in The Netherlands (educational institution or employer) can apply to the Aliens Police. Both methods ordinarily take 3-6 months; however, many educational institutions, companies, and organizations promoting cultural exchange are allowed to submit MVV applications under an accelerated schedule. Check

Buying Books at Oudemanhuispoort

Using Pulleys to Move In

Wertheim Park

with your Dutch sponsor (employer or educational institution) to see if they can apply under the accelerated procedure (they are allowed to do so if they submit at least ten MVV applications to the Immigration and Naturalization Service per year). South African citizens may not enter The Netherlands during the application period, not even as tourists. The application fee is €50.

WORKING

For an extensive listing of "off-the-beaten-track" and specialty travel opportunities, try the Specialty Travel Index, 305 San Anselmo Ave. #313, San Anselmo, CA 94960, USA. (☎888-624-4030 or 415-455-1643; www.specialtytravel.com. US$6.) Transitions Abroad (www.transabroad.com) publishes a bimonthly on-line newsletter for work, study, and specialized travel abroad.

AU PAIR

Au pairs are typically young women who work as live-in nannies, caring for children and doing light housework in exchange for room, board, and a small spending allowance. In The Netherlands, au pairs must be between 18 and 25 years of age and are not allowed to work more than 30 hours per week in the household. Au pairs can stay in The Netherlands for a maximum of one year. They must be unmarried, must have no dependents, and must not have been granted a Dutch residence permit before. Working as an au-pair requires a residence permit (and a Dutch entry visa, depending on your passport).

Most former au pairs speak favorably of their experience. Drawbacks, however, often include long hours of constantly being on-duty and the somewhat mediocre pay. Much of the au pair experience really does depend on the family you're placed with. The agencies below are a good starting point for those looking for employment as au pairs.

Activity International, P.O. Box 7097, 9701 JB Groningen, The Netherlands (☎050 313 06 66; info@activity.aupair.nl, www.activity.aupair.nl). Places au pairs throughout The Netherlands.

Accord Cultural Exchange, 750 La Playa, San Francisco, CA 94121, USA (☎415-386-6203; www.cognitext.com/accord).

Au Pair Homestay, World Learning, Inc., 1015 15th St. NW, Ste. 750, Washington, DC 20005, USA (☎800-287-2477; fax 202-408-5397).

Au Pair in Europe, P.O. Box 68056, Blakely Postal Outlet, Hamilton, Ontario L8M 3M7, Canada (☎905-545-6305; fax 905-544-4121; aupair@princeent.com; www.princeent.com). Places au pairs in 21 countries, including The Netherlands. Airfare reimbursement. Administrative and referral fee US$425.

Childcare International, Ltd., Trafalgar House, Grenville Pl., London NW7 3SA, UK (☎+44 20 8906 3116; fax 8906 3461; www.childint.co.uk). UK£100 application fee.

interExchange, 161 6th Ave., New York, NY 10013, USA (☎212-924-0446; fax 924-0575; info@interexchange.org; www.interexchange.org).

TEACHING

Amsterdam and The Netherlands are home to a large number of English-speaking schools, be they international, American, British, or Dutch with an international section. The two largest English-speaking schools in Amsterdam are the International School of Amsterdam (www.isa.nl) in the suburb of Amstelveen and the British School of Amsterdam (britams@xs4all.nl). The Hague is home to many English-speaking schools, including the American School of The Hague (www.ash.nl), the British School in The Netherlands (www.britishschool.nl), the International School of The Hague (www.ishthehague.nl), and the Rijnlands Lyceum Oegstgeest (www.rijnlandslyceum.nl/oegstgeest), between The Hague and Leiden. There are also English-speaking schools in Rotterdam, Eindoven, Groningen, Hilversum, and Maastricht. For employment information, contact the schools directly. While some schools interview and hire directly, most hire through recruitment fairs run by International Schools Services and the European Council of International Schools (see below). Most schools require at least a few years of teaching experience for employment, although some do welcome student teachers.

European Council of International Schools, 21 Lavant St., Petersfield, Hampshire GU32 3EL, UK (☎+44 1730 268 244; fax +44 1730 267 914; www.ecis.org). An association of international schools (over 500 member schools worldwide) that organizes four annual hiring fairs, in London, Vancouver, and Melbourne. Website has directory of English-speaking schools in The Netherlands.

International Schools Services, Educational Staffing Program, P.O. Box 5910, Princeton, NJ 08543, USA (☎609-452-0990; fax 609-452-2690; edustaffing@iss.edu; www.iss.edu). Recruits teachers and administrators for American, British, and international schools in The Netherlands. US$150 program fee.

Office of Overseas Schools, US Department of State, Room H328, SA-1, Washington, D.C. 20522, USA (☎202-261-8200; fax 202-261-8224; www.state.gov/www/about_state/schools/). Keeps a comprehensive list of schools abroad and agencies that arrange placement for Americans to teach abroad.

Teach Abroad (www.teachabroad.com). Posts listings of available positions for English-speaking instructors.

INTERNSHIPS

International Internships (www.internabroad.com). A webpage that searches international internship postings and directs you to links.

VOLUNTEERING

Volunteer jobs are readily available, and many provide room and board in exchange for labor. You can sometimes avoid high application fees by contacting the individual work camps directly.

Service Civil International Voluntary Service (SCI-IVS), 814 NE 40th St., Seattle, WA 98105, USA (☎/fax 206-545-6585; www.sci-ivs.org). Arranges placement in work camps in Amsterdam for those 18+. Registration fee US$65-150.

SIW Internationale Vjiwillgersprojekten, Willemstraat 7, Utrecht (☎231 77 21; info@siw.nl; www.siw.nl), organizes project in The Netherlands for volunteers from other countries.

Volunteers for Peace, 1034 Tiffany Rd., Belmont, VT 05730, USA (☎802-259-2759; www.vfp.org). Arranges placement in work camps in The Netherlands. Annual *International Workcamp Directory* US$20. Registration fee US$200. Free newsletter.

Volunteer Abroad (www.volunteerabroad.com). A webpage that searches and posts listings of volunteer opportunities worldwide.

Vrijwilligers Centrale, Hartenstraat 16 (☎530 12 20). The main volunteer agency in Amsterdam.

RECRUITMENT AGENCIES AND TEMPING

Amsterdam is full of recruitment and temp agencies that can find you short-term work. Dutch is required for many jobs.

Undutchables, P.O. Box 57204, 1040 BC Amsterdam (☎623 13 00; fax ☎428 17 81; office@amsterdam.undutchables.nl; www.undutchables.nl). The most useful job recruitment agency for foreigners, recruiting for jobs that require command of a language other than Dutch. Temporary and permanent jobs available.

Other temp agencies: Content, Van Baerlestraat 83 (☎676 44 41); **Manpower** (☎305 56 55); **Randstad,** Dam 4 (☎626 22 13).

OTHER OPTIONS

Agriventure (International Agricultural Exchange Association), 1000 1st Ave. S, Great Falls, MT 59401, USA (☎406-727-1999; fax 406-727-1997; usa@agriventure.com; www.agriventure.com). Runs an agricultural and horticultural exchange program. Participants are placed with a Dutch host family, receive room, board, and allowance, and learn about Dutch agricultural and horticultural techniques. Exchanges last 4-15 months.

STUDYING

Amsterdam is a popular destination for study abroad because of its wealth of programs and its proximity to other major European destinations. Depending on the needs and desires of a given student, many options are available. Some study abroad programs are affiliated with universities in Amsterdam or The Netherlands and allow students to take classes directly through the university; others are more self-contained programs for foreigners, with instruction in various combinations of English and Dutch, or only in Dutch. These programs may be affiliated with an American university but open to other students as well. While these programs have a reputation for creating self-contained social circles void of Dutch nationals, they often offer great benefits. They usually arrange housing, with a family or in a dorm, and excursions, both within the city and throughout The Netherlands. Some also offer an internship placement program for part-time work.

Study-abroad students will need to contact individual programs and universities to apply to them directly and find out the requirements for their stay. Study for 90 days or more requires a student visa, to be procured at least two months in advance; the program in question should provide all the necessary paperwork.

UNIVERSITIES

Most American undergraduates enroll in programs sponsored by US universities. Those relatively fluent in Dutch may find it cheaper to enroll directly in a local university. Some schools that offer study abroad programs to foreigners are listed below. Websites such as www.studyabroad.com are excellent resources, as are the following books, available at most libraries and many university career/study abroad offices: *Academic Year Abroad 2001-2002* (Institute of International Education Books; US$47); *Vacation Study Abroad 2000-2001* (Institute of International Education Books; US$43); and the encyclopedic *Peterson's Study Abroad* and *Summer Study Abroad 2001* (Peterson's; US$30 each).

American Institute for Foreign Study, River Plaza, 9 West Broad Street, Stamford, CT 06902-3788, USA (☎800-727-2437; www.aifs.com/college/semester/holland/index.htm). Organizes programs at the Holland International Business School and the Vrije Universiteit, both in Amsterdam. Courses offered include economics, law, history, political science, and social science. Classes are taught in English for college juniors and seniors.

Central College Abroad, Office of International Education, 812 University, Pella, IA 50219, USA (☎800-831-3629; studyabroad@central.edu; www.central.edu/abroad). Offers semester- and year-long programs in Leiden. US$25 application fee.

School for International Training, College Semester Abroad, Admissions, Kipling Rd., P.O. Box 676, Brattleboro, VT 05302, USA (☎800-336-1616 or 802-258-3267; studyabroad@sit.edu; www.sit.edu). Semester- and year-long programs about sexuality, gender, and identity run US$13,100. Students stay with host families in The Netherlands and take intensive Dutch. Open to college sophomores, juniors, and seniors.

International Association for the Exchange of Students for Technical Experience (IAESTE), 10400 Little Patuxent Pkwy. #250, Columbia, MD 21044-3510, USA (☎410-997-2200; www.aipt.org). 8- to 12-week programs in The Netherlands for college students who have completed 2 years of technical study.

University of Amsterdam (www.uva.nl/english). Programs for economics, philosophy, history, linguistics, film studies, international affairs. Open to college and graduate students. Students live either in university dormitories or apartments.

Amsterdam Maastricht Summer University, P.O. Box 53066, 1007 RB Amsterdam (☎620 02 25; fax 624 93 68; office@amsu.edu; www.amsu.edu). Located on Keizersgracht 324, the Summer University offers courses in cultural studies and art history, economics and politics, health sciences and medicine, language, law and public policy, media studies and information science, and performing arts.

OTHER OPTIONS

Keizer Culinair, Keizergracht 376 (☎427 92 76; www.keizerculinair.nl). Choose between a sumptuous Dutch or Italian five-course feast–then learn to cook it and eat it–at this school in a lovely canal house (€53,50). Their is also a more intensive workshop that focuses on specialty skills (€59), or you can take an extended course over five weeks (€235).

MONEY MATTERS

BANKING

The major banks in Amsterdam are ABN-AMRO and Rabobank. Standard banking hours are between 9am-5pm on weekdays and often include extended hours (9am-7pm) on Thursdays. See **Banks,** in the **Service Directory,** p. 297.

CUTTING CORNERS

There are always ways to cut corners, whether in rent, utilities, food, or transportation. To save money on **rent,** start by looking in less expensive neighborhoods like De Pijp, the Oude West, or the East—the farther you get from the city, the cheaper rent will be. If you need to be in a certain location where the rent is still too steep, look for a **roommate.**

When you rent an apartment, find out what **utilities** are included in the rent. If no utilities are included, it's up to you to keep costs down. Now's the time to remember all those things your parents nagged you about, from turning off lights when you leave the room to not wasting water; not running the A/C while the windows are open; investing in blankets so you can keep the heat down, etc. In addition, you may want to look into getting a **cell phone** instead of a phone in your apartment—often, a cell phone gets you cheaper local service, and you can get plans in which long-distance is included as well. Not to mention that you'll look more trendily European, too.

With some creativity, you can cut corners on your **food bills** without having to starve. The most obvious option is to avoid eating out—even making your lunch in the morning instead of buying it can save you a bundle. When going grocery shopping, head for big suburban chains like Albert Heyn and outdoor markets like the Albert Cuypmarkt for basics instead of opting for the more convenient but more expensive specialty shops.

For **transportation,** avoid cabs, and if you can, avoid getting a car as well. Take public transportation, walk whenever possible, or find yourself a bike and get around the city like a true local.

HEALTH

Should you require a house call for a condition not requiring hospitalization, contact the appropriate number from the list of emergency numbers listed in the **Service Directory,** p. 301. Any hospital should be able to refer you to a dentist, optometrist, or ophthalmologist. Request documentation (including diagnoses) and receipts to submit to your home insurance company for reimbursement.

EU citizens can get reciprocal health benefits, entitling them to a practitioner registered with the state system, by filling out a E111 or E112 form before departure; this is available at most major post offices. The Dutch medical system will generally treat you whether or not you can pay in advance. EU citizens studying in The Netherlands also qualify for long-term care. Other travelers should ensure they have adequate medical insurance before leaving; if your regular insurance policy does not cover travel abroad, you may wish to purchase additional coverage. With the exception of Medicare, most health insurance plans cover members' medical emergencies during trips abroad; check with your insurance carrier to be sure.

If you need a **doctor** *(dokter)*, call the local hospital for a list of local practitioners. If you are receiving reciprocal health care, make sure you call a doctor who will be linked to the state health care system. Contact your health provider for information regarding charges that may be incurred. Note that the same medicines may have different names in The Netherlands than in your home country; check with your doctor before you leave.

USEFUL WEBSITES

The following websites provide helpful information about relocating to, living in, and working in The Netherlands.

www.undutchables.nl. The website of the Undutchables recruitment agency is full of practical information for foreigners living and working in The Netherlands.

www.howtosurviveholland.nl. Undutchables runs this website, too, which is less practical in nature, but rather contains humorous essays about and introductions to various elements of Dutch culture, written by foreigners.

www.expatica.nl. Devoted to the expatriate community in The Netherlands, this website is geared towards wealthier and older expats but still contains interesting articles.

www.transartists.nl. An information clearinghouse website for artists seeking jobs, lodgings, and studios in The Netherlands. Features classifieds postings and festival and workshop info.

LIVING IN AMSTERDAM

LONG-TERM ACCOMMODATIONS

STUDENT HOUSING

Many **colleges and universities** open their residence halls to travelers when school is not in session; some do so even during term-time. These dorms are often close to student areas—good sources for information on things to do—and are usually very clean. Getting a room may take a couple of phone calls and require advanced planning, but rates tend to be low, and many offer free local calls.

The Universiteit van Amsterdam guarantees housing for students in its International Study Programme. Students in these programs should contact their coordinators about housing, as they cannot apply directly to the Universiteit themselves. Other international exchange students can try entering themselves into housing lotteries organized by the Office of Foreign Relations and a student accommodations cooperative (☎525 29 26), provided that they meet certain criteria. Lotteries are held on certain days of the month; call for more information.

RENTING

Take care; for renting an apartment in Amsterdam from abroad is very difficult. If you have connections in Amsterdam, ask them to check a local paper (especially on Wednesdays) or to consult a rental agency. The website **www.housingonline.nl** might also prove useful. Another website to try is **www.amsterdam-ts.nl/apartments.html,** which is a bit pricey—apartments go for $850 per month and up, but if you have a group of people this website might be a good bet. Below are a few rental agencies to try in Amsterdam.

REAL ESTATE AND RENTAL AGENCIES

A4U, internet-based at www.apartments4u.nl.

Accommodation Home Agency BV, Singel 402 (☎422 30 20).

Amsterdam Housing, Singerbeekstraat 29 (☎671 72 66).

Apartment Services AS, Maasstraat 96 (☎672 30 13).

Dutch Housing Centre BV, Valeriustraat 174 (☎662 12 34).

Horst Housing Service, Elandsgracht. 86 (☎627 63 90).

OTHER OPTIONS

HOME EXCHANGES & HOME RENTALS

Home exchange offers the traveler various types of homes (houses, apartments, condominiums, villas, even castles in some cases), plus the opportunity to live like a native and to cut down on accommodation fees. For more information, contact **HomeExchange.Com** (☎888-877-8723; www.homeexchange.com), **Intervac International Home Exchange** (☎800-756-4663; www.intervac.com), or **The Invented City: International Home Exchange** (☎800-788-CITY or ☎415-252-1141; www.invented-city.com). These organizations charge a fee to view listings and are most useful to those who have homes to exchange.

Service Directory

AMERICAN EXPRESS

Damrak 66 (☎504 87 70). Open M-F 9am-5pm, Sa 9am-12pm.

BANKS

In general, banking hours in Amsterdam are M-F 9am-5pm, Th 9am-7pm.

ABN Amrobank: Branches at Dam 2 and Leidsestraat 1 (☎523 29 00). Open M 11am-5pm, Tu-F 9am-5pm.

GWK: Centraal Station (☎627 27 31). Open M-W and Sa-Su 7am-10:45pm. Julianaplein 1 (☎693 45 45). Open M-Sa 7:30am-8pm, Su 10am-6pm.

Rabobank: Nieuwmarkt 20, Frederiksplein 54, and Dam 16 (☎777 88 99). Open M 1-5pm, Tu-W and F 9:30am-5pm, Th 9:30am-6pm. For Dam 16, opening hours same, except M 9:30am-5pm.

BICYCLE RENTAL

It's not the drivers in Amsterdam who are crazy, it's the bicyclists. Bike (or, occasionally, moped) is the preferred means of travel for a great number of the city's residents; outside of a popular bar at night, you're more likely to find hundreds of parked bikes than parked cars. Theft is almost as common; be wary of buying "twenty-dollar bikes" from salesmen on the street—they are most likely stolen, and you can get in trouble with the law for buying one. You're better off renting a bike for a short stay in the city, and you'll be able to see twice the sights in half the time. Remember to use classic hand signals when you turn, or you'll have the unenviable task of explaining yourself to the fellow bicyclist you just wheeled into.

Beware if you rent a bike that you'll be looking at a €300-600 replacement fee if yours gets stolen. If you're not planning on being careful, some establishments will let you buy bike insurance when you rent.

Bike City, 68-70 Bloemgracht (☎626 37 21; fax 422 33 26; www.bikecity.nl), in the Jordaan. Bike City offers reasonable rates on 1-, 3-, and 5-speed bikes, from €3,50 for 2hr. to €29,50 for 5 days on the more inexpensive models. Bike rental comes with 2 good locks: use them! Be sure to bring a passport or other government-issued ID and the €25 deposit for each bike. Open daily 9am-6pm. Accepts major credit cards with 5% surcharge.

Damstraat Rent-a-Bike, Damstraat 22 (☎625 50 29; rent@bikes.nl; www.bikes.nl). Head south down Damrak from Centraal Station until you hit Dam Sq.; from there, go left across the square onto Damstraat. Good deals on all different kinds of bikes. Rentals from €7 per day, €31 per week. Credit card imprint or €25 and an ID required as deposit. Open daily 9am-6pm.

Frederic Rent a Bike, Brouwersgracht 78 (☎62 45 509; www.frederic.nl), in the Shipping Quarter. From Centraal Station, head down Damrak and turn right at Nieuwendijk. Turn left after you cross the Harlemmersluis bridge, and follow along the Brouwersgracht for about 7 blocks; it's on the right. Part bike rental establishment, part tourist office, Fred's is well worth the 10min. walk from Centraal Station. In addition to renting bikes, the friendly and helpful staff provides street maps, cycling know-how, and information suited to customers' particular interests. Bikes €10 per day, which includes lock and theft insurance. Online reservations available. No deposit (though ID or credit card imprint is required). AmEx/MC/V.

Holland Rent-a-Bike, Damrak 247 (☎622 32 07), in the basement of the Beurs de Beurlage. One of the cheapest places around, and right by Centraal Station. Bikes €6,25 per day, €32,50 per week; €100 or €30 plus an ID for deposit. Open M-F 7am-7pm, Sa-Su 9am-6pm. AmEx/MC/V.

Mac Bike, Marnixstraat 220, Weteringschans 2, Mr. Visserplein 2 (☎626 69 64, www.macbike.nl). This popular chain of bicycle rental stores offers a variety of options, from same-day rentals (€6,50) to 6-day stints (€27,25). Be sure not to rent one of the bikes that has a garish "Mac Bike" logo on the front, lest you brand yourself a tourist. For 50% of the rental price, you can insure your bike against theft and avoid paying the replacement fee of €300-600; locks cost extra. Requires €30 deposit. Open daily 9am-6pm. Visa.

BODY PIERCING

Body Manipulations (☎420 80 85; piercing@body-madam.demon.nl; www.bodym-europe.com), on Oude Hoogstraat in the Oude Zijd. Very helpful staff will assist you in all your desires to be punctured and adorned at this careful, hygienic establishment. Most body piercing €27,50, ear €5, nose €16, plus the price of the jewelry (€3,50-31). 5% off if you show this book and 10% off for a repeat piercing. Women and gay friendly. No appointment required. Open M-W and F-Sa 11am-6pm, Th 11am-8pm.

BOOKS

A Space Oddity, Prinsengracht 204 (☎427 40 36). Storeowner Jeff Bas has assembled an impressive assortment of sci-fi and comic book paraphenalia, from old action figures to movie promos. The young at heart will find old and rare toy incarnations of their favorite movies and comic books, from *Star Wars* to *Spider-Man*. Some as cheap as €10, others as expensive as you can imagine. Open M 1-5:30pm, Tu-F 11am-5:30pm, Sa 1-5pm. V.

American Book Center, Kalverstraat 185 (☎625 55 37; www.abc.nl), discounts 10% for students and teachers. Open M-W and F-Sa 10am-8pm, Th 10am-10pm, Su 11am-6:30pm.

Arcitectura and Natura, Leliegracht 22 (☎623 61 86; www.archined.nl/architectura), in the Canal Ring West. Can't read Dutch? Well, it doesn't matter, because it's the pictures that make these coffee table books extraordinary. Enough of them are in English, anyway. Heavy and beautiful, the tomes here tend to be expensive. Open M noon-6:30pm, Tu-Sa 9am-6pm. V/MC/AmEx.

Athenaeum Boekhandel, Spui 14-16 (☎622 62 48; www.athenaeum.nl), at the bottom of the Nieuwe Zijd in the Spui. Everything from your most obscure literary needs to cultural criticism and philosophy to beautiful art coffeetable books; most are in English. Also maintains a newsstand with a very extensive selection of American and British magazines. Open M 11am-6pm, Tu-W and F-Sa 9:30am-6pm, Th 9:30am-9pm, Su noon-5:30pm. AmEX/MC/V.

The Book Exchange, Kloveniersburgwal 58 (☎626 62 66), between the Oude Zijd and the Jodenbuurt, deals in used texts and has a friendly, tasteful, knowledgeable staff. Frightfully good selection of used English-language books, from the basic fiction and nonfiction to the more esoteric. Any book you could want to pass the time at the many canal-side cafes, all reasonably priced (paperbacks €3-11). You can also drop in to sell those old paperbacks; true to its name, the Exchange offers a more favorable deal if you're willing to trade. Open M-F 10am-6pm, Sa 10am-5:30pm, Su 11:30am-4pm.

English Bookshop, Lauriergracht 71 (☎626 42 30), in the Jordaan. Renovated and reopened in July 2002, it now offers coffee and tea to sip while you browse its strong selection of books and American magazines. Open Tu-Su 10am-6pm.

Waterstone's, Kalverstraat 152 (☎638 38 21), carries a wide selection. Open Su-M 11am-6pm, Tu-W 9am-6pm, Th 9am-9pm, F 9am-7pm, Sa 10am-7pm.

BUDGET TRAVEL AGENCIES

Eurolines, Rokin 10 (☎560 87 88; www.eurolines.nl), will book coach travel throughout Europe. Open M-F 9:30am-5:30pm, Sa 10am-4pm.

CONSULATES AND EMBASSIES

Most of the foreign embassies in The Netherlands are in **The Hague,** area code 070:

Australia, Carnegielaan 4, 2517 KH (☎310 82 00). Open M-F 8:45am-4:30pm.

Canada, Sophialaan 7, 2514 JP (☎311 16 00). Open M-F 9am-1pm and 2-5:30pm.

Ireland, 9 Dr. Kuyperstraat, 2514 BA (☎363 09 93). Open M-F 10am-12:30pm and 2:30-5:00pm.

South Africa, Wassenaarseweg 40, 2596 CJ (☎392 45 01). Open daily 9am-noon.

UK, Lange Voorhout 10, 2514 ED (☎427 04 27). Open M-F 9am-1pm and 2:15-5:30pm.

US, Lange Voorhout 102, 2514 EJ (☎310 92 09). Open M-F 8am-4:30pm.

CONSULATES IN AMSTERDAM:

American Consulate, Museumplein 19 (☎575 53 09) is open to visitors M-F 8:30am-noon and takes calls M-F 8:30am-5pm. Embassy and Consulate information at www.usemb.nl.

British Consulate, Koningslaan 44 (☎676 43 43), is open for visitors M-F 9am-noon and 2-3:30pm. The switchboard is open M-F 9am-12:45pm and 1:45-5pm.

CURRENCY EXCHANGE

American Express, Damrak 66, offers the best rates, no commission on American Express traveler's checks, and €4 flat fee for all non-Euro cash and non-American Express traveler's checks. Open M-F 9am-5pm, Sa 9am-noon.

GWK, in Centraal Station, with **Change** locations at Damrak 86, Leidsestraat 106, and Kalverstraat 150, offers good rates, charging €2,25 plus 2.25% commission. Students with ISIC card get 25% discount. Those changing traveler's checks will pay

3% commission. Open M-W and F-Sa 8:30am-7pm, Th 8:30am-9pm, Su 10:30am-6pm. Location at Schiphol open 24hr.

Pott-Change, Damrak 95 (☎626 36 58; open daily 8am-8pm) or Rembrandtplein 10B (☎626 87 68; open M-Sa 9am-5pm), charges no commission on cash, €1,50 flat fee on traveler's checks.

EMERGENCY

*See also **Health and Medical Assistance.***

Emergencies: ☎112 (police, ambulance, fire brigade), free from all pay phones.

Police: Headquarters, Elandsgracht 117 (☎0800 88 44), at the intersection with Marnixstraat. Call here to get connected to the station nearest you or the rape crisis department.

Crisis Lines: General counseling at **Telephone Helpline** (☎675 75 75). Open 24 hr. **Rape crisis hotline** (☎612 02 45) staffed M-F 10:30am-11pm, Sa-Su 3:30-11pm. **Drug counseling, Jellinek Clinic** (☎570 23 55). Open M-F 9am-5pm.

AIDS Helpline (☎080 00 22 22 20). Offers advice and information about AIDS. M-F 2-10pm.

HIV-Plus Line (☎685 00 55). Phone line operated Tu and Th 8-10:30pm and M, W, F 1-4pm.

ENTERTAINMENT INFORMATION

Amsterdams Uit Buro (AUB), Leidseplein 26, (☎09 00 01 91, €0,40 per min.; www.uitlijn.nl.), through the entrance on the left-hand side of the building, is stuffed with fliers, pamphlets, and guides to help you sift through what's being offered at any given time. The AUB also sells tickets and makes reservations for just about any cultural event in the city. Pick up the free monthly *UITKRANT* (in Dutch) or the English-language *Day-by-Day* (€1,50) at any AUB office for a breakdown of what's on. Open M-W and F-Sa 10am-6pm, Th 10am-9pm, Su noon-6pm.

VVV's theater desk, Stationsplein 10. Makes reservations for cultural events. Open M-Sa 10am-5pm.

EXERCISE AND ADVENTURE

Squash City, Ketelmakerstraat 6 (☎626 78 83; www.squashcity.com), take bus #18 or 22 to Ketelmakerstraat, dir. Haarlemerplein, offers squash courts, a gym, and sauna, about a 5-min. busride, or 15-min. walk, west of Centraal Station. Squash for 2: before 5pm, €13,60 for 45 mins.; after 5, €18. Rent a racket for €2,50. Gym: before 5, €8; after 5, €9,50. Special student rates if you show up before 5pm. Open M-F 8:45am-midnight, Sa-Su 8:45am-9pm.

Garden Gym, Jodenbreestraat 158 (☎626 87 72; info@thegarden.nl), offers competitive rates to tourists and residents. Its central location in the Jodenbuurt renders working out a true convenience. Open M, W, and F 9am-11pm; T,Th noon-11pm; Sa 11am-6pm; Su 10am-7pm. Call or email for deals.

Borchland Sportscentrum, Borchlandweg 6-12 (☎563 33 33). Take the metro #54, to Strandvliet and follow signs to Borchland. This is the city's largest sporting center and a great place to spend a rainy day. Tennis (€20 per hour), squash (€17), badminton (€9,75), and bowling (14,50-22,50 depending on time) are all available and you can even rent a racket for €2,75. Located next to the impressive Amsterdam ArenA, this gorgeous complex also has a restaurant and cafe. Open daily 8am-11pm.

De Mirandabad, De Mirandalaan 9 (☎546 44 44), is a veritable waterpark, with a wave pool, beach, and indoor and outdoor pools. Admission is €3, 12 entries for €30. Open daily 9am-midnight.

Avonturenbaai Sloterparkbad, Pres. Allendelaan 2-4 (☎506 35 06), take tram 14 to its end, is complete with indoor and outdoor pools and costs €3 for admission. Open daily 10am-6pm.

Flevoparkbad, Insulendeweg 1001 (☎692 50 30), take tram #14. Has a great outdoor pool, open daily May-Sept. 10am-5:30pm. Bring your bathing suit and get wet for €2,25.

Bungy Jump Holland, Westerdoksdijk 44 (☎419 60 05; www.bungyjump.nl), from the back entrance of Centraal, turn left and follow for about 10 mins. Take

Amsterdam by air, with a 75m waterside jump from a crane. €50 for one, €90 for two, and €250 for ten. July-Aug. daily noon-9pm; May-June Th-M noon-9pm; Oct Th-Su noon-9pm.

Klimmuur Centruum, De Ruyterkade 160 (☎427 57 77), about a 10min walk to the right of Centraal Station; it's the enormous corrugated tilting block. An incredible indoor wall climbing facility. Open weekdays after 5pm and on weekends.

Deco Sauna, Herengracht 117 (☎330 35 65; www.saunadeco.nl) Pamper yourself amidst fabulous 20s art deco style with massage, Shiatsu or reflexology (e27 for 25 min, e44 for 55 min). Also offers facials, manicures and special "beauty days" from e100.

GAY/LESBIAN RESOURCES

The monthly **Culture and Camp** provides info on gay venues and events. The **Gay Krant** and the fortnightly **Shark** also provide excellent and thorough listings of what's going down in queer Amsterdam.

COC, Rozenstraat 14 (☎626 30 87; www.cocamsterdam.nl), exists as a social network and information center. Maps designed specifically for the gay traveler available in the lobby. Office open M-Tu and Th-F 10am-5pm, W 10am-8pm. The cafe on the ground floor turns into a multicultural discotheque on F and Sa nights. Café open Th 8pm-midnight, F 8-10pm; disco F-Sa 10pm-4am (Sa is women-only). For more on the COC, see p. 297.

Vrolijk, Paleisstraat 135 (☎623 51 42; vrolijk@xs4all.nl; www.vrolijk.nu), claims to be the largest gay and lesbian bookstore in Europe. With an excellent selection of literature and periodicals, it's an ideal place to stop in for tips on what's hot and what's not in gay Amsterdam; shop online for books as well. Open M 11am-6pm, Tu-W and F 10am-6pm, Th 10am-9pm, Sa 10am-5pm.

Gay and Lesbian Switchboard (☎623 65 65) is available to answer questions, suggest events, or listen to personal problems. All switchboard volunteers speak English and some speak other languages. Phone staffed daily 10am-10pm.

Gay Krant Reisservice, Kloveniersburgwal 40 (☎421 00 00; reis@gaykrant.nl; www.gaykrant.nl/reis). A travel service devoted exclusively to gay and lesbian travelers. Also features an impressive display of magazines and newspapers for gay travelers. Newsletters available. Open M 2-6pm, Tu-F 10am-6pm, Sa 10am-4pm.

SAD/Schorerfoundation, P.C. Hoofstraat 5 (☎662 42 06). A counseling center for gay men and women. Open M-Th 10am-5pm.

Xantippe Unlimited, Prinsengracht 290 (☎623 58 54; xantippe@xs4all.nl; www.dds.nl/~xantippe). General bookstore, but with a specialization in women's and lesbian issues. Open M 1-7pm, Tu-F 10am-7pm, Sa 10am-6pm, Su noon-5pm.

HEALTH AND MEDICAL ASSISTANCE

*Also see **Emergencies.***

Academisch Medisch Centrum, Meibergdreef 9 (☎566 91 11), is easily accessible by taking bus 53 from Centraal (just ask the driver to announce the medical center). Arranges for hospital care.

Tourist Medical Service, Sarphatistraat 94 (☎592 33 55). After hours, call the number to get connected to the doctor on call. Otherwise, check into the clinic by taking tram #9 or bus #22 to Tropenmuseum, crossing the canal to the north, and turning left on Sarphatistraat. Open M-F 9am-5pm.

Kruispost Medisch Helpcentrum, Oudezijds Voorburgwal 129 (☎624 90 31). This walk-in clinic offers first aid daily 7-9:30pm. From Centraal Station, head out and turn left at the Victoria Hotel, and follow the street until Oudezijds Voorburgwal, on your right.

Centrale Doktorsdienst (☎0900 503 20 42, €0,75 per min.). For 24hr. medical help, this service will direct you to appropriate treatment.

STD Line, Groenburgwal 44 (☎555 58 22), offers phone counseling and, if you call ahead for an appointment, a free test-

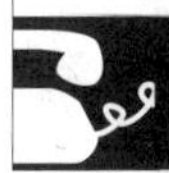

ing clinic. Open for calls M-F 8am-noon and 1-4pm.

INTERNET ACCESS

Internet access in Amsterdam leaves much to be desired. There are a few copious cyber areas—the best bet may be a cozy coffeeshop with a single computer in the back. The following all have more than five computers and have Internet access as their main attraction.

easyEverything, Reguliersbreestraat 22, off Reguliersgracht south down that street from Rembrandtplein. Smaller location at Damrak 34, just south of Centraal on the west side of the street. Both house hundreds of PCs and webcams on several floors. €1 for 26min., or longer-term deals (24hr. for €5, 1 week for €8, 20 days for €20) using a password given, appropriately, by a machine.

Cyber Cafe Amsterdam, Nieuwendijk 17. From Centraal, turn right at the Victoria Hotel, left at Martelaarsgracht, and right on Nieuwendijk. This is a comfy little cybercafé with Internet at 12 computers (€1,50 per 30min.) Open Su-Th 10am-1am, F-Sa 10am-2am.

Free World, Nieuwendijk 30 (☎620 09 02; info@cafe.euronet.nl; http://cafe.euronet.nl). From Centraal Station, turn right at the main street, left at Martelaarsgracht, and right on Nieuwendijk. Quality Internet service (€1 for 30min.) and a slick computer-age interior meet at this very fresh cyber coffeeshop. Open Su-Th 9am-1am, F-Sa 9am-3am.

Internet Cafe, Martelaarsgracht 11 (627 10 52; www.internetcafe.nl). From Centraal, turn right at the Victoria Hotel and then left on Martelaarsgracht, near the intersection with Nieuwendijk. 20min. free with a drink (€1,75-4,90), max. 2hr. free. Otherwise, €1 for 30min. Open Su-Th 9am-1am, F-Sa 9am-2am.

LAUNDRY

If you're running out of clean clothes, you should have no trouble finding a *wasserette* (laundromat) in your area.

Rozengracht Wasserette, Rozengracht 103 (☎638 59 75), in the Jordaan. Go west down Rozengracht from Westermarkt. You can do it yourself (wash €5,50; dry €8 per 5kg load) or have it done for you (€8 for 5kg). Open daily 9am-9pm. Cash only.

Wasserette/Launderette, Oude Doelenstraat 12. From Dam, take Damstraat toward Oude Zijd and the laundromat is on your right just before Oudezijds Achterburgwal; good location if staying in the Red Light District, Oude Zijd, or the northern half of Nieuwe Zijd. Wash a load for €5,80 and dry it for €7. Open M-F 8:30am-7pm, Sa 10am-5pm. Cash only.

Aquarette, Oudebrugsteeg 22, off Damrak just south of Centraal Station. Self-serve only. Wash a load for €5, dry it for €1 per 12min. Cash only.

Wasserette-Stomerij 'De Eland', Elandsgracht 59 (☎625 07 31), in the Jordaan. From the Westermarkt tram stop, turn left at Prinsengracht; after the second bridge, turn right at Elandsgracht. Self-serve only. €4 for 4kg, €6 for 6kg. Open M-Tu and Th-F 8am-8pm, W 8am-6pm, Sa 9am-5pm.

LIBRARIES

Openbare Bibliotheek Amsterdam, Prinsengracht 587 (☎523 09 00). The main branch of the city's public library system is the only one in the direct city center. Free Internet access. Sign up for a 30min. slot at the information desk. Check out the reading room and catch up on the latest issue of the *Herald Tribune* over a cup of coffee at the inexpensive cafe. The library has a fair selection of English magazines and fiction. Open M 1-9pm, Tu-Th 10am-9pm, F-Sa 10am-5pm; Oct.-Mar. Su 1-5pm.

HOME GOODS

De Emaillekeizer, 1e Sweelinckstraat 15 (☎664 18 47; www.emaillekeizer.nl; emaillekeizer@zonnet.nl), a block and a half off the Albert Cuypmarket in De Pijp. Selling bright baskets, colorful woven deck chairs, a handsome beaded door divider, and other knicknacks primarily from Ghana. Incredibly cheap dishware and teapots. If you're in town for a little while

and realize you might like a plate, mug, or teapot, this is the place to go. Open M 1-6pm, Tu-Sa 11am-6pm.

Gallerie Casbah, 1e Van Der Helstraat (☎671 04 74), in De Pijp. Beautifully ornate imports from Morocco. Mostly serious pieces such as tiled fountains, 1m vases and rugs although there are also some wonderful plates and book bindings. Open daily 11am-6pm. Cash.

Maranon Hangmatten, Singel 488-90 (☎622 82 61; www.maranon.net), in the Central Canal Ring. Right off the flower market, this is the best temporary refuge in the city. Come in for a rest to "test" the colorful, comfortable hammocks hanging from the ceiling. Open M-Sa 9am-6pm, Su 10am-5:30pm. V/MC/AmEx.

The Purple Onion, Haarlemmerdijk 139 (☎427 37 50), in the Shipping Quarter. Step into this incense-filled shop to a world of eclectic goods imported from India. The owners, a Dutch anthropologist and an Indian scientist, select items using natural materials, such as wooden sculptures and handmade bedspreads. Open Tu-Sa 11:30am-6pm. V/MC.

MAIL

Post offices are generally open M-F 9am-6pm, and some are also open Sa 10am-1:30pm. Larger branches may stay open later. Mailing a postcard or letter to anywhere in the EU costs €0,54; to destinations outside Europe, postcards also cost €0,54, but letters (up to 20g) cost €0,75. Mail takes two to three days to the UK, four to six to North America, six to eight to Australia and New Zealand, and eight to ten to South Africa. Mark envelopes "air mail," "par avion," or "per luchtpost," or your letter or postcard will never arrive (surface mail and mail by sea take one to four months at best).

Main post offices: Singel 250, at the corner of Radhuisstraat (open M-W and F 9am-6pm, Th 9am-9pm, Sa 10am-1:30pm); Oosterdokskade 5, just east of Centraal Station (open M-F 9am-9pm, Sa 9am-noon); St. Antoniebreestraat 16, near Nieuwmarkt; and Waterlooplein 2, in the Stadhuis (open M-F 9am-6pm, Sa 10am-1:30pm).

MUSIC

Africa & World Music Record Shop, Kinkerstraat 294, (☎412 17 76). Tram #7 or 17 to Ten Katestr. A unique look into the diverse musical styles of North Africa, from Fela Kuti to the wildest extensions of world beat. The shop carries a wide selection of world music. Open M 1-7pm, Tu-W and F-Sa 11am-7pm, Th 11am-9pm, Su noon-7pm. AmEx/MC/V.

Back Beat Records, Egelantierstraat 19 (☎627 16 57; backbeat@xs4all.nl). In the Jordaan, tightly packed collection of jazz, soul, funk, blues, and R&B. Most prices are a bit steep, but there are some bargains to be found. New CD's as well as new and used vinyl. Open M-Sa 11am-6pm.

Concerto, Utrechtsestraat 52-60 (☎623 52 28; info@concerto.nu), in the Central Canal Ring. Around since 1955 and arguably the best music store in Amsterdam, Concerto sells a broad selection of CDs from five adjoining houses: second hand, dance, pop, jazz/world, and classical. Records downstairs. Listening station where they'll play anything. Open M-W and F-Sa 10am-6pm, Th 10am-9pm, Su noon-6pm. V/MC/AmEx.

Dance Tracks, Nieuwe Nieuwstraat 69 (☎639 08 53). This record/CD shop advertises as "strictly dance music," and that's exactly what it means. Expect to find all sorts of cuts in the dance genre–bootlegs, rare records, and tons of hip-hop and house music. Open M 1-7pm, Tu-W and F-Sa 11am-7pm, Th 11am-9pm, Su 1-6pm. Credit cards accepted.

De Plaatboef, Rozengracht 40 (☎422 87 77; www.plaatboef.com), in the Jordaan. Big selection of new and used CDs (around €11). Credit cards accepted for purchases over €40. Open M noon-6pm, Tu-Sa 10am-6pm.

Roots Music, Jonge Roelensteeg 6 (☎620 44 70). If you're want reggae, Latin, or African beats, look no further than this mousehole-sized music shop. Roots houses a great selection of vinyl, 7-inches, and CDs at very affordable prices. Open Su-M 12:30-6pm, Tu-W and F-Sa 10:30am-6pm, Th 10:30am-9pm.

Soul Food, Nieuwe Nieuwstraat 27c. Specializes in dance music, both CD and vinyl.

Wide selection of new and old cuts from Europe, the US, and abroad. Open M 1-9pm, Tu-W and F-Sa 11am-7pm, Th 11am-9pm, Su 1-7pm.

Schot CD Shop, van Baerlestraat 5 (☎662 37 59), between P.C. Hooftstraaat and Vossiusstraat. From the Museumplein, walk away from the Rijksmuseum and take your first right on van Baerlestraat; it will be 2 blocks down on the right. Diverse selection of music, with everything from world music to classical, opera, New Age, jazz, soul, and a larger selection of pop. Prices vary widely, but there are many special deals. Outside are some good jazz, classical, and world music as well as corny '70s hits (€4,60, 3 for €12,00). Open daily 10:30am-7pm. Credit cards accepted.

Wenterwereld Records, 13a 1e Bloemwarsstraat (☎622 23 30). If you've ever wanted to round out the "Nederpop" section of your record collection, this is the place to do it. A wonderful assortment of used and new records (€8,50-17,50); most are Dutch, and many of the American records are quite obscure. Also has an impressive collection of old comic books for sale, most in Dutch. An in-store turntable lets you listen before you buy. Open M-Sa, noon-5:30pm. No credit cards.

PHARMACIES

Look for an *apotheek* sign. Most are open M-F 8:30am-5:30pm. Most pharmacies sell toiletries, first aid supplies, and condoms in addition to filling prescriptions.

RENTAL AGENCIES

A4U, Internet-based apartments at www.apartments4u.nl.

Accommodation Home Agency BV, Singel 402 (☎422 30 20).

Amsterdam Housing, Singerbeekstraat 29 (☎671 72 66).

Apartment Services AS, Maasstraat 96 (☎672 30 13).

Dutch Housing Centre BV, Valeriustraat 174 (☎662 12 34).

Horst Housing Service, Elandsgracht 86 (☎627 63 90).

SUPERMARKETS

Albert Heijn supermarkets line the streets in Amsterdam. Check for locations at www.albert.nl

Dirk van den Broek, Marie Heinekenplein 25 (☎673 93 93), in De Pijp, just behind the Heineken Brewery. Big, basic supermaket that's significantly cheaper than Albert Heijn. A similarly low-priced liquor and drug store share the complex, so load up on munchies. Open M-F 8am-9pm, Sa 8am-8pm, Su 1-7pm.

TOURIST OFFICES

VVV, Stationsplein 10 (☎0900 400 40 40; phone number €0,55 per min.; open M-F 9am-5pm). When exiting Centraal Station, the office is across the tram tracks to the left. Once there, if you make it through the hefty lines, you can get help with hostel/hotel reservations (€3 per person). You can also buy tickets for museums, canal boat tours, and the Circle Tram 20. Open daily 9am-5pm. Expect a long wait here and at the other offices at platform #2 inside **Centraal Station** (open M-Sa 8am-8pm, Su 9am-5pm); **Leidseplein 1,** around the corner on Leidsestraat. (open M-Th 9am-6pm, F-Sa 9am-7pm, Su 9am-5pm); and **Stationplein,** Argonautenstraat 98. (Open M-F 9:30am-5:30pm, Sa 10am-4pm.)

GVB, across from Centraal Station and to the right of the VVV, with a "Tickets and Service" sign, specializes in bus, tram, and metro information, and has much shorter lines than its neighbor. Buy a *strippenkart* get good excursion information from the helpful staff. Open M-F 7am-9pm, Sa-Su 8am-9pm. Info line ☎0900 92 92; €0,30 per minute; open M-F 6am-midnight, Sa-Su 7am-midnight.

Eurolines, Rokin 10 (☎560 87 88; www.eurolines.nl) is one of Europe's leading coach services, offering incredibly cheap transport to destinations across Europe. Paris (one-way, low season €36; high €39). Berlin (€55 and €60), Brussels (€15 year-round), and Prague (14 hours, but only €70). Backpackers know Eurolines, with prices less than 1/3 that of train or cheap air transport. Open M-F 9:30-5:30, Sa 10am-4pm. You can also purchase tix when you depart, at the Eurolines bus depott, at Amstel Station (call first to ensure availability; take the metro, any line, to the 5th stop; open daily 6am-10pm; same contact details as Rokin store).

Holland Tourist Information at **Schiphol Airport.** Open daily 7am-10pm.

TRANSPORTATION

BY PLANE

Amsterdam's sleek, glassy **Schiphol Airport** (☎800-SCHIPHOL or 72 44 74 65; www.schiphol.nl) serves as a major hub for cheap transatlantic flights. Major carriers include KLM/Northwest (☎800-447-4747; www.nwa.com), Martinair (☎800-627-8462; www.martinairusa.com), Continental, Delta (☎800-241-4141; www.delta-air.com), United ☎800-241-6522; www.ual.com), Air Canada (☎888-247-2262; www.aircanada.ca), and Singapore Airlines (☎800-742-3333; www.singaporeair.com).

BY TRAM

See **Once In Amsterdam,** p. 23 for more information.

Circle Tram 20, traces a loop around the city, with stops at 30 attractions. (Every 10min. 9am-7pm, last train leaves Centraal Station at 6pm.) Great way for tourists to travel, with hop-on and hop-off service at most main sights around the city. Although it's simple, it may be less expensive to just buy a *stippenkaart*. One-day pass €5; ages 4-12 and seniors 65+ €3,50; 2-day pass €8; 1-week €20.

Appendix

LANGUAGE

Dutch is the official language of The Netherlands, however in Amsterdam most natives speak English fluently. To initiate a conversation in English with natives, politely ask "spreekt u Engels" (pronounced, "sprekt oo angles," meaning "do you speak English?"). Even if your conversational counterpart speaks little English, they will usually make every effort to communicate, which you can acknowledge by thanking them for their bilingual assistance: "dank u wel" ("thanks!"). In such a case, knowing a few words of Dutch can't hurt, particularly in smaller daytrip towns where English is not spoken as universally as in Amsterdam. Fill up on *dagschotel* (dinner special), *broodjes* (bread or sandwich), *bier* (beer), and *kaas* (cheese). Dutch uses a gutteral "g" sound for both "g" and "ch." "J" is usually pronounced as "y"; e.g., *hofje* is "HOF-yuh," "ui" is pronounced "ow," and the dipthong "ij" is best approximated in English as "ah" followed by a long "e."

PHRASEBOOK

ENGLISH	DUTCH	ENGLISH	DUTCH
NUMBERS			
1	een	**15**	vijftien
2	twee	**16**	zestien
3	drie	**17**	zeventien
4	vier	**18**	achttien
5	vijf	**19**	negentien
6	zes	**20**	twintig
7	zeven	**30**	dertig
8	acht	**40**	veertg
9	negen	**50**	vijftig
10	tien	**60**	zestig
11	elf	**70**	zeventig
12	twaalf	**80**	tachtig
13	dertien	**90**	negentig
14	veertien	**100**	honderd
DAYS, TIME			
Monday	maandag	**April**	april
Tuesday	dinsdag	**May**	mei
Wednesday	woensdag	**June**	juni
Thursday	donderdag	**July**	juli
Friday	vrijdag	**August**	augustus
Saturday	zaterdag	**September**	september
Sunday	zondag	**October**	oktober
January	januari	**November**	november
February	februari	**December**	december
March	maart		
PHRASES			
Hello	hallo	**...the bathroom**	...de badkamer
Good morning	goedenmorgen	**...the bank**	...de bank
Good afternoon	goedenavond	**...the church**	...de kerk
Good night	goedenacht	**...the hotel**	...het hotel
Goodbye	tot ziens	**...shop**	...de winkel
Please	alstublieft	**...the museum**	...het museum
Thank you	dank u wel	**...the market**	...de markt
You're welcome	alstublieft (like please)	**...the pharmacy**	...de apotheek
Excuse me (to get someone's attention) **Excuse me (to apologize)**	pardon neemt u mij niet	**...the hospital**	...het ziekenhuis
I don't speak Dutch	ik spreek geen Nederlands	**I do not understand**	ik begrijp het niet
Do you speak English?	sprekt u Engels	**Do you have...?**	heeft u...?
Where is...?	waar is...?	**...any rooms**	...ook kamers vrij?
...for one	...voor een persoon?	**What time is it?**	hoe laat is het?
...with bathroom?	...met badkamer?	**yes**	ja
May I see the room?	mag ik de kamer zien?	**no**	nee
How much is it?	wat kost het?	**day return (tickets)**	dagretour

ENGLISH	DUTCH	ENGLISH	DUTCH
one-way (tickets)	enkele reis	**round-trip (tickets)**	retour

CLOTHING SIZE AND METRIC CONVERSIONS

WOMEN'S CLOTHING

US SIZE	**4**	**6**	**8**	**10**	**12**	**14**	**16**
UK SIZE	6	8	10	12	14	16	18
EUROPE SIZE	36	38	40	42	44	46	48

WOMEN'S SHOES

US SIZE	**5**	**6**	**7**	**8**	**9**	**10**	**11**
UK SIZE	3	4	5	6	7	8	10
EUROPE SIZE	36	37	38	39	40	41	42

MEN'S SUITS/JACKETS

US/UK SIZE	**32**	**34**	**36**	**38**	**40**	**42**	**44**
EUROPE SIZE	42	44	46	48	50	52	54

MEN'S SHIRTS

US/UK SIZE	**14**	**14.5**	**15**	**15.5**	**16**	**16.5**	**17**
EUROPE SIZE	36	37	38	39	40	41	42

METRIC CONVERSIONS

1 in = 25 mm / 1 mm = 0.04 in	1 ft = 0.30 m / 1 m = 3.28 ft	1 lb = 0.45 kg / 1 kg = 2.2 lb
1 mi = 1.61 km / 1 km = 0.62 mi	1 gal = 4 qt = 3.78 L	1 L = 1.06 qt = 0.264 gal

DUTCH FOOD

krokette: a kind of deep-fried croquette
stamppot: a mashed potato stew made with vegetables and sausage
patates frites: french fries, typically served with mayonnaise
bitterballen: deep-fried meatballs, served with mustard
erwtensoep: a traditional pea soup served with sausage and bacon
herrings: a type of fish eaten raw
pannenkoeken: pancakes served for dessert and topped with syrup *(stroop)* or fruit
Limburgse Vlaia: a pie made with bread dough and fruit-filled; served hot or cold
brood: bread
hoofdgerechten: main course
kaas: cheese
nagerechten: dessert
sla/salade: salad
suiker: sugar
vis: fish
vlees: meat
voorgerechten: appetizer
vruchten: fruit
zout: salt
soep: soup
rood: rare
half doorbakken: medium
doorbakken: well done

Index

A

B

sights
museums
shopping
entertainment
food & drink
coffeeshops
nightlife
accommodations
daytrips
hiking
festivals

CCR canal ring **CRW** canal ring west **DP** de pijp **J** the jordaan **JP** jodenbuurt and the plantage **LP** leidseplein **MV** museumplein and vondelpark **NZ** nieuwe zijd **OZ** oude zijd **RLD** red light district **RP** rembrandtplein **SQ** shipping quarter

H

sights · museums · shopping · entertainment · food & drink · coffeeshops · nightlife · accommodations · daytrips · hiking · festivals

K

L

M

sights | museums | shopping | entertainment | food & drink | coffeeshops

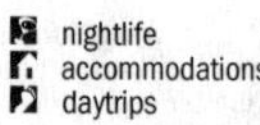

nightlife | accommodations | daytrips | hiking | festivals

O

P

Q

R

CCR canal ring **CRW** canal ring west **DP** de pijp **J** the jordaan **JP** jodenbuurt and the plantage **LP** leidseplein **MV** museumplein and vondelpark **NZ** nieuwe zijd **OZ** oude zijd **RLD** red light district **RP** rembrandtplein **SQ** shipping quarter

S

T

sights · museums · shopping · entertainment · food & drink · coffeeshops · nightlife · accommodations · daytrips · hiking · festivals

U

V

W

Y

Z

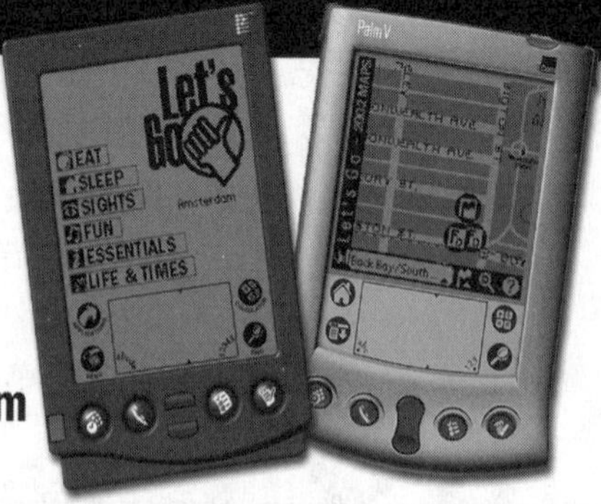

Maps

INSIDE:

MAP LEGEND

Hospital
Police
Post Office
Tourist Office
Bank
Embassy/Consulate
Site or Point of Interest
Telephone Office
Theater
Library
Airport
Bus Station
Train Station
TRAM STOP
Ferry Landing
Church
Synagogue
Mosque
Castle
Mountain
Museum
Hotel/Hostel
Camping
Food & Drink
Shopping
Entertainment
Nightlife
Coffee Shop
Internet Café
Pedestrian Zone
Park
Beach
Water

The Let's Go compass always points NORTH.

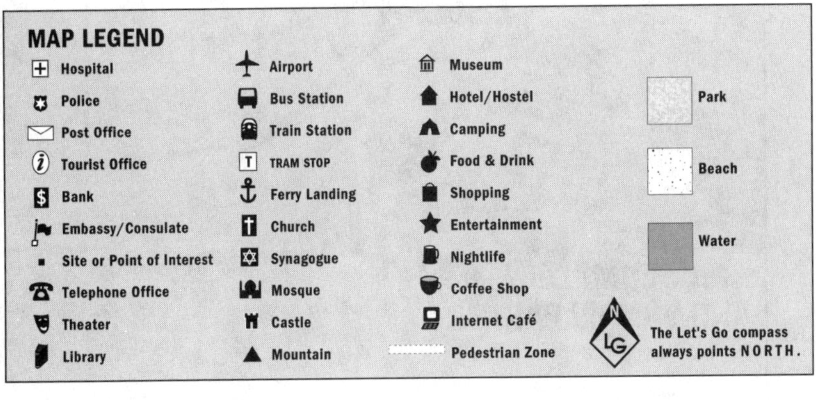

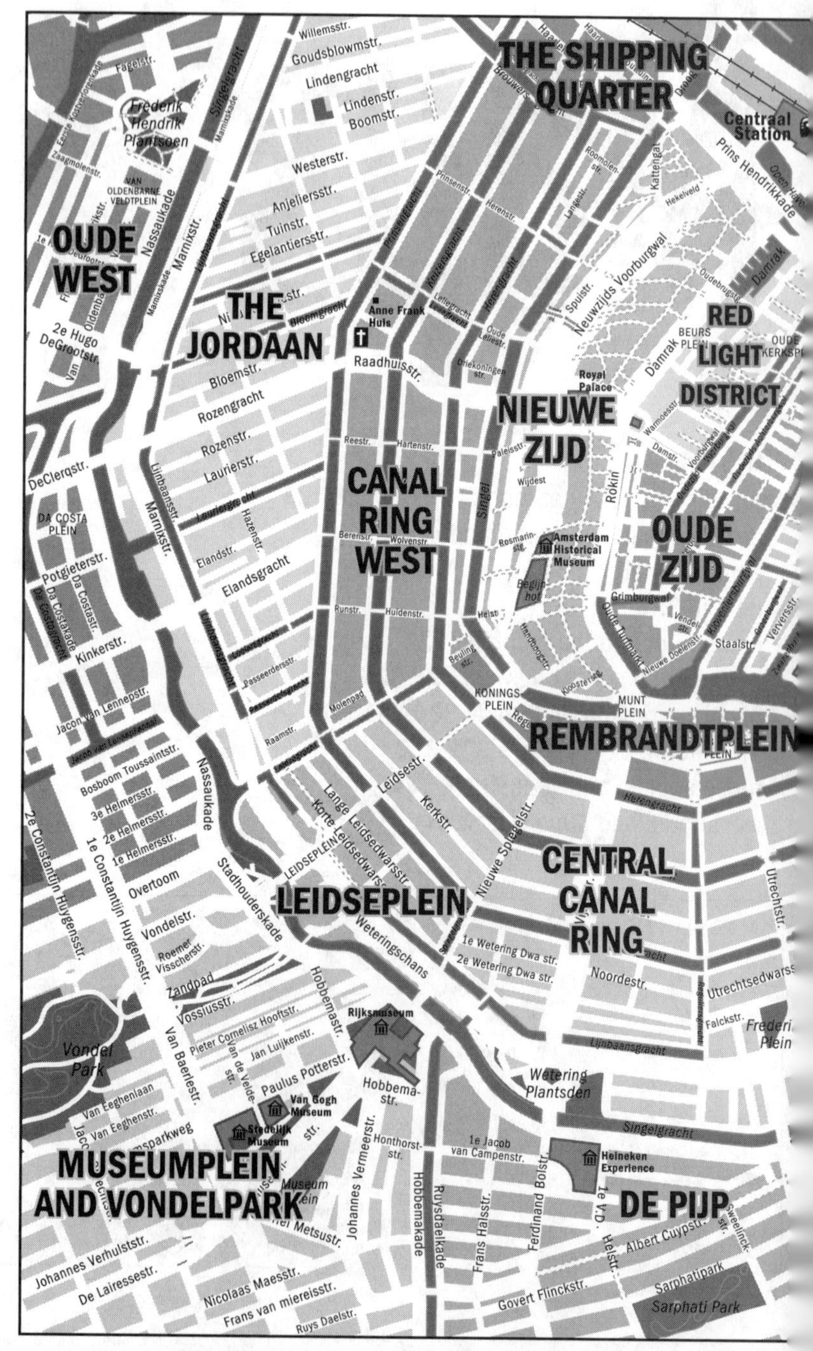
THE SHIPPING QUARTER
Centraal Station
OUDE WEST
THE JORDAAN
Anne Frank Huis
CANAL RING WEST
NIEUWE ZIJD
Royal Palace
RED LIGHT DISTRICT
OUDE ZIJD
Amsterdam Historical Museum
REMBRANDTPLEIN
CENTRAL CANAL RING
LEIDSEPLEIN
Rijksmuseum
Van Gogh Museum
Stedelijk Museum
Heineken Experience
MUSEUMPLEIN AND VONDELPARK
DE PIJP
Vondel Park
Sarphati Park
Frederik Hendrik Plantsoen
Wetering Plantsden
Raadhuisstr.
Rozengracht
Elandsgracht
Prins Hendrikkade
Damrak
Rokin
Singel
Nassaukade
Marnixstr.
Leidsestr.
Kerkstr.
Nieuwe Spiegelstr.
Weteringschans
Stadhouderskade
Overtoom
Vondelstr.
Hobbemastr.
Paulus Potterstr.
Van Baerlestr.
Johannes Vermeerstr.
Ruysdaelkade
Hobbemakade
Ferdinand Bolstr.
Frans Halsstr.
Albert Cuypstr.
Sarphatipark
Govert Flinckstr.
Utrechtsestr.
Singelgracht
Lijnbaansgracht
Kinkerstr.
Nicolaas Maesstr.
De Lairessestr.
Johannes Verhulststr.
Westerstr.
Lindengracht
Bloemstr.
Rozenstr.
Laurierstr.

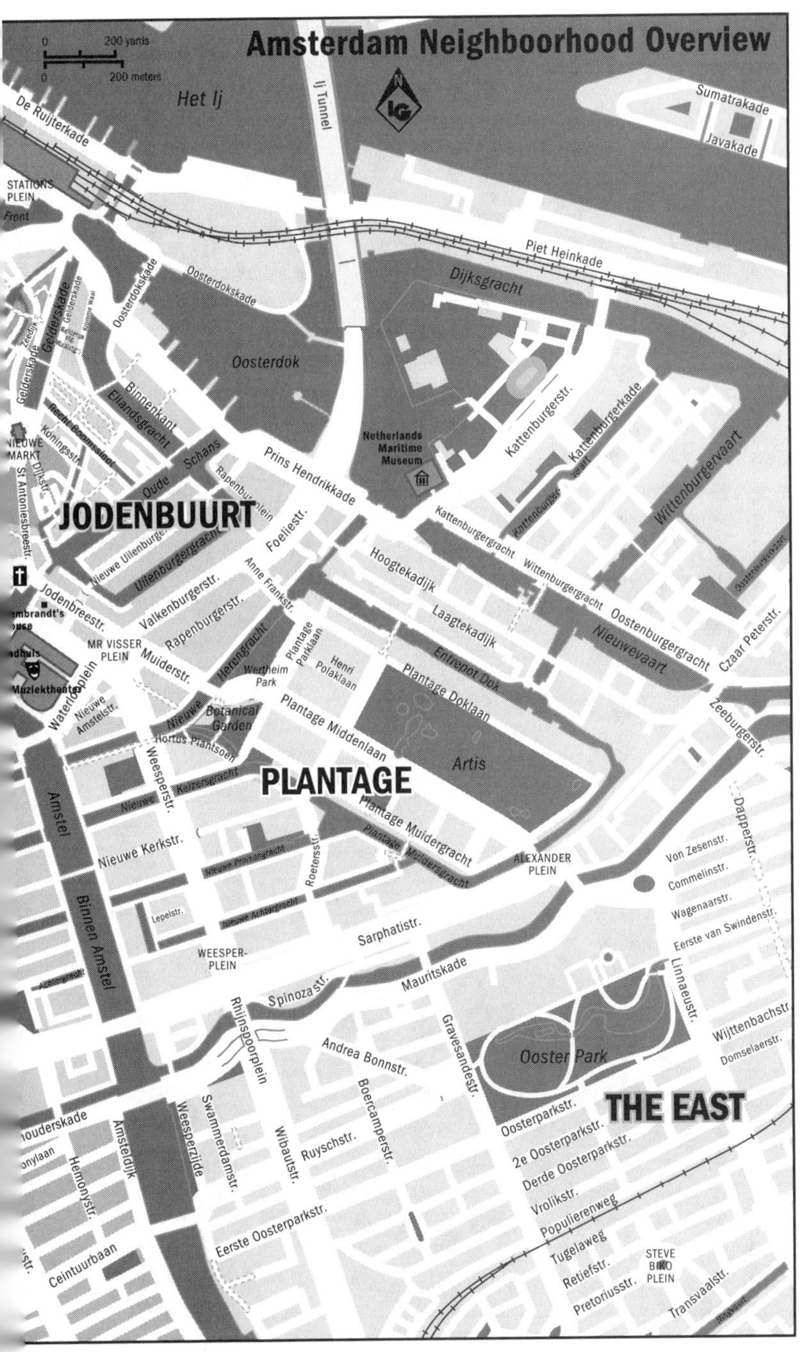
Amsterdam Neighboorhood Overview
0 200 yards
0 200 meters
Het Ij
Ij Tunnel
Sumatrakade
Javakade
De Ruijterkade
STATIONS PLEIN
Piet Heinkade
Dijksgracht
Oosterdokskade
Oosterdok
Netherlands Maritime Museum
Kattenburgerstr.
Kattenburgerkade
Wittenburgervaart
Gelderskade
Zeedijk
Binnenkant
Recht Boomssloot
NIEUWE MARKT
Koningsstr.
Oude Schans
Prins Hendrikkade
Rapenburgerplein
JODENBUURT
St Antoniesbreestr.
Foeliestr.
Kattenburgergracht
Hoogtekadijk
Wittenburgergracht
Nieuwe Uilenburgerstr.
Uilenburgergracht
Anne Frankstr.
Laagtekadijk
Oostenburgergracht
Nieuwevaart
Czaar Peterstr.
Jodenbreestr.
Rembrandt's House
Valkenburgerstr.
Rapenburgerstr.
Entrepot Dok
MR VISSER PLEIN
Muiderstr.
Herengracht
Wertheim Park
Plantage Parklaan
Henri Polaklaan
Plantage Doklaan
Muziektheater
Waterlooplein
Nieuwe Amstelstr.
Nieuwe Herengracht
Botanical Garden
Hortus Plantsoen
Plantage Middenlaan
Artis
Zeeburgerstr.
Weesperstr.
Nieuwe Keizersgracht
PLANTAGE
Amstel
Plantage Muidergracht
Nieuwe Kerkstr.
Nieuwe Prinsengracht
Roetersstr.
ALEXANDER PLEIN
Dapperstr.
Von Zesenstr.
Commelinstr.
Wagenaarstr.
Eerste van Swindenstr.
Binnen Amstel
Lepelstr.
Nieuwe Achtergracht
Sarphatistr.
WEESPER-PLEIN
Achtergracht
Mauritskade
Spinozastr.
Linnaeustr.
Rhijnspoorplein
Gravesandestr.
Wijttenbachstr.
Andrea Bonnstr.
Domselaerstr.
Ooster Park
Boerecamperstr.
THE EAST
Swammerdamstr.
Weesperzijde
Amsteldijk
Hemonystr.
Wibautstr.
Ruyschstr.
Oosterparkstr.
2e Oosterparkstr.
Derde Oosterparkstr.
Vrolikstr.
Populierenweg
Eerste Oosterparkstr.
Ceintuurbaan
Tugelaweg
STEVE BIKO PLEIN
Retiefstr.
Pretoriusstr.
Transvaalstr.

Central Canal Ring, Rembrandtplein and Leidseplein

ACCOMMODATIONS

City Hotel, **62**
Euphemia Budget Hotel, **35**
The Golden Bear, **14**
Hans Brinker Hotel, **26**
Hemp Hotel, **70**
Hotel Asterisk, **38**
Hotel de la Haye, **1**
Hotel de Lantaerne, **2**
Hotel Kap, **37**
Hotel la Boheme, **10**
Hotel Monopole, **52**
Hotel Titus, **4**
International Budget Hostel, **34**
Quentin Hotel, **8**
Radion Inn Youth Hostel, **69**

COFFEESHOPS

Coffeeshop Little, **33**
Dreamlounge Smartshop, **25**
Free I, **48**
Global Chillage, **15**
The Noon, **31**
The Other Side, **39**
Rookies, **20**
Tatanka, **21**
The Saint, **51**
Seeds of Passion, **64**
Stix, **65**
Tops, **24**

FOOD & DRINK

Axum, **68**
Bojo, **23**
Bombay Inn, **12**
Carousel Pancake House, **36**
Coffee and Jazz, **67**
Curry Garden, **59**
De Smoeshaan, **9**
Golden Temple, **71**
NOA, **11**
Santa Lucia, **22**
Tashi Deleg, **66**
Tomo Sushi, **49**
Wagamama, **29**
Rose's Cantina, **46**

ENTERTAINMENT

Alto, **17**
Bourbon Street Jazz & Blues Club, **27**
Paradiso, **30**

BARS & NIGHTLIFE

Arc Bar, **45**
Aroma, **16**
The Back Door, **60**
Bamboo Bar, **13**
De Beetles, **28**
Café April, **40**
Café de Koe, **6**
Café Menschen, **58**
Escape, **54**
La Esquina, **43**
Exit, **47**
The iT, **61**
K2 Apres-Ski Lounge, **56**
Kamer 401, **6a**
Lellebel, **63**
Lux, **7**
M Bar, **41**
Mankind, **32**
The Ministry, **42**
Montmartre, **53**
Mr. Coco's, **50**
Pirates, **18**
Soho, **44**
Vive la Vie, **55**
Weber, **5**
You II, **57**

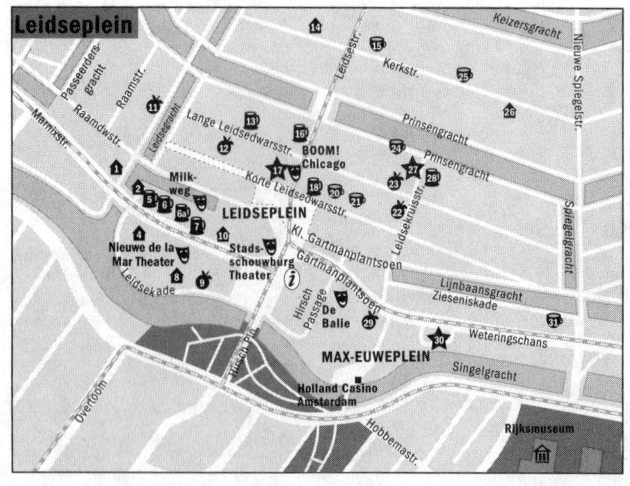

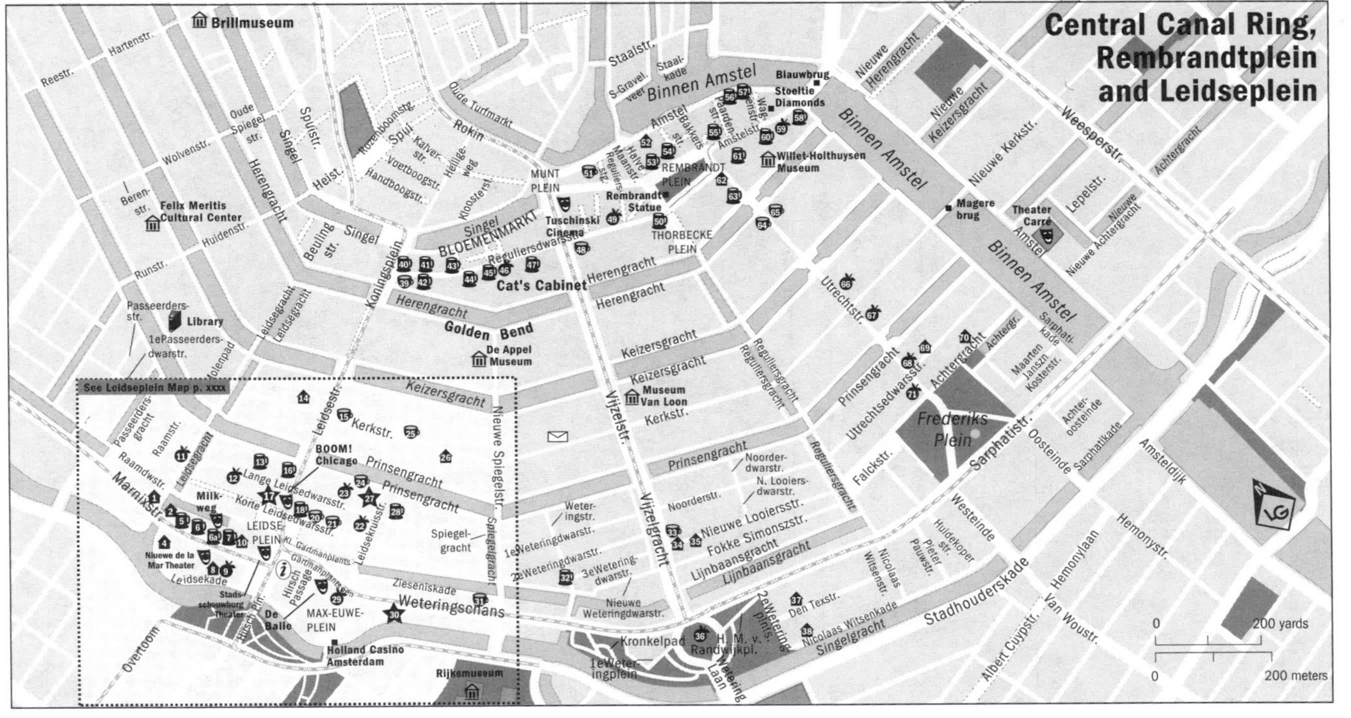
Central Canal Ring, Rembrandtplein and Leidseplein
See Leidseplein Map p. xxx
Brillmuseum
Felix Meritis Cultural Center
Library
Golden Bend
De Appel Museum
Cat's Cabinet
BLOEMENMARKT
Tuschinski Cinema
Rembrandt Statue
REMBRANDT PLEIN
THORBECKE PLEIN
MUNT PLEIN
Museum Van Loon
Willet-Holthuysen Museum
Stoeltie Diamonds
Blauwbrug
Magere brug
Theater Carré
BOOM! Chicago
Milk-weg
Holland Casino Amsterdam
Rijksmuseum
LEIDSE PLEIN
MAX-EUWE-PLEIN
De Balie
Hirsch Passage
Stadsschouwburg Theater
Nieuwe de la Mar Theater
Frederiks Plein
Herengracht
Keizersgracht
Prinsengracht
Singel
Leidsegracht
Reguliersgracht
Spiegelgracht
Lijnbaansgracht
Binnen Amstel
Amstel
Weteringschans
Stadhouderskade
Singelgracht
Vijzelstr.
Vijzelgracht
Utrechtsestr.
Leidsestr.
Koningsplein
Rokin
Spui
Kalverstr.
Sarphatistr.
Weesperstr.
Overtoom
Marnixstr.
Leidsekade
Nieuwe Spiegelstr.
Kerkstr.
Nieuwe Looiersstr.
Fokke Simonszstr.
Den Texstr.
Nicolaas Witsenkade
Albert Cuypstr.
Van Woustr.
Hemonylaan
Hemonystr.
Amsteldijk
Nieuwe Keizersgracht
Nieuwe Herengracht
Nieuwe Kerkstr.
Lepelstr.
Achtergracht
Falckstr.
Westeinde
Oosteinde
Sarphatikade
Reestr.
Hartenstr.
Runstr.
Huidenstr.
Wolvenstr.
Berenstr.
Oude Spiegelstr.
Spuistr.
Heiligeweg
Kloosterst.
Oude Turfmarkt
Staalstr.
Kronkelpad
H. M. v. Randwijkpl.
0
200 yards
0
200 meters

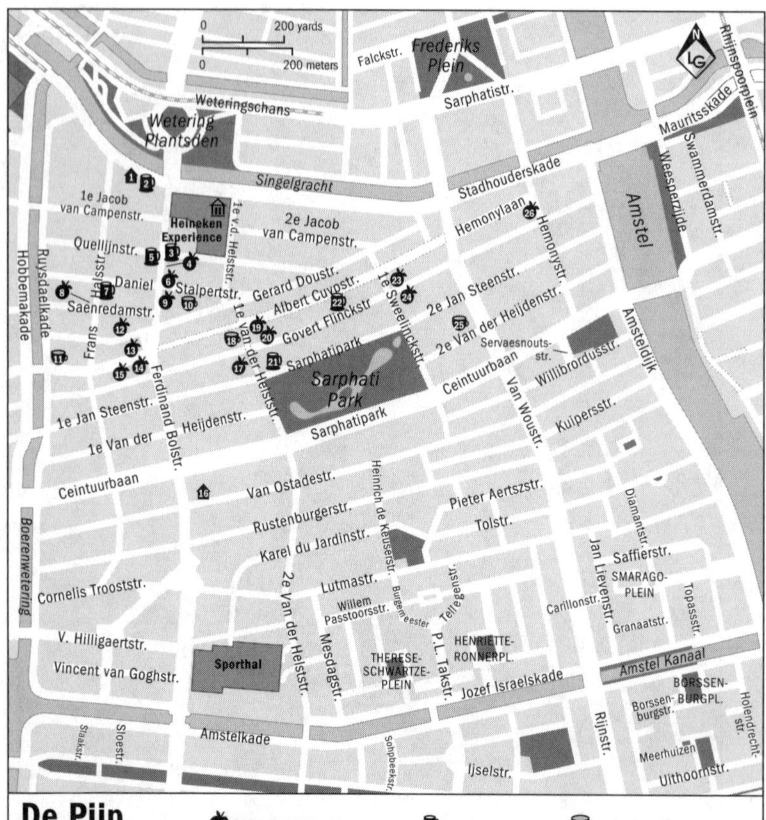

De Pijp

ACCOMMODATIONS
Bicycle Hotel, **16**
Hotel de Stadhouder, **1**

FOOD & DRINK
Albina, **13**
Bar Soup, **20**
Cambodja City, **15**
Eufraat, **17**
Granny's, **19**

FOOD & DRINK (Cont.)
L'Angoletto, **26**
Mas Tapas, **8**
Moksi, **9**
De Ondeugd, **4**
Peppino Gelateria, **23**
Saray, **12**
De Soepwinkel, **24**
Zagros, **14**
Zento, **6**

BARS
De Engel, **22**
Café Berkhout, **2**
De Duvel, **21**
De Vrolijke Drinker, **7**
Kingfisher, **5**
O'Donnell's, **3**

COFFEESHOPS
Bom Shankar Chaishop, **11**
Katsu, **18**
Media, **10**
Yo Yo, **25**

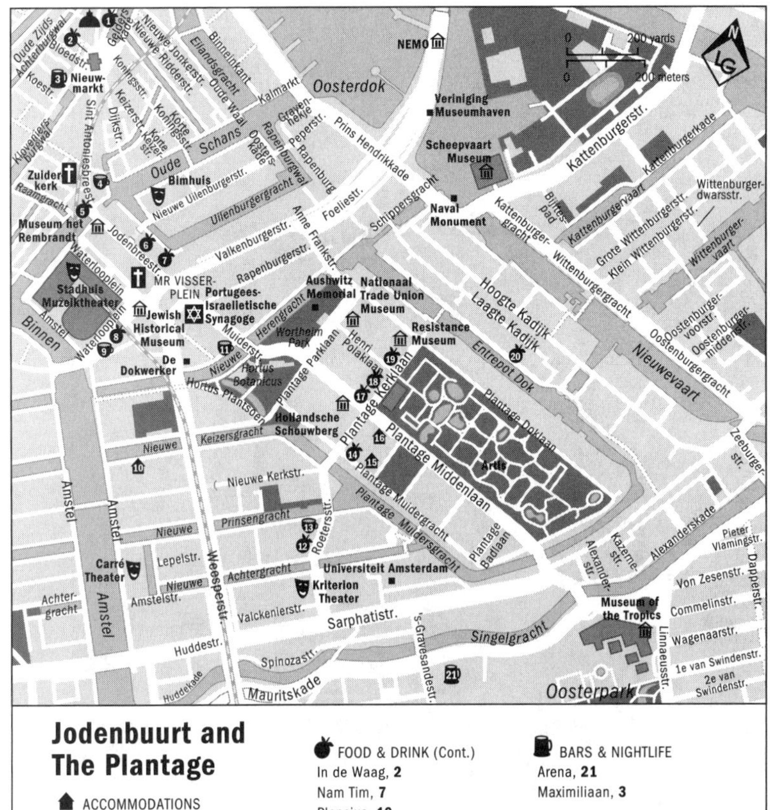

Jodenbuurt and The Plantage

ACCOMMODATIONS

Hotel Barbacan, **15**
Hotel Fantasia, **10**
Hotel Pension Kitty, **16**

FOOD & DRINK

Abe Venito, **14**
Aguada, **12**
Café Koosje, **17**
Café Latei, **1**
En'tre Dok, **20**
King Soloman Restaurant, **8**

FOOD & DRINK (Cont.)

In de Waag, **2**
Nam Tim, **7**
Plancius, **19**
Restaurante La Sala Comidas Caseras, **18**
Soup En Zo, **6**
TisFris, **5**

BARS & NIGHTLIFE

Arena, **21**
Maximiliaan, **3**

COFFEESHOPS

Bluebird, **4**
Het Ballonnetje, **13**
De Overkant, **11**
Smoesie, **9**

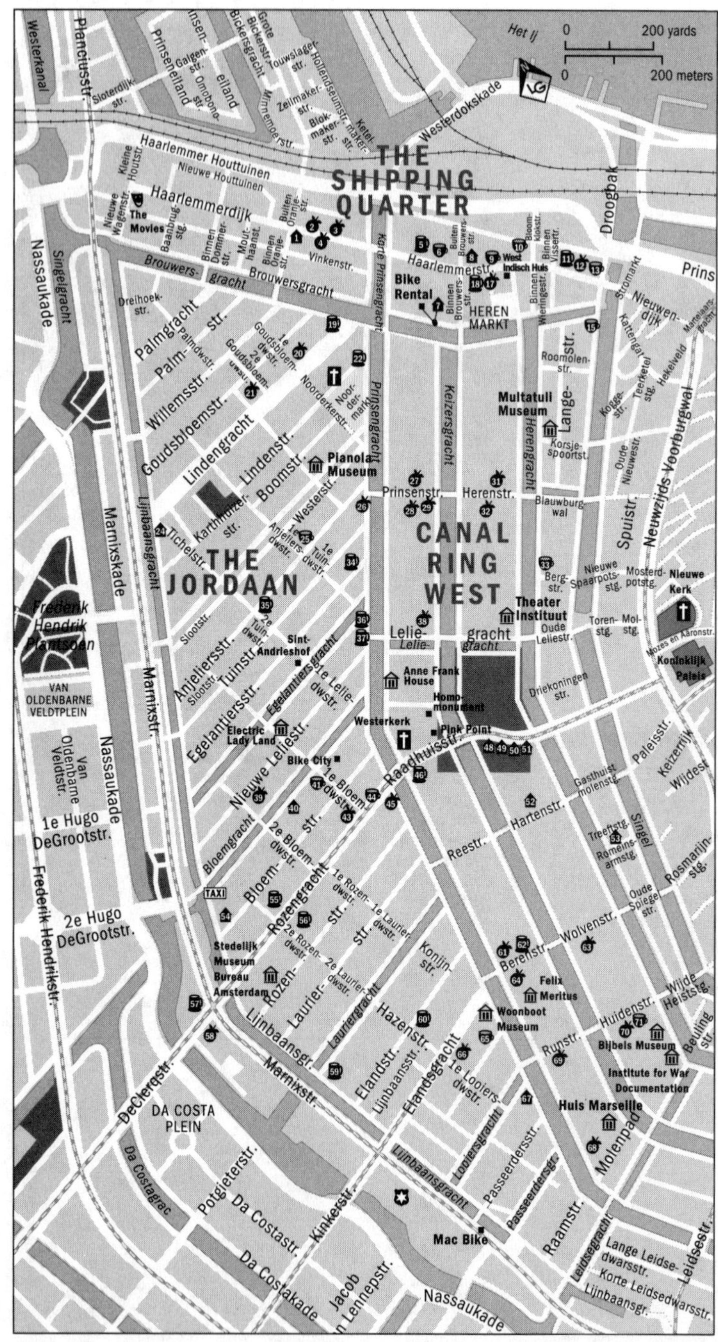
THE SHIPPING QUARTER
THE JORDAAN
CANAL RING WEST
Het IJ
200 yards
200 meters
Westerdokskade
Haarlemmer Houttuinen
Nieuwe Houttuinen
Haarlemmerdijk
Haarlemmerstr.
Brouwersgracht
Prinsengracht
Keizersgracht
Herengracht
Singel
Lijnbaansgracht
Marnixstr.
Nassaukade
Westerstr.
Prinsenstr.
Herenstr.
Raadhuisstr.
Rozengracht
Bloemgracht
Egelantiersgracht
Lindengracht
Leliegracht
Spuistr.
Nieuwezijds Voorburgwal
The Movies
Bike Rental
Multatuli Museum
Pianola Museum
Theater Instituut
Anne Frank House
Homomonument
Pink Point
Westerkerk
Electric Lady Land
Bike City
Sint-Andrieshof
Nieuwe Kerk
Koninklijk Paleis
Stedelijk Museum Bureau Amsterdam
Felix Meritus
Woonboot Museum
Bijbels Museum
Institute for War Documentation
Huis Marseille
Mac Bike
DA COSTA PLEIN
VAN OLDENBARNE VELDTPLEIN
Frederik Hendrik Plantsoen
HEREN MARKT
TAXI

The Shipping Quarter, Canal Ring West, & The Jordaan

see map p. 328

ACCOMMODATIONS

Frederic Rent-a-Bike, **7**
Hotel Acacia, **24**
Hotel Aspen, **51**
Hotel Belga, **52**
Hotel Clemens, **48**
Hotel Hegra, **53**
Hotel My Home, **8**
Hotel Pax, **49**
Hotel van Onna, **40**
Ramenas Hotel, **1**
The Shelter Jordan, **54**
Wiechmann Hotel, **67**
Westertoren Hotel, **50**

FOOD & DRINK

Bakkerij Paul Année, **69**
Balraj, **3**
Ben Cohen Shawarma, **58**
Bolhoed, **26**
Broodje Mokum, **45**
Cafe de Pels, **70**
De Vliegende Schotel, **39**
Dimitri's, **29**
Duende, **20**
Harlem: Drinks and Soul Food, **17**
hein, **61**
Het Molenpad, **68**
Jay's Juice, **12**
Jordino, **4**
Lunchcafé Neilsen, **64**
Manzano, **43**
Padi, **2**
Prego, **32**
Rakang, **66**
Ruhe Delicatessen, **28**
Spanjer en Van Twist, **38**
Snackbar Aggie, **21**
Top Thai, **31**
Vennington, **27**
Wolvenstraat 23, **63**

COFFEESHOPS

Amnesia, **33**
Barney's Coffeeshop, **6**
Black Star Coffeeshop, **44**
Blue Velvet Coffeeshop, **9**
Extreme Amsterdam, **71**
Pablow Picasso, **13**
Paradox, **41**
Pink Floyd, **10**
Siberie, **15**
Spirit Coffeeshop, **25**
La Tertulia, **65**

BARS

Bar 8, **62**
Cafe Thijssen, **19**
Cafe de Tuin, **35**
Cafe de Wilde Zee, **11**
Cafe Kalkhoven, **46**
Cafe P96, **34**
Cafe 't Smalle, **36**
Club More, **56**
De Blauwe Druife, **18**
Dulac, **5**
Korsakoff, **59**
Mazzo, **55**
Proust, **22**
Saarein II, **60**
Sound Garden, **57**
Wil's Cafe, **37**

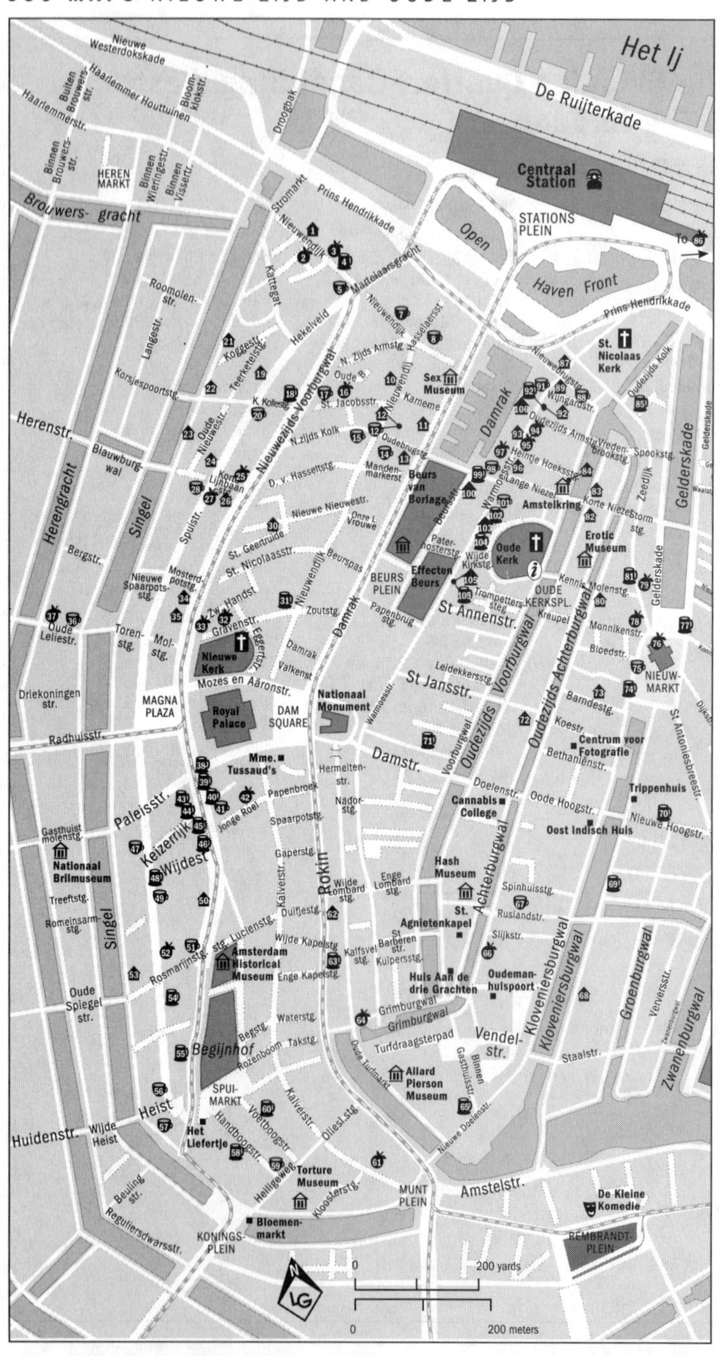
Het Ij
De Ruijterkade
Centraal Station
STATIONS PLEIN
Open Haven Front
Prins Hendrikkade
Nieuwe Westerdokskade
Haarlemmer Houttuinen
Haarlemmerstr.
Brouwersgracht
HEREN MARKT
Droogbak
Nieuwendijk
Martelaarsgracht
Roomolenstr.
Langestr.
Korsjespoortstg.
Herenstr.
Blauwburgwal
Herengracht
Singel
Nieuwezijds Voorburgwal
Damrak
Sex Museum
St. Nicolaas Kerk
Beurs van Berlage
Amstelkring
Oude Kerk
Erotic Museum
Effecten Beurs
BEURS PLEIN
St Annenstr.
OUDE KERKSPL.
Nieuwe Kerk
Royal Palace
MAGNA PLAZA
DAM SQUARE
Nationaal Monument
St Jansstr.
Oudezijds Voorburgwal
Oudezijds Achterburgwal
NIEUWMARKT
Centrum voor Fotografie
Trippenhuis
Oost Indisch Huis
Cannabis College
Damstr.
Radhuisstr.
Mme. Tussaud's
Paleisstr.
Keizerrijk
Wijdest.
Nationaal Brilmuseum
Hash Museum
St. Agnietenkapel
Rokin
Kalverstr.
Amsterdam Historical Museum
Huis Aan de drie Grachten
Oudemanhulspoort
Kloveniersburgwal
Groenburgwal
Zwanenburgwal
Begijnhof
Vendelstr.
Allard Pierson Museum
SPUI-MARKT
Heist
Huidenstr.
Het Liefertje
Torture Museum
MUNT PLEIN
Amstelstr.
De Kleine Komedie
Bloemenmarkt
KONINGSPLEIN
REMBRANDTPLEIN
200 yards
200 meters

Nieuwe Zijd, Oude Zijd, & The Red Light District

see map p. 330

ACCOMMODATIONS

ANCO Hotel, **82**
Anna Youth Hostel, **19**
Bob's Youth Hostel, **26**
Budget Hotel Tamara, **34**
Christian Youth Hostel "The Shelter", **73**
City Hostel Stadsdoelen, **68**
De Oranje Tulp, **84**
Flying Pig Downtown, **10**
Frisco Inn, **100**
The Greenhouse Effect Hotel, **96**
Hotel Brian, **23**
Hotel Brouwer, **22**
Hotel Continental, **13**
Hotel Cosmos, **30**
Hotel the Crown, **83**
Hotel Groenendael, **1**
Hotel of Heart of Amsterdam, **72**
Hotel Hoksbergen, **53**
Hotel Internationaal, **89**
Hotel Mevlana, **35**
Hotel Nova, **50**
Hotel Rokin, **62**
Hotel Royal Taste, **80**
Hotel Singel, **21**
Hotel Vijaya, **11**
Kabul, **93**
La Canna, **12**
Nelly's Hostel, **105**
Old Nickel, **87**
Old Quarter, **106**
Stable Master, **92**
Tourist Inn, **24**
De Witte Tulp Hostel, **103**

FOOD & DRINK

Aneka Rasa, **94**
Foodism, **37**
Hoi Tin, **78**
In de Waag, **76**
KinderKookkafe, **66**
La Fruteria, **33**
La Place, **61**
Mr. Coco's, **3**
New Season, **95**
Old Highlander, **16**
Orvieto, **2**
Pannenkoekenhuis Upstairs, **64**
Ristorante Caprese, **52**
Sea Palace, **86**
Sie Joe, **32**
Stereo Sushi, **42**
Taste of Culture, **79**
Tasty and Healthy, **25**
Theehuis Himalaya, **97**
Usama, **27**

BARS

Absinthe, **40**
Belgique, **31**
Bep, **45**
Blarney Stone, **4**
Cafe de Jaren, **65**
Cafe de Engelbewaarder, **69**
Cafe de Stevens, **77**
Cafe Heffer, **99**
Cock and Feathers, **85**
Cockring, **104**
Danse Bij Jansen, **58**
Durty Nelly's Pub, **105**
Getto, **102**
Gollem, **54**
Harry's Bar, **55**
Cafe de Hoogte, **70**
Item, **38**
Lime, **81**
Lokaal 't Loosje, **74**
Meander, **60**
NL Lounge, **39**
Seymour Likely Lounge, **45**
Stablemaster, **92**
The Tara, **63**
Vrankvijk, **48**
Wijnand Fockink, **71**
Why Not, **18**

COFFEESHOPS

Abraxas, **41**
Cafe de Kuil, **14**
Cafe Del Mondo, **75**
Coffeeshop Any Day, **20**
Conscious Dreams Kokopelli, **91**
Dampkring, **59**
Dutch Flowers, **57**
The Essential Seeds Company Art and Smart Shop, **5**
Funny People Coffeeshop, **88**
The Greenhouse Effect, **8**
Grey Area, **36**
Hill Street Blues, **98**
Kadinsky, **51**
La Canna, **12**
The Magic Mushroom, **49**
Magic Valley, **28**
Old Style, **17**
Route 99, **101**
Rusland, **67**
Softland, **47**
De Tweede Kamer (The Second Room), **56**
Wolke Wietje, **15**

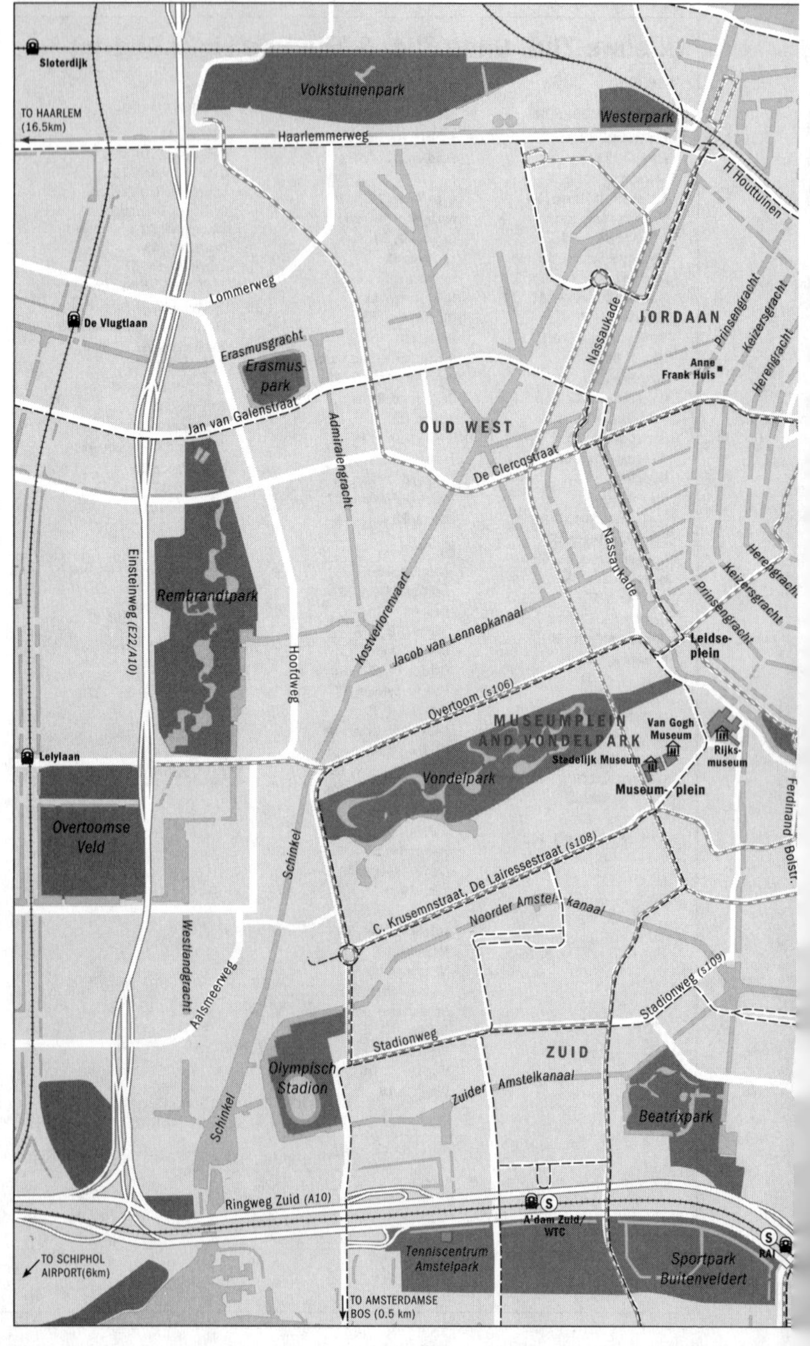
Sloterdijk
Volkstuinenpark
Westerpark
TO HAARLEM
(16.5km)
Haarlemmerweg
H Houttuinen
Lommerweg
De Vlugtlaan
Nassaukade
JORDAAN
Prinsengracht
Keizersgracht
Herengracht
Erasmusgracht
Erasmus-
park
Anne
Frank Huis
Jan van Galenstraat
Admiralengracht
OUD WEST
De Clercqstraat
Einsteinweg (E22/A10)
Rembrandtpark
Nassaukade
Herengracht
Keizersgracht
Prinsengracht
Kostverlorenvaart
Jacob van Lennepkanaal
Hoofdweg
Leidse-
plein
Overtoom (s106)
MUSEUMPLEIN
AND VONDELPARK
Van Gogh
Museum
Rijks-
museum
Lelylaan
Stedelijk Museum
Vondelpark
Museum-
plein
Overtoomse
Veld
Ferdinand Bolstr.
Schinkel
C. Krusemnstraat, De Lairessestraat (s108)
Noorder Amstel- kanaal
Westlandgracht
Aalsmeerweg
Stadionweg (s109)
Stadionweg
ZUID
Olympisch
Stadion
Zuider Amstelkanaal
Schinkel
Beatrixpark
Ringweg Zuid (A10)
A'dam Zuid/
WTC
RAI
TO SCHIPHOL
AIRPORT(6km)
Tenniscentrum
Amstelpark
Sportpark
Buitenveldert
TO AMSTERDAMSE
BOS (0.5 km)

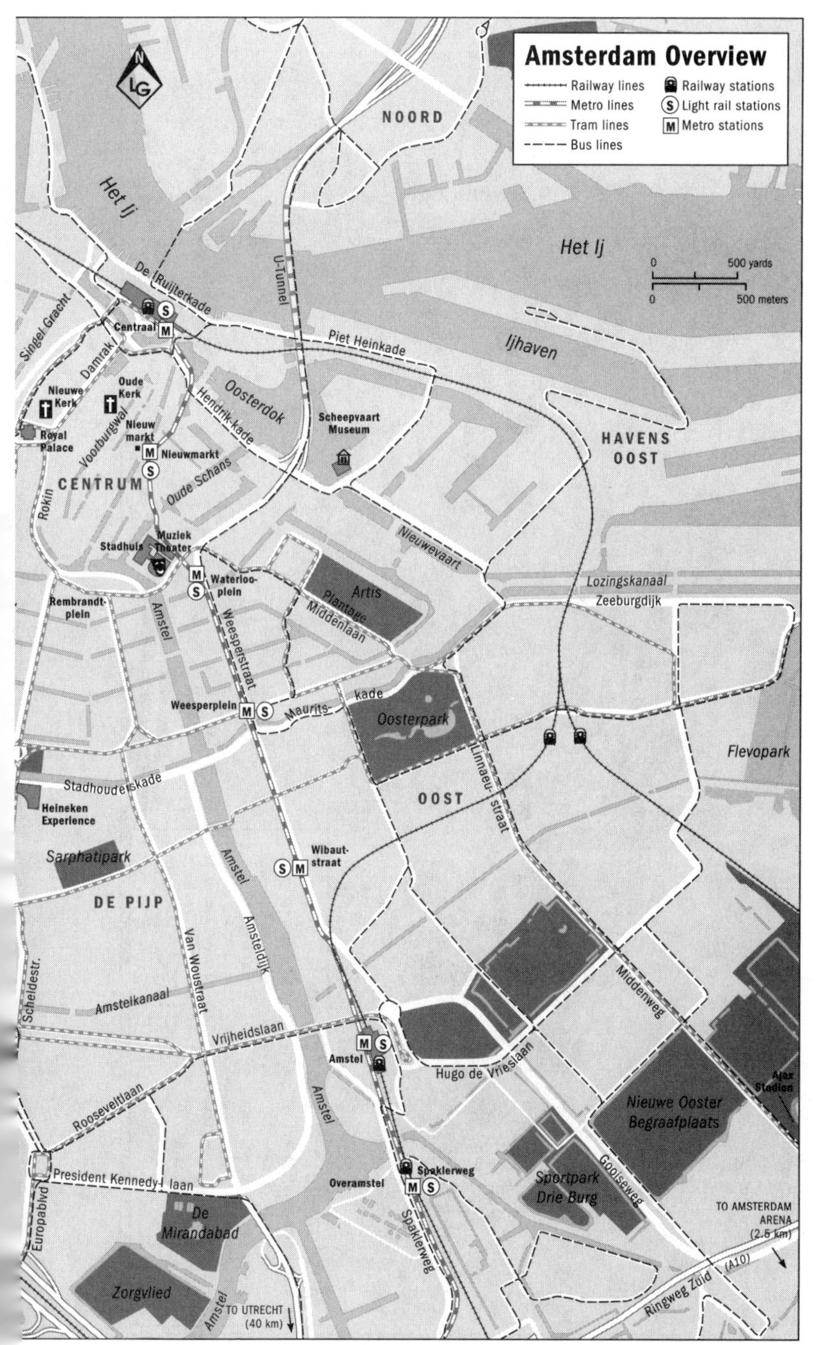
Amsterdam Overview
Railway lines
Metro lines
Tram lines
Bus lines
Railway stations
Light rail stations
Metro stations
0 500 yards
0 500 meters
NOORD
Het Ij
Het Ij
Ijhaven
HAVENS OOST
De Ruijterkade
Centraal
Singel Gracht
Damrak
Piet Heinkade
U-Tunnel
Nieuwe Kerk
Oude Kerk
Royal Palace
Voorburgwal
Nieuw markt
Nieuwmarkt
Oosterdok
Hendrik-kade
Scheepvaart Museum
CENTRUM
Oude Schans
Rokin
Stadhuis
Muziek Theater
Waterloo-plein
Nieuwevaart
Artis Plantage
Middenlaan
Lozingskanaal
Zeeburgdijk
Rembrandt-plein
Amstel
Weesperstraat
Weesperplein
Maurits-kade
Oosterpark
Linnaeu-straat
Flevopark
Stadhouderskade
Heineken Experience
OOST
Sarphatipark
Wibaut-straat
DE PIJP
Amstel
Amsteldijk
Van Woustraat
Scheldestr.
Amstelkanaal
Middenweg
Vrijheidslaan
Amstel
Hugo de Vrieslaan
Ajax Stadion
Nieuwe Ooster Begraafplaats
Rooseveltlaan
Amstel
Spaklerweg
Overamstel
Sportpark Drie Burg
Gooiseweg
President Kennedy-laan
De Mirandabad
Europablvd
Spaklerweg
TO AMSTERDAM ARENA (2.5 km)
(A10)
Ringweg Zuid
Zorgvlied
Amstel
TO UTRECHT (40 km)

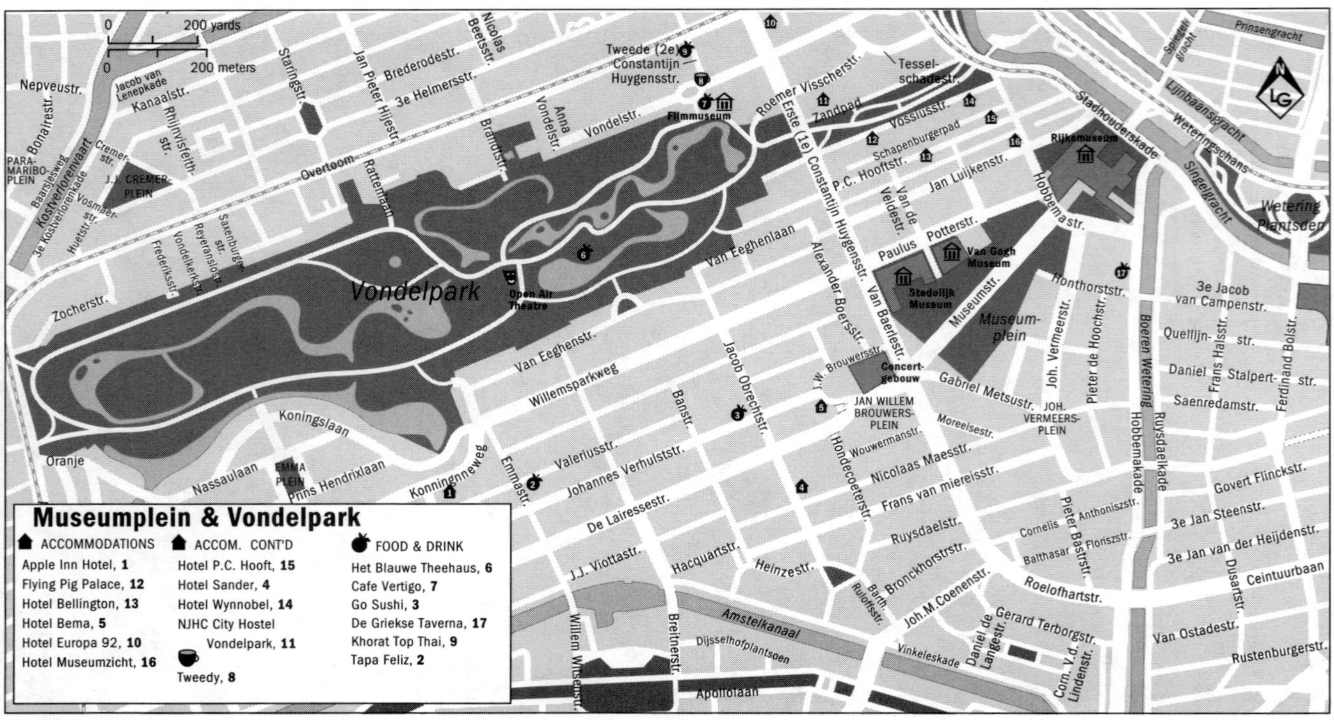
Museumplein & Vondelpark
ACCOMMODATIONS
Apple Inn Hotel, 1
Flying Pig Palace, 12
Hotel Bellington, 13
Hotel Bema, 5
Hotel Europa 92, 10
Hotel Museumzicht, 16
ACCOM. CONT'D
Hotel P.C. Hooft, 15
Hotel Sander, 4
Hotel Wynnobel, 14
NJHC City Hostel Vondelpark, 11
Tweedy, 8
FOOD & DRINK
Het Blauwe Theehaus, 6
Cafe Vertigo, 7
Go Sushi, 3
De Griekse Taverna, 17
Khorat Top Thai, 9
Tapa Feliz, 2
Vondelpark
Museum-plein
Rijksmuseum
Van Gogh Museum
Stedelijk Museum
Concertgebouw
Filmmuseum
Open Air Theatre
Stadhouderskade
Singelgracht
Lijnbaansgracht
Weteringschans
Prinsengracht
Spiegelgracht
Wetering Plantsden
Boeren Wetering
Ruysdaelkade
Hobbemakade
Hobbemastr.
Museumstr.
Van Baerlestr.
Paulus Potterstr.
P.C. Hooftstr.
Jan Luijkenstr.
Van de Veldestr.
Vossiusstr.
Schapenburgerpad
Tesselschadestr.
Roemer Visscherstr.
Zandpad
Erste (1e) Constantijn Huygensstr.
Tweede (2e) Constantijn Huygensstr.
Alexander Boersstr.
Van Eeghenlaan
Van Eeghenstr.
Willemsparkweg
Jacob Obrechtstr.
Banstr.
Valeriusstr.
Johannes Verhulststr.
De Lairessestr.
J.J. Viottastr.
Emmastr.
Konninginneweg
Koningslaan
Prins Hendrixlaan
Nassaulaan
EMMA PLEIN
Oranje
Zocherstr.
Overtoom
Rattenlaan
Staringstr.
Jan Pieter Hijestr.
Brederodestr.
3e Helmersstr.
Nicolas Beetsstr.
Brandtstr.
Anna Vondelstr.
Vondelstr.
Amstelkanaal
Dijsselhofplantsoen
Apollolaan
Breitnerstr.
Willem Witsenstr.
Gabriel Metsustr.
JAN WILLEM BROUWERS-PLEIN
J.W. Brouwersstr.
JOH. VERMEERS-PLEIN
Moreelsestr.
Wouwermanstr.
Nicolaas Maesstr.
Frans van miereisstr.
Ruysdaelstr.
Bronckhorststr.
Barth. Ruloffsstr.
Roelofhartstr.
Pieter Bastrstr.
Cornelis Anthoniszstr.
Balthasar Floriszstr.
Gerard Terborgstr.
Daniel de Langestr.
Corn. V.d. Lindenstr.
Joh.M.Coenenstr.
Vinkeleskade
Joh. Vermeerstr.
Pieter de Hoochstr.
Honthorststr.
Hondecoeterstr.
Heinzestr.
Hacquartstr.
Ferdinand Bolstr.
3e Jacob van Campenstr.
Quellijn-str.
Frans Halsstr.
Daniel Stalpert-str.
Saenredamstr.
Govert Flinckstr.
3e Jan Steenstr.
3e Jan van der Heijdenstr.
Dusartstr.
Ceintuurbaan
Van Ostadestr.
Rustenburgerstr.
Kostverlorenvaart
3e Kostverlorenkade
Baarsjesweg
PARA-MARIBO-PLEIN
Bonairestr.
Nepveustr.
Jacob van Lenepkade
Kanaalstr.
Rhijnvisfeith-str.
Cremerstr.
J.J. CREMER-PLEIN
Vosmaerstr.
Huetstr.
Saxenburgerstr.
Reyeranslostr.
Vondelkerkstr.
Frederiksstr.
0
200 yards
0
200 meters

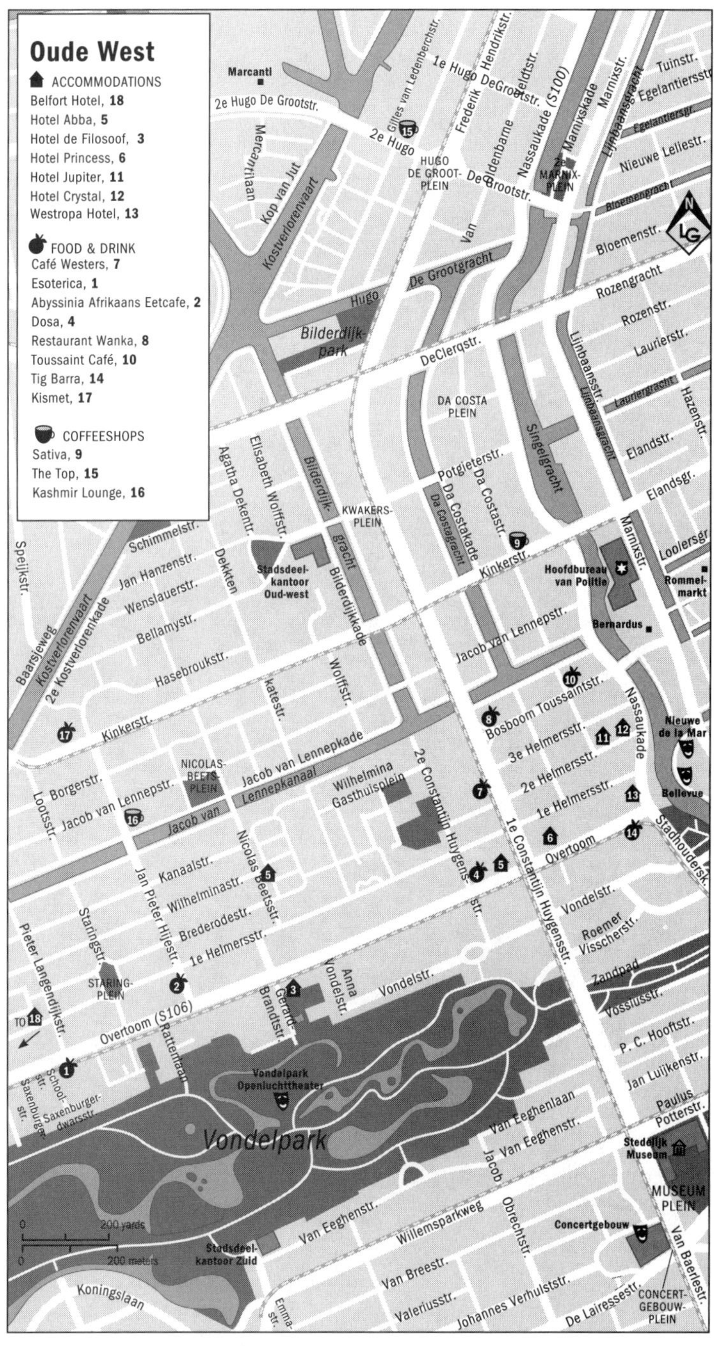
Oude West
ACCOMMODATIONS
Belfort Hotel, 18
Hotel Abba, 5
Hotel de Filosoof, 3
Hotel Princess, 6
Hotel Jupiter, 11
Hotel Crystal, 12
Westropa Hotel, 13
FOOD & DRINK
Café Westers, 7
Esoterica, 1
Abyssinia Afrikaans Eetcafe, 2
Dosa, 4
Restaurant Wanka, 8
Toussaint Café, 10
Tig Barra, 14
Kismet, 17
COFFEESHOPS
Sativa, 9
The Top, 15
Kashmir Lounge, 16
Marcanti
2e Hugo De Grootstr.
1e Hugo De Grootstr.
HUGO DE GROOT-PLEIN
2e MARNIX-PLEIN
Bilderdijk-park
DA COSTA PLEIN
KWAKERS-PLEIN
Stadsdeel-kantoor Oud-west
Hoofdbureau van Politie
Bernardus
Rommel-markt
Nieuwe de la Mar
Bellevue
NICOLAS-BEETS-PLEIN
Wilhelmina Gasthuisplein
STARING-PLEIN
TO 18
Overtoom (S106)
Vondelpark Openluchttheater
Vondelpark
Stedelijk Museum
MUSEUM PLEIN
Concertgebouw
CONCERT-GEBOUW-PLEIN
Stadsdeel-kantoor Zuid
0 200 yards
0 200 meters
Koningslaan

WHO WE ARE

A NEW LET'S GO FOR 2003

With a sleeker look and innovative new content, we have revamped the entire series to reflect more than ever the needs and interests of the independent traveler. Here are just some of the improvements you will notice when traveling with the new *Let's Go.*

MORE PRICE OPTIONS

Still the best resource for budget travelers, *Let's Go* recognizes that everyone needs the occassional indulgence. Our "Big Splurges" indicate establishments that are actually worth those extra pennies (pulas, pesos, or pounds), and price-level symbols (❶ ❷ ❸ ❹ ❺) allow you to quickly determine whether an accommodation or restaurant will break the bank. We may have diversified, but we'll never lose our budget focus—"Hidden Deals" reveal the best-kept travel secrets.

BEYOND THE TOURIST EXPERIENCE

Our Alternatives to Touism chapter offers ideas on immersing yourself in a new community through study, work, or volunteering.

AN INSIDER'S PERSPECTIVE

As always, every item is written and researched by our on-site writers. This year we have highlighted more viewpoints to help you gain an even more thorough understanding of the places you are visiting.

IN RECENT NEWS. *Let's Go* correspondents around the globe report back on current regional issues that may affect you as a traveler.

CONTRIBUTING WRITERS. Respected scholars and former *Let's Go* writers discuss topics on society and culture, going into greater depth than the usual guidebook summary.

THE LOCAL STORY. From the Parisian monk toting a cell phone to the Russian *babushka* confronting capitalism, *Let's Go* shares its revealing conversations with local personalities—a unique glimpse of what matters to real people.

FROM THE ROAD. Always helpful and sometimes downright hilarious, our researchers share useful insights on the typical (and atypical) travel experience.

SLIMMER SIZE

Don't be fooled by our new, smaller size. *Let's Go* is still packed with invaluable travel advice, but now it's easier to carry with a more compact design.

FORTY-THREE YEARS OF WISDOM

For over four decades *Let's Go* has provided the most up-to-date information on the hippest cafes, the most pristine beaches, and the best routes from border to border. It all started in 1960 when a few well-traveled students at Harvard University handed out a 20-page mimeographed pamphlet of their tips on budget travel to passengers on student charter flights to Europe. From humble beginnings, *Let's Go* has grown to cover six continents and *Let's Go: Europe* still reigns as the world's best-selling travel guide. This year we've beefed up our coverage of Latin America with *Let's Go: Costa Rica* and *Let's Go: Chile;* on the other side of the globe, we've added *Let's Go: Thailand* and *Let's Go: Hawaii.* Our new guides bring the total number of titles to 61, each infused with the spirit of adventure that travelers around the world have come to count on.

Do You
Yahoo!
?